Imaneq's Conversion to Christianity, watercolor by Aron (ca. 18

Source: J. Meldgaard (1982: 10–13), Greenland National Museum a

1. Imaneq is encountered and cut up by the smiling giant, *Qungussutariaq*.

2. Reassembled and supported by his grandparents, Imaneq rides or glides on his kayak sitting skin toward land. He is blinded/enveloped by his bladder float.

WORLDVIEWS OF THE GREENLANDERS

WORLDVIEWS OF THE GREENLANDERS

An Inuit Arctic Perspective

Birgitte Sonne

UNIVERSITY OF ALASKA PRESS

Published by
University of Alaska Press
P.O. Box 756240
Fairbanks, AK 99775-6240

Cover design by UA Press.
Interior design by Rachel Fudge.
Author photo by Zsuzsanna Willkan.

This publication is supported by the Velux Foundation.

Figures 1–8 redrawn by Lisa Devenish for printing.

Cover and endsheet images: Imaneq's conversion to Christianity, watercolor by Aron.
1. Imaneq is encountered and cut up by the smiling giant, Qungussutariaq.
2. Reassembled and supported by his grandparents, Imaneq rides or glides on his kayak sitting-skin towards land. He is blinded/enveloped by his bladder float.
3. Imaneq is saved and brought back to life by Southerners, who know the correct ritual procedure.
4. Back home Imaneq dreams about the life and light of heaven. Notice that the hunting bladder and the light from heaven are painted in the same yellow, luminous color.
Source: J. Meldgaard (1982: 10–13), Greenland National Museum and Archives

Library of Congress Cataloging-in-Publication Data

Names: Sonne, Birgitte.
Title: Worldviews of the Greenlanders : an Inuit Arctic perspective / by Birgitte Sonne.
Description: Fairbanks : University of Alaska Press, 2017. | Includes bibliographical references. | Identifiers: LCCN 2017007893 (print) | LCCN 2017033908 (ebook) | ISBN 9781602233393 (ebook)| ISBN 9781602233386 (hardback) Subjects: LCSH: Inuit—Greenland—History. | Inuit—Greenland—Social life and customs. | Greenland—History. | Greenland—Social life and customs. | BISAC: SOCIAL SCIENCE / Anthropology / General. Classification: LCC E99.E7 (ebook) | LCC E99.E7 S6425 2017 (print) | DDC 998.2004/9712dc23
LC record available at https://lccn.loc.gov/2017007893

Contents

Illustrations

Preface

Having studied Greenland, Arctic Canada, and Alaska for most of my adult life, my primary focus has been on the precolonial Greenlandic worldview, its key symbols, and changes brought about by early colonial trade and Christian missions. As no such exploration of the topic has been conducted since William Thalbitzer and Knud Rasmussen made their contributions almost a century ago and because fairly recent publications about the cosmologies of Canadian Inuit and Alaska Iñupiat and Yupiit call for a Greenland "companion," I feel that the time has come for a thorough presentation of the Greenlandic material. While some authors who write about Alaska and Canada make stray references to Greenlandic sources in English, German, and French translations, the extensive corpus in Danish and Greenlandic remains a closed book to most "foreigners." These rich and revealing sources invite study, comparisons, and contemplation.

A Note on Terminology

Inuit in Greenland, Arctic Canada, and northern Alaska speak the Inuit languages or, rather, dialects, because they form a linguistic continuum (Michael Fortescue pers. comm.). The older Yup'ik languages are spoken by the Yupiit in Southwest Alaska, from Unalakleet in the north to Kodiak Island in the south, in the north on St. Lawrence Island in the Bering Strait, and by a very few native speakers among the Yupiit on the Chukotka Peninsula in northeast Siberia. The Aleut language is the oldest related language (Krauss 1988) and is probably mixed with a now-extinct Indian language (Fortescue 1998). The term "Inuit" has been established as a politically correct term for these people, but because not all Yupiit are thrilled to be called Inuit, I use Inuit/Yupiit—both in the plural—as a common term. The recent ban on using "Eskimo" is thus followed (except of course in quotations from older sources). "Yup'ik" in the singular is today the accepted term used for cultural characteristics of the Yupiit in Alaska ("Yupik" refers Chukotka and St. Lawrence Island). I rarely refer to the Unangan (Aleut Islanders), because they were not affected by the same Thule Culture influences that reached all the other Inuit and Yupiit in the twelfth to fourteenth centuries. The term "Eastern Inuit" credits striking cultural differences between Inuit west and east of the Mackenzie River in Canada (Burch 1988b; Lantis pers. comm.). The Eastern Inuit thus include the vast majority of Canadian Inuit plus Greenlanders. In late historic times, however, the dividing line moved slightly east due to the immigration of "western" Inuit from northern Alaska (Usher 1971). Ethnic names of Canadian Inuit groups are used except for those of the Labrador Inuit (Nunavimmiut of the Nunatsiavut agreement 2005) and South Baffin Island (the southern Nunavummiut of the Nunavut agreement 1995). My distinctions between Greenland group names, outlined below, follow historic-linguistic criteria.

■ ■ ■

Introduction

This introduction opens with a survey of regional names. Next it takes the reader through relevant points in prehistoric and historic times of Greenland's changing inhabitants, climatic changes, and exchanges within the region and with foreigners such as whalers, colonial traders, and missionaries. I discuss the term "worldview" and describe my method in comparison with those employed in recent research on Inuit and Yupiit worldviews. My method is similar to the Anthropological Field Study (AFS) method, which covers an entire field of related cultures (e.g., of Inuit and Yupiit). But because I also consider ethnohistorical issues, an outline of the contact histories of Arctic Canada and Inuit/Yupiit Alaska ends the section on method. The following evaluation of the sources, a longtime necessity in the Danish humanities, pays particular attention to the stepwise colonization of Greenland, region by region, from 1721 to its completion in 1894 and 1910 with the establishment of trade and mission in Ammassalik (East Greenland) and Avanersuaq (Thule), respectively (see fig. 4, p. 9). Thus the impacts of trade, mission, and colonial administration differ according to time and place as do the discourses of the authors. Together such differences offer knowledge about changes in Greenlandic worldviews.

Then I will present my chosen theories—those of practice, perception, and perspectivism—and finally make content summaries of chapters 1–5.

Greenland: Regions and Place-names

Two hurdles must first be overcome by new readers of Greenland's history and prehistory: the name Thule and the varying premises for changes in regional names.

Thule is the name of both a *region* and a *culture*. The region Thule is north of Melville Bay, which is now called Avanersuaq. The name "Thule" was indirectly given to the region by Knud Rasmussen, who in vain tried to persuade the Danish government to colonize this northernmost part of the country with mission and trade. He took on the responsibility himself, obtained funding, and in 1910 named his trading post the Thule station.

The Thule culture developed along the Arctic coast in northern Alaska and northwest Arctic Canada. It started to spread eastward about 1000 AD and reached northern Greenland by 1200. The

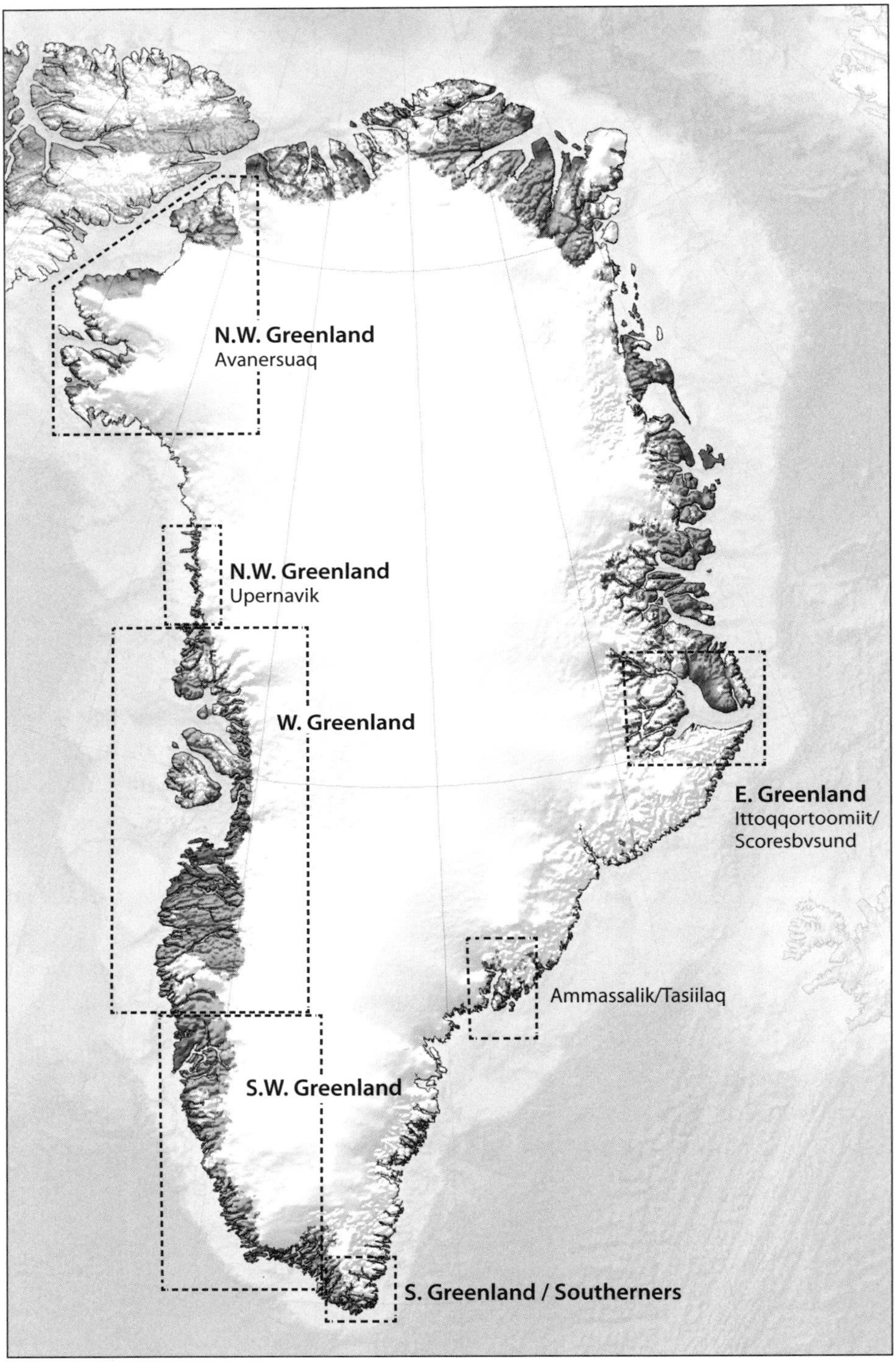

Fig. 1. Regions of Greenland: Avanersuaq, Northwest Greenland (Upernavik district); West Greenland; Southwest Greenlandl Southerners, Southest Greenland (depopulated in the year 1900); East Greenland (Ammassalik/Tasiilaq and Ittoqqortoormiit). *Redrawn for print by Lisa Devenish.*

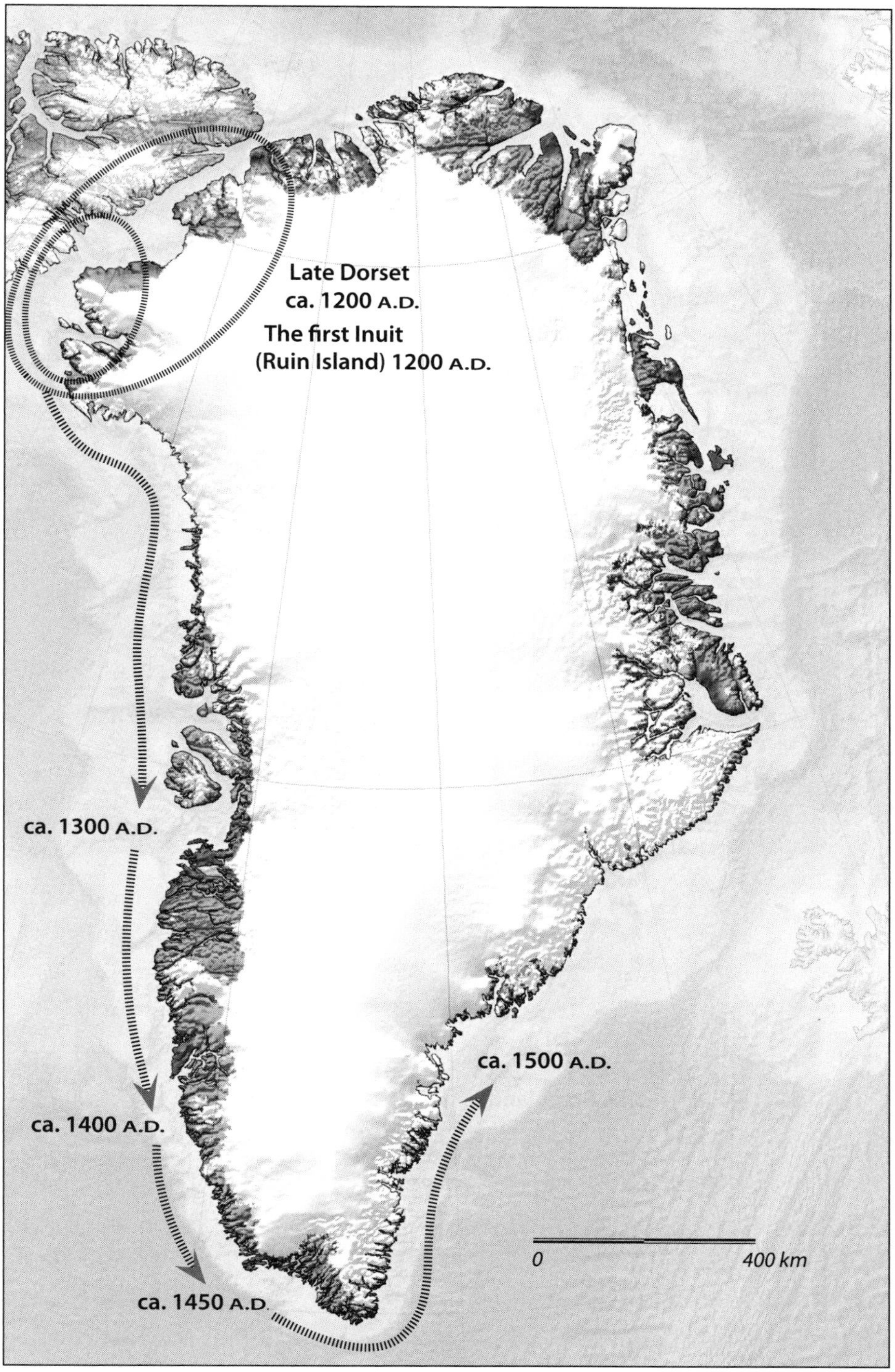

Fig. 2. The Thule pioneers. The first Inuit, the Ruin Island people, appear to have traveled nonstop from North Alaska and arrived in Avanersuaq about 1200 AD. These pioneers most probably met with Late Dorset (in Avanersuaq since ca. 800 AD), but they quickly expanded south along the west coast and likely met with the last Norse in the south. The vanguard continued round Cape Farewell and north along the southeast coast. Arrows and years show the findings of their earliest winter settlements. *Gulløv (2012: 138), courtesy of H. C. Gulløv. Redrawn for print by Lisa Devenish.*

members of this culture became the Inuit ancestors of present-day Greenlanders. The Thule culture was named in compliment to Rasmussen, because the first artifacts were excavated at Cape York (Comer's Midden) during Rasmussen's Second Thule Expedition (1916–18). The actual naming and first thorough description of the Thule culture, however, was done by Therkel Mathiassen based on his rich findings at Naujan, Repulse Bay, during the Fifth Thule Expedition (Gulløv 2016: 148–51). I shall reserve the name Thule for the culture and use Avanersuaq to describe the region.

On the official map of Greenland, or Kalaallit Nunaat, the country consists of three parts: Avannaa (North Greenland), Kitaa (West Greenland), and Tunu (Backside, or East Greenland). The Danish colonization of Kitaa started in 1721, close to Nuuk, and was by and large accomplished by about 1800; Tunu (Ammassalik and Ittoqqortoormiit) followed in 1894 and 1925, and Rasmussen's Thule station in Avannaa in 1910. From the very beginning of colonization, the Royal Mission College was tied to the colonies (roughly the cities of today) located all along the coast. The German Moravians, who got permission to missionize from 1733 to 1900, extended southwards from Nuuk to Friedrichsthal/Narsamijiit in competition with the Danish Royal Mission.

For nearly 200 years, from 1782 to 1953, the colonies of the west coast were divided into two provinces: South Greenland stretched from Sisimiut to the southernmost trading annex near Cape Farewell, and North Greenland extended north from Sisimiut to Melville Bay, including Upernavik. Apart from references to H. J. Rink, the superintendent of South Greenland from 1855 to 1868, my references to this division in provinces are scarce.[1] The transformation of the colonies into municipalities (beginning in 1911 and still changing) is largely beyond the scope of this book.

Greenlanders, Kalaallit, Inuit

Within Nordic history, the Western term "Greenlanders" used to be the appellation conferred on Norse settlers, who also gave Greenland its name (Nørlund 1967: 10; Arneborg 1997: 43).[2] The vanguard arrived from Iceland about 985 AD, settled in the south (Eastern Settlement) and moved consecutively farther north into the fjords east of today's Nuuk (Western Settlement). They remained for 400 to 500 years, abandoning first the Western Settlement and then, in about 1450, the Eastern Settlement.[3] The term "Kalaallit" (Kalaaleq in the singular), as the present Greenlanders call themselves, most probably derives from exchanges between the Norse settlers and the vanguard Inuit along the west coast.[4]

The Norse and the Inuit no doubt met. They did fight at times and they may have mixed to some degree. Be that as it may—except perhaps for the change in self-appellation from Inuit to Kalaallit—the Norse did not demonstrably change the Inuit worldview. The Greenlanders' own stories about the Norse cannot be trusted as historical testimony. They make sense only in contemporary colonial contexts, and I shall treat them accordingly. In modern Greenland, the term "Inuit" has been revived

1. For those interested in Greenland's political development from colonial to autonomous status (2009) within the Kingdom of Denmark, basic information is available online. Numerous in-depth titles can be found on the academic market; for a start, see articles in the journal *Études/Inuit/Studies*.

2. The two quotations differentiate between Greenlanders (the Norse settlers) and the Skrælings (the Kalaallit).

3. Besides an unlikely war hypothesis (the Inuit attacked and eliminated the Norse), the main theories set forth regarding the abandonment of settlements are climatic changes (the Little Ice Age) making the region unfavorable for farming and the discontinuation of the trade and administrative connections with Norway about 1370 (Jørgensen et al. 2012; Arneborg et al. 2012).

4. Discussed at length in "Holdningsændringer," *Fortolkningsmuligheder*, Sonne (2011), linked to Sonne (2005): http://sonne.arktiskleksikon.dk/index.php?id=50/Fortolkningsmuligheder_basen.pdf/.

for political reasons several times in order to promote the achievement of rights of autonomy. The first political party of 1963, the Inuit Party, did not succeed. But the term still makes sense in the name of the radical political party known since 1976 as Inuit Ataqatigiit, in the Inuit Circumpolar Council (ICC), and in ongoing discussions of identity that take place on the internet. Some Inuit advocates also prefer Nunarput, which means "our land" and is the name of the national anthem,[5] to the formal name Kalaallit Nunaat, "the land of the Greenlanders." From their perspective, Inuit signifies traditional self-sufficiency while Kalaallit implies dependence on the Qallunaat (Danes/Europeans).

As I am not bound to the ethnopolitical issue of identity, I shall use the Western term "Greenlanders" instead of Kalaallit or Inuit. By "Inuit," I refer to the prehistorical Thule culture people including their present descendants in Canada and North Alaska. By "Inuit/Yupiit," I refer to Greenlanders, Inuit and Yupiit alike. For dialectal-historical reasons,[6] within Greenland I distinguish between the following populations: the Inughuit or Polar Inuit of Avanersuaq; the Northwest Greenlanders of the Upernavik region; the West Greenlanders; the Southwest Greenlanders (Nuuk-Nanortalik); the Southerners (Qavat or Qavanngarnisat) of the Nanortalik–Cape Farewell region; the Southeast Greenlanders south of Ammassalik (depopulated by 1900); and the East Greenlanders of the Ammassalik region.[7] The East Greenlanders of Ittoqqortoormiit/Scoresbysund, which was established in 1925 north of Ammassalik/Tasiilaq, are rarely mentioned due to a minimal number of relevant sources.

"Traditional" and "Static" versus Movement and Development: Precolonial and Early Colonial History of the Greenland Inuit

Since I find the adjectives "precontact" and "precolonial" clumsy, I often resort to the much-debated term "traditional" to refer to precontact ways of thinking, such as idioms reflected in statements and stories. The concept came under discussion in Hobsbawm and Ranger's introduction to their book *Invention of Tradition* (1963). As the term "traditional" fell into disrepute, it became necessary for scholars to define that term if they used it (e.g., Brimnes 2004).[8] Several definitions appeared until

5. In 1916, the anthem "*Nunarput utoqqarsuanngoravit*" ("Our Country, Which Has Become So Old"), with lyrics by Henrik Lund and music by Jonathan Petersen, was officially adopted. For an English translation, see Wikipedia: http://en.wikipedia.org/wiki/Henrik_Lund#National_anthem, accessed 6 June 2013.

6. The Inughuit arrived from Canada during the 18th century into the apparently depopulated Avanersuaq (see p. 22); the Northwest Greenlanders of the Upernavik district emigrated from Avanersuaq during the 15th century and speak the so-called "i-dialect" similar to the East and Southern Greenlanders. The Southwest Greenlanders received a great number of southerners, who left the southeast coast vacant during the first two centuries of colonization. They joined the Moravian missions at Nuuk and along the southwest coast. Their descendants told H. J. Rink the majority of his collection of stories about 1860.

7. The self-appellation of the polar Inuit is Inughuit ("fine Inuit"): *-huit*, pl. of *-huaq*, "big," apparently in a self-glorifying sense; but in this context *-huaq* means "fine" as in the answer to "How are you?": "I am fine, thank you" (Qaavigaq & Diklev 2000). Inughuit is still the official name of the Inuit people in Avanersuaq, but it has to some degree lost its former ethnopolitical appeal of the 1970s (Hastrup 2015: 8, 89).

8. The meaning of "traditional" varies with context. In Denmark these days, "traditional farming" means industrialized farming in contrast to ecological farming (reusing several old-fashioned methods). In his book about Saqqaq, the settlement considered by Saqqamiut and other Greenlanders to have remained a traditional hunting community, Jens Dahl points to this tradition as a "modernized" one in the sense that the Saqqamiut have been able to adopt technical innovations and use them for cultural development. In defining his use of "traditional," Dahl refers to those cultural elements that have relatively old historical links or are considered "original" cultural traits," such as the Danish flag and the Lutheran Church (Dahl 2000: 8f).

the term became relativized according to the ways people put traditions into use, inventing, reinventing, invoking, or simply unconsciously repeating them (e.g., Fienup-Riordan 1990). My usage of the term "traditional" refers to neither original nor static. Like other people, the Greenlanders took a considered, creative part in the ongoing changes, a fact to which both prehistory and their oral lore also give strong testimonies.

With regard to former connotations of traditional, stagnant, static, and original, the development and expansion of the Inuit Thule culture, the culture of the Greenlanders' Inuit ancestors, speaks to the contrary (e.g., Gulløv ed. 2004; Morrison 2001). Continuous development has been documented in Alaska from circa 3000 BC (Denbigh, Arctic Small Tool cultures) via the Old Bering Sea and Ipiutak cultures to 1000 AD (Punuk and Birnirk Thule cultures) (Gulløv 1999; Morrison 2001). Nor would "static" be a correct characterization of the immigrant Thule Inuit's subsequent adaptations to the climatic changes in Arctic Canada and Greenland from their arrival about 1200 AD and on. The Little Ice Age (peaking about 1650) caused a decline in Inuit whaling, the main source of subsistence for the immigrating Inuit. Whaling remained possible only along the middle part of the west coast (McGhee 1984; Birket-Smith 1959; Gulløv 1997) and to a minimal degree in East Greenland.[9] The impossibility of whaling in South Greenland created a dependency on the baleen used for deep-sea fishing rods because halibut was the main resource in that region. Travels thus became urgent to whaling grounds at Amerloq (close to Sisimiut) and Disko Bay. Similarly, soapstone deposits for lamps and pots were limited to a few areas; caribou were not equally accessible everywhere (Gulløv 1986a; 1987), and neither were beluga, lumpsucker, guillemots, or halibut. The animals' seasonal arrivals in big numbers at certain limited locales drew people from near and far. Consequently, the Greenlanders were connected in a long line of places of assembly arranged like a string of pearls, which grew in importance with the annual visits of European skipper merchants in the 17th century and whalers in the 18th century. These travels to places of assembly led to intermarriages across territorial boundaries and long-distance partnerships. All in all, the term "static" would not suit the cultural changes and movements of the "traditional" Greenlanders.

Changes brought about by trade and mission can be followed as soon as written sources are at hand. The European skippers and whalers, Dutch in particular, arrived every summer, caught whales, traded with the West Greenlanders, and returned in autumn.

This traffic was a main reason why Danish colonization, from its onset in 1721, immediately met with economic difficulties. The commodities offered by the Danes could not compete, and since the trade was supposed to finance missionary activity, the entire project was on the verge of being abandoned. Missionary Hans Egede petitioned the king of Denmark, which brought about a change in politics, and gradually, from 1734 to 1797, colonies were established along the entire west coast.

The competition in trade and whaling came to a halt in 1777, when the Dutch whalers suffered a devastating shipwreck on their way home. After that, the monopoly enjoyed by Den Kongelige Grønlandske Handel (KGH, the Royal Greenland Trading Department) prevented unlicensed foreign entrepreneurs from settling or participating in Greenlandic production and trade until 1953, when Greenland was opened up by law. From 1810 to the end of the Napoleonic wars in 1814,

9. Exactly when the Ammassalimmiut stopped whaling remains an open question insofar as dead whales intermittently hit their coasts during the 17th-century Dutch whaling in the Greenland Sea off the east coast. Some East Greenlanders traded baleen to the southerners in 1726 (H. Egede 1925: 109; 1971, 1: 240).

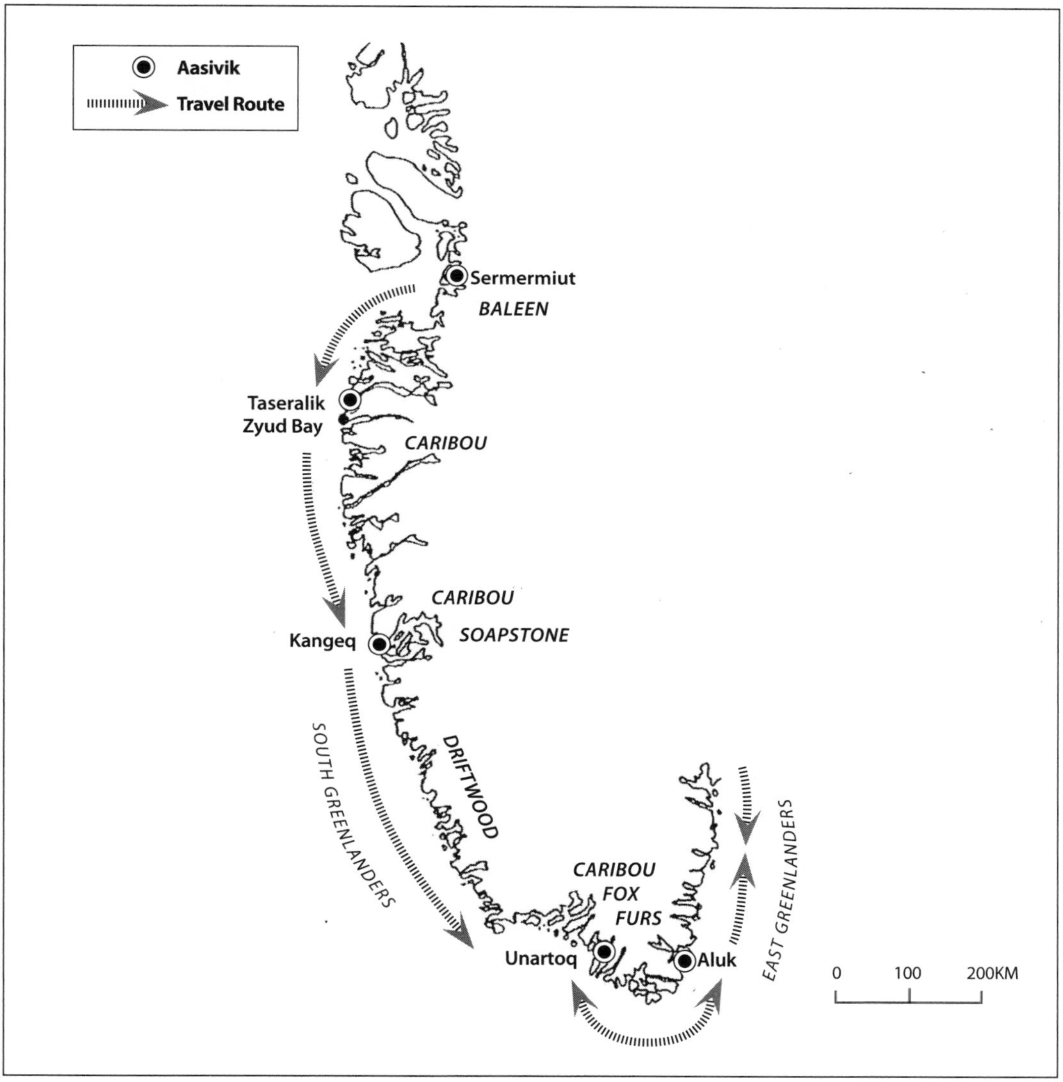

Fig. 3. Pre- and early colonial trade routes and goods exchanged after ca. 1650 AD. *Gulløv (1997: 406), courtesy of H. C. Gulløv. Redrawn for print by Lisa Devenish.*

however, Greenland and the Faroe Islands came under the patronage of Great Britain. Supplies were to pass via Leith, and British whalers, who hunted off the Greenland west coast, apparently continued to do so annually right into the 20th century. Individual Greenlanders' contacts and trade with these whalers are well documented, as are larger-scale festive summertime gatherings (e.g., Sonne 2005: ID 443, 869, 1897, 1952, 1953; Gad 1984: 202; Giescke 1910). Indeed, *kalattuut*—quick hybrids of British dances—have survived as a vivid symbol of Greenlandic legacy and identity. Otherwise, the Danes (and, until the 1814 treaty of Kiel, also Norwegians) were the only foreigners to impact Greenlandic views and ways of life—and they did so thoroughly.[10]

At first, Hans Egede, who led the colonization efforts, planned to convert the remaining Norse settlers from popish Catholicism to Danish Lutheranism. However, he met with no Norse, only pagan Inuit, upon whom he turned his zeal. In compliance with Luther's ideas, the Lutheran church demanded literacy as a ticket to baptism. The language had to be Greenlandic, which Hans Egede never came to master, but after a couple of years he managed to convert the main articles of faith into some intelligible written Greenlandic (H. Egede 1925: 132–42). His son Poul, who was 12 in 1721, became eloquent and helpful. By 1800 the majority of Southwestern and Western Greenlanders could read, and some could write.

Hans Egede first met with strong opposition from the Greenlanders, mostly from men and shamans, but after a decade he also faced competition from the German Moravians. These nonacademic craftsmen got royal permission to assist Hans Egede in 1733, but the intended cooperation ended in bitter strife on theological matters. On their side, the Moravians also learned and used Greenlandic and taught literacy. They attracted predominantly Southerners to their station Noorliit at Nuuk, first those who passed by on their travels to the whaling grounds and later, when the region became largely depopulated by a 1733–34 smallpox epidemic, a good number of immigrant families. The island of Kangeq, off Nuuk, also became predominantly populated by Southerners. The Moravians expanded southward with additional stations (Akunnat/Lichtenau in 1758; Alluitsoq/Lichtenfels in 1774) right on to Cape Farewell (Friedrichsthal/Narsaq Kujalleq/Narssarmijit in 1824), and in 1861 and 1864 they added two annexes, one at Uummannaq in the eastern interior of the Nuuk fjords an one at Illorpaat (not marked on fig. 4) north of Narsaq Kujalleq/Narssarmijit, respectively.

As Danish colonization extended into settled trading posts, travel between neighboring colonies declined, whereas outlying posts remained attractive to those without such opportunities. Depopulation of the southeast coast, starting in the 18th century and completed in the year 1900, was the most impressive migration. Similarly, after the repopulation of Avanersuaq in the 18th century by the Inughuit (Polar Inuit), they received a few families originating from Southeast Baffin Island in 1863.

Colonization of East Greenland and Avanersuaq in the far north lagged behind until 1894 and 1910, respectively.

Movements from East to South and Southwest Greenland left the Ammassalimmiut isolated from their former Southeast Greenlandic trading partners and waiting for a trading station to be

10. The *Instruks* (Instruction) of 1782 only set rules for the KGH staff and their relations with Greenlanders, and introduced fixed prices. Nonetheless, personal relations had an influence: The majority of Danish and Norwegian (Norway was part of the Danish kingdom until 1814) employees learned to speak Greenlandic, and those who got permission to marry Greenlandic women then had to stay in Greenland for the rest of their lives. (See Seiding [n.p. forthcoming] for a PhD dissertation on this subject.) Their children were predominantly taught and employed by KGH.

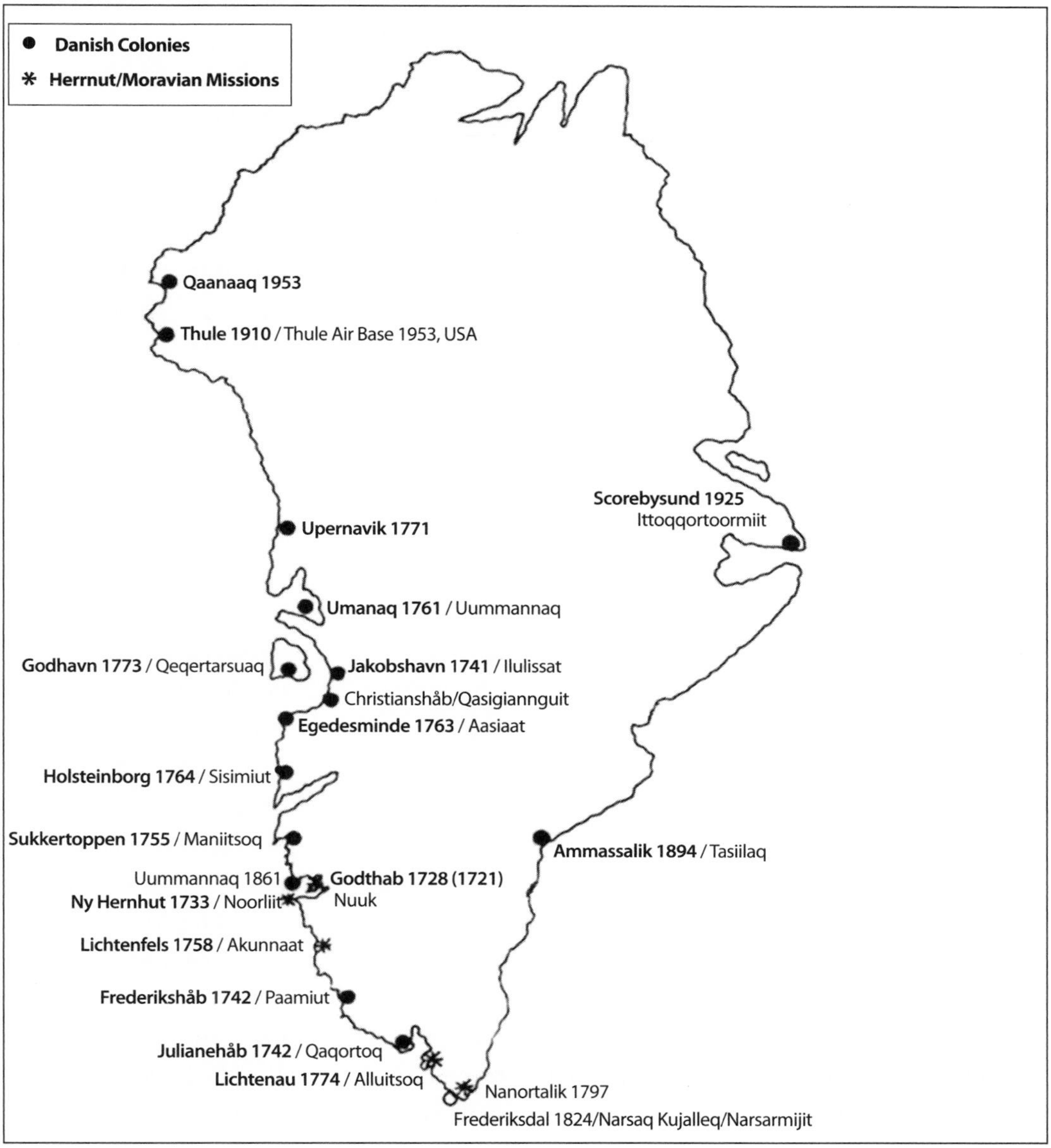

Fig. 4. Colonies and Moravian missions. The Danish missions were part of the colonies. The Inughuit/Polar Inuit of the Thule settlement were relocated to Qaanaaq in 1953 due to the establishment of the US Thule Air Base. *Lidegaard (1991: 105 with additions by BS). Redrawn for print by Lisa Devenish.*

established. They were promised one in the near future when visited in 1884–85 by Gustav Holm's Konebådsekspedition (Women's Boat Expedition). But the promise was not immediately fulfilled. In the meantime, the Ammassalik region's population was reduced by nearly one-third (from 413 to 294 persons) in 1892. The decline has been interpreted in various ways, but a complete repopulation enumerated in 1896 points to the attraction exerted by the eventual establishment of the trading station in 1894.[11] The second missionary to Ammassalik, the West Greenlander catechist Christian Rosing, was highly effective. He arrived in 1904, and he baptized the last pagan East Greenlander in 1921.

The Polar Inuit of Avanersuaq had been offered Western commodities in trade by the explorer Robert Peary, who from 1891 time and again went in search of the North Pole. In 1909, when he claimed to have finally reached it, he stopped his expeditions north and also ceased trade with the Polar Inuit. By that point the Danish government was reluctant to colonize the region, so first Ludvig Mylius-Erichsen, leader of the 1902–4 Literary Expedition, and after his death his traveling companion, Knud Rasmussen, took the initiative (Michelsen 2014). He raised the money and established a mission in 1909 and a trade station in 1910. In 1937, four years after Rasmussen's death, the Danish state eventually took over.

In the evaluation of the sources below, as well as throughout the book, I will add several details will to this short outline of Greenland prehistory and colonial history.

Worldview and Method

In my attempt to relate precolonial Greenlandic ideas about their way of life and its conditions to the cosmologies of the other Inuit and the Yupiit, I use as my point of departure the extensive and fairly recent spread of the Inuit Thule culture to the entire area. I look for orientation in space, in time reckoning, for meanings of rituals, myths, stories, key words, symbols, and body analogies. And I look for changes—"remakings of cosmologies" (Barth)—in treating my selected issues.

"Worldview" has long been in dispute as an anthropological term along with the related "folk models" and "cultural models." Half a century ago, Ong strongly advocated the thesis that people of oral cultures conceived of the world "as something dynamic and relatively unpredictable, an event-world rather than an object-world, highly personal, overtly polemic, fostering sound-oriented traditionalist personality structures." Worldviews are thus produced exclusively by literate cultures (Ong 1969: 634; 1982). Boyer partly follows suit, attacking the anthropological (mis)conviction that repetitive behavior (religious rituals in particular) presupposes static traditions based on a coherent worldview. Rejecting the descriptor "static, Boyer admits that a worldview may exist but not as the base for people's communication. Instead, people think using concrete situations, not by employing general abstractions or symbols. Rituals are repeated not in order to uphold ideas but because precise repetitions are considered decisive (our ancestors told us to do so; we always did it that way). In every-

11. The clergymen said it was because blood feuds were about to annihilate the population. They thus interpreted the introduction of Christianity as the event that saved the people from obliteration (e.g., Sonne 1982b). Gessain, followed by Robert-Lamblin, considered that the deep impression made by the trade goods brought by the Konebådsekspedition caused a mass migration to the trading post in South Greenland, Pamialluk. But epidemics in the south also took their toll (Gessain 1975b: 129f; Gessain & Robert-Lamblin 1974; Robert-Lamblin 1986: 11–12). In objection, Robert Petersen, looking into some of the same archives, concludes that very few Ammassalimmiut families went that far. The majority remained on the east coast, and some wintered at the places left vacant by the Southeast Greenlanders, and then returned with the good news about the trading station of 1894 (R. Petersen n.p.: 152–54).

day communication, people exchange not ideas but events, which can narrate a myth or elicit ritual guidelines. However, nobody interprets the myth or explains why the ritual should follow those lines. The sequence of ritual events is remembered, and in case anybody should cherish lofty ideas about the aim of the ritual—for example, that the knowledge conferred in puberty rites is comprehended by the young—the discrepancy between ideology and practice is astounding (Boyer 1990).

Obviously, both Ong and Boyer are right in rejecting the existence of a conscious, coherent worldview in oral or small-scale (and by most people in large-scale) societies. The unconscious worldview that Boyer grants such illiterates must be based, he maintains, on common practice following certain grammatical and syntactic rules like those of a language. Analyzing practice, the most salient verbal and bodily acts, as both stereotypes and in contexts, must be the method of coming to know that worldview (Boyer 1990). Using that method on the implicit Greenlandic worldview would necessitate conducting fieldwork in the past.

Keesing's view is less rigid. Rather than favoring noncontradictory "models" he sees a folk model "as representing a set of opening strategies for using cultural knowledge in the world; they comprise sets of shortcuts, idealizations, and simplifying paradigms that work just well enough yet need not fit together without contradiction into global systems of coherent knowledge." These sets can hardly be considered constituents for cultural knowledge; rather, they appear only as its surface manifestations. On the other hand, Keesing does not deny people the drive and tendency to consider things and think through rules, although such rules may be the outcome of the conversations between informant and anthropologist (Keesing 1987).

Tim Ingold, whose goal is to combine anthropology with biology, accepts neither rules nor the term "worldview" in reference to small-scale, oral societies like premodern hunter-gatherers. They do not make a view of the world but take up a view *in* it. They relate to space from the inside as if existing within a sphere, not from the outside as if looking upon a globe. Their "life-world," Ingold's preferred term, is not a matter of transmitted constructions. It is not like a cognitive schema of collective representations ordering an otherwise chaotic mess of perceptions, transmitted through the generations and available for application independently of one's bodily activity in the world. It is not a "worldview" (Ingold 2000: 225). By contrast, "life-world" is a matter of engagement in the environment, where people "dwell," sense, and act in relationships with its other beings, humans and nonhumans alike. They achieve their skills, capabilities, and knowledge in learning by doing, imitating the movements of those who know how. Through coming to know by body-mind, they "grow" their skills. People "grow" with one another, continuously, from infancy right into very old age. Perception, activity, bodily movement (including those of one's eyes in seeing), awareness, the inseparability of mind and body: those are the key words of Ingold's theory of agency-in-the-world. He quotes Bourdieu, of course, whose *habitus*, the embodied dispositions and knowledge of one's society's way of life, can be likened to the "skills" of Ingold. Yet Ingold further includes the skilled knowledge of one's whole environment, which is comprised of land, tasks, and relationships. Knowledge, he stresses, is gained through revelation—that is, experientially, for example by staying aware of any movement and change in one's environment. This is in contrast to gaining knowledge through the control over nature that is sought and apparently accomplished by modern Western reason and technology.

Concerning method, the common critique has it that Bourdieu failed to translate his theory of practice into operative variables. The same is noted by Ingold about the phenomenologists on whom he relies, Merleau-Ponty in particular (Ingold 2000: 171). So, what are we to do then, unable as we are to do fieldwork in the past and having to rely upon written statements and stories in our attempt at coming to know or becoming skilled in the oral life-world of the Greenlanders? Ingold himself actually accepts the term "worldview" in one particular case and the neighboring term "cosmology" in some others. "Worldview" passes unquestioned in his quotation of Hallowell's attempt at understanding the Ojibwa attributes of personhood: "[They] form part of a comprehensive worldview that is projected onto reality-as-we-know-it. His [Hallowell's] concern is to understand the worldview, not the fundamental nature of reality" (95). This is exactly my concern with regard to the premodern Greenlanders. Furthermore, "cosmology" carries a positive value in the following declarations with which I agree: "Traditional cosmology places the person at the centre of an ordered universe of meaningful relations... [it serves] as a foundation for proper conduct towards the environment" (216); "pre-modern and non-Western cosmologies are anthropocentric in the strict sense of placing the human beings at the hub of a dwelt-in world, a centre of embodied awareness that reaches out, through the activity of the senses, into its surroundings" (218). Still, because (?) the multiple meanings of *sila*—namely world, space (the outside), weather, reason, and its "way," *silap ingerlasia*—point to "view" more than to scientific logic, I prefer "worldview" to a term ending in -logy, such as cosmology. However, in compliance with academics, I use the adjectival form, cosmological.

"Culture" is another term that suffers a sorry fate in Ingold's effort to combine biology with anthropology and mind with body and to break down the dichotomy between subject and object. Ingold declares that cultural constructions are prefabricated by the anthropologists, who then attribute them to "their" objects of research. In treating metaphors and symbols I shall drop the anchor into tangible contexts and strictly follow their associations of practical logic; I will remain on earth but—against Ingold—I will, when flying with the shaman, have to ascend from the dwelt-in hub and adopt the imagined bird's-eye perspective bestowed on both him and the *inua* (the being, person, owner, indweller) of the moon (hereafter Moon) in many stories. This perspective must be rooted in the views gained from the local lookout and from climbing the mountains in one's own environment.

Recent Research on Inuit Worldviews, Methods, and Applicability

For good reason, Ingold draws heavily on Ann Fienup-Riordan's analysis of the Southwest Alaska Yup'ik cosmology. Apparently, however, these Yupiit do not seem to agree with his theory of living-in-the-world but rather with the possibility to "think out rules" allowed by Keesing. Having successfully observed and analyzed the structures of practice within the seal parties of the Nelson Islanders in particular, Fienup-Riordan continued asking about practice when she got the job of interviewing the elders about the (traditional) ways of their parents and grandparents: "You *kass'at* [White people] always want to know about the things we do, but it is the rules that are important" (Fienup-Riordan 1994: xiii). The superior rule, which Fienup-Riordan was taught time and again, both explicitly and through metaphors, concerned passages being opened and closed in the boundaries between the two worlds: those of humans and nonhumans (6f). Eventually, paying heed to this discourse and thus in consonance with more recent anthropology, Fienup-Riordan analyzed practice accordingly. Following that train of thought, all sorts of descriptions and statements made sense on topics like upbringing, rites of passage, the treatment of illness, the ceremonies. Taken together they showed a coherent world with an extensive potential for explaining most occurrences in life. This was a convincing version of the Yup'ik worldview but hardly the only possible one that could be rendered probable, as Fienup-Riordan admits.

The same conscious, superior rule cannot be pursued in the Greenlandic sources. They do mention boundaries set by, or to be overcome by, travelers between this and the "Other World" that similarly show a clear division between humans and nonhumans. Devices for opening up or overcoming boundaries, as well as involuntarily setting individual new ones, will be discussed in chapter 6, "Conclusion." However, other oppositions are also at play, and additional ideas and metaphors have been shown to be more promising in outlining aspects of the Greenlanders' worldview. One such aspect is "balance," although not every relevant issue can be subsumed under this concept. So, neither a complete structure like the one that Fienup-Riordan has described, nor the following system proposed by Saladin d'Anglure, have been achieved with regard to the Greenlandic early colonial worldview.

Academic discussions about the relevance of worldviews in small-scale oral societies apparently never bothered the French anthropologist Saladin d'Anglure. Taking as his point of departure the structuralism of Lévi-Strauss and a lifetime of fieldwork in Arctic Canada, Saladin d'Anglure has explored the traditional world of the Inuit and come up with an impressive result: a schematic outline of Inuit orientation in space and time. It combines the annual round with the life cycles according to the most salient binary oppositions in ritual and myth. Three levels are interconnected by analogy with the fetus in its mother's womb at the center on the lowest level, the igloo (snow house) on the next, earthly level, and the space beneath the heavenly vault on the third. The annual round of light and darkness, the temporal coming and going of game animals, the prevailing winds that are opposed by gender-associated corners of the world, the imagined worlds above and below the one in the middle—all fit within a space-time outline that reflects the ongoing transformations between the binary oppositions of light and darkness, heat and cold, land and sea, and gender symbolism. Naturally, this outline is not a "universal," considering the distinct Arctic conditions of that world; although "house = visible space" is common to most cultures, the fetus in its womb is not a worldwide analogy.[12] The notion that the fetus receives its skeletal bones from its father's semen, its blood from its mother, and its flesh from the animals eaten by both parents is probably also culture-specific (Saladin d'Anglure 1986).

Saladin d'Anglure's outline is inspiring for my analysis insofar as similar oppositions are at work in Greenlandic myth, ritual, and orientation. I do make use of several of its points, especially those that seem to throw new light on otherwise obscure statements and stories. The center of the outline, the fetus in its womb, is particularly revealing with regard to my far-reaching analysis of a certain initiation of East Greenland shamans, the *angakkut puullit.* But otherwise the Greenlandic sources, belonging to highly differing historical periods as they do, must be analyzed in their historical contexts of transformation. In that regard, J. G. Oosten's (1945–2016) method comes closer to the one I use.

Starting out with firm structuralist conviction that a worldview is based on an ideological theory (Oosten 1976), Oosten moved away from this belief and on to employing a method including changes over time and covering an extended ethnographic field. Focusing on variations and transformations, he still looks in part for binary oppositions, especially their mediating agencies. The

12. But, for example, the innermost holy room of an Indian temple is sometimes called the mother's womb (Sand 2005).

method, called anthropological field studies (AFS), was developed at the University of Leiden and was originally inspired by Marcel Mauss's way of eliciting the seasonal variations present within the common Inuit and Yupiit sociocultural heritage. The two main features of this shared heritage were those of language and of periods of assembly that intensified ritual life (in contrast to times of dispersal into smaller groups with hardly any religious manifestations at all). Despite flaws in empiricism due to limited sources at that date, Mauss's idea of focusing on variations and not on identical "traits" within a cultural field (not to be confused with Bourdieu's "field") has proved fruitful by the Leiden anthropologists in analyzing Indonesian cultures. Oosten uses the method on the Inuit field (e.g., Oosten 2006), covering related people from Chukotka to East Greenland and from the Arctic to the Subarctic in Alaska, Canada, and Greenland.

Apart from my particular interest in metaphors, symbols, differences in social organization, and historical issues, agreements between the AFS method and my own (throughout some decades) are striking. Whenever relevant I similarly look for variations all over the Inuit/Yupiit field, and basically, I presuppose that "inside the region the data become mutually interpretative" (Oosten 2006). Relationship in language and prehistory defines the Inuit/Yupiit area as a "field." This means that practices, metaphorical references, motifs, and so on that are found among related groups widely distributed over time and space represent a common substratum. By "basically" I make a reservation, because the data do not always appear on the same level of explicitness. In many cases they become mutually interpretative only in the way that explicit connotations or meanings in one locale may offer a key to understanding implicit connotations in another. In other words, variation provides a field of data from which, by inference, you can tease out underlying principles. Parallels in themes appear in multiple contexts that inspire interpretations with reference to what else you know about the society, environment, and culture in question. Take for instance this clear statement among the Polar Inuit that observing the taboos[13] keeps the threatening powers of the world in balance and then the examples they offer of the effects of breaking them: a tsunami may swallow up the houses or an avalanche bury the entire settlement. I see overbalance one or the opposite way implied in these movements. Restoring the balance means that the effect of the breaks must be neutralized. In many other Inuit and Yupiit groups, where the rationale may be less explicitly stated, this was brought about by public confession, a ritual frequently led by a shaman. In South Baffin Island, the confessional ritual was held at the equinoxes, led by a shaman representing a raven figure. The confessions were communicated to the Sea Woman (*Nuliayuk* or *Sedna* or *Senna*, "the one down there in front") and were meant to clean the land of hindrances for the coming season's hunt. Curiously, these points in time, the equinoxes, coincide with the highest tides of the year, symbolized by these Inuit with strong movements: "the earth made a somersault." In widely dispersed locales of the Inuit/Yupiit field, somersaults imply renewal of life and good hunting. And since the raven is generally counted as a master of somersaulting, I venture to draw a parallel in meaning between the raven figure's renewal of the land by leading the confessions, the

13. The word "taboo" has become taboo in academic circles (e.g., Steiner 1967). Oosten prefers "injunctions"; Fienup-Riordan's "prescriptions" and "proscriptions" are preferable insofar as the unwritten "rules" were of both kinds, "do nots" and "dos." Applied to an oral culture, however, "-scriptions" feel odd, for which reason I frequently relapse to using taboo in the ordinary meaning of "do nots."

turning of the earth at high tides, and the havoc the breaks will cause by tipping the balance of the world, one way or another, as stated by the Polar Inuit.

Another parallel can be drawn in regard to variants of cleaning practices: the ritual killing of Sea Woman, done by a shaman in South Baffin Island as a prelude to the winter festival, was explicitly said to clean her and renew her life—that is, implicitly, with the same effect as the shaman's ritual acts of fighting and combing her hair in West Greenland. The wished-for outcome in Baffin Island was the calming of storms for a solid ice cover of the sea to permit hunting at breathing holes, whereas in West Greenland it was hoped that a storm would rise to break up the ice, thereby giving way to the spring hunt at sea. These removals of disturbing taboo breaks vary and do not have identical effects. But the effect is to balance the powers of *sila*, which favors a life-saving hunt.

Oosten puts variation in front. Generalizations and basic ideas, the desired outcome of the comparative method, are of secondary importance. True, because it demands identity of compared phenomena. But by focusing on variation, I contend, you may arrive at some basic idea anyhow, like the one above of breaks that disturb the balance of the world and demand ritual restoration. A basic idea may also serve as a rewarding tool for analysis of stories, rituals, sayings, etc. that have the object of your investigation in common. In Oosten and Laugrand's own illuminating article investigating the connotations of Raven among the Canadian Inuit, the title of the article offers one (or perhaps the basic) idea of that bird: "The bringer of light." They conclude the analysis with an outline of the ontological structures at work (Oosten & Laugrand 2006). When I looked to Raven and ravens in the Greenlandic sources, the "bringer of light" and other connotations were of immediate use. And some more could be added. Nor did structures (explicated in the end) guide my analysis, but they showed an additional outside/inside dimension to the structures pointed out by Oosten and Laugrand. So, connotations in their contexts first, structures later. On the other hand, structures *may* help support hypothetical findings. Thus, the structural axes of Inuit/Yupiit orientation of the entire "field," as uncovered by linguist Michael Fortescue (1988), are very helpful analytical tools in treating stories and statements about movements over land and at sea.

I look for manifold objects for variations: variation in ritual and myth; symbolic meanings of stars; ideas about the powers of land and sea, heaven and underworld; connotations of animals and plants, of life essences and of manufactured objects and ritual paraphernalia. Movements and body movements in particular are of central concern in tracing the connotations of balance, which often simultaneously express mental states. Comparisons of story variants with several episodes in common demand analysis in depth because, despite similarities in course of events, the agendas may vary and thus throw light on variations in meanings of episodes. With regard to selected key words like *pooq* (bag) and *sila* (air, world, reason, weather, outdoors), their meanings are restricted in *taartaq* (mother) and *aniivik* (exit place), respectively, whereas in daily speech they are both numerous and changing with context.

Regrettably, I do not have sufficient knowledge of Greenlandic to decipher every possible meaning in daily use. Also, some meanings have either fallen into oblivion or been changed at present. Thus, when Karen Langgård asked her students and friends at Ilisimatusarfik at Nuuk about meanings of *pooq*, she received only a single extraordinary one: a condom. As will be clear from analysis in chapter 5, the main connotation of a protective bag is still valid (Sonne 2017). On the other hand, the paradoxical idea of protection against both death (HIV) and birth (pregnancy) is modern not only because HIV is new but because pregnancy used to be desired. In fine consonance with tradition, however, one of my students, Eleonora Jacobsen, a Southerner, used *pooq* to mean a pregnant woman, a usage derived from the pre-Christian spirit language (*taartaq*).

The equally polysemous *sila*, a root of countless words, has retained its meanings of outdoors, reason, weather, and world. At present, my proposed additional meaning of balance (e.g., Sonne 1984) is a common association that reflects a cosmological order. But today *sila* rarely calls to mind one of its personifications, the androgynous figure of *Nalikkatteeq* ("Big Crotch"). Nevertheless, this figure still provokes artists who look to tradition for inspiration. Thus, a drawing of the world, *silarsuaq*, combines heaven, earth, sea, and underground in an annual circle, and it has Raven, signifying *sila* as balance, occupy spring and *Nalikkatteeq* as autumn (Lauridsen 2015). I have no answer to the placing of *Nalikkatteeq*.

Since stories constitute a major part of my sources, it would seem appropriate to use methods of interpretation deriving from theories of performance. They consider relations between storyteller and audience, the teller's intentions, the reactions of the listeners, the competence in communicating the intended message of the story in consonance with the "culture" of audience, etc.[14] "My" stories are all written text that allow for next to no application of these theories. In order to demonstrate their limited relevance, let me apply the model of SPEAKING concerning the "speech act" as proposed by Dell Hymes (1974). It raises more questions than can be answered:

(S) Setting and scene: Most rewarding in this regard is the setting of stories recounted in diaries, where the occasion for telling a story is described as also the points of the following conversation between teller and collector. Otherwise the scene is limited to either the teller writing down his/her own story in the family's common room, or to teller and collector alone in the same place or in the temporary house of the collector, the school, or some quiet room at the station.

(P) Participants: On rare occasions when listeners are present, their reactions are barely noted. The slow dictation and repetitions of sentences demanded of a collector writing down the story is too boring. If the story is told fluently and in company, the collector resorts to taking notes that will be filled out later. Listeners' comments are rarely encountered in the manuscripts. If the recording was done by electronic device, listeners were generally unwanted.[15] So, since no reaction from a possible audience is on record, the listeners' differing understandings of a story cannot be studied (e.g., Nayani 1989: 90ff).

14. Narayan (1989) offers excellent examples and discussions of the storyteller Swamiji's variations of a story according to his intentions and interplay with his audience.

15. Holtved, Thalbitzer, and Jens Rosing collected sound recordings. Sandgreen destroyed his after publication (pers. comm.). Thalbitzer worked with his main informant, Missuarniannga, one-on-one (2014: 71f). His only reference to an audience mentions people's joy of listening to the phonograph outside the telling of stories and without further comments (124). Rasmussen stuck to handwriting, a slow procedure without listeners. Holtved had great problems with the techniques of recording in the utterly cold climate of Avernersuaq. "[T]he essential thing was, however, that the narrators should be quite unimpeded in their speech, and during the recording process they sometimes made quite a dramatic display as if telling their tales to a listening crowd, and this in spite of the fact that they did not like anyone but myself to be present at the proceeding. If there happened to be an audience, they immediately became shy, and here they seemed to respect each other's feelings. They quickly realized what it was all about, all the more as several of them, as time went on, had tried to perform" (Holtved 1951, I: 11). Jens Rosing does not mention any listeners in his publication of selected stories (1963).

(E) Ends: Sometimes the storyteller's goals are explicated or can be found out; other times they remain uncertain. One goal is to tell the story completely as heard from another person (some variation can be expected but is rarely checked). Another is merely to tell as much as one remembers, adding that others know the story better. The payment alone may be the teller's incentive; or perhaps to (unconsciously) gain respect from the collector or just brace oneself. The teller's positive/negative attitude to the collector's goal of knowledge, surmised cultural background, and personality may lead to omissions or, to the contrary, additions in order to explain assumed misunderstandings. Is the collector a catechist or a missionary, a Dane or a Greenlander, an old friend or a foreigner, open-minded or narrow-minded, trustworthy or suspicious? Another issue to consider could be the moral lesson to learn from a story, such as the "stalking with stories" among the Western Apache. Their elders would "attack" somebody's indecent behavior by telling a certain well-known story in public with the "target" present and left for herself to ponder (Basso 1990). This was apparently not common in Greenland. Several stories did of course implicate morals (see, e.g., Kaassassuk, pp. 97ff), but to my knowledge they were not told with similar intentions. Yet the so-called *ileqqorsuut*, songs about many topics that included reprimands against actual persons, were composed and sung into circulation to a point when the wrongdoer could not avoid realizing the hint (Robert Petersen pers. comm.). More direct moral lessons were "taught" through accusations of wrongdoings in song duels (see Kleivan 1971a and Rosing 1970).[16] One example is recorded of a sort of collective song duel between people of two locales, the baptized Qasigiannguimmiut and a large group of pagans visiting from the south.[17]

(A) Act sequence: Form and order of the event. See (S) and (E) above.

(K) Key and (I) Instrumentalities: Transmission of "tone, manner, or spirit" of the speech act, such as direct speech, is poorly communicated by dictating a story and better described by both electric recording and the writing down by the teller. Again, the outcome of the latter depends on the writer's competence in literacy varying from little more than oral sentences to the use of literary grammar, of the orthography introduced in 1860, and the ability to keep track of the unfolding of the story (Thisted 2006).[18]

(N) Norms: Social rules governing the event and the participants' actions and reaction. Stories were not individual or family property, but the teller could pay respect to the person from whom he heard his variant. No rules prevented a person from telling a story anytime, but storytelling with adult listeners usually took place in the evening, especially in winter. In this case the collector without an electronic device was, as mentioned above, obliged to make do with notetaking. He might do the filling in by memory or catch up on the story later without listeners. Sometimes the archival notes will tell the procedure.

(G) Genre: The common Inuit and Yup'ik distinction between *oqaluttuat* (old stories without known kin relations to its characters) and *oqalualaarutit* (legends and accounts) is used for categorizing stories in publications and sometimes also in handwritten collections. At present *aliortukkat*

16. E.g., http://www.kb.dk/e-mat/dod/115308011418.pdf. I have not studied the song duels and moral *ileqqorsuut* ("about custom") in depth. Some *ileqqorsuut* are about the King and Greenland, others are about more personal subjects, some of which are quite "juicy" (R. Petersen pers. comm.).

17. The visitors reproached the Qasigiannguimmiut for imitating the customs of the Qallunaat but were totally beaten and pursued far out on the ice with songs about the way they would go weeping to hell while the hosts themselves would go singing to heaven (N. Egede 1939: 195; 1971: 112).

18. Applying theories of orality versus literacy on every single story exceeds the scope of this publication.

(stories about experiences with ghosts, other beings, and inexplicable events) are still told among friends, on radio, and on TV. As examined by Thisted (1997), the West Greenlanders used to choose among a series of starting words in dating a story: *itsarsuaq* (a very, very long time ago); *itsaq* (a long time ago, or more precisely, as "the time when nobody was baptized, and the Qallunaat were still strangers, because the whalers were the only Qallunaat to be encountered"); *itsaalluarsimanngitsoq* (once in the not very old days, referring to the period of transition when some were baptized and others remained heathen); or, finally, *itsangajaq* and *itsarsuunngitsoq* (not that very long ago, referring to the Christian era). This refined chronology must have been an outcome of colonial time reckoning insofar as similar datings are absent from pre- and early colonial stories taken down in East Greenland and Avanersuaq. The affix *-goq* (it is told) is the most frequent starter no matter the type of a story (see search for archival references in Sonne 2005 by the words Berthelsen Ammassalik; Holtved 1951, I).

All in all: Performance theory is extremely interesting (e.g., Baumann and Briggs 1990), but apart from stray questions stirred by some of the authors in that field, its applicability is nil.

The Inuit/Yupiit Field: Pre- and Early Contact History[19]

As mentioned above, I also look for ethnohistorical aspects of the variations. They support analysis of changes in worldview and demand knowledge of the movements of prehistoric Thule culture. Transformations due to acculturative changes, be they the outcome of changing intertribal communication and/or colonial impacts, are part of my investigation as well. I consider differences between Greenlandic, Canadian, and Alaska Inuit/Yupiit in social organization, in resources available and used, and in marked documented changes in both trade and rituals of exchange (Burch 1988a; Sonne 1988a). Comparisons are supported by the expansions of the Thule culture to the entire Inuit/Yupiit field.

As far as archaeology goes, the Thule culture developed during the latter half of the first millennium AD through interaction between people on both sides of the Bering Strait and its islands. Improved means of transport and hunting on the open sea, decked-in kayaks, *umiat*, and collaboration in whaling yielded a surplus of meat for a growing number of dogs harnessed to bigger sledges. Starting in the 11th century, a warmer climate gave impetus to the expansions from North Alaska both south and east to every part of the Inuit/Yupiit world except the Aleuts.

In Alaska, south-going waves pushed the Yupiit south to Unalakleet (at Norton Sound), where their Yup'ik language merged with the Northwest Alaska Iñupiaq language. Embracing the Thule technology, the Yupiit south of Unalakleet pushed farther south and came to dominate the coastal stretches and lower runs of the rivers right on to the Pacific Rim except the Aleutian Islands. Some myths and perhaps ideas followed suit. In this regard, Fortescue et al.'s (1994; 2010) etymological Inuit/Yup'ik dictionary is very informative. Derivatives of proto-Inuit/Yup'ik word roots are listed region by region. Some turn out to be pan-Inuit/Yup'ik and thus most probably "old"; others are restricted to the Yup'ik languages, some to the Inuit dialects, and some to the Eastern Inuit (east of the MacKenzie River) exclusively.

Among the Thule extensions eastwards, which reached Greenland about 1200 AD, it's worth noting the pause in immigration that lasted from sometime in the 17th century until the arrival of the Polar Inuit in the 18th century. Until the colonization of Avanersuaq in 1910, very sporadic

19. For Greenland colonial history in detail until 1782, see Gad (1973–82).

contacts can be verified between the Polar Inuit and the Northwest Greenlanders, the earlier arrivals situated south of Melville Bay. Therefore, the cultural agreements shown in the sources between Greenlanders and the other Inuit and Yupiit in Canada and Alaska can be considered basically precolonial, whether recognizably transformed in their historical contexts or not.

Of further importance for comparison are two movements inside Greenland, one of some Baffin Islanders into Avanersuaq about 1860 and another of Southeast Greenlanders to South and Southwest Greenland in the 18th and 19th centuries. I shall go into details below.

Thule and Late Dorset

In Arctic Canada and Avanersuaq (but apparently not other parts of Greenland), some of the early Thule immigrants encountered the less mobile Dorset, a pre-Inuit culture developed in Canada from the same technological basis as the forerunner of the Thule culture in North Alaska. The forerunner, the Arctic Small Tool tradition, has been dated to about 3000 BC and has been excavated all over the Inuit/Yupiit region. Named Saqqaq in West Greenland and Independence in the uppermost north of Greenland, no visible development took place during the millennium of their stay until their disappearance from the scene (Grønnow 1991; 1994; 2017). Subsequently, stages of Dorset arrived from Canada into Avanersuaq. They spread, remained, and disappeared, leaving Greenland depopulated for about 500 years until the arrival of the Late Dorset in the 9th century from Arctic Canada to Avanersuaq. These Late Dorset, a thriving culture in Avanersuaq and Ellesmere Island, were probably engaged in trade with the widely traveled Norse at the arrival of the Thule culture people, the Inuit, in the 13th century (Appelt & Gulløv 2009; Appelt, Gulløv & Kapel 1998). One branch of Thule people remained in Avanersuaq and received cultural impacts from the Dorset. Later they expanded east along the north coast and then south along the east coast to Ammassalik. The west coast became populated by the so-called "pioneers," who seem to have traveled almost nonstop from Alaska to Avanersuaq and from there south along the west coast. They were most probably attracted to trade with the Norse, whose settlements they took over when the Norse left in the 14th and mid-15th centuries. The expansion continued around Cape Farewell right on to Ammassalik (see also fig. 2), where about 1600 the aforementioned Dorset-impacted immigrants arrived from the north. Back in Avanersuaq, life became intolerable with increasing cold. About 1700 the last (or most; see p. 22) inhabitants moved south across Melville Bay and settled in the Upernavik district (Northwest Greenland). This movement explains the curious correspondence in dialects between the Northwest and East Greenlanders as well as some cultural ideas.

After about 1650, the Southeast Greenlanders, attracted to possibilities of trade, began their new migrations "backwards" south and west around Cape Farewell into South Greenland. The last Southeast Greenland families arrived at Narsarmijiit/Friedrichstal in 1900 (Appelt & Gulløv 2009; Appelt, Gulløv & Kapel 1998; Gulløv 2012).[20] These movements explain the differences in Greenlandic dialects, namely the so-called u-dialect and i-dialect and some mixes.[21] These last emigrants left

20. According to Petersen (n.d.: 152–54), families of the Ammassalik region moved to vacant settlements until the establishment of the trading station at Tasiilaq in 1894 caused their return.

21. The u-dialect is the oldest and is closely related to that of the Alaska Iñupiat—i.e., the dialect of the "pioneers" and still the dialect of the mid-west coast. Kleinschmidt's Greenland orthography of 1860 reflects this dialect (1871). The younger i-dialect could be due to impact from Late Dorset (Gulløv 2012). It is spoken by the East Greenlanders and, overlaying the u-dialect, also by the SE Greenlanders (now the Southerners) and some of the southernmost SW Greenlanders. This mix is due to the movements of the SE Greenlanders to South and Southwest Greenland.

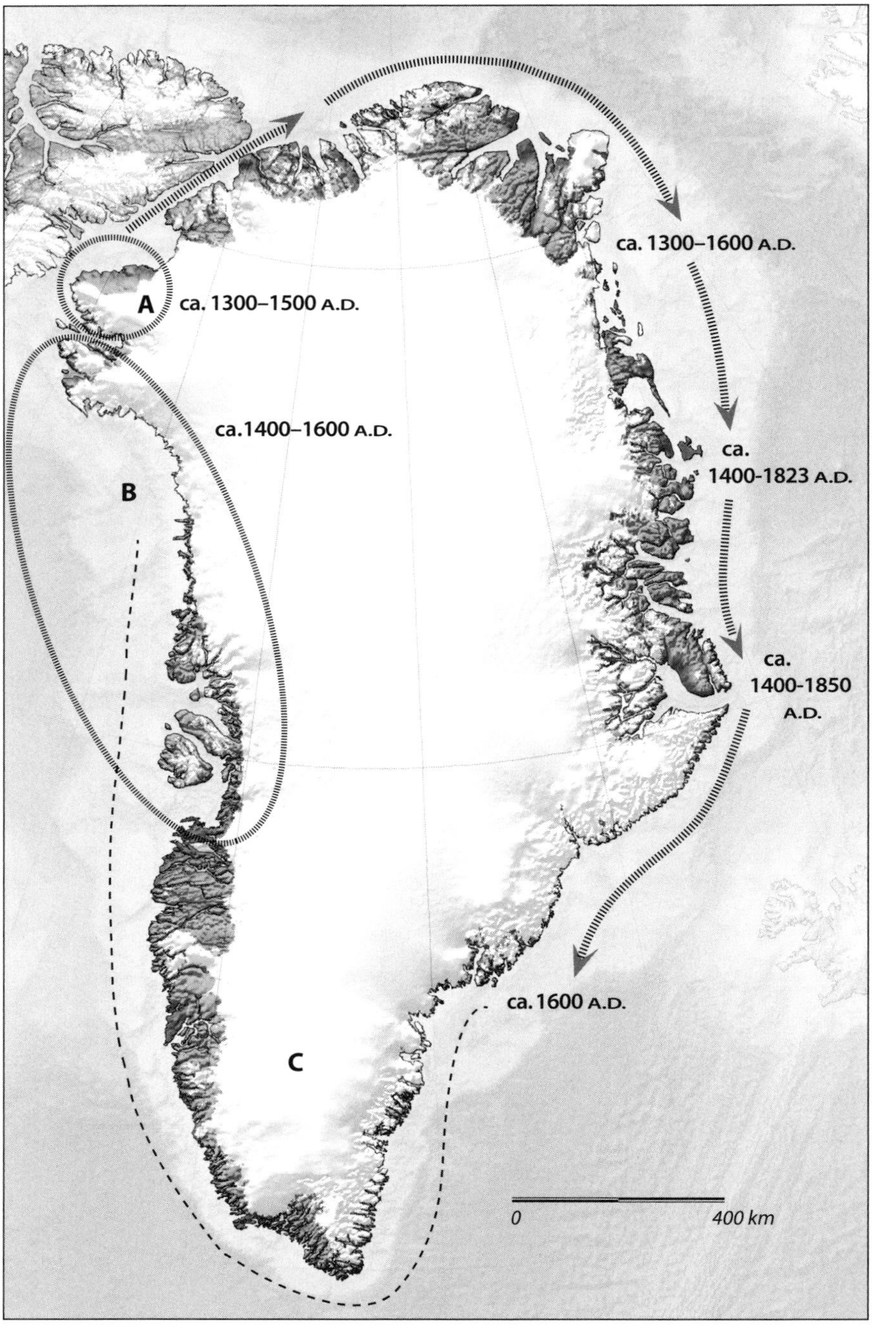

Fig. 5. The map shows the extensions of three archaeologically documented phases, A, B, and C of the Thule culture in Greenland between 1300 and 1600 AD. The arrows departing from A (in Avanersuaq) indicate the Inuit who, impacted by Late Dorset, moved north, east, and then south along the east coast. Their settlements existed for 400 years along the northeast coast. B indicates the southernmost extension of this Thule culture impacted by Late Dorset on the west coast. The same impact is found in Canada south to Baffin Island and around Fox Basin. C indicates the extension of the original Thule culture, the "pioneers" (see fig. 2). *Gulløv (2012: 140), courtesy of H.C. Gulløv. Redrawn for print by Lisa Devenish.*

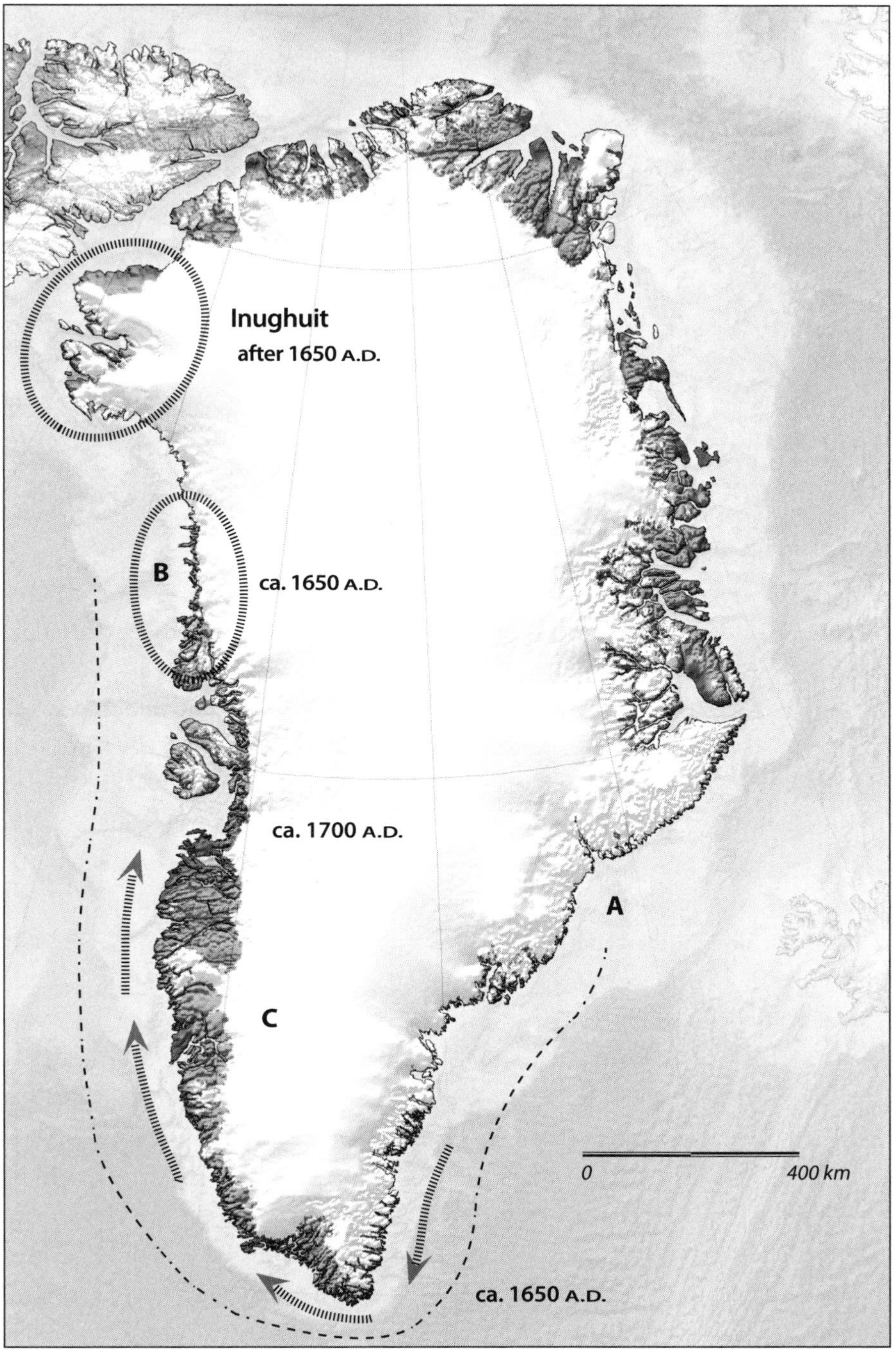

Fig. 6. Population movements from about 1650 AD. "A" indicates the continued extension of the Dorset-influenced Thule culture south along the east coast and its encounter with descendants of the Thule "pioneers" in the Ammassalik region. "B" (= B in fig. 5) Avanersuaq becomes depopulated, and the last emigrants settle in the Upernavik district south of the Melville Bay. About a century later, new immigrants to Avanersuaq, the Inughuit/ Polar Inuit, arrive from arctic Canada. The arrows of "C" indicate trading voyages up the west coast undertaken by the Southerners and some Southeast Greenlanders. *Gulløv (2012: 143), courtesy of H. C. Gulløv.Redrawn for print by Lisa Devenish.*

Avanersuaq empty until the arrival of the Inughuit sometime in the 18th century. This is how far the archaeologists and linguists have agreed until recently. New finds point to surviving groups (Hastrup 2015: 98, 423–25) whose descendants received immigrants from the Kitlinermiut/Copper Inuit area (Fortescue 1986).

Despite convincing impact from Late Dorset, speculation about meetings between the Thule culture immigrants and possible surviving pockets of Dorset people in Ammassalik proper remain only hypotheses. They are based on the impressive artistic skill displayed by some precolonial Ammassalimmiut (J. Meldgaard 1960: 31–32; J. Rosing 1963: 49).[22] The last Dorset of the Ammassalik area had been extinct for at least five centuries at the advent of the Inuit from the north.

Thus, any possible traces left by illiterate Dorset on the Thule worldview are, except from plausible dialectal evidence, difficult to take into account. Stories about Dorset people were transmitted in Greenland, and I shall treat them on par with stories about other fictive "Others" in their actual colonial contexts. Similarly, as mentioned above, probable changes in Inuit worldview due to encounters with the Norse will remain hypothetical.

Histories of Contact in Inuit/Yupiit Canada and Alaska

Western activities of any importance reached the Canadian Inuit first, beginning with sporadic trade from 1616 with the Hudson's Bay Company's annual supply ships passing through the Hudson Strait en route to York Factory at the bottom of James Bay (Ross 1975). Next, the establishment of the trading post at Churchill in 1718 involved Inuit as customers and middlemen to both Indians and other Inuit (Burch 1978). Euro-American whaling, however, made the greatest impact from 1860 to 1910, particularly on those Inuit living along the east and south coasts of Baffin Island and along the west coast of Hudson Bay. Cooperation in whaling, the possibility of jobs supplying the wintering crews with food (mostly caribou), the chance to develop trading relations, and the desire to participate in festive get-togethers attracted Inuit from near and far (Ross 1975). Incipient Christianity also made itself felt at an early date in the same areas, in effect impacting the worldview (Sonne 1990). The Moravians brought about decisive changes along the Atlantic coast of Labrador from about 1770 onward, but apart from their diaries (see Garth Taylor 1989, 1997) sources regarding these Inuit appear sparse. The main sources of the early-contact Canadian Inuit are Franz Boas (1901–7; 1964), Diamond Jenness (1922), and Knud Rasmussen's reports from the Fifth Thule Expedition (1929; 1930a; 1930b; 1931; 1932; 1942). Due to the minor effects of colonial administration until the 1970s, more recent fieldwork has yielded valuable supplements (Saladin d'Anglure; Therrien; Oosten & Laugrand).

Beginning with the Aleutian Islands in 1743, the southernmost part of Yup'ik Alaska was occupied by Russian fur traders, who a century later extended both their trade and their Russian Orthodox religion northward to Southwest Alaska. Here the effects were already strongly felt, due to a Russian trading post established in 1789 in Northeast Siberia. Intertribal trade, which had been going on since time immemorial in alternation with raids, was intensified and extended to include a

22. A later hypothesis by Gulløv goes against that of Dorset impacts on the Ammassalik Thule culture. Instead he points to the stress on resources and climatic conditions in the 19th century that led to a last resort to religious means, viz. the richer decorations of gear and artefacts (Jensen et al. 2011; see also pp. 62 and 296 and note 131). Another hypothesis set forth by Anne Bahnson places the development in Holm's demands in objects bought during the wintering of the Konebådsekspedition in 1884–85 (Seminar at the Danish National Museum, Jan. 2001).

vast range of commodities such as soapstone objects from the Kitlinermiut, Siberian caribou skins, and valuable furs from Southwest Alaska (Burch 1988a). The trading communications put an end to the wars, and ceremonies of exchange grew in importance and underwent transformations. The latter can be superficially followed in the sources (e.g., Lantis 1947; Sonne 1978; 1988a; Fienup-Riordan 1984; 1990). Catholic and Protestant missions that came to operate after the sale of Alaska to the United States in 1867 eventually succeeded in banning the ceremonies. Information on the last ones celebrated in the 1930s has been collected, analyzed, and published by Lantis (1947), Morrow (1984), and Fienup-Riordan (1984; 1990) with regard to Southwest Alaska and Rainey (1947). Rainey has published valuable details concerning Tigara, one of the places in Northwest Alaska where whaling societies previously gathered in both spring and autumn.

Evaluation of the Essential Sources: Descriptions, Statements, and Stories

Dating a statement or story to points in time when no European impact is present is very difficult. All statements are parts of written texts, and the Greenlanders had no written language until it was literally spelled out by the missionaries and then taught to the Greenlanders. Only with an extended corpus in hand, which permits comparisons between sources from early and later colonized regions, can we arrive at approximate suppositions about a precontact worldview(s).

West Greenland

The cultural biases of the main Western accounts of traditional West Greenland are sometimes striking, sometimes less transparent, and sometimes of minor importance (see, for example, the historical outlines in Sonne [1986b]). The diaries of Hans Egede (the first missionary to the region, who worked there from 1721 to 1736), his two sons, Poul (a missionary from 1735 to 1741) and the younger Niels (a colonial trade and whaling manager) were published at early dates, 1738–41 (Hans Egede) and 1741 (Poul and Niels Egede) in attempts to draw public attention to the urgency of the Greenlanders' salvation. Hans Egede appears particularly prejudiced in religious and moral matters (1971, 1; 1925), whereas his son Poul, who was a young boy of 12 in 1721 and consequently fluent in Greenlandic as an adult missionary, did his best to understand the ideas of the Greenlanders. However, Poul did this less out of pure tolerance than with the zeal for disproving their "wrong" ideas by using Christianity as well as the natural sciences. His edited diaries were published shortly after an eye disease forced him to leave Greenland in 1741 (P. Egede 1971; 1939). At the same time, his father wrote his Perlustration (Enlightenment) about Greenland and the Greenlanders (H. Egede 1971, 2; 1925). Here Hans relies heavily on Poul's observations in most matters of particular interest for this book. The apparently less broad-minded Niels Egede presents good examples of the clash of cultures, offering—like his father and brother—the individual contexts of the Greenlanders' statements; these are invaluable for this particular analysis.

The diaries of missionary H. C. Glahn (from 1763 to 1769) were published posthumously and are still only partially available. They present Glahn as a tolerant enlightened person, who takes Greenlandic ideas and beliefs to be "natural"—i.e., the effects of "God in Nature" (Glahn 1921; Sonne 1986a). Of greater public interest were Glahn's commentaries, published in 1771, on the *Historie von Grönland* by David Cranz (1765–70; 1820), the historian of the Moravians in Greenland and Labrador. Glahn was asked by the authorities to give these commentaries. They appeared anonymously, harsh in critique but also in defense of the Danish mission and colonization. Yet the deviations in information between Cranz and Glahn should be read with care for at least two reasons. First, differences in local customs can be assumed between the Southerners (the Moravian proselytes) in Nuuk and those of Glahn a good distance to the north at Amerloq and nearby Holsteinsborg/Sisimiut. Second, Cranz is not an independent source. Quite a few statements clearly reflect either Hans Egede's Perlustration or Lars Dalager, whose *Second Continuation of the Relations about Greenland* (Dalager [1752] 1915) is an indispensable source regarding South/Southwest Greenland and its immigrants from the east coast around 1750. This enlightened, humorous, intelligent, and outspoken manager, who considered Voltaire and Holberg his preferred authors, was also belligerent and argumentative; this was especially evident in his critique of the Danish Royal Mission to the advantage of the rivaling Moravians. Some years after his arrival in Greenland in 1742, Dalager was put in charge of the recently established southernmost colony of Paamiut/Frederikshåb, from 1746 to 1748 and again from 1750 to 1754. Subsequently he became appointed to Godthåb/Nuuk, but, despite his successful reforms in promoting hunting to the profit of both hunters and colonial trade, he was dismissed in 1767. Quarrels with the colony's Danish missionaries had become unbearable (Dalager 1915: Preface by the editor of that second edition, L. Bobé). Dalager's description, published in 1752, is clear, informative, frequently amusing, and transparently biased (e.g., he awarded Greenlandic women little respect) but rarely condescending in the way of Hans Egede's Perlustration (1971, 2). Dalager highlights the unwritten rules of upbringing, aspects of sharing and exchange, rites of transition, beliefs, murder and revenge, heritage, manners (which he learned by trial and error), dinner courses, and shamans and their varying individual credibility. One shaman who became a very close informant was a thoughtful, honest, well-reputed person. Apparently Dalager was not, like most Qallunaat of high colonial standing, excluded from attending the shamanic performances, but unfortunately he had little to report on that topic.

Moving on to the next century, H. J. Rink (1819–1893), the inspector of administrative South Greenland (1853–1867), stands out as our most important source. Rink had a degree in the natural sciences, traveled both inspectorates while writing his description of Greenland (Rink 1974), was widely read in literature about the Inuit/Yupiit, engaged in correspondence with Franz Boas, and came up with his own answer to the question of Inuit/Yup'ik origins (Rink 1887–91). Culturally he was biased less by Christian concepts than by the political ideas of his time (Sonne 1986a).[23] Struck by the contemporary poverty and powerlessness of the Greenlanders (later to be questioned by Marquardt 1992; 1999), Rink made reputable hunters discuss and write down proposals for improvements and brought about the Greenlanders' first (partly) self-governing councils. He also started a printing press for publications in Greenlandic; this produced the first monthly journal, *Atuagagdliutit* ("reading for free"), in 1861, and several books, including four volumes of selected stories taken down by the Greenlanders themselves. Those stories were among the first of about 500 sent to Rink as the successful outcome of a circular call for stories that Rink dispatched in 1858. Some were written down by the storytellers themselves, others by the local catechist or colonial

23. Namely, the early nationalism engaged in collecting *gesunkenes Kulturgut* to meet a low self-esteem as also the first Danish democratic constitution of 1849. Rink further blamed the mission for having deprived the traditional Greenland society of their authorities, the shamans, leading to said misery (questioned by Sonne 1982a; see also Oosten 1989: 331–41).

manager, and the remaining ones by Rink, who, when sufficiently versed in Greenlandic, took down word-by-word approximately seventy-five stories told by some very good narrators in Nuuk in 1867 (Thisted & Thorning 1996).[24]

Rink himself produced an analysis of the traditional worldview based on the Egede journals and the Perlustration, Dalager, Glahn, Cranz, and the stories received, as well as his own interrogations collected throughout his southern inspectorate (administrative South Greenland; Rink 1866–71, II: 180–233; 1975: 35–69). Besides some bizarre speculations on prehistoric Inuit/Yup'ik religion (Sonne 1986a), his description treats relevant topics, but cross-checking takes an intimate knowledge of his sources, to which he makes next to no references. He treats stories on the same level as historical sources, and rarely considers statements in context. Furthermore, in the first volume of the stories translated into Danish, Rink repeatedly mixed several variants into a single story, although with commentaries on the storytellers, their provenances, and on which variant(s) take(s) the lead in his mix (Rink 1866–71, I). The original manuscripts (some only in fair copies) can be accessed at the Royal Library in Copenhagen, where Rink's meticulous registration of the type and themes of each story is a great help in studying them. In preparation, one should first consult the Greenlandic transcriptions and translations into Danish published by Kirsten Thisted (Thisted & Thorning 1996; Thisted 1997; Thisted & Grove 1997; Thisted 1999; Thorning et al. 1999; Danish summaries and references in Sonne 2005) with very useful introductions to the biographies and cultural environment of the storytellers. Research is also facilitated by using the database of some 2,300 Greenlandic stories, including the Rink collection by Sonne (Sonne 2005).[25]

When evaluating a Rink story, provenance helps one estimate how deeply rooted in tradition the story may be. For instance, missionaries had had little effect in the 1860s in Northwest Greenland (Upernavik region) and in South Greenland only since 1824. Avanersuaq and East Greenland were still beyond colonial administration, whereas the Nuuk region had been at the center of missionary activity for 140 years. Nevertheless, stories were transmitted through generations, as can be seen by comparing stories from East and South Greenland collected from 1885 to the 1960s with those told by the Moravian followers at Nuuk. In fact, some 75 percent of the Rink collection was told by storytellers belonging to the Moravians, and their East-Southeast Greenland ancestry quite often shows through, if tuned to the new Christian key. Consequently, effects of acculturation are traceable, even more so in comparison with the younger generation of these Nuuk families, whose stories are in Knud Rasmussen's collections.

Knud Rasmussen, the famous collector of Inuit stories, personally took down a good number of stories in Greenland, especially in Avanersuaq, among the immigrant Southeast Greenlanders and along the west coast from Nuuk and north to Upernavik. A considerable number of the stories published in his name had been taken down by others, including several by descendants of Rink's Moravian-baptized storytellers (search "herrnhut" in Sonne 2005). Their competence in writing is excellent, leaving nothing to be desired in comparison with those Rasmussen personally recorded.

---

24. As the ability to read was a prerequisite for baptism, baptized Greenlanders were literate at different levels. Both missions stuck to using Greenlandic from the very beginning. Spelling varied considerably until the introduction of Samuel Kleinschmidt's orthography of 1860 (revised in 1973; see Berthelsen et al. 1990).

25. All texts are in Danish except a few in English (the earliest myths as retold by Poul Egede). A manual in English accompanies the database.

East Greenland

From East Greenland[26] we derive the richest sources of the precolonial worldview, collected as they were at early points of acculturation by persons who met less-biased scientific standards than the early authors of 18th-century West Greenland. This does not mean, of course, that source criticism is irrelevant. News about the Qallunaat and their Christian ideas was heard at an early date in exchanges with the Southeast Greenlanders, who traded with the Southwest Greenlanders and took part in the trading expeditions mentioned in the Introduction. Christian knowledge increased with the sermons preached by Hanseeraq, or Johannes Hansen, a catechist from South Greenland and steersman of the Konebådsekspedition (Thalbitzer ed. 1933; Holm 1914; 1972). Hanseeraq's southern dialect, like that of the young Johan Petersen (Gustav Holm's interpreter), facilitated communication considerably. This resulted in both the brilliant ethnographic sketch of the Ammassalimmiut and the earliest collection of stories from that part of Greenland (Holm 1957).[27] Well educated and informed by Rink beforehand about which topics to cover, the open-minded, rational marine officer Gustav Holm managed to complete fieldwork and produce a report that would match the above-average ethnographic descriptions of his time. Holm's close representation of the performance of the shaman Sanimuinnaq, who later entrusted to him knowledge of the tricks that shamans employed, is quoted time and again in readers on shamanism. The census completed by Hanseeraq, which was conducted settlement by settlement, longhouse by longhouse, family by family, and named person by named person, is of unsurpassed value for demographic research (e.g., by Robert-Lamblin 1986; Holm 1888; 1914). In 1921, a follow-up of the sketch appeared, offering more detailed descriptions of the Ammassalimmiut's annual round, their movements, ever-changing settlements, and early colonial history. Johan Petersen—who was manager of the trading post from 1894 to 1915—and Holm were the authors. Petersen (Uujuat) also produced a diary, published by Thalbitzer (Holm 1957), and the first missionary Rüttel wrote another (1917).[28] Both were less prejudiced than Rüttel's successor in 1904, the West Greenlandic educated catechist Christian Rosing, who wrote a disparaging description after his very first year on duty (C. Rosing 1906; 1946). Rosing, who baptized the last East Greenlander in 1921, did change his opinion of the Ammassalimmiut and turned to collecting statements on traditional religion and stories himself (e.g., E. Rosing 1994).

William Thalbitzer (1873–1958), who was trained in several languages as well as the field of linguistics, was the very first person who did anthropological fieldwork in a way comparable to that of Malinowski (Høiris 2009). Instructed by Marcel Mauss, who furnished him with a questionnaire, Thalbitzer spent the year 1905–6 in East Greenland collecting valuable ethnographic information. An atheist, Thalbitzer was moved as much by the Greenlanders' traditions as by their prospective political autonomy. Like Rink's, Thalbitzer's personal engagement came to color his speculations about the origin of the Inuit/Yupiit culture, and like Rink some of his thoughts go completely astray, as does his presentation of the Inuit religion on the model of Greek Olympian mythology (Thalbitzer

26. See R. Petersen (1984) for a historical and cultural overview.

27. These stories are fairly short, as they were taken down by Holm in Danish at the dictation of the interpreter, Johan Petersen. Because length and personal style differ in variants of the same story and the entire collection appears unrevised in the files, these facts suffice to make them useful, in my view (search "Holm" in Sonne 2005).

28. Despite the lack of fluency in Greenlandic that yielded Rüttel poor results in baptisms, he is a fine observer and offers a multitude of cases in context. Petersen appears thoroughly impressed by the intelligence and quick learning of the East Greenlanders (Holm & Petersen 1921: 622, 637).

1926; 1928; 1941; Sonne 1986b). Linguistics, however, supports his tracing of Inuit/Yupiit shamanism, far back in time and place, to environments of Lake Baikal (Fortescue 1998). Following the hypothesis of Fortescue (1998), a glance at the Yukaghir cosmology and shamanism would be worthwhile. Here Bogoras (1907), Jochelson (1910), and Lehtisalo (1924; 1937) are definitely relevant (see chapter 4 on shamanism), as they were mentioned by Thalbitzer in support of his hypothesis.

In 1905–6, when Thalbitzer wintered in Ammassalik, the majority of the population was still pagan (Thalbitzer 2014). He managed to collect a considerable number of songs of all kinds: pet songs, story songs, songs of derision, songs for entertainment, and, for the masked dances, *uaajeertut* (Thalbitzer 1923) (pronounced *ooaayeertut* in English). Among his collected stories he selected all variants of the most well-known myths together with a few more for publication, storing the remainder in the files. The latter are even less easily read than the printed ones, studded as they are with notes. Similarly, the published biography of the female shaman Teemiartissaq remains obscure in many passages due to note upon note referring to words and phrases (Thalbitzer 1923).[29] East Greenlandic is no easy dialect to learn in a short time. Thalbitzer was familiar with West Greenlandic, and in his attempt to solve the problems of his texts he went to South Greenland in 1914; there he met with Kuannia, one of the last immigrated Southeast Greenlanders, who did his best to answer Thalbitzer's numerous questions (Thalbitzer 1923; Vebæk 2006: 83–85).[30] Fewer difficulties meet the reader of Thalbitzer's (1941) section on the East Greenlanders' social customs and mutual aid, a unique outcome of his survey in 1905–6 by means of the questionnaire created and recommended by Marcel Mauss. A kind of relief is felt by the sociologically minded reader, who will miss similar early studies of traditional West Greenland society.

Thalbitzer was deeply impressed by his successor in East Greenland, Knud Rasmussen, who returned with a considerable number of stories and drawings after a stay of only three weeks in the summer of 1919. That's how those who know the language can get along, he remarked. Perhaps, but Rasmussen neither knew East Greenlandic nor were the majority of stories collected his own recordings. His East Greenlandic friend, Kaarali Andreassen, a catechist educated in Nuuk from 1910 to 1914, took down thirty-three stories; Kaarali's wife, Johanne Andreassen, wrote twenty-two of them, and the young Sofie Jørgensen at the Ammassalik colony collected twenty-seven, fifteen of which have been filed with decent West Greenlandic translations (not signed). As for those in Rasmussen's own handwriting, eight stories are in Danish, two are partly in Danish, two consist of Danish notes alone, and thirteen are in West Greenlandic (Sonne 2005, search foab [Rasmussen, Knud] Ammassalik). As stated in the introduction, Rasmussen relied heavily on the collections by the missionary Christian Rosing recorded in West Greenlandic for his own sections on religious rites and ideas (Rasmussen 1921–25, I). Evidently, Rasmussen did not pick up East Greenlandic during his stay—nor did he like to admit the fact. These facts shine through in his apology for the shortcoming that no storyteller's name figures at the end of any story, as the standard demands. Rasmussen's explanation states that all these East Greenlandic stories were taken down at one and at the same

29. Generally raising more questions than they answer, some notes nevertheless do open up a more relevant interpretation.

30. Due to his outspoken critique of the swift colonization and baptism of the East Greenlanders, Thalbitzer was forbidden to reenter East Greenland and permitted only to visit the recently immigrated Southerners around Cape Farewell (Høiris 2009).

settlement; they were told by three women, named by their Christian names in the opening story of the volume, which is a bombastic description of a boat trip in a threatening storm. Fascinated by their reactions, Rasmussen presents them as Children of Nature, still firmly rooted in the old beliefs, and still incapable of pronouncing their new Christian names despite baptism (so why bother?). Like Kaarali and Johanne Andreassen, these ladies may very well have been dwellers of the boat trip's destination, Kuummiut—a mission established in 1915 that had a total of forty-seven residents by January 1, 1920 (Holm & Peteresen 1921: 647). They may have been the narrators as well, but visitors from other places came by at regular intervals. They came not only to hear Kaarali preach the Gospel but also to sing their songs and tell their stories (Vebæk 1990: 105–6). Such get-togethers would have been welcome opportunities for Kaarali and Johanne Andreassen to take down the impressive pile of manuscripts that were handed over to Rasmussen; this collection included approximately forty drawings by Kaarali, which illustrate a good number of the stories.[31] These get-togethers were hardly casual. Kaarali, who started drawing at the age of ten, was fifteen when he told a story to Thalbitzer wintering in Ammassalik in 1905–6. His drawings motivated sculptor Ellen Locher Thalbitzer, Thalbitzer's wife, to teach him during their stay (Geertzen 1990: 9). In 1914, having finished his education as a catechist at the teacher's college in Nuuk and returning to East Greenland, Kaarali had to winter in Denmark due to traveling conditions. He was invited to stay with Knud Rasmussen's parents: Christian Rasmussen—formerly a missionary to Ilulissat—and his wife. Consequently, it seems that Knud Rasmussen asked Kaarali Andreassen to collect and draw, and he would have done so with the approval of the missionary, Christian Rosing. Kaarali also did extensive collections of descriptions and stories for Rosing, as well as his sons and successors, Peter and Otto (O. Rosing 1957–61; J. Rosing 1960; 1963; 1970; 1993).[32]

In short, Rasmussen was not present at the telling of most of the East Greenlandic stories he published in 1921. If he had been, he likely would have listened and taken down the narrators' names. Judging by the stories in Rasmussen's own handwriting, his informant in Kuummiut was not one of the three ladies but rather Kaarali Andreassen himself. Kaarali knew West Greenlandic, recounted the extended narrative about his father Missuarniannga's development into a shaman (Sonne 2005: ID 2283), and most probably also told the stories about his grandfather, the shaman Akku, as well. Kaarali's manuscripts are in West Greenlandic, whereas his wife Johanne mixes East with West Greenlandic and shows a fairly good competence in writing, which she likely learned during her preparation for baptism. Finally, Sofie Jørgensen, only eighteen years old in 1919, was raised at the colony led by West Greenlandic managers and was therefore well versed in both West and East Greenlandic. Rasmussen asked her to take down stories from elderly visitors to the colonial shop in the attic of the building. Her two younger brothers were asked to do the same, but it seems that they did not leave any readable stories worth filing. Rasmussen was sometimes present, but other times he was not (Margarida Hermann, daughter of Sofie Jørgensen, pers. comm.). According to an obituary, Sofie "used to tell how she both interpreted the stories told by elders from East Greenlandic into West Greenlandic and took those stories down for Rasmussen who had them

31. In his publication on the artistic skill and display of Kaarali Andreassen, Ib Geertsen wonders how the cooperation between the two in just three weeks could yield the total of forty drawings brought home by Rasmussen (Geertsen 1990: 11). See my qualitative guess above.

32. Peter Rosing was Kaarali Andreassen's classmate in Nuuk.

published in 1921" (Smidt 1989). Part of this cooperation took place in 1920, when Sofie Jørgensen wintered in Copenhagen en route to her training as a midwife in Qaqortoq, West Greenland (Smidt 1989; e.g., Sonne 2005: ID 812).

The smoke screen laid down by Rasmussen shakes one's trust in him and calls for checking the files whenever possible.[33,34] This does not completely devalue the East Greenlandic stories of Rasmussen's collections, but Kaarali Andreassen's bias is worth considering due to his attempt to raise the reputation of the East Greenlandic traditions in the eyes of both West Greenlanders and other Christians (Jens Rosing pers. comm.). The West Greenlanders' disdain conferred on the pagans to the east was offensive and very pronounced by missionary Christian Rosing in his *Tunuamiut* (1906, see above), which was read at the teacher's college in Nuuk—that is, by Kaarali Andreassen and his classmates as well.

France "received" East Greenland for research in the International Polar Year of 1932. Ever since then East Greenland has been "their" field, counting names as P. E. Victor and Robert Gessain in the mid-1930s, Joëlle Robert-Lamblin and Pierre Robbe a generation later, and fairly recently Nicole Tersis in linguistics (2008). Victor had to rely on interpretation during the first season but ended up well versed in the dialect during his next stay.[35] Unfortunately, nothing resembling a consistent orthography is used in his published notes (Victor & Robert-Lamblin 1989–93), thus making a great number of glosses in his otherwise extremely valuable list of *taartaq* words (the language spoken by and used in communication with the beings of the "Other World") difficult to translate in their own literal sense. Only their equivalents in ordinary human language are rendered into French (Victor & Robert-Lamblin 1989–93, II: 252–63). Despite such deficiencies, Joëlle Robert-Lamblin is the one to thank for the eventual edition of Victor's rich information on stories, rites, and ideas of a precolonial past that still loomed large in adult memories. Robert-Lamblin herself has made her own very useful contributions in topics of demography, traditional medicine, shamanic data and biographies, and basic information that spare the analyst a host of speculations.

Robert Gessain, alone and in cooperation with Victor, has published valuable, unique bits of information about East Greenland masks, ideas about the moon, the drum, and a particular bisexual figure, *uizerq*. He taunts colonizers in general with their devastating impacts on non-Western societies (Gessain 1970: 15–16) and the Danes in particular with their prejudiced approaches to the East

---

33. Further casting doubts about Rasmussen's honesty is own description of his principles of recording in his introduction to the first volume of his *Myter og Sagn fra Grønland*, which contains East Greenlandic stories exclusively. The principles would have better suited the following volumes, II (West Greenland) and III (Avanersuaq and Northwest Greenland): "The method I employed in recording these tales was to let the narrator tell the whole story from beginning to end, without interruption. Then I wrote it down, getting him to repeat it sentence by sentence. Daily occupation with the same kind of material engenders a great facility for grasping and remembering, the result being that one memorizes the tale on hearing it the first time. Consequently, if the narrator became weary of my necessarily slow recording and tried to abbreviate or scamp his original tale, I was able to step in immediately and lead him back to his first form" (Rasmussen 1921–25, I: 69–70, translation in Rasmussen 1939: 5–6).

34. Sonne (2005) offers references extant in the archives to each story, whether published or not. Most nonpublished stories are presented in Danish translations. Numerous handwritten West Greenlandic stories were sent to Rasmussen, whose untimely death prevented him from finishing additional publications. For posthumous publications of both his own recordings and those received from others, see Rasmussen (1938; 1981, I–III; 1981–82, I–IV).

35. Sara Helms, a doctor in Ammassalik at that time, once told me about her job of translating the East Greenland informants' songs into German, which someone else (I do not recall who) translated into French (published in Victor 1991). Quite a few songs that were taken down also by Thalbitzer (1923) show no serious deviations.

Greenlanders. In contrast, he claims, the tolerant French researchers knew how to become friendly with their informants and thus received a lot of information that was withheld from both the Danes and the West Greenlanders in their inquiries (Gessain 1984). Gessain may be right about his latter accusation to some degree.[36] However, the information collected by Kaarali Andreassen and the Rosing family (see above), which was later translated and supplemented by Otto Rosing's son Jens, who later conducted fieldwork in 1961 (1957; 1963; 1970, 1993), is no less valuable and informative. Rather, the two sets of sources supplement each other, with the text published by Jens Rosing showing how well stories, songs, etc. were still sung and retold around 1960.

Similarly and simultaneously, a West Greenlandic minister, Otto Sandgreen, was able to record the biographies of four shamans during the 1960s. Two were autobiographies (Kukkujooq/Apulu, Georg Qúpersimân) and two were biographies, one (Naaja) going back to the first half of the 19th century and the other, of a female shaman (Kaakaaq), dating to the turn of the 20th century. Kaakaaq was born in 1884, was baptized in 1917, and died in 1942 (Robert-Lamblin 1997). All four biographies must be read with care. The autobiography by Georg Quppersimaan, published with only a few remarks added by Sandgreen (Qúpersimân 1972; 1982), is hardly a completely true telling of Georg's own experiences.[37] He was notorious for borrowing stories about other shamans and transforming them into his own (Pierre Robbe pers. comm.); furthermore, his claim of never having practiced as a shaman is not true (Sara Helms pers. comm.). The same holds true for the shamanic practices of both Kaakaaq and the other autobiographer, her son Kukkujooq, who told most of the stories about his mother as well (Sandgreen 1967; 1987; Jens Rosing pers. comm.; Gessain 1975a: 324). To admit practicing shamanism both before and after baptism was apparently embarrassing, if not dangerous, when face-to-face with the minister Sandgreen. However authentically problematic Quppersimaan's autobiography is, his stories still reflect tradition, ways of thinking, and lifestyles. The stories of the remaining three, given the common title (in translation) of "An Eye for an Eye and a Tooth for a Tooth," appear edited in both sequence and in composition. Collector and editor Sandgreen was convinced of the early belief among Greenland ministers and catechists that blood feud would have wiped out the East Greenland population had the Christian mission not put an end to paganism in time. The feud running in "An Eye for an Eye" covers five generations with only a single physical murder, in retaliation for suspected sorcery, in the first generation. The remaining "murders" (deaths) are explained as acts of sorcery. That unending chain of vengeance constituting Sandgreen's red thread appears exaggerated; the local ideology considered a single retaliation just, and in practice such an act usually appeared to bring about satisfaction and peace of mind (Sonne 1982b). Nevertheless, the published version of "An Eye for an Eye" was fully approved by Juserf, son of the youngest narrator Kukkujooq/Apulu (Robert Petersen pers. comm.), possibly because the series of West Greenland missionaries since 1904 had repeatedly communicated their conviction about the cause and effects of feuding. In my opinion, these stories tell less about blood feud than about sorcery in actual social life, a topic to which I shall return in due course.

---

36. His discussion of sexual matters is not commonplace but is important (Gessain & Victor 1973), whereas he has little news to reveal in his article on East Greenlandic masks (Gessain 1984).

37. Several passages were cut from the translation into Danish (Qúpersimân 1982). The editor made such decisions for unknown reasons (Sandgreen pers. comm.).

Among the second generation of French ethnographers in East Greenland, Pierre Robbe has also enriched our knowledge of settlement life and its natural conditions (climate, temperature, etc.) in the 1970s. At this point, the number of settlements was drastically reduced and many people moved into one of the remaining ones, the sealing community of Tineteqilaq. Lacking strong relations of blood and affinity, they had to create a common way of life. In this and other respects, Robbe's chapter on sharing is particularly revealing. Sharing—as much as, or even more than, intermarriage and naming—seems to have been the main operator; the rules of sharing, which stress individual ownership, throw unexpected light on Inuit sharing in general. The Dutch ethnographer Gert Nooter, who conducted periodic fieldwork from 1965 to 1986 at Tineteqilaq, investigated material-*cum*-social culture, focusing on changes brought about by new technology. His treatise on leadership is a classic (1976, 1978). More recently, his daughter-in-law, Cunera Buijs, did a thorough study regarding changes in clothing, pointing out a surprisingly early general use of Western fabrics (Buijs 2004).

Southeast and South Greenland

As mentioned above, the Southeast Greenlanders all immigrated to the southern parts of West Greenland. Some of them told Knud Rasmussen a good number of valuable memories, legends, and myths during his short stay at Narsamijit and Illukasik at the end of the Danish Literary Expedition 1902–04 (published posthumously by Ostermann in English and Søby in Danish: Rasmussen 1939; 1981, III; 1981–82, III). I cannot imagine how Rasmussen managed to understand these recently arrived immigrants without difficulty. Their dialect had developed into a now-extinct mix of West and East Greenlandic called *qavaq*; this variant of the language was documented in several of the stories tape-recorded by Mâliâraq Vebæk in the 1950s and 1960s. Her recordings consist mostly of memories, both those personally experienced by the speaker as well as accounts received from others. By the time her transcribed and translated texts (into Danish) appeared in a bilingual Greenlandic dialect/English publication including a CD-ROM (Vebæk 2006), she was close to celebrating her 90th birthday (search Vebæk in Sonne 2005). Her informants confirmed some of the alarming memories about brutal murders which Rasmussen had received and then published only in Danish (Rasmussen 1906). In contrast, the less shocking memoirs collected among the Polar Inuit were published in both Danish and English (Rasmussen 1905; 1908; see also Sonne 1988b).

The Southerners came to color both the East Greenlandic and the West Greenlandic sources. First, in continuous trading contacts with the East Greenlanders, they passed on elements of the Christian faith that, together with the hellfire sermons by the steersman Hansêraq/Hanseeraq of the Konebådsekspedition, caused worry and some changes to the East Greenlandic worldview. Second, as outlined above, groups of Southerners went north on trading expeditions to the whaling grounds at Disko Bay and Amerloq, and from about 1740 they moved to the Moravian mission in Nuuk in increasing numbers. The Southerners who took turns going north would frequently winter in Disko Bay at today's Ilulissat. They would stop at Nuuk to buy pots and lamps carved in soapstone by local Greenlanders and pay visits to the Royal Mission (Dalager 1915; Gulløv 1983; 1987; 1997: 400ff). When settled at Noorliit,[38] the Moravians, who were despised by the local Greenlanders for

38. Noorliit, "the outmost foreland," Neu Herrnhut, 1733–1900.

their poverty (Cranz 1765–70, I), received Southern visitors who passed by in steady numbers. So when the Southerner Qajarnaq, who visited Noorliit in 1739, became deeply moved by the story of the Passion, the Moravians immediately turned to that story for winning followers. Soon they attracted an increasing number of Southerners who also arrived due to the depopulation of the region. After being baptized, these Southerners were then ordered to remain at the mission. This success was followed by the establishment of several missions on the stretch from Nuuk and south to Cape Farewell. Close to Cape Farewell, Friedrichsthal/Narsarmijit, the Moravian mission established in 1824, received and baptized the stream of Southeast Greenland immigrants, with the last families arriving in 1900. Another early stronghold was the island of Kangeq off Nuuk, and in 1861 the Uummannaq annex was established in the eastern interior of the Nuuk fjord, where Moravian-baptized families from the overpopulated Noorliit had moved. With their mission thus completed according to contract and their request for a continuation on the east coast refused, the Moravians had to leave the country. Their success, however, left their East-Southeast Greenland marks on a good number of stories on record from the 1850s to the 1930s, which have been collected from Nuuk and south to Cape Farewell. Their eastern origin and transformations in the new Christian key are recognizable godsends to the analyst, who fortunately has the rich lore of the East Greenlanders for comparison.

Northwest Greenland

Moving north along the west coast to the region of the Northwest Greenlanders, we find a district that had been the object of discontinued mission until 1833, when Christianity eventually took root. The last baptism occurred in the 1850s, but it did not eliminate the legends and memories about parents, grandparents, and great-grandparents. An epidemic in 1814, which prompted some inhabitants to flee to Uummannaq in the south and a single family to head north to the Polar Inuit, left an estimated one-third of the total population alive (R. Petersen 2003a: 28–29). The fugitives to the south later returned, resumed their daily lives, and continued telling their legends, myths, and memories. The collections from that district show differences according to the interests of the collectors. Those in Knud Rasmussen's archives consist predominantly of variants of the well-known myths and legends. They were taken down by Greenlanders, three named and one anonymous, during the Danish Literary Expedition in 1902–4 (search Rasmussen Upernavik in Sonne 2005).[39] The names of the storytellers are not mentioned except for one. Among the few historical narratives, one about the prophet movement of "Maria" (Sonne 2005: ID 934) has been excellently treated by Inge Kleivan (1986), who supplemented it with other sources. By contrast, memories—both secondhand and personally experienced—dominate the collections by Hans Lynge and the published accounts of one of his main informants, catechist Martin (Martêraq/Marteeraq) Nielsen in the 1950s (H. Lynge 1955; 1967; Søby 1973; search Hans Lynge and also Martêraq in Sonne 2005). Together these narratives are fascinating testimonies to both pre-Christian and acculturated ideas, and to exchanges with the Qallunaat (Europeans), be they colonists or British whalers. Regarding the assumed cultural kinship with the East Greenlanders (see above), a few of these

39. The stories by a member of the expedition, Gaba, and the anonymous person (probably Jørgen Brøndlund, another member) await translation from Greenlandic.

Northwest Greenland stories help interpret obscure points in some of the East Greenlandic ones that are not recorded in variants from West Greenland.

Avanersuaq

Following the first "pioneers," Thule Inuit may have continued to arrive for centuries in Avanersuaq from Canada (Gulløv 1997), but at the onset of extremely low temperatures during the 16th century, human life may have become impossible in that region. The explorer William Baffin, at least, did not meet anyone there in 1616 (but see above p. 22). Then, in the early 18th century a new group, the Polar Inuit, moved into the area (Rischel 1986a; 1986b); rumors about their presence reached Poul Egede in 1771 (P. Egede 1988 [1788]: 157), and John Ross met some of them in 1818.[40]

Dialectally, the Polar Inuit are related to the Kitlinermiut (Fortescue 1986), and since their exchanges with Greenlanders south of Melville Bay appear to have been sporadic until colonization (Gilberg 1984; R. Petersen 2003a), one should look west to the Kitlinermiut (and Nattilingmiut) for close cultural relations. In addition, looking southwest is equally relevant, because in about 1860 the Polar Inuit received a small group of families that originally started out from southeast Baffin Island. They stopped over for some time in Pond Inlet/Mittimatalik, then Iglulik, and then several years on Devon Island, before moving on to Avanersuaq. Although they soon left again heading for their previous home, a couple of families managed to get back to Avanersuaq. Their companions had been lost to starvation, bitter fights, and cannibalism (Inuutersuaq 1976; 1985; Mary-Rousselière 1980; Rowley 1985; R. Petersen 2000; 2003a). The returning Baffin Islanders certainly made their impact on the Polar Inuit culture, through both technology and lore. They taught the Polar Inuit how to build a kayak, make bows and arrows, hunt caribou, and make leisters for catching trout.[41] Only the immigrants' dogsleds did not match the Polar Inuit's much longer one with uprights (Sonne 2005: ID 11; Gilberg 1974–75). The stories brought and transmitted by these Baffin Islanders are still recognizable in those collected at later dates by Rasmussen in 1903–4 (1908) and Holtved in the 1930s and 1940s (1951). In particular, the stories told by Amaunalik, a granddaughter of one of the immigrants, Ittussaarsuaq, are amazingly similar to some of those received by Franz Boas half a century earlier from south and southeast Baffin Island (Holtved 1951; Boas 1964; 1901–7; Sonne 1990; R. Petersen 2000; 2003a). Euro-American whalers anchoring at Cape York during the 19th century traded wood and spread epidemics among the Polar Inuit; Robert Peary took over until 1899, whereafter Rasmussen saw to the colonization with a mission and a trade station established in 1909 and 1910, respectively. Still another earlier impact is of interest, namely the flight of Hans Hendrik in 1855 into Avanersuaq from E. K. Kane's Second Grinnell Expedition, which stopped over at Cape York in its search for John Franklin. Hans Hendrik, who originated in the far south of Greenland (Fiskenæsset, Qeqertarsuatsiaq), married Mequ and settled for five years among her Polar Inuit. During his stay, Hans Hendrik, a follower of the Moravian mission at Lichtenfels, did his best to spread the Gospel,

---

40. For a description of the district, see Rasmussen (1921) and Rasmussen in Vahl et al. (1928–29).

41. People reported that the lost knowledge of kayak building was due to a severe epidemic (Sonne 2005: ID 11). Other ecological causes may have been either that the walrus and other sea mammals caught at the ice edge offered sufficient food (Birket-Smith 1961: 119f), or that the kayak used by ancestral Kitlinermiut and Nattilingmiut, which was only for hunting caribou in lakes, was less useful in Avanersuaq (R. Petersen 2003a).

though with little success according to his own memories (Rink 1878a: 287; 1878b; Lidegaard 1986: 49).[42] However, traces are left in several stories including some about the Norse.

Collections from the Polar Inuit in Avanersuaq were taken down by Knud Rasmussen, who wintered there in 1903–4, and by Erik Holtved, who visited in 1937 and 1946. During this and later visits Rasmussen learned the local dialect, which, related as it is to the Kitlineq and Nattilik dialects, would later help him understand the Inuit he encountered during the Fifth Thule Expedition (Rasmussen 1905; 1908; 1921–25, III; 1981–82, IV). However, his Polar Inuit handwritten originals, myths, legends, and memories are partly in West Greenlandic, and at times they differ from the texts in translations, pointing once again to the need to check Rasmussen whenever doubt is raised. The published Holtved collection (1951) has turned out to be in need of linguistic revision, a job done by Arnaq Grove, PhD, and Robert Peary, a Polar Inuit descendant. The result (Grove 2000) still awaits publication. Concerning comparisons of Polar Inuit with both other Greenlandic and Canadian Inuit stories, the latter are frequently more promising due to the late immigration of some Baffin Islanders, as mentioned above.

The Stories

The majority of the Greenlandic stories I use are translated or described in Sonne (2005). There are variants, of course, and they differ without exception to a degree, that in case two written texts prove identical, one quotes the other. I make use of written stories alone, because the only sound recordings extant from the period in question, Thalbitzer's and Holtved's, both suffer from inadequate recording technique, and the dialects spoken are not my competence. For the same reason I had to leave out the tape recordings Jens Rosing made in 1961 and make do with the printed stories. Questions of interpretation will be dealt with below in the section titled "Method."

Theory

Connections between ritual and myth are obvious, and looking for them has long been second nature for me. Also trained in the historical philological method, I became fascinated—if also repelled—by structuralism, and so I looked to cognitive anthropology for the treatment of symbols (e.g., Basso 1990: 52–79; Keesing 1993; T. Turner 1991). I was then taken in by theories of praxis and others emphasizing sensing and perception, and so my theoretical outline is a mixed, probably self-contradictory one. Call me an outdated positivist, but when time and again I have looked to natural surroundings for interpretation of many a symbolic meaning, this method has been rewarding. Indeed, observations of nature (*sila*) used to constitute the main part of Inuit knowledge and legacy.

Allow me to present my use of theories step by step during my prolonged attempt to discover the meanings of the East Greenlandic *angakkoq puulik*, shaman with (*-lik*) a bag (*pooq*): In the 1970s, when structuralism turned a multitude of disconnected statements and badly sustained generalizations into beautiful, convincing, and static patterns, history either disappeared from the scene or was moved way back in time to prehistory. Since the same tendency to look into a distant past also governed the treatment of Inuit/Yupiit cultural similarities and differences by

42. His topics were the creation, Jesus, redemption by Jesus, the crucifixion, the resurrection, and Judgment Day. The latter especially scared the Polar Inuit (Rink 1878a: 287).

the cultural-historical method, research into Inuit traditional religion was left in a remote past. Despite centuries of well-known changes, religion was apparently considered less changeable than any other aspect of culture. In an attempt to break the stasis, I undertook (and, I believe partially succeeded) an analysis of the changes in the origin myth of Sea Woman (*Nuliayuk, Sedna, Sassuma Arnaa, Arnaquassasuaq, Immap Ukuua*), relating the variants to local, contemporary events (Sonne 1990). On the other hand, to completely discard either method is not recommended. Comparisons within the Thule culture area of similarities in varying contexts and settings offer insights to be tested in situ as mentioned above. Structuralism may help one to get hold of stories, ritual descriptions, and other statements in the first run and in the second, but rarely in the third, that is, as an analytical tool.

The contexts of binary oppositions lead one into chains of associations (here, I am thinking of the associative logic of Bourdieu's theory of praxis that I understand as abcd ↔ abce ↔ bcde etc.), and they may open up new, fruitful ideas to pursue. This was what happened in my search over the years as I attempted to come to terms with the particular East Greenland initiation of an *angakkoq puulik* (*pooq* "bag" + *-lik* "with"), or "a shaman with a bag." Cultural historical research pointed to Alaska, not to West Greenland or Canada, but it revealed no useful interpretation of that "bag" (*pooq*). The well-known land (freshwater) versus sea (saltwater) opposition of the Inuit next became a fine guide in comparing the *puulik* initiation (at sea) into becoming *invisible* with that of the inland initiation into the ability to *see* the Other World. This comparison led to a partial understanding through still another comparison with a distant cosmological myth of origin from the MacKenzie region: the origin of the sun. It followed the same schema as the ritual myth of the *puulik* initiation, stressing identical elements of bodily activities. At this point, both symbolic analysis and the importance of the course of events entered the scene, pointing to thematic variations of midwinter and annual renewal. But still, why *pooq*? Pursuing symbolism, the very polysemy of *pooq* invited in-depth analysis. Besides "bag," *pooq* means not only "cover," "skin," and "caul" but also, in the spirit language (*taartaq*), "mother" (uterus). All Inuit spirit languages (spoken by nonhumans) on record elicit this meaning. Furthermore, the polysemy of *pooq* turned out to involve associations with other bags, artifacts, which have their own names but are synonymous in concept. In other words, *pooq* was a key symbol (Ortner 1973) or a multivocal one (V. Turner 1974: 29–30). Finally, however, the perspectivism as advanced by Viveiros de Castro (2002) widened the scope. He puts forth the argument that there is no ontological difference between humans, animals, and other beings. In "spirit" or "soul" every living being is a humanlike being, seeing itself and others of its own kind as humans. But they (animals) differ (by species) in their manifest bodies. In other words, they differ particularly in their "clothing," the privileged means for transformation, the very cover that, as Tim Ingold puts it, "identifies the capabilities, skills, dispositions that serve the being who can thereby *carry on a particular kind of life in the world*" (2000: 94). *Pooq*, apparently, could conform to the "clothing," that part of the body that holds (expresses, symbolizes) the distinct capabilities, senses, and intentions of its owner more than any other part; if so, the *pooq* would reveal the owner's perspective and serve as the preferred means for transformations, namely, in contrast to the common human constitution of every live being, its "soul" or "spirit." However, the soul part of the theory proved less applicable to Inuit ideas.

Obviously this spirit could be the possessive form of *inuk*, *inua*, its "*inuy*" (prototype), its owner, master, indweller, or person.[43] Yet, as is discussed in the section on *inua* in chapter 3, pursued in chapter 4 on shamanism, and reconsidered in chapter 6, the conclusion, the notions do not completely fit Viveiros de Castro's perspectivism. As I searched further for some applicable theory, Terence Turner's critique of late structuralism (2009) helped clear my thoughts to an acceptable point, which allowed me to stop worrying and leave further theorizing to brighter academics. My main gain, however, was a spinoff focus on clothing versus nakedness, on dressing and undressing, the significance of a few animal species born as naked as the human baby, and the differing vulnerability of differing covers. In short, these were acts and powers that turned out to be of recurring significance in the build-up of a good number of stories. The symbolism of covers, whether inborn like pelts or manufactured like clothing, made sense in the analysis of not only traditional stories but also those that were acculturated. The symbol of the cover literally served as a vehicle in the transformation of older ideas into newer ones, as evidenced in the end of chapter 5 on the polysemous *pooq*.

The Greenlandic sources do not invite studies of changes that are not due to movement, colonization, and missionizing, like those brought forth by Frederic Barth (1995). Nevertheless, his study inspires my treatment and presentation of the ways some select stories employ tradition in new keys. If worldviews cannot predict future events, they can still help us come to terms with changed premises.

Similar to the way I once learned some finer nuances of German by listening to the idioms used by a native speaker of German speaking Danish, acculturated statements and stories may reveal more about tradition than traditional ones. This will be exemplified throughout the following chapters.

Contents: An Overview

Chapter 1: Space and Time

Perceptions of space and time merge in the Inuit/Yup'ik languages, and sometimes in the same way as in the European languages. Thus, like "here" the affix *-vik/fik* means both place and point in time. Similarly, *silap ingerlasia*, "the way the world moves," covers the annual round in both time and space. It reveals circularity in time, whereas events elicit linear time. Experiented, or so-called biocultural time, merges cyclic and linear time, and this meddling provides our acts with their meaning (Munn 1992). I present structural models of space and time, and consider the applicability of the one sketched by Saladin d'Anglure. My foci on body analogies, orientation, and movement are emphasized.

Sila has a "partner," *silam aappaa*, the Other *sila* of a couple. It is the invisible world, with its own space and time. It is seen and traveled by shamans, deceased humans, and sometimes by ordinary people in dreams and extraordinary experiences. Boundaries between the two worlds are passed at certain points in time, the *naar* times at dusk and at dawn (in the language of the Other World, see below pp. 157ff). Spatial passages are manifold and they will be described as they become relevant in context.

43. Spirits, animals, humans, things, concepts, and most anything can be seen as an *inua*. Phonological equivalents are *yua*, *shua*, *chua* in Southwest Alaska.

Orientation

To respect, understand, and follow *silap ingerlasia*, the cosmic "way of the world" in all situations of life, was to use one's *sila* in the meanings of being sensible and clever: to have *sila*. One Canadian Inuit personification of Sila, a giant baby, had its counterpart in East Greenland. The annual round, starting with the appearance of the star *Aassuutit* (Altair and Tarazed in the constellation Aquila) in late December (among all Inuit and Yupiit), counted four seasons and twelve or thirteen moons. Sometimes the moons bore names of the hunt of a certain animal or a recurring event in its life cycle. The week was introduced by the missionaries. Linear time was not counted by years but kept track of by events and by the naming of babies for related ancestors. Greenlandic is rich in suffixes that distinguish between past, present, and future. The past became further divided by the events of colonization and the adoption of Danish numbers greater than twenty.

The Greenlanders used to hold apparently conflicting views of the spatial world. One was seen from the inside of a house, the other from the outside looking at movements of the heavenly bodies. Because only the perspective changed, these views did not collide, whereas the heliocentric view preached by the missionaries did. Due to still another view, the view from above, I partly denounce Ingold's theory, that the shaman's view *always* penetrates its object, sees it from the inside. But in order to discover the many meanings of *sila*, I prefer the perspective advanced by Ingold of "being in the world" rather than a single philosophical synthetic meaning of *sila*.

Like other Inuit, the Greenlander identified her- or himself by "dweller" (*-miu*) of a named place, usually one's birthplace, and the time of one's arrival into This World with a cry (*ungaa*) was marked by the weather of that day.

The Greenlandic spatial center of orientation is placed at the coast facing the sea, and localizers denote upwards behind you, downwards in front, and right and left along the coast (see figs. 7–8). In West Greenland, right agrees with north, left with south, etc. This sometimes causes errors in translation of the localizers in texts from the east coast, where the mirror effect means that the word for north in West Greenland means south in East Greenland, etc.

In "Making a Living from Land and Sea" (p. 58) I describe the annual round as a cyclic series of moving and hunting activities without much ado, while events are treated in the ways they speak to variation and changes in diaries and stories, be they mythic, legendary, or close to fact. Identifying personal agendas demands a comprehensive corpus of stories for comparison of variants, which are fortunately at hand in Sonne (2005).

Balance

Although the missionaries' Christian ideas of This and the Other Worlds distort the earliest statements, they point to the Greenlandic view of the earth as a disk with access to the underworld at the shore, and also through cracks and lakes. Right below shore live the prehumans, the "big fire people," *innersuit* (sing. *innersuaq*), who ended up there long ago, when a big (tsunami) flood turned the earth around. The missionaries identified the flooding with the biblical deluge and thus made their impact on some of the variants.

The fear of a possible end of the world, or a return to some primordial state by a fall, is my point of departure for further investigations of balance in the world analogous to balance in body and mind. Christian preaching about doomsday aggravated this fear, which brought some structures

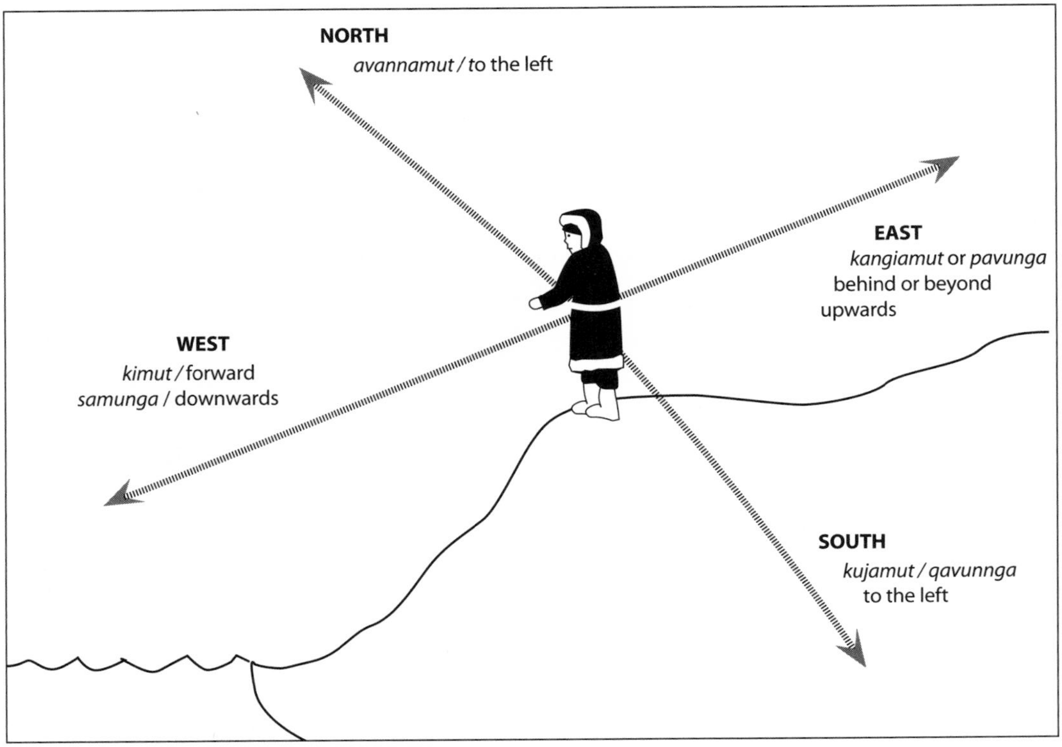

Fig. 7. The mirror effect of the localizers (right, left, up behind, down in front). Pictured here: Orientation on the west coast. *Experimental drawings by the author. Redrawn for print by Lisa Devenish.*

of the building out into the open: pillars kept heaven and earth apart and might become rotten, fall down, or get loose in their sockets like bones in their joints. Just as frightening, the earth itself might capsize, tilting as it apparently does with the tides. A full turn or somersault, however, bears positive connotations of life renewal and luck in hunting, and Raven is a master of this sport. The world is kept in balance by observing the rules, the Polar Inuit declared. It prevents avalanches from ruining settlements and the earth from being swallowed up by the sea. Tilt and tide turn out to be interchangeable body-mind metaphors.

I approach the ideas of an ideal human balance in body and mind from various angles: the development from birth to adult, and then as a balanced upright being, awake and aware of changes in *sila*. Next I compare the human with the other balances in the body of animals and especially the humanlike land spirits, which reveals a humancentric perspective. Finally, I investigate statements on loss of balance in both body and nature to uncover other insights, starting with focus on kayak dizziness: a recommended cure, to sit down with a bare rump on a young raven until it dies, sets in motion a far-reaching survey of raven's connotations. The course of events of an East Greenlandic origin myth compares favorably with the parts played by a raven figure of Canadian Inuit seasonal rites. Hints in both myth and rites to the oscillating balance of the tide ask for comparison with the mythic Raven who sees to the stabilization of this balance among the Tlingit. Applied to comparable statements from places along the subarctic coasts of Alaska, Canada, and Greenland, the findings

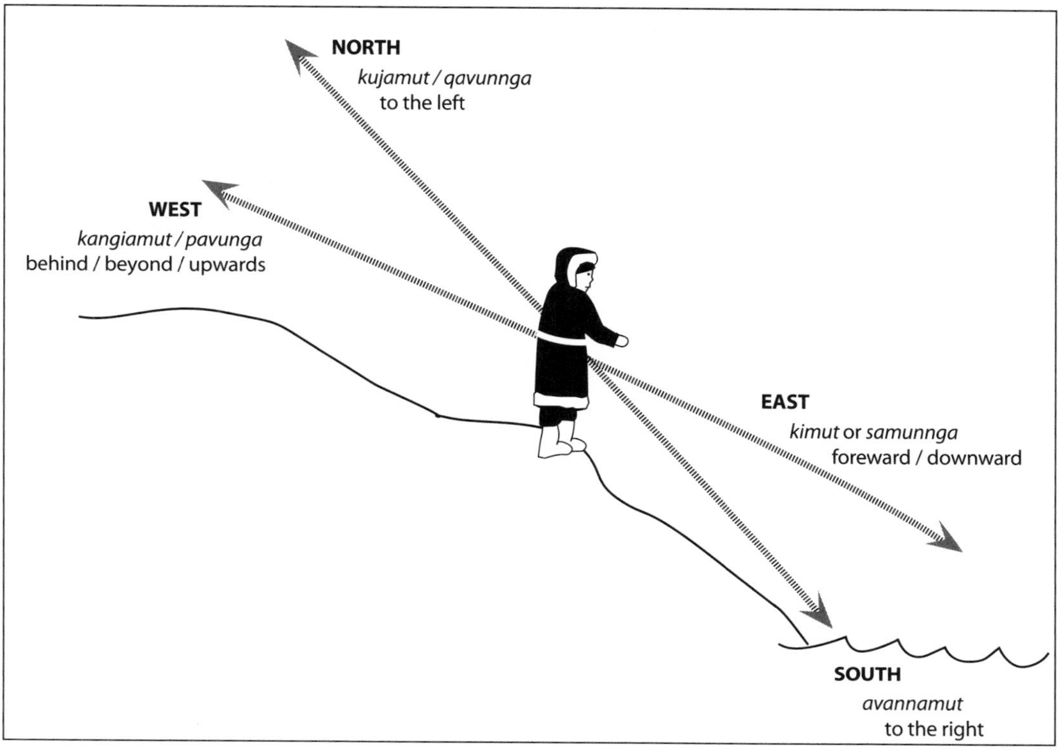

Fig. 8. The mirror effect of the localizers (right, left, up behind, down in front). Pictured here: Orientation on the east coast. *Experimental drawings by the author. Redrawn for print by Lisa Devenish.*

point to the tide as a central phenomenon in coastal worldviews in places where the tide runs high.[44] Further connotations of raven as revealed by Oosten and Laugrand (2006) in Arctic Canada are then applied to Greenlandic statements. They fit very well but lead to a crux, because Raven—although a bird of transitions—has its structural limits. It belongs out of doors, to *sila*, exclusively. Following up on "balance" in space as in the body and senses, the contours of human identity begin to emerge. It points to balance as an additional meaning of *sila* that exists alongside its other well-known meanings such as world, space, reason, awareness, and weather. This hypothesis is substantiated from various points of view by subsequent analyses.

Human Foreigners and Powers of the Sea and the Land

Parts of This World that lie beyond ordinary view are traveled in oral lore by a few (extra)ordinary humans who succeed by will, intelligence, and knowledge of magic means. They remain on the surface of This World, and unlike shamans they do not visit the realms below and above of Sea Woman, Moon, and deceased humans. They circumnavigate Greenland, or cross the inland ice, or they get across the winter sea ice to the opposite coasts of Labrador and Baffin Island, alias the mythic Akilineq of precolonial Greenland. They tell about dangerous passages, monsters, and foreign but

44. Significant flooding at high tides—covering some 30 miles of land—in Yup'ik Southwest Alaska does not inspire ideas about a tilting land (Fienup-Riordan & Rearden 2013: 43, 110).

more or less real human beings. The bearings of the separate social agendas of the stories are treated in correspondence with traceable changes in history.

Other travelers cross the sea to Akilineq on a drifting floe, by sledge in winter, or by kayak. They brave storms, maelstroms, and other powers of the sea. Kivioq travels by kayak, and variants abound in both Greenland and Arctic Canada (Kiviuq). The main findings of the Canadian variants (as uncovered and discussed by Oosten) are compared with the corresponding issues of the Greenlandic variants. A frequent claim that the Inuit are constantly on the move due to love of adventure is tested and not confirmed by these travelogues. Social conflicts or neglect are the personal motivations for traveling far and wide. Powerful beings of the sea may have been staged as ritual figures.[45] Their sexual and dangerously laugh-provoking characters, who had their edges rounded off by Christian influence, remained bogies that are still remembered by adult Greenlanders of today. Among these figures is Qungussutariaq, "the smiling giant of the sea." He ends up an acculturated laughingstock, as will be discussed in chapter 5 on *pooq*.

The powers of the sloping land, moving with the tide and setting boulders on the move in spring, are at play in the story about the maltreated orphan Kaassassuk. He receives powers from an inland giant or a huge land predator that enable him to pick up boulders and uproot plants or large objects frozen to the ground. In addition he achieves an improved balance in body and is in various ways associated also with *sila* and its upholding. The analysis calls for a lengthy treatise on the ambiguous meanings of stones, in general and as a means for acculturative changes. The particular development of Kaassassuk in Greenland shines through in the Canadian variants recorded and published by Knud Rasmussen, where he identifies *Silap Inua* (the person of *sila*) with Kaassassuk's empowering land animal. This identification is discussed and asks for a closer look on ideas of *sila* as both a concept and a characteristic of a person (*inua*).

Chapter 2: Seasonal Rituals and Rituals of Crisis

The Greenlandic sources on winter feasts are scant, especially those from the early colonial days in West Greenland. The Christian Christmas and Easter soon became popular and took over. Nonetheless, New Year used to occasion visits, feasts, dances, wife exchange, and also, in East Greenland, masked dances. The roles of shamans, central as they were in Canadian Inuit New Year celebrations, do not appear in the Greenlandic sources. Shamans' travels to *Sassuma Arnaa* ("the woman down there in front of you at the center of orientation," the coast, hereafter called Sea Woman) and *Qaammatip Inua* (Moon) were not part of this annual festival. They took place in situations of crisis, the former in spring and the latter around New Year. But winter solstice was the ideal time for great shamans' public initiation. The famous East Greenlandic shaman Ajijak was said to have gone flying and been caught and tortured by the sportive people of heaven. The events of this séance call for a comparison with the Iglulik shaman's *ilimmarneq* (flying) to the Northern Lights, akin to Ajijak's ball-playing torturers. Correspondences abound in ritual details, but the agencies differ considerably.

Moon used to be the main *inua* of the East Greenlanders. Séances were held at full moons, and statements on historical shamans' flight to Moon are dated close to New Year, but then the occasion

45. Sea Woman was not staged in Greenland, but in the 1970s the play *Inuit*, produced by the Tuukkaq theater, had Sea Woman emerge as the Greenlanders' savior from the devastating effects of colonialism.

is a crisis. One winter, several East Greenlandic shamans staged an impressive actual fight with the descended Moon Man. Naturally he was driven out and back to his heaven, a thrilling show. His loss of authority caused by the Christian mission comes alive by analysis of stories, where only his powers over tide and reproduction are, for good reasons, retained.

Spring could demand a shaman's ritual of crisis in East Greenland, as far as myth can tell. The giant boulder called "the person who goes for the stomach" (*Aqajarormiorsiorpua*) got loose on top of the mountain and came thundering down with the intention to smash the longhouse. The shaman's particular helping spirit, an *equngasoq* ("wry mouth")—i.e., a fulmar that connotes spring—defeats the boulder. Another situation of crisis in spring is a heavy layer of snow that covers the breathing holes. Myth has the shaman travel to the *inua* of precipitation, *Asiaq*, who is persuaded to let her baby-husband pee for days of rain to do away with the snow. The baby reminds one of *Naarjuk* (the Iglulik *inua* of *sila*, a giant baby), and the shaman Naaja was said to have managed the trip.

Turning to Sea Woman, *Sassuma Arnaa, Sedna/Nuliayuk, Nerrivik*, she had a great say among the Inuit of Canada, West Greenland, and Avanersuaq, but less so in East Greenland. I consider also another figure, *Ni-givik*, at the whaling point Tigara in Northwest Alaska, because she shares her name ("place of food"), her residence, and some of her powers with *Nerrivik*, the Sea Woman in Avanersuaq. Three kinds of texts are compared: 1) statements on and descriptions of historical shamans' visits to Sea Woman; 2) the same event in a mythic frame of reference; and 3) variants of her origin myth. A question has been raised in regard to 1 and 2: was the shaman's ritual confrontation an annual—i.e., calendric—event, or was it only provoked by a crisis? I sketch the research provoked by this question and can echo the satisfying answer offered by Oosten and Laugrand: the shamanic ritual was provoked by a crisis. In Greenland, the three texts all agree on both the occasion, a crisis caused by a prolonged winter, and on the outcome of the ritual confrontation: to have the sea ice cover removed so the sea animals and seabirds can reappear. Stories and statements are predominantly of southern provenance, a peculiarity that may be explained by an intimate connection between Sea Woman and whaling. This link, between whaling and *Ni-givik*, is also recognized among the Iñupiat of Tigara and fully among the Canadian Inuit who cooperated with Euro-American whalers. In my view still another link to this cooperation comes to the fore in the exchange of women at the winter feast at Iglulik, which was said to produce the children of Sea Woman. Perhaps they included the actual children birthed by the Qallunaat whalers. If so, they may have been legalized during the winter feast, *tivajuut*.

The individual rites of transition were recurrent, expected events. They concerned birth, abortion, naming, "ritual firsts," sometimes marriage, but always death with its demanding taboos. A boy's *pernarneq* (first catch) was celebrated with feasting and the generous dispersal of gifts. On a smaller scale the girl's first berry picking and her similar firsts were recognized in public. They were welcome signs of development into responsible adults. The development of children's intellectual firsts was observed by seemingly identical phrases among most Inuit and Yupiit, but the stages were not celebrated as far as the sources go. Michèle Therrien presents an interesting analysis of firsts. Besides the ordinary firsts, it also covers initiation of shamans and extraordinary experiences and demonstrates the importance the Inuit attribute to firsts as a continuous series of stages in life. A prominent issue in research on Inuit rites of passage has been the sometimes perilous effects of the multitude of connected taboos, such as the mortuary taboo on going out to hunt during a period of starvation. The contributions are merely described and I side with none of the hypotheses, which all sound reasonable.

Greenlanders paid respect to the animals killed along the same lines as other Inuit and Yupiit. The strong taboos observed at birth, abortion, and death served to keep human and animal life cycles apart. Rules observed by other Inuit for the treatment of slain animals were in force also in Greenland, but apparently on a more reduced scale. But the killed animals were not feasted annually and collectively as they were in most Inuit and Yupiit groups in Alaska. Only the East Greenlandic *uaajeertut* bear a faint resemblance to the more elaborate mask rituals in Southwest Alaska.

Chapter 3: The Other World(s) and Its Beings

The issues treated are the interdependence and boundaries between This and the Other World(s), space and time of the Other Worlds, and the timelessness of origin myths. Humans were the responsible part of the interdependence, but the Others, *inuat* (sing. *inua*), spirits and deceased humans, were also subject to limiting rules. In body terms the Other World was a stomach, *naaq*, the interior, invisible part of This World, seen involuntarily in dreams and by shamans at will. The shaman passed through a period of blurred sight either way between the worlds. Similarly, times of reduced sight, dusk and dawn, were *naar*-times (see p. 82) and the right times for shamans' and spirits' travels between the worlds. There were several spatial boundaries. The nearest one, right beyond sight from human habitation, worked in case you were out alone, frightened, or absorbed in grief. And it worked for spirits as well. They never passed that limit, unless invited or with evil intentions. The majority of relations with beings of the Other World were established by shamans with the spirits of the land, the spirits of the surface, and below the shore. I argue in various ways for the existence of a clear ethnocentric or humancentric perspective on these relations.

The Christian creed about eternal afterlife in either Heaven or Hell caused reorganization of the Other World, above and below. Changes came gradually, from clear opposition into acceptance, most probably because the shamans paid recurrent visits to both realms of death. The idea of eternal afterlife in either realm asked for solutions to the eternal separation after death from one's dear relatives who had ended up in the opposite place. Timelessness is next considered as regards myth. It is discussed in light of some combinations of origin myths into a chronological course of events, which meet with difficulties. So do investigations of the "Others" in terms of *inuat*, by means of the theory of perspectivism advanced by Viveiros de Castro. He postulates that the Amerindians in his "field" hold the view that all live beings share with humans a common humanlike ontological essence. At home in their own world they look human in body. In their manifest bodies they differ, as do their habits in getting food and shelter and in reproducing. He names these differentiations in bodies "multinaturalism." A critique put forward by Terence Turner appears useful, and as far as my analysis goes, Viveiros de Castro's theory also falls short when applied to Greenland (and Southwest Alaska). However, more can possibly be added to the theory by giving more thought to a so-called intermediate plane between essence and body. Viveiros de Castro mentions this plane but does not sufficiently define it, and I do not have the knowledge to engage in further speculation (see below pp. 191ff).

Another possibility for testing Viveiros de Castro's theory on the Greenland worldview is *taartaq*, the language "of darkness" spoken by the beings of the invisible Other World. Although the lists of words on record are not all just transparent, some general characteristics can be identified. Among these multinaturalism finds no support, whereas Saladin d'Anglure's theory on a gendered worldview does. In my view, *taartaq* reveals an Inuit perspective on the perspective of the Others on humans and the world.

Chapter 4: *Angakkut* (Shamans)

Angakkuuneq

Within research, definitions of shamanism (*angakkuuneq*, in West Greenlandic) are not all in concordance. Among the "fathers," Hultkrantz (1973; 1989) emphasized common cultural-historical roots, whereas Lewis (1975: 50; 1981) stressed structural-functional issues. I look to both. Neither of the two adopts the research of altered states of consciousness (ASC), which began in the 1970s. I don't either because the main distinction between ASC states, the shaman's possession by spirit and his travels in spirit, does not apply. Unlike Lewis, however, who sticks exclusively to etic criteria for research, I make emic aspects a prominent part of my own approach. Thus, a reliable list of East Greenlandic shamans, together with biographies of several of them, permits us to verify and discuss the definition proposed by Hultkrantz from an emic perspective. Not unexpectedly, his generalizations meet with uncomfortable counterexamples, which are nonetheless useful for opening up new vistas. Emic statements similarly disprove stereotypes about shamans that still haunt the Internet, such as mental disorders being a condition typical of shamans. Instead, the statements give insight into the East Greenlandic psychology of motivations, such as the high value placed upon becoming a shaman despite the ambiguities of the position; the young person's free will to ignore a call from the spirits; the experiences of apprenticeship; and criteria for ranking shamans. Gender turns out to be a decisive criterion—female shamans rarely ended up at the top of the rankings, because motherhood was an obvious hindrance in ideology as well as also in practice. Nor did female shamans, as far as the sources go, pay visits to Moon, and when visiting Sea Woman in the stories, they are supported by another shaman, always a close relative like a brother, a husband, or a mother. Male shamans went alone (in company with one or more helping spirits and never as bachelors). Only they visited Moon and the Northern Lights, competed with each other, and cooperated in impressive performances.

Turning then to the thesis forwarded by Saladin d'Anglure, of shamans representing an androgynous "third sex," its social criteria are not met by any of the named and well-known Greenlandic shamans. Children dressed in odd clothes, *piaaqqusiat*, could be accorded bisexual magic abilities but were not raised contrary to their biological sex. Curious about the social basis of a "third sex" in Greenland, I continue the analysis of the criteria one by one in society at large: an assumed change in gender at birth (*sipineq*), cross-gender naming, bringing up girls as boys, and vice versa. In general, the findings point indisputably to a greater value placed upon boys than girls. All in all, male dominance in pre-Christian Greenlandic society and shamanism cannot be talked away. Since some recent research on Inuit gender stresses equality between the sexes, I look for an explanation in the significant changes brought about by the missionaries' effective bans on feuds, polygamy, and taboos. Beyond discussion, however, is the fact that women—or, rather, mothers, especially those with sons—used to gain considerable authority with age. At this point in life equality, or dominance, was apparently obtained by this *ningiu*, the female leader of the household. Actual examples of women opposing male authority are all from polygamous marriages, which statistically absorbed a surplus of women due to a high death rate among able-bodied men. At the lower end of the scale, women who were not provided for were liable to be accused of sorcery and might be lynched in periods of crisis. Destitute men were in the danger zone as well, but they figure less often as victims.

Ilisiinneq

Ilisiinneq, sorcery, the order of the day in premodern small-scale societies, was not distinguished from shamanism by the first 18th-century missionaries. Although Poul Egede came to realize a difference, both arts remained equally condemned. Actually, as Thalbitzer realized during fieldwork in 1905–6, it was as mandatory for shamanic pupils to obtain means of sorcery as knowledge about shamanism. Both kinds of knowledge were precious commodities transferred in secrecy and carried a considerable price. A curious demand on East Greenlandic pupils to obtain an equal number of future helping spirits and means of sorcery appears fairly new and may have served as a defense against the missionaries' disdain. Sorcery is hard to dispense with in small-scale societies, but although sorcery was invariably meant to harm, it also had its social advantages. When practiced in defense, as a means of just (ideal) revenge, and also as a way of removing a person turned dangerous to his surroundings, sorcery was an indisputably moral act. Furthermore, the need for secrecy together with a belief in the boomerang effect of failed attempts constituted a built-in social control, which could afflict the unsuccessful practitioner with insanity. Confessions sometimes cured the maniac, eliminating the effect of sorcery, and consequently brought a secret personal network of enmities into the open.

Angakkussarneq (Apprenticeship)

The main object of apprenticeship (*angakkussarneq*) was to obtain "light" (vision) and helping spirits, *toornat*. The difference between *inuat* and *toornat* has been a longstanding, bewildering issue in research.[46] The simple distinction made by the Canadian Inuit: a *toornaq* is an *inua* attached to a shaman (Oosten et al. 2002; Saladin d'Anglure & Morin 1998: note 37). Or, in Greenlandic terms, a *toornaq* is merely an attached "alien," *allanaq*.

Secrecy was a general precondition for shamanic apprenticeship. Disclosure at the wrong moment could spoil the entire endeavor. Yet, as always, generalizations meet with exceptions.

No strict course was followed through apprenticeship. The scholars accord differing meanings to the same kind of experiences with spirits, and the biographies rarely live up to generalizations made by scholars and informants alike. Tuition was common but descriptions are astonishingly scarce. Only one is sufficiently detailed, and it describes knowledge communicated on shamanism and sorcery on par with tuition in hunting methods and taboos. The same source also contests the common theory in research that learning in small-scale societies occurred exclusively by silent imitation.

The acquisition of helping spirits was a must for any apprentice, who *ujarlerpoq* (went in search of spirits) for several years, roaming the land in summer. The sources supply us with useful

46. Probably due to the fact that the *inuat* of the moon, the sea, and the air did not appear as anybody's helping spirits, Thalbitzer made a distinction between *inuat* and *toornat* and became entangled in hopeless speculations about prehistoric origins (e.g., Sonne 1986a; Thuesen & Sonne 2005). Merkur picked up the thread with no greater success (1985; 1991).

information on the spirits' differing characters and inclinations for becoming a shaman's familiar. Some offered the apprentice service on their own, attracted as they were by the apprentice's interior light, a source of reenlivening heat on entering his body during future performances. In contrast, dangerous individual spirits, whether used for particular initiations or for frightening spirits at performances, had to be sought out, called upon, and sometimes permitted to devour the pupil's skin, flesh, and entrails. Relations with friendly helping spirits are well described. The pupil/shaman was expected to pay recurrent visits to their families, could be called on in order to cure a spirit family member, and an insulted spirit might attack his master. Still, as mentioned above, no merging of human with spirit society was permitted; dyadic relations reigned. To illustrate this rule, a long story about the failure of a helping spirit to steal an adoptive son of Naaja is extremely entertaining. Other stories and statements show that relatives of neither shaman nor spirit could benefit from the alliance on their own accord. Nor were any of the helping spirits per se an object of collective worship. The shaman remained the mediator, and the sources stress the shaman's individual ownership of his helping spirits. The sources also permit us to test and question a couple of allegations in research. One postulates a complete equality between Inuit and nonhuman beings. In fact, asymmetry reigned. The other assumption stresses the liberty enjoyed by the spirits to transcend any boundary of space and time. Yet they are seen to respect *naar*-times and boundaries of human habitation. A third question of sexual relations with the spirits resumes the issue of the intimate character of the relationship between a shaman and his spirits. But the examples are few. The embryo–mother relationship takes precedence in consonance with the urge of "seeking a mother," which used to take up a prominent part of Inuit "ontology." I resume this issue later.

Initiations

The Greenlandic shamans went through several initiations, in isolation as a pupil and in public as a shaman. They all follow the tripartite sequence proposed by van Gennep to cover all sorts of rites of passage. J. P. Schjødt (1986), who takes into consideration earlier research by Mircea Eliade, Lauri Honko, Victor Turner, and Terence Turner, defines, in accordance with T. Turner, the initiation rituals as the only kind yielding a "gain." In contrast, rituals of crisis and season merely restore normalcy (see Figs. 15–17). I follow T. Turner's definition as expounded by Schjødt in my extended treatment of the East Greenlandic initiations. My first issue, *qaamaneq* ("light"), the means of seeing the Other World, was the necessary and sometimes sufficient "gain."

The connotative identification between light, sight, and insight may be a human universal (basic metaphor in Lacoff and Turner's terms). And although the ways of obtaining the shaman's light, *qaamaneq*, were culturally specific, in most cases they are at least intelligible to Westerners. Thus, the heavenly lights of night were the prominent sources. The moon, the *innersuit* (the "great fires") who reflected the light of the moon, the stars, and the Northern Lights looked into the dark world (stomach, *naaq* in the spirit language) at night, as did the shaman by means of his "light." He looked into the Other Worlds (of darkness)—including the dark interior of humans. But nobody, be he shamanic pupil, initiated shaman, or an ordinary dreaming human, was able to see both worlds at the same time. A clearly described period of blurred (liminal) sight either way illustrates this Inuit principle of complementarity. The polysemy of light in Inuit origin myths reveals intimate associations with movement, heat, and attraction. These associations render the pupil's way of summoning future helping spirits perfectly intelligible when combined with the process of making fire by means of stones. The apprentice used to rub a small stone in circular movements on a bigger flat one for hours on end, following the way of the heavenly bodies, the lights of the worlds. *Qaamaneq* rarely dawned upon the pupil once and for all. Instead, training, newly obtained spirits, and experiences like the most frightening one of being devoured by the so-called "freshwater bear" stimulated its growth. Frequently, an emphasis on "light" events within a shaman's legendary biography added to the fame he left behind.

As to the symbolism of being devoured by an animal, the simplest interpretation points to a reversal of no great surprise: hunters who kill and eat animals then see to their revival by ritual means. In the light of Maurice Bloch's theory of "prey into hunter,"[47] there is more flesh involved with this reversal, though not many supporting instances of a Greenlandic pupil going berserk after recovery. A direct focus on the East Greenlandic metaphors is more rewarding, because the eaters, the so-called "freshwater" animals—the polar bear and the dog—explicitly belong to Moon. In my interpretation they act as his extended potency, by the association of sex with eating: the polar bear or dog of the Moon satisfies its appetite on the pupil and ejaculates his flesh, a quick conception that has the pupil wake up as naked as a newborn baby. As liminal beings, the polar bear of sea and land and the dog of animals and human beings serve these transformations well. They are culture-specific, as Schjødt proposes they should be. The same is true of another kind of initiating creature, the water beetle and the larva. They transform from larva to pupa to beetle or insect. In contrast to the male *inua* of the moon, the larva is more closely associated with the female role in procreation, whereas still another figure, a devouring giant of the inland ice, must be male. Be this as it may, the more interesting part of this myth conferred on the shaman Naaja offers an explanation to the interlude between the acts of being devoured and "reborn." Namely, it puts the neophyte on the dark path through the ice cover in clear analogy with the difficult passage of the baby from the dark interior of its mother out into the light of the day. Finally, copulation is the way the androgynous spirit, *Uersaq*, initiates the pupil, who loses and later regains consciousness and clothing. This figure, studied by Gersain, is discussed at length.

A particular helping spirit, *toornaarsuk* (*toornaq*, helping spirit + *arsuk*, special), who holds initiating power in West Greenland, is less easily defined. Identified with the Devil by the first missionaries, this "apotheosis" has its own story of development to tell. The East Greenlandic statements cause some confusion because they suffer from both spelling errors and instances of overinterpretation. Yet the identification of two kinds of wing snails with *toornaarsuit* (the plural of *toornaarsuk*) is possible, whereas a third, a certain *ululoo* (pronounced *ooloolo-o* in English), calling spirit of the sea, points to a sea mammal figure with significant ritual functions. I return to this spirit in the chapter on *pooq*.

Traveling Abilities

Flying, gliding, and walking were the shamans' ways of traveling. Contradicting statements are discussed and I either find ways to harmonize them or rule them out. In general, the statements are

47. Being tortured and devoured, the prey (i.e., the apprentice) becomes one with the predator, an identification that turns him into a hunter himself. By violence he has to recapture his daily life in order not to lose the benefits gained from the initiation, defined by Bloch as the overcoming of the transitoriness of life (Bloch 1992).

fewer on the acquisition of traveling abilities than on obtaining the shaman's "light," *qaamaneq*, the sine qua non of any performing shaman at any level of competence. Gliding, rarely mentioned in research, attracts attention due to the attire required, socks or boots and sometimes the gutskin anorak, *ikiaq*. Finally, it takes a long time to discover Maratsi's peculiar outfit for his last visit to the heavenly realm of death.

Saqqummerneq, Initiation in Public

The pupil's public initiation, *saqqummerneq* (coming forward, disclosure), coincides with winter solstice in the biographies of the great shamans. In social terms, marriage before the event was a requirement, provoking an explanation for a singular deviance. The master of ceremony was seldom a shaman; rather, the father or the eldest man of the household is the chosen support. Only a few candidates follow the ideal series of first a "delivery," *ueerineq*, which turned the candidate insane or unconscious, followed by the actual "first" performance, *saqqummerneq*, and finally, a presentation of the helping spirits acquired during apprenticeship. There are many variations, but the impressive staging managed by the talented few offer a sample of rituals, which draw upon well-known ritual games and particularly spectacular performances. A less convincing *saqqummerneq* could be augmented by subsequent glorifying performances, a possibility greatly exploited also by the talented few. Even failed attempts would enhance one's reputation. Treating the descriptions from some "haughty" distance, I may not please the descendants of the storytellers or whomever it may concern. But by dealing with the performances as well-prepared and staged theatrical events, which successfully create the illusion that makes them work, I do justice, I hope, to the artistic genius of these great shamans. At the same time, my approach brings to the fore the personal agenda of the shaman in question, as recognized by either his contemporary surroundings or, in retrospect, by the storyteller. Ending this chapter, a discussion of nakedness versus clothing is supplied with another about the "spirituality" of the traveling shaman. He loses neither identity nor consciousness, and his bodily senses remain intact. Would this, my question goes, correspond to "the intermediate plane," a poorly defined proposal by Viveiros de Castro, between a differing body and a proposed undifferentiated "soul"?

Among the East Greenlandic ways to elevate one's reputation post-*saqqummerneq*, the initiation to an *angakkoq puulik* ranks the highest. While enigmatic because it has been insufficiently explained by the informants, it asks for thorough analyses in several directions. Consequently, they are placed in a chapter on their own.

Chapter 5: *Angakkoq Puulik* (Shaman with a Bag)

Pooq (bag, cover, envelope) is a rich, polysemous word. Its superordinate meaning denotes the protection of any object or life essence. Named as the "gain" of a post-*saqqummerneq* initiation to an *angakkoq puulik*, it connotes a process involving a cooperating couple of a polar bear and a walrus and, judging from ritual descriptions, an *ululoo*-calling spirit as well. Among Canadian Inuit, the animal uttering this call appears identified with the narwhal (not extant in Alaska and encountered for the first time by the Thule culture immigrants along the Arctic coast of Canada). In East Greenland, however, it may be identified as a bearded seal. The ritual demands on carrying out the initiation of an *angakkoq puulik*, along with the meanings and cosmological positions of these three animals, take up the first part of the chapter. For a start, the unusual cooperation of polar bear and walrus demands some attention to their range in daily life and myth. Next, the bearded seal takes us all the way through Inuit/Yupiit cultures from East Greenland to Nunivak Island in the Bering Sea, due to its importance not only as a deliverer of skins and guts for almost any kind of handmade *pooq* but also as a ritual bogey of New Year celebrations. The bearded seal's character of a libidinous male calling *ululoo* is encountered across the Inuit Arctic. Among the Eastern Inuit, additional associations of the bearded seal include the center of the open sea in summer, the open sea beyond the ice edge in winter, an ability to cut through the ice or find a lead at the turn of winter, and the power to travel right on to the horizon, beyond which the ritual polar bear and walrus belong. I name the polar bear/walrus/bearded seal grouping the *pooq* complex, and include the *inua* of the bearded seal as the bogey that in myth kills noisy children. The corresponding ritual play is performed at winter ceremonies. Finally, I embark on a treatment of *pooq* as a symbol of facilitating acculturative rearrangements of cosmology. Conversion to Christianity is one early theme, its creed and the presence of Qallunaat authorities another, whereas a third directs the course of a story composed by the great storyteller Aron into the Christian area of West Greenland. It tells about a particular male sculpin in the figure of a humanlike hunter. Implicitly he can be identified with the dangling "phallus" of the Entrails Snatcher and along the way combined with several *pooq* objects of differing kinds and meanings. Aron ends up turning the traditional meaning of invisibility obtained by getting *pooq* on its head by describing the light emitted by two *puuat*, a gutskin anorak and the dressing of the great seamark south of Nuuk—the mountain Kingittorsuaq—in perpetual snow.

The final discussion focuses on the role of tide and raven, on boundaries, body symbolism, and the power of my select Inuit key symbols—light and *pooq*—in order to come to grips with acculturative changes.

CHAPTER ONE

■ ■ ■

Space and Time

Introduction

Corresponding to theory of practice, Inuit do not separate time and space in actual life; in indicating time they live up to Ricoeur's thesis that time markers would not exist if there was no "right time" (or place) for an activity (cf. Munn 1992; Adams 1994). Similar to Western idioms such as "space of time" and "a long time," the Inuit use the affix *-wik*/ *-vik*/*-fik* to indicate time and place for both a usual human activity and a recurring event in nature (Fortescue et al. 1994: 398; 2010: 440).[1] Aspects of the polysemous *sila,* such as both the annual round *silap ingerlasia* and its use to refer to one's close environment, similarly cover both time and space.[2] Indeed, Inuit and Yupiit have no words for abstractions of space and time (*ibid.*; see also Nagy 2006). The Greenlanders have *piffissaq*, the time for something going to be done, and *pivik*, for doing something. The spatial meanings of *sila* are the "out of doors": the environmental field of vision of land, sea, and, in particular, the airy space between earth and the heavenly vault, *qilak*. The great *sila*, *silarsuaq*, is the world.

Space and time are combined in structuralist representations of worldviews such as Bourdieu's of the Kabyle world.[3] Like most perceptions of spatial world, the house or dwelling serves as the model while the annual round of nature and human activity structures the changes in time. The basic Kabyle opposition is man versus woman and the opposed key metaphors are wet versus dry (Bourdieu 1990a [1972; 1977]: 155–57).[4] Saladin d'Anglure provided a similar detailed exposition of the Canadian Inuit worldview on three levels of "houses," the biggest one being the outside world, the middle one the human house on earth, and at the lowest level the much smaller interior "house" of the fetus in its womb. The basic opposition is similarly that of genders united in building the skeleton and blood of the fetus by male semen and female blood, respectively, and its (mediating) flesh from

1. Nuttall's "memory scape" is another example of the coincidence of time and space, namely the content and meaning conferred on localities from experience by his Greenlandic informants (Nuttall 1992).
2. "Spacetime" of the physicists—time as the fourth dimension—is not an issue here.
3. The Kabyle example holds even though here Bourdieu is theorizing against structuralism.
4. Not included in Bourdieu (1980; 1990b).

the animals eaten by both parents. The key metaphors are light versus darkness and heat versus cold (1986: 39). The Greenlandic sources may permit substantiation of a replica, but this time-consuming job must be completed by people younger than me. My analysis, though not avoiding the numerous binary oppositions encountered, will be a structurally less ambitious one, context-dependent as my method primarily is. One central focus is on the analogies of bodily positions, movements, and the senses, which dominate relations between This World and the Other World(s). Meanings of standing erect, awake, conscious, and keeping one's balance are my main concern, as are orientation and movement—in general the sign of life versus death. Among the senses, sight and vision stand out as decisive means for keeping up the relations between This and the Other World. Fienup-Riordan's emphasis on the senses has been of inspiration (1990: 49–67; 1994: 356), but I do not treat taste, touch, speech, hearing, and thinking as thoroughly as sight, which is tantamount in the perception of "light," the Inuit shaman's metaphor for vision and a means of seeing the Other World.

Being in *Sila*

The polysemous *sila*—which means weather, reason, sight, and second sight beyond its primary meanings of space, air, and the visible world—is in my view best grasped by theories of the human body's being-in-the-world (Heidegger's Dasein and Ingold's life-world): moving, lying down, and rising, with its senses and mind of perception. I prefer this approach to attempts at having *all* meanings of *sila* unite in a single philosophical synthesis. The ordered way of the world may cover such a synthesis, but it does not tell how this order works or might implode. The body-centered way of orientation appears reflected in binary ideas about the balance of the world, of light versus darkness, movement versus nonmovement, and in sayings about *sila* that are about body-sense perspectives of humans in contrast to that of nonhumans (and practicing shamans). Similarly, theories of praxis govern my focus on aspects of time. *Sila* includes the cosmography of the Other Worlds traveled by shamans, depicted in stories, and peopled with beings related to humans in binding ways.

The Other World, *Asia* or *Silam Aappaa*

The Other World was invisible, and its inhabitants spoke *taartaq*, the language of darkness, which named the space of This World *naaq*, stomach (O. Rosing 1957–61, I: 92). Admittedly, my concept of the "Other World" is in part a biased abstraction. According to the reactions of Teemiartissaq, a female East Greenlandic shaman apprentice cut off from her carrier, there is no *one* Other World. She told Thalbitzer that "*Asia* ['the other side'] means all the other countries [lands] inhabited by beings touching us without being together with us... for instance another place to which one is bound out of interest or kinship or other" (Thalbitzer 1930: 84–85, tr. BS).[5,6] These bindings are precisely expressed in the West Greenlandic term *silam aappaa*, meaning the other *sila* of a couple.[7] *Silam*

5. I can easily follow her way of perceiving first one, then another "country," be that on or inside earth, below the foreshore, beneath the outer skerries, the realms of death and Sea Woman far away down below and the realms of death and Moon above.

6. The original quote in French reads, "*Asia*, c'est-à-dire ce qui nous touche sans être avec nous : « l'autre côté », par exemple, un autre endroit où l'on est lié par un intérêt, une parenté ou autre."

7. *Silam aappaa* is mentioned once as "the other world" without further qualifications in an Avanersuaq text (Holtved 1951, I: 73–74).

aappaa is one reason for my use of the (Western) shorthand term the Other World. Another reason is the idea of a common language, *taartaq* (belonging in darkness) spoken by all residents in the Other World, be they the *inuat, allanat* ("aliens," or *allanertat*), or deceased relatives, and no matter to which "country" of the Other World they belong. A third decisive reason is the idea of changing sight from This World to the Other World, which could be experienced unintentionally by laypeople and mastered by shamans. The shaman's *silaninneq*, or coming to see (acquiring the knowledge of) the entire Other World, as called forth while alone in the wilderness was also staged and obtained in public during *saqqummerneq*, the shaman's public initiation (see chapter 4). This mental process of *silaninneq* corresponded to the change in sight between This and the Other World, experienced by pupils and shamans on a smaller scale, no matter which part of the Other World they approached. So while the Other World was separated from This World by its language (*taartaq*) and its invisibility, mutual dependency reigned between the "couple" or pair of *sila*s. Similarly, on the symbolic house level, its *interior* was related to the *outside* and vice versa by the common word *taqqama*, meaning the opposite "world" of either. The responsibility of keeping the relationship with the opposite world in balance rested with humans, who were to observe pre- and proscriptions placed at decisive points in time of the annual round and individual life cycle. Consequently, when I discuss ritual behavior in chapter 2 (under the heading "Times of Ritual"), my distinction between the two worlds cannot help becoming blurred. I discuss the particular "geography" and "times" and language of the Other World separately in chapter 3.

Biocultural Time

Experientially, theories of praxis about lived time appear evident. To quote Munn: "In practice... calendars or similar nature-bound 'collective representations' [cannot be distinguished] from the personal 'time,' the stream of consciousness (Bergson's *durée*) in our minds. This does not mean that calendars do not exist, or that grammars including our own do not distinguish between past, present, and future. But cognitively we cannot put back the clock. No time is static. Present and future meddle with remembered past, and past and present into our (always) future-oriented 'projects.' This meddling provides our acts with their meaning" (Munn 1992). Along the same line of thought, Adams contrasts our Western dominant clock time, the "machine time" objectified into a commodity, with four common aspects of time that are still in use, albeit "invisibly" and that refer to biocultural rhythms of nature and society. "Temporality" is the course of our irreversible life. "When time"—which refers to concepts such as "bedtime," "springtime," "childhood," and "opening hours"—can be fixed by clock and calendar but usually refers to the rhythms of nature, or social norms, or political decisions. "Timing" appears analogous to *kairos*, or Ricoeur's "right time." Finally, "tempo" is the subjective feeling of time that runs, flies, or drags on (Adams 1994). These ways of experiencing time are probably as universal as the mingling of circular and linear time, annual rounds, and the irreversible time of events. Ritual celebrates the first, biographies the latter, though rarely in a linear order until put into writing.

Visibility governs ideas about the dependency between space and spatial time in This and the Other World of the Greenlanders. Space visible to humans out of doors is *sila*, or the environment. Arching over *sila* is *qilak*, the sky arch, which is traveled by the sun during the day and at night by the other heavenly bodies who look into *naaq* ("stomach" in ordinary speech and "night" in the spirit language). Fading and growing visibility similarly mark the liminal *naar*-times, dawn and dusk. Both are announced audibly by the raven's cry, and they mark the when-times of both shamans and nonhumans for crossing the border between the two worlds (O. Rosing 1957–61, I: 92; Victor & Robert-Lamblin 1989–93, II: 241, 249; for details, see chapter 3). Places and devices for passing or open up spatial boundaries are numerous. They will be described all along and summed up in chapter 6, "Conclusion."

Orientation

The Way of the World in Time and Space

Silap malillugu, "following the way of the world" (i.e., the ritual circling following the direction of the sun), was a pan-Inuit/Yupiit term (R. Petersen 1966/67: 262; Saladin d'Anglure 1986; 1990a; Fienup-Riordan 1994: Chap. 12) for a panglobal ritual. Alternately, the West Greenlandic *silap ingerlasia* means the annual round of changing seasons, of weather, light, and life cycles of nature's beings (e.g., Sonne 2005: ID 769). To respect, understand, and follow this cosmic order in whatever situation of life was to use one's *sila* in the meanings of being sensible and clever, as underlined by Saladin d'Anglure (1991: 28). It took a lifetime of experience to understand the way(s) of *sila*, especially to learn the signs of changing weather, personified by Canadian Inuit as a giant baby, raging at times *silaittuq* (without *sila*)—like any baby beyond pedagogical reach (A similar figure, the baby-husband of the East Greenlandic *inua* of precipitation, *Asiaq*, received more restricted connotations, see p. 134.) The annual round of *sila*, *ukioq*, a year, also meant "winter" in the same way that Danes and other Europeans used to count years in summers. I shall refrain from further comparisons in symbolic meanings of Inuit winter versus European summer and merely point to the Inuit genderizing of the two half-years, assigning men the upper hand. Winter, in *taartaq* (the language of the spirits of the Other World), is "the time of men," *angutaaneq/angitaaneq*, in contrast to summer, "the time of women," *arnaavoq* (O. Rosing 1957–61, I: 87; Victor & Robert-Lamblin 1989–93, II: 255; Saladin d'Anglure 1997: 46). The subject of summer, *arnaavoq*, however, is also male: "the time when the men [males] have to do with the women [females], or are much occupied with them" (Thalbitzer 1923: 488).

The seasons were four like ours, *ukioq* (winter), *upernaaq* (spring), *aasaq* (summer), and *ukiaq* (autumn) (West Greenlandic), if slightly differently named among the Inuit groups. For more precise reckonings, affixes like *-ssaq*, or "approaching," are used. In this context *-ssaq* literally means that one season is considered the material for the next, as in the statement *Ukiassariartorami ukialerpoq*: "Having used (*-riartorami*) the material for autumn, *ukia-ssaq* (approaching autumn = late summer), *ukiaq* (autumn) *-lerpoq* (began)." In short, "late summer is the material for autumn" (Sandgreen 1967, II: 26). The appearance of the twin stars *Aassuutit* (Altair + Tarazed in the constellation Aquila) marked New Year among all Inuit and Yupiit (Holm 1972: 137; 1914: 105; MacDonald 1998: 44).[8] At the turning of the sun in December, Greenlanders can actually feel the earth tremble, the stronger the farther north (Juuaka Lyberth pers. comm.). In Ammassalik the two stars were said to save the sun from drowning at winter solstice (O. Rosing 1989), and in the view of the Yupiit of Southwest Alaska they lifted up the sun continuously from December to March (Fienup-Riordan & Rearden 2013: 66). About the same time, in April, when the rising sun took over their point of rising on the horizon, they marked spring in

8. This is also true of the Chukchi, who were under the influence of the Siberian Yupiit (Anisimov 1963: 212).

Ammassalik (Holm 1972: 137; 1914: 105). The altitude of the sun marked equinox as did forceful high tides in spring and autumn; the farther south in Greenland, the higher the flood (see below).

April usually meant moving out of the houses and camping at places for fishing, sealing, and caribou hunting as well as occasional travels to places of assembly and trade. At freeze-up in September, houses were repaired or fresh ones built for wintering; these were mostly longhouses in the period of our concern.[9] Regarding the Greenlandic names of moons, little is known compared to the recurrent Inuit and Yupiit ones that refer to events in nature (e.g., MacDonald 1998: 192–98; Lantis 1946: 171; Fienup-Riordan & Rearden 2013: 73f). "They have no calendar," Hans Egede reports, "nor do they compute or measure the time by weeks or years, but only by months; beginning their computation from the Sun's first rising above their horizon in the winter; from whence they tell [count] the month [months], to know exactly the season, in which every sort of fishes, sea animals, or birds seek the land, according to which they order their business" (1818: 212).[10] Holm was informed by the Ammassalimmiut that they counted the new moons, twelve or thirteen, as they came (Holm 1972: 137; 1914: 105), while the more detailed information collected by Dalager in South-Southwest Greenland reveals a mix of counting and seasonal events. The first three or four moons were counted until the move from house to tents, followed by the moon of the ravens laying their eggs and the arrival of the snow buntings. The fifth moon was the time of seals and capelin, followed by the time of sealing, the eider ducks hatching their young, and the calving of caribou. At that point in summer the moon became invisible, and time was reckoned in relation to the growth of the young eider ducks and the ripening of the crowberries. Time for wintering (September) approached when the velvet was shredded from the caribou antlers, the terns left, and the seals had grown fat.[11] At that point nobody cared for dividing up moons until New Year, "because nothing else was hunted but seals" (Dalager 1915: 54–55). In short, in this part of the Inuit/Yupiit world events in the annual round of hunting and movements served as the points of reference; however, because more than one activity was mentioned for some moons, it remains uncertain whether these events actually named the moons. Colonization soon introduced the European calendar, as well as the week (*sapaatip akunnerana*, the in-between Sabbaths), which was indispensable for keeping track of the "forbidding" Sundays.

In their reckoning of linear time, the Greenlanders made no use of their numbers, which referred to fingers and toes, twenty being *inuk naallugu*, "a complete human being."[12] Days were broken into morning, midday, afternoon, evening, twilight, and dawn, and the years (*ukiut*, "winters"), as in most oral cultures, were accurately remembered by their main events in nature and/or family life. The age of humans was divided into childhood, youth, adulthood, and old age, as well as relationally, by kinship terms.[13] For obvious reasons the ages of important game animals were quite precisely differentiated by appellations meaning "one year old," "two years old," and "adult."

---

9. Longhouses for several families, separated on the main platform by partitions. See Sørensen & Gulløv (2012) for the possible origin of the construction.

10. The Danish original has "*tæller alle måneder*" (H. Egede 1925: 401; 1971, 2: 124).

11. The shredding of caribou antlers is a pan-Inuit/Yupiit name for that moon.

12. Would the counting of moons throughout the annual round be considered a linear or a circular time reckoning?

13. "For instance, asking the age of Utuak's son, he [Utuak] enumerated their places of wintering and the ensuing summers since the birth of his son, 13 years ago. At a later repetition, and still without using numbers, he arrived at the same result" (Holm 1972: 139; 1914: 112).

For relating mutual points in time, Greenlandic is quite rich in possibilities: apart from the verbal inflected when-suffixes (past and future), the affixes *-reer*, *-sima*, *-qqu*, and *-li* refer to the past; *-ssa*, *-ngor*, or *-gu/-ru* to the future; and the directing *-mut* to both time and space (Trondhjem 2009). Particulars such as *ippassaaq* and *ippaasaani*, for instance, mean yesterday and the day before yesterday; *siorna* and *siornaaq* mean last year and the year before last; *siornal-li*, several years ago; *itsaq* or *qannga*, a long time ago; and *itsar-suaq*, *qaanga-li*, a very long time ago. Insofar as the examples of the modern dictionary show, the future appears less rich in particulars: tomorrow is *aqagu*, day after tomorrow is *aqaguagu*, whereas *aappaagu* or *ukioq ataaseq kangiuppat* (when one year has passed) both mean next year. In fact, research regarding premodern dating is scarce,[14] but judging from the up-to-date dictionary, no Danish loan words except the names of months and the unending series of numbers have been necessary for constructing all sorts of dating (Berthelsen et al.; Jones & Petersen). But you may notice that a Greenlander less fluent in Danish grammar will use the present in telling about past events, owing to their Greenlandic when-grammar, which follows other rules of cause-and-effect dependency. Events in the lives of individual persons were remembered in stories transmitted within the family; the more extraordinary ones in wider circles. As to relational chronology, the naming of babies for deceased relatives kept track of the extended network of ancestors through the generations. This network went back some four or five generations according to MacDonald (1998: 194) or up to ten, trusting Dalager, who in a very matter-of-fact way adds, "which means great support for many poor families" (1915: 56). Indeed, realistic expectations were meat gifts from well-to-do relatives (compare with Bodenhorn 2000; Nuttall 2000).

The common Inuit and Yupiit distinction between very old and more recent stories or accounts, *oqaluttuat* and *oqalualaavit* in West Greenlandic, is used for categorizing stories in publications and sometimes also in handwritten collections. At present *aliortukkat* (stories about experiences with ghosts, other beings, and inexplicable events) are still told among friends, in radio, and on TV. A detailed chronological typology used by West Greenlandic writers in starting a story will be described and commented on below.

Perceptions of Space and Land

Being out of doors, especially on a starry night, one could see the heaven circling on top of a high mountain in the north (P. Egede 1971: 57, 59; 1939: 43–44), a notion in fine agreement with the idea of *silap ingerlasia*, "world," moving continuously with the sun. The East Greenlanders noted that it spirals like the winding of a conch (Thalbitzer 1930: 83). From another center, inside the dwelling, and in analogy with the house, the heavens (i.e., the roof) did not circle, supported as they were by wooden pillars. No need was felt to reconcile the two views, one giving rise in some contexts to the idea of the heavenly realm of death as a bad place due to the dizzying effect of the constant circling (P. Egede 1971: 97–98; 1939: 67–68), the other to the impending downfall of heaven, which was supported by the Christian preaching of doomsday (see below). The logic works, depending on perspective. Westerners too do not feel the urge to root out every "when-time" time idiom of our language referring to the perceived movements of the sun, despite our highly esteemed knowledge of the sun, which neither rises

14. See Therrien (1996 and p. 150) for the multitude of suffixes used for "first-time acts" and their importance.

nor sets. Perception and scientific knowledge coexist, disassembled by context. Some Greenlanders were alarmed, however, by the new heliocentric worldview taught by enlightened missionaries. One Greenlander even accused the colonists of having introduced the new confusing order: it made the seals miss their old routes and reduce the number that arrived in spring and summer (N. Egede 1971: 31–32; 1939: 146). Another complaint was that the continuous rotation of the earth, apparently started by the mission, had brought extremely bad weather, halved the course of life, made everybody an easy target for all kinds of illnesses, and promoted aging and the depopulation of the land, especially that in the north (N. Egede 1943: 51). It is a peculiar argument insofar as it retains the explanatory value of both the traditional and the Western views. Or to quote Munn, who quotes Connerton, "the present derives its meaning as a departure from earlier ways, but the latter are then dialectically implicated in the very idea of the new" (Munn 1992: 110–11; Connerton 1989: 7–8). My own comment furthers this idea: how are we to deal with such intricacies if words like " worldview" or "cosmology" are ruled out?

Whereas the Greenlandic shaman was able to see only one world at a time, either This World of ordinary human sight or the Other World of their second sight (see p. 278), various *inuat* (*inua* in the plural) of the Other World could follow the doings of humans in This World without losing sight of their own. Thus the Yup'ik *Ella* (*Silap Inua* in Inuit dialects), partly influenced by Christian ideas, watches the world and reacts with roaring gales and other calamities to wrongdoings, especially toward game (Rasmussen 1927; Fienup-Riordan 1994). In Greenland this role is only rarely attributed to the *inua* of *Sila*.[15] Most frequently, the watchful eye on high is *Qaammatip Inua*, the man in the visible moon. In myth his perspective was the land and sea below; on a reduced scale, his gaze was centered on the littoral region with its human settlements in close succession and the distance between the houses reduced, so that they looked like dogs around a feeding trough (e.g., Sonne 2005: ID 1812). The human visitor to the Moon witnessed that view, a view that in a way contradicts the ideas set forth by Ingold about "mapping" one's land. The land has no surface, Ingold claims, in contrast to cartography; in other words, "a totalising vision above and beyond the world.... [P]eople's knowledge of the environment undergoes continuous formation in the very course of their moving about in it" (Ingold 2000: 233–34). In the same way Ingold understands the precise wood carvings made on request and from scratch by East Greenlanders of the extended littoral zones they knew from their travels: "For Inuit mappers it was the performance that mattered—the recapitulation of environmental features" (232–33). Ingold may in a sense be right, but it is first important to remember that the same Inuit immediately "read" European maps of the lands they knew (Holm 1972: 140; 1914: 107–8). Second, I contend that imagination did work on another level, too. By climbing a high mountain on a clear day, the perspective of Moon was easy to imagine and enlarge, at least on a reduced scale. Knowledge of the land gained by long travels along the coast was similarly reproduced in a bird's-eye view in stories about flights of shamans (e.g., Sonne 2005: ID 350).[16] Yet seeing the

15. "[T]he shamans make people believe that a person in the air, allowing itself to be seen only by them, is called Inerterrirsok (Inerteritsoq), the person who forbids" (P. Egede 1971: 67; 1939: 47).

16. Andreas Roepstorff (2003) has made the same objection from the point of view of *Sassuma Arnaa* (Sea Woman), according to a late variant of her origin (Sonne 2005: ID 1882). In personal communication by e-mail, Ingold has tried to convince me that both Roepstorff and I are wrong in our understanding of the view of the shaman (identical with that of either Sea Woman or Moon). Ingold contends that the shaman does not outwardly overlook but rather penetrates whatever is being looked at. I agree insofar as the Other Worlds seen by the shaman are interior worlds, be that

world as a full *globe* from the outside, the view of modern cartography, was not part of Inuit tradition.[17] The Inuit in both Canada and Alaska objected that the water would fall off that globe, as they perceived the earth as a disk (MacDonald 1998: 24–25; Gubser 1965: 193; Boas 1901–7: 173; Saladin d'Anglure 1990a: 81; Fienup-Riordan 1994: 259, 264). Similar perceptions were current in Greenland as will appear in the section "Balance."

Being in Space

Sila, in the meaning of "out of doors," environment, has a center: the point where you are at the moment (Kleinschmidt 1871). *Sila* is thus your life-world, to quote Ingold, the sphere surrounding you in contrast to the cartographic view of the globe from the outside (2000: 230ff). Obviously Ingold could have looked to Inuit/Yupiit phrasing in thinking out his theory of environment, dwelling, and awareness (a hunter is constantly aware of his environs, natural and social).[18]

A human being's entrance/birth into This World was an event of spatial dimension. Like any Inuk, a Greenlander identifies herself by *-miu*, the dweller of (a named *nuna*, land [locality], or today, a city or settlement), predominantly the birthplace. Formerly the *sila*-time of one's birth was simultaneously the decisive when-point in life, to which a person could refer in an attempt at changing the weather: "*nauk silaga, ungaa*," or "where is (*silaga*) my weather? (*ungaa*) baby cry"—i.e., let the weather change to that of the day I was born, when my (creative) "words" were those of a baby's cry (*ungaa*). Saladin d'Anglure picked out that ritual sentence (1986: 72; 1990a: 94), which commonly appears among Eastern Inuit; it is also recorded in Avanersuaq and South and East Greenland (Sonne 2005: ID 1556, 1728, 658; F. Lynge 1981: No. 77; Victor & Robert-Lamblin 1989–93, II: 390). In the perspective of the East Greenlandic spirits as expressed in their spirit language, humans belong at the border of the land but still at the center of the middle world—i.e., as coast-dwellers (*sijaa ijivata*, Sandgreen 1967, II: 28; *cilat* (W. Grl. *sissat*), Victor & Robert-Lamblin 1989–93, II: 255).

The Coastal Center

From atop the lookout at the coast and looking back, the mountainous land rises from the coast upwards to the inland ice, and is in most places used only during summer travel and hunts. It covers the greatest part of the inland region and touches the sea at the bottom of the icefjords. Looking the opposite way, the shore below is seen to continue slanting and then disappear under the sea. Skerries are visible, and they are known to be numerous along the west coast. Some are inhabited only in

---

of "nature" as among human beings, in the same way that Moon, in myth as in actual life, looks right into rooms of human houses (through the windows) observing whatever "deeds of darkness" are committed. But first, the reduced scale on which Moon and the visiting shaman (or any human visitor to Moon) see the entire littoral zone and the actual activities of humans on earth is very clearly depicted in myth; second, the second sight of the shaman usually excludes that of the ordinary one (see the section on initiation of shamans in ch. 4). Of greater import, however, is that the basic or source metaphor is the ability to see whatever darkness hides to the ordinary eye: the Other World of darkess, *taartaq*, and This one as well—*at night*: thus, in a completely dark room the shamans could see people as clearly as "when all lights were burning; and not only could they see their fellow-beings, but they could see quite clearly through clothing and skin and flesh into their very innermost" (Rasmussen 1938: 110).

17. One late variant opening the view from the moon to "the entire earth" may reflect Western impact by binoculars or pictures seen of the globe, but no concrete limit to this "entire world" is given (Sonne 2005: ID 341).

18. In common use, the relational *eqqaa*, "her close by," means "her nearest environment" and with the reinforcing affix *-leq* "her close kin," sometimes "her neighbor" (Kleinschmidt 1871).

spring, whereas other sizable ones are lived upon all year round, like Kangeq off Nuuk and the island of Disko farther north, the largest of them all. It has flora similar to that around Nuuk, which is reflected in the myth about its relocation from the south to the north (P. Egede 1971: 68; 1939: 50). The horizon of the sea sets the outer limit and continues to do so for kayakers hunting beyond the outermost skerries, because Akilineq, the opposite land, lies beyond the ordinary field of vision. The heavenly vault, *qilak*, is marked off by the movements of sun, moon, and stars, whereas the Northern Lights, believed by most Greenlanders to be produced by the movements of deceased relatives playing ball, connect earth with heaven. So does the place for the lookout, offering a convenient position for consulting the Northern Lights (N. Egede 1971: 87; 1939: 180) and used by the man in the moon (*Qaammatip Inua*, hereafter Moon) for a stepping-stone on visits to earth (Sonne 2005: ID 1343).

Thanks to MacDonald's copious research in Inuit orientation, we can learn to find our way in their world (1998). Fortescue (1988) has advanced a hypothesis about the quarters of the prevalent winds of pan-Inuit/Yupiit extension. Saladin d'Anglure (1990a), Oosten and Laugrand (2004–5), Michèle Therrien (1987), and Raymond Gagné (1968) have each used their own approach to contribute to our understanding of orientation in the Canadian Arctic. Saladin d'Anglure and Oosten and Laugrand underline that the dominant orientation among the Canadian Inuit with whom they worked is toward the south—the position of the sun at the times it disappears and reappears on the horizon at the beginning and end of the polar night. Consequently, the mapping of Inuit Canada is oriented toward the south, the opposite direction of Western maps. Greenlanders too looked south for annual arrivals of game and European ships; above the polar circle they searched for the reappearance of the sun (in the south). The confrontation of "southerners"[19] versus "northerners" was also the way of distinguishing between people from mutually distant locales, who met for competitions (see p. 236). However, the center of their localizers was standing at the coast, facing the sea. Gagné, together with his copyist, Zeilich-Jensen (see below), and certainly Fortescue, are of particular relevance for my presentation of some aspects of the Greenlandic worldview. Fortescue maps out the "logical" variations of a pan-Inuit/Yupiit orientation system, and traces its origin to the (Alaska) Norton culture (prior to the Thule culture) in the Bering Strait region. From the summary of that intriguing and well-argued hypothesis, I shall quote the points of relevance to Greenland: "The essential framework... consisted of an 'up/down' dimension away from and down to the shore...; a 'left/right-along-shore one'... deriving ultimately from within the house; and a 'major wind' axis, originally down through the Bering Strait region, which would have provided a more 'absolute' frame of reference than the first two dimensions, more closely bound to the configurations of the shoreline" (Fortescue 1988).[20]

Being selective I shall stick to the right/left and up/down dimensions. The first involves a mirror effect that complicates translation. The latter is treated by its extensions upward and downward, which concern the movements of the tripartite world.

Right and Left in East Greenland

A comment must be made on differences between terms for Greenlandic and Western directions that refer to facing the sea and the sun, respectively. The translations of Greenlandic "right" and "left"

---

19. Used here as a general, relative term, not the "Southerners" of the Cape Farewell–Nanortalik region.
20. Gagnée considers "here/there," "outside/inside," and "up/down" to be the dominant dimensions (1968).

into our cardinal points north and south work well for West Greenland but not for the east coast. There is a mirror effect not realized by the Greenlander, who to this day faces the sea as his point of orientation. He calls the direction to the right *avannamut*, to the left *kujamut* or *qavunnga*, behind or beyond upward *kangiamut* or *pavunga*, and forward or downward (sloping) *kimut* or *samunnga*, respectively. Greenlanders who know Danish are rarely aware that translations of the directions into Danish are to be laterally reversed for the east coast, where *avannamut* (to the right) means south. Facing the sea, right is *avannamut*, left is *kujamut*, etc., no matter the position of the sun. Even Danes who have lived for a long time in Greenland similarly look to the dictionary and get the translations wrong as regards East Greenland (e.g., Rasmussen 1921–25, I: 252–53; J. Rosing 1963: 218 in transl. of O. Rosing 1957–63, I: 128). In my attempt to solve that problem while translating a large volume of texts, I had to ask the author, Otto Sandgreen (1967; 1987). Sandgreen, a West Greenlandic minister who had taped the stories in East Greenlandic but had them printed in West Greenlandic, was unable to help. He had never thought that way. Greenlanders face the sea having *avannamut* to the right and *kujamut* to the left regardless of our cardinal points, and so my problems remained unsolved.[21]

Making a Living from Land and Sea

While the missionaries preached spiritual versus material values and trust in God's providence, 19th-century West Greenlanders were simultaneously accused of merely living in the present and abandoning themselves to fate by never doing any planning or saving and never worrying about the future. During the mid-19th century, when poverty seemed to take root, spread, and worsen, Inspector H. J. Rink blamed missionaries who, by banning the shamans, had stripped the Greenlanders of their former authorities (1866–71, II: 202; 1975: 59f). Taking measures to ease the misery, he saw to the establishment of the first local councils, which were the basis for the Greenland Home Rule of 1979 and its extension into self-government on June 21, 2009. I have questioned the maintained authority of the shamans (Sonne 1982a), while Marquardt (Marquardt 1992; 1999; 2009) has examined the claimed causes for the poverty and also its actual extension and the Greenlanders' alleged laissez-faire attitude to contemporary climatic changes. In actuality, the critique of Rink began earlier with Dybbroe and Møller (1980; n.p.), who argued that the visible poverty was a result of a set of innovations introduced by the Kongelige Grønlandske Handel (KGH, the royal Danish trade monopoly): a money economy, an increased assortment of tempting goods, and an urge to replace the longhouses of sod and stone with wooden one-family houses. At that time buying blubber was one chief aim of the KGH, which thus gained a surplus partly by breaking up sharing habits between the families of the longhouse and partly by replacing blubber for heating the longhouse with coal mined and sold by the KGH. So, the alleged laziness of the locals combined with an overconsumption of trade goods triggered an endemic shortage of skins for the production and repair of kayaks and *umiat* (sing. *umiaq*, "women's rowboat"). Rink was right in some measure, but the stories tell that traditions of putting up winter supplies did not become extinct in the mid-19th century (Sonne 2005: ID 1207, 13, 2043, 299, 349, 1893, and search still more documents in Sonne 2005 by *forråd**). So altogether the Greenlanders did not stop caring about the future.

---

21. Thalbitzer and Victor & Robert Lamblin can be trusted, but as for other translations where no East Greenlandic original remains, one may never know.

For good reasons, orientation has its center at the coast facing the sea; this is the main source of life in Greenland and is exploited for the greater part of the year. Nevertheless, one resource of the land was all-important: fresh drinking water. There were no succulent plants, and drinking animal blood would not suffice. The water of lakes and small streams was brought indoors, along with snow and ice to be melted, the latter cut out from old icebound icebergs shut off from the inland ice. Houses for wintering were build on solid ground, but otherwise the land was used primarily in summer, combined with simultaneous sealing except for the season of caribou hunts by some families in certain parts of the West Greenlandic hinterland.

Evidently the annual round of hunting and fishing differed along a coast of 2000 km stretching from the subarctic to the high Arctic. In addition climatic changes and the increase in visiting Qallunaat played their parts. The Polar Inuit even had a remarkable ecocultural history of their own. Since at some point in the past they had lost knowledge and technology for building kayaks, as also for hunting caribou and trout, they relied on dog sledge and ice-hunting techniques until a small group of Baffin Island Inuit arrived about 1860 and widened the horizon (e.g., Holtved 1967: 8).[22] Fear of caribou was then overcome, but as it was preferred for food by anchoring expeditions and whalers, the stock shrank almost into extinction by 1912 (Rasmussen 1921; Rasmussen in Vahl et al.; Muus et al. 1981: 392). Reintroduction of semi-domestic reindeer has been fairly successful in West Greenland, including Avanersuaq. In East Greenland caribou became extinct due to climatic changes at some point in the 14th century, before the first ancestors of the Ammassalimmiut arrived about 1500 AD (Møbjerg 1994: 132–34; M. Meldgaard 1986).

The ecohistory of caribou in West Greenland shows dramatic fluctuations on par with those of the Canadian Arctic.[23] The number of Arctic hare differs as well, ranging from zero in East Greenland due to prolonged thick layers of snow to numerous in both the far north with its insignificant precipitation and around the interior of deep fjords possessing milder climate in the far south. Hare used to be caught in snares, and its dry flesh eaten with blubber; the skin was used for making socks. Arctic fox caught in stone traps were valuable primarily for the skin, which was first sold to the Dutch whalers and later to the colony. Grouse meant a minor if welcome change in diet, especially in winter. In July, Arctic char caught in streams behind the entire coast were eaten fresh, whereas capelin, harvested in great quantities in April–May, were dried for storing up and formed a stable part of the starvation diet in winter. Caribou skin was relied on for clothing part of the year in some places, along with the skins of seal and seabirds in most regions. Polar bear, occurring in the north, east, and around Cape Farewell in the south (arriving with the pack ice), were sometimes encountered on the land but most frequently at sea, walking the solid ice or the ice floes, or swimming. It was primarily sought after for its skin, and secondarily for its meat, and in no small measure for the prestige accorded a great bear hunter. Eggs were collected in summer, along with dried willow twigs for outdoor fires, straw for lining boots, berries (mostly crowberries), and roseroot, the latter two both important edibles for immediate consumption or adding to meat conserved in blubber and stored.

---

22. For hypotheses, see the Introduction.

23. See http://www.natur.gl/fileadmin/user_upload/PaFu/Raadgivning/Landpattedyr/Caribou%20Raadgivning%20preliminary%202010_Dansk_rev.pdf

The meat and blubber of sea mammals formed the mainstay of the Greenlandic diet, with blubber providing the main source of light and heating as well. The Southerners partly differed in their dependence on halibut for meat and fat. The meat of seabirds (guillemot in the south, little auk in the far north) and the flesh of fishes (especially capelin, halibut, and lumpsucker) not only added to the diet but also offered the main opportunities for great assemblies of people at the points where and when they arrived in great quantities. Similarly, the hunt for big whales, still possible along the mid–west coast in early times of contact, attracted people from afar, as did perhaps the tidal hunt of belugas at Qaquk near Nuuk (Muus et al. 1981: 436). On a small scale the latter bore resemblance to the Mackenzie Inuit hunt of beluga (McGhee 1974), as the animals were brought in by the high tide and were thus easy to catch when stranded in shallow waters at the receding of the tide. An East Greenlandic story describes this method as something that the shaman Naaja heard about when he allegedly made a flight to the west coast in ancient times (Sonne 2005: ID 1666, 1673). So does an episode in most Greenlandic variants of the widely traveled mythic hero, Kivioq. He visited among other strangers a mother and daughter living alone but subsisting luxuriously by hunting various species of sea mammals in the following way: at low tide they planted their bladder harpoons into stranded live animals, which were subsequently carried to the shore by the high tide. Significantly, because the Southerners used to rely on halibut as their primary source of food and fat for fuel, their variants of the Kivioq story include halibut among the stranded seals as the catch explicitly preferred by Kivioq (ID 41, 344, 595, 1478, 1556, 1796, 1878). Other edibles left by the tide (which was known to be caused by the moon), like mussels and seaweed, were especially relied on by the East and South Greenlanders. Thus, in their variants of the myth about an obstinate hunter who fights Moon to the point of killing him, these Greenlanders mention the fatal disappearance of this resource in case the threat is realized (ID 350, 555, 596, 752, 1827).

Animal bone and skin, baleen, stone, and driftwood (save in Avanersuaq) made up the materials for creating means of transport, hunting gear, and utensils. The kayak was used everywhere except for Avanersuaq for hunting at sea. Hunting caribou by kayak in lakes was not practiced. Open water throughout most of the winter in Southwest Greenland stimulated the art of kayak building and the perfection of kayaking skills. In East Greenland the wintering ringed seal was hunted at breathing holes; in spring mothers and their young were obtained in the birth caves of snow that lay close to the breathing holes. Dog sledges were in use in East Greenland and from Sisimiut north in West Greenland, whereas women's boats (*umiat*) were the common means all over for travels in summer, save Avanersuaq. People followed the coast and crossed the sea to islands, which were at close quarters to the passing schools of migrating seals in spring. The skilled hunters went well beyond the skerries, but even in clear weather they rarely went so far as to lose sight of the land. In the opposite direction, deep into the fjords, capelin were scooped up while the seals pursuing the same little fish coming in from the sea were hunted simultaneously. Women did the rowing, with the men escorting the boat in their kayaks and hunting seals as they floated along. When used in the whale hunt, the *umiaq* was rowed by men, but they would ask a woman or two to pull an oar if undermanned.

When leaving the longhouse in spring, the roof was pulled down for airing out the room. The inhabitants, split by extended families each having their own tent and *umiaq*, headed for their choice places of hunting and fishing, and changed camp at intervals. The caribou hunt in early autumn meant traveling extended fjords by *umiaq* for optimal access to the hinterlands. The beloved berry picking

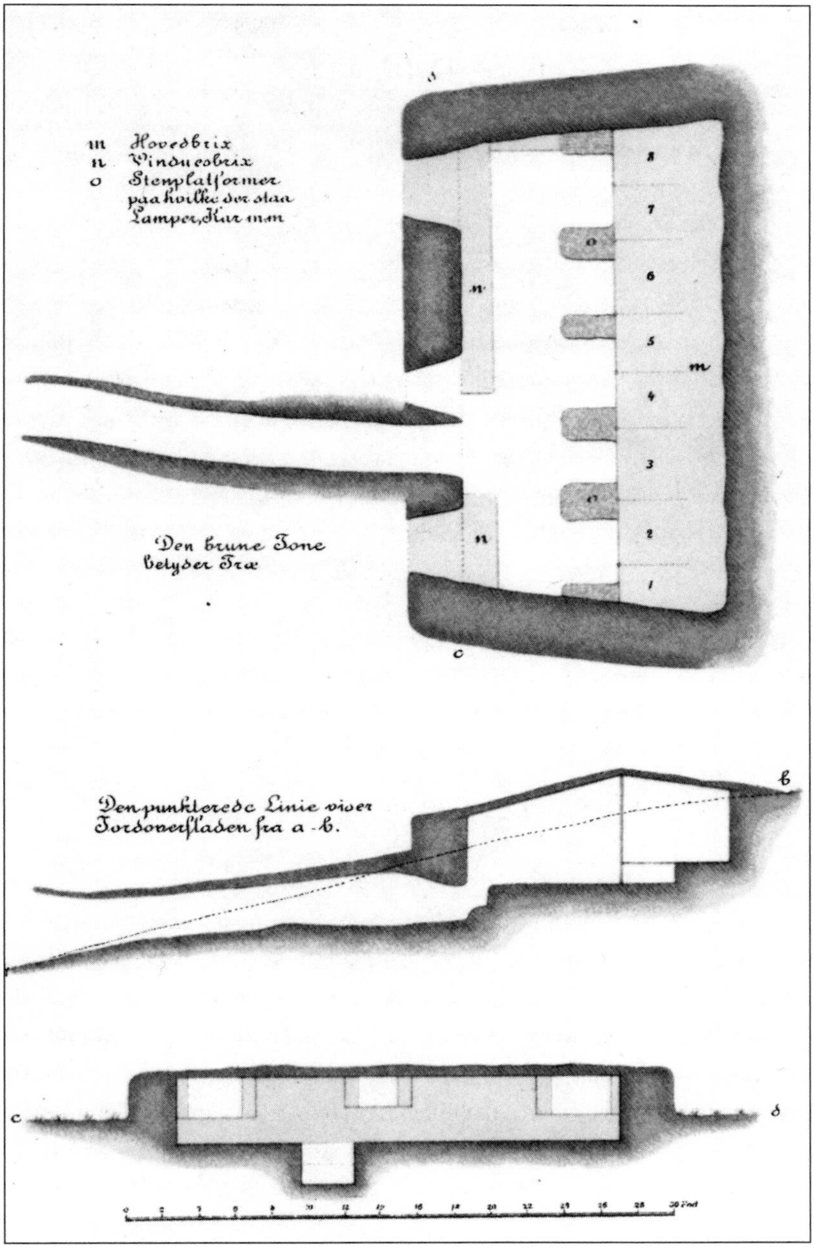

Fig. 9. Longhouse in Ammassalik/Tasiilaq, 1885, showing 38 named persons distributed in eight households. *Courtesy of The National Museum of Denmark, Copenhagen.*

was done by women during a short season in August. Reassembling in September before freeze-up, the women repaired the longhouse or built a new one from scratch, always at the coast with the windows facing the sea. Stones, turf, and driftwood (for the pillars) were the materials (whale bones in Avanersuaq). Snow igloos were made only for an overnight stay in the northern locales. The men still hunted seals for some months and whenever possible during winter. Thus they added fresh meat to the stores of dried, mature, and blubber-preserved meat, dried fishes, and berries prepared in summer. The last months of winter, February and March, frequently meant an end to both the stores and fresh catches. A prolonged winter leading to a missed summer, like the one from 1880 to 1881, meant starvation and deaths in appalling numbers, as did the previous one of 1816 caused by the 1815 eruption of Mount Tambora in Sumbawa, Indonesia (J. Rosing 1993). Few details have survived in stories on record about the latter catastrophe, whereas the recollections of the prolonged winter of 1880–81 are numerous and detailed, put to paper as they were by Kaarali Andreassen (J. Rosing 1963: 99–153; O. Rosing 1957–61, II). They tell about highly differing behavior in twelve settlements, ranging from clever leadership to absolute anarchy, depending on the personal qualities of the leaders and inhabitants. All in all, standards of living declined along the east coast during the 19th century; this was due in some part to climatic changes, but in much greater part to the Norwegian sealing that followed the near extinction of big whales by the 17th-century European whalers. As hypothesized by Gulløv in opposition to former hypotheses of Dorset reminiscence, these hard times seem evidenced in the development of a flourishing art—i.e., in an increasing number of carvings and decorations for religious purposes (Gulløv in Grønnow 2009b and Jensen et al. 2011).

Summary

Silap ingerlasia, "the way the world moves," or the way of the sun, or its annual order of changes in light and temperature, covers the annual round in both time and space. The movement was "evidenced" outside by the starry sky circling around a mountaintop in the north, and reflected a geocentric worldview. The heliocentric view introduced by the missionaries was perceived to cause calamities in the "order" of transmigrating animals, weather, human health, and their life span. From another, inside perception the world was likened to the interior of the house, and the roof/sky did not move. It was supported by pillars, which were said to need repair with the threat of doomsday preached by the missionaries. *Silam aappaa* means the "Other World" of a couple, stressing the mutual dependency between live humans and the lives of their deceased relatives and the other beings of the Other World. The latter was seen and traveled involuntarily in dreams by ordinary people and at will by shamans. Responsibility for keeping up harmonious relations (by observance of rites and taboos) rested with humans. Time was marked by the rising of the twin stars of the New Year, the four main seasons, and the moons counted and/or descriptively named. Above the Arctic Circle, polar night was observed by the disappearance and return of the sun. Night and day were separated by the liminal *naar*-times, dusk and dawn, the times for departure to and return from the Other World. The day was divided according to the movements of the sun. Missionaries introduced the concept of the week and caused some finer divisions of the past. The comings and goings of transmigrating animals were crucial to the movements of humans, who settled together in winter, parted by extended families in spring, and moved about in summer to hunt, fish and pick berries. Places of assembly, where animals temporarily arrived in big numbers, drew people from near and far. The

Fig. 10. Members of a household on the move by umiak (women, children, and pick-pack) and kayaks (men). *Photo by W. Thalbitzer, 1906. Danish Arctic Institute, Copenhagen ID 23564.*

Fig. 11. Spring camp at Qinngeq, Ammassalik. *Photo by W. Thalbitzer, 1906. Danish Arctic Institute, Copenhagen. ID 23558.*

point of orientation is (still) at the coast facing the sea, with the sea down in front, the land back up behind and right and left along the coast. As previously discussed, these directions (localizers) do not refer to the movements of the sun. So, in translation into Western terms of north, south, etc., as was done first in West Greenland, they are inverted when centered on the east coast. Not every translator is aware of this mirror effect.

Balance

Movement signifies life, and so too does the movement of the world. Although the Greenlanders opposed the heliocentric movements of the earth preached by the missionaries, the Greenlandic earth seemingly (implied in various statements) *did* move—or, rather, the relations between sea and land and between earth, heaven, and underworld changed continuously.

The Earth Is a Disk

The earliest information to be found on the West Greenlanders' perception of the earth became mixed up with the missionaries' own Christian identification of the underworld with Hell (Sonne 1986b). Poul Egede thus placed the dwelling of *Sassuma Arnaa* ("The woman down there"—i.e., "in front of you facing the sea," Sea Woman) and the realm of death at various locations, first deep down inside earth as well as the farthest point down inside the earth. Later, in better agreement with the Greenlandic perception, the site became the farthest point down inside the earth beneath the sea (P. Egede 1971: 26, 45–46, 68; 1939: 23, 36–37, 50), but the latter is still not definitive (1971: 71–72, 73; 1939: 52, 53). Muddling the picture even further, it remains uncertain in which sense Poul Egede employs the Danish word *jord* (earth), meaning either the land or the world. Most probably he meant the "world," because Poul Egede reacts strongly to a shaman's understanding of a hell inside the earth. This shaman had been told about that place by Poul's father, Hans Egede, long before, and later when he became a shaman and made a trip down there, "no 'Death' [or dead person, according to P. Egede 1988: 75] was seen and everything was well." [24] To this Poul Egede replied, "My father never taught you that the souls of the dead live inside the earth, or that any human being could pass through the hard ground" (P. Egede 1971: 52–53; 1939: 40, tr. BS). No easy endeavor either, but necessary nonetheless for curing the sick, as declared by another shaman in defense when accused by Poul of overcharge; necessary, that is, for bringing back a lost soul from beneath the earth (P. Egede 1971: 90; 1939: 64). Similarly, a dying person placed on the floor would follow the same difficult route through the earth to the other side (of the disk) (1971: 128; 1939: 86). This idea of a disk also presents itself in the origin myth about the capsizing of the world. It turned upside down and thus placed the former humans called *innersuit* ("big fire spirits") on the underside, which was flat as a plain (1971: 96–97; 1939: 67). Access to their land was via rock caves and coastal clefts. The East Greenlandic sources leave no doubt about the idea of the earth as a disk. "The biggest [souls] are those of the back, almost the size of a wagtail; when these drop down from human beings, they proceed right through earth to the opposite side" (C. Rosing 1946: 39). They pass not through solid rock but through the cracks formed by a primordial earthquake (98). Otherwise the "main road" of shamans and deceased

24. *Død* means both "death" and "dead person" in Danish.

humans starts at the boundary between land and sea (O. Rosing 1957–61, I: 80–81; J. Rosing 1963: 188–89; Rasmussen 1921–25, I: 71). Stories about shamans tell that the first part is either pitch dark or suffocating and narrow, but leads on to the light prevailing in the underworld (Sonne 2005: ID 1600, 1196, 1697, 420; see also Fienup-Riordan 1994: 228 about deceased Yupiit). Identical experiences were had by West Greenlandic, Iglulik, and Nattilik shamans as well (P. Egede 1971: 67; 1939: 50; N. Egede 1971: 36–37, 1939: 149; Sonne 2000a; MacDonald 1998: 29; Rasmussen 1931: 317–18). Other access to the underworld was through lakes and ponds as documented for East Greenland, at Pond Inlet/Mittimatalik, Canada, and at Kushunuk, Alaska (e.g., Sonne 2005: ID 1686; Zeilich-Jensen 1974: 33, 39–40; Nelson 1899).[25] As declared by a Mittimatalik informant in explanation of a sketch drawn of the world as seen from an outlook at the coast, "the world (*nunarjuaq*, the big earth) is flat and slightly slanting causing the sea to be on a lower level than the land, which caused by its sloping continues down below and constitutes the bottom of the sea. The sea itself continues beneath the land, and where the land is low-lying, lakes are formed" (Zeilich-Jensen 1974: 33, 39–40, tr. BS).[26] In East Greenland lakes were considered to be in open connection with the sea below, thus permitting spirits to emerge for the initiation of the shamanic apprentice, as is most clearly shown by a story about Maratsi. Maratsi's teacher took him to a shore at some distance from the camp, filled a mitten with water, went far inland, emptied the water into a giant cauldron, had it covered by a tile-like stone, and churned the rubbing stone for a while. When he next removed the cover, a small, highly vivacious wing snail had arrived. Teacher and pupil returned to the shore, where the wing snail, transformed into a being as big as the sleeve of an anorak, lay waiting, staring at them with two big luminous eyes (Sonne 2005: ID 1686). The text offers no explanation as to how the creature had managed to get into the cauldron and return to shore; I maintain that it traveled through some passage from the sea below. Georg Quppersimaan, who told a version of the story (as his own experience), maintained that the wing snail was already in the water that filled the mitten. He said the snail, a being of the sea, complained about being brought inland, but he did not offer an explanation of its return to the shore (Sonne 2005: ID 1163).

Primordial Events

Some Greenlanders declared that the world has always been like it is today, in opposition to the Genesis story preached by the first missionaries (H. Egede 1971, 1: 156–57; 1925: 151; N. Egede 1971: 44; 1939: 154; 1943: 43). This statement did not take into account myths of origin; rather, the objection concerned the idea of creating something out of nothing. Whether recognized at the moment by the objecting Greenlanders or not, several different beginnings had occurred, either in separate stories or paired together in different narratives. No single mythic construction covered all mentioned beginnings. One myth has it that once upon a time the earth had turned upside down, exchanging the flat surface for the mountainous underside (Sonne 2005: ID 1678; P. Egede 1971: 96; 1939: 67). The event just happened spontaneously, or may have been due to a storm surge (*ibid.*). Another beginning states

25. Nelson observed a Bladder Feast in 1879 at Kushunuk. The bladders were thrust down through a hole made in the ice of a pond. In most places the hole was made in the sea ice (1899: 389).

26. The reconstructed Siberian world of the proto-Altaians by Napolskikh (1992) similarly slants from heaven to the underworld.

that the surface cracked (Avanersuaq, Sonne 2005: ID 1722), leaving ravines going right through to the other side (Holm 1914: 82f, 106f; C. Rosing 1946: 39). Or, in the beginning, heaven and earth were still not separated, in that the primeval flood raised heaven from its former position of resting on top of the mountains to its present position; shells found high in the mountains confirmed this belief (P. Egede 1971: 89; 1939: 63). Still another statement declares that *Nalikkatteeq* ("Big Crotch," the Entrails Snatcher) helped raise the pillar supporting heaven (Sonne 2005: ID 1596, E. Grl.). In another case, the earth was formed by earth and stones falling down from heaven (ID 1517, Avanersuaq).

In fact, events in nature supported these ideas. Considering them from the last mentioned to the first, we can note that stones and earth did come down, especially in the melting of spring, from the inland places touching heaven far up there behind one, facing the sea at the coast. The farther north you travel, the nearer the heaven is felt to be to earth, the stars becoming threateningly close. You better bring a whip for scaring them off (P. Egede 1971: 59; 1939: 44). Earthquakes were and still are quite common, especially in East Greenland; furious gales or the tsunami effect of a huge calving iceberg can send high waves ashore, swallowing up entire settlements (J. Petersen 1957: 105; Rasmussen 1908: 124). Avalanches come sliding down with a similar destructive effect (*ibid.*). The movements of the tide could be perceived as a tilting movement of earth, as I shall demonstrate in detail below. Rituals performed to prevent the supporting pillar from giving in are explicated later as well.

Since the early missionaries immediately identified the flooding with the biblical deluge, it may or may not have left its influence on some variants. This apparently happened to an East Greenlandic variant imported (as stated by visitors) from the Christianized South. "The one up there behind you" (*pinnga, pissuma*),[27] the story goes, ruined the earth with earthquakes and subsequent rain because *he* did not like the doings of the humans.[28] Later the earth came about anew, but then it became completely covered by a glacier. As the ice disappeared little by little, two humans (a man and a woman) fell down from heaven and from them the earth became populated (Holm 1972: 139; 1914: 106–7; see also Thalbitzer ed. 1933: 85, 86–87, 93–94; Rasmussen 1929: 252; 1931: 208–9). Rasmussen was unable to have this *pinnga*, who punishes the wrongdoings of humans, identified except that it was the taboo word used for both the moon and the sun (KRH, 52, 2, booklet 405: 1). However, despite possible Christian impact, common ideas were shared over vast distances of a threatening imbalance restored to balance by rituals of neutralizing breaks of taboo.[29]

Primordial Events Strike Back

No sooner were these primordial world orderings established than disorder might recur. Ordering was not merely a question of ritual performance in, e.g., New Year ceremonies, but was done in the belief that the world might actually be ruined for good. Doomsday preached by the missionaries who mentioned foreboding signs in sun and moon raised dormant fears (H. Egede 1971, 1: 133; 1925: 115; Thalbitzer ed. 1933: 86–87). They made topical both a repeated capsizing of the earth and its complete falling into pieces, but the most frequent fear was the downfall of heaven for which

27. That is, placed above the inland. See "Orientation" above.

28. *Pinnga* or *pissuma* is gender-neutral.

29. This is a pan-Inuit myth. See Nelson (1899: 452); Rasmussen (1908: 101, 1929: 252, 1931: 208–9); Boas (1964: 229–30); P. Egede (1971: 96–97; 1939: 67).

heavy storms, eclipses, and meteors were alarming signs (H. Egede 1971, 1: 143, 207; 1925: 123, 190; P. Egede 1971: 103, 121; 1939: 71, 82). Among the shamans some opposed and others submitted to the news. They made exploring travels to heaven, where Moon would either deny or confirm a dangerous rotting of the supporting pillar (H. Egede 1971, 1: 143; 1925: 123; P. Egede 1971: 32; 1939: 27; N. Egede 1971: 80; 1939: 176). One obtained the knowledge that God had sent one of his servants with the message of the downfall (P. Egede 1971: 66; 1939: 49). Another had righted the sloping pillar (P. Egede 1971: 69; 1939: 51). Besides the downfall other causes mentioned were the bursting of the big dam in heaven, from which the rain came (P. Egede 1971: 51; 1939: 39); a storm like a hurricane which raised the fear of a capsizing of the land; and a renewed cracking of the earth as foreshadowed by a lunar eclipse (P. Egede 1971: 101–3; 1939: 70). In the remaining cases the way of the feared ruin is not mentioned, only that gales and eclipses provoked fear of the impending doomsday or "end of the world" (P. Egede 1971: 135, 140, 159; 1939: 91, 94, 106; N. Egede 1971: 39; 1939: 150; 1943: 20–21). Let us take a closer look at earthquakes, gales, and pillars.

Earthquakes in East Greenland

In addition to eclipses of the moon, Moon was believed, especially in East and South Greenland, to be the cause of both earthquakes and thunder. If the darkened moon touched the top of a mountain, the end of the world might be near (F. Lynge 1981: No. 319). More common were small earthquakes, usually heard as a buzzing beneath the surface of the earth (C. Rosing 1946: 59; Thalbitzer 2014: *passim*). The colonial manager Johan Petersen mentions two bigger ones, one in December 1904 and another in December 1905, but adds in a note that earthquakes occur most frequently in autumn and spring (J. Petersen 1957: 80, 87, 167, n. 45). In 1904 people expressed fear that the world had come to its end (*ibid.*), whereas a generation later Christianized informants told Victor that earthquakes, called forth by breaking taboos, could smash a house or blow out the windows although no wind was blowing. The inhabitants would die, one after another (Victor & Robert-Lamblin 1989–93, II: 393).

The buzzing sound of a minor earthquake may have been the noise announcing the arrival of Moon's dog, heard by Aadaarutaa when he was a small boy. The dog approached the house from below, but fortunately Aadaarutaa's mother found out the reason in time, namely her worn-out pair of trousers that ought to have been discarded long ago. So she threw them out and the dog went away (Sonne 2005: ID 971). When the punishing Moon visited earth in person, threatening to smash the longhouse with his weapon, a stick or a whip, he was sometimes fought by shamans and their helping spirits during splendidly staged performances. I shall deal with one such event in detail in chapter 2 under the subheading "Fighting Back Moon in Actual Ritual." Another variant, if less historical, is told about both Naaja and another shaman; they managed to stop a boulder rolling downhill that was intending to smash the longhouse, an event caused by the snow melting in spring (Sonne 2005: ID 1192, 807). This story too shall be dealt with later.

The Threat or Boon of Gales

Furious gales were frequent, and they could cause great havoc by either raising the sea—and thus washing away houses, boats, kayaks, and stores—or throwing around and smashing every object in its path (Google "piteraq" for impressive photos). The fall winds blowing from the inland areas meant a sudden breakup of the sea ice, either by its strength in East Greenland or by its sudden dramatic rise in temperatures in Southwest Greenland, known as the *nunasarneq* (the *foehn*, "wind from the inland"). Hunters on the ice at the time were sent adrift away from the shore, in actual life as in myth (to be treated below). Yet in spring the same *foehn* had a beneficial effect by opening up the sea for the returning migrant birds and seals. In fact, the removal of the ice by raising a storm was the explicit goal of the shaman's visit to *Sassuma Arnaa* (Sea Woman) in West Greenland (e.g., Sonne 2005: ID 340, 1445, 1492). Consequently, during one prolonged winter, people repeatedly asked Poul Egede to create a strong wind for the removal of the ice. No, he answered, I cannot do that, only God can, etc. But some of our shamans can, the Greenlanders objected (P. Egede 1971: 63; 1939: 47). In East Greenland, besides earthquakes, devastating gales from the inland region (the female *piteraq*) and the northwest (the male *ningeq*) (Victor & Robert-Lamblin 1989–93, II: 390) brought a prolonged cover of snow and hid the breathing holes in spring.[30] This could arouse a fear of the impending end of the world. While earthquakes might cause a further splitting up of the earth by causing still more clefts to open up right into the world below, the snow cover meant starvation and ultimate death. Rain, not wind, was the means for removing the snow. To obtain this needed rain, the shaman (in myth) went flying to *Asiaq*, the *inua* of precipitation (more below).

Gales and the Support of Heaven

Rink heard about pillars separating both heaven from earth and earth from the underworld (Rink: 1866–71, II: 182), but regarding the rotting or sloping pillars mentioned above, none of those supporting earth were at stake and most frequently only a single one is mentioned to support *qilak*. My distinction between gales and the support of heaven is actually an artificial one; among the eastern Inuit they certainly overlap. The Greenlandic Entrails Snatcher, for instance, *Erlaveersiniooq*, or *Nalikkatteeq* (literally "Big Crotch"), who aided in raising the pillar(s), has power over mountains as well. She can make big boulders come rolling down by merely kicking the mountains, or she knocks the mountain down right away (Sonne 2005: ID 1596). The latter variant identifies her as *Silap Inua*, as did a West Greenlander when asked about the identity of *Sila*. And Egede adds: "[the name of] this figure (Erloersortoq/*Erlaveersiniooq*) and the Air (Sila) are used indiscriminately" (P. Egede 1971: 87; 1939: 62).

In Canada, among the Nattilingmiut and South Baffin Island Inuit, the *inua* of the wind, not *Ululirnang* ("owning an *ulu*," women's knife for cutting out entrails like the Entrails Snatcher), was credited with the power of kicking down mountains. On the other hand, like *Erlaveersiniooq* this *inua* of the wind was identified with *Silap Inua* (also called *Naarjuk* in the abovementioned figure of a giant baby among the Nattilingmiut). Or similarly this figure would someday kick down *silap ajaguktaak*, the pillars of the world (Rasmussen 1931: 231).[31] Gales were a frequent plague, but however tempting

30. In East Greeenland called *piteraq* if it is furiously strong. The directions of the winds that most fatally rise into devastating storms differ from one region to another along the Greenland coast. The effects of the fall winds from the inland region like the *piteraq* in East Greenland and the *foehn* in Southwest Greenland are as dramatic as a sudden northwestern gale around Cape Farewell (e.g., Sonne 2005: ID 2028). But no matter the direction, a gale forces the human being to his knees, on all fours, or rolling along. Such losses of bodily balance coincide with the threatened balance of the world whether by capsizing, by losing its air, or by having the support of heaven overturned.

31. Rasmussen adds the following note: *Silap ajaguktäk*: this is the only place in the tradition of the Netsilingmiut [Nattilingmiut] where the pillars of the world are mentioned. In Greenland they occur much more frequently (*ibid.*).

an elimination of that *inua* of the wind could be, it was not advisable. Air and wind were one and the same, and if this person of the air were killed the expanse of heaven would collapse (Rasmussen 1929: 71–72). Considering the common notion of heaven circling on top of a mountain, the act would have a similar effect in South Baffin Island, where the killing would level all mountains with the earth (Boas 1901–7: 537); this idea is similar to another about how an eclipsed moon would cause destruction if it happened to touch the big mountains in South Greenland (F. Lynge 1981: No. 319).

So irrespective of its medium—air, pillar, or mountain—the support of heaven was not a fixed support. Nor for that matter was the rainbow, *ajagutaq*, as perceived by the Kitlinermiut, as it separates heaven from earth and changes height with the seasons (Rasmussen 1932: 23). The balance of the world was a tricky one. *Naarjuk* of the Nattilingmiut would let the pillars come down, as confirmed by an East Greenlandic song that reads: "The supportive pillar (*sugaaq*) of heaven is bound to come loose" (Victor & Robert-Lamblin 1989–93, II: 393). Observing the rules was the Polar Inuit way of postponing that calamity (Rasmussen 1921–25, III: 13; 1908: 124).[32] Furthermore, a renewed capsizing of the earth that would return the flat land of the underworld on top and the supporting mountains to the underside was still another threat. As I read these statements the movements of an iceberg or a large ice floe come to mind. Apparently fastened to the bottom, it may suddenly either turn around or dissolve into pieces.

The Earth Is a Tilting Disk

One may say that on the surface of the disk, the Greenlanders lived on a slippery slope, in that the perceived profile of the land is slanting and felt as slightly tilting. The slanting, already touched on above, is realized by anybody descending from the inland mountains down to the lookout above the shore, from where the similarly slanting seafloor is seen to disappear into invisibility. When served a dish of food on earth, the one-legged star people, on a visit to earth from the horizontally circling sky, flee, exclaiming, "But the dish tilts!" (Sonne 2005: ID 103, 1782, 1788, 1977; Danielsen 2006; Robert Petersen pers. comm.).[33] When at the lookout, the aforementioned localizers draw the same line: *pavunga*, behind upwards, and *samunga*, in front downwards. Not only does the bottom of the sea slant, but according to Gagné the surface of the sea is perceived to be on a lower level than the shore, because an Inuk pointing from the shore to an object floating on the sea will refer to it as "the one down there."[34] Zeilich-Jensen, trained by Gagné, used his insights and was able to confirm them

32. "*We observe our old customs, in order to hold the world up, for the powers must not be offended.*" (I have translated the word *sila* the first time as "world" and the next as "powers." The sentence in the Polar Inuit language is as follows: *Sila najûmivdlugo, sila ajuatdlangnertôrssûngmat. Sila* means not only "the whole," "the universe," but likewise "the individual powers of forces of Nature," for instance, in the sentence *sitdlardlupagssualeqi-mioq*: Bad weather has come on.) "*We observe our customs, in order to hold each other up; we are afraid of the Great Evil, perdlugssuaq. Men are so helpless in face of illness. The people here do penance, because the dead are strong in their vital sap, and boundless in their might.*" "*If we did not take these precautions,*" say the Eskimos, "*we believe that great masses of snow would slide down and destroy us, that snowstorms would lay us waste, that the sea would raise in violent waves while we are out in our kayaks, or that flood would sweep our houses out into the sea.*"

33. In a different context and meaning, the Yupiit of Southwest Alaska similarly liken their bowl to their land (Fienup-Riordan & Rearden 2013: 111).

34. This "optical illusion" makes Gagné refer to the Whorf hypothesis, which states that our language decides our perceptions. Why not the other way round?

at Mittimatalik/Pond Inlet. This was shown in his drawing of a man on the lookout above the shore seeing the water on a slightly lower level (Zeilich-Jensen 1974: 33).[35]

The continuation of the sea beneath the land corresponds nicely with a common Inuit myth of the primordial earth disk as a floating island that lost its balance due to overpopulation. Death was introduced for a better equilibrium (Rasmussen 1908: 101; 1929: 92; Boas 1901–7: 173; Sonne 2005: ID 1517), and this new balance was upheld by rules to be continuously observed, as quoted in note 32 above. The surge of an avalanche, a violent spring flood, an onshore storm—each implies a tilting slope. According to the Iglulingmiut, the island became fixed in place but the balance remained a delicate one (Saladin d'Anglure 1990a: 80). The Nattilik and East Greenland spirits saw every island afloat like an ice sheet, *puttajoq* and *puttalivatsiaq*, respectively, in their spirit languages (Rasmussen 1931: 312; O. Rosing 1957–61, II: 93; Victor & Robert-Lamblin 1989–93, II: 254).

The equinoxes seem to have been the turning points of the continuous tilting. Thus, a Southern shaman told Poul Egede that the autumnal equinox was the ideal time for travel to the heavenly realms, because at that point the distance from the horizon to the rainbow (leading to heaven) was the shortest one possible (P. Egede 1971: 13; 1939: 14).[36] The opposite downward tilting in spring can be indirectly concluded from various statements wherein one relates the fear that doomsday would renew the capsizing of the earth. The fear was raised by a furious gale on New Year's Eve in 1738 and was soon increased by the much too early calving and plummeting of the inland ice in January (P. Egede 1971: 101–2; 1939: 70). Obviously, the sloping had become alarmingly steep for that time of the year. Normally the calving starts in spring as does the thaw that causes roaring streams and rumbling boulders to come rushing down the mountainsides. As will be treated below, one such boulder, in the mythic figure of a stone *inua*, threatened to smash the house and had to be stopped by the shaman assisted by his strongest spirit of spring (Sonne 2005: ID 1192, 1527, 807). Nor does an iceberg keep quiet when, having lost gravity, it capsizes and turns bottom up. The capsizing kayaker is still another experience of an intricate balance. I shall return to these latter issues—boulders, icebergs, and kayak dizziness—in a while.

Corresponding to the Greenlandic "sloping downwards" in spring, the southeast Baffin Island Inuit were convinced that the underwater abode was at that point much nearer to the earth than at any other time of the year. But here the earth not only rocked; it turned around once in both autumn and spring (Boas 1901–7: 130–31). Identical statements are not, to my knowledge, on record from among the other Inuit, only similar ones such as the recently mentioned statement from Iglulik: that

---

35. Zeilich-Jensen had already been awarded his PhD when long quotations without references (to Briggs 1974a) were discovered in his thesis, and he was consequently removed from his academic position. But the information he received during his fieldwork was not "stolen," and the sketch he made of the Mittimatalik world appears closer to the Greenlandic view than the "layer cake" reproduced by Rasmussen of the Iglulik world (published in Saladin d'Anglure 1990a: 81).

36. Poul Egede calls that equinox *solstitium autumnale* (P. Egede 1971: 12; 1939: 13), which is nonsense. In a note to the 1939 publication Ostermann understands it as summer solstice, *solstitium aestivale*, but Hans Egede, who draws heavily on the journals of his son, Poul, translates the misnomer into "fall" (1971, 2: 111; 1925: 394; 1818: 189), i.e. *aequinoctium autumnale*. The latter sounds reasonable, since travels to heaven (and the underworld) were rarely undertaken in summer (P. Egede 1971: 35; 1939: 29–30). Yet winter solstice is more likely the time, because at this point in the year the distance to heaven, marked by the arching of the rainbow, was the smallest, as also it marked the public initiation of several shaman apprentices, among whom at least one, Ajijak, went to heaven.

the balance of the earth island is still delicate, and that observing the prescriptions explicitly upheld the balance of the world in Avanersuaq.[37]

Why, I kept asking myself, is this idea of a pendulous balance like an inclined shuttle between equinoxes?[38] For an initial explanation I looked to the sun and the stars. In Iglulik, as in South Greenland (and most probably among the Inuit generally), the rising and falling altitudes of the sun were observed as well as its movements along the horizon (MacDonald 1998: 114; Saladin d'Anglure 1986: 39ff; Dalager 1915: 54; Holm 1972: 137; 1914: 108). Being halfway up twice during the year, at the equinoxes—moving upward and "forward" in spring and downward and "back" in autumn—these recurrent movements alone could give the impression of a tilting earth in a geocentric world-view. Similarly, because the Inuit compared the rising of stars with the rising of the sun along the horizon (but granted that the circling of the heaven was considered invariably horizontal), the obliquity that we call ecliptic between the movements of the sun and the fixed stars could be explained by a tilting earth. Strained speculations aside, the most obvious explanation of a tilting movement would be observations of the tide. The tide was in Greenland known to be caused by the moon, as it perpetually floods the shore and withdraws twice a day plus at night and it grows in force at the equinoxes. At new and full moons in spring, the difference in levels between low and high tide are at their maximum, and the farther south along the coast the bigger this difference becomes (Fabricius 1946: 39–40).[39] Actually, the tides reach twice the normal difference at springtide (N. Egede 1943: 52–53). But did the land seesaw or did (only) the sea rise and fall? Both perceptions are reasonable. The springtide that breaks the impenetrable ice on lakes and at shore (*ibid.*) points to the first conception, and the idea of a primordial capsizing to the latter formation. As Hans Lynge remembered from his youth in Nuuk: "at the flood of springtide the tremendous swelling of the sea makes Akia (the opposite land of the fjord) sink to a degree that gives you the reverse impression, namely, that the land is going down" (H. Lynge 1978: 19, tr. BS).[40] A similar perception is stated by a Paamiut dweller in describing the kayaker caught in the inward current of *innersuit*, fire spirits living beneath the shore, in their attempt to capture him. He sees the shore rise and slope down *as made by the tide*, but at a much faster pace, because, like a mouth, the sea opens and shuts (Rasmussen 1979: No. 167, emphasis BS).

Turning to body-mental terms, the feeling of being flooded was considered a warning signal. As is well known, mental states impact those of the body, such as becoming red in the face when

---

37. The occasion was a storm surge, allegedly caused by an offense to a recently deceased Inuk by the Danish Literary Expedition. In the Danish edition, Rasmussen translates the statement "*Sila najûmivdlugo*" into "uphold the balance of the world" (not just uphold the world), and he explains it as such in the English edition: "I have translated the word *sila* the first time as 'world'" and the next as 'powers'" (Rasmussen 1908: 124).

38. Fienup-Riordan and Rearden strongly emphasize that the Yupiit of Southwest Alaska have no idea of a tilting land: "the land does not move." Nor is the tide that high (Fienup-Riordan & Rearden 2013: 110, 233). Leach mentions pendulum movements in the time reckoning of some oral cultures; however, they do not point to a tilting earth (Leach 1963: 133–34).

39. In response to my presentation of the powers of Moon in stories, some Greenlandic students told me about the fun of placing a cup filled with water on the windowsill at springtime and observing how the full moon would make the water spill over.

40. In the same region was Qaquk, the place where, in spring, belugas were chased in and fenced off for an easy catch at low tide (Muus et al. 1981: 436). The East Greenland stories about historical shamans visiting the "land of the high tide," meaning West Greenland, most probably refer to that particular place (Sonne 2005: ID 806, 1667, 1673).

ashamed (e.g., Sahlins 1976). In Greenland, the tilting or flooded earth could express mental states, as in the cases of both the great shaman from Karra near Nuuk and Uillaq from Upernavik. The former shaman, who would not give in to the missionaries, ended up being the only unbaptized person in the region. Remaining stubborn, he nevertheless suddenly felt the shore shrink beneath his feet. He very nearly fell and eventually he gave in, if with no success because he knew no other letters than A (literacy was a prerequisite for baptism) (Sonne 2005: ID 356). Similarly, Uillaq became the last convert in his area; in ripe old age he felt the tide rise and rise, leaving him no higher place of refuge (ID 1961). And in still a third example, a man's imminent death was declared by a shaman who in his vision saw the water approach the sickbed (J. Petersen 1957: 73). Tilt and tide were interchangeable body-mind metaphors.

The uninterrupted tilting would make the earth somersault around, as imagined by the southeast Baffin Islanders to happen twice a year at equinoxes (Boas 1901–7: 131). This turning around, if only halfway, happened long ago in Greenland, when the primordial storm surge flooding the land made the earth capsize with the first people, who thus came to dwell in the flat land underneath as *innersuit* ("big fire spirits"). According to a West Greenlandic version, the mountainous surface subsequently became populated by the Inuit, starting with one man having a beard like trees. Nobody knew where he came from, but he walked about and then copulated with a hummock that bore a girl whom he later married (P. Egede 1971: 96–97; 1939: 67; Sonne 2005: ID 2295).[41] Egede did not ask further questions about the primordial event of the capsizing, but fortunately, a complete story was told in East Greenland. The informant, Saajooq (Odin Maratsi), told Jens Rosing that the great (historical) shaman Ajijak had received the story from the "horse's mouth": his helping spirit, *Uniagaq*. This *Uniagaq*, who belonged to the outermost island, used to live on the mainland at the time when people suddenly panicked, because the earth began to capsize and turn around. At that point, both he and his younger brother, orphans who were fed but given no clothing, got the idea to run up the rising bottom of the sea toward the light, in the opposite direction of the people who took to the mountains. But they needed clothing in order to go outdoors. Promptly shredding discarded blubber-skin bags, *Uniagaq* wound a long, broad strap around the entire body of his younger brother. He then did the same to himself, and along they ran, on dry land in continuous daylight, all the way to the outermost island.[42] Completely alone and with nobody to feed them, they started to wish for things to use. From invisible hands they thus received driftwood, an axe and a knife for making the skeleton of a kayak, skins for cover, next a woman who arrived from out of the blue, and finally her tools for the covering. Proceeding with this cultural development, *Uniagaq* wound off their "clothing," tied the two straps together, and fastened one end to the kayak. He then made his younger brother enter and begin to practice kayaking, while *Uniagaq* saw to

41. Evidently they both came out of the earth: the woman from the hummock, the man probably through the earth from below as evidenced by his beard made of trees. I cannot evaluate a similar statement about a capsized earth among the Canadian Inuit, because no reference has yet been made (Saladin d'Anglure 1991: 26).

42. A late variant of "Visit to Moon" offers a particular interpretation of the straps. Having returned to earth, the hero travels to the faraway hunting place of moon, where he fights Moon and then *Nalikkatteeq*, followed by the giant ice-covered polar bear. The latter episode is a variant of the story about a hero who lets himself be swallowed by a monstrous bear. He cuts his way out, completely bald due to the interior heat of the bear. The hero of this variant has sensibly prepared for the feat by bandaging himself from top to toe in straps, which explicitly makes him invisible and apparently protects him from becoming scalded all over the body. This is an example of the *pooq* effect (see chapter 5), as it were (Sonne 2005: ID 350).

his balance by holding the other end of the strap. Soon the younger brother became an excellent seal hunter, while *Uniagaq* himself remained a minor hunter of eiders. As a consequence of his sibling's hunting ability (I suppose), *Uniagaq* let his younger brother marry the woman; however, he then fell in love with her himself. She turned him away, so he cast a spell on her that rebounded and ruined his hips (Sonne 2005: ID 1678). To my knowledge, variants are not on record from Arctic Canada, whereas amazingly similar ones were told about the origin of Nunivak Island in Alaska (Lantis 1946: 265–67; Himmelheber 1951; 2000: 33–35; Curtis 1930: 74–75, 77–78). The Yup'ik variants do not include the tipping of the earth and the winding of the two naked brothers in straps.

A parallel for the peculiar outfit, however, is found in a drawing of one of three masked shamans of the Sedna feast at Iqaluit, southeast Baffin Island. That figure, called *Noonagikshown*, is similarly completely wound up in broad lashings of (bearded seal) skin when, at the Sedna feast in November–December he distributes the women among the men (contrary to marriage bonds; see Boas 1901–7: 141–42). He also appears in spring and autumn, bringing health and good weather to the people. Bilby, who spells the name *Nunagisaktut*, identifies him as a raven figure that cleans and renews the land at equinoxes by communicating people's confessions of offenses to Sedna (Bilby 1923: 222; cf. Oosten & Laugrand 2006: 196; Laugrand & Oosten 2015: 102–5). These are the times for the said turning around of the land and further aligns with the statement communicated by Saladin d'Anglure: that the spring equinox meant the suspension of the taboos in force during the winter (1990a: 108). Or, as stated by Laugran's informant: "*Nunagiqsaqtuq* [correctly spelled, 'the one who shall beautify the land'] is when the shamans would try to perform a ritual in order that people in the land and in the camps could have good weather and good hunting area" (Laugrand 1997: 107; cf. Oosten & Laugrand 2006: 196; Laugrand & Oosten 2015: 102–5).

Therefore, not only the correspondence in bandaged clothing but also the events for the rejuvenation of the land, place *Nunagiqsaqtuq* in line with *Uniagaq*. While the former both transmits confessions to Sea Woman and re-creates good hunting conditions at the turning points of equinoxes, the latter re-creates the core of the sealing culture by kayak in the new land of daylight. It rises toward the east of the capsizing world and, due to his attraction to the light, *Uniagaq* shares also another epithet with *Nunagiqsaqtuq*, the raven who in Inuit Canada brought light into the world (*ibid.*). The Greenlandic origin is due to a quarrel between two women about getting light in exchange for eternal life in darkness, a quarrel that sounded like ravens, I suppose. Actually, a story among the oldest collected in West Greenland (Aasiaat in the 1820s) points to raven as the advertiser of light in spring. The story has three birds announce a visit by a person with important things to tell to a woman alone at home: first a snow bunting, next a *kussataq* (? *kussaq*, wheatear), and then a raven. The person to arrive is the sun and her message turns out to be first, her story of origin—i.e., about the incest committed by her brother and their flight to heaven. Right now, however, she will rise to a higher position in order to give warmth to the poor children (lacking sufficient clothes). In other words, she brings summer in. Every event in the story points to spring: the woman alone at home and her husband (out hunting at the moment) have children who have left for their summer travels.[43] The snow bunting symbolizes the onset of spring (in West Greenland). The meaning of the *kussataq* remains obscure,

43. A human, being alone, invites "Others" to visit. Similarly, a married couple without children and neighbors have the same attraction.

but that of the raven does *not*. In the spirit language *taartaq*, the raven is characterized as the only bird to be seen moving about throughout winter—i.e., he knows what is going on in *sila*. So, raven is the person to forebode the coming of light. Maybe the origin of Sun and Moon was in some places retold at some ritual in spring.

Taking *Uniagaq* to be a raven figure, who brings about the hunting culture anew after the capsizing of the earth, this is due to his attraction to light, his magic of having his wishful thinking about material, tools, and a woman come true, and his genius in training his brother to balance in the kayak using their common clothing, the unwound lashings tied together. As will be shown later, this "clothing" is a *pooq*, meaning "mother" in the spirit language. Raven thus comes out an East Greenlandic culture hero. This is a prominent characteristic of raven in the complex shared by Natives of the Alaska West Coast and across the Bering Strait in northeast Siberia. The other raven figure of a trickster clown is usually emphasized as the only one present (left) among the eastern Inuit (Hultkrantz 1962). Yet Thalbitzer (1930), Inge Kleivan (1971b), and Oosten and Laugrand (2006) have all pointed to its creative connotations, and to me the *Uniagaq* story adds strong evidence. But the trickster figure is part of this story as well. Despite his marvelous deeds of procuring the basics of light, balance in body of his brother at sea, division of labor by sex, and reproduction, *Uniagaq* himself ends up on the margin of society. Being no kayaker of the deep sea, only of the coast, he has no right to marry. His spell rebounds. The refused suitor ends up a bachelor, reduced in bodily balance by his disabled hip. As will be shown below, although raven is a master of balance in the air, he is no bird of the deep sea, he looks limp hopping along on the earth, and he is never permitted indoors among humans.

Whether the East Greenlanders and the southeast Baffin Islanders used to share a common Thule tradition about equinoxes is hard to tell. They live at roughly the same latitude of high tides. Be this as it may, when turning the focus on tides, ideas about Raven, tides, and balance are very similar to those of the Northwest Coast Tlingit. There a devastating flood, a punishment for wrongdoings created by "the old woman down there," forces Raven to dive for sea urchins (instead of picking them on the beach at low tide, I suppose). Angered, the old woman asks him where and at which (low) tide he happened to get hold of this food. Provoked, Raven cuts open the cliff with the knife for opening the shells. He then descends and wounds her buttocks with the spikes of the sea urchin. He continues until she has made the flood recede and promised to let it rise and recede in the ordinary balanced way that brings food to the coast (Swanton 1902: 9–10). This origin myth was told at funerals for restoring the mental balance of the mourning relatives (Swanton 1970 [1902]; cf. Tybjerg 2008: 105–6). So, if we take balance as the key symbol and the tidal movements as proof of a seesawing land, we can assemble elements of a complex that suits the Inuit as well: breaking the rules disturbs the balance of the world in a way similar to a mind disturbed by the death of a close relative. And, to repeat, the Polar Inuit kept the world in balance by observing their taboos. In East Greenland the flood capsizing the world is sent by somebody above (*pinnga*) as a punishment for wrongdoings. *Nunagiqsaqtuq* is concerned with punishment as well. He transmits the confessions of breaking taboos to Sea Woman, *Sedna*, or *Sana* (Boas 1964: 175)—i.e., *Sanna*, "the one down there in front"—and he also cleanses the land at the highest tides at equinoxes, which are said to make the world turn a somersault. The parallel ritual of wider Inuit extension has the shaman kill or clean Sea Woman of the offenses, whereas the Tlingit Raven, by its threats to hurt a similar female figure "down there" with the spines of a sea urchin, has the flood turned into the beneficent tide.

Uniagaq, having escaped the turning around of the earth by running towards the light (like the Inuit Raven), reintroduces the Inuit hunting culture from scratch. This story does not explicate a conversion of the flood into the balancing movements of the tide. Instead, balance is the element stressed in the kayak-hunting culture inculcated into the little brother. Nor is this story associated with Sea Woman, with whom the East Greenlanders were not particularly concerned. The connection is rather with Moon, the "somebody up there," *pinnga*, in the spirit language, *taartaq*, who reacted to wrongdoings by turning the earth around. Moon causes the tide, which, like the Tlingit high tide, explicitly brings edibles to the coast. In short, the powers of heaven and underworld are to be balanced by ritual means at the times when one of them visibly gets too great a say, due to the rule breakings of humans. The coastal cultures of Greenlanders, Canadian Inuit, and the Tlingit seem to have shared such fundamental ideas centered in the movements of the tide.

Somersaults

A recurring idea among the Inuit is that somersaults had the power to renew life and procure good hunting in the near future. In addition to the horizontal circling in imitation of *silap ingerlasia* usually referred to in scholarly literature, somersaulting used to be a body movement of cosmological value. In analogy with the turning around of the world at equinoxes or at the beginning of time, a somersault was, in East Greenland, simply called "a sun"—i.e., a full circling of the world (Victor & Robert-Lamblin 1989–93, I: 208–9), or in South Greenland the full course of a day and a night (Sonne 2005: ID 1892). Farther north at Uummannaq, old dwarves (W. Grl. *inuarullikkat*, sing. *inuarulligaq*) obtained rejuvenation by rolling headfirst down a slope. Five times they managed to do so with success, but on the sixth turn they were to die like all mortals. Their success, however, depended on experienced awareness in that the young (inexperienced—i.e., less balanced) dwarves were at risk of getting killed, as they could be caught in an avalanche (Sonne 2005: ID 163, 148 [see "Hist."]; Thalbitzer 1923: 531 n. 5).

In the south, famous for its excellent kayakers, a peculiar way of somersaulting in the kayak was practiced—i.e., pitchpoling,[44] where the kayak turns end over end (Kaalund et al. 2006a: 261; 2006b: 261). In contrast to the "ordinary" feat of rolling a kayak, pitchpoling was practiced by only a few Greenlandic kayakers. Knud Rasmussen knew about that competence and planned to include a filming of this practice in his *Palos Brudefærd*.[45] But he fell seriously ill and had to remain in hospital in Qaqortoq/Julianehåb, and so he never turned up in Nanortalik, where the weather soon turned too bad for filming (*ibid.*). Nothing is said about when or why the trick was played, but it may have been a way of coping with heavy surfs, because in this region an astonishing exercise was practiced for exactly this end. It consisted of rolling, head protected by a bag, head over heels down a steep hill. Ungaralaq, who provided a description of the practice, had tried it once himself and ended up lying unconscious for five days and spending an entire summer in bed (Berthelsen & Langgård 1983: 51). This practice is made fun of in East Greenlandic stories, for example in a variant of "Qasiassaq" and in another about a tiny dwarf (E. Grl. *ijaajavaatsiaq*, pl. *ijaajavaatsiat*) with a strong tendency to lose his balance. Qasiassaq, a poor hunter who excelled at playing dirty tricks (which first made his wife proud and then, when exposed, deeply embarrassed), becomes as damaged as Ungaralaq by letting himself roll down a steep hill

44. The right word communicated by Phyllis Morrow.
45. Shot in 1933 in Tasiilaq/Ammassalik. Search YouTube.

(Sonne 2005: ID 1100, 1101). The tiny dwarf who loses his balance and tumbles down a cliff receives a huge bump for an eyelid (ID 554, 594, 1452). In my understanding of these stories, both Qasiassaq and the dwarf reflect Raven, Qasiassaq its bragging, trickster character, whereas the coastal dwarves are, especially in East Greenland, explicitly identified with or likened to ravens (ID 2283, 1290). First and foremost, Raven is the expert in somersaulting, as I once happened to observe in Iceland. From atop a steep cliff, a number of ravens had fun somersaulting downward toward the sea then letting the wind carry them back upward. In a pan-Inuit myth, when Raven is married to a goose, he, a resident bird, quickly tires out during the migration and ends up drowning. The geese had warned him in advance, of course, but he insists, and in one variant he even brags that he will turn somersaults backward all along (ID 40). Somersaulting ravens signify humans in the vicinity (ID 191), and a raven somersaulting above your head brings luck in hunting (F. Lynge 1981: No. 97; Rasmussen 1979: No. 498). Like ravens in winter, the tiny dwarves live close to humans at the coast. And like ravens braving storms in low flight over coastal waters, the dwarves make a smooth path through the rough sea along the coast, but as they are unable to catch even the smallest young of a seal, they make a living stealing from humans. Not only as thievish but also as filthy as ravens, the dwarves nevertheless have shamans as white and clean as you may wish. This, I suppose, is an allusion to the white, primordial Raven before he was blackened by loon (Sonne 2005: ID 423, 1364; J. Rosing 1963: 184; O. Rosing 1957–61, I: 77; Kleivan 1971b).[46]

Other examples of significant somersaults are no doubt to be found all over the Inuit/Yupiit area. Besides those of southeast Baffin Island I have come across some far away from Greenland, on Nunivak Island. One is a myth about Raven introducing death among humans, the second concerns two rituals at the close of the Bladder Feast, and the third is a myth about starvation.[47]

In the first myth Raven suddenly made mink stop its pleasant habit of letting people roll down a hill for their recurrent rejuvenation. Next he caught a crab, buried the creature close to the village, put up two sticks in a cross, simulated weeping, and told the disappointed mink that it (the village?) looked much nicer (with a graveyard?). From that day on people began to die (Lantis 1946: 186–87).[48] At the Bladder Feast, right after the returning of the bladders' "life" to the sea, the men and young boys removed their boots and ritual gutskin parkas and rolled somersaulting toward the rear platform, where the frightened small children took flight. Next followed a game of tag around the entrance hole in the floor, children first, leaving the circle one by one when tagged and replaced by an older runner right on to the oldest men. The meanings of both rolling and circling are not completely clear. Did they concern the renewal of human and animal life generally or the return of the animals for a renewed catch, or both? Anyway, somersaulting could procure game as demonstrated by my last example, the story about a starving man. He came across a house full of seals guarded by two whales, where a man told him to roll somersaulting three times on his way out in order to drag a whale along to the village.[49] And so

46. "Whenever they [the Greenlanders] believe that something they are waiting for will not happen within reasonable time they use the expression 'when the ravens get white' (*tulugkat qaqortigpata* [*tulukkat qaqortippata*]" (cf. Kleivan 1971b: 38).

47. The Bladder Feast was a five-day celebration of feasting during which the stored urine bladders of all the animals slain that year were inflated, brought out to holes in the ice, then stuffed into the holes; the animals were asked to come back the following year.

48. The longer variant received by Rasmussen also has Raven instructing people in mourning rites (1952: 261–62).

49. The sea mammals of the Yupiit world lived like humans in their own species' village beneath the sea.

he did (Lantis 1946: 186–87, 297, 288). In the same line of thought, a Greenlandic caribou hunter will get a big bull if it happens that a raven turns somersaulting over his head (Rasmussen 1979: No. 498).

Raven shares its somersaulting ability with the sand hopper, which is simply called *napalariaq* (the somersaulting one) in East Greenland. We shall return later to this creature, as well as to other symbolic meanings of Raven.

To recap: A great number of sayings, statements, and stories indicate perceptions of a regularly seesawing earth like a movable disk, with a slanting profile from up behind you standing on the coast facing the sea and down under along the bottom of the sea. The regularity was disturbed by breaks of taboo, causing flooding and avalanches read as overbalance, and the mythic turning around of the earth as a new beginning or rejuvenation of human life (and culture) in This World. The perception of seesawing seems evidenced by the observations of both the tide, rising to extreme heights at the equinoxes, and the repeated growing and reduced altitudes of the sun. Ideas about the tide in places where it runs high are comparable from Greenland to the Northwest Coast Tlingit. Another association with both the beginning and possible end of the world rested with the changing altitude of the sky, supported like a roof by pillars, by the rainbow of changing altitudes, or by the air becoming dangerously disturbed by gales. The latter caused havoc at sea as on land: kayakers drowned, houses were smashed, and people were forced to crawl along on their knees.

The Balanced Upright Human Being

"Upright" balance is central to Inuit body symbolism. The balanced human body, when awake, is upright, as also expressed by Umingmaktoormiut, the Muskox People, a branch of the Kitlinermiut, who called the soul *nappan* ("it keeps one upright"). One delicate example of this analogy is *sila*, as the *inua* of weather, being in charge of the upright support of the heavens.

Humans are comparatively slow in developing into upright beings. A baby will turn around from lying on her back to lying prostrate at an early age; soon, encouraged by the adults, she will lift herself onto her arms and look around. Next she will get along by crawling (like an animal), and only then raise herself using some support to an upright (if still unsteady) position and eventually walk her first step from one embracing adult to another. This step in becoming an upright human being was a recognized "ritual first" to be celebrated socially among all Inuit. Coming to master one's body, however, meant some more years of encouraged practice.

When animals, birds, and humans die, they fall over. When they lose consciousness, they fall over. When they fall ill, they lie down. Humans and mammals sleep lying down. The Inuit and Yupiit were not all too happy about that position, it seems, judging from the fact that generally Inuit and Yupiit children were warned against sleeping for too long: "We children were always woken up early in the morning" (Mathias Frederiksen, Nuussuaq/Kraulshavn, pers. comm.). After someone had died, Aupilaarjuk's father, who wanted a long life for his children, made them rise at an early hour: "He did not want us to be like dead people" (Oosten et al. 1999: 14). Similarly, in Southwest Alaska, getting up early kept sickness away from Yup'ik children and counteracted laziness (Fienup-Riordan 1994: 149–52). And the Aleut children were sent out of doors to the light and air at daybreak for the sake of their longevity and health (Veniaminov 1984: 211, note 37, cf. Atkinson 1992). Rising early was the usual moral practice everywhere, and the ideal human being—alert and healthy—was the upright one.

Animals and birds, when at home in their own worlds (the Other World) or when visiting humans, might appear in their human forms. Yet at the moment the visitors took leave, they changed into their manifest appearances of This World. Birds in particular were hardly capable of running at any useful speed in their human forms. It is true, when compared with all other beings in the Arctic and sub-Arctic, only human beings can run on two feet in an upright position, if slightly stooping (Sonne 1996). Among Polar Inuit, Iglulingmiut, and Umingmaktoormiut, the polar bears refer to human beings as "the upright" or "the living ones" (*makitajut*, Sonne 2005: ID 1551; Rasmussen 1929: 270; 1932: 110). This is surprising in a way, because polar bear can also stand on its two hind feet and remain upright for some time, just as the ermine can (Muus et al. 1981: 388). Still, both polar bear and ermine walk the land on all fours. From the perspective of a Nattilik polar bear, the owl is always *standing* upright, and from the perspective of the owl the polar bear always gets along walking (Rasmussen 1931: 402). The lemming is another mammal capable of standing on its hind feet, as also observed by Rasmussen once in company with a party of Polar Inuit: "On a big stone right in front of us is a small lemming eyeing our bed for the night with genuine astonishment. There it stands, raised on its hind legs like some small *sensible* two-legged being, looking at us" (Rasmussen 1915: 136–37, tr. and emphasis BS). Since the context refers to the knowledge gathered by the Polar Inuit on lemmings by observing their ways, Rasmussen most probably quotes his companions. They also stress the lemming's very human arrangement of its dwelling with both platform and a neat little dunghill at one end (*ibid.*). So, the upright being looks sensible, as it uses its *sila*. Moving about is another matter. For most species, it means to walk on all fours. Birds certainly do walk and hop around on their two feet, and sandpipers can even run, but the moment they flee they take flight. (There are no ostriches in Greenland, the great auk has become extinct, and during molting in spring the guillemots ride the waves.) One apparent deviation is stated by the Umingmaktoormiut in a story about polar bears and a human being. The polar bears call themselves Inuviit, genuine humans, in distinction from human beings, those with their staggering ("*chancellent*") walking (*ulrunnapiaraluin*), according to the translation by Métayer (1973: 440). Etymologically, however, *ulrun* does not mean staggering from side to side, but rather it means stooping, or the gait of an interrupted falling forward, as it were (Fortescue et al. 1994; 2010).

In comparison not only with animals, birds, etc. but with the spirits as well (from whom the shamans got their helpers), human beings possess bodily abilities of their own. In an analysis of East Greenlandic traditional identity, the objects of my comparisons were the faunal species and also the spirit species of the shaman performances (Sonne 1996). The spirits were suitable for analysis, because in precolonial East Greenland, Qallunaat, or the West Greenlanders, were not very often at hand for comparison in the ongoing formation of one's identity, whereas many individual spirits were well-known mythic and ritual figures. Several helping spirits appeared time and again during performances because they were inherited or acquired by the up-and-coming young shamans when the old ones passed away (e.g., Sonne 2005: ID 1692; Gessain 1984). Naturally, the East Greenlanders identified themselves as Inuit (E. Grl. *Iviit*), but why did the spirits in their spirit language call human beings "coast dwellers" despite the fact that two subspecies of spirits, the tiny dwarves and the *innersuit*, were coast dwellers too?[50] Apart from the disproportionate short hind part of their kayaks,

50. *Eqqarlivut*: our closest neighbors (KRH, 52, 2, booklet 405). Thalbitzer translates Teemiartissaq's "*erqarsivun*" into "our relatives" (1923: 481).

they even used hunting equipment like those of human beings. A fine systematized presentation of the spirit species done by Kaarali Andreassen, together with a good number of stories, called my attention to decisive differences in bodily weight distribution. Thus, when running downhill the tiny dwarves stoop; the other dwarves and the giants do not succeed in learning how to kayak. Similarly, the *innersuit*, the unsurpassed hunters of sea mammals, cannot raise their "unbalanced" kayak like humans when they turn over. By capsizing they remain hopelessly bottom up, until saved by a human kayaker (Sonne 2005: ID 950, 1386). Taken together with some other points, these characteristics led me to the following conclusion:

> All the spirits surpass humans in one way or another as regards hunting and movement. But none of them possesses the balance of humans when it comes to travel on both land and sea with body or torso erect, *and*, turning around in a kayak to get on an even keel. Neither spirits nor animals can be taught this balance. Humans can learn from animals and spirits, even to fly as is the case of shamans. Animals and spirits are dependent on the shaman, and the shamans depend on the abilities of the spirits and animals when the balance of the world needs restoring. These balancing abilities may be the basic meaning of being a "coast dweller." (Sonne 1996: 249–50)[51]

Kayak Dizziness

It takes some training to acquire balance as second nature when paddling a kayak. Greenlandic children were carefully taught kayaking; they rarely just learned by imitating adult kayakers. Usually an adult would hold on until balance was incorporated, and then always remain close by in his own kayak. Young children were not permitted to set off alone or far away from the shore until well trained. Almost anybody could learn, and some were definitely talented and excelled, though kayak dizziness, *nangiarneq* (fear), could still strike the best of all. Losing balance from dizziness, the kayaker became paralyzed with fear at the point of capsizing, and more often than not he subsequently had to give up kayaking for good.

The concept of *nangiarneq* invokes both social and cosmological issues, which means that the following considerations will be of some length. In his treatise on this subject, K. G. Hansen first advances that *nangiarneq* must be a recent substantivizing of the verb *nangiarpoq*, in translation of the diagnosis made by Western medicine of kayak dizziness as an illness. And second, Hansen suggests that the Greenlanders themselves considered the malady not an individual illness but rather the effect of sorcery. Encountering a *tupilak*[52] at sea would most certainly bring about kayak dizziness.[53]

---

51. One exception has two of the biggest dwarves successfully learn to paddle a kayak but remain miserable hunters at sea (J. Rosing 1963: 186; O. Rosing 1957–61, I: 79–80). Another is apparently thought out by the West Greenlander Ajaqak, one of Rasmussen's intelligent informants, who declares that an *innersuaq* succeeds in turning around without help if he wears a *kapitak*, a waterproof jacket, and is decorated with carvings of walrus tusk (Sonne 2005: ID 1598).

52. A *tupilak* was an artificially made being used for sorcery. It was meant to hurt the person to whom it was sent. It looked like and was the same size as a seal and was made of bones from various animals plus sometimes the skull of a child, filled in with peat and covered with skin. The *tupilak* was brought to life by magic songs and made to grow by suckling the genitals of its maker. The peculiar change in meaning of a *tupilak* into an auspicious talisman feels absurd. The production since about 1900 of small *tupilaks* carved in bone and sold as curios is to blame.

53. Simply hiding something from the land in the kayak (belonging to the sea sphere) could do the trick (Sandgreen 1967, II: 134; 1987: 365).

Consequently Hansen proposes that kayak dizziness ought to be treated by solving social conflicts that involve (expectations of) sorcery. Traditionally, the *angakkoq* could neutralize the conflicts by pointing out the "sorcerer" during a performance; means of defense like amulets, *aarnussat* (sing. *aarnuaq*), and spells, *serratit* (sing. *serrat*), were also believed to prevent dizziness (K. G. Hansen 1994).

Greenlandic sayings on kayak dizziness emphasize the bottom of the body as the point of its balance at sea: "A boy who prefers the rump of birds will sit safely in his kayak" (F. Lynge 1981: No. 267; Rasmussen 1979: No. 388). However, both boys and men who eat the tail bone of the seal will capsize (F. Lynge 1981: No. 140, 197; Rasmussen 1979: No. 86, 24; 1921–25, III: 327). This is likely because kayakers are seen to be like seabirds riding the waves and not like seals, which dive and swim beneath the surface. Another association to the tail bone refers to weather, in that a kayaker who is weather-bound is said to have broken his tailbone (F. Lynge 1981: No. 471). Furthermore, whenever the kayaker begins to feel dizzy, he should get hold of a young raven, pull down his trousers, and sit on the bird until it dies (No. 400). Since the anus was considered the exit and entrance of the *tarneq* ("soul"), the sitting meant free access for the characteristic essence of the animal being (F. Lynge 1981: No 92; Rasmussen 1921–25, III: 331; 1979: No. 86, No. 493). Why, then, is stabilizing balance in body the essence of Raven? An answer has been given above in treating Raven's part in ritual and myth in the balancing of tide and flooding. Nevertheless, let us take a second, more detailed look at this mediating figure.

Sila and Raven as Mediators of Transition

The mythic figure of Raven is less prominent among the Eastern Inuit than the culture hero Raven is among western groups in Alaska, in northeast Siberia, and among Northwest Coast Indians (see e.g., Kleivan 1971b). Nevertheless, Raven's Eastern Inuit epithets are much the same. As shown by Oosten and Laugrand (2006), in Arctic Canada Raven is a provider of knowledge and the "bringer of light." He is associated with both the beginning and the end of life, with tattooing (raven's claw) as related to the fertility of women and the renewal of the land by the abovementioned ritual raven figure, *Nunagiqsaqtuq*. The comparable *Uniagaq* of the East Greenlandic story about the turning around of the land is not explicitly identified as a raven, but he is indeed explicitly attracted by the light at the renewal of the world (and implicitly a reinventor of the kayak culture). The balance of the earth restored, and another balance, namely that of the younger brother in his kayak, is initiated by *Uniagaq*. He keeps the younger brother in control of the kayak by means of their "clothing," the straps that protected their naked bodies when being outdoors (Inuit dressed when going out, and undressed when coming in). Unlike *Nunagiqsaqtuq*, *Uniagaq* was not connected with Sea Woman, but like *Nunagiqsaqtuq*, Raven was associated with breach of taboo, as demonstrated once by Aqqasaaq during a horrid famine in 1888. The starving household of Aqqasaaq happened to get hold of a newly killed hooded seal, which, being one of the big species, could not be eaten for three days (see, e.g., Søby 1969/70: 60–61). Aqqasaaq stepped in, pushed his long hair forward, plaited it into the likeness of a beak, and then hopped and danced like a raven around the meat, exclaiming, "[S]o by now the black one has tasted the meat, and every taboo is lifted" (J. Rosing 1963: 137). Neutralizing taboos or the breaches of them turns out to be a job of raven figures, because, as emphasized by Oosten and Laugrand, raven is not subject to the taboos of humans (2004–5; 2006).

The association of Raven with female fertility seems to explain the behavior of the young South Greenlandic mother in celebrating her luck in bearing sons. "[S]he braids some hairs into the shape of a horn on her forehead" (Dalager 1915: 59). The horn means a raven's beak, I suppose. Even more significant Raven's call, *qaut*, meaning light, and repeated four times, announces the transformation into a human or social being of a newborn baby by its name—Kiivi, for instance:

> *Qaut-Qaut-Qaut-Qaut!*
> Kiveetaaqaut.
> They have, they have, they have
> They have got a Kiivi!
> (Rasmussen 1921–25, I: 37; 1938: 181)

This basic idea runs implicitly as the red thread in a story about a dumb woman whose newborn babies die from bleeding, one after the other. When consequently the poor mother is thrown out by her husband, she gains the use of speech at the moment she leaves the house, and now she can tell the reason why they died. They bled to death because their little finger was cut off by their grandmother, who was babysitting. The mother goes in search of her children, whom she finds as young ravens far away in the inland mountains. They transform into their human shapes and follow her back home to a happy life hereafter (Sonne 2005: ID 362). The cut-off fingers no doubt refer to the ritual of naming, when the name of the baby is clearly pronounced for the first time and not used in public hereafter. Naming used to be the privilege of the grandmother. She would use her own little finger (or fourth finger) to let a drop of water fall into the baby's mouth, and then would take hold of the baby's right little (or fourth) finger while reciting the above formula (Rasmussen 1921–25, I: 37). Of even greater import is that the story also refers to the beginning of times, the time of reversals, when a man was able to become pregnant and bear a child.[54] In search of a cure for his infertile wife, this man travels the entire west coast, first north and then south, until he comes upon an old woman in the farthest south, who hands him dried capelins, a male and the roe of a female. The wife is to eat the former to bear a son, the latter for a daughter. On his way home the man runs out of food, eats the roe, becomes pregnant, and, having been opened below by a midwife who smears him in the crotch with a dead grouse and some blue mold from beneath the floor stones, he bears a dumb daughter. She is left to grow up and later marry at her birthplace, and she remains dumb until thrown out of the house. Since, as will be shown presently, raven definitely belongs outdoors, this mother of young ravens remains dumb until thrown out of the interior space of human relations. Outside she can intelligibly *qaut* or speak; that is, she can disclose the unspoken secrets. Eventually named by their liberated mother, the children transform back into human beings.

Raven's associations with *sila* in the meaning of "weather" abound in plain sayings. Troubled waters, which can also be likened to the mental state of an irresolute person, *aalasoq*, can be calmed by a beheaded raven, blown up and thrown out on the sea (F. Lynge 1981: No. 79).[55] In contrast, plundering

54. My reference here is not to a Greenland text but to the Canadian Inuit origin myth of two men, shamans, living as a married couple, one getting pregnant and the other making him split below to bear the child (Saladin d'Anglure 1990a: 84–85).

55. Other means of similar effect are things from the land, such as the kokleare growing on the midden or an inflated grouse, the bird of the land par excellence (Rasmussen 1979: No. 157; F. Lynge 1981: No. 81, 86, 80).

a raven's nest will raise a storm, which will come from the north when the nest faces north and from the south if that is the direction (F. Lynge 1981: No. 230; Rasmussen 1979: No. 193, 378). The kayaker, who together with his son found shelter in a storm with ravens in human form, later warned his son: "You see, our hosts were ravens. Never mention our visit to anybody. Holding your tongue you can always take refuge with them in bad weather. Those are my refuge whenever the weather turns bad during my kayaking." The son of course lets his tongue run away at the first opportunity (Sonne 2005: ID 825).

Raven belongs in the neighborhood of human dwellings of Inuit as of Semites. Like biblical Noah, who first sent out a raven as a scout to see if the floodwaters had receded, the story is also in acculturated Greenlandic versions connected with ravens (Sonne 2005: ID 78, 485, to be treated below). Sayings bear witness as well: the traveler who sees ravens will know that people are around (ID 41, 191, 292, 1434, 1825), and people at home know that guests are arriving when they hear the raven's cry (Rasmussen 1979: No. 1; 1921–25, III: 325; F. Lynge 1981: No. 288). Nevertheless, although close to humans, Raven absolutely belongs to the outside/out of doors, to *sila*. Thus an East Greenlandic couple told Victor that when one night they heard a raven on the roof, they went out and scared it away. It followed them into the entrance tunnel. They chased it out and Odarpi went out with his gun. But then it was gone. The same evening it had been first in Tasiilaq, and then in Kulusuk, and then in Noortiit. If it had come into the room and had puffed out its feathers, it would have suffocated everybody in the room (Sonne 2005: ID 2009). There is too much outdoor weather (*sila*) in Raven, who normally respects the human boundary between inside and outside. However, on another occasion:

> [S]hortly after the return of the sun, a raven entered and flew around in the living room; people did absolutely nothing, and the bird got out by itself. People were paralyzed from terror, and the effect, was soon to follow. A man who had been sick since autumn suddenly exclaimed that he was cured. Hungry from a long period of no eating, he asked for food, and ate in company with his fellows, but then one among them called out: "He has gone mad!" Crawling away under the platform he was seized in time by the men who with much effort managed to get him back to the platform again. (Rasmussen 1938: 168–69)

So, although Raven is associated with the ascending sun and brings a sudden clarity to the patient, he simultaneously causes his outbreak of insanity by its indoor hopping and screaming.

In the meaning of a clear mind, Raven is confounded with *sila-cum*-light in various ways. There's a saying about a person who has for a long time been soft and then returns to a normal state of mind: "A raven flew over his head" (F. Lynge 1981: No. 472). But a raven crying in darkness of evening forebodes madness (No. 468). Among the Iglulingmiut the cry of raven, *qauq qauq* ("light"), was associated with the origin of daylight and its alternation with the darkness of night (Oosten & Laugrand 2006; Laugrand & Oosten 2015: 85f).[56] In Greenland, besides being uttered at the onset

56. Holtved (mistakenly) gives the translation "my platform skin" of the raven's cry *qâ-qâ* in his summary of Amaunalik's version (1951, 2: 92f). The original offers no translation (1951, 1: 232). Nor does the version taken down by Niels Egede give a translation of the *ka-ka-ka* ending his version (1939: 257). The remaining Greenland versions quoted in Kleivan (1971b) do not mention the cry. Here Raven's black color is the only point of the story.

of the naming ritual (transforming a nonhuman into a related human), the cry announces more precisely the transitions between day and night: twilight and dawn. At these *sila-* or *naar-*times an *angakkoq* sets out or returns: "He (the shaman) tied himself up (for the spirit flight) and rose. He headed for home and he arrived at the point when the ravens started to cry (i.e., just before sunrise)" (Sonne 2005: ID 187). "The light put out, she sat down on the floor and said: 'Throughout the night nobody must neither move nor blink... Not until the ravens start crying shall I rush through the air!'" (ID 258). Raven is *sila* in transition, the bringer of light at dawn, the remover of light at dusk, and accordingly it restores the balance of the dizzy kayaker and the mind of the mentally disturbed, but at the same time it serves as an omen of a darkening mind at twilight or, if it happens to slip indoors, causes insanity right away.

The above examples are of both West and East Greenlandic provenience. Peculiar for the East Greenlandic shaman tradition, a particular helping spirit—a coastal dwarf (*ijaajavaatsiaq*), acquired early in apprenticeship—saw to the return of the pupil (lying unconscious through initiation in solitude) by *waking him up* at the time right before sunset. Among several instances of this situation at sundown (Victor & Robert-Lamblin 1989–93, II: 241, 249, I: 92; Sonne 2005: ID 1981, 575, 2283, 966, 1236, 1241, 1153), the story about Naaja's last initiation is complete in the symbolism of rebirth. In search of a very strong helping spirit he called forth the giant *inua* of the inland ice and let himself be eaten up by the monster. Hardened, because he had gone through the course of being eaten several times, he remained conscious throughout the consumption of his flesh right until the point when the monster opened him up, took hold of his heart, and removed it. At that point he passed out. "And while passing out he remembered that the sun was still shining, at its meridian altitude in fact..." No poor feat of memory, considering that no shred of meat was left on his body! Backstage the storyteller sets time correctly. When the dwarves wake him up, there are two of them circling his body; he is whole and hale, but in darkness. He lies inside the giant's cave. He wants to go back, immediately, out into the light. "Don't," the dwarves tell him. "You shall perish." So they take him along in the opposite direction, through a long, long tunnel to a point where the light from the other end seeps in through an opening between two big stones that slide together at the moment he tries to pass between. "Close your eyes!" the dwarves encourage him. He succeeds and continues right out into the sunlight. The dwarves do not feel like going outside; they quickly turn around in the sunlight and return to the darkness of their tunnel. The ray of the sun is dazzling, and then it sets (Sonne 2005: ID 1215).

The birth symbolism of this story hardly needs comment, recognizable as it is from stories of initiations all over the world. It should be added, though, that the two big stones—a common motif, (i.e., "Symplegades" in Greek mythology)—at the end of the tunnel have their counterparts in reality. In another rebirth story the main character is explicitly to pass between *patsitsit*, the name[57] of the two big stones placed at each side of the entrance from the tunnel into the house (Thalbitzer 1923: 112–13). They supported the outermost beam of the roof and were used in treatment of madness, a highly feared unbalance of mind, and probably for other ritual means too (Sonne 2005: ID 996, 1238). Yet of particular interest in Naaja's story is the specification of points in time that appear

57. Other spellings are *patdisat, pattisat, pallisat, patitsit.*

important: first his half-conscious noticing of the position of the sun in its highest altitude, then the full daylight that would kill him in case he returns the way he came in; next the boundary of the still-shining sun in This World, to which the dwarves do not belong, and finally, the sunset immediately following Naaja's symbolic rebirth or return to This World. This is the very transitional *naar*-time of ill fate in case you, a shaman or a pupil (or a spirit), miss it.

Although the two dwarves approaching Naaja are not likened to any other beings, dwarves of this kind, the *ijaajavaatsiat*, are usually compared to birds in general and most frequently to ravens. With ravens, with which they share the characteristics of being dirty and thievish, and of living close to human dwellings at the coast, they also possess ravens' intimate association to *naar*-times, in the figure of a life-saving wake-up helping spirit.

Turning to structuralism, as mediators between life and death, the tiny dwarves and the ravens roughly live up to the position of Raven among the Northwest Coast Indians in the analysis by Lévi-Strauss. He points to Raven's creative potentiality as a coastal bird mediating land and sea, as a scavenger between meat-eating hunters and herbivorous farmers, and thus between life and death (Lévi-Strauss 1963: 224). It should be mentioned, though, that in real life raven complements its carrion with young birds hunted on the cliffs, eggs from their nests, and the collecting of plants (Muus et al. 1981: 330–31). Nor does the Inuit (Greenlandic) Raven mediate outside versus inside. It belongs out of doors and it causes death by suffocation if let in. As a coastal being Raven, which breeds, plays, and hunts at the cliffs, is less a bird of the sea than one of the land. In myth Raven, a nonmigrating bird, dies by drowning in the sea by his in-laws, the geese. He is not reborn from Sea Woman's house in spring like the migrating seabirds. Rather, as a bird of the land, Raven belongs in heaven. Indeed, ravens seem to be the only species of bird encountered in the heavenly realm of death. In the early days of the missions, some West Greenlanders turned down the promise of a pleasant afterlife in heaven by emphasizing its lack of food (seals), its continuous rotation making you dizzy, and the ravens becoming entangled in your hair. By and by, when the shamans from personal inspection could promise seals for food in heaven, their countrymen then obliged (Sonne 2000a). In East Greenland the problem of eternal life without food was solved in a more reasonable way. The deceased humans who ended up in heaven were said to live exclusively on young ravens, easy as they were to catch, because they got so fat by eating all those human corpses (Sonne 2005: ID 1698, 1818, 1991; J. Rosing 1963: 280; KRH, 52, 2, booklet 405: 5).[58] Recycling in an old key, as it were! And perhaps they also took away the West Greenlanders' assertion about the dizziness caused by the rotating heaven. The missionary must have asked the East Greenlanders about this effect, because the shamans explicitly denied it, that is, unless one suffered from dizziness when alive on earth (KRH, 52, 2, booklet 405: 5).

Let us return once more to the cure of kayak dizziness by the essence of a polysemous young raven. We can by now consider this restoration of balance to be in closest association with the relightening of *sila* announced by raven at dawn. As stated, one meaning of *sila* includes clearness of mind, and so the reason why a raven *young* serves as the remedy against a body-mind paralysis could be explained by the presence in heaven of young raven. In a perfectly balanced relationship of exchange, they live on the meat of human bodies and serve as food for the deceased. Additional associations

58. Although sealing is the most frequent way of hunting in the lower realm of death, a single story mentions young raven as a prey easy to kill in that place as well (Sandgreen 1987: 195).

should be considered, since unnamed babies can transform into young ravens in myth; thus, the babies that are fetched from Moon in heaven by the shamans can be likened to young ravens, all the more so because some East Greenlanders had their own ideas about the Northern Lights. This light was not the pan-Inuit effect of deceased humans playing ball with a walrus skull, but was produced by miscarriages and unnamed babies left out to perish. They played ball with their placentas (Holm 1914: 82; 1972: 121). So, did the babies derive from heaven? Some did, since an infertile woman could make use of a particular white stone said to have come down from heaven (see p. 105). Or did babies come from the sea? This is the message of most versions of the myth about a man or woman who took up residence in one animal species after another and finally entered the womb of a woman as the soul of a seal just caught and brought home by her husband (e.g., Blaisel & Arnakak 1993). Since the East Greenlanders also told this story ("Navagiaq" in Sonne 2005) about the "transmigrating soul," babies apparently derived from either place, above or below. In support of this idea, there is a warning that a child born after the death of former child (an *angerlartoqut*)—and thus considered to have returned home—should never be offered meat from either the fetus of a seal or a raven (Rasmussen 1979: No. 293). But still: Why was a dizzy kayaker cured by the soul of a young raven? Because, by sitting on the young raven until it dies, he inhales its restoring balance through the anus (the way of the soul). Finally, Hansen's assertion that kayak dizziness is thought to be an effect of sorcery—a social thing—is in line with the general belief, presented below, that rebounding sorcery brought forth imbalanced behavior in both body and mind.

A Balanced Body = A Clear Mind: Sorcery and Insanity

"If an old person tends to fall down while walking (s)he has 'sent something off'"—i.e., sent off some means of sorcery addressed to a certain person (F. Lynge 1981: No. 359). An absentminded person mumbling with closed eyes could arouse suspicion (e.g., Sonne 2005: 757). Indeed, attacks of insanity were feared. The stricken person who acquired immense physical strength was thought to have been hit by his/her abortive attempt at sorcery. It had returned with the effect of a boomerang but might be neutralized by confession (Holm 1972: 132; 1914: 98; Sonne 2005: ID 1238, 9, 1257, 1268, 2007, 2113). On the other hand, a foolish person might be of quite some use in foretelling and making a diagnosis. As reasoned by Rink concerning *imaanaanngitsut*, or "the not just so ones," "the more sense and good judgment of everything visible is lost, the more the person concerned becomes enabled to see the Unveiled of present and future" (Rink 1868–71, II: 198, tr. BS). Shamans, who were experts in coming to see the Unveiled and were thought to be acting sane outside of their performances, operated on a thin line between mental worlds.[59]

For an example of suspicion of sorcery, we can look to an autobiographical story, also quoted at length by K. G. Hansen in treating kayak dizziness. Kukkujooq recollects the paralyzing dizziness that befell him by first touching with his paddle and then seeing a big trout remaining immovably still at his kayak. It remained for a long time until, after a moment of his inattention, it disappeared. At the point of capsizing, he managed to concentrate sufficiently in order to gradually paddle along and get ashore. Somebody had tried to hurt him by sorcery—there was no question about it. Later

59. See also Jakobsen (1999: 99).

he was told that such a big trout was no *tupilak* (see above p. 79 and note 52) but was known as another means for sorcery that made a peculiar sound: "*naar, naar, naar!*" (Sonne 2005: ID 1278). Kukkujooq, a shaman, suspected his mother, Kaakaaq, also a shaman, to be the sorcerer, a shocking suspicion but rendered probable by an earlier account (by Kukkujooq) about how Kaakaaq time and again failed in her attempt to hit Kukkujooq's wife with sorcery. Having realized her defeat and that her daughter-in-law was immune (too hyperaware) to her attempts at sorcery against her, and thus by sheer mental strength cut them off, Kaakaaq became intermittently dazed, sometimes saying nothing but "*naar, naar!*" And so she decided to hit her own son, because destroying his skill in hunting would mean hard times for his wife (ID 1268). Exactly how to explain *naar* in this context of sorcery, uttered by both the huge trout and the shaman Kaakaaq in her blurry mental state as her alleged means for sorcery, escapes my understanding.[60] *Naar* is, as will be shown below (p. 157), the spirit word used for *sila* in its transitional states, but lacking examples of *naar* in other Greenlandic contexts (except in the everyday meaning of a belly), one has to make do with the concept of *naar* as being a liminal thing (like Kaakaaq's blurred mental state) that can imply good or evil depending on context.

As for the *sila* of shamans, the similarity between their accepted, dissociated states of mind and the suspicious ones could put them at risk. The performing shaman who went into ecstasy did the right thing, whereas a similar state outside ritual could be interpreted in various ways: as insanity (the boomerang effect of failed sorcery); as the state of doing sorcery by murmuring spirit words in secrecy; as a sign of inborn abilities for becoming a shaman; or, as will be discussed later, the prelude to a shamanic initiation in public. Still more confusing or paradoxical are the *meanings* of *sila* in shamanic contexts. The practicing shaman was described as a *silaatoq*, of being out of his (ordinary) mind, whereas at the same time, by means of this same ecstasy, he was supposed to receive *sila*: *silanippoq*. He thus got the light, *qaamaneq*, the sight for seeing the Other World, *silam aappaa*, entirely. Like *naar*, the even more polysemous *sila* cannot be formularized. The flow of meanings overlaps by combining mind, body, space, breath or air, and This World with the Other World.

Sila as Balance of Mind and Body

Reason is one meaning of *sila*, and possessing *sila* in the sense of being reasonable is depicted by a spherical metaphor: *Naak silavit qeqqerta?* ("Where is the center of your *sila*?") This is a common phrase meaning "Are you out of your mind?"[61] Here Ingold's concept of the "world as a sphere" is of relevance, as is Anthony P. Cohen's (1994) discussion of identity in his critique of structural functionalism reducing identity to "roles" and social structure read small. Quoting Ralph Turner, Cohen declares that throughout life every person has a consistent self that comes about through engagement in, but not dependence on, the social structure. Cohen shows that balance is the recurrent ideal of a person's sense of being him- or herself in the world, as he tests the thesis on notions about that self in premodern, small-scale societies. An ideal expressed by the Mbuti in Central Africa covers the Inuit image to the letter: only if you rest at the center of that spherical bubble which is the world

60. Stories of giant fish are very common. The film *On Golden Pond* tells one; the North Alaska Inuit tell several others (Burch 1971).

61. I am indebted to my former student Eleonora Jacobsen for that phrase.

(and society), your balance is perfect. Confusion removes you from that center, and in that case you better move to another band, an ever-present option within the Mbuti social network of extensive classificatory relatives (Cohen 1994).

Intelligence and knowledge, so highly valued by the Inuit, were in many ways identified with the work of one's *sila*. Coming to know by practice—either consciously or "half-consciously" (Bourdieu)—is achieved through "awareness," or the Yup'ik meaning of *ella* (phonological equivalent to *sila*), which in this sphere of life refers to reason, sanity, and sensibility in Greenland. More than anything, the other meaning of *sila*, weather, was, and still is, at the center of constant awareness (Tejsner 2013), the first thing to be observed in the morning and throughout the day, on the sea in kayak, on the treacherous ice, or far inland among mountains and ravines (see also Fienup-Riordan & Rearden 2013: 60). Since dead calm can change into a gale in minutes, familiarity with the signs of impending storms is as appreciated as the knowledge of points in time and place for the coming of game, and of how to get there in time (e.g., Burch 1975: 51ff, 73ff). Children were taught to be aware—and a shamanic pupil to be constantly so—of anything *strange* when moving about. The small Naaja half-consciously followed that inculcated advice when suddenly he became aware of a cascade running upward in the stream. He stopped, looked intensely, and saw the horrid figure of a huge dog take form in the water; he took flight, stumbled, and lost consciousness, but the dog devoured him. It thereby had him initiated to the shaman's "light," *qaamaneq*, and thus to seeing and being seen in the Other World (Sonne 2005: ID 1236).

As advocated above, the metaphor of balance in body is associated with that of *sila*, air, whether upheld by pillars, mountains, or simply the air itself. Although *sila* does not denote "balance" per se, and *sila* body analogies are rare—such as being dizzy, *sila kaavittoq* (one's *sila* rotates)—balance is associated with *sila* in the meanings of several words.

In the vernacular, a person having *sila* (*silaqartoq*; *silalik*) is clever, considerate, and sensible; behaves properly; and is in possession of all her faculties (P. Egede 1750: 168; Fabricius 1804: 422; Saladin d'Anglure 1990a: 94). The person lacking *sila* in every way (*silaqanngitsoq*) is dotty, naïve, still a mere child, or drunk, talking nonsense, and reeling (Kleinschmidt 1871: 323–24); that is, that person is also bodily out of balance.[62] To be bereaved of one's *sila*, *silaeruppoq*, means being drunk, or reeling along. Eleonora Jacobsen, who called my attention to the metaphor of being at the center of one's *sila* world, stresses *sila*'s meanings of reason: that is, it is intellect, not body. But back in the 1860s the semantically very sensitive Kleinschmidt saw a direct relation between *sila* and body. Among the five meanings in his list of *sila* two concern that topic: "4) metaphorically: that which relates to the human body almost like the air (see 5) to the body of earth: reason, willpower… 5) The air personified, or the air animated due to its changeability and according to the pagan Greenlanders a sort of demigod or independent spirit: the spirit of the air, the cause or origin of change of weather" (Kleinschmidt 1871: 323; tr. BS). So the ability to master one's activities of both mind *and* body seems

62. The Greenlanders did not take to drinking at the beginning of colonization: "but they do not much care for our liquors; yet, notwithstanding, some of them, who have lived some time among us, have learnt to drink wine and brandy, and never refuse it, when it is offered them" (H. Egede 1818: 39; 1925: 372). At that time the Greenlanders still observed with wonder the employed Europeans' yelling and reeling when drunk. Why all that trouble brewing beer instead of drinking water and keep up your *sila* at that, they wondered (N. Egede 1943: 43). By and by the Greenlanders learned to appreciate drinking from the Danes (Nellemann 1962).

to have been his idea of the analogy. The same idea is obtained from his translation of having *sila*: *silaqarpoq*—he knows how to act, consciously and deliberately (324; tr. BS).[63]

To recap: The well-balanced upright moving (and running) body of a human being appears—in contrast to the movements of animals, birds, and spirits—to be an Inuit ideal. So does a balanced mind, awake, aware, and settled at the center of one's world, *sila*.[64] Thus "concentrated" one can cope with whatever happens in environment and social life. Being drunk, performing sorcery, or becoming hit by its boomerang effect visibly spoils both bodily balance and presence of mind. Raven, the bird of *sila* in the meanings of "outdoors," intelligence, and balance, lives close to humans but, although a being of transitions, it is never allowed indoors. As a being of transitions between This and the Other Worlds, Raven is attributed particular powers of restoring balance in both humans and a defiled world. It announces the coming into being of both day and night and of a newborn baby by its naming and potential human ability to speak.

Human Foreigners and Powers of the Sea

Travelers to the more or less mythic countries of This World rarely enter the worlds above and below of deceased humans, Moon and Sea Woman. They travel north, south, around, and across Greenland; they go inland and they cross the sea to Akilineq, the "land over there." They encounter awkward-looking objects, animals, and humans of differing sizes and characters. The Kivioq stories reflect ideas about powers of the sea and Akilineq; the Kaassassuk stories point to forces of the land.

Encircle the World and Circumnavigate Greenland

Ordinary humans—or, rather, extraordinary nonshaman humans—succeeded in traveling far and wide and returned with news about the world. This world was a circular one, according to two Polar Inuit men, who started off (each with his family) in opposite directions and met again in old age, their grandchildren leading them along and their drinking cups of musk ox horn completely worn out: "The world is very large," they declared (Rasmussen 1908: 102–3; Sonne 2005: ID 1537). They traveled by sledge at a time when people were still numerous, a prerequisite perhaps of being able to travel that far. Nothing, however, is told of people encountered en route, or about how the route was imagined, except that the world was encircled. More restricted in scope was the circumnavigation of Greenland by the legendary East Greenlander Uiarteq ("the one who rounded the promontory") and his wife. Starting out southward from Ammassalik, accompanied by another couple, Uiarteq forced his way past the dangerous Cape Farewell, which the other couple did not manage to pass by. Uiarteq continued north along the west coast, turning east along the north coast and then south

63. *Silap Inua*, in the figure of a giant baby in Canada and by mythic epithets recognized in the husband of *Asiaq*, the *inua* of precipitation in East Greenland, could be visited by shamans and is thus dealt with under "Times for Ritual."

64. Briggs focuses on *ihuma* (W. Grl. *isuma*) and excludes *sila*, although the definitions of *ihuma* would fit *sila* as well: "[*ihuma*] refers to all functions that we think of as cerebral: mind, thought, memory, reason, sense, ideas, will" (1974a: 375). And: "When a child begins to respond to the social world around him; when he begins to recognize people and to remember, to understand words and to talk, when he begins to be shy and self-conscious . . . to learn restraint in self-expression, and to want to participate in socially useful activities, people remark affectionately that the child is acquiring *ihuma*" (11–12).

following the northeast coast to Ammassalik. Not much is told about the humans encountered en route. Uiarteq meets with humans only along the southeast coast and at Cape Farewell, and he either kills or avoids them due to their giant look or cannibalistic manners. Nor are the differing localities along the way described in any detail except Cape Farewell and some northeastern places. The former is the point of troubles. A strong current has carved caves in the cliff, swallowing up Uiarteq's travel companion, or a sculpin (*qivaaqi*) attacks and bites his dog in half, or he passes the cape by sledge. The west coast is exclusively and incomprehensibly characterized by its equal numbers of seal and grouse, the former emerging at the latter's call. The northernmost coast offers no way of getting ashore, only a steep cliff to which Uiarteq "anchors" the *umiaq* by means of a bung of congealed seal blood. This and a couple of other places mentioned by name along the northeast coast are localized by Gulløv, who, supported by archaeological findings, connects the story's knowledge of the localities with the movements of the northern branch of the Thule culture people into the Ammassalik area in the 1600s and 1700s. Here they met with the southern branch, which arrived in the 1500s. The Uiarteq story shows historical knowledge of both the immigration from the north, which was still partly traveled at intervals at Holm's time for wintering, and the southern travel route rounding Cape Farewell (Gulløv 1995; Jensen et al. 2011; Sørensen & Gulløv 2012). But the story takes Uiarteq all the way round Greenland (Sonne 2005: 418, 419, 578, 993, 434).[65] So, by which transmitted bits of knowledge had the northern branch of the Ammassalimmiut come to know that Greenland is an island? Gulløv feels sure that encounters and communications with the southern group at Ammassalik may have given rise to this idea (Gulløv pers. comm.). Probable frictions between the two groups are not evident except for Uiarteq's aggressive attitude to people encountered en route to and in passing Cape Farewell. Nevertheless, the Southeast and Ammassalik Greenlanders met at *aassiviit*, traded, and intermarried.[66]

Across the Sea to Akilineq

During the 19th century, mythic speculations about dangerous people living in Akilineq, "the opposite side (of the sea)," were modified by news received about real Inuit living over there.[67] These were the Inuit of Labrador and Baffin Island, and since there was still another century to pass before archaeologists unearthed the true prehistory of the eastern Inuit, stories were told to explain the evident likeness between Greenlanders and real Akilinermiut. The knowledge led to changes in attitudes that can be followed in the stories. Thus, stereotypes of disparagement and hostility determine the traditional type of stories about the Akilinermiut. The latter are clearly mythic humans and nonhumans. More recent versions reflect bits of knowledge mediated by Greenlandic companions to traveling Qallunaat, who had encountered and realized that the Akilinermiut were Inuit of some

---

65. The translation of the variant Kaarali told to Rasmussen, which pays no heed to the mirror effect of the localizers on the east coast, causes confusion (Sonne 2005: ID 434).

66. The trading route from East to West Greenland is also mapped in a story about the shaman Naaja, who went flying along the coast with some of his helping spirits to "the land of the high tides," somewhere up the west coast. They encountered no West Greenlanders, but visited and made friends with spirits, who subside on sea mammals hunted at low tide. The story is discussed in chapter 4 on shamans.

67. The Moravians received letters from the mission in Labrador; the Moravian missionary Warmow visited Cumberland Sound Inuit in 1856–1857 and returned with news about the "Akilinermiut." See also Lidegaard (1999).

sort.[68] The transformations can be followed in variants of a type I shall name "Qilaatuaq" (W. Grl. Qilaasuaq) after the East Greenlandic main character, but with quite differing agendas. Apart from the variants that stick to the traditional type, others have it followed by or mixed up with less discriminating views on the Akilinermiut. They allow Greenlanders and Akilinermiut to marry and stay married, unless closer bonds demand a breakup, while some merely refer to both actual knowledge and rumors.

In the following, first a variant of the traditional type is resumed, next a simple story, told by Moravian Luutivik combining the traditional with the new ideas, and then the variants told by Hendrik are analyzed. Hendrik, also at the Moravian mission, was a descendant of a fugitive Southerner, Singajik, who settled on Kangeq. Hendrik told stories of all types, traditional and mixed. Finally, one very late variant, which includes episodes from another travelogue, the one about Kivioq, leads to a comparison of the Greenlandic with Canadian Inuit variants as analyzed by Oosten (2002).

Traditional "Qilaatuaq"

Paraphrase: A prolonged winter of an icebound sea has the old, clever, industrious man Qilaatuaq climb the nearby highest mountain every day in order to look out.[69] One day he can just make out a small cloud of evaporation in the distance. It signals a *sassat*—i.e., some water kept open by either seabirds or some locked-up beluga or narwhals crowding there to breathe. The old man's journey out there, accompanied by his sons and either a son-in-law or adoptive orphan, takes time, but the catch is rewarding. Returning across the ice the old man keeps an eagle eye on the distant mountaintops, which all of a sudden disappear from sight in a snowstorm, an offshore gale that arrives in no time and starts to break up the ice. The little group of hunters is sent off across the sea on an ice floe for adventures in Akilineq, the mythic opposite land of cannibals, etc. They prove stronger, more intelligent, and better armed with amulets than their Akilinermiut enemies for overcoming the threats, and they return in the fully developed spring by means of either a women's boat or transformed by their amulets into polar bears for swimming across the sea. The son-in-law turns into a walrus and the adoptive orphan into a snow bunting (e.g., Sonne 2005: ID 1099, 1434). Back home they have a story to tell, of course, but they have made no lasting relationships abroad.

Acculturated Variants of "Qilaatuaq"

Luutivik of the Nuuk congregation honored the new knowledge about related Inuit "over there" by having his main character, Tungujorlersaat, and a travel companion stay in Akilineq after their complete extermination of the evil Akilinermiut. They came to another house of a very nice man, who in stark contrast to the former people lived up to the Greenlandic standards of a friendly host. After

68. Actually, Hans Egede reported earlier Inuit encounters on the ice between Disko Bay and Baffin Island. Still, they were only on hearing distance: "According to the relation and opinion of those Greelanders, that inhabit the gulf of Disko, in 69°, Greenland is an island, which they infer from the strong current that runs from the North, and keeps the ice open even into the midst of the sea: they will also tell you, they have spoken with people different from themselves on the other side of the ice, and hailed them. Their language, they say, is the same, but the persons different, so that a small strait only divides Greenland from America. The said straits are so narrow, that men on both sides can shoot at once one and the same fish. The continent farthest to the North is all covered with ice: the islands only uncovered, where reindeer, as well as geese and other wild birds, are found in great numbers" (H. Egede 1971, 2: 2; 1925: 313; 1818: 2–3).

69. A search for Qilaasuaq in Sonne (2005) offers the relevant hits and the hero's differing names in other versions.

a prolonged stay, when Tungujorlersaat and his buddy became homesick, they were kindly urged to take leave. They paddled for days without further hindrances (Sonne 2005: ID 54).

Hendrik featured the Akilinermiut in several stories, some legendary: one apparently reflecting his own family history, one offering a "date" for the tying of the bonds. But one, which denies such bonds, remains at little variance from tradition.

In his attempt to date the bonds of ancestral kinship, Hendrik has the traveler Isigaarsigaaq and brother travel from Nuuk north and then in the company of the local people up there cross the sea to hunt caribou in Akilineq. The boat needs two layers of cover, meaning that the distance is of quite some length (the fairly narrow Smith Sound of Avanersuaq is thus ruled out). They meet with very friendly people over there, song contests are held, and Isigaarsigaaq's brother marries and remains among the Akilinermiut. So, having divided and shared their common amulet, a piece of coal, between them, Isigaarsigaaq bids his brother a last farewell, returns to Greenland, and travels south. Back in Nuuk Isigaarsigaaq stays vigorously alive, surviving one generation of descendants after another until finally he grows old, loses strength, and becomes liable to weep whenever teased good-naturedly by his great-great-grandchildren (Sonne 2005: ID 1801). Hendrik makes no attempt to date Isigaarsigaaq's death, but the latter's absurdly high age offers some chronological idea of the hypothetical origin of kin relations with the Akilinermiut.

In his other stories about Akilinermiut, Hendrik stresses the gigantic size not only of the Akilinermiut and their hunting gear but also the animals of their imagined country. Of two accounts based on hearsay, one relates the experience of a group of Southerners, who a long time ago ended up "over there" because they got off course. They arrived at a steep nesting cliff of the great auk (*pinguinus impennis*) (extinct at Hendrik's time). In a valley close by, they slept overnight in shavings of wood left by Qallunaat, and a giant gull asleep on the sea was luckily passed by on the return journey (Sonne 2005: ID 1766). The other story relates how Nakunnguaq, the exceptionally capable hunter (i.e., hunting in the outer sea beyond the skerries), harpooned a giant specimen of a haired seal that looked like an oversize young of a common seal. Overwhelmed by its speed and strength he had to let it go, whereafter he came upon a hunting bladder the size of a skerry. Both seal and bladder were imagined to belong to Akilineq and their giant humans (ID 1759).

Three of Hendrik's remaining stories refer, like "Isigaarsigaaq," to *kinship ties* with the Akilinermiut. One plainly rejects this relationship in being a variant of the traditional type, which negates the possibility of lasting ties with nonhumans: A Greenlander's beloved cousin is kidnapped by a giant Akilinermiu; he goes in search of her across the ice by means of imaginary monsters used as sledge dogs. He is received in a friendly manner, and thus realizes that his cousin suffers no harm. Nevertheless, when politely invited to his in-laws in Greenland, the giant, who has to go to sleep halfway into the entrance tunnel, becomes easy prey to the monstrous sledge dogs set on by the brother-in-law. The couple's baby is killed as well, after which the two cousins, who used to be together day in and day out, resume their former habits (Sonne 2005: ID 1784). Though marriage between first cousins was prohibited in West Greenland, love affairs before marriage cannot be ruled out.

An even closer, more intimate relation between sister and brother is indicated in another variant. It starts out with the flight northward of their father, the Southerner Anertorsuaq, who involuntarily killed one of his cousins. Far up north he stopped and settled down at the boundary of the never-melting ice. His son, brought up to take (or stand up to) revenge, goes hunting at breathing holes on the ice together with his sister. Every other night they stay on the ice in a snow hut. When one day an Akilinermiu manages to steal the sister, her brother gets hold of peculiar sledge dogs—namely, a giant hare, a giant fox, and an *avaqqiaarsuk*, "the far north living special one" with teeth strong enough to crush stones.[70] He crosses the ice, shows his superior strength, and retrieves his sister, whose one-eyed giant husband follows on a visit. The remaining episodes all demonstrate the superior powers of the Greenlandic in-law, but in a gentle manner, in that he never fights his Akilinermiu in-law. Quite on the contrary! The two relatives travel south for adventures, and when the *naalagaq*, the colonial authority of a settlement, insults the Akilinermiu, his strong Greenlandic brother in-law kills the offender.[71] Back in the north the Akilinermiu goes home across the frozen sea (Sonne 2005: ID 1741), and he probably brings along his human wife, as proposed by Thisted in her edition of Hendrik's stories published in Greenlandic. Like me she senses a hidden hint of incest in the sister-brother couple staying overnight alone in a snow hut (Thisted & Thorning 1996: 332). Maybe baptized Hendrik considered the northern people represented by this story's main character less "civilized." Anyway, he sides not only with this Northerner, like himself a descendant of a fugitive Southerner (in fact), but also with the related Akilinermiu against a representative of colonial authority, a *naalagaq*.[72] The latter, whether a Qallunaaq or an educated Greenlander of mixed descent, ought not to insult the one-eyed giant related to a Greenlander by marriage. Was the seed to the Inuit Circumpolar Council (ICC), the pan-Inuit organization of 1977, already sown by Hendrik?

Nonetheless, some ambiguous feelings against the foreigner who needs defense are felt, and they also emerge at the end of Hendrik's story about a shaman who, while visiting in Akilineq, is asked to procure seals. The shaman makes his helping spirit bring in an iceberg that has seals on one side, but the concealed *anngiaq* (a baby born and killed in secrecy) of a young girl causes havoc. Having seen the *anngiaq* but making up his mind that these foreigners, who were none of his kind, may follow other rules, the shaman does not interfere. The iceberg turns around and smashes the house, and the shaman escapes at the last moment. Back home, he immediately and ashamedly admits this shortcoming, pitying the many people who have died. Nonetheless, a vengeful shaman approaching from Akilineq is not allowed access. For five nights he is kept at bay by lighting up the house and swinging a whip in the air (Sonne 2005: ID 1901). Empathy has its limits, after all.

Even less serious is the story told to Hendrik by the Southerner, Daniel, about Inuussaarsuk, "the little doll," a maltreated orphan. Fleeing his tormentor, the orphan ends up in Akilineq, where he avoids being "stung" by the knife tail of an evil bumblebee woman, then flees again and stays for some time with a nice mother and her daughter hunting seals and halibut at low tide. A slip in the story leaves out the reason why he flees these benevolent ladies, who in most versions of "Kivioq" upset this hero by their use of either a penis called up in a lake and/or the knotty pillars of their house for "dildos." Kivioq may even kill the ladies, while Inuussaarsuk, seemingly content with merely paddling away, enters the last episode by mistaking a giant kayaker for a skerry. Caught by

70. Prof. Robert Petersen (pers. comm.) proposes big "limb" (*avatit*).

71. This is the meaning of *naalagaq* at the time in translation by Rink, who took down the story straight from the horse's mouth.

72. His great-great-great-grandfather Singajik (Gulløv 1986b: 173; Sonne 2005: ID 50 (told by Hendrik), and 1450 by Hendrik's son, Esajas Martensen).

the giant and handed over to the latter's equally giant daughter as her amulet or toy (his name, "Dear Doll"), at night he attempts an unsuccessful escape across her thighs, a juicy and malodorous affair. Realizing the actual needs of his daughter, the sensible father transforms Inuussaarsuk into a giant for his daughter to marry. Finally, on a return trip of revenge, Inuussaarsuk the enlarged "doll" finds his adoptive parents' house in ruins (Sonne 2005: ID 1796; see also Thisted's comment in Thisted & Thorning 1996: 328).

Reconsidering Hendrik and the Akilinermiut

All in all, Hendrik is, with slight reservations, kindly disposed toward the Akilinermiut, strictly following tradition only in the story about the cousins who are reunited in the end by killing off the Akilinermiu husband and child. Following the new trend, Hendrik has the one-eyed Akilinermiu sent up but defended by the Greenlandic in-law at the moment a colonial representative puts the Akilinermiu to scorn. On the other hand, one senses a deeper contrast made between pagan and Christian Inuit. Thus, the unproblematic kinship ties between the Greenlanders and the Akilinermiut, which is judged an established event, took place in very remote times when no Inuk was baptized on either side. Next, the suspicious incestuous relationship between brother and sister takes place in the far north, where still no mission was established at Hendrik's time. Pagan versus Christian ideas are also at play when an *anngiaq* spoils the procurement of seals by the Greenlandic shaman. But I am uncertain about in how many ways, except morally, because clandestine birth was condemned on both sides if for differing reasons. Anyway, when the clever Greenlandic shaman does not interfere when he sees the *anngiaq* clinging to the young girl, this is because the hosts are not of his kind, and thus might have their own rules. Evidently they did not differ in their rules. So he both denies the relationship and has to realize that they are his relatives. He feels guilty and confesses when back home, but since he and his fellow men permit no vengeance in return, no further conflicts arise: both the Moravian and the Royal Danish mission succeeded in their ban on blood feuds (see also Sonne 1982b).

Kivioq

Returning to "Inuussaarsuk" as a "Kivioq" variant, this Kivioq is another traveler to Akilineq who usually has to overcome difficulties like tree-eating lice attacking his paddle, a very strong maelstrom, and a hardly passable school of seal; then, in Akilineq, first he meets the bumblebee woman, whose deadly "sting" he avoids, and then the two kind but lonely women, a mother and daughter. The latter are well off from their rich hunting at low tide, but in most variants they satisfy their sexual appetite in ways that make Kivioq leave in disgust. They use the knotted house pillars as dildos or copulate with a penis of a lake. Kivioq's longing for home is another cause.

Canadian Inuit variants were analyzed by Oosten, who underlines the lesson obtained about the bad morals of the female characters abroad. He sees in Kiviuq (Inuktitut) a shaman, whose adventures neither serve nor threaten society. Sent across the sea by a gale, Kiviuq uses his powers of intelligence, second sight, and a single helping spirit. He escapes the bumblebee woman and then kills the mother, who has killed her daughter in jealousy. In the end he either returns home for a reunion with his wife and a good social life like Odysseus, or he departs from society by transforming into an immortal being like Heracles (Oosten 2002). By comparison, the Greenlandic variants show differing agendas. In these versions, Kivioq is not in possession of a helping spirit and is not pictured as a shaman except in one deviant East Greenland variant told by Kaarali (Sonne 2005: ID 1360). Nor is "Penelope" patiently waiting for years on end in expectation of his return. The Polar Inuit variants, although closely related to the Canadian ones, have Kivioq's wife remarry in his absence in the—according to Greenlandic morality—reasonable belief that he has died. The story either ends at this point or Kivioq has to content himself with the bachelors' platform in his ex-wife's house (ID 657, 658, 659, 1556). This latter Kivioq is hardly a true Heracles type. In most West Greenlandic variants the bad morals of Kivioq's wife overshadow those of the women abroad. Pretending to be dead and thus buried, she steals away to marry another man. The deceit is disclosed by the little daughter or son left with Kivioq, who sneaks away depressed. He leaves society like a *qivittoq*, heading not for the hinterland in the ordinary way of *qivittut* but for the open sea.[73] Hence, instead of Kivioq he is in one version called Qivikkaluartoq, "the actually leaving society one" (ID 41).[74] Compared to these problems at home, those met with abroad are less serious in the Greenlandic than the Canadian variants. Apart from one variant (ID 1478), the mother-in-law over there does not kill her daughter, nor does Kivioq kill the mother in any variant.

To repeat: The most frequent reason why Kivioq eventually leaves both women is his disgust for the women's "dildos." Another cause sometimes given is his longing for the son, left at home as a small boy. In fact, one repeated "problem" dealt with by the Greenlandic variants appears to be male sexual rights in return for provisions. Thus in the final duel between the bumblebee woman armed with an *ulu* (women's crescent-shaped knife) and Kivioq with his harpoon, the latter comes out the winner by means of his "meat"-winning gear. The two ladies know perfectly well how to provide for themselves, sexually as well as in the way of hunting at low tide. Sometimes the latter theme is repeated by a great number of eiders offered them in gratitude by the penis of the lake. The same issue is underlined in a couple of endings: hearing while close to shore that his wife has remarried, Kivioq turns around. But somebody, an old woman or his wife, manages to get hold of the point of his kayak—i.e., *usuussaq*, "like a penis." The wife throws out her new husband, whereas the variant about the resoluteness of the old woman leads to a single combat with the new husband. Victorious Kivioq gets back his ex-wife (Sonne 2005: ID 595, 1360), who thus wins the better provider. The old woman most probably wins shares of his future catches, and society at large will benefit as well. This is apparently a happy return in line with the Canadian Odysseus. Yet the idea of a "Penelope" remaining both unmarried and in her senses would overstep the mark in a Greenlandic context. One may speculate no end on the difference in social morals between "Kivioq" and "Kiviuq." Anyway, the more recent Greenlandic variants delight not unexpectedly in making fun of the sexual issue. In one, the unfaithful wife has died for no apparent reason, but in spirit she reproaches the returned Kivioq for the pleasure he seeks in the house of the young unmarried people. He abides and takes up an elder man's life in residence with his married children (ID 1478). Similarly, "Inuussaarsuk" regales the audience with beloved ambiguities.

---

73. Unrequited love seems to have been the most common cause for those actually becoming *qivittoq* in premodern Greenland.

74. The issue of *qivinneq* is emphasized by the storyteller's final comment: although he fled the company of people, he happened to be together with people continuously (Sonne 2005: ID 41).

Reflections on Real Threats and Imagined Beings of the Sea

The "Qilaasuaq" family, possessing amulets of bear and either walrus or snow bunting, travel to Akilineq without meeting any obstacles other than thirst and the dwindling of their ice floe. They are sent off by a spring gale, whereas the gale in "Kiviuq" in the Canadian and Polar Inuit variants is caused by a human act of revenge. Storms and sudden gales are real threats to kayakers, whereas tree-eating lice belong in myth. They attack the paddle of the provident Kivioq, who saves it by dressing the ends/blades in old mittens collected in advance and brought along.[75] Subsequently, a maelstrom, the navel of the sea, very nearly sucks him under. He escapes by no other means but paddling hard. So, by way of (body) symbolism, the sea is revealed as an enormous stomach. In one variant, some water-filled guts of a bearded seal soaking in front of the navel most probably allude to its umbilical cord (to be discussed later), and sometimes Kivioq has to pass through droves of harmless seals encountered out there where they apparently belong (Sonne 2005: ID 252, 344, 595, 1360, 1478, 1796, 1878). But the seals' "mother," Sea Woman, remains invisible below.

As pointed out in the beginning of this section about Greenlandic globe travelers, they are generally not pictured as shamans (in contrast to Kiviuq in Canada). Like most respected elders in real life, the main characters excel by possessing presence of mind and knowledge, including magic means. While traveling, they do not encounter any of the beings usually approached by shamans, such as deceased humans or Sea Woman, but they do sometimes meet with monsters. Uiartoq's dog is attacked at Cape Farewell by a mysterious giant male sculpin, a *qivaaqi*, and in one version Kivioq comes upon an abnormal creature stranded at low tide in Akilineq. The mother and daughter tell him to leave it alone. It is called an *unneraarsuk* (etymology?), and belongs in the world below (Sonne 2005: ID 344). Although a well-known bogey of the tide, this figure is rarely mentioned in the stories.[76] Yet in an account of some rituals at Appat (a settlement on Disko Bay, north of Ilulisssat), a ritual relationship was kept going with *Unneraarsuk*, who was offered lots of fresh water to drink during performances. In return, it sent seals for people to hunt (ID 336, 337). They came with the tide, I suppose, because both as a bogey and as encountered by Kivioq, *Unneraarsuk* was associated with the tide.

The *qivittoq* motive of Kivioq for leaving society due to unrequited love prevails in the Greenlandic variants except among the Polar Inuit. Here, as in Canada, he is sent off by a gale, as is Qilaatuaq. The latter experience is not all that uncommon to hunters in actual life. Stories are told all over the coastal Arctic and subarctic. Outside the skerries they might have to fight strong currents as well as schools of seal, or even walrus. In the 18th and 19th centuries the latter used to bar the way along the West Greenlandic coast between Attu, south of Aasiaat, and Maniitsoq from September to February (Muus et al. 1981: 407). The tree-eating lice (most likely shipworms), however, hardly reflect anything else but rotten paddles. Crossing the sea to Akilineq by kayak or *umiaq*, however, was an event reserved for myth.

---

75. Similarly the main characters of other stories secretly collect boot soles for their travel over land.

76. According to Prof. Robert Petersen (pers. comm.), born and raised as a child in Maniitsoq: "I used to hear *unneraarsuk*'s squeak when the pieces of ice in the tide at Kuuttartoq (the fjord by our house) rubbed against each other. This sound may explain the etymology of the word *unnerpoq*: making oneself known. Another proposal is *unneq*: white skin. We never saw them. I cannot tell their colou, because we never saw them. We only heard their squeaking sound." I support the former explanation.

The Land, the Hinterland, and Heaven

The Inuit were absolutely aware that their land provided them with the fundamental source of life, drinking water. The slain sea mammal was offered a drink, suffering from thirst as it had to. The newborn baby received its name with drops of freshwater. As experienced by the shaman Akku, the realms of death, above and below, were also land-based and provided drinking water; it was lukewarm below and refreshingly cold above (Sonne 2005: ID 1324, 1818).[77]

Travels Across the Land

Legendary Greenlanders traveling across the land—that is, the inland ice—were less common in lore. The few who are told about remain anonymous, and the knowledge they reflect about inhabitants on the opposite coast is rooted in fact but seasoned with slander. When news traveled along the coastal trading route about the extremely hard winters on the east coast that led to a few instances of cannibalism, all Tunuamiut were turned into cannibals in the view of many West Greenlanders (H. Egede 1971, 1: 110; 1925: 98). A single story holds the same view (Sonne 2005: ID 529); others have the West Greenlandic travelers well received except for the tyrannical leader of the settlement, whom they then eliminate to everybody's relief (ID 182, 1735). One exceptional story takes on the characteristics of an origin myth in being dated prior to the formation of the inland ice, caused by a conflict between close kin, and ending in tragedy. A mother's greed (for the prettiest skins) and a brother's excessive love for his sister (he tolerates no critique on part of her husband) are the familiar causes. In order to provide his sister with beautiful skins, he urges her and another brother to leave their greedy mother. Having crossed the land to the east coast, they happen to arrive at the tent of immigrant West Greenlanders, an old childless couple. Consequently, they are well received in the settlement, and so they stay and intermarry—except for the jealous brother. Due to his quarrelsome nature, they split up and leave on his command, much to the great sorrow of the sister and her in-laws. The latter take up pursuit without success because the evil brother kills his sister's youngest child when the child begins to cry. The sister too dies of grief: "So, in this way the evil brother caused his sister's death" (ID 1612). Apparently this story tells that long ago, when no ice barred the crossing of the land, there used to be people moving from the west to the east coast, taking up residence and intermarrying. The West Greenlandic mother by her greed and her son by his envious character bring this to a sore end. Still, before the breakup, the East Greenlanders nonetheless counted as foreigners with whom peaceful relations could only be established by means of earlier immigrants from the west coast. The bad moral of this story's West Greenlanders is not said to have caused the formation of the inland ice, but some bad conscience shines through. It may reflect the new ideas forming among West Greenlanders at the time of telling the story, in 1902, when an emerging national identity brought the still partly pagan East (and Northern) Greenlanders into focus (Thuesen 1988). Nonetheless, to this day the West Greenlanders generally look down upon the "Backside Greenlanders" (Tunuamiut). They still meet with difficulties in being accepted by the West Greenlanders inhabiting the front side according to their perspective. The name Tunuamiut has also been accepted by the East Greenlanders (E. Grl. Tunumiut).

---

77. Early West Greenlandic statements opposing Christian ideas run down the quality of water in heaven in sheer contrast to that of the realm below (e.g., P. Egede 1971: 26, 28; 1939: 23, 24).

No trace of this condescension is found in the very small number of East Greenlandic stories about crossing the inland ice. A girl who walks the ice all alone rejoices, because she marries a hunter of caribou (extinct on the east coast) and receives all sorts of nice utensils, such as an iron pot of far greater value than the copper sewing needle she owned on the east coast (Sonne 2005: ID 1133). Another overdramatic story shows, for good reasons, a great respect for the inland ice. It takes a sledge made from an entire platform, with a tent placed on top for wife and child, as well as two bewitched dogs, and several serious threats to be overcome before the sea becomes visible on the other side. People in the west are kind, they live in small houses (in contrast to the longhouse of the East Greenlanders at the time of telling, 1885), and they hunt all kinds of sea mammals in great numbers. The travelers continue north to meet real foreigners, that is, cannibals, whom they trick and kill by means of the fantastic dogs. They then return to the east coast without further adventures (ID 585). This story seems to reflect rumors that Southerners of East Greenlandic origin were well received by relatives in the Moravian congregations. People living north of Nuuk, whether Christianized or not by the Royal Danish Mission, were apparently considered less trustworthy.

Into the Land

The ordinary travelers of the stories on record are West Greenlanders who remain on their own side of the ice. As in real life, they are hunters of caribou, or *qivittut,* who are said to have survived in the wilderness. The nonhuman figures we meet in these stories are dwarves and giants, living in families or alone, all of whom are described in their relation to the part of the land in which they dwell (see pp. 160–63). Aqissiaq, whose family moved to the inland Tunit branch of their kin, is a rare figure of mixed human and nonhuman origin; he appears in stories told along the southern half of the west coast and in East Greenland. These Tunit (known in Canada as Dorset people), might of course refer to Inuit encounters with Late Dorset people who actually were in Avanersuaq at the arrival of the first Inuit immigration. Too many loose ends, however, offer nothing but pure speculation (Kleivan 1996). Instead we shall turn to a widely known story, "Kaassassuk," which, by taking changes in versions into account, points very clearly to the powers of land and its strong connections to those of heaven, and finally, events featuring these land powers in confrontation with those of the sea.

Analysis of Kaassassuk's *Pinnga* Forces[78]

Analysis of "Kaassassuk" convincingly shows that *Pinnga,* the one up there behind you, is closely associated with the forces attributed to the inland. "Kaassassuk" still enjoys amazing popularity in Greenland; this is primarily due to changes made first by Aron about 1860 and then by Jaakuaraq two generations later (Thisted 1990). Knud Rasmussen, who received the latter version, made his own contribution by identifying the story's particular *inua* of the land, a land animal or a giant, with *Pinnga,* "the one up there behind you," as explained by the Caribou Inuit shaman, Igjugaarjuk. The animal or giant of the inland transformed Kaassassuk from a poor weakling into a strong, incorrigible, murderous outlaw. The storyteller Aron resocialized this figure into the hero who is still admired

78. Presented abridged in Sonne (2010).

today.[79] Several splendid interpretations have been made (see below), but the symbolic meanings of the boy's bodily peculiarities, his acquired physical powers, and ways of showing them off remain to be analyzed. Stemming from the power-embodying *inua* of the inland, these powers offer insight into the Greenlanders' "land" thinking as the very part of space in which they are "rooted." So, having noted the contribution made by Rasmussen, I give an overview of the variants, then describe the significance of the following issues: breathing, stones, the pillar(s) of uncertain balance upholding the world, and the balance in body obtained by Kaassassuk. The last three issues undergo marked changes in the development of variants influenced by ideas of Western origin.

Pinnga and Rasmussen

Personifications like *Silap Inua* and *Naarssuk/Naarjuk* (giant baby) share common characteristics of weather with the entrails snatcher *Nalikkatteeq*, *Asiaq* (the *inua* of precipitation), and Moon. They all belong "up behind," either on or above earth. *Pinnga*, or *Pissuma*, is still another being on high, if more difficult to pin down. In my following attempt at unraveling ideas of *Pinnga*, I shall have to make a long detour of historical discourses.

In Inuit orientation marked by localizers, *pinnga* is "up there behind your back" (Gagné; Schultz-Lorentzen 1969: 40). The person *Pinnga* is thus an inland figure in partial distinction from *Sila* in the meaning of air, which covers both land and sea. Correspondingly, *Pinnga* was the mistress of caribou among the Caribou Inuit, but in East Greenland, a place poor in inland resources, *Pinnga* was hardly a figure. The correspondence between inland and heaven comes to the fore by its use as a substitute for both Moon and Sun by people under taboo (KRH 52, 2, booklet 405). Similarly, the distant inland (up there behind you) was said to be the land of Moon (Thalbitzer 1930: 80). In an apparent remake of the biblical deluge story mentioned above, the East Greenlanders had *Pinnga* send the storm surge *out of annoyance with the behavior of people on earth.* Knud Rasmussen made inquiries about *Pinnga* during his visit to East Greenland in 1919, but nobody really knew much about this being (KRH 52, 2, booklet 405). Three years later, during the Fifth Thule Expedition, Rasmussen came to know *Pinnga* of the Kivallirmiut. His main informant, Igjugaarjuk, explained that *Pinnga* was his source of shamanic power; in the role of a mistress, he identified her with both *Hila* (*Sila*) and *Nuliayuk* (the Gadabout, Sea Woman). Rasmussen explicitly finds *Nuliayuk* out of place (among inland people, in his siding with Birket-Smith's theory, see below), and he prefers *Sila* to *Pinnga* as Igjugaarjuk's source of shamanic power (Rasmussen 1930a: 51–52). Certainly, Rasmussen received a revelation about the elevated position of *Silap Inua* during the Fifth Thule Expedition, which has been discussed at length (Sonne 1986; 1988b; Thuesen & Sonne 2005). In light of the theory advanced during the expedition by Birket-Smith—namely, that the Caribou Inuit (Kivallirmiut) represented the proto-Inuit/Yupiit culture—*Sila* received the title of primordial high god of the Inuit and Yupiit (Sonne 1986; 1988b; Thuesen & Sonne 2005).[80] When Birket-Smith's theory about Caribou Inuit (Kivallirmiut)

---

79. Interestingly, Angaangaq Lyberth, a Greenlander who moved to Canada and created an evangelic religion by mixing Inuit myths with ideas of Christianity and New Age, takes Kaassassuk as his role model. That is, the Kaassassuk transformed by Aron. Lyberth calls him, in Inuktitut, Kaujjajjuk (Laugrand & Oosten 2008a: 65), but he was not transformed. He remained a brute and a wife tormentor.

80. Viz. Rasmussen (1929: 73): "Sila was the principal spirit on which all religious ideas were based. The original world power when the Eskimos had not yet become a coastal people and were dependent on the sea."

origin was eventually disproved by Burch (1978), the argument for the identification of *Sila* with a primordial revelation of God disappeared. But for fifty years following the Fifth Thule Expedition, the high position accorded *Sila* by Rasmussen provided immense support to the appreciation of pre-Christian religion by educated Greenlanders (Thisted 1990; Sonne 2010). The latter had no need to read Rasmussen's report in English (Rasmussen 1930a), as they were already able to read about the events of the expedition in Danish (Rasmussen 1925–26). In this publication, however, *Nuliayuk* has disappeared from the passage presenting Igjugaarjuk's identifications. *Pinnga* is relegated to a commentary made by another person, not Igjugaarjuk, and only *Sila* remains. It reads: "In religious terms the word *Sila* is used about a power to be achieved by humans—a power personified in *Silap Inua*: the *Lord of Power* or literally, the proprietor of power" (Rasmussen 1925–26, I: 178, tr., emphasis BS). Surprisingly, this appellation can be unreservedly identified with *Pissaap Inua* (the *inua* of power), the giant land predator who gave physical strength to Greenlandic Kaassassuk. However, this occurs exclusively in the Southern variants. So two questions arise: why did Rasmussen identify *Pinnga* or *Sila* with this particular *Pissaap Inua*? And which particular powers did Kaassassuk receive from this otherworldly *inua*? The answer to the former question tells a story on its own, which has been unraveled by me and Kirsten Thisted (Sonne 1988b; Thisted 1994); now I shall try to clear up the second.

The "Kaassassuk" Story

The poor Kaassassuk is a dwarfish, outcast boy who, tormented by his fellows, receives physical strength from an inland being of the Other World. He takes a terrible revenge and, unless he is killed, he remains a threat to his surroundings. This awe-inspiring story was told from East Greenland to North Alaska, but due to Aron's changes made around 1860, "Kaassassuk" became one of the most popular "traditional" stories in Greenland. Aron, a proselyte of the Moravian congregation at Nuuk, was skilled in literacy and was the first Greenlandic illustrator of stories. Then, in about 1920, Jaakuaraq—who was positioned at an even greater distance from pre-Christian paganism—left his personal stamp of humor on the story. Aron's variant was one among a total of nine "Kaassassuks" received by H. J. Rink in response to his circular in 1858 urging whomever it pleased to write down their oral stories. Impressed by its highly literate qualities, Rink selected Aron's variant for the first printing in Greenlandic (Rink 1859–63, II; Sonne 2005: ID 93).[81] The number of copies was small, but two generations later the version of Aron's variant recorded by Jaakuaraq became more widespread and added to the story's popularity (Sonne 2005: ID 1395). His manuscript was received, translated into Danish, and published by Knud Rasmussen in 1924 (1921–25, II: 34–52) and in Greenlandic by Kristoffer Lynge in 1938 (K. Lynge 1978: 21–38; Thisted 1994).[82] As pointed out by Thisted, Aron's decisive contribution was to have Kaassassuk develop from the mass-murdering character of folklore into a "modern" individual who recognizes his limitations—i.e., into a new role model for Christian Greenlanders (Thisted 1994). Indeed, through the years this ideal Kaassassuk has continuously been referred to and used by Greenlandic writers, artists, sculptors, politicians, and even psychotherapists

81. Van London (1999: 113–16) quotes Rink's (1975: 93–99) English version, which for the most part follows Aron.

82. From 1925 an increasing number of educated Greenlanders learned to read and speak Danish. Jaakuaraq's variant is translated into English in a trilingual edition (Rasmussen 1967). The title incorrectly lists Knud Rasmussen as the recorder. Jaakuaraq did the writing himself and had it sent to Rasmussen (see ref. in Sonne 2005: ID 1395).

(A. Larsen 2008). The changes made by Aron ameliorate the ending of the "traditional" variants that either let Kaassassuk remain a mass-murdering brute, have him killed or tortured, or, in East Greenland, subdued into a womanish figure who loses a duel on dogs to a masculine hero (Thisted 1994; Sonne 2005: ID 134, 195, 278, 285, 315 [E. Grl.], 434 [E. Grl.]).[83] Aron has Kaassassuk lose a duel to another very strong man, *Ususaarmiarsunnguaq* ("the little penis with the capacity to grow big"), whose father stops his son from throwing Kaassassuk into the sea by mentioning the old saying "Seemingly lonely persons may, when killed, turn out to have relatives (for taking revenge)" (Sonne 2005: ID 93). Aron's variant thus lines up with a recurrent theme in contemporary West Greenlandic storytelling of putting an end to feuds through baptism (Sonne 1982b). Admittedly, resocialization also occurs in one variant from Moravian Labrador, by the simple act of Kaassassuk getting married (L. M. Turner 1894: 265–66), and in Northwest Alaska by order of *Silap Inua*, the empowering being. The latter had asked for blood offerings from the hero's murders in return, but eventually it became fed up. In line with Alaska Poor Boy stories (van Londen 1999), this North Alaska figure, which by the way is no orphan but certainly maltreated, develops into a great and respected hunter by means of a magic object, received in this case from *Silap Inua*. But neither variant shows comparable signs of self-reflection.

When Knud Rasmussen identified *Pinnga* and *Sila* with *Pissaap Inua*, he was, indirectly, among the first to reuse Kaassassuk in print. When translating Jaakuaraq's variant—prior to the Fifth Thule Expedition—Rasmussen raised *Pissaap Inua* into a higher spiritual position than the original manuscript vouches for (Thisted 1994). Rasmussen thus had his own discourse to which not all Greenlanders might agree. Hans Lynge (1906–1988) for one embraced Igjugaarjuk's identification of *Pinnga* with *Sila* raised to the position of a God-like high god by Rasmussen, but Lynge did not accept the latter's further identification of *Pinnga* with *Pissaap Inua* (Sonne 2010). The big fox empowering Kaassassuk in Aron's and Jaakuaraq's variants doesn't match contemporary elevated ideas about the Christian God. Nor would Aron have agreed either, as I shall show at a later point.[84]

83. A few South Greenlandic variants offer special solutions, such as having Kaassassuk killed by a *tupilak* (sorcery figure) made from his own shit (Sonne 2005: ID 269, 352). Another praises the happy life led by Kaassassuk, his wife, and his adoptive mother after the massacre, meaning that nobody dares continue the feud (the ideal hero of oral tradition; Sonne 1982b). A third version, strongly influenced by Christianity, evades the entire problem by declaring that Kaassassuk abstained from taking any revenge whatsoever (Sonne 2005: ID 1837). The Polar Inuit either have Kaassassuk develop into an invincible mass murderer (ID 1060) and have him killed because of that (ID 1552), or they present him with only one tormentor, the revenge on whom ends the story in just retaliation (ID 660, 661). For "just retaliation," a traditional ideal, see Sonne (1982b). In the Canadian Inuit variants he generally ends up an incurable wife tormentor. Most East Greenlandic variants have Kaassassuk and/or his son defeated by a stronger person or mass murderer, but the defeat does not cause the self-reflection that turned Kaassassuk into a role model on the West Coast (Thisted 1994).

84. Rasmussen not only identified *Pinnga/Sila* with *Pissaap Inua* but also associated the latter with Moon in both his title and translation (and reproduction?) of an Iglulik variant that has Moon impart the power to Kaassassuk: "The *Lord of Power* makes the miserable Kâgjaghuk invincible and mighty among his fellows." And Rasmussen concludes the story thus: "So the miserable Kâgjagjuk became a strong man and a great fighter, because the Moon Spirit came to him *as the Lord of Power* and cleansed him from his mother's breach of taboo (explaining why Moon's treatment makes the boy vomit female combings and fragments of female breeches)" (Rasmussen 1929: 88–90, emphasis BS). This variant is not found among Rasmussen's phonological presentation of his Iglulik texts, which includes another variant mentioning no Lord of Power. The power-imparting spirit is plainly Moon, but under its title "ka.bjäkjuk" Rasmussen adds the West Greenlandic phonological equivalent "Kâgssagssuk" (orthography until 1973). Obviously then, in his search for common Inuit traditions, Rasmussen took Aron's or Jaakuaraq's variants to be the model, or better the "original" one; that is, the first variant you happen to come to know.

Turning to the second question of the particular powers received by Kaassassuk, I find an answer in a symbolic analysis of most variants on record from all over the Inuit area. Following from a structural analysis by van Londen of Inuit/Yupiit Poor Boy stories, including several about Kaassassuk, I shall take some recurrent elements as my point of departure. However, I shall only touch upon her main focus—the ecological reasons for differences among western and eastern ways of acquiring Inuit identity as an adult hunter (an amulet in the west, physical strength in the east)—in passing. From Thisted's comprehensive analysis of the original Greenlandic manuscripts, which considers evidences of literacy theory, folklore theory, and historical changes (1994; resumed in Thisted 2008), I take both her conclusion about Aron's variant and her investigation of the remaining variants from this particular point of view. Thisted's publication is in Danish, as is the unpublished thesis by Aviaja Larsen (2008), who treats the outcomes of Kaassassuk as a role model in Greenlandic art and literature. Her particular psychological concern, however fascinating, is not mine, nor is an analysis by Knud Wentzel (1990), who compares Kaassassuk with the personality and life of Knud Rasmussen. The focus of my inquiry is the spatial symbolism of the powers imparted to Kaassassuk by the Other Worldly *inuat* of the variants. My findings have already been published in an abridged version (Sonne 2010), but a detailed presentation of these *pinnga* forces is placed here where it rightfully belongs, that is, among an exploration of spatial issues.

Kaassassuk Variants

Among the twenty-odd variants on record from East Greenland to Northwest Alaska (the latter to be dealt with separately), some do not name the hero, whereas some Canadian ones that do call him (phonological equivalents of) Kaassassuk relate a differing sequence of episodes. I shall leave out the latter and stick to the Greenlandic variants: Kaassassuk, an abused orphan, starved and smeared with shit, is given physical strength and growth by some otherworldly *inua*.[85] When enabled to throw boulders around, Kaassassuk demonstrates his strength, first in secrecy, then by single-handedly killing three bears (a mother with two young) in public. Shocked at his immense powers, people curry favor with Kaassassuk, but in vain. He takes a terrible revenge on his tormentors, sparing only his old adoptive mother and another helpful relative. He continues to kill at random and thus reminds the listeners of the risky consequences of maltreating orphans. Aron, as already mentioned, brings the series of murders to an end and eliminates further evil consequences. Jaakuaraq follows suit.

The main difference between the Greenlandic and Canadian variants is Kaassassuk's excessive killings in the former and his development into a nonstop wife tormentor in the latter. Within Greenland the differences are smaller, if regionally clear, between Northern (Avanersuaq), East, and West Greenland, but the most interesting ones for this analysis are the elements that set apart the variants from Nuuk southward to Cape Farewell from those to the north of Nuuk. The southern variants, including those of Aron and Jaakuaraq, have these elements in common: the name of the power-imparting being *Pissaap Inua* and Kaassassuk's marriage to the daughter of Qaassuk, another

---

85. Sonne (2005: ID 93, 134, 195, 269, 278, 285, 315, 352, 434, 600, 660, 661, [1013], 1060, 1395, 1552, 1837 [strongly acculturated]); Boas (1964: 222–25; 1901–7: 186–88); Rasmussen (1929: 88–91; 1930: 52–55; 112–13); L. M. Turner (1894: 265–66); Métayer (1973: 116–23). Left out are Sonne (2005: ID 1734); Boas (1964: 220–22); Rasmussen (1930b: 121–23; 1932: 193–98; 1942: 99ff).

strong figure of oral tradition. Furthermore, they share with a few East Greenlandic variants (Sonne 2005: ID 315, 434) Kaassassuk's secret demonstration of his strength by carrying a huge trunk of driftwood from the shore and either raising it in a threatening position at the common longhouse or plugging it inside its entrance tunnel. Evidently, these agreements point to the emigrations during the 18th and 19th centuries from Southeast and East Greenland via South Greenland to the Moravian congregations (see Introduction and, e.g., Sonne 2001a). Aron was among the descendants whose stories frequently reveal their East Greenlandic roots (Sonne 2001a). On a wider scale, including the Canadian variants, the most recurring elements are his growing nostrils, the name Kaassassuk, a power-imparting *inua*, and the throwing of boulders as proof of an increase in physical strength.[86,87,88]

Growing Nostrils, No Social Name, the Power-Imparting *Inuat*

The nostrils are Kaassassuk's only body parts that "grow," not of their own accord but because every time the dwarfish boy wants to join people in the common room, he is lifted up from the entrance tunnel by somebody hooking two fingers into these openings. A heavy breath (alluding to *sila*, signifying air) would be the outcome as visualized once by the incessant waves his breathing calls forth in front of his kayak (Sonne 2005: ID 1013). In Greenlandic myth, heavy breathing is the epithet of both the polar bear and the biggest giants of the inland ice, as emphasized by the following opposites: the polar bear swims on the surface most of the time in contrast to walrus, which dives for long hours, whereas the heavy breath of the biggest giants forms into bridges of fog in contrast to the lack of breathing of the noseless *innersuit* ("big fire spirits") who dwell beneath the foreshore (see Sonne 1996). Kaassassuk matches polar bears in strength as demonstrated by his killing of a mother and two young, and in cosmography he seems placed somewhere on level with the biggest giants that inhabit the innermost inland region, far "behind on high." His fellowmen caused both epithets of breathing and strength to develop by their rough handling, whereas his parents added to his peripheral fate by giving him no real human name.[89] Having lost all their previous children as babies, they had little faith in the boy's survival (the explanation offered by Rasmussen; Thisted 1994, II: 193). In other words, they did not want to insult a deceased relative by having the boy named for him or her. So Kaassassuk was from the very beginning not a genuine part of human society. His eventual growth into a young man is alternately pictured by either the actual growth of his body or by toys falling out of his body due to the rough treatment bestowed upon him by the powerful being.[90] This latter *inua* belongs either to the distant inland area or in the heaven above that inland region.[91] The former is, in West Greenland, an oversize land predator, like a fox, dog, or wolf, called *Pissaap Inua*

86. Lacking in Rasmussen (1929: 88–91); L. M. Turner (1894: 265–66).

87. Lacking in L. M. Turner (1894: 265–66); Rasmussen (1952: 188–90).

88. Lacking in Boas (1901–7: 186–88).

89. Attempts at clearing up the etymology of Kaassassuk tend to turn a linguist's hair gray (Birgitte Jacobsen; M. Fortescue pers. comm.).

90. An Iglulik variant has the boy vomit female combings and bits of female clothing due to some break of taboo by his mother, who is thus made the culprit of the story (Rasmussen 1929: 88–91).

91. As argued above, Greenland's profile slopes from highest mountains of the inland area or the *nunataks* of the inland ice downwards toward the coast from where it continues sloping beneath the sea. Facing the sea, the point of orientation in Greenland, *pinnga* thus points to "something" up behind your back.

in the Southern variants. This animal recurrently hurls the boy by its tail, somersaulting along the ground. The East Greenlandic giant who treats Kaassassuk roughly and may have a voice like thunder also belongs to the distant inland region. This leads us to the heavenly figures (otherwise confined to Canadian versions), namely, either the *inua* of Moon or a star *inua* operating in the light of the full moon, both of whom use a whip (in mythic equivalence with the predator-tail element). So, at both a structural and an environmental level, the ambiguous powers belong (as does Kaassassuk's growing nose) to something of the inland "up there behind and above," *pinnga*.[92]

Boulders and Pebbles

Kaassassuk's heavy breathing and boulder play bring to mind the mythic figures with the power of gales to kick asunder mountains and/or to overthrow the pillar upholding the heavenly vault: *Nalikkatteeq* or *Erlaveersiniooq* (Entrails Snatcher) in Greenland, *Naarjuk/Naarssuk* (Giant Baby) and other *inuat* of gales in Canada. In mythic fact, the Nattilik origin myth of *Sila* or *Naarjuk* comes close to the message of Kaassassuk, because this giant baby, who was orphaned and mocked by a giant of another kind, *Inugpagssusuk*, "became an evil spirit, a spirit of the air, destined to revenge himself upon those who had no compassion for the orphaned" (Rasmussen 1931: 230–31). The stones per se, however, bear various meanings, be they boulders, pebbles, or sand.[93]

In analogy with Inuit body symbolism, the mountains make up the long-lasting skeleton of their land, which nevertheless undergoes changes. Roaring boulders break away and come down in a shower of sparks and stinking smoke (Sonne 2005: ID 485); smaller stones come sliding with rain and melting snow. In a dream leading to his conversion, Akamalik met with severe hindrances, among these stones sliding down, en route to the heavenly abode (ID 1819). The tsunami effect of a huge calving iceberg swallows up a boulder from the shore (ID 835). Weather and tidal waters erode bigger stones into smaller ones. Crumbling stones, said to be "rotten," have strange mythic beings living on and among them (ID 811, 812). Frost glues stones firmly to the ground, yet in some variants Kaassassuk tears some stones loose, in mythic equivalence with his handling of a big trunk of driftwood.[94] All such observable facts occasion a number of mythic issues, most frequently associated with fertility, which can be beneficent or devastating in differing contexts. In practice, Stone Age Inuit used stones for many ends: houses, caches, graves, cairns, weirs, weapons, utensils, striking fire, lamps, pots, etc. Boys continuously practiced their strength and marksmanship by lifting ever-bigger stones and throwing smaller ones at targets and small birds. Young apprentices could obtain a new helping spirit the same way (ID 2283).

In everyday practice, fire could be produced by hitting stones, and in myth, lightning (Boas 1901–7: 498). In ritual practice, stones mediated connections with the Other World, for sacrifice

92. "Nose" means "up" in Greenlandic body symbolism: *qingaq*, nose, denotes the smoke hole in the roof, and both Moon and *Silap Inua* turn up their nose, *qinngarpoq*, get angry, in reaction to breaks of taboo (Thalbitzer 1926: 60–61; 1928: 408; Kleinschmidt 1871: 146).

93. The rich tradition of boulders and cairns marking places of religious importance, signposts, and memorials among the Canadian Inuit (Hallendy 2009) is less pronounced in Greenland, where they seem to serve primarily as signposts (Lauridsen 2015). In my treatment of stones, I chiefly use Greenlandic sources, and refer to the Canadian Inuit ones for comparison.

94. Big objects like *umiat* frozen to the ground are pulled loose in northern variants.

and for the shaman pupil's calling forth spirits. The latter would rub a small stone in circles on the flat side of a rock or on a gravestone, or he might skim small stones along the surface of a lake (e.g., Sonne 2005: ID 2283, 1241). Among the South Baffin Islanders, a shaman apprentice might be addressed by a large stone rolling down a slope with the following offer to become his helping spirit: "I jumped down in long leaps from my place on the cliff. As the snow melts, as water is formed on the hills, I jump down" (Boas 1964: 183). Myths like this concur not only with the origin of stones from above, from heaven or the uppermost inland region behind you, but also with their ambiguity. In Avanersuaq the earth was originally formed by fallen earth and stones of either beneficent or malignant nature (Sonne 2005: ID 1517). Indeed, the three big meteors at "the place for knife-material," Savisivik (until Peary carried off these rare boulders), did in fact come down, whether realized by ancestors of the Polar Inuit or not. The East Greenlanders have observed meteors (Victor & Robert-Lamblin 1989–93, II: 390–91). In East Greenlandic myth a boulder rolling down the mountainside in spring could be dangerous when threatening to smash the longhouse at the coast. It was called *Aqajarormiorsiorpua*, "striving to get into the stomach"—i.e., the interior of the house in common analogy with the world. It had to be stopped by the shaman and his helping spirits among which only *Equngasoq*, the spirit kayaker from the outermost islands, matched the boulder in strength. Chasing the boulder upwards, *Equngasoq* managed to lift it up, then let it fall, and the terrifying boulder smashed and dissolved into small and harmless stones (Sonne 2005: ID 807, 1192). Which, given time, is the way of stones. So, the fertilizing powers of spring could be dangerous as was indeed the equivalent descent of Moon on a punishing expedition. He similarly threatened to ruin the longhouse using his long black (phallic) staff, and he was also overpowered by *Equngasoq* (ID 1343, 1344, 1353, 1675). *Equngasoq* means "twist mouth," which in most East and South Greenlandic contexts can be identified with a fulmar. This seabird, the first to arrive with open waters in spring, is remarkable for its peculiar "twisted" beak; it hovers above the sea some distance from shore and never breeds on the land (Rasmussen 1938: 210; Muus et al. 1981: 174; Sonne 1990).[95] In East Greenland, he fights both *Aqajarormiorsiorpua* and Moon; in South Greenland he turns up in his kayak at the sudden breakup of the sea ice in spring in order to carry a shaman, stuck on an iceberg, along to the opposite land of Sea Woman (Sonne 2005: ID 340, 1445). In West Greenland, where the great *Asiungasungaaq* ("the big destroyer") corresponds in myth to *Aqajarormiorsiorpua*, Raven, not *Equngasoq*, enters the story in an acculturated variant, which combines a Greenlandic young girl with both a Qallunaaq (European) and a renewal of the world. When the big destroyer, *Asiungasungaaq*, comes sparkling down the steep mountainside, producing a heavy smell of smoke, this boulder disturbs a raven mother in telling the biblical story of Noah and the deluge, as witnessed by her raven forefathers. Her "audience" is a human girl who missed her chance to travel abroad with her beloved Qallunaaq captain when, due to excessive love-making at night, she overslept on the very day of the ship's departure. The raven mother offers her help and invites the crying girl to her place, but while busy sweeping the floor and relating her story, the rumbling noise of *Asiungasungaaq* sets

95. Apart from the multifarious representations in masks of beings with a twisted mouth from all over native North America, another twisted mouth comes to mind, "the paradoxical smile," half smiling and half wry, made by Iglulingmiut at the reappearance of the sun in mid-January, another important turning point in time (Saladin d'Anglure 1990a: 105 and front page of the issue).

her to flight with her children. She leaves the maiden to make her way out alone, described using the metaphors of a birth—i.e., through a difficult passage made partly clear by the sweeping and fleeing ravens. Evidently this act is in analogy with the Greenlandic ritual of promoting a delivery by having all inhabitants quickly leave the house through the entrance tunnel.[96] The young girl forgets about her captain; I propose that this is due to her rebirth to Greenland, stated in the story as being the land first seen by the raven sent out by Noah (ID 485). Thus, implicitly associated with the primordial storm surge (which was identified by the missionaries with the biblical deluge), this story, based on a mix of biblical and traditional life-renewing episodes, would serve as an early origin myth of Greenlandic national identity.[97]

Not every boulder comes down of its own accord. Giants of the distant inland region are particularly busy with huge stones, rolling them downwards (Sonne 2005: ID 248, 434) and also using them as a means to fertility and producing no end of children. One giant married to a human wife tried to be helpful at her delivery by placing big stones on her body, but stopped when told that this method was not used in her (human) world (ID 826). Another giant called *Aningaangujuk* ("like Moon" [*Aningaaq*+ -*ujuk*] or "minor Moon") called forth menstruation by throwing big stones on his little human wife from the coast (ID 92).[98] Moon, the fertilizer of the human world (e.g., Thalbitzer 1926, 1928), usually performs that job, if by other means (e.g., Sonne 2005: ID 159), but the giant is by its name obviously likened to Moon. Similarly, ambiguous fertility recurs with the boulders like *Aqajarormiorsiorpua*, or with Moon whose children with human women rarely survive (see below and p. 112). But he has babies in store for the mediating shaman to ask for without risks and to receive when dropped on request by Moon (Rüttel 1917: 39–40). Similarly, in mythic exaggeration a giant is told to produce a swarm of children overnight, kill them in the morning, but promise to let a litter survive at the end of his life (Sonne 2005: ID 361); I imagine him smashing big stones into small ones and then crushing them into sand.

Small white stones were children's toys for playing "house" in summer. Children used these stones to "draw" their world, the outlines and interior lines of houses, kayaks, etc., on the ground. Among adults certain small white or light-colored stones were attributed great fertility powers. Thus, a barren East Greenlandic woman would try to remedy her flaw by placing such a small white stone in her briefs and murmuring the following lines: "Creep in! Let me now get you for my embryo! As you begin to accustom yourself to creep in, I have ceased to menstruate. You round (rare) stone! Come hither from beyond the heavens! Creep into my interior, having your effect" (Thalbitzer 1923: 274).[99,100] In

96. In Greenland births took place in the common longhouse, not, as in Arctic Canada, in an isolated hut.

97. The acculturated Kreutzmann calls a similar phenomenon *Toornaarsuk* (the Devil, in Christian terms) in his variant of the Big Fire (*Innersuaq*) who usually arrives across the sea and scares noisy children to death. The event takes place in spring but it may refer to some lightning and not to a boulder coming down, because Kreutzmann has the spirit appear as fire springing to and fro between two very steep cliffs (Sonne 2005: ID 237).

98. -*ngujuk*, "like" or "little," is not a productive post base (Fortescue pers. comm.).

99. The space beyond the heavenly vault or horizon according to Thalbitzer (1923: 274, note 6).

100. Another version of the spell has the stone emerge from its place of origin, the interior of the earth (Thalbitzer 1923: 273–74). Still, it may have been associated with *sila*, as were particular big white stones, the "eggs of the earth," found on the ground by the Canadian Inuit. These were called *sila*, *silaat*, or *silasaat* (becoming *sila*, or *sila* fetuses) but certainly *not* used by humans for fertilizing ends. When hatched they developed into much-feared oversize albino animals, mostly polar bears, bearded seal, and caribou (Saladin d'Anglure 1990a: 96ff; Boas 1964: 232; 1901–7: 492–93). In NW Greenland, a married couple, the informant's close of kin, once found such a *nunap mannia*, no bigger than the

perfect agreement an idea was held of a big translucent stone in heaven, much like ice but too hard to be scratched by a nail (Rasmussen 1938: 106). This was most probably quartz, producing sparks when hit as in the East Greenlandic myth about *orsugiaq*, a big-bellied woman, who when smashed either vomits fire or transforms into a halibut entering the sea through the entrance tunnel of a house.[101] Her husband supplies a visitor, a human hunter, with a never-failing stone point (made from *orsugiaq*?) for a weapon and then transforms into a grenadier (*Macrouridae*), following the wife into the sea (Sonne 2005: ID 1105, 1104). Both kinds of fish are deep-sea species; the grenadier figures as a favorite helping spirit, whereas the halibut was caught for both consumption and fuel, especially by the Southerners, who were downright dependent on halibut fat for feeding their lamps (Gulløv 1983: 254). Fat, sparks, fire, and effective weapon points are the mythic connotations of *orsugiaq* in association with the sea, whereas a ball of quartz of whichever place of origin, heaven or earth, was chosen by some shaman apprentices for their rubbing in circles *sila malillugu* (following the movement of the world) in order to call forth a spirit from the Other World (Underbjerg 1984: 145). Among the Nattilingmiut, small, very pretty white stones were available in heaven for shamans to fetch, as did Atungait. Starting out from atop a very high, steep cliff, he traveled the entire circle of the Other World. Atungait brought along his only dog (bearing his own name) harnessed to a sledge and an old childless wife with a bad breath. His first visit was to some people of heaven who did nothing but play *ajagaq* (ring and pin) with such lovely stones, one of which he got hold of to take home (Rasmussen 1931: 300ff, 391ff). These heavenly stone players were no doubt deceased humans whose playing produced light of some heavenly kind, a mythic reference, I presume, to both the ball-playing Northern Lights and the playing of *ajagaq* on earth. Thus, placed on a grave, a piece of quartz, which also corresponds to the Northern Lights, transformed in the beholder's mind "into a spiritual object known as *qaummaqquti*, a manifestation of the *innua* [*sic*, life force] of the deceased as he or she travels through the sky" (Hallendy 2009: 42). As for the *ajagaq* playing, it was ritualized by the Iglulingmiut. They began to play at the return of the sun in January (Saladin d'Anglure 1990a: 104–5). And the dog bearing the shaman's own name, *Atungait* ("boot soles," connoting movement) has both phallic (Saladin d'Anglure 1980a; 1990b; Randa 1986) and border-transcending connotations (Oosten 1989). Finally, the childlessness of Atungait's wife must in some way allude to the fertility power of the white stones. But I dare not guess the reason why her breath was that bad (short or foul?) and her age that high.

---

egg of a *taateraq* (kittiwake), at the edge of a stream. Nourishing earth stuck to it and they brought it home, sensibly it seems, because if it remained in place, the dweller of the egg would hatch, enter the sea by the stream, and grow into a giant polar bear-like monster, a *qoqqoriaq*. This beast, with fat like that of a polar bear but of immense thickness, feeds on sea mammals and remains underwater; it has no gills, and so at new moons it emerges for breathing. It was once attacked and killed by sharks, leaving a thick layer of fat to be easily gathered in great quantities (Sonne 2005: ID 772). The Iglulingmiut associated their *silaassaq* with the forbidding poor sight of the thick fog that would result from breaking the "egg" (Saladin d'Anglure 1990a: 97).

101. Etymologically, *orsugiaq* means "of blubber," but *orsugiaq* should not be translated into Danish as *fedtsten*, (lit. blubberstone) or soapstone in English, nor to *ukkusissaq* (soapstone) in W. and E. Grl. Most probably, *orsugiaq* looks like blubber and behaves like burning blubber by sending out sparks when hit. Thalbitzer identifies *orsugiaq* as feldspar, and in West Greenland *orsugiaq* is cryolite, but cryolite is not found in East Greenland, and the sparkling makes geology professor Minik Rosing identify *orsugiaq* as quartz (pers. comm.). Quartz is *aligoq* in W. Grl. and the Canadian Arctic (Fortescue et. al. 1994: 18), but the word is not to be found in the East Greenlandic dictionaries (Robbe and Dorais 1986; Tersis 2008).

Anyway, the Polar Inuit who shared part of their lore with Southeast Baffin Islanders (see "Introduction") held the idea that prior to sexual reproduction, the primordial women found their babies in the form of small stones lying at the edge of big stones, which were rare all the same (Sonne 2005: ID 1296). Similar small, light-colored stones found around a boulder were believed by the Nattilingmiut to be the shit of beings living inside the boulder. The "shit" is called *uvivigtut*, the "fidgety" ones, according to Rasmussen (1931: 246–47, 388) but hardly correct. The dictionaries offer more precise translations like "naughty, thievish, lecherous ones," who steal their way into houses and, with Christianity, they became identified with devils or demons (Robert Petersen pers. comm.). So, *en miniature* the *uvivigtut* head for the interior of the houses on their own like the boulder *Aqajarormiorsiorpua*, whereas the barren East Greenlandic woman invited the rare white stone into her womb, and her primordial forerunner, who collected babies from the earth, nursed it "raw." All three kinds of postprimordial stones head for the interior of houses (wombs), be it for desirable or disastrous ends. In addition, the two myths of *Aqajarormiorsiorpua* and the *uvivigtut* each tell their story of erosion, the former as an instantaneous breaking into small stones in one crash, the latter protracted by the stone-consuming *inuat* of the stone, digesting and shitting the *uvivigtut*. Obviously, context and discourse determine the understanding of fertilizing stones as being beneficial, disastrous, or satanic. There is also the recollection of a West Greenlander, who emphasized the devastating powers of white pebbles from heaven. When told the story about the seven plagues of Egypt, with the shower of hailstones as the last one, he agreed. That's a true story, he said, because people tell about such stones that came down like snow in the old days and killed a lot of humans and animals (P. Egede 1971: 40; 1939: 32–33). In still another context, a big stone that looked like a woman received stone offerings in exchange for success in hunting. Once a human woman who refused to take a husband, she turned into stone bit by bit as she called in vain for some kayakers to stop, approach her, and marry her. Her stone figure used to be seen in full, but because people offered small, light-colored stones to her in order to receive game in return, she was almost completely covered up. People were sure she would fancy such lovely pebbles (as her babies? or toys?), because she herself had turned into stone (Rasmussen 1931: 243–44, 386–87).

Turning our focus now to sacrificial boulders, these were common with the Nattilingmiut (Rasmussen 1931: 225) as with other Canadian Inuit (Boas 1964: 183; Rasmussen 1925–26, I: 425; Hallendy 2009). East Greenlandic *Aqajarormiorsiorpua*, we are told, used to be such a sacrificial boulder when still in place "up there behind" (Sonne 2005: ID 1192), and several were in regular use along the Greenlandic west coast way into the time of Christian mission (F. Lynge 1981: No. 247, ill. p. 82; Hans Lynge 1978: 43–44). One such boulder, called *Naartuup pissiffia*, the big *Naar*'s sacrificial place, was situated near Nuuk, at Qaquk, the place of strong tides and beluga hunts. It received offerings right up until 1900 (*ibid.*). *Naartooq*, Big Belly, is indeed a significant name, as it is related to *Nätsuk* or *Naarjuk*/*Naarsuk*, the giant baby identified with *sila* among the Nattilingmiut and Iglulingmiut (Saladin d'Anglure 1980b; 1990a; Rasmussen 1929: 71–73). *Naaq* means "belly" in ordinary Greenlandic, but in the language of the spirits *naar* means "night" in space (as inside a belly) and, as we know, both dawn and dusk are transitional *naar*-times (O. Rosing 1957–61, I: 92; Rasmussen 1930b: 77; 1931: 310; 1932: 112). So, *naaq* signifies transitional *sila*, alias space, in the reversed perspective of the spirits, and stones are both polysemous and ambivalent, associated as they obviously are to *sila* ideas, to successful hunting, to annual renewal in spring, disaster, adultery, and fertility. You should not exchange a stone for bread, but for Inuit stones were excellent "food for thought"—i.e., for coherently relating ways of life to environmental options (Sonne 2010).

By according Kaassassuk a mastery of stones on par with that of the biggest giants, the non-social values come to the fore. Due to maltreatment, he turns forever vengeful by the powers received from the Other World. On the other hand, if not killed (Sonne 2005: ID 269, 352) or losing his powers with age (ID 434, 1116), Kaassassuk fulfills the traditional ideal of a hero who eliminates his enemies to a degree that nobody ever dares to attempt a counter-revenge (ID 600; Sonne 1982b). The issue of revenge, an ideal duty in pre-Christian Inuit society and evoking a discourse of never-ending feuds, looms large not only in oral tradition but also in Greenlandic literature right through the 20th century (e.g., H. Lynge 1967; see Sonne 2010).[102]

Remaining on the topic of Kaassassuk, several Greenlandic versions are, as demonstrated in Sonne (2010), particularly concerned with stones. Kaassassuk builds an unusually huge stone trap for catching polar bears (Sonne 2005: ID 134, 278, 418, 434, 1115). He smashes boulders to pieces, and may even kick his way into mountains using both his feet and head (ID 1552). Aron scatters stones throughout his narrative. First, Kaassassuk is likened to a stone because he never grows. Families who take turns in adopting the orphaned boy utter, "Let's take him. Since he is not a stone he shall sooner or later start to grow" (ID 93). But they all throw him out in disappointment. Eventually an old, marginalized woman adopts him for good, and when hurled along like a rolling stone by *Pissaap Inua* his stony nature is transformed by the power he receives into a master in handling stones.[103] He has overcome his inborn nature. Aron also introduces the sexual aspect of stones in association with eating (the nearly universal association of sex with eating is also genuinely Inuit).[104] He has the boy hide a small piece of flint under his foreskin. Stealthily, he tries to use this for chewing, because his tormentors knock out his teeth whenever he grows new ones. So, not only his nose but also his teeth grow: one by maltreatment, the other "by nature." When detected in its conspicuous place, the piece of flint is also removed. With the physical powers he gains, Aron's Kaassassuk behaves like a gale, overturning every object encountered on his way down from the inland region. He even budges steep rock walls by a push with his shoulder. Finally Aron ends his narrative with stones in a most significant way. Having lost the single combat to his opponent Ususarmiorsunnguaq, Kaassassuk demonstrates his recognition of the defeat by squeezing a white stone—soft like himself—into sand, whereas he shows the superior strength of his opponent by squeezing a black stone into nothing more than an oblong form (Sonne 2005: ID 93).

As emphasized by Thisted (1994), here Aron clearly demonstrates Kaassassuk's self-reflective development and final recognition of his limitations. So Aron, by employing symbolic meanings of stones, has managed to have Kaassassuk socialized in accordance with contemporary changes in ideology. In the sense of self-reflectiveness, the pulverizable white stone representing the powers

---

102. The traditional ideal of revenge was nourished by a lack of legal institutions except the song duels (banished by mission) together with, as stressed in recent Greenlandic literature, a strong tendency to let envy get the upper hand (e.g., Brandt 1971; Villadsen 1996 [1965]).

103. In some East Greenlandic variants, this happens by making him grow (Sonne 2005: ID 315, 434).

104. Thus, for instance, most variants of the Inuit origin myth of Sun and Moon have Sun, after detecting her brother Moon as her secret lover, cut off her breast, throw it to his feet, and declare, "I seem to be to your taste, eat this as well!" (Sonne 2005: ID 180, 1086, 1087, 1088, 1123, 1519, 1595; Rasmussen 1929: 81; Boas 1964: 189–90; 1901–7: 173).

of Kaassassuk bears some desirable connotations in contrast to the black one.[105] Subdued, he stops killing indiscriminately. Apparently then, in Aron's Kaassassuk, the stones have retained their symbolic potential with changes in history. Among these changes, the annihilation of feuds stands out at the time of Aron, who lets the stone speak with effortless ease.

Forces of Spring and Playing with the Pillar of Support

In some versions, Kaassassuk marks his powers in secret by tearing up plants and tearing loose big pieces of frozen meat or women's boats put up for the winter, or kicking stones frozen to the ground into pieces. The latter are either securely hitched and/or similarly frozen to the ground (Sonne 2005: ID 134, 278, 285, 352, 660, 1013, 1395). Either act signifies, in my interpretation, the melting forces of spring that send both stones and plants and also people on the move, the former down the mountains and the latter on their travels throughout summer by their women's boats. The sexual analogy of both spring and threatening boulders comes to the fore when Kaassassuk breaks the frozen roof of the entrance tunnel with his back (always passed through by crawling, and signifying in myth and ritual the vagina of the house as part of the analogy of a womb) (ID 134, 278). The huge trunk of driftwood, however, that he manages to drag from the coast single-handedly and raise either behind the longhouse or barring the entrance brings to my mind the unstable support of heaven. The storyteller Noah has Kaassassuk plant it leaning, and Aron first leaning and then falling, and Jaakuaraq first leaning, next catching it falling, and then putting it up again leaning, and finally crashing (ID 315, 434, 600, 269, 195, 93, 1395).[106] All in all, this is a frightening omen for the cruel revenge to be taken by Kaassassuk. But although the trunk episode matches Kaassassuk's other secret trials of strength, which point to devastating forces of spring, would the pillar(s) threaten to come down in spring as well? Or, more likely, would they need to be (ritually) raised again?

Pillars Raised or Strengthened?

The one-legged giant, Ittuku, living on an island in the far south, has to prop up the pillars (*ajagutat*) of his house several times, first in autumn to defy the shit of a multitude of seabirds passing by and next past midwinter, when a huge migration of polar bear and then an enormous migration of walrus pass by, crawling over both land and house (Sonne 2005: ID 1325). So from autumn to late winter the house is in danger of having its roof come down by the weight of passing hordes of game. The story is East Greenlandic, and the one-legged Ittuku is most probably a star being living on an island passed by the seasonal migrations of birds and animals, and I take his house to symbolize the world writ large. I shall deal with this story in detail toward the end of chapter 5. Less obvious is a magic song about the pillars sung by a lonely Kitlinermiut caribou hunter for a safe return in the falling of night.

---

105. For the subdued phallic humor of both the name Ususaarmiarsunnguaq ("the little penis with the capacity of growing big") and these stones, see Sonne (2010).

106. The only Canadian Inuit variant that has this element plus a couple of others in common with Aron's and Jaakuaraq's variants is one recorded by Métayer among the Kitlinermiut (1973: 116–23). I suspect Knud Rasmussen to be the importer during the Fifth Thule Expedition.

He seems to invoke the following dawn by comparing getting up in the morning with a turning over of the supports of heaven:

> The great sky's its enormous pillars
> That keeps it up, as we overturn them (*ajägpägdlugit*/*ajappallugit*)
> Down there and up there
> They are upright as pillars—we overturn them
> Rising from our bed.
> Big dwelling! Rest on your arms,
> Hold fast!
> Platform! Rest on your arms
> Hold fast!
> I hold on to it, I faithfully hold on to it, to the island
> Like a gull, anxiously screaming for its young.
> (Rasmussen 1932: 118)

Since neither Rasmussen nor his informant offer an interpretation, I'll take the liberty and point to the light dizziness you may feel by getting to your feet too quickly in the morning due to the turn in perspective from horizontal to vertical. Since by analogy you overturn the pillars supporting the island (the world), you should rise slowly, resting your arms on the platform, and, despite the risk involved, cling to it like a gull screaming for its endangered young. My interpretation may be wrong, but regardless the movement from horizontal to the upright position seems to be likened to overturning the pillars. It might also relate to pushing (propping up) the pillars in analogy with raising your body at an arm's distance and pushing off with your hands on the platform, or *ajappallugit* in Greenlandic. If so, we arrive at the opposite meaning—that is, of propping up heaven in concordance with the light opening up the world in the morning. The pillars themselves, *ajakutat*, etymologically have precisely that function: to keep apart two sides (Fortescue et al. 1994: 58; 2010: 63) as for example the cross-beam, *aajaq* (W. Grl.) of a kayak. Assisting or imitating a similar rising of heaven from earth could very well be the idea of *ajagaq* (the ring-and-pin game), played by the Iglulingmiut at the reappearance of the sun in mid-January (see above; Saladin d'Anglure 1990a: 104–5). The event simultaneously marked a stop in the playing of *ayaRaRaR* (Saladin d'Anglure 1990a: 104–5; Fortescue et al. 1994: 58; 2010: 64), or string figures, restricted to the period of "night" (no sun) and meaning thus that the distance (between heaven and earth) is "little, barely," or *-RaRaR* (*ibid.*). If that stop was ignored, the string figures could turn into tripwires, and in consequence make the reappearing Sun lose balance, stumble, and wound her knees so that they bleed (Saladin d'Anglure 1990a: 105). Balance in body is a must, of humans as of *inuat* traveling the entire world. Another *aja* word used by the Kitlinermiut, *ayaɣutaq*, means "rainbow" (Fortescue et al. 1994: 58; 2010: 63), which, when highly vaulted gives pleasure but when low induces the opposite feeling (Rasmussen 1932: 23).[107] So, as mentioned above but worth repeating: the rainbow of changing heights adds

107. Related in meaning is the Greenlandic rainbow, *neriusaq*, "inspiring hope." As a route to heaven, the rainbow was said by a shaman to be perfect at the autumnal equinox when low on the horizon (see above).

still another perception to pillars, air, and mountains in that they all *keep heaven and earth separate.* Each of these pictures is easily visualized—and sensed—but like metaphors in poetry they cannot be harmonized by formal logic. Taking into account myths and ideas about the separating means, the common denominator could be the potential of change in distance between heaven and earth with the seasons, or weather, or erosion, along with the descent of boulders in spring.

Kaassassuk's Own Balance

The issue of bodily balance gained by Kaassassuk is particularly prominent in the West Greenlandic variants. They offer fine illustrations of its achievement, when time and again he is being surrounded by the long tail of the land predator and hurled along like a top. Somersaulting (connoting revival/rebirth, see above) along the ground while toys drop out of his body and sometimes losing consciousness as well, he eventually gets to his feet. The last time he is hurled, neither toys nor consciousness are lost. Swiftly getting upright, he hops on one foot for a short while, stops, tests his strength on big stones, and descends feeling light in body—the right feeling of mastering one's body in Greenlandic lore. Nevertheless, in the end Aron questions the value of the balance in body of Kaassassuk. Not trained in kayaking from childhood, and like the failing ability of inland giants to master kayaking, the invincible Kaassassuk is overturned by a gale coming from the inland. Or, to put it another way, he paradoxically loses balance by land powers like his own when out at sea. Furthermore, had it not been for the intervention of his last opponent's father, his foe would have killed Kaassassuk by throwing him into the sea. As with his powers in handling black versus white stones, his balance in body appears to be insufficient as well.

The North Alaska variant puts the balance of body in front. The boy named "Fright," who receives help from above, from *Silap Inua*, is born handicapped, with his feet turned the wrong way. As he is ordered to train his muscles, his feet are set right (Rasmussen 1952: 188–90). This simple message about coming of age by making yourself the master of your upright body runs parallel to "Fright"'s culture-specific (Alaska) necessity of acquiring an amulet for achievement of adulthood.

Aspects of *Silap Inua* and Similar Figures in Ritual and Myth

Rasmussen's identification of *Pissaap Inua* (the *inua* of power) with *Pinnga* and *Sila* in his presentation of Canadian Inuit versions of Kaassassuk asks for further scrutiny of the sources. *Pinnga* is identified with the *inuat* of the Sun and the Moon in the East Greenlandic language of the Other World. They are depicted as oversize but recognizable humans, a woman and man in myth. The latter is an active ritual figure as well, but how is the figure of *Silap Inua* imagined? As a mythical figure, *Silap Inua*, or just *Sila*, has been an object of research for a very long time. Only Rink—without further speculations—mentions the identification drawn by Poul Egede's informant of *Sila* with the Entrails Snatcher (*Nalikkatteeq*) in myth (Rasmussen 1866–71, I: 88). Thalbitzer looked into prehistory but lacked solid basis for his nomination of *Sila* to the eldest Inuit/Yupiit deity with Big Raven as the reorganizing, reformative representative (Sonne 1985; 1986b, 1988b). Speculations on prehistory similarly supported Knud Rasmussen, Pater Schmidt, and Holtved in their exaltation of *Sila* to, respectively, a mythical, initial power à la mana, an *Urgott*, and a High God. All three based their speculations on Birket-Smith's mistaken theory about the origin of Inuit/Yupiit culture in the inland of Arctic Canada (Burch 1978; Sonne 1997; Thuesen & Sonne 2005).

Sensibly leaving prehistory alone, Saladin d'Anglure has paved a better way to understand this force by his studies of *sila*'s meanings, "*les sens de Sila,*" among the Inuit in Canada. His emphasis on *sila* as the medium of transition especially resonates in pre-Christian Greenland, as does his analysis of the paradoxical *Narssuk/Naarjuk*, weather *Sila*—i.e., the giant baby who is deprived of *sila*. He is *silaituq*, out of his wits and self-control (Saladin d'Anglure 1986: 73, 1990a: 102–3). As will be shown later, in bodily abilities he shares characteristics with the baby-husband of East Greenlandic *Asiaq*, the local *inua* of precipitation. On the other hand, when Saladin d'Anglure appoints certain aspects to avatars of Sila (1990a: 99), I get inappropriate associations with Indian gods. There certainly are overlaps in characteristics and abilities accorded to various figures of air and heaven, especially above the distant inland area, located beyond, and upwards. But not much of a theology or a mythology helps us differentiate among them. Since they are interchangeable in myth, the recurrent characteristics are in my view of greater importance to interpretation than the raising of one or the other to a dominant position. Also, different criteria could represent dominance: authority (in relation to other *inuat* or humans), raw strength, ritual representation, or . . . ? As to ritual, the shamans were said to visit *Silap Inua* in order to subdue storms (Holm 1888: 117, 1972: 133; 1914: 96; Rasmussen 1932: 28–29). However, no ritual descriptions or ritual myths are on record.

Fienup-Riordan's copious analysis of the Yup'ik *Ella* as a sentient, comprehensive keeper of morality (1994)[108] is not applicable to Greenland without further explanation. As stated above, the "Eye on High" was more frequently ascribed to the visible Moon, who primarily watched behavior in reference to game and less to social morality among humans. In ritual the angered Moon was fought, as was *Sassuma Arnaa*/*Immap Ukuua*/Sea Woman in the ritual myth when she became enraged by the breaches of prescriptions that soiled her body and then trapped the sea mammals in her house.[109] On the other hand, Moon did, in mythic fact, interfere directly with social morals when he took care of neglected boys (though never young girls, for unknown reasons) and women beaten up by their husbands. The results, however, were rarely happy. The Canadian Kaassassuk whipped strong by Moon turns into an incurable wife tormentor, and a son (never a daughter), fathered by Moon and born by the maltreated woman when back on earth, either ends up an asocial brute or dies (e.g., Sonne 2005: ID 179, 407, 1128, 1520; Boas 1901–7: 198–200, 555; Rasmussen 1929: 85–86, 87–88).[110] Consequently, myth does not permit Moon the position of a socially integrated father among humans. Shamans were the preferred go-betweens, who could safely go to Moon for babies, for game, and sometimes for the "light" they needed for seeing the Other World (see chapter 4, "Shamans").

Summary of Sea and Land Forces

In order to discover ideas about the powers of sea and land, I look to stories about travels by people who (in Greenland) are not shamans. One traveler covers the entire world, another (named

108. Less personified on the model of God in Fienup-Riordan and Rearden (2013: 60): a genderless, sentient force constantly aware of and reacting to humans' mutual behavior in their relations to all parts of the world.

109. Historical stories tell about fighting Moon (Sonne 2005: ID 1343, 1344, 1353), whereas visits to the Greenlandic Sea Woman are only encountered in ritual myths (search Havkvinde* in Sonne 2005).

110. The only Greenlandic exceptions are a Polar Inuit variant, where the son of Moon develops into a mighty hunter of polar bears (Sonne 2005: ID 616), and a late (probably of Christian influence) West Greenlandic one that has Moon take the son to his home in heaven (ID 179).

"Uiarteq"), the entire coast of Greenland. They are not particularly revealing on the topic. The globe-trotters who travel a lifetime have only one comment upon their return: "the world is very large." Uiarteq passes a couple of difficult coastal stretches. He encounters a monstrous sea scorpion and some evil cannibals at Cape Farewell but no other humans along the entire coast. Yet the interesting issue of the story is its possible reference to a prehistoric immigration to East Greenland. Two types of stories, "Qilaatuaq" and "Kivioq," relate travels across the sea to the opposite land, Akilineq. Both focus primarily on the Akilinermiut.

Qilaatuaq's family is blown out to sea on an ice floe. They suffer from thirst, the ice floe melts with the coming of spring, and they encounter aggressive cannibals in Akilineq; and all threats are overcome by their individual amulets and Qilaatuaq's awareness, magic knowledge, intelligence, and lithe body. The course of events is structured by ordinary changes in *sila*, weather, from midwinter to spring.

Kivioq leaves home due to his wife's adultery. Among the hindrances he encounters across the sea, some are ordinary natural obstacles, but one—a maelstrom at the center of the sea, its navel, with some water-filled intestines in front—points to the idea of the sea as a pregnant stomach. In Akilineq Kivioq visits first an aggressive, humanlike bumble bee and then a mother and daughter living alone but without any material troubles due their rich catches at low tide. Kivioq leaves the ladies, either repelled by their sexual habits or longing for home. In some variants, he gets his wife back, and sometimes he has to settle as a bachelor. The issue discussed appears to be the relation between hunting abilities and sexual matters. The tone in most variants is humorous in contrast to the "Kiviuq" stories of the Canadian Inuit as analyzed by Oosten. A comparison reveals differences beyond my clear understanding. Still a third type (various personal names) concerns kin relations established with Akilinermiut who are encountered on the ice in midwinter. Some versions stick to the traditional "rule" (see p. 172) that no mixing of human and spirit societies will work. Here the Akilinermiut are "Others." But stories made up by the Moravian proselytes Luutivik and Hendrik reflect the news, received by the Greenlanders during the 19th century, that the Akilinermiut were related Inuit (of Labrador and Baffin Island). This fact apparently called for speculations on how and when they became related and later split without enmity.

The land powers are treated in stories about travels across the inland ice and the pan-Inuit variants about Kaassassuk. Naturally, the former stories relate the extremely long distance and ordinary dangers of crossing the ice. The focus, however, is on relations between East and West Greenlanders in the perspective of either. "Kaassassuk" offers a far better point of departure for analysis of land powers, because he, a poor maltreated orphan, is empowered by either a predator or a giant of the inland, called the "*inua* of power" in the southwestern variants. Kaassassuk of the "traditional" variants ends up a brute, a lust murderer or a wife tormentor. In some variants he gets killed. The message is clear: do not mistreat poor orphans. During the 19th century, however, some Greenland storytellers, Aron in particular, had Kaassassuk resocialized. Ever since this figure has been a hero, the "Greenlander" who trained and overcame oppression, but, finally overpowered, he realized his defeat and refrained from further revenge. The powers he receives are those of the inland, "up there behind you," the forces of *pinnga*. They include its air and heaven. They appear ambiguous, fertilizing and/or destroying depending on the situation. The loosening warmth of spring sets them on the move, fresh waters in loudly streams and stones, boulders in particular, thunder and lightning. They are set off by giants or let loose by themselves. Figuratively, the heaven is coming down, threatening the lives of humans. The threat must be kept ritually in check. The down-rolling boulder (*Aqajarormiorsiorpua*) must be crushed into small stones (see fig. 25, p. 392), the descended Moon returned to heaven, or the heaven must be propped up, its pillars restored. White pebbles from heaven are "godsends," others produce light when rubbed hard for fire by ordinary humans; some are used for getting *qaamaneq* (light, vision) by the pupil, or for creating lightning by *inuat* in the sky. They connect land with heaven, and as sacrificial *naar* (liminal or interior *sila*) stones they also link *sila* with the sea mammals. I analyze the imagined powers of stones in many details by means of other stories and statements, because they figure not only symbolically in the traditional "Kaassassuk" versions but with amazing numbers in the acculturated variants, which transform Kaassassuk into a self-reflective, social human being. So, in regard to transformations: as a key symbol, stones take on that multitude of meanings, which appear particularly useful for acculturative mythopoeic transformations. Besides the numerous occurrences of stones, also the balance in body, which Kaassassuk gradually achieves, is put to a significant test in the acculturated versions: strong, adult Kaassassuk, but still a beginner in kayaking, is overthrown out at sea by his own powers—a storm from the inland. This episode fits my above conclusion on balance: the particular balance of a human being permits him to move about over land as also at sea. My final exposition of *Sila*'s aspects is caused by Knud Rasmussen's problematic identification of *Sila* with the *inua* of power, *Pissaap Inua*, in his translations of Canadian Inuit variants.

CHAPTER TWO

■ ■ ■

Seasonal Rituals and Rituals of Crisis

Introduction

In my younger days I was taught that, apart from the shamans' séances, pre-Christian Greenlanders had few significant rituals. Indeed, in comparison with the Yupik "time for drumming," which covered about four months of ceremonies in winter (e.g., Morrow 1984), this was true.[1] My professor's keen interest in rituals above all was no incentive either. Yet stubbornly staying with Greenland I turned my focus to all kinds of ritual acts, be they proscriptions or prescriptions, obligatory or recommended, observed or violated, and the use of spells, amulets, and sorcery. In short, I focused on all acts attributed to "supernormal" effects. The number was overwhelming and the attributed effects frequently obscure. However, considered in the light of seasonal changes in nature, the ideas of its beings, its demands on making a living and on social organization, together with associative and symbolic thinking in general, my focus on these acts helped me to arrive at some understanding. Gradually they came to form parts of a whole, a worldview. Interpretations of these acts speckle the text in all its parts, and in this regard the presentation below may appear cursory. It follows the conventional division into seasonal and life-cycle rites, because the poor Greenlandic sources on this topic are enriched by comparisons with well-described ritual patterns among other Inuit and Yupiit.

Among all Inuit and Yupiit, changes in *sila* as in human physiology and development of skills decided the times for regularly returning rituals. Marked events in the annual round of seasons (the coming and going of light and thus game), as in the life of individuals (birth, "firsts" in production, reproduction, and the initiations of shamans, death) were considered to be of utmost concern to the relations of humans to nonhumans, be they game animals, particular *inuat*, or deceased relatives. Generally midwinter or New Year called for more comprehensive rituals.

The pre-Christian Greenlandic celebrations of New Year and some minor collective rituals in autumn and spring appear negligible. Nor are the sources impressive, scanty and hardly recognizable

1. In comparison with the Eastern Inuit, the Yupiit ritual calender reflected their riches in resources, a higher complexity in social organization of lineages, and a less prominent part played by the shamans.

as they are as statements on such events. Only descriptions of the East Greenlandic New Year have some substance. I shall do my best first in regard to winter festivals and, later, in references to rituals of both the other seasons and the individual rites of passage in contexts that support such analysis. Shamanic performances dominate the pattern of collective rituals in Greenland and Canada. They sometimes coincide with, but more frequently took place outside, the "calendric" collective rituals. Full moons (i.e., in winter) and winter solstice seem to have called for shaman performances (Gessain 1978; Gessain & Victor 1973; Sonne 2005: ID 1687, 1211, 1212, 1311, 1312, 1676). Otherwise, séances were occasioned by any critical event asking for a curing, by a shaman's desire to raise his reputation, by visits from other settlements, or by mere boredom in the long, dark evenings of winter.[2] Shamans' travels to the main *inuat* like *Qaammatip Inua* (Moon), *Sassuma Arnaa* (Sea Woman), and *Asiaq* (East Greenlandic *inua* of precipitation) may once have been annual events, as were the late-19th-century South Baffin Island Sedna cult and the springtime visits to the *inua* of the weather (*Sila*) and *Ni-givik* ("the woman who feeds people") at Tigara, Northwest Alaska, about 1900 (Rainey 1947: 258).[3] But according to both myth and actual statements, the occasions in Greenland were invariably some crisis, and the season would be spring in the case of Sea Woman and *Asiaq*, whereas historical statements on travels to Moon are centered in the period around the New Year. In myth, visits to Moon follow more or less the same course no matter the kind of traveler, whether a shaman, a great, obstinate hunter, or a maltreated wife (in Greenland, this is never a female shaman or, for that matter, a child).[4] As for visits in the other direction, by these *inuat* to earthly humans, none is on record for Sea Woman. In East Greenland *Asiaq* was invited to help herself, unseen at nights, by hook from opened bags of food (Thalbitzer ed. 1933: 164), while Moon came down all over inhabited Greenland for hunting during his dark quarters, for raping a young woman who slept on her back at full moons, or in East Greenland in order to ruin the house of humans in punishment for some break of taboo. He could arrive in person or just send his dog or polar bear, an event usually portended by earthquakes. In either case it could occasion a shaman's performance in East Greenland, which was apparently dependent on the abilities of the shaman or of one or more shamans in a well-prepared cooperation. A couple of such performances will be dealt with below.

New Year Celebrations

Masked figures leading an exchange of wives turn out to have been the minimum ritual marking a new annual round or New Year in Canada (Kleivan 1960; Blaisel & Oosten 1997; Saladin d'Anglure

2. Mauss's hypothesis that the Inuit religion is a collective matter in force only at the winter settlements has lost its appeal. Prescriptions concerning birth, abortion, and death, for instance, were in force all year round; assemblies that formed during spring and summer for the arrival of migrating resources presented shamans with the occasion to perform, compete, and be consulted. In fact, in the East Greenlandic ethnography, on which Mauss heavily relied, people came together throughout summer in numbers far surpassing those of the individual winter settlements. Almost the entire population gathered for harvesting the *ammassat* (capelin) in May, came together at a few other places for sealing in July, and at still others for fishing Arctic char in August to September (Holm & Petersen 1921: 588ff).

3. *Nuliayuk* ("the gadabout") is the common term in Canada. *Nerrivik* (the place of food) in Avanersuaq stories; *Sassuma Inua* or *Arnaqquasaarsuaq* (giant woman) in pre-Home Rule West Greenland, presently *Sassuma Arnaa*; and *Sattuma Eeva*, the phonetic equivalent to *Sassuma Inua* or *Immap Ukuua*, the "mother of the sea," in East Greenland. For more information, see most references in Weyer (1932: 351–52).

4. One exception to the common course of events, to be treated later, is a variant told by the baptized former shaman Missuarniannga (see pp. 128f).

1990a; Boas 1964: 201; 1901–7: 138–42). In his analysis of the North Baffin Island festivals, Saladin d'Anglure emphasizes the monopoly possessed by the masked shamans in choosing the most desirable women for themselves and the older men, the amount of violence they used, and the ban put on laughing at the mock sexual act they repeated in front of each selected couple (1990a; 1993). Masks, sexual themes, violence, and occasionally a ban on laughing were also common in the East Greenlandic New Year *uaajeerneq* (W. Grl.; *uaayiiniq*, E. Grl.) that most likely were completed with "a putting out of the lamps" (*qaminngaarneq*). No conspicuous violence is seen in the meager West Greenlandic descriptions of the ritual wife exchange or other feastings; and, as far as the sources go, women had greater liberty in the choice of partners than in Arctic Canada. Furthermore, neither in West nor East Greenland did shamans take the lead. On the other hand, individual shamans might take sexual advantage of both the fear and the appreciation their powers gave rise to.

West Greenland: Wife Exchange and Feasting

Hans Egede received the earliest description published of the ritual exchange of wives from an eyewitness in 1729. The time of year was mid-January, pointing to a celebration of the New Year:

> In one of the houses I was forced to levy execution against somebody about whom I had heard that they had recently had the usual whore-game going off as follows: Men and married women get together as if a party. One man takes the floor, plays his drum and sings an erotic song whereby he invites one of the women to a whore-play, after which he puts down the drum on the floor and withdraws behind a curtain put up for that particular purpose in one end of the house. The woman who feels like playing with him joins him without any bashfulness, and when ready (through?), another man immediately steps forward doing the same thing, et cetera. But no young and unmarried participate, because they are more bashful… (H. Egede 1971, 1: 252; 1925: 217; tr. BS)

Egede's "execution" consisted of both reprimands and a solid thrashing (*ibid.*). The abridged description in Hans Egede's Perlustration ends with the addition that the play culminates in a rich feast, and that:

> those are reputed the best and noblest tempered, who, without any pain or reluctance, will lend their friends their wives… Especially the women think themselves happy, if an angekkok, or prophet [shaman], will honour them with his caresses: there are even some men so generous, that they will pay the angekkok for it, chiefly if they themselves can get no children; they fancy that an angekkok's child will lead a happier life and become better qualified for business than others. (H. Egede 1971, 2: 79; 1925: 373; 1818: 141–42)

So, trusting Hans Egede, reputation, rather than violence or plain authority, would lend the shamans their share in sexual pleasures.

Poul Egede's son-in-law, H. C. Glahn, a missionary to Sisimiut in 1763–1768, was the first to comprehend the religious import of the ritual wife exchange, but he mistakenly thought that its range was limited to his own district and inspired by lecherous shamans alone (Glahn 1771: 223).

Glahn never found information on celebrations of winter solstice or New Year. In his annotations to the Moravian historian David Cranz's *Historie von Grönland*, Glahn vehemently overrules its description of feastings at solstice (Cranz 1765–70, I: 229). Banquets, he objected, are extremely common throughout the dark months, simply because people need variety in the long evenings (Glahn 1771: 271). So, obviously, then, there was a lot of feasting at midwinter! Otherwise, Cranz's report is quite detailed: people gorge themselves on rich food, entertain one another through evenings and nights with merry drum dancing and singing, with four songs accorded each participant. They also play ball in the light of the full moon and compete in physical strength. The songs of the drum dances are about hunting, the achievements of the ancestors, and the joy felt at the return of the sun. The comical touch is predominant in that the dancer who lets himself go in the most entertaining contortions is considered the champion singer (Cranz 1765–70, I: 229–30). I would call this a basic Inuit/Yupiit way of feasting. Cranz mentions no masking, nor shamans playing any roles, nor any ritual exchange of women. Merriment comes to the fore and playing ball outdoors in the light of the full moon sets a "date." It further reminds one of the ball game that used to end the Sedna cult in South Baffin Island, recognized by Blaisel and Oosten as reflecting the ball game played by the deceased humans of the Northern Lights. Returning to West Greenland at a fairly late point in 1931, the carpenter Josva at Nuuk—who built the first Christian chapel at the former place of the festival house, *qassi*—told Thalbitzer that in heathen times it was the custom of the inhabitants (of Saarloq) on the shortest day of the year, when the New Year stars *Aassuutit* appeared in the eastern sky, to dress themselves in new fur coats and proceed in couples to the festival house to celebrate solstice (Thalbitzer 1941: 671–72). Both the term *qassi* and the stars marking the New Year evince a past when church and Christmas were still not the place and time for celebrating winter solstice.

Moving on to the stories, a variant of the Singajuk legend (about a Southerner who fled north) informs us that the people of the island Kangeq opposite Nuuk (a stronghold of the immigrant Southerners) dressed in new clothes on New Year's day (not Christmas) for some untold festivities, and put a ban on hunting on that day. In other words, this was a religious feast![5] Finally, two variants told by (Moravian) Hendrik and his co-religionist, Luutivik, of the story mentioned above about a shaman's visit to some starving Akilinermiut, combine the procession in couples with the shaman's attempt to procure seals on request. The people line up in the festival house, married couples first, unmarried young boys and girls last, but at some point everything goes wrong. The shaman's helping spirit attracts a huge iceberg, which brings along the wished-for seals, then suddenly turns around and smashes the house to pieces. In one variant the offender is a young woman who conceals a secret abortion or birth, an *anngiaq*, and in the other it is an evil spirit passing by outside the window (Sonne 2005: ID 370, 1625). Still, the impetus is hunger, not a "calendric" feast, and no date is mentioned, nor is Sea Woman visited or lured up for a fight. For the procurement of seals, the shamans may thus have had other ways out than fighting Sea Woman.

The lack of masking in the above descriptions is—although at a much later date—richly compensated for by those of the *mitaartut*, the grimacing figures in disguise with blackened faces, oversize penises, and batons in the mummers' play described by Kleivan (1960), Nellemann (1960),

5. H. C. Petersen collected information on midwinter feasts in West Greenland (pers. comm.). His notes can be studied in the archives of the National Museum of Greenland in Nuuk.

Nooter (1975), Nuttall (1992), Kielsen (1996), and continuously on the internet. They arouse a joyous mix of laughter and horror, partly as mute dancing guests in every house, where they receive small gifts, and partly as monsters chasing others between the houses. Children scream when captured and slapped, and young girls squeal in being rolled over and hugged in the snow. The usual "dates" are the week between Christmas and New Year's or the following week. Regrettably, the sources are late (Kleivan 1960). The oldest source of disguised merrymakers at Christmas goes back to the 1820s, and they may or may not have been called *mitaartut.* The place is Aasiaat, at the house of the manager where the invited local Greenlanders make fun of the Southerners by dressing and acting like them (Kragh 1875). Did they also make fun of *qavaq*, the derogatory name for the dialect of the Southerners? If so, they were not *mitaartut*, who were not supposed to talk. Correspondences are more striking—if far from complete—between *mitaarneq* and the East Greenlandic *uaajeerneq*.

East Greenland: Masked Dances, Wife Exchange, and Feasting

Uaajeerneq (pronounced *ooaayeerneq* in English), the masked dances celebrated at New Year and possibly also at later get-togethers in winter, differed in one important way from *mitaarneq* in being no mummers' play but more like turns of a revue.[6] The *uaajeertoq* sang, danced, and drummed, and whether disguised or naked the performer was recognizable. The actor's talent in playing roles was admired, as much as his being two persons at the same time: his familiar figure and that of the role (only male actors were dressed up). Among the very detailed sources of the *uaajeerneq* plays (Thalbitzer 1923: 291–318; 1933 (ed.): 95, 107, 199–200; Gessain & Victor 1973; 1984; J. Rosing 1957; 1963: 301–3; Victor 1991; Victor & Robert-Lamblin 1989–93, II) sexual references abound, as do gross acts of violence, two of the themes emphasized by Saladin d'Anglure (1990a) in Canadian Inuit winter feasts.[7] Regarding the exchange of women, few European sources on *uaajeerneq* dare insist on an ensuing "extinction of the lamps," *qaminngaarneq*. Jens Rosing expects it (1957), Gessain alone was directly told so (1984: 88), Victor does not touch upon the topic (1991), and Holm merely reports that the dances usually ended in a feast (1972: 111, 150; 1914: 129). Thalbitzer does not know exactly, but refers to Hansêraq's information that the game would take place, for example, at New Year when visitors from other locales arrived, as also in the middle of May. A full or a new moon marked the "date" (Thalbitzer ed. 1933: 69; 1941: 667). The "date" in May coincides with the gathering at the capelin fisheries at Qinngu, and the date at New Year to the regular time for *uaajeerneq*. Thalbitzer's own informant, the immigrant Kuannia to South Greenland, described the "extinction of the lamps" in 1914 as:

6. The word means "rocking," "balancing." The body rocks while dancing. This may figuratively refer to balancing of the New Year, but I have no definitive answer.

7. Eleven of 70 dances described by Victor were sexually stimulating, and a similar number both titillate and end in thrashing (1991: 228–45). One particular dance bears a striking likeness, if differing in the amount of violence, with the tug of war between those born in summer and those in winter at the Baffin Island Sedna cult: "a dancer, masked or made up with soot, sang and asked everyone in turn when they were born, in summer or in winter (*attiwa*, up, the sun is up; *qattiwa*, down, the sun is low). Thus, the population was divided into two groups, or moieties. Those who did not belong to the same group as the dancer were beaten with his stick" (Gessain 1984: 88).

> The challenge is set by one of the ordinary men of the congregation; it would be considered too ridiculous and unseemly if a woman made the first advance. When the lamps are extinguished for this part of the game, a skin curtain is hung in front of the inner end of the house passage and one of those who take no part in the exchanging of wives rattles the curtain in such a way that it drowns the sound of what takes place in the dark. In the meantime, the children remain on the window-platform. When the lamps are lit later on, each man has to be back again with his wife on their common platform place, making pretence that he has not been elsewhere. But the next day, the children will tattle about what they have noticed. (668)

According to Georg Quppersimaan/Qúpersimân, who actually combines *uaajeerneq* with a sexual postlude, the women's prescribed modesty did not characterize the preliminary steps to the drawing of the curtain:

> A hitting with batons also occurred at *uaajeerneq*, where they [the actors] beat people using a *kammiut* (baton for stretching skin boots) as a club. Those brave ones who merely remained sitting were gently hit, but the fearsome others who tried to get away were pursued; when caught the latter received a severe thrashing, no, they were not spared, they could get severely hurt. I know about one person who fled to another wintering settlement, because he was hit that way. But adults alone were treated that way, children never. The women and the men started to become lustful, and they all started to dance and drum. This was both a game and of use [for reproduction] and also a laugh of course. The women did like this: as soon as they became aware that a man tried to catch a woman's attention, she approached him and said: "You got a sweetheart! You got a sweetheart!" Then she turned her back on him and while withdrawing said: "I am mad about becoming your sweetheart," and then she left him.... Previously a woman who began to feel lustful would do something like this: she would approach those sitting on the platform and portend mishap (or death), telling one after the other, "Take me on your lap!" When one person agreed and the others did not want to, she was supposed to hit the reluctant ones with her drumstick on their bodies, never the head. And when a man felt lustful he frequently did something like this: He clenched a drill between his teeth and behaved like a tern facing those who were lined up in a row and said: *piaa, piaa*, and then he prodded at them, yes, sometimes they received cuts.[8] And he continually approached the women and said: "I will give you a kiss because you are so lovely!" If they did not agree he put down his drum and kissed them, on the tip of the nose. (Qúpersimân 1972: 196–97; tr. into Danish by Stig Bjørnum, into English by BS; omitted by editor Sandgreen in Qúpersimân 1982)

Actually, the erotic aspect structured the drum dancing and may have been the untold reason why the mission put a ban on it. As reported and illustrated with photos by Gessain, the male drummer went through prescribed motions and facial expressions ending with exclamations of joy, *qatewaarteq* (at its highest pitch), "repeated thrice, which requires the evocation of an orgasmic

8. It means "one's (my) property."

progression. This sexual aspect ought not to be underestimated because the semantic analysis of the term *tiwavoq* reveals content of the same nature. *Tiwavoq* signifies that he dances with the drum, he jumps, and scampers (like a bird flapping its wings, a hopping gesture of courtship). *Tipavoq* means that he makes hugging gestures, bows to someone, he flatters, he tries to insinuate, he is gay, sportive, lascivious, indecent, lewd" (Gessain & Victor 1973: 145, tr. BS) Although the women's drum dancing was comparatively more subdued, the process was orgasmic as well. It led to a visible trembling ecstasy all through the body, but the expression of joy, the *qatiwaarteq*, was inaudible: "the repeated triumphant cry heard during the *qatiwaarteq* [was] the property of men" (144, tr. BS).

Comparisons

A second look at the man behaving like a tern prodding the lined-up persons (only women, or mixed?) is strongly reminiscent of one of the masked figures with the Nugumiut in Frobisher Bay, *Nunagiqsaqtuq* (see above pp. 73f, 80), who uses his "beak," a long pointed hood (like the big hood of the woman's anorak, *amaat*, twisted and set up), for exactly the same purpose (Boas 1901–7: 142). The fertility aspect is prominent in both attacks. But the flirting and independence in choice accorded to the women in East Greenland have no noticeable parallel in Arctic Canada. The same holds true for the women's liberty to make their own choice in Hans Egede's environment in 1729. Violence and sex went hand in hand in East Greenland as in Arctic Canada, but shamans do not visibly present themselves as leaders in Ammassalik. Thalbitzer, who in 1914 had read Boas, asked Kuannia, who strongly denied that the shamans had any deal whatsoever in ritual wife exchange. They did not even participate (Thalbitzer 1941: 667). I doubt that this was the case; since some 20 percent of the adult population were shamans, they certainly did participate, albeit not in the role of shaman. Some shamans were reputed goats in East Greenland, where their assumed sexual privileges had a good cause (Robert-Lamblin 1997: 286). They capitalized on them when procuring babies for barren women; when being paid for teaching female pupils, as did Kunnak (Sonne 2005: ID 1249); or when they simply took the liberty of the awe assigned to them due to their knowledge in sorcery.

The combination of teasing, tickling, and violence seems to be a pan-Inuit/Yupiit issue, to which I shall return in the treatment of bogies. In Georg Quppersimaan's mind, they were simultaneously a source of fun and also great use, because the ensuing extinction of the lamps served procreation.[9]

The Fate of the *Uaajeerneq* Masks

At the beginning of colonization at Ammassalik (1894), most masks fell out of use. They were replaced by a blackening of the face with soot, a cross-stick in the mouth distending the cheeks, and a strap tied across the face from ear to ear and below the nose. Masks were only used for scaring the children, Kruuse was told about 1900, a statement dismissed by Gessain, who blames the mission for people's reluctance to talk (Kruuse 1912: 44, cf. Gessain 1984: 82–83). Previously, as somebody told Thalbitzer in 1905–6, some masks could represent helping spirits of the shamans at *uaajeerneq* (1923: 291).

9. In his own memory and when confronted with the interviewer, missionary Otto Sandgreen, Georg stressed his shyness and reluctance in sexual matters (Qúpersimân 1972: 147; 1982: 141).

The shamans may or may not have used masks while performing; however, the statement that during his public shamanic initiation Ajijak presented his helping spirits in a dim light that made the audience dizzy supports the idea that carved masks could be used for representing helping spirits (Sonne 2005: ID 1676). So does the fact that masks were used in "playing shaman," a very popular entertainment among both adolescents and adults (Holm 1972: 129; 1914: 93). They knew quite well how to do shamans' tricks and to imitate those familiar characters among the helping spirits, which recurrently appeared during the genuine performances (Gessain 1984: 88). In representing helping spirits, carved masks at *uaajeerneq* would correspond to those in use at Yup'ik New Year ceremonies in Southwest Alaska (Lantis 1946; Rosing 1957; Gessain 1984; Morrow 1984; Sonne 1988a; Fienup-Riordan 1996).

The French ethnographers who began fieldwork at Ammassalik in 1935–36 and won the confidence of the East Greenlanders bought an impressive number of wooden masks, carved on Victor's commission and placed at the Musée de l'Homme in Paris. Gessain completed a comprehensive publication on these masks, identifying a few of them with the corresponding *uaajeertut* "roles," whose songs and dances Victor took down simultaneously (Victor 1991). Gessain, however, offers little information not available in other published sources (Gessain 1984).

Gessain's proposal that the mission's ban on the use of carved masks gave way to the blackening of faces remains a hypothesis. Jens Rosing, who observed two sedentary drummers wearing wooden masks during an *uaajeerneq* in the late 1930s, is inclined to think that, because the masks were very heavy to dance with, the blackening of the face was preferred (J. Rosing 1957). This is possible. However, skin masks would be a third option, unless they made breathing difficult. At all events, blackening was neither a new invention nor more secular than the masks. Blackening with soot would protect the Yupiit participants in ceremonies against the guests from the Other World (Fienup-Riordan 1994), and the distortion of one's features by thongs, from ear to ear and under the nose, has also been witnessed among Yupiit (seen by Morrow in 1978 at a Halloween party, pers. comm.) and at Tigara, where the wives of the *umelit* (whaling crew captains) would dance, one by one, in front of a small burning lamp:

> Across their faces the women tied strings which passed under the nose and over the ears. Then they kneeled near the lamp, and, as they looked up toward "the daylight" [the painted board across the end of the *qalegi*] so that all could see their faces, they licked the edge of the lamp. At a certain point in the second song they leaned forward to smother the flame with their tongues. The husbands of those women who were not burned would get a whale during the ensuing spring hunt. It was a very serious performance and although the young wives were often embarrassed no one was permitted to laugh. (Rainey 1947: 251)

Again we encounter this prohibition against laughing. Was *uaajeerneq* "cult" or entertainment? Victor classifies *uaajeerneq* songs as entertainment, and so does Kleivan (1960), regarding both *mitaarneq* and *uaajeerneq*. However, Kleivan is convinced of their religious function at an earlier date. At a distance, the discourse seems odd in maintaining that solemnity is religious and fun is merely entertaining. In that line of thought, one of the inventive *uaajeertoq* roles played by the former shaman Maratsi escapes proper characterization. It took place several years after his baptism, and he mixed old with new in an ingenious way: Maratsi performed the dance of

Nalikkatteeq (the Entrails Snatcher) with distended mouth, straps across the face, and a phallic dog's head in his crotch. During the dance, he instructed a grandchild to announce, after a short trip outside, that a star (most probably the *Aassuutit* of the New Year) had disappeared. It was a threat of doomsday, because, being a star, *Nalikkatteeq* had the power to overthrow the support of heaven. At that message, the audience immediately changed into their Sunday best in order to receive Jesus in a decent way. Maratsi danced on, unaffected, until interrupted by his wife, who made him understand that the end of the world was imminent. A little later he was seen sitting with folded hands muttering the Lord's Prayer out of his distended mouth while the dog in his crotch bobbed up and down. The grandchild was sent outside once more, and returned with the glad tidings that the star had reappeared. The world would endure! By his mixing of solemn prayer with the tilting of his dog, Maratsi had pressed all the buttons. People were killing themselves with laughter, explosively relieved, and laughing for hours and hours (J. Rosing 1957). Neither missionary nor catechist were present, of course, and nobody can tell for how long *uaajeerneq* with or without masks were continued in secret with references to the new faith appearing in shocking interactions with the old. Today wooden masks are carved for tourists and mostly analyzed as objects of art (Geertsen 1994).

Shamans' Travels to and Fighting Visitors from Heaven at New Year

The heavenly lights of night were naturally in focus around New Year. In myth, Moon was closely associated with the ritual wife exchange in winter. He saw his chance in a "putting out of the lamps" to sleep with his sister, Sun, who fled to heaven with a burning light, pursued by Moon, whose light lost its flame. He never caught up with her. Nevertheless, Greenlandic variants of a human's visit to Moon have Moon and Sun share the same house, but not as a married couple. A partition wall separates their places on the platform, and she may be the one who serves the human visitor his meal. Apparently the big hunter, Moon, could not be imagined without female household support. Before arrival, the visitor to Moon usually encounters *Nalikkatteeq*, sharing epithets with *Ulurlirnang* ("supplied with an *ulu*," women's lunar knife) in Canada, who rips open his/her front and removes the lungs and/or entrails at the moment her indelicate dancing provokes the slightest hint of a smile on the visitor's face. In myth Moon will come to his guest's rescue, whereas during *uaajeerneq*, the masked *Nalikkatteeq* would, at the moment people burst into laughter, hit left, right, and center with her stick (J. Rosing 1957). Although variants of mythic visits to Moon continued to be told in Christianized West Greenland, statements on punishing visits by Moon to earth are sparse.

No statement leads to the conclusion that Sea Woman was at play during New Year celebrations in Greenland. Nor are references made to the abode of the deceased humans en route to her dwelling at that time of the year. More likely the deceased relatives of heaven were associated with the ball-playing people of the Northern Lights, as proposed by Blaisel and Oosten (1997) in their interpretations of ball games that ended the South Baffin Island winter feasts.

As for ritual visits to heaven around New Year by West Greenlandic shamans, the Egedes' diaries offer several examples. In how far these travels reflect tradition remains an unanswered question, for the evident reason that the majority were undertaken in response to the missionaries' preaching. At any rate, apart from two trips, one in March and one in June (N. Egede 1971: 83–84, 7; 1939: 177–78,

132), they all occurred in winter.[10] One took place around January 24, 1723, in order to get some sign or (literal) trace of Hans Egede up there, but he (the shaman) saw only an old hag walking around with the head of a Qallunaaq and a dog gnawing some Qallunaaq bones (H. Egede 1971, 1: 77; 1925: 63).[11,12] On January 11, 1740, a shaman could confirm the preaching of Poul Egede about the pleasant realm in heaven. By personal inspection he had seen lots of people and caribou. But Poul was hardly correct in indicating a vertical ascension in this case. The preferable and much easier route went across the sea, following the waves to the horizon and upwards from there (P. Egede 1971: 134–35; 1939: 90–91). Another shaman had nothing to tell about his visit about the same time of the year. He did not succeed in taking off and was later found frozen to death outside the house (P. Egede 1971: 137; 1939: 94). A group of Southerners on their return from the north mocked Niels Egede for his inability to travel to heaven. A shaman among them told how the preceding winter he had been on his way to heaven but got lost in the fog and ended up in Holland, where he witnessed their carving of dolls that they made alive by breathing. In this way he came to know why that country was so densely populated (N. Egede 1971: 22; 1939: 140). A visit to Moon in order to procure seals in a time of crisis was carried out by a local shaman in January 1739, but, according to his neighbors, without any success (at that time they were perfectly aware that Poul appreciated derogatory stories about shamans) (P. Egede 1971: 101; 1939: 69). Finally, as an effect of the preaching about Doomsday, Moon was consulted by a shaman in the winter of 1723–24. Moon assured the shaman that heaven was not going to fall down (H. Egede 1971, 1: 143; 1925: 123). A less-soothing answer was received by another shaman in mid-February 1742, when Moon could appoint the end of the world to the approaching summer, because one of the pillars of heaven was rotting away. The shaman even brought back a piece of rotten wood as evidence (N. Egede 1971: 80; 1939: 176).

Still, one legendary version of a visit to Moon and one statement on a similar trip are worth considering. Kanak, apparently a historical shaman, is said to have been initiated by Moon. Taken to heaven by his helping spirit and welcomed by deceased humans of heaven (producing the Northern Lights) by handshakes the European way, Moon asked him to enter his house. He is threatened by the Entrails Snatcher, *Nalikkatteeq*, who arrives with her bowl for cutting out his entrail; but, advised by Moon to avoid smiling at the Entrails Snatcher's dancing, Kanak's entrails are not cut out. The disappointed *Nalikkatteeq* asks several times in vain for her bowl back, but when she threatens to let the pillars supporting heaven collapse, Moon gives in, and *Nalikkatteeq* retreats. Moon lets Kanak see the entire world below, and has him returned to earth a great shaman (Sonne 2005: 159). Visitors to

10. Although a shaman's travel to heaven in midsummer seems unlikely, the purpose was to be informed about God, who turned out to be shining like the sun, having a voice like thunder or sometimes a strong wind (common characteristics of Sila) but difficult to understand for those with no learning (nonshamans) (N. Egede 1971: 7; 1939: 132). The journey in March actually went to the king and his son in Copenhagen. On the way outward the shaman took the route across the sea, but on the way back he preferred the less dangerous (and shorter) way through heaven (*qilak*), where some Qallunaaq duel-singing gentlemen told him to urge his fellow men to try to end up in that lovely realm (N. Egede 1971: 83–84; 1939: 177–78). Most probably the sky arch, *qilak*, also made a shorter route judging from the quick speed of the stars throughout a night.

11. Since Hans Egede constantly praised heaven, he would know from visits up there, and thus would have left traces. Shamans could see the traces of former travelers in the Other World. This was how they traced either lost souls, shamans who never returned, or persons robbed by spirits.

12. The 1925 edition of the original has a dog gnawing an old hag and a young girl carrying around the head of a Qallunaaq. In either case, the vision is not exactly friendly toward the Qallunaat.

Poul Egede on New Year's Day 1737 mention a recent performance by a newly fledged shaman, who had succeeded in getting the walrus skull—the ball of the Northern Lights—for his helping spirit. He had it enter and furrow the floor with its tusks, which inspired the head of a falcon hung up above the entrance to scream and a small doll to speak Dutch. Consequently he planned a trip to heaven in the near future (P. Egede 1971: 44; 1939: 35). Neither the purpose of this flight nor its course is on record. Yet the short description calls for comparisons with statements on visits, actual or in myth, to the Northern Lights by shamans in Arctic Canada and East Greenland.

Ilimmarneq to the Northern Lights

Some of the great East Greenlandic shamans were initiated in public at winter solstice (New Year), which involved a flight to the Northern Lights. This of course was no annual event, considering the small number of great shamans. But the point in time, the returning light, is significant, and the ritual described appears to be a variation of the Canadian Inuit shaman's flight to the Northern Lights, *ilimmarneq* (i.e., flying). Bound with thongs for flying, the Iglulik shaman went directly to the Northern Lights, who were merry people who played ball with the delighted shaman and his thongs. In the end the thongs fell down and hit the floor in elaborately tied figures like a polar bear or a sledge driver complete with sledge and dog team (Rasmussen 1929: 129–31; Kublu & Oosten 1999: 125; Saladin d'Anglure 2001: 86–87, 156–59). Apart from the ingenious trick of producing these figures, they can be considered promises of future support from the relatives of heaven, an interpretation in consonance with that by Blaisel and Oosten (1997) of the ritual ball game ending the Sedna feast in South Baffin Island. It goes like this: while ghosts haunting the settlement were fought at the beginning of the ceremony, peace with the dead relatives of heaven was restored with the ball game at the end. The same interpretation cannot be applied to the heavenly people catching the East Greenlandic shaman Ajijak. As many as three versions (Kaarali, Sandgreen, and Saajooq) describe the event that was staged at winter solstice as a prelude to his recognition as a shaman in public, or his *saqqummerneq* (Sonne 2005: ID 1311, 1674, 1271, 1676). Laced up for flying with two thongs, he takes off into the air, where he mistakenly ends up with the so-called *qulummiin* spirits, "the people of sports and song duels."[13] These can only be the Northern Lights, though not recognized as such in the Ajijak variants. The performance turns out to be dramatically exciting, because these spirits are far from nice.[14] Their ball-playing with Ajijak is extremely rough, causing him to bleed to the point

13. *Qulummiq-* (hold athletic or song festival) + *-miut* (dwellers of a place) (Fortescue et al. 1994: 316; 2010: 344).

14. It is difficult to draw a distinction between pre-Christian and Christian attitudes to the ball players. Etymologically they have fun, as did the Iglulik shaman on his visits up there (Rasmussen 1929: 95). East Greenlandic Naaja, who was credited as an *ilimmarneq* to *Asiaq*, the *inua* of precipitation, almost forgot his errand (to ask her to send rain), delighted as he was to attend the song duels of the heavenly people (Sonne 2005: ID 1200). Their nasty treatment of Ajijak is a complete contrast. Either the fear of a sudden death by being caught by the Northern Lights or the story's character of an initiation (implying pain) may have got the better of the description. Anyway, the mission caused confusion. Aasiaat's (1820s) story about Kanak identifies the inhabitants of heaven with friendly, hand-shaking (European) deceased humans (Sonne 2005: ID 159). In 1738 Poul Egede apparently hit the nail on the head in opposition to the perpetual complaints that no food was to be had in the heaven of the missionaries. He compared its blessings with the mood created by the song festivals on earth, which made one forget any cravings for food and drink (P. Egede 1971: 94; 1939: 66). Nevertheless, the Moravian Hendrik of East Greenlandic heritage told a story about 1850 that distinguishes between two peoples of heaven, one constituting the baptized dead, who are well fed, blissful, and dressed in white clothing, and the other who are disgusting, meager ball players in rags and tatters (Sonne 2005: ID 1764).

of dying, while (in the Sandgreen version) one of his two thongs ends up twisting wildly in front of the audience. His father (as a master of ceremony) gets worried but is soon relieved, because the other thong, with which Ajijak is laced up, does not come down. If it fell, the father states, Ajijak would never return.[15] Trapped in a difficult situation, Ajijak calls in (through his thoughts) one helping spirit after another, which do not scare the *qulummiin* spirits (hereafter the Northern Lights). But when at long last he comes to think of his ghost spirit of a very strong deceased female relative (grandmother/mother), the spirits become terrified, and she liberates him. One variant ends at this point, which, apart from the rough handling, appears very similar to the *ilimmarneq* of the Iglulik shaman, the tricks with the thongs included.[16] Another, older Ajijak variant (by Kaarali) has him present his helping spirits afterward, the performance being a *saqqummerneq*, which used to take place at winter solstice. The most recent variant by Jens Rosing's main informant, Saajooq, has it that Ajijak was on his way to Moon when, by sticking his neck out at the calling of the *qulummiin* spirits, was drawn immediately into their midst, etc. During the subsequent performance he succeeded in reaching Moon, where he went through the torture of having his entrails cut out by *Nalikkatteeq* but was brought back and restored by Moon. From this *ilimmarneq* Ajijak returned with the surplus of helping spirits needed for the carrier of a great shaman. Almost like Kanak, who also had the heavenly dead humans as a stepping-stone for a similar propitious visit to Moon.

The contexts of the three versions of Ajijak's painful visit to the ball-playing *qulummiin* spirits differ. In Sandgreen's version the coming shaman Kukkujooq/Apulu is about to go flying to a distant part of the land, when fortunately he remembers the story he knows from hearsay. The recollection helps him avoid the nasty spirits en route (Sonne 2005: ID 1271). Kaarali's version has the event take place during Ajilak's initiation in public, a *saqqummerneq*. His helping spirits decided in midsummer that preparations were to be made, namely that Ajijak was to catch two particular seals and his wife was to cure the skins. They were meant to cover the entrance hole during the actual public initiation, which took place at winter solstice when a great number of guests had arrived for a song feast (ID 1311).[17] Saajooq's "modern" version, however, postpones Ajijak's *saqqummerneq* because he is short of a sufficient number of helping spirits. The delay makes room for the addition of several ritual and mythic ideas about Moon. Ajijak encounters first the Northern Lights, then *Nalikkatteeq*, and finally Moon, who supplies him with the helping spirits he needs to become a great shaman. Also the prelude, resumed below, is couched in the framework of Moon: in childhood Ajijak and his older sister practice together as pupils. They train their muscles by bringing still bigger lumps of ice to the house

15. Kaarali's version has Ajijak return, get seated on the floor, blow the thong loose, and make it switch, hammering into the wall skins.

16. An interesting, if partly obscure, variant about an anonymous shaman, actually a pupil, taken down by Kaarali's wife, Johanne, points to winter games or rituals in still another way. Before a visit to the nasty ball-playing people or the figures of small people whose wrists are broken by either the pupil or his helping spirit (?), a visit to another spirit's house involves lines or thongs being fastened from the main to one of the side platforms. The pupil is caught in this snare and has his leg broken by the usual suspect in this type of story: his helping spirit's malevolent housemate. The reference may have been to the play with string figures. See p. 391 about the ban on this play with the return of the sun in Iglulik (Saladin d'Anglure 1990a: 104–5).

17. There is a correspondence with the newly fledged West Greenlandic shaman who obtained the walrus skull, the Northern Lights' ball, as a helping spirit during a séance shortly before the New Year. He then planned a follow-up by an *ilimmarneq* (P. Egede 1971: 44; 1939: 35). So, the ideal time for a *saqqummerneq* at winter solstice was not restricted to East Greenland.

(for drinking water), and the sister becomes the stronger of the two. She, however, neglects an old lamp in her charge. It catches fire, and Moon reacts not only by taking her soul but also by a punishing expedition to earth. He is successfully fought back by the famous Karraq/Uitsaleqanngitseq in a performance witnessed by the child, Ajijak. We shall turn to this in a moment, but it is interesting to realize the storytellers' differing intentions. Ajijak's *ilimmarneq* tales place in the early 19th century. Kukkujooq tells, in about 1960, how he made use of the story for his own benefit. Sometime between 1910 and 1932 Kaarali wrote down a complete ritual description divided by the two turning points of the year, summer solstice for the preparations and winter solstice for the actual *saqqummerneq*. The reason why Saajooq has the *saqqummerneq* postponed may be, as I shall return to later, that very few stories were transmitted about Ajijak's apprenticeship. Anyway, the postponement allows for the insertion of ideas about Moon and rituals connected with Moon. To one outstanding ritual event among the latter, I shall turn in the following.

Fighting Back Moon in Actual Ritual

Although Saajoq's description of the performance, the one of chasing away Moon as witnessed by Ajijak, is rather concise, a better choice for analysis is the oldest of the four versions. It was told during the Women's Boat Expedition by Angitinngivak,[18] who was closely related three generations back to Karraq/Uitsaleganngitseq, as well as to some other participants identified in the notes. The event takes place sometime in winter when Karraq, on a journey to Moon, has been warned that Moon shall arrive on a punitive visit if the women disregard their prescriptions.

In Angitinngivak's version, two old women have already broken the rules by talking about the men being away hunting. They live at Puilortuloq/Puulortuluk on the island of Kulusuk, where they show utter disbelief in Karraq's message mentioned above. Karraq, who lives at Tasiilaq on the mainland, gets angry. He visits Puilortuloq/Puulortuluk with another shaman from the Sermiligaaq fjord and takes the opportunity to perform a séance while all the adult men are away hunting. Moon portends his arrival by panting like a hurricane through Karraq's hair. Soon he arrives in person, in the entrance tunnel in his bearskin dress, and the women push out into the tunnel and throw themselves upon him with harsh blows. Moon clears out in a flash and settles on the nearby lookout, while Moon's escort, *Nilaarsik* (Vega), appears on an island in his water skin suit. When later both Moon and *Nilaarsik* have disappeared, a local shaman, Angiseq, enters the house and asks his wife to pack in a hurry. They leave, and the next day the oldest man of the house fixes a hammer and a lampstand above the entrance hole. In the evening they begin to stir. The hammer rocks and the lampstand falls onto the floor, where it spins. Everybody flees in terror to a settlement farther inside the fjord, where in the evening they hear Moon's dogs barking in the air and his giant "freshwater bear" growling underneath the ice. Returning the next day, the people see for themselves that the tunnel has collapsed, the roof is down, the platform is ruined, and the floor is a mess of littered bits

18. Angitinngivaq told his version to Holm in 1885 (Sonne 2005: ID 1343); Pitiga transmitted a shorter and less accurate one to Holm the same year (ID 1344); Rasmussen transmitted a somewhat bombastic and moralizing one in 1919 (ID 1353); and finally, Saajooq told the shorter, more mythic one to Jens Rosing in 1961 (ID 1675). Since Karraq/Uitsaleqangitseq acted as a shaman in the first half of the 1800s, Angitinngivak, aged about 55 in 1885, may have been an eyewitness himself (Holm 1888: 195; 1972: 145 (photo), 146; 1914: photo lacking). The reason for Moon's descent differs from one version to another.

and scraps. *Nilaarsik* did that, they agree. The next evening Moon is seen atop the lookout, attempting to break the house down with his long stick. At long last two of Karraq's helping spirits, a giant from a distant island, *Ipak* (*Inupak*), and an another islander, *Ikilerfik*, get Moon where they want him. The giant islander plainly asks him to stop, and when the other islander captures his spear, intending to break it to pieces, Moon finds himself hard up: "Shall the water [tide] never fall anymore? Must seals bear no young anymore since you want to break my spear?" Moon gets his spear back, takes off and disappears.

Analysis: Three shamans cooperated to get everything running: Karraq/Karrak/Uitsaleqanngitseq from Tasiilaq/Ammassalik, an anonymous shaman from the Sermiligaaq fjord, and local Angiseq of Puilortuloq at the island of Kulusuk. The eldest man of the household, who places the hammer and lampstand above the entrance, is a fourth fellow player, and no shaman. His role is decisive, though, because the sudden movements of hammer and spinning lampstand, which make the participant flee, portend the coming ruin of the (trembling) house, symbolizing the world in ritual terms. Local Angiseq most probably played the role of *Nilaarsik* (Vega). He left in a hurry with his wife at an early point, pretending that he sensed something brewing, and then returned in order to damage the deserted house. The Sermiligaaq shaman would fit the part of Moon, while Karraq acted in his own shamanic role, leading the women's defeat of the Moon figure in the tunnel. Producing the sounds of dog and polar bear outside at night was an easy job to be performed by either Angiseq or the anonymous shaman, while the final chasing away of Moon by the two helping spirits was either reported by Karraq or faintly observed through the windows when acted out by the two other shamans (or some pupils).

This final fight forcing Moon to beg for his own, and consequently everybody's, life recurs in all variants of the "obstinate hunter," an (extra)ordinary human man who neglects some particular rule set down by Moon. Consequently Moon arrives enraged, demanding that the culprit meet him out of doors for a single combat. Moon loses, saves his life by uttering the phrases about tide and reproduction, and then invites his match for a visit to the moon (e.g., Sonne 2005: ID 555, 752). The close connection between myth and the description of Karraq's performance using Moon as a frightening spirit is worth considering. Karraq may have staged the myth. Or he may have reproduced a traditional performance, or just expanded on an ordinary frightening spirit act.[19] It is impossible to tell, because the only local performance with which to compare it is a less impressive attempt made by Missuarniannga sometime before his baptism (in 1901). He presented a séance that had Moon's dog arrive. It was on the way, a rusty voice announced, and everybody fled to the next settlement. But on their return the following day, their house was untouched, just as they had left it (Sonne 2005: ID 1930). This was somewhat disappointing, it appears, in comparison with the great predecessor Karraq's/Uitsaleqanngitseq's wonderfully staged show in cooperation with several colleagues.

Missuarniannga also made an *ilimmarneq* (flight) at some full moon to Moon's house in heaven (Sonne 2005: ID 1812). However, the course of events is unusual and peculiar. Instead of

19. In essence, if on a smaller scale, the above performance did not differ from the frequent one of calling in a dangerous frightening spirit at the opening of a shaman's performance. The arriving spirit might make the audience panic and flee from the house, be it the deadly serious dog-headed Amoo, the baby-spirit crying *ungaa*, or the blubber-eating ghost (J. Rosing 1963: 182–83; Sonne 2005: ID 1109, 1194, 1195, 1674).

the confrontation with *Nalikkatteeq*, Missuarniannga and his helping spirits are to pass by dangerous dogs, including a watchdog like that of Sea Woman's, in front of the entrance and several others inside the tunnel. Contrary to his usual kind reception of guests from earth, Moon, like Sea Woman, is in a very angry mood, but is later appeased by the visitors' promise to clean his house. Like the dirt removed from Sea Woman for the release of sea mammals, the dirt of Moon's house transforms into animals, but not only land animals. Sea mammals are included. So, upon closer inspection, Missuarniannga's story reveals a mixing up of the two myths: one regarding the shaman's journey to Sea Woman, the other about a visit to Moon. To my understanding, the Christian bedeviling of Sea Woman's abode had by then made a visit to her realm a risky undertaking. And because Moon, like Sea Woman, punished breaks of taboo and could deliver game animals, a cleaning of his place had become a safer way out. In control of both sea and land animals, inviting no fight, and appeased by the mere promise of purification, Moon furthermore turns out to be a more favorable being to approach than Sea Woman. I take it that the message of a God forgiving sins in heaven has left its mark on this story.[20]

The Acculturative Fate of Moon and *Nalikkatteeq* in Oral Lore

The above mixture of stories is not the only example of the acculturative fate of Moon in Greenland. With Christian beliefs getting the upper hand, Moon and his consorts—dog, polar bear, and *Nalikkatteeq*—become butts of teasing fun. All the same, especially in East Greenland, Sea Woman fades away. Her origin myth holds its ground in South Greenland, and stories were still told in the 1960s of legendary West and South Greenlandic shamans fighting and cleaning her for "removing the ice." She seems never to have been visited by ordinary people, not even in their dreams about meetings with deceased relatives below. Moon, however, is visited by shamans and ordinary humans alike, the latter (the obstinate type) going to extremes in letting him down. The East Greenlandic variants tell about a hunter who commands his wife to ignore her taboos, which, due to her recurrent abortions, prevent her from mending his kayak and clothing. The offense makes Moon come down in a very bad temper. He challenges the hunter to a fight, but when ending up second best he invites the offender to pay him a visit. Moon tells the hunter how to get sledge dogs flying and warns him, to no avail, against *Nalikkatteeq*. The hunter has his entrails stolen by *Nalikkatteeq* and restored by Moon, who, when showing his guest the view of the earth through a tube, complains about people breaking taboos, which make his floor tiles rattle with an irritating noise. Unharmed, the hunter returns with this message to earth (Sonne 2005: ID 555, 752). The lonely Ilulissamiu (from Ilulissat at Disko Bay, W. Grl.) is not that lucky. He steels the catch of an *innersuaq* (pl. *innersuit*), forces it into fleeing, kills Moon's dog sent in punishment, and finally forces the descended Moon to flee.[21] He is neither invited nor taught any lesson by Moon, and dies within a year. This variant, written down about 1825, takes no liberties with Moon (ID 169), but the same cannot be said for Moravian Hendrik's variant about Manguaraq

20. Rasmussen took down the story in Danish in 1919. The storyteller was no doubt Kaarali Andreassen, who was baptized in 1899 and was a trained catechist who knew West Greenlandic. He was the son of Missuarniannga, baptized Andreas in 1901.

21. The reason why Moon acts on behalf of the *innersuaq* must be their connection to the light of the full moon, which made the light of the *innersuit* visible to the ordinary eye.

told some forty years later at Nuuk. He has exchanged the usual fight between the hero and Moon for a boasting competition in which the characters enumerate their earliest catches one by one. Through with the small birds, Manguaraq boasts about his first catfish. Moon hesitates. Then, embarrassed, he has to admit that the frightening sight of this fish baring its teeth above the gunwale made him flee to the other end of the boat and prevented him from ever trying to catch one. This very nice Moon takes Manguaraq along on his sledge. Absorbed in cozy conversation, they pass by *Nalikkatteeq*, who gets no chance to tempt Manguaraq into smiling. She[22] takes up pursuit but is violently whipped away, as she is again when she insistently enters Moon's house; he throws her out, flinging her dish after her. So, implicitly, contrary to her traditional bevior (Sonne 2005: ID 1676, 333, 1596, 616), she has no reason left for threatening to let heaven come down in case she does not get back her dish. Deeply offended, she stays away. Manguaraq is fed and entertained the usual way and shown how Moon, by sending down whittles of tusk, covers houses and land with snow (ID 1769). This fine snow, explains Jaakuaraq in his very similar version of about 1920, curbs people's thoughtless behavior (ID 341). How gentle!

A Southern version told by baptized Nicolai at Narsarmijit/Frederiksdal about 1860 was taken down in Danish by Ulrik Rosing, who intersperses his own mocking comments from an educated point of view (ID 1827). Fortunately, a more complete version was sent to Rasmussen by an anonymous recorder at a later, unknown date. The qualifications of the hero, rightly called Uteriitseq (W. Grl. Uteriitsoq), "the obstinate one," are a bit difficult to make out. He starts out an ordinary hunter who, upon concluding his visit, is named a shaman in embryo by Moon. The appointment, however, is given no cause such as a death and rebirth initiation by losing and getting back one's entrails. Nor can any consequences for the remaining part of the story be detected. In other words, the frame looks like an initiation but without recognizable consequences. More striking is the thread of the story, which takes every opportunity to mock Moon together with all his associates: his dog, *Nalikkatteeq*, the giant polar bear. It starts out the East Greenlandic way by Uteriitseq objecting to the taboos incessantly befalling his wife, whose newborn babies, one after another, die right after birth. He orders her to mend his kayak. Moon reacts by sending his dog, only for Uteriitseq to kill it. When in the subsequent fight with Moon Uteriitseq proves himself to be stronger, he forces stifled Moon to beg for its life the usual way: if Moon dies, light shall never return, the movements of the tide shall stop, and the seals bear no young. Never mind the light and tide, Uteriitseq frankly retorts, but gives in at the last threat. At this point the story takes a new turn. Uteriitseq is not invited by Moon; instead, Uteriitseq insists on visiting his defeated opponent. Moon refuses: "No! You will never be able to visit me as long as you remain living in your own body. Only the souls of the dead come to my place." Uteriitseq won't take no for an answer. Well then, Moon gives in, but be careful not to follow the sunny side of the mountain! Uteriitseq finds out (or knows from older versions) how to train his dogs for flying by throwing them, time and again, up into the air. It takes five days of training to take off. Naturally, he chooses the sunny side of the mountain. When ugly *Nalikkatteeq* enters the scene, she appears as a beautiful woman! Singing, dancing, and guffawing, she invites him to look into her crotch with plank bed and

22. *Nalikkatteeq* (literally "Big Crotch") is a woman with male genital symbols (see e.g., Rasmussen 1921–25, I: 92). One of my readers is convinced that *Nalikkatteeq* is a man. So was the minister Sandgreen. But Rasmussen, informed by Kaarali, did not think so (*ibid.*). *Nalikkatteeq*'s weapon is usually an *ulu*, but in his drawing Kaarali has provided her with a knife. As an *uaajeertoq* (*ooaayeertoq*) figure, a man disguised as a woman most probably played her part.

pendant. He does absolutely nothing in the way of smiling. Deeply scared after all, he attacks her by ruining both her dish and *ulu* with his whip handle. She bursts into tears and he leaves her crying. Inside the house of Moon, mythic time has passed with acculturative changes into a new standstill, in that Sister Sun, turned as pale as a white shadow, hardly can be seen when serving Uteriitseq a meal. She has grown old and slow, and Moon explains that this is the actual reason why she can hardly be seen in winter, when she sits down most of the time, grieving the suffering humans. As for Moon's way of calming down the thoughtless rule-breaking people on earth, his behavior is not dressed in discreet symbolism. He lets out some urine, a turbid fluid (semen; slushy snow). The following episode promises another visit, namely to the lower realm of death. Moon becomes absorbed by the view of his private distant hunting field, rich in seals and small whales at a coast with only a single house. "I want to go there," says Uteriitseq. "No, if you do, you shall turn old and feeble." "But I want to go!" Upon dispatching Uteriitseq, Moon hands him two tusks (Moon's less offensive material for making "snow"), saying, "Take these as a proof of your story. If you are a genuine shaman, you will know how to bring them home." Clever Uteriitseq hides them in his trousers, where, connoting phalli, they significantly belong. It takes Uteriitseq five years of traveling by *umiaq* to arrive with his wife and household to Moon's distant hunting field. The house is peopled with very humanlike beings, who suffer no privation except for the days when Moon is around, or *Nalikkatteeq* pays a visit, or the giant polar bear threatens them all. Only by remaining indoors do they feel fairly safe. The visiting Moon leaves them in peace, as he is visibly occupied outside with hunting at a *sassat.* Uteriitseq of course does not adapt to the people's timid behavior. He walks out to meet Moon on the ice. "You said I could not make it. But now I am here, and therefore I want part of your catch." Moon denies him such a part, as it will prevent him from taking off for heaven. Uteriitseq cuts and removes his half, to the expected effect: Moon cannot get off the ground. Skipping all further nonsense, Uteriitseq seizes Moon's gear, kills a narwhal, cuts it in half, offers one half to Moon, who then starts to rise, but not until people troop out for a carefree look, encouraged by Uteriitseq. It takes Moon five days to rise, just like it took Uteriitseq that length of time to train his dogs for his flight to Moon. *Nalikkatteeq* is not all that harmless this time, and staying indoors does not help the poor people. She enters with her roar of laughter, dancing and singing her frivolous invitation. Observant Uteriitseq becomes aware how people, having pulled down their trousers, shamelessly pick at their private parts in order not to smile. He bursts into laughter and calls to *Nalikkatteeq*: Come on! She comes close, and then he grabs and breaks her wrists, splits her dish, breaks the handle of her *ulu* and traps it in her armpit. Crying, *Nalikkatteeq* leaves the scene. The episode of fighting the giant polar bear does not vary from tradition: Uteriitseq lets himself be drawn inside the monster's body by its heavy inhale, works hard inside, and cuts his way out. The only rare element is the precaution taken against being scalded to death inside the hot stomach: allowing him to be bandaged in thongs from top to toe (*pooq* protection like that of *Uniagaq* and *Noonagikshown*). After his great feats Uteriitseq remains with his wife and household among the deeply grateful people for some years until, growing older, they get homesick. They travel for another six years and enjoy well-deserved leisure at their former settlement (Sonne 2005: ID 350).

The radicalism of this story is notable. Courageously, Uteriitseq fights down the "windmills" of both former taboos and frightening figures of ritual and myth with success and tickling humor. By his own will and persistence, Uteriitseq visits both above and far beyond the horizon in the *sassuma* (down there in front of you) direction, implicitly the underwater realm of death. No mention is made of Sea Woman, the *inua* usually fought in this environment. Instead Uteriitseq fights the three great visiting *inuat* from above and thus removes the inhabitants' plagues forever. Did he eliminate the plagues of Hell preached by the missionaries? Anyway, despite the prospect of a shortened and feeble life by going there, as also a certain death by visiting Moon, he visits both realms without loss of life or lifespan. Moon names him a prospective genuine shaman, but simultaneously guarantees him a quick aging in case he should visit below. Naturally Uteriitseq and his wife grow old with the years—they spend eleven years alone just traveling—but in no way do they become feeble. Nor would any (Greenlandic) shaman bring along his household.[23] He would travel accompanied by helping spirits and go swiftly, leave and return at the cries of the crow. Altogether the excursion to the realm beyond/below with its timid inhabitants is a novelty, as is the way in which Moon is turned—temporarily—into an ordinary human being. The trick is done by a forced "balanced exchange" of the catch from Moon's private game, which, in the variants told along the southwest coast, catalyzes the entire course of events. Uteriitseq cuts the narwhal caught by Moon into half lengthwise, the way two cooperating hunters share an animal. The impudence literally turns Moon into an earth-bound being. Not until he receives a half from another of his private narwhals, caught by Uteriitseq with Moon's own gear, is Moon reinvigorated for flying. But again, being mocked by the people who used to fear him, he, like the ordinary Uteriitseq, needs five days of training before he can take off. Uteriitseq has made Moon start all over again. A second break with timeless myth! Supposedly Moon, when he eventually returns to heaven (from his new moon visit, below), resumes his way of causing the tide, the light, and the reproduction of seals, but is bereaved of his license to punish. One senses an opposition to some authority. It may be the usual target, the colonists, unwilling to share or lend beyond balanced exchange at prices set by themselves. Simultaneously, however, the opposition is in line with a changed worldview. It annihilates the dread of traditional figures, however much the terrifying spirits used to make people feel "togetherness" and raise their sexual appetites. If this is a bit blasphemous for your taste, then perhaps take a second look at baptized Maratsi playing *Nalikkatteeq* and mumbling the Lord's Prayer against an advancing Doomsday.

By raising the question of Moon's unwillingness to share his animals with ordinary humans, the Uteriitseq version could be a belaboring of already acculturated versions like Moravian Hendrik's Manguaraq. So could a less detailed version of Uteriitseq told in 1904 by an immigrant Susanne, from Southeast Greenland. She twists this subject by having Moon offer Uteriitseq a single walrus caught from a swarm revealed in a pit below the threshold of his house. Refusing the offer, head-strong Uteriitseq catches first one, then a second walrus to bring home from the pit (Sonne 2005: ID 596). "The Lonely Ilulissamiu," the only version on record north of Sisimiut, may have been based on the Manguaraq type as well, reacting conservatively in accordance with the pre-Christian idea that only shamans had the "passport" for opposing and fighting Moon. The Lonely Ilulissamiu, Uteriitseq, and Manguaraq are all ordinary humans. The former is punished by death, the second comes out the winner, but the successful Manguaraq is placed in an extraordinary relationship with Moon. His name Manguaraq, "the little root," is derived from the name of his father, Mangorsuaq, "the big root," who was killed by Moon as punishment for having caught one of Moon's game animals. Manguaraq's

23. However, there are always exceptions. I must admit that a Nattilik shaman did bring an aged infertile wife along for his travel through the Other Worlds, including the realms of foreigners (Rasmussen 1931: 300ff, 391ff).

repetition of his father's transgression is explicitly said to be a matter of revenge (ID 341). So, retaliation, a human social ideal introduced by nobody, human or nonhuman, opens the way for this legalized attack on Moon. His authority has ebbed away, while *Nalikkatteeq* is left to mourn the loss of both her cause for removing the pillar upholding heaven and her tools for cutting out people's entrails.

Summary of New Year or Winter Festivals

On differing scales winter festivals were celebrated all over the Inuit/Yupiit area, greatly elaborate in the west, less impressive in the east. Masks and/or contortions by strings of the blackened face were most likely in use everywhere. They were prominent in the East Greenlandic *uaajeertut*, where individuals danced in representation of various mythic figures and animals. Obvious comparisons with the use of masks in Southwest Alaska have been attempted by Gessain, but his information on most *uaajeertut* masks is scant. The antiquity of the West Greenlandic *mitaartut* plays in disguise is another problem. I have left both questions unanswered. Christian mission meant an end to the *uaajeertut*, but masks are still cut and sold to tourists. Wife exchange was part of the festivals in both Arctic Canada and Greenland. It was led by disguised, authoritative shamans representing mythic figures in Canada but merely following certain rules of conduct and free choice in Greenland. The combination of teasing, tickling, sexual hints, and violence present in these masked games are prominent. They are dealt with in the sections on bogies in chapter 5.

Legend or history has it that the public initiation of the great East Greenlandic shamans took place at winter solstice. This could be no annual event, but the association of shamanic fame with the return of light is significant. Some went flying to the Northern Lights and/or Moon as described in a ritual myth showing great similarities with the Iglulik *ilimmarneq*. In East Greenland Moon was the punishing *inua*, sometimes staged by the shamans to descend and smash the house in company with another "eye on high," the star that measured time during the dark quarters of the moon. The ritual character of Moon and his companions seems to have offered a good cause for telling mocking variants about their loss of authority with the coming of Christianity.

Rituals of Spring, Summer, and Autumn

In most of Greenland the hard times of the year were the couple of months preceding the sealing in open waters of spring or, in East Greenland, at breathing holes in early spring. In West Greenlandic lore, the shaman's journey to Sea Woman was meant to remove the ice; in East Greenland the *inua* of precipitation, *Asiaq*, was appealed to. In the latter region Moon or the boulder might come down, threatening to smash the longhouse. I shall comment on the latter first, and thereafter discuss *Asiaq* and finally Sea Woman.

Aqajarormiorsiorpua and Moon

The aforementioned performance when the helping spirit *Equngasoq* warded off the smashing of the longhouse by *Aqajarormiorsiorpua* was beyond doubt an event of the spring melt; this was the time of stones to come down as also *Equngasoq*, a fulmar, was the sign of spring. The truth of the stories about this impressive deed cannot be ascertained. It was no annual event, nor that of chasing off the visiting Moon, which actually did take place once, maybe around New Year, maybe in spring. But the correspondence in myth of the two events is obvious.

Asiaq

East Greenlandic *Asiaq* appears confined to this exceptionally rainy and snowy part of Greenland, where a thick layer of snow covering the breathing holes at the end of a prolonged winter portends starvation. *Asiaq*, who dwells up there behind at the border of the inland ice with her baby-husband, is appealed to for sending rain. Since her husband does no hunting at all and she thus depends on human offerings of food, people used to open up their bags of blubber for *Asiaq* to help herself (Thalbitzer ed. 1933: 164). Both Ajak (Ajijak) and Naaja reputedly carried out travels to her abode (Sonne 2005: ID 1016, 1361, 1200, 2012). When *Asiaq* needs food for serving her guests (shaman and helping spirits), she helps herself from the stores below by means of a mitten fastened to a long rope. She takes vegetable food for the coastal dwarf, *mattak* (delicious whale skin) for the undershore *innersuaq*, and dried meat for the inland spirit (ID 1355). After the meal she shakes her husband's napkin with overwhelming effect (ID 1355, 1016, 1200, 1361, 1200).[24] She has the power to clap her husband from a baby into a big man and back at will. Rasmussen's variant offers a fine description of this husband, a very big man sitting on her platform with beautiful bracelets around his arms. Sympathetic listeners will know why *Asiaq*, embarrassed, hurries to make her husband small. Furthermore, there are two napkins, one filled with snow and refused by the intervening shaman, and another, the right one, for producing rain (ID 1355). Teemiartissaq's variant is interesting in sharpening the focus of the breathing hole sealing, because the heavy rain obviously melts not only snow but also the ice, and thus Moon is asked to bring about the necessary fine, thick cover of ice (ID 1016). In contrast, reopened waters were the desired outcome of the visit to Sea Woman in spring along the west coast.

I shall take the liberty of identifying the snow as semen in this context in line with Saladin d'Anglure's interpretation of another weather baby, *Naarssuk/Naarjuk*, who had a penis that could change size; this exposition makes perfect sense when applied to *Asiaq*'s baby-husband. In the state of a big man (provoking laughter) he would produce snow, and in that of a baby, melting rain (ID 1355).[25] The same variant tells how, long ago, *Asiaq* stole a crying baby from its babysitter, its blind grandmother. *Asiaq* had since the beginning of the world been constantly on the move in fruitless search of a husband, ugly as she was. She always saw to make fine weather for her traveling, but ever since she had stolen that baby and settled down, the weather had turned bad. One of two versions about Naaja's visit to *Asiaq* places her house in heaven next to that of the deceased humans. They are engaged in continuous drum dances, described at length and not unlikely inserted by the editor, Sandgreen, from his other readings. The other variant, most probably told by the same informant, does not mention the place of *Asiaq* and her husband. Regarding the couple's origin, this version puts shame on the boy's father, who, irritated by the intolerably crying baby, asks someone to take away

24. The variants do not agree on who is called *Asiaq*, the wife or the baby-husband. Because Teemiartissaq, an informant of Thalbitzer's, named the wife *Asiaq*, this became her identity in Thalbitzer (1926: 68–69; 1928: 414–15). In the same section Thalbitzer rightly corrects Rasmussen, who had *Asiaq* the wife do the urinating (Sonne 2005: ID 1355). Perhaps Kaarali, Rasmussen's storyteller, named the baby-husband *Asiaq*.

25. Robert-Lamblin (1996: 123) rejects the identification of the East Greenlandic with the Nattilik-Iglulik baby figure, arguing that *Asiaq* dominates her baby-husband but is subordinate to the dominant Moon, whereas *Naarjuk* or *Sila* are presented as the dominant *inua* in Arctic Canada. Such ahistorical and hierarchical positioning in an Inuit worldview appears artificial to me. I prefer correspondences in metaphors—body metaphors in particular—as analytical points of departure for treating the leaderless "egalitarian" cultures of the Eastern Inuit.

the boy. By this lack of empathy with his own son, he apparently invites the kidnapping *Asiaq*. Many years later, at Naaja's visit, the baby has grown into an old man with a beard, but he still cries *ungaa, ungaa* like a baby (Sonne 2005: ID 2012). Other examples of mixing up contrary descriptions are found, such as the features of *Asiaq* being upside down (ID 1355, 1016, 1200; see also Kaarali's drawing in Rasmussen (1921–25, I: between pp. 104 and 105). Sometimes the baby-husband may have a twisted mouth (Sonne 2005: ID 1016). All of these details may point to previous representations in masks among which both types are recognizable (Gessain 1984: fig. 16 with inverted features and, among the numerous twisted mouths, perhaps especially the bearded one fig. 52).

A third ritual, described only once, may have been performed at spring. This was hardly an annual event but more likely occurred in a situation of crisis. It has a shaman summon his "somersaulter," *napalariaq/napasariaq*, a sand hopper (*gammarus*) spirit. Heeding his call, it came rolling along, eventually growing into the size of a women's boat. This was a perilous performance that demanded a particular kind of house called *ajangalisaq* (propped up). It had solid rock for floor and rear wall, and was buttressed with long tent poles, some of which would stick out horizontally through the entrance to prevent the spirit from getting inside (J. Rosing 1963: 180–81; O. Rosing 1957–61, I: 83). So, like the other somersaulter of the "liminal" coast, raven, the sand hopper was also denied access to a human house. I see a likeness with the turning around of the earth at equinoxes in South Baffin Island, the times for a cleaning of the land by the raven figure, *Nunagiqsaqtuq*, but no somersault occurs in the only Greenlandic story on record about an actual use of a sand hopper. Only the time may be the same, the spring equinox, when a prolonged thick cover of snow hides the breathing holes. The sand hopper spirit belonged to the wife of the great shaman Naaja, who at this point in his career is said to have lacked any remedy for removing the snow. At that critical moment, a man weakened from hunger went to the lookout, came back, and told of a polar bear visible at a great distance. Immediately Naaja's wife performed and by *qilaneq* (divination method) made her sand hopper spirit push the bear within reach of the emaciated hunters. The following day the impression of a women's boat was seen in the snow right outside the entrance (Sonne 2005: ID 1200).[26] There is no mention of either an *ajangalisaq* or tent poles, but the sand hopper *umiaq* has left its trace out of doors and dragged the polar bear within reach. Thus all three shamanic rituals of keeping an *inua* or a spirit at bay, whether invited or not, *Aqajarormiorsiorpua*, Moon, and the somersaulting sand hopper, point to the riotous forces of spring, the most critical time of the year.

Visits to Sea Woman: *Sassuma Arnaa, Sedna/Nuliayuk, Nerrivik*, or *Ni-givik*

Shamans traveled to Sea Woman's abode in times of need in order to have the seabirds and mammals liberated or symbolically reborn from her house into this world. In a confrontation, the shaman usually had to fight the angry woman and then clean her of the dirt that accumulated from neglecting game-handling rules. The Greenlandic and Iglulik shaman combed her long, tangled hair; the Kitlinermiut shaman could call her up and let her enter his body, acting wildly, and have the other

---

26. *Kingugg*, the giant sand hopper at Nunivak Island, served the shaman Kapooran as a very strong helping spirit. Kapooran obtained protection against attacks by letting himself be devoured by the sand hopper. Any human's attempt to kill this being meant death by rebound (Sonne 1988a: 164–65, 337). Concerning the both lethal and reviving powers accorded such small creatures, see Laugrand and Oosten (2010; 2015: 113–47).

men fight her down; and the South Baffin Island shaman either traveled to her place below or made her arrive at some artificial breathing hole in the floor and had her killed with the same cleansing effect: a renewal of her life that reopened the way for the sea mammals.

The time for the Inuit shaman's confrontation with Sea Woman has been a longstanding issue. Did it take place annually at a fixed "calendric" point or accidentally, caused by a situation of crisis?

It would seem the shaman's visit to Sea Woman, or the latter being called up, formed the first part of the annual ceremony in December (or November). Among the Southeast Baffin Islanders her cleaning or killing (revival) was followed by various rituals, among which masked shamans led an exchange of wives (Boas 1964: 195–98; 1901–7: 138–42, 489–90). The latter invites comparison with other Inuit winter feasts combining mask rituals with wife exchange. The *tivajuut* of the Iglulik New Year and some Iñupiaq and Yup'ik ceremonies in Alaska show conspicuous parallels. They do not, however, include any confrontation with Sea Woman. Neither do the Greenlandic winter celebrations, *uaajeertut* (masked dancers), and the feasting at winter solstice described by Cranz. The West Greenlandic *mitaartut* (grimacing figures in disguise) of a probably more recent date does not refer to Sea Woman either. Nevertheless, the parallels made Inge Kleivan propose a common Inuit/Yupiit tradition of which the Greenlandic masked games, *uaajeertut* and *mitaartut*, were attenuated reminiscences of a Sea Woman cult in line with the one celebrated by the Southeast Baffin Islanders (Kleivan 1960). Merkur frankly turns away that hypothesis on the questionable grounds that the shamans' confrontation with Sea Woman among the Southeast Baffin Islanders occurs the day before the actual ceremony (Merkur 1991: 171). Blaisel and Oosten, who in their comparison of the South with the North Baffin Island winter ceremonies point to the lack of a Sea Woman ritual in the latter, do not consider the likelihood of Kleivan's hypothesis. They merely refer to her article and misconstrue some of the facts by reporting that the (West) Greenlandic mask festival took place only at situations of crisis (Blaisel & Oosten 1997). They are wrong because first, *mitaartut* still takes place annually around Christmas, at New Year, or at Epiphany,[27] but no evidence exists until the late colonial times, when Nordic mummeries at Epiphany had become mixed with Greenlandic traditions. The decisive point, however, is that they elicit no shaman's confrontation with Sea Woman, whereas a situation of crisis might bring about that latter performance at any point in winter and spring.[28] Actually, as Blaisel and Oosten (*ibid.*) make clear, only among the South Baffin Islanders did the ritual of the killing/cleaning of Sea Woman take place as an annual "calendric" event in Arctic Canada. And then, in a more recent publication, Laugrand and Oosten (2008b: 103) support the former conclusion by resolving any doubts. Although the Sea Woman ritual was an apparent annual event in the south, it was occasioned by a crisis—wild storms that time and again broke open the newly formed ice, preventing people from moving out on the ice for breathing-hole hunting (Boas 1964: 195; see also Rasmussen 1929: 123–24; 1932: 24ff). I fully agree.[29]

27. Google *mitaartut*.

28. *Mitaarneq* has more recently been spread to East Greenland, causing some of the old *uaajeerneq* customs to be revived.

29. The North Baffin Island winter feasts took place at winter solstice, dated by the stars, as did a particular one in South Baffin Island, in Frobisher Bay, some twenty-five years earlier than the first description by Boas from Cumberland Sound. Back in the 1860s, Hall was informed by the baptized Tookoolita about this celebration occurring in December close to our Christmas; that is, it was not provoked by autumnal storms, but coincided with the North

Turning to early colonial West Greenland, we shall compare the ritual myth of the shaman's travel to Sea Woman with the scant information on historical shamans who did go in actual life. In myth the journey takes place *in spring, in a situation of crisis*, when a prolonged winter ice cover prevents the migrating sea mammals and birds from returning into open sea. The shaman's journey starts inside the house, proceeds down through the earth to the shore, where the shaman is seen to pop up and then to descend through a crack in the ice at the shore. He/she follows the route beneath the sea, hampered by dangerous obstacles, the last one being to fight the furious woman and clean her of dirt. These acts give way to the storm needed to break the ice cover, which arrives the night or some days after the shaman's return.

The removal of the ice seems to be aimed for also *in actual, ritual practice.* Among the few West Greenlandic statements on that feat, one quotes a Southerner returning from his wintering at Disko Bay, who bragged that he had "removed the ice" prematurely up there; in Greenlandic terms, that would mean a successful visit to Sea Woman in early spring (P. Egede 1971: 12; 1939: 14). Poul Egede himself was asked to do the job; however, it was not implied that he would do the traveling but rather that he would procure the wind that could remove the ice. God alone can do that, he declared. Well, some of our shamans can as well, they replied. The date was May 1737, and the place Disko Bay (P. Egede 1971: 63; 1939: 47). In January 1741, or "out of season," Niels Egede, Poul's younger brother, received the news of a shaman who had fought Sea Woman, shared a meal of halibut with her, and made her promise to resume sending seal and fish. The text makes perfectly clear that this was a situation of crisis, in that the rough weather keeping seals and fish away was caused by the Jutlanders in Denmark, who had made fun of the blubber coming from Greenland the previous year (N. Egede 1971: 38; 1939: 150). So, not only to have the ice removed but also to calm down the unruly sea could be the purpose for visiting Sea Woman, in Greenland as in South Baffin Island. Nothing can be concluded, though, from a statement in October 1737, when Poul was told about a shaman from the far south, who *planned* to descend to Sea Woman by means of an extremely long line tied together by whatever pieces of thong were available. There are no other details, so we can only ask when, and why, in vain. And finally, both time and errand deviate, according to the talk Niels Egede had with a female shaman in June 1741, who had (recently?) shared a meal of halibut with Sea Woman. This shaman had two husbands, both shamans, and she was barren and so her errand was to have children. She called Sea Woman both Our Lord and the Spirit of the Earth, and instead of fighting Sea Woman she mitigated her anger by promising her all her future children.[30] Sea Woman accepted her offer, telling her to put her future newborn babies, mounting up to ten with the years, into the container for her lamp drippings and train every one of them to be shamans. Otherwise they would

---

Baffinland feasts. It did not involve a shaman's confrontation with Sedna. The participants prayed to Sedna, thought of Sedna, and asked her for a happy new year bringing a lot of game, in the same generous way the participants exchanged gifts on that day. Some days later, the new sun was welcomed by the extinction and rekindling of every lamp in the settlement (Hall 1864, I: 528). Perhaps the prelude of the Sedna cult, the cleaning or killing of the Sea Woman was a fairly recent development. Blaisel and Oosten similarly call attention to the lack of this ritual in another description of the winter ceremony in Frobisher Bay in about 1900 (1997: 36).

30. Perhaps the mission's identification of a particular helping spirit, *toornaarsuk*, with the Devil of Christianity—considered by Hans Egede to rule the lives of the Greenlanders (Sonne 1986b)—lies behind this unreasonable identification with an earth spirit feasting on deep-sea halibut. Some mixing up of figures did happen in both Greenlanders' and colonists' attempt to come to terms with religious matters (*ibid.*).

die (N. Egede 1971: 3–4; 1939: 129). In my view this female shaman's agenda is threefold in her confrontation with the missionizing Niels. He opposed shamanism as much as polygamy and she was undoubtedly ashamed of being childless. Hence she tried to cover up her shame by having Sea Woman in the authoritative figure of God legalize not only her marriage to two men but also the continuation of shamanism. Both this detailed errand and the halibut eating, however, invite further commentary. Male shamans would go to Moon for babies and afterwards have sex with the childless woman, just to make sure. But female shamans do not go to Moon on their own free will in any Greenlandic story or historical statement. In fact, the above statement is the only Greenlandic information on Sea Woman as a source of getting children. But why not, as long as in myth (Navagiaq, "the transmigrating soul"), the pregnancy of a wife was caused by the soul of a seal caught by her husband (e.g., Sonne 2005: ID 1089), and as long as a newborn baby did not differ from an animal as a live being until it was named (e.g., Kleivan & Sonne 1985).

Concerning halibut, extremely long fishing lines were needed to catch them. Halibut live at depths of up to 1500 meters (Muus et al. 1981: 149), and the line had to be made from the only suitable baleen, namely that of the Greenland right (bowhead) whale. As investigated and shown by Gulløv (1983: 254; 1997: 400–7), the Southerners in particular had become dependent on halibut during the Little Ice Age. They did not practice breathing-hole sealing, as they preferred fishing to sealing, and so halibut ensured their survival in winter; they also generally used halibut fat instead of blubber for their lamps. But because at that time the Greenland right whales were accessible only to the north (Sisimiut to Disko Bay), acquiring baleen was a main objective of the Southerners' trading and whaling expeditions to the north (*ibid.*). So, in the worldview of the early-18th-century Southerners, Sea Woman, who was accessible by means of such long lines and served her guests halibut, had become closely associated with the complex of acquiring baleen for deep-sea fishing on trading expeditions.

Judging by the West Greenlandic historical shamans visiting Sea Woman, we can conclude that the above statements point to *no* celebration of an annual feast. The first, about removal of the ice at an early date the preceding winter at Disko, reveals nothing about the cause, crisis, or possibly the shaman's own self-serving boasting. Crisis was certainly the cause in May 1737, when the sea ice created havoc and Poul Egede was attributed the abilities of a great shaman who could have set things right by procuring the necessary strong wind for the removal. The third statement, dated January 1741, was explicitly said to solve a crisis caused by Danes who did not know how to treat the seals with respect. But nothing can be concluded about the fourth incident, the planned descent to Sea Woman by the shaman with the long line, and as for the fifth female shaman, she acted solely in her own interests. All things considered, most often practice fits myth when caused by a crisis in sealing and fishing in spring and with the purpose of having the ice removed. But practice could also match the opposite goal of having the storms subdued by fighting Sea Woman, just as in the late-19th-century winter feasts of South Baffin Island.

Turning to East Greenland, some early-19th-century shamans were said to have visited Sea Woman in situations of crisis: Karraq (or Uitsaleqanngitseq, "The Blind One"), Naaja, and Aaqqii (Sonne 2005: ID 1354, 1196, 29). Since none of the courses of events differ from the ritual myth in any noticeable way, not much can be concluded. There are only two interesting peculiarities: one ends the Aaqqii variant, the other is an order given to Karraq by the giant woman to return once a year for a renewed cleaning (ID 1354). The Aaqqii version has the ice formed again in the end, due to one hunter's offense against the prohibition of catching only one seal the first day. In the West Greenland variants, only the offender is punished. On the other hand, to have Moon form a fine clean layer of ice for breathing-hole sealing was, as we know, the idea of warding off the crisis in spring according to Teemiartissaq's general version of the shaman's journey to *Asiaq* for rain. So, apparently the hunter who spoiled Aaqqii's efforts did right on East Greenlandic terms. The second peculiarity, the order given to Karraq, can be read as a confirmation of an annual ritual event. None of the younger generation of shamans, however, managed to carry out that order (Holm 1972: 121; 1914: left out). Well, Missuarniannga did, or so he confided to Thalbitzer (1910; 1930), but the mission's bedeviling of Sea Woman may have prevented others from openly admitting similar feats. The common statement that no contemporary shamans match those of bygone days was heard in Ammassalik as everywhere. Nevertheless, the only shaman of some great reputation at the time, Akku, actually could have managed, they say, had he not preferred a visit to the realm of death, which was otherwise passed by en route to Sea Woman. He had set a limit that he could never go beyond during any later attempt at visiting Sea Woman (Sonne 2005: ID 1324). Kukkujooq made that story his own as well (ID 1287). At this point in time the question of life after death, provoked by the mission and heard about at places of assembly, seems to have stolen the scene from Sea Woman, if she had ever had much of a say in humid East Greenland.

To my knowledge, no particular source refers to a historical Polar Inuit shaman's visit to *Nerrivik* (place of food) in Avanersuaq. Soqqaq, who went downwards through the earth during a performance observed by Freuchen (1935: 133–37), is a possible exception. Turning to myth, local tradition became enriched with stories brought along in about 1860 by the immigrants who were originally from Southeast Baffin Island (see Introduction). Consequently, the variants told by Amaunalik, the granddaughter of an immigrant, bear amazingly strong resemblances to those published by Boas in 1888 (Boas 1964; 1901–7; Sonne 1990). Both Amaunalik's origin myth of Sea Woman and the ritual myth of the shaman's visit to her abode are clearly recognizable, although her name is the Polar Inuit "Nerrivik" (place of food), an appellation that makes one look west to Tigara, North Alaska. Within this area of both the origin and also continuation of the Inuit Thule whaling culture, the objective of the shaman's journey in preparation of the whaling in spring was twofold: it served both to have a storm break up the ice and to secure ensuing calm waters. The fine and detailed description received by Rainey in 1940 shows a surprising similarity to the Eastern Inuit shaman's journey to Sea Woman, except the fixed time and occasion of the performance: each whaling *umelik* (leader) hired a shaman who acted on behalf of him, his crew, and their families:

> At the house of the patron *umelik* people were gathered to hear the *angatkok*'s story of his visit to the *itiviyai* and the *nuwunmiu.* According to his tale his [helping] spirit found in the underground house of the *itiviyai* a creature like a man, but with very long ears who heard everything said in Tigara ("a kind of radio operator," according to the interpreter). The *angatkok* sought the spirit of someone then living in Tigara, but because of the crowds of spirits moving about in the *itiviyai* igloo, that particular spirit could not be found. When he went down through the shore crack near the igloo of the *itiviyai,* that *angatkok* found the undersea whaling camp of these same people and saw that they had already killed a whale. At this camp below the ice there was a married couple, the man having a tail like a dog. This man told the *angatkok* that he was going

up into the air, the source of the weather, so that he could change the wind to the north. His wife, he said, was going down into the sea to the house of the *ni-gevi* (*a woman who feeds people*), and she would make the sea calm. When the *angatkok* went to the underground house of the *Nuwuk* people he found them so lazy that they sat in shavings and scraps of seals up to their chests. The *angatkok* cleaned up this place before returning to tell his tale. (Rainey 1947: 258, emphasis BS)

I shall take the liberty of interpreting this course of events through a Greenlandic frame of reference: in spirit the shaman seeks his helping spirit, the "radio operator" or oracle among the *itiviyai* (resembling the Greenlandic *innersuit* living beneath the foreshore), among whom he looks for some deceased human who was either stolen by these *innersuit* or paused there en route to the realm of death below. This person cannot be seen in their crowd and thus cannot be brought back to earth by the shaman. He leaves their underground house (inside a little mound close to the real lagoon) and takes the route downwards to their whaling camp underneath the shore through the crack in the ice next to their igloo. In their undershore camp he receives the glad tidings that the whales have already arrived and are being caught (like Greenlandic *innersuit*, the *itiviyai* appear to be excellent hunters at sea). A married couple among the *innersuit* in their whaling camp then agree to go: the dog-tailed man upwards to *Sila* for the northern wind to break up the sea ice, and his wife downwards to a figure called *Ni-givik* (phonological equivalent of *Nerrivik* [Sea Woman] of the Polar Inuit) to ask her to appease the unruly sea. The calmed sea permits the humans to hunt the whales arriving in the opened sea—i.e., the leads opened by the northern wind of the Bering Strait. The shaman finally visits the spirit people living below the tip (*nuuk*) of the tongue of Tigara (*nuwumiut*), who have no precise Greenlandic counterpart except that the mess of dirt and remnants needs cleaning in the same way as does the defiled Sea Woman. At Tigara the whales are to pass by this point of strong currents, whereas among the Eastern Inuit their passage is the tunnel river sending garbage into Sea Woman's house. Through her cleansing, this river is simultaneously cleaned and its course reversed (Sonne 2005: ID 1354, 1882).

Later, when comparing the stories of tide and the turning around or capsizing of the world among East Greenlanders, Baffin Islanders, and Northwest Coast Tlingit, we shall see in the Tigara case a similar balancing of the powers; in this case, the *Sila* storm from above and the calming *Ni-givik* winds from below serve as the procurement of beneficial hunting conditions.

Sea Woman and Whaling

Correspondences are evident across the Inuit Arctic between the shaman's journeys to the world of sea mammals for clearing the latter's access into This World. How these travels were ritually performed and imagined during the development of the Thule culture and later, no one can tell. But what strikes one by comparison is a close connection with whaling, not only at Tigara as memorized by Rainey's informants in 1940, but also in the 18th-century Disko Bay and Amerloq (near Sisimiut) of West Greenland. As stated above, both places attracted families from along a wide coastal stretch, including considerable numbers from the far south. For untold reasons Greenlandic variants of the *origin myth* of Sea Woman are scarce on record (Avanersuaq excepted). There are four, all told by Southerners, the oldest told to Poul Egede in October 1737 by some passersby at the whaling grounds, one to colonial manager Lytzen (1874) at Qaqortoq/Julianehåb in about 1870, one sent to Knud Rasmussen from the south in about 1900, and one collected by Mâliâraq Vebæk in the same region in 1965 (Sonne 2005: ID 547, 1882, 2070, 2304). If the persistence of this myth in the south seems due to the migrations to whaling in the north, this supposition is confirmed by the distribution of the Greenlandic variants of the *ritual myth* (the shaman's journey to Sea Woman). They are numerous, and in West Greenland the majority show a similar affinity to whaling. Among sixteen variants registered in Sonne (2005), the provenance of four is Disko Bay, one Sisimiut, five the far south (in need of baleen), two the Moravian congregation at Nuuk (of "southern" origin), three north of Upernavik (no whaling), one Ammassalik (stray dead whales washed ashore from Dutch whaling during the 17th century), and one uncertain. In further evidence, one of the southern variants has the shaman liberate not only ordinary seals but also a big "genuine Greenland (right) whale" not available in the south (Sonne 2005: ID 511), and the two "Moravian" variants of a story explicitly connect the ritual myth of the shaman's journey to Sea Woman in a southern locale with subsequent travel to the Amerloq (Sisimiut) whaling in the north (ID 340, 1445).

No whaling-based explanation can be offered for the Upernavik variants. Narwhal and beluga were hunted locally, and whaling was conducted by Scottish whalers in the 19th century, who added to their outcome by a lively trade with the Upernavimmiut. All of which amounts to the proposal that at Disko Bay and Sisimiut, the common interests of local people and wintering Southerners in getting access to whales and their baleen for deep-sea fishing may explain the particular importance they attributed to Sea Woman in myth. But concerning the question of why Southern shamans predominate among *actual* travelers to Sea Woman at the times of Poul and Niels Egede, several answers are possible. One could be the quickly growing reluctance among the local Greenlanders to be laughed at by the missionaries, whose authority was felt to be less oppressive by the migrating visitors from the south.

In Arctic Canada the importance of Sea Woman seems to have increased with Euro-American whaling from about 1840 to about 1910, as argued in my treatise on that subject (Sonne 1990). At that time I focused on myth alone, which in its shortest course relates how a marginalized girl was thrown into the sea and then had her fingers chopped off when she clung to the gunwale. She transformed into Sea Woman and her fingers became species of sea mammals. This mythic girl became identified with not only the Inuit mother of Indians and Qallunaat (the Whites) fathered by a dog ("Dog Husband") but also the girl who married fulmar, the true follower of the whalers, who caused that bird's actual extension into the Canadian Arctic (*ibid.*). In entering the mythic scene, fulmar brought about (fathered?) the sea mammals by raising a storm in pursuit of his wife, who had been fetched by her family. These identifications in myth of Sea Woman as the marginalized girl thrown into the sea with the girl who married a dog, and later with the girl who married a fulmar, can be explained by the cooperation in whaling between the whalers (Qallunaat) wintering in the Arctic and the Inuit, local and immigrating. In Greenland the whalers neither wintered nor employed Greenlanders to any noticeable extent. This explains in my view why no such identifications occurred in their variants of Sea Woman's origin myth.

The impact of the cooperation and trade with the whalers on ritual remains to be dealt with. I shall describe first the situation of exchange between the Inuit and whalers at the time and place of the Sedna feast described by Boas, and next discuss some possible impacts. Here, two very clear analyses made of the feast come in handy, and I have some comments to add.

In the conclusion of my thesis in the 1980s, I sided with contemporary Inuit anticolonial oppositions, probably strongly influenced by Flaherty's movie *Nanook of the North*, and deemed the whalers' intrusion fatal to the affected Canadian Inuit. Given the choice, they would have preferred to do without

(Sonne 1990). I was wrong. By and large the Inuit were grateful, as concluded by Eber, who traveled the entire whaling area in the 1980s doing interviews by showing people old photos: "For the moment there are still Inuit who recall the times 'when the whalers and Inuit worked together, helping each other out.'... 'We used to call the whalers the Arctic Postmen, because they brought many things'" (Eber 1989: xvi–xvii) Also, I might add, they literally were told to bring such things by their Inuit mother in the compound myth of their origin. "The whalers brought new equipment, new concepts, new attitudes, new delights... wage labour, new diseases, and new genes. The relationship between Inuk and whaler was close and intimate; it is a rare Inuk who has no whaler ancestor, said an interpreter who helped to collect the interviews" (xxii).[31]

In the 1880s, when overwhaling left few Greenland whales to be hunted in Cumberland Sound (Boas 1964: 60), trade and cooperation between the Inuit families and the Qallunaat continued. Attention was turned to seals, which boasted enormous populations in the sound. Trade for sealskins and seal blubber increased. In addition, the kitchen of the station at Kekerten, Cumberland Sound, received a share of every seal caught by the employed Inuit hunters. In return, on Saturdays the women "came into the house of the station, at the blowing of the horn, to receive their bread, coffee, syrup, and the precious tobacco" (59).

So this was the situation when the so-called Sedna cult, the cult of Sea Woman, took place at the Qeqerten/Kekerten station in 1883. Boas, who published a detailed description (1964: 194–98), did not himself observe the course of events. He spent the time reading three books, as he noted in his diary, but in the end he took part in the Qallunaat throwing of trinkets (pearls in his case) for the Inuit men to scramble for (Laugrand & Oosten 2002b: 207; Müller-Wille 1998: 137). Boas left this event out of his description, along with some visits by the Inuit to the houses of both Captain Mutch and the cooper of the station. Blaisel and Oosten did the same in their ingenious analysis of this ritual description published in 1997, because it appeared the same year as Müller-Wille's publication of Boas's diaries. Their analysis is centered on exchanges: the Inuit with one another, with their deceased relatives, with game, and with the animals' mother, Sedna, to whom the entire ceremony was dedicated. At the very beginning she was confronted, killed, and then revived by the shamans. The masked shamans directing the subsequent ritual exchange of wives were her representatives; the resulting children were said to be "children of Sea Woman." So were in myth, I shall add, the Qallunaat. And since the issue concerns exchanges, I miss at least some comment on exchanges with the Whites in the analysis. They were part of the Inuit families as biological fathers and obviously recognized as meat-sharing partners by the share they regularly received. For instance, Eber's chief informant about Kekerten, Leah Nutaraq, was the daughter of the cooper, Tom, employed at the station around 1900 (Eber 1989: 8, 12). Blaisel and Oosten do raise the question of naming the children fathered by the Whites. Did they receive the names of Inuit ancestors as did any "genuine" Inuit baby (Blaisel & Oosten 1997)? They offer no answer, but Leah Nutaraq apparently did receive an Inuit name, in addition to the Western Leah. Another question could be: Did this very offspring of mixed descent, young, adolescent, or adult in 1883, for example, participate in the Sedna ceremony's drinking rite of

31. Both Ross and Boas (1975) testify to the "perfect revolution in the trade between the Eskimo tribes... that the constant contact between the whalers and Eskimo brought about" (Boas 1964: 60). Trading opportunities were the main attraction directing the intense mobility of the Inuit (Boas 1964: 59ff; Ross 1975).

self-identification by name and birthplace? I suppose so, since in this ritual "everybody participated, beginning with the oldest man, next the oldest woman . . . and then all the others do the same down to young children who are represented by their mothers. Only the parents of children born during the last year are forbidden to partake in this ceremony" (Boas 1964: 197). According to the compound myth combining the origin of Sea Woman with both "Dog Husband" and "Fulmar Husband," the dog fathered the Whites whereas the fulmar, alias the whalers, fathered the sea mammals. All were the children of Sedna, as were the Inuit themselves in the youngest variant on record (Sonne 1990). Which leads to still other questions: Did the Whites at the station participate in the entire ceremony, as fathers and/or sharing relatives? They did participate as witnesses at the very least, as it turns out in Boas's Appendix, where he attributes the information received on the ceremony celebrated in 1886 at Umanaqtuaq, Cumberland Sound, to the whalers: "The witnesses of this festival describe it exactly the same way as I described it above. . . . According to the description of the whalers . . ." (Boas 1964: 261, note 6) At a minimum, then, it is safe to assume that the children fathered by the Whites—children of Sedna—became legalized as genuine Inuit in the course of the cultic events.[32]

Returning to Greenland, no compound myth identifies the mother of sea mammals with the mother of the Qallunaat, because as argued above, the whalers did not overwinter, nor did they employ the Greenlanders to any significant degree. Among the versions of "Dog Husband" one has the Inuit mother ask the Qallunaat to return with nice things (commodities). Indeed, trade was brisk with the whalers, predominantly Dutch in the 18th century along the west coast including Disko Bay, and Scottish in the 19th century farther north. Sexual relations occurred as well. Obviously husbands and fathers, like Inuit and Yupiit everywhere, initiated trade relations by asking their wives and daughters to visit the ships. Memories of 19th-century contacts with Scottish whalers in the Upernavik district evoke lively trade, visits to the vessels by the women, caretaking of shipwrecked whalers, and the names of some Upernavimmiut who acquired English at a fairly high level (Sonne 2005: ID 1951, 1953; search Hans Lynge hvalfanger*; Marteeraq hvalfanger*). Older stories of the west coast farther south tell of long-lasting friendships between individual Greenlandic hunters and captains returning annually for trade (ID 212, 1739, 1765, 1797). See, for instance, the previously mentioned humorous story about a girl in love with a captain. She overslept on the very day of the ship's departure due to excessive love-making (ID 78). Others tell of Qallunaat being unsuccessful in their attempts to rob crafty Greenlanders (based on actual events that happened long before), and they delight in made-up stories like Pukitsulik, about a Greenlander who visits a Dutch vessel with a fascinating pendulum clock, surprising mirrors, and, in the end, a cross-eyed sailor missing his mark. This mark is Pukitsulik, caught, tied up, and hoisted in the top of the mast. Apparently invulnerable and thus a great shaman, Pukitsulik leaves the vessel in his kayak, overloaded with gifts. His nose alone is abovewater (ID 517, 545, 1774).[33] In contrast to the whalers, the Danish (including

32. As commented on by Morrow (pers. comm.): Whether or not these Inuit were delighted with absolutely all aspects of the relationship with whalers at this time period, they were certainly dealing with a lot of changes and novelties. And it is the Inuit way to use kinship/naming as the tools to view, explain, define, and shape social relations and unprecedented encounters. The Sedna myth and ritual would seem to form an ideal core for all that.

33. A comprehensive analysis of Greenlandic stories about the European whalers would be most rewarding, and I regret having to leave it out here. *Pukitsulik* means "with *pukitsut*, shoes" in the shape of a Dutch vessel. Its crew or inmates, *-miut*, are *Pukitsumiut*, Dutchmen.

Norwegian) colonists represented another crux, the alleged extinction by the Greenlanders of the Norse (about 1450).[34] Consequently the Norse came to represent the Qallunaat in the earliest variant on record of "Dog Husband." But, as stated above, no compound course of events identified the Inuit mother of the Qallunaat with Sea Woman, the "mother" of sea mammals. The Norse "problem" is dealt with later in reference to origin myths.

Other Possible Ritual Figures of the Deep Sea

Dealing with the variants of Kivioq who traveled to Akilineq, we met with *Unneraarsuk*, who was closely associated with the tide as both a bogey and a receiver of fresh drinking water during performances in return for sending seals. Other beings of the deep or distant sea with the ability to attract sea mammals may similarly have been summoned or rounded up as helping spirits. Relying on stories alone, one big worm is caught by a mythic childless, infertile Southerner. While he paddles far beyond the skerries, he obtains a wormlike creature in order to complete the fertility effect of an old fisherman, whom he has asked his wife to seduce. Pulling out the worm from the bottom of his kayak, he whips his wife's naked back. Consequently, the son, when born, develops into an unsurpassed hunter. He attracts sea mammals like a magnet from his very start as a small kayaker, and when grown, he brings in walrus and even a bowhead whale up north at Amerloq (close to Sisimiut). When harpooned, the big animal, instead of fleeing to the open sea, heads toward the shore. For obvious reasons this hero is called Qujaavaarsuk ("welcomed with thanks"). Mission accomplished, the worm disappears from the story. It is not asked for further contact nor is it needed for repeated invigorations of sealing capacities, and so no lasting relationship is established (Sonne 2005: ID 258, 1445). In a younger version, the fertility being is named *Qungussutariaq*, "the smiling one." According to Rink this being is a bogey who scares noisy children (1866–71: 189); that is, it is similar to *Unneraarsuk*.[35] Aqajak, who told a variant about *Qungussutariaq* as a fertility being in 1902, dates his variant back in time beyond Rink, to the period of transition when most Greenlanders around were already baptized. The tone is humorous, even ironic, and *Qungussutariaq* is explicitly said to be not all that dangerous. The infertile hunter's son who gained powers from *Qungussutariaq* is called *Usuusooq* ("big penis"). He reveals the abilities of a shaman and owns a *serrat* (spell) for stilling the storm—for a short while. The subsequent storm will blow with increased force. Nevertheless, once caught in a storm out at sea, *Usuusooq*'s repeated singing of the *serrat* and some simultaneous birthlike rituals performed by his parents at home save his life (Sonne 2005: ID 1613).[36] Similarly associated with fertility in another story, *Qungussutariaq* reveals in person the reason why the wife of the hero, Qivaaqiarsuk (analyzed in chapter 5), remains childless (ID 69). Smiling *Qungussutariaq* of course invites others to smile, but, like *Nalikkatteeq*, he tends to react dangerously to a smile in return; the farther back in history this occurs, the worse the situation. In about 1900, Aqajak, as we know, deemed him harmless. Not so for Kristian, who around 1860 (the same time as Rink), makes *Qungussutariaq* the helping spirit of the historical shaman Imaneq. Imaneq was cut up by this helping spirit due to his haughty manner and a break of taboo; this led to Imaneq's baptism in 1768. The

34. Norway was part of Denmark until 1814.
35. Bogies are dealt with in depth in chapter 5 on *pooq*.
36. An in-depth analysis of this late story of sexual allusions would take us far beyond our present scope.

cutting up was done in a particular way: body and kayak were first sliced lengthwise and then dismembered. Reassembled and steered by his deceased grandparents, emerging from below, Imaneq returns to shore, where people know the ritual for revival. He then receives recurrent revelations of light from heaven until he eventually decides on baptism (ID 506; see illustrations on the cover and endsheets). Closer to "tradition" in our relative chronology, Aadaarutaa (Southeast Greenland) knew the dangers of encounters with the smiling merman from personal experience as a shaman. He calls the figure *kittormoortoq/killormoortoq*, "the contrary or awkward one." He identifies it as an *innersuaq*, and has it emerge with a big smile amongst several ice bubbles. Due to some obscure question, Aadaarutaa invokes the anger of the spirit, which reacts by paralyzing his arms. He needs the speed of two of his strongest helping spirits to return home (ID 971). Like Aqajak, however, the acculturated Jens Kreutzmann (W. Greenland) presents the figure as a benign person of the sea. In need of a foxtail, it emerges next to a kayaking shaman, who happens to be in possession of such a tail. The latter is asked all sorts of questions about his hunting gear. Suddenly the figure, upon hearing the wrong term for some lashings, falls backwards into the sea, calling out, "*Qilaavakka* (my lashings)!" (ID 226) The gift of foxtail evokes a ritual offer, but of uncertain meaning. Similarly, neither this nor any other story solves the riddle of the words uttered by Kreutzmann's shaman, nor of the fatal words uttered by Aadaarutaa. They may, I think, point to some former ritual act or play, all the more so because dangerous laughter-provoking ritual figures like *Nalikkatteeq* are common in Inuit and Yupiit ritual and myth. To take one obvious mythic example, the giant merman of some Canadian Inuit has a striking resemblance to *Qungussutariaq* as a phallic being of the deep sea. Laughed at when harpooning his own distant penis that he takes for a beluga, he falls backwards, causing a tsunami to flood the land (Rasmussen 1931: 153; Saladin d'Anglure 1986: 73). *Qungussutariaq* similarly falls backwards at hearing the wrong term for lashings. Although *Qungussutariaq* was already losing relevance by this point, this deep-sea being remained useful for acculturative purposes in mid-1800s West Greenland. This will be demonstrated in chapter 5 on the polysemous *pooq*, where the possible reminiscences of ritual plays are taken up again. Later, in about 1920, when the storyteller Jaakuaraq takes the liberty of making fun of traditional figures, no trace of ritual speech is left. In his variant of "Imaneq," even the smile has disappeared, in that the serious look of the reproaching executor makes its cheeks hang down as if they were hitched (ID 470).

Moving In

No ritual on record is connected to moving out of the houses into tents in spring, whereas during the return at freeze-up in September, when old houses were repaired and new ones built, an East Greenlandic ritual of moving in took place. It was supposed:

> [T]o protect it for the winter against evil magic, sickness, bad hunting and all kinds of adversity by saying, slowly, the following *serrat* (spell) [by whom?]:
>
> *Iaa-ijaa*
> *What is it that would pursue me?*
> *Ijaa-ijaa*
> *A misfortune would pursue me!*
> *Misfortune, death and sickness would pursue me!*

Ijaa-ijaa
Look here, look here, look here!
I have covered up my face
And put over it a mask!
Ijaa-ijaa
What is it that would pursue me?
Misfortune, death and sickness would pursue me.
Look here, look here!
I have covered up my molars
And use them as arms!
Misfortune turns its back on me!
Ijaa-ijaa.

This was recited slowly and with great stress on every single word. It was concluded in the ordinary voice as follows:

"You always go away! Then go!"

on saying which one had to stand out in the open air with an amulet.[37]

This *serrat* (spell) was to be pronounced while standing on the roof of the house, whereafter the passage-way was blessed with the following *serrat*:

Ijaa-ijaa
Just look, a torch!
Ijaa-ijaa
A torch up here!
A torch up here!
Ijaa-ijaa

and, this having been said with emphasis on every word, one then had to repeat in one's ordinary voice:

ukuuko—ukuuko—ukuuko!
Those there—those there—those there!
walking round the house repeating these words all the time.
(Rasmussen 1938: 177–78; 1921–25, I: 62–63 [in Danish]; 1979: No. 325 [in Danish])

The effects of the first formula uttered while holding an amulet in one's hand on top of the roof needs no explanation, except for the way the molars are used as arms.[38] Some identification would also be welcome concerning the torch (representing the moon?) and of the "those there." But the mask is interesting. It points to a use of masks not mentioned in any other source: a mask representing some spirit suitable for keeping all sorts of misfortunes at bay. The conjecture that this moving ritual coincided in time with the autumnal equinox cannot be proved.

37. The translation into Danish has "swinging an amulet in the air."
38. It is unclear if this refers to weapons or limbs, though the translation into Danish has "arms"—i.e., limbs.

To conclude: the rituals of spring were performed by shamans, irregularly, and caused by crises. They differed in substance by ecological conditions: snow covering the breathing holes in East Greenland and a prolonged layer of ice in West Greenland. The East Greenland *inua* of precipitation, *Asiaq*, was offered food and sometimes (in myth alone?) visited by a shaman in order to make her produce rain by shaking her baby-husband's diaper. By his epithets of bad weather and phallic connotations, he bears strong resemblance to the giant baby *Naarjuk* of the Canadian Inuit. In West Greenland the idea of the shaman's fight with and cleaning of Sea Woman was to have the ice cover removed by a strong wind, whereas the Southeast Baffin Islanders sought the opposite goal, to calm the storms and leave the ice cover unbroken. Like the East Greenlanders they were dependent on breathing-hole sealing, that is, in November, not in spring. An actual majority of Southern myths and statements about Sea Woman in addition to some from Disko Bay may point to a relation between this figure and whaling. The Southerners used to go north to about Sisimiut and the Disko Bay for whaling in order to secure the baleen necessary for making long lines. They were dependent on the fat halibut, a deep-sea fish, for food, heat, and light. In Arctic Canada (as argued in Sonne 1990) Sea Woman became intimately connected with whaling with the advent and wintering of Euro-American whalers in the latter half of the 19th century. Originally the mother of sea mammals, she became in myth identified with the mother of the Whites. On their part they both cooperated with the Inuit and fathered many a baby of mixed descent. During the winter feast, during which the exchange of wives was said to produce the children of Sea Woman, these babies may have become legalized by the naming ritual of the same feast. No such mix of myths occurred in Greenland because, as I argue, the whalers always left in autumn and made less use of Greenlandic labor. Another connection of whaling with a figure resembling Sea Woman is seen in the whale cult performed at Tigara in spring. The shaman descends into the sea and has a married couple of submarine spirits do the job of procuring the right winds. The husband (with a dog's tail) rises to *Silap Inua* for the northern wind to break up the ice. His wife descends and visits *Ni-givik*, "the place of food," for her to calm down the ensuing waves. *Silap Inua*/*Ellam Yua* is a pan-Inuit/Yupiit being, whereas *Ni-givik* apparently had her phonological equivalent, *Nerrivik*, the Sea Woman among the Polar Inuit.

Life Cycle Rites of Transition

The Multitude of Taboos

Indeed, to anyone familiar with the multitude of rules that used to control Inuit and Yupiit life crises there is little new to consider about the very similar ones of pre-Christian Greenland. In essence they do not differ in their predominant focus on individual birth (and abortion), menstruation, "ritual firsts," the death of a relative, and the life-renewing rites of individual animals (Kleivan & Sonne 1985; Søby 1969/70). Individuality reigned in puberty rites. No age groups were extant, nor did a common feasting of the slain animals like that of the Yup'ik Bladder Feast take place.

Theories have flourished around the countless taboos impeding and sometimes endangering the lives of the Inuit in Canada and Greenland, where few ceremonies steal the scene as in the more affluent parts of Alaska (rich in whales and/or salmons). Weyer (1932) saw their cause in the fear of ghosts. Balikci (1970), who filmed the Nattilingmiut traditions, considered the taboos the outcome of the perilous life in a hostile environment, which gave rise to fear, wicked human deeds, and notions of a multitude of evil beings. Fienup-Riordan, an expert on Southwest Alaska, focuses on the goals of pre- and proscriptions, namely to set and open boundaries between humans and nonhumans. The idea was to prepare the path for game to arrive and to keep in check any nonhuman guest, whether unwelcomed or invited to the ceremonies (Fienup-Riordan 1994). David Riches (1994), looking to both Fienup-Riordan (1983) and Balikci (1970), applies a deductive model in an attempt to arrive at a reasonable understanding of the multitude and diversity of the often fatal rules (taboos) set by shamans and laypeople in interaction. His focus is on the premodern Canadian Inuit, where the diversity in rules between the groups around 1900 points to the continuous making of fresh ones. Riches compares this ongoing process to the similar one in Barth's *Cosmology in the Making* and defines as the goal of the shaman to augment power by succeeding in his "profession"; for laypeople, the aim is to acquire health, a happy life, etc. Failures on part of the shaman result in new rules fitting the situation, which are legalized by the lay audience during the process of "public confessions." The social basis of the deductive model is the "communitas" of small-scale societies combined with the cosmological or religious notion that any catch depends on the animal's willingness to get caught. This leads to the egalitarian view that no hunter surpasses anybody else due to his excellence in hunting, because ultimately it depends on the attitude of the animal.[39] Rules of sharing see to economic equalization, but the shaman is nevertheless recognized as the specialist, the only one with access to the knowledge to be obtained in and from the Other World (Riches 1994). Testing this theory in a Greenlandic frame of reference would be of little use because information is scarce. Furthermore, as will be dealt with later, the dividing line between shaman and layperson in regard to rule setting was far from sharp in actual life.

Birth, Puberty, and Death

The tripartite phases proposed by van Gennep as generally constituting rites of transition were fulfilled insofar as the separation and isolation of the person under prescriptions were carried out within the symbolic analogies of body, clothing, and house. Unlike in Arctic Canada, in Greenland no separate hut was required for either first menstruation or birth. At puberty both girls and boys started to wear breeches (*naatsit*) indoors, the boy for no stated reason, and the girl at her first menstruation, after which she put up her hair in a topknot, the sign of a safe adult woman. At any later menstruation, at the birth of a child, and the death of a close blood relative, she would signal her perilous state by loosening her hair—perilous, that is, to human relations with game. Menstruation, birth, abortion, and death were the main occasions for warning the hunters to keep a distance until the young girl or woman, "reborn," had her topknot redone. At births the inhabitants of the longhouse were sent outdoors through the entrance tunnel in analogy with the baby being born through its difficult passage into the world. Removable objects were brought outdoors in time in order to escape defilement and being discarded, because a stillbirth was an invariable possibility. Any death meant severe prescriptions for those who had to touch the dead body. Only close kin (blood relatives), including both parents at the death of a child, were to observe strict prescriptions in isolation, which lasted three days in East Greenland and five in West Greenland and Avanersuaq. Strict isolation meant

39. Riches of course is aware of the following an able hunter was prone to acquire.

staying indoors and remaining on the common platform, but either prostrated or sitting facing the back wall, fully dressed, hood drawn up, silent, being fed by others, and doing absolutely nothing. Using the East Greenlandic way of mourning a deceased child as the better-described example, the mother's movements remained restricted for a year, while the father's immobility was shortened by gradual environmental reintegration led by an elder pronouncing the appropriate *serratit* (spells). Both parents washed the entire body after the three days, when the husband was reinitiated behind the house to the land. After a month, at which point his wife cleaned her body a second time, he was reinitiated to the sea but restricted to remain along the coast and, finally, a third time, to go *avamut*, outwards, to the deep sea. His first catch was fetched by cohabitants at the shore and like a *pernarneq*, the "first catch" of a young man, everybody had a share except the hunter himself.

Prescriptions were harder and of longer duration after a death than after a birth or first menstruation; but altogether they were harder on women than men. During a whole year the mother was to wail morning and night, and she was hampered in both movements and talking, in eating varied food, and joining games and common merrymaking. When at the end of the period she had washed her entire body and dressed in new clothes, the eldest member of the household announced her reintegration and, if a widow, her liberty to remarry: "*Tassa una arnaq nutaanngorpoq*: This woman has become new" (C. Rosing 1946: 89–96; Rasmussen 1938: 188; 1921–25, I: 42–44; Victor & Robert-Lamblin 1989–93, II: 326–34). Her counterpart in myth and ritual is Sea Woman, buried in dirt with tangled hair and furious when visited by the shaman, but calmed down when cleaned and her topknot redone. Grateful, she had seabirds and animals liberated for a fresh life in the sea of This World (e.g., Sonne 2005: ID 29; 1975; Kleivan & Sonne 1985: 27). Nevertheless, the earthly woman naturally felt sick not only during but also for a long time after the year of restrictions (C. Rosing 1946). Considering numerous miscarriages, stillborn babies, and the high rate of mortality among small children, it was no wonder that the women took to baptism with gratitude. Released from taboos, the lives of women in particular became lightened.

Naming and "Ritual Firsts"

On the more pleasant side of the rules, the naming of a child after one or more deceased relatives was decisive in turning the nonhuman baby into a real human, that is, into a social being. Naming, to which I shall return in relevant contexts later, was to be done right after birth by the mother or midwife. By and by "ritual firsts" like the first tooth, first step, new clothing, etc. were happy events celebrated by feasts of varying dimensions, with the *pernarneq* of a young man's first catch ranking the highest. Social recognition was a must. Spirits were heightened by some older relative who, at the moment the returning kayaker towing his first booty was spotted, performed a funny dance of welcome, sometimes in rags, on the shore (Jensen 1968). Every member of the settlement was supposed to take part in the feasting of ritual firsts, no matter how apparently small the occasion and the servings of food. At a young man's *pernarneq* they were obliged to eat and loudly appreciate the taste of his first catch (Dalager 1915: 4), as well as from less significant edible "firsts" like a handful of berries symbolically said to be the *pernarneq* of a baby girl (Søby 1983). Søby has called praiseworthy attention to *symbolic* celebrations of "firsts." These are claimed by the parents to have been achieved by their babies and small children. Coincidence could decide the occasion, such as Nukaaraq's first impressive catch of a big narwhal having a fetus. Communal eating of the *mattak* followed, with servings of coffee by his parents, after which people were invited to another *pernarneq* in the neighboring tent of a young married couple. There everyone ate a tiny bit and appreciated the taste of the fetus placed on the floor, said to be the *pernarneq* of the couple's one-year-old, Simon (*ibid.*). The fetus belonged to the world of children, I suppose, not only by its comparable stage in development, but also because fetuses were given to children as toys like any other adult thing produced in miniature for children to play with.[40] A deliberate creation of a symbolic *pernarneq* could even be effected by, for example, bringing the clothes of a young son along on a hunt and attributing the catch to the boy (*ibid.*). Similarly, an East Greenlandic father could serve people a symbolic *pernarneq* in case his newborn son had received an *ukutsuk*, a seal's snout, as a protective amulet against *tupilaks* (Rasmussen 1938: 182). In any case, the subsequent feasting—meaning social recognition—made the symbolism come true. On the other side, the prestige gained from such celebrations might create jealousy or disdain, as I happened to witness when living in a small settlement with a family not related to any other family of the place. "NN is really getting high and mighty," my hosts chuckled, when NN had celebrated first some big catch of his own and then his young son's first shot with a rifle. The shot possibly wounded the seal, subsequently killed by NN. Another aspect of *pernarneq* concerns the child's relation to the animals, berries, or other edibles, in that neither boy nor girl were permitted a taste of their *pernarneq*. With regard to the first catch of a seal, the avoidance was said to establish a close relation between the boy and this particular seal, which hereafter would return to him personally throughout his hunting life. In support, or in the sense of a consecration, the communal welcome and appreciation of the tasty meat were meant to please the animal and thus further its desire to return (Dalager 1915; B. Jensen 1963).

Besides symbolic *pernarneq*, an analysis made by Michèle Therrien highlights a particular kind of "firsts." She considers all well-known life-cycle and seasonal "firsts" together with the initiation of shamans and fortuitous supernatural experiences by ordinary people. The latter were considered beneficial, and all three kinds move the individual on from one stage to a new one in relation to the religious and social world. In order to show the importance the Inuit attribute to "firsts," Therrien further lets us into the impressive number of suffixes that mean "to do something for the first time" in a multitude of contexts. "Firsts" occur to everybody as a series of continuous movement throughout life (Therrien 1996: 22–41). This latter part of the analysis could be applied also to Greenland, but not by me at this time. But I would like to contest the meaning attached to misfortunes, whether cured or not. Fitting Therrien's thesis are first the following: a small child who revealed an unusual experience to a parent could be told to keep it secret, because it was a sign that the child was attractive to spirits and might become a shaman (e.g., Sonne 2005: ID 1152). Similarly, apprentices were asked to notice anything unusual happening in nature and to keep silent until initiation. Otherwise their future helping spirits would terminate the agreement. Contrary examples concern unusual experiences heralding death (ID 911) and others that did harm until they were fully revealed and/or treated. Here sorcery could be implied, as in the case of Angajulleq. His quid had been stolen by a woman who later appeared to him in the figure of a paralyzing caribou. Baptized, he mumbled the first parts of "Our Father" twice, when eventually he remembered the complete prayer and got through the

40. Nothing is said about the implicit intention of this symbolic *pernarneq*. Most probably it either confirmed or created a close relationship between the young couple and the celebrated young hunter.

paralysis. He hurried back home in order to tell about the event, but suddenly he did not remember. He got violent swelling of the face until somebody placed the back of a book along his spine. His memory came back, he told the whole story, and the swelling disappeared (ID 792).[41] *Arnanneq*, a third kind of extraordinary experience (dealt with below), meant that some deceased person slipped into a living person, made the hostess sick, and become identified with the intruder. The latter was treated with food served by its close relatives, left, and the hostess recovered. I am uncertain about how such cured misfortunes—not to mention those not cured—were judged.

Marriage

As among other Inuit, a young Greenlander's first catch of a seal did not mean the permission to marry. In some places, a first catch of all recognized species was a prerequisite. In Greenland it seems that no particular catch, nor, for that sake, a ritual, marked a young man's eligibility. Rather, accomplished skills mattered most, not only in hunting but also in the making of all kinds of hunting gear (e.g., Dalager 1915: 4). Nevertheless, the young man's *pernarneq* seems to have been considered the admission card to sexual relations, as also mentioned by Dalager. After the festivities the young man was brought to a young virgin and was supposed to "touch her in a particular place" for enhancing his luck in hunting (4–5; see also B. Jensen 1963: 275).[42]

Although in the language of the spirits (*taartaq*), the birth of the first child was called the *pernarneq* of a young woman, no noticeable public celebration is on record, nor was there any event marking her social reintegration as "a new woman." *Pernarneq* of a boy is still celebrated in the few remaining hunting communities, but in a modern context the festivities are held for either sex, namely on the first day of school and on confirmation at about age fourteen. I have not come upon statements that combine the latter event with permission to have sex. In apparent consonance with a fairly liberal view on sex, the Greenlandic church neither encourages nor at present explicitly bans premarital sex.

The close connection between sex and luck in hunting also seems emphasized in the young Greenlander's rape of his bride, a fake ritual in most instances (and no longer practiced). Although the couple (and their parents) had agreed on the liaison, she was supposed to resist and remain extremely unwilling while he dragged her roughly out of the house and along to their future virilocal residence. In marking her social transition she immediately placed herself on the platform with her back to the room and her hair let down like a woman enduring mourning prescriptions. After two days the young man succeeded in persuading her to have sex, thus sealing the marriage (P. Egede 1971: 102; 1939: 71; H. Egede 1971, 2: 79–80; 1925: 373–74; 1818: 143–44). The young man's rough handling of his chosen bride was eagerly observed by everybody present. The more unwilling she acted and the more severe the bruises she received, the greater her virtues.[43] After the period of

41. Baptism demanded literacy as well as to have learned by heart both prayers and the answers to questions of the catechism.

42. The introduction of rifles has lowered the age of a boy landing a *pernarneq*, as well as, perhaps, the age of his sexual debut. Thalbitzer made references to youth houses reserved for the practice of premarital sex (especially at places for whaling), which appear convincing but are difficult to substantiate (Thalbitzer 1941: 656–57). A late West Greenlandic variant of Kivioq refers to such a house (Sonne 2005: ID 1478).

43. Both groom and bride, especially the latter, were hard put to express the affirming "yes" in public requested at the Christian wedding.

chaste "mourning," she was expected to abide to his will. I see an analogy in the young man's killing, bringing home, and not tasting the first seal. Also this "spoil" was supposed to let itself be "caught" time and again throughout the life of the hunter, who, after *pernarneq*, was free to eat from his subsequent catches. Basically or ideologically, the husband possessed the sexual rights to his wife. Stories from actual life most often confirm this right, even if sometimes they do not. Also, not every man had the physical and mental strength needed for robbing his bride (H. Egede 1971, 2: 79; 1925: 373; 1818: 143). Nor was every marriage agreed upon by the "bride." Saabye mentions girls opposing a proposal accepted by her parents. Such a girl would cut her hair, run away, and take refuge in the mountains for the rest of the day. Upon her return she had it her way, but at the same time she ruined her chances of ever getting married.[44] Saabye's other examples concern unwilling a bride's recurrent attempts at running away during the days of transition. Fetched back each time by the groom, she risked being cut on the soles of her feet, and after the period of transition any act of reluctance was severely reproached by the other women of the household (Saabye 1942: 17–18). I postpone the matching issue of male dominance to the discussion of social aspects of shamanism related as it is to Saladin d'Anglure's hypothesis of a "third sex."

Comparisons of Life-Cycle Rites in Societies with and without Ranking

Summing up the life cycle rites of the small-scale bilateral Greenlandic society, a comparison with the conclusions reached by the late Margaret Lantis's analysis of Nunivak rites of transition are of relevance. They agree in principle despite the difference in "affluence" and social structure, the Nuniwarmiut being generally better off and structured by lineages. But they differ in the stress put on the Nunivak boy's puberty rite. Lantis distinguished between three kinds of passage rites. The first category covered the physiological changes at birth, puberty (first menstruation), and death; these were not of communal but only "supernatural" concern. To the second category belonged the change in status with regard to food getting by ritual "firsts," which concerned both parties, the "spirits" and society. By contrast, the third category of change in social status by marriage, divorce, and adoption demanded neither "taboos" to be observed nor communal rites to be performed. The border case of first catch—or, better, the locally decisive one of a big bearded seal—Lantis placed in both the first and second categories. Like physiological change, it required equally strict and demanding taboos to be observed and public recognition by the gifts spent by the father at the subsequent Bladder Feast (Lantis 1946: 229–33). Similar distinctions can be made regarding Greenland. Social recognition was definitely required of first catches, be they "real" or "symbolic,"[45] with collective backing making the wishful thinking effective, as it were. But the negligible obligations put on the young Greenlander at his first catch ask for some considerations in comparison to the prolonged and severe ones endured by the Nunivak young man. First, at about the age of sixteen the latter had received his complete heritage of hunting amulets/*inogos* and songs of his paternal lineage. At about twenty he had proved his eligibility to marry by having caught at least one specimen of each species of seal and then been isolated in a separate hut for an extended period (*ibid.*). The Greenlandic boy received some individual

44. Which I doubt.

45. But fortuitous experiences were apparently not celebrated, except perhaps a lucky hunt bringing big game into the settlement.

amulet(s) considered suitable at birth and perhaps later by a parent and/or another elder of the family, but he was rarely older than sixteen at his decisive *pernarneq* of a seal, no matter the kind, at which he became acknowledged an adult in relation to game and probably also to women. However, he was not encouraged to marry until he had proved himself to be a reliable provider. Dalager set the average age to about twenty-seven (1915: 5). The excellent provider, a *piniatorsuaq* (great hunter), naturally enjoyed a high if unofficial reputation in Greenland, whereas on Nunivak the rankings of hunters were public affairs. Honorific titles were attributed, one annually to the hunter who had caught the most bearded seal in the previous year and, at intervals, another temporary title of "chief." He earned the title by adding lavish gifts to the common pile at local ceremonies, which were distributed by others according to certain rules of seniority and/or need. By his capable, industrious hunting and generosity he had provided for the poor, and in "potlatches" between villages he raised the reputation of his own village (Lantis 1946: 248). In Greenland, apart from feasting one's guests, the hunter celebrating a son's *pernarneq* would throw valuables for everybody, adults and children, to scramble for. On top of feasts and the obligations of sharing he would give personal gifts of meat for particular reasons to personally selected persons. By comparison, then, "social matters" were at stake to a higher degree in the Nunivak system of ceremonies structured by lineages of religious import and prestige-giving feasting. Apart from skills in hunting, the prestige to be gained was absolutely dependent on the relation of the hunter (and his wife) to game and "the supernatural" as expressed in the heritage of *inogo*s and prolonged liminal period of severe prescriptions that marked his coming of age and eligibility to marry. I shall resist the temptation to compare Greenlandic ritual "firsts" with those of even more complex social structures. Suffice it to restate common knowledge: in comparison with Nunivak, the number of Greenland life-cycle taboos and rites appear small, if no less burdensome as regards the women, in this leaderless, "egalitarian" society. In both, however, the three categories made by Lantis apply by stressing physiological change and procurement of food.

Mental Development

Physiological changes, status changes in relation to food procurement, and changes in civil status are striking and fairly easy for an outsider to observe. Changes in mental development, however, as Briggs (1974a) richly calls attention to, and as I have discussed above, did in fact cause serious changes in parents' behavior toward their children. Yet they seem not to have called for ritual.

Whereas adults would comment on a child's growing *isuma* and progressing *sila*, an individual Inuk would refer to the development of her memory. The first event remembered is experienced as a "becoming aware of oneself," *ilisimarisseqqaarpunga*. For some time afterwards only some stray events are remembered until a complete working memory is obtained; from that particular event and on "he remembered everything" (Sonne 2005: ID 1252). This particular way of checking up on one's mental development turns out to be a common Inuit/Yupiit heritage (e.g., Sonne 2005: ID 1252; Lantis 1960: passim; Fienup-Riordan & Rearden 2013: 33; Nagy 2006). Most probably the phrases were learned by listening to adults relating their autobiographical events. Generally the first remembered event happens about the age of two, and the second that marks the complete developed memory at about five (Nagy 2006). Coincidentally or not, at the age of five a West Greenlandic girl would have her first topknot done (J. Petersen 1957: 178, note 192). This hairdo used to signify the ordinary adult female, but was let loose during mourning and other critical transitions (occasioned by the first menstruation in most places). Since the Greenlanders, like other Inuit, did not count the years, one would like to know which acquired skill called for a topknot at this early age. Would it be the complete telling of an experience or a dream, proving both a working memory and the mastery of speech? The telling of memories was greatly appreciated, especially memories of an earlier existence, a recognized phenomenon in myth as in actual life. The Inuit myth about the human who lived the lives of one animal after another is one case in point. Reborn a human, (s)he could relate the ways of moving around and eating habits of these species (e.g., Sonne 2005: ID 1089, 1523). Similarly a South Greenlandic story is told about the human dwarf, baptized Peter Ranthol, who was sold by his biological father, a spirit dwarf, to a human shaman, but transferred into and reborn by a human mother. Coming of speaking age, he could tell the complete migration history of his former relatives, the spirit dwarves, *inuarullikkat* (ID 163).

The memory of a five-year-old East Greenlander was not considered sufficiently mature for remembering terrifying encounters with aggressive spirits. The small shaman apprentice was supposed to be protected by a failing memory; it was protected because telling about such experiences would ruin his/her chance of ever becoming a shaman. More details on this will be provided in chapter 4, on shamans.

To repeat: Although mental development of the child, of its *sila* or *isuma*, seems to have been recognized and valued in similar ways among all Inuit and Yupiit, ritual markings are next to absent from the sources.

Greenlandic "Animal Cult"

Greenlanders did not celebrate anything like the Alaska hunting ceremonies (Lantis 1947), which honored game by masks, bladders, or similar representations. People dressed up in their finery for the whale hunt (H. Egede 1818: 102–3; 1971, 2: 57; 1925: 354–55), and certain dances mimicked the behavior of various game animals during the masked dances, *uaajeertut*. The animals caught by individual *pernarneq*s were collectively honored, and rules were observed against cutting up large-sized species for three days in East and five in West Greenland.

On a smaller scale than in parts of Arctic Canada, in Greenland some taboos concerned cooking and eating meat from sea and land animals together (the statements are scant, Søby 1969/70). Any catch of seal was given a drink of water and some drops of urine smeared on the head, whereas the treatment of the skeletal remains varied, depending on the size and social importance of the catch. Thus, in the south, the unbroken bones of a young man's *pernarneq* were given back to the sea or Sea Woman (Dalager 1915: 4), and in East Greenland so was the skull of the bigger species (Holm 1972: 86; 1914: 49). Polar bear skulls were placed indoors and given gender-appropriate gifts (Sonne 2005: ID 893, 1806; Søby 1969/70). Not much can be added to Søby's meticulous article, except the following East Greenlandic origin myth of the gifts offered to a polar bear (named "The Deal" for later analysis): In a dream a woman under taboo visits a family of polar bears in human form living with their two sons-in-law, a walrus and an Arctic fox. The bears propose a deal to exchange their skins and meat for the particular skins prepared by humans for boot soles. *Pisuartartut*, "the always wandering ones," was a common epithet of the polar bears, which thus were in constant need of prepared skin for soles. The walrus stays outside the negotiations, but the Arctic fox, a regular visitor to human settlements, has a big say. Humans have sharp knives, he objects, and the garbage between their houses stinks. While the young bears lose heart, the oldest among them accepts the deal by showing the woman a broken tooth in his mouth for identification when killed. Waking up, but still under taboo, the woman informs her husband by signs about the approaching bear. So, when killed and recognized, it receives the precious gift of skins for soles to take home by his returning *tarneq* (Sonne 2005: ID 1806).

The question of why the bears do not produce the soles themselves will be dealt with in due course—i.e., when discussing theories of animism and perspectivism in an Inuit context. Besides, the tone of this little myth of origin is in no way serious. The differing characters of the animals are humorously sketched. The woman entering into the deal is no shaman. As a married Inuit woman she sees to the relations of exchange (e.g., Robbe 1994: 341ff). Her "placing" is her being under taboo (on the outer limits of society), which facilitates encounters with the "Others" who, like these polar bears, may take the initiative to negotiate a deal of balanced exchange.

Conclusions

In the research, the sketchy descriptions of West Greenlandic collective rituals at New Year have been denied any value. Nonetheless, the statements on their wife exchange, feasting, and drum singing look genuinely Inuit/Yupiit. The far better described get-togethers with mask dances, feasting, and wife exchange of the East Greenlanders are comparable with both the Canadian Inuit *tivajuut* at New Year and the Yup'ik "time for drumming." In Greenland winter solstice appears to have been the ideal time for public initiation of new shamans, who might *ilimmarneq*, go flying to heaven, to the Northern Lights, and/or Moon as did the Iglulik shamans in winter. In contrast to the latter's authoritative parts in the Iglulik *tivajuut*, who decided the pairing off for the ritual exchange of wives, the Greenlandic shamans did not direct the ritual wife exchange, and the Greenlandic women also had much freer choice of partner.

Late winter and spring were the times of empty stores and few accessible resources. Crises were likely to occur, and in Greenland—as everywhere among the Inuit—people asked for the shaman's help. In East Greenland, the Moon or a boulder let loose with the melting in spring might descend and threaten the lives of the dwellers of the longhouse, and *Asiaq* (the *inua* of precipitation) was asked to send rain (in myth at least). In West Greenland Sea Woman was visited and cleaned so that a storm would arrive and rip open the frozen sea. This *inua* of the sea appears to have had some strong connection with whaling. Southerners, who took turns going north for whaling at Sisimiut and Disko Bay, dominate in the Sea Woman sources. Whaling and Sea Woman are also related in parts of Arctic Canada, where cooperation and exchanges, both material and sexual, with Qallunaat whalers became intense. Here, Sea Woman was identified in myth with the mother of the Qallunaat. Also, as I hypothesize, the Iglulik winter feast, *tivajuut*, celebrated in the name of Sea Woman's children, could have served to transform the children fathered by the Qallunaat into genuine Inuit. In Tigara, Northwest Alaska, preparations for the spring whale hunt included a shaman's visit below in the sea in order to have the man of a married couple of spirits persuade *Silap Inua* (weather) to rip open a lead in the ice and the woman to ask *Ni-givik* (lit. "the place of food") to calm the ensuing turbulent waves. I cannot avoid the temptation to name *Ni-givik* a prototype of Sea Woman, especially because she was called the phonological equivalent, *Nerrivik*, in Avanersuaq. Her connection with whaling at

Tigara is evident.[46] Furthermore, the undersea space traveled by the Tigara shaman makes perfect sense in a Greenlandic frame of reference.

Taken together, access to sea mammals through the surface of the sea was the main purpose of visiting, killing, or cleaning Sea Woman: to have the ice removed in West Greenland and the opened surface calmed in Northwest Alaska. Among the South Baffin Islanders, the goal was to have the ice cover form in order to hunt at breathing holes, and the ritual took place in November, ravaged by storms. In spring the East Greenlanders depended on sealing at breathing holes as well, but due to their humid climate they were to look inland, to *Asiaq*, for rain to melt the heavy layer of snow hiding the holes, and then, in case the rain also did away with the ice, ask Moon for solid ice to form. The other powers of the inland—such as a boulder let loose and coming down in spring—occasioned the shaman to call on his *Equngasoq*, the fulmar spirit connoting spring, and the only superior of both boulder and Moon.

With the introduction of Christian ideas, Moon was changed into a laughing stock, whereas Sea Woman slowly changed attitude toward Inuit and became the loving mother of original Greenlanders.

The Greenland life-cycle rites differ only in degree from the Inuit/Yupiit pattern in general. One main object was to keep separate the recycling, through death and rebirth, of humans and animals. Hence, birth, menstruation, abortion, and death were demanding in taboos. Women suffered the most. Men were reintegrated step by step into the free life of a hunter after some months of mourning. Women were ritually declared a "new woman" after a year on the platform. (The multitude of taboos hampering the lives of the Eastern Inuit has been vividly discussed by academics. The Greenlandic sources do not permit a testing of their proposals.) Another goal of the life-cycle rites was to create beneficial relations with the animals. Most "ritual firsts" concerned production, such as the celebration of a boy's first catch, his *pernarneq*, a happy communal event. Here his adult relationship with the sea mammals became established by the duty of everyone but himself to taste the animal's meat and, later, by the return of its bones to the sea. But he did not become socially adult until he was able to provide for a family. Also "symbolic first catches" were to be socially recognized in order to have the imagined initiating effect. The girl's first menstruation was not celebrated. She posed a danger to the hunt. After the period of taboos, she put up her hair in a topknot as her sign of being safe. During all her subsequent periods she was obliged to let her hair hang loose. Marriage sometimes took the (false) appearance of a rape but with a course of events that reflected the boy's *pernarneq*. It marked his free access to and ownership of his wife's sexuality. The birth of a young woman's first child was recognized as her *pernarneq* by the "Others" in their spirit language. Thereby she eventually became an adult in relation to the game animals with the right to cut them up.

46. No whaling took place in Avanersuaq. They were only visited by European whalers who were en route to the whaling grounds in Arctic Canada.

CHAPTER THREE

■ ■ ■

The Other World(s) and Its Beings

Introduction: Transitional Aspects of Sila

Naaq denotes "night" in the language of the Other World (*taartaq*) and "belly" or "abdomen" in the ordinary language of This World. The connotations are spatial, temporal, and corporal, that is, corporal in the human sense of an interior, invisible physical part of the body. Big *naaq*, or *naartta*, means air, heaven, atmosphere, and night in *taartaq*, and *sila* in ordinary language; in Canada *sila* is personified as the giant dwarf *Naarssuk/Naarjuk*. Jakob Sanimuinaq, the grandchild of three shamans, told Joëlle Robert-Lamblin that this *naartta* was of decisive importance to the shamans. Robert-Lamblin, who had never heard *naartta* used in the East Greenlandic vernacular, turned to the spirit language, where she came upon *naartta magipo* ("*le jour se lève*"), *naartta qamiderpo* ("*il commence à faire sombre*"), and then to the spirit languages of the Nattilingmiut, Iglulingmiut, and Kitlinermiut, where the corresponding *naarjuk/naarsjuk* mean "the day that lies down or sits down" (Rasmussen 1930b: 77; 1931: 310; 1932: 112; cf. Robert-Lamblin 1996: 127).[1,2,3] Why Jakob Sanimuinaq considered *naarta* of crucial importance is not clarified (*ibid.*), but fortunately *naarta* occurs in a few texts in reference to exactly those transitions in time, when the shaman apprentice, whether fainting or visiting in the Other World, must wake up or leave to get home in time. Otherwise, he is at the mercy of the "Other World" (Qúpersimân 1972: 59–61; Sandgreen 1967, II: 22; Sonne 2005: ID 1666, 1677). The reverse demand was obviously in force for the spirits visiting the human world (O. Rosing 1957–61, I: 109; J. Rosing 1963: 242; search *naarta* in Sonne 2005). Corroboration of the

---

1. In both East and West Greenlandic *naaq* means "belly, abdomen" (Fortescue et al. 1994: 205; 2010: 224). In West Greenlandic *naartu* means "embryo," and *naartuvoq*, "she is pregnant." Thus *Naartee*, the pregnant one, is a *uaajeertoq* man dressed as a pregnant woman who asks every onlooker for some food (Thalbitzer 2014: 121).

2. *Nârta makípoq* (*naarta makippoq*) and *Nârta qamigpoq* (*naarta qamippoq*), respectively (O. Rosing 1957–61, I: 92). See also Therrien (1987: 134).

3. An interesting parallel is *Pon* of the Yukaghirs, the weather, light, and darkness of the world, a nonpersonified "something" and not the object of either cults or prayers. *Ponyulec* (like *naarta qamillerpoq*) means that "something" gets light, *pon-emi'dic* that "something" gets black (night), and *pon-ti-boi*, "it rains" (like *sila-llerpoq*) (Jochelson 1910: 140, 235, additions in parentheses BS).

same idea using colors is beautifully sketched by the Canadian Inuit artist William Noah from Baker Lake/Qamaniktuaq of a skeletal figure of a shaman in Hessel (1998: 49). More information is had in a black-and-white reproduction in Goetz (1977: 216). Goetz offers this legend quoted from Butler, who was informed by the shamans of Baker Lake: "Late in the evening when the sun sets behind the horizon, in the half red and half blue darkness his (the shaman's) shadow can work loose, acquire life and disappear in the twilight. At that moment the shaman becomes transparent" (Butler 1973–4: 157). Blurriness means ignorance, but transparency means knowledge, according to M. Therrien's striking commentary on this statement (1987: 122). It supports my present focus on the *naar*-time.

The use of *naaq* verbs for transitions between day and night—that is, those between the Other World and This World—is significant, because *in other contexts* the spirit words used for *sila-* + suffix are not *naaq*. One word is *aniivik*, or "the exit" or "place for out of doors" (O. Rosing 1957–61, I: 87); others include *nunarrartewa*, "the great land," and *eqqartewa* "environment" (Victor & Robert-Lamblin 1989–93, II: 253).

Silam Aappaa *and* Asia

Silam aappaa, literally "the other *sila* (in grammatical dual) of a couple (*aappaa*)," is the invisible world of the "Others" seen involuntarily in dreams or extraordinary experiences, and at will by shamans. Mutually dependent, events and activities in one *sila* affect those in the other. In most records, *silam aappaa* is predominantly applied to the realm of death below by the West Greenlanders (P. Egede 1988: 100; Fabricius 1804: 422), whereas the East Greenlandic term *asia* in most contexts refers to the Other World of the land and its spirits. Dwarves and giants lived inside hummocks, hills, and mountains; the *innersuit* (big fire spirits) lived upside down under the foreshore and skerries.[4]

Spatially, the Other World—with its plains, hills, and river—is no void. Time is sometimes ruled out, but sometimes still valid, depending on context. I shall enumerate the aspects of space first and then turn to time and questions of timelessness concerning both the afterlife of humans and the "chronologic" time of myth. In preparation of the latter issue, the earliest Greenlandic myths of origins are quoted and discussed separately. The theoretical questions of *inuat* and then the special language of the Other World serve as an overture to the next chapter on shamans. One cannot, however, avoid the subject of shamans in an attempt to describe the main field of their experiences, the Other World.

Environment in Changing Perspectives

The Other World of This, the middle, World possessed several boundaries beyond which humanlike beings, *inuat*, were encountered; most frequently these borders were crossed by the shaman apprentice in search of helping spirits, or *toornat* (sing. *toornaq*).

The change in vision, a temporary splitting up of one's view into layers (see below p. 278), overcame one boundary in making way for a clear sight of the Other World, but several were in force in both space and time. In space the boundary most frequently trespassed without perceptible consequences in daily life began beyond the range of vision centered at human habitation: the summer

4. Also mentioned once in Polar Inuit texts (Holtved 1951, I: 73, P. Egede 1988: 100, note: *Sila—silam aapaa, Sillam aipane:* realm of death; Fabricius 1804: 422: "*Sila—Sillam aipa*: den anden verden" [The other world]).

camp at inland streams and fjords, the coastal settlement in winter. Summer was the preferred time for going in search of helping spirits in any part of the uninhabited inland and beyond human sight. As well, empty settlements were liable to be haunted by ghosts (e.g., Sonne 2005: ID 1802, 451). Heading for the inland region, little Kaakaaq (ca. 1865–1917, renowned female shaman), became anxious at the point when she was out of sight from the tent but was also elated, as the possibility of meeting something extraordinary increased (ID 1243). The spirits did not swarm the inland country to the ordinary eye. A spirit might approach a lonely human in This World with the intention of becoming a helping spirit. Sometimes a new helping spirit would invite the little pupil on a visit to its dwelling place and later see him home, but rarely all the way (e.g., ID 1218). Unless invited by a shaman for a performance, spirits usually respected the boundary of ordinary human sight and habitation. The small Naaja (famous great shaman of the early 19th century), however, when in danger of being killed by a relative of his two first helping spirits, was flown by his helpers right on to his family's tent. Immediately, in gusts of wind, the spirits then hurriedly encircled the tent and disappeared in a rush (ID 1234). Another variant respects the boundary set at the washing place outside the camp. Crossing that boundary would turn the spirits from helpful to aggressive, this storyteller warns us. So in one big throw they sent Naaja along through the air from this place right on to the tent (ID 1668). For spirits related to a human shaman, visiting humans in an almost pitch-dark house during a shamanic performance is not felt to be that risky. Indeed, literally This and the Other World are like day and night changing at *naar*-times, which also have an effect on the still-immature mind of the very young child, who easily forgets about one world by entering the other. Little Kaakaaq's return from having been devoured and thrown up again by the "freshwater bear" is a fine instance. Awakened by her "waking up" dwarf at sunset, she sets off for home naked, cold, and terrified. Gradually she recovers by receiving back her clothes, piece by piece, and at the moment the tent is within sight, her fear evaporates and she forgets about the whole event. This was a fortunate mental block, because apprenticeship was to be kept secret. At night, however, she wakes up among the sleepers, remembers the mighty bear, and promises to tell everybody in the morning. Light wakes her up and cleans her memory once again (ID 1241).

Outside performances, the shaman could travel the Other Worlds on his own in company with one or more familiars by changing sight and taking off from somewhere in the wilderness. During public performances, access to the Other Worlds started inside the house, with the lamps extinguished and windows covered. For spirit flight, a corner between wall and roof was said to open up to the shaman as he circled the room. He apparently drilled his way out since he left in a shower of sparks together with a good number of his spirits (e.g., Sonne 2005: ID 1666). Even more like "bow drilling" (spinning on the big toe), it would open a passage down through the floor to the shaman heading for the worlds below. He would proceed under the earth to the shore and then upwards into This World; at this point he became visible to the audience for a short while and was then seen diving through a crack in the ice (e.g., ID 467).[5] For roaming the surroundings and the surface of

5. Unlike the Yup'ik *qasgi*, the semisubterranean entrance of the Greenlandic longhouse had no winter passage below the ordinary one. Like shamans, spirits would also enter and depart through the earth, emerging and disappearing through the floor at the place corresponding to the *qasgi*'s fireplace. The former is reminiscent of the latter, I suppose.

the sea, whether open or covered with ice, the entrance tunnel was a sufficient way out (and in; see *angakkoq puulik*).

In myths as in the dreams of all humans, be they shamans or laypeople, the Other Worlds bore earthly characteristics with their plains, rivers, bogs, ravines, etc. In search of helping spirits, the pupil saw This World, the middle one, differently, due to his changed sight. It disclosed the Other World(s) of This World. The home of certain dwarves or giants became visible and accessible, and the flat shore land of the *innersuit* became unveiled below the steep cliff (e.g., Sonne 2005: ID 1287). These *innersuit* underneath the foreshore and skerries belonged to the Other World of the middle world, living as they did as coast dwellers vertically opposite human habitation. In human perspective they belonged in reversed world, upside down spatially as well as in seasonal time: winter above meant summer below and vice versa. Besides such familiar oppositions known from cultures all over the world, in Greenland the character of the land—inhabited by a species of spirits—clearly put its mark on a species' appearance, size, way of life, hunting techniques, and abilities. This emerges from Kaarali Andreassen's ordering of potential helping spirits (O. Rosing 1957–61, I: 76–85; J. Rosing 1963: 179–92). My analysis (Sonne 1996) showed that the decisive criteria are the relations in space of the species' place to both air (*sila*) and human habitation at the coast. Thus the distance of a species' dwelling from the coastal point of human orientation in *sila*, along the sloping profile of the land, serves as the primary criterion. It determines both relative size in body of the spirit species and its way of breathing. The *innersuit* beneath the shore (and human dwellings) are the size of humans, while those beneath the skerries (used by humans for the spring hunt) are bigger. The land is peopled by three sizes of dwarves and three of giants. They belong, depending on relative size, to their part of the land: the coastal, the middle, and the uppermost inland region at the border between worlds and on the nunataks of the inland ice. As for breathing, no wind blows in the abodes of the *innersuit*. Consequently, they have no visible noses, and they do not breathe (nor would you in a submarine world).[6] At the other extreme, the biggest dwarves and giants most probably have big noses (like the equivalent *innersuit* of the far inland region of Arctic Canada [Rasmussen 1929: 210]), due to their heavy breath (like your breath in the thin air of that height). In the icy air, their exhalations form into visible bridges of mist used for crossing from one mountaintop to another. Like humans, these spirits live in families and make their livelihood from hunting, but their technology and methods differ. The *innersuit* are fairly similar to humans. They are excellent kayakers who hunt sea mammals with great success. But they hunt exclusively at sea and fear everything from the land, which they fastidiously avoid (in East Greenland).[7] The land spirits' ways of hunting differ considerably. Actually, this is where the mirror effect of reflexivity (Willerslev 2007) comes to the fore. They get around with great ease by various nonhuman means, but like humans they hunt trout, grouse, and polar bear along with *sea mammals*. The latter are caught inland by several spirit species, which pursue small or big specimens corresponding to the size of the hunter. The lack of caribou in this part of East Greenland

---

6. Aadaarutaa owned three *innersuit* with noses and one, a stronger type, without, according to his son in-law, Amos (Sonne 2005: ID 2032).

7. Statements are insufficient for a similar West Greenlandic systematization. Aadaarutaa mentions *innersuit* of the land, mountain spirits (Sonne 2005: ID 971).

could have triggered that peculiar way of making a living on the land.[8] Furthermore, their hunting methods are also strange, and this is where the true reversal occurs. Apart from the tiniest dwarves, who are fine kayakers but too small for coping with even the smallest seal in the stories, the land spirits are not kayakers at all.[9] They remain on land, but they can reverse the course of streams and rivers by their whistling, which makes the seals swim backwards, up the river. Next, they stop the course with the effect of tipping the balance of the animal, whose raised tail is easily lassoed. This is the method applied by the biggest dwarves and the smallest giants. The medium-size and largest giants hunt in the outer or inner cracks of the inland ice. Besides making seals go upriver, they draw narwhals and whales from the innermost parts of the ice fjords inwards underneath the inland ice. At times this can create a *sassat*, an opening in the ice cap crowded with narwhals or belugas. Thus, the greater land spirits orient themselves as do the humans, by facing the sea, but their sea is that of the inland ice. According to some, this ice cover is the remnants of the primordial flood that immediately froze but later partly withdrew, making room for humans to live along the coasts (Holm 1972: 139; 1914: 106–7). The tiny dwarves, previously discussed in their likeness to ravens, lasso trout by the tail (as do human boys), hunt grouse with difficulty, and steal from their neighbors, the humans. But like all land spirits, they move quickly. Paddling their kayaks, they make a smooth lane for themselves through the towering waves of a stormy sea (Sonne 2005: ID 423, 827, 1364). The medium-size dwarves have powers of their own. They do not turn around the course of rivers while hunting. Rather, they hunt seals at rest on coastal rocks or basking on the ice, seabirds resting in flocks, and fox and polar bear on the land. They put the resting prey to sleep, and they slow down the escape of the fleeing land animals by literally stealing their speed. Furthermore, they facilitate their travel by leveling out the mountains and drawing the land together. The giants of the inland ice cover and its nunataks travel, as mentioned above, long distances by forming bridges of fog from one mountaintop to another.

Looking for some "natural" inspirations for these behaviors, the giants' heavy, frosty breath up there on the inland ice testifies to the bridges of fog. The reversed water courses would be the enlarged effects of high tide that bring in edibles of the sea (beluga in some places, and narwhals into the ice fjords in winter). Spring tide in particular reverses the movements of waters. When they travel at full speed, both the small dwarves in their kayaks at sea and the others across the land move like sea and land birds, respectively, to which they are frequently likened in stories. Also, the peculiar balance in body of these spirits is like that of birds, having their focal point in the tail vertebrae in contrast to the supple loin vertebrae of humans. The tiny dwarves tend to stoop downhill (ID 1364). In figure, both the *innersuit* and their kayaks have bodies like seabirds, a heavy forepart/breast and a small hind part or thin legs (J. Rosing 1963: 188; O. Rosing 1957–61, I: 80). All in all, their speedy, birdlike nature makes them particularly useful to the shaman.[10]

---

8. Bad winters finished off the caribou between the 13th and 15th centuries (Møbjerg 1994: 132–34; M. Meldgaard 1986).

9. Sonne (2005: ID 1364, 1336); Thalbitzer (1923: 475).

10. A draft in Danish on body symbolism treats the issue in more detail and of wider bearings than Sonne (1996). Maybe later I shall have time to produce an English version.

Kaarali's systematization of potential helping spirits is not a "spirit theology" transmitted through generations but rather the outcome of his attempt to create one, partly for communication to the missionaries and partly for heightening the reputation of his father's religion. People visited from all over and told him their stories (Vebæk 1990: 105), most probably the sources of the impressive collection taken down by both Kaarali and his wife and handed over to Knud Rasmussen in 1919 (see "Evaluation of the Essential Sources," above). The logic of his criteria makes sense, particularly in regard to environmental facts; it makes sense to us, as it might have done to any "traditional" East Greenlander. But the criteria did not work as smoothly in everybody's mind. Although the section on the dwarves is in part confirmed by the statements Victor received, his editor, Robert-Lamblin, may have read Kaarali (Victor & Robert-Lamblin 1989–93, II: 241, 362–66). In fact, Teemiartissaq, one of Thalbitzer's main informants, uses the criterion of size according to distance in a different but analogous way. She places representatives of all three species of dwarves within the same house (world analogy) on the upper, middle, and lower part of the platform, respectively (Thalbitzer 1923: 475). Otherwise people told their stories about encounters with the spirits of the land and beneath the shore without overly strict distinctions in characteristics, except for the *innersuit*'s lack of noses (they were called "the noseless ones") and the giants' lack of kayaks. As for one instance of overlapping, in two stories about visiting dwarves they are the size of the smaller ones but their way of life is that of Kaarali's medium-size ones (Sonne 2005: ID 1233; Rasmussen 1921–25, I: 27–28 in Sonne 2005: ID 2283).[11] Still, the criteria of distance, breathing, and reversals reflect the points of interest to a human perspective of the world.

Besides the coastal *innersuit* and the six species of land spirits, Kaarali mentions several single living spirits of the land, the skerries, the shore, and the fjords as potential helping spirits. They serve ritual functions such as being means for calling on other helping spirits, saving their master (the shaman) from exceedingly dangerous situations, and serving as frightening spirits, *qimarratit* ("which make you flee") for increasing the thrill at the opening of performances (common thrill was highly appreciated as entertainment, outside of shamans' performances as well as within them). These individuals are identified as animals, birds, mollusks, and insects, oversize or same size as in nature, and, according to Grønnow's analysis, the farther inland they dwell the more dangerous they can be (Grønnow 2009a). Why Kaarali left out deceased humans as potential helping spirits remains an open question. Nor does he mention the still much-feared *qivittut* (sing. *qivittoq*), although for more comprehensible reasons. First, they apparently rarely served as helping spirits, and second, according Holm they were not encountered in precolonial East Greenland (Holm 1972: 176). *Qivittut* are humans who, for depressing reasons, have left society. They are believed to receive superhuman powers and continue their lonely lives in the wilderness. They abound in West Greenland and are mentioned by Niels Egede in 1742 and 1743 at Qasigiannguit (N. Egede 1971: 73, 128; 1939: 171, 206). Seemingly with the spread of the Christian creed, they came to receive their powers from the Devil and are consequently doomed. Simultaneously, the multifarious spirits receded into the background

11. At the Teacher's College in Nuuk, Kaarali heard West Greenlandic stories that provided a possible explanation for the fact that among the East Greenlanders, Kaarali is the only one to mention the evil (devilish?) *innersuit* of younger West Greenlandic stories, the *allit* or *alliarusit*. They live farther out and below the ordinary *innersuit*, underneath submerged reefs (Rink 1866–71, II: 188; 1975: 46; O. Rosing 1957–61, I: 81; J. Rosing 1963: 189).

and the number of stories about *qivittut* increased at the expense of stories about offended humans, who were either stolen by spirits or asked by spirits to become shamans.

The Routes to the Realms Above and Below

The difficulties to be overcome en route to the realms above and below were of an earthly nature; they included wide rivers, slimy or circling stepping-stones, boglike grounds, a steep cliff to be either ascended or descended, a wide ravine, a passage as sharp as the edge of a knife above a river, and slippery steps turned the wrong way and drenched in blood (Sonne 2005: ID 1015, 1992). Great shamans who covered long distances by flying or gliding, walking, or using something like a wind-filled gut were not exempt from the "difficult passages," but on their return all hindrances were eliminated. Deceased humans were definitely not supposed to return unless attached to a shaman as a helping spirit and directed by his calling.

Going into detail with the shaman journeys downwards to Sea Woman and upwards to Moon, we are fortunate that Poul Egede recorded descriptions as told by a still-unbaptized Greenlander during his early years of mission in Qasigiannguit/Christianshåb:

> [Jan. 19, 1737:] . . . two Greenlanders arrived by sledge from the innermost part of the ice fjord [at Ilulissat] called Tasiusaq. One of the two told me this weird story: Farthest down in earth lives a big, bad woman (the Devil's Great-Grandmother, without a doubt) in a giant house too big for shooting an arrow across.[12] This very woman governs all creatures of the sea; they all belong in her household, such as whales, unicorns [narwhals], seals, etc. The basin placed under her lamp, into which the waste oil of the lamp drips, swarms with all kinds of sea fowls, and the guard at the entry of her abode is made up of flocks of seals, standing erect and snapping at any intruder. Nobody can enter except Angekut [*angakkut*, shamans], and they must be escorted by their Tornaq [*toornaq*, helping spirit]. Along the route they are first to pass by the souls of the deceased humans, who look exactly like live humans on earth and are very well off [or suffer no pains]. Passed by that region they arrive at a very long, broad and deep gap that they are to pass over, but the only means for doing that is a big wheel, slippery as ice and continuously revolving with great speed. The spirit must help the shaman or wizard to get across. Having next passed by a big kettle with seals in boiling water, they eventually arrive at the residence of the Devil's Great-Grandmother. At that point the spirit takes the shaman by the hand through the strong guard of seals. The entrance is wide, but the accessible road is as narrow as a thin rope; on both sides there is nothing to lay hold on, and underneath a most frightful and bottomless abyss opens up. Inside, the goddess of hell, offended at this unexpected visit, sits in great confusion, grumbling, perspiring with sheer anger and tearing her hair. Immediately she grasps hold of the wing of a water fowl, sets it on fire and claps it to their noses, after which they are completely powerless and become her prisoners. But previously instructed by his tornaq [*toornaq*] or familiar, the wizard takes hold of her by her hair and drubs and bangs her for a long time, until she loses her strength and yields, and in this combat his familiar lends a hand. Around her face hang

12. "Farthest down in earth" is in Hans Egede's "Perlustration" corrected to "the lower parts of earth under the seas" (H. Egede 1818: 202; 1971, 2: 118; 1925: 397–98).

> *agleruttut* (since the significance is something natural, it is left out. In another meaning they are the clothes worn by a woman during an abortion. Such clothes are never to be used again, or mishaps will befall the hunt). These *agleruttut* are torn away because they have caused the sea mammals to leave the land and return home to this Female Devil. No sooner have they cleaned her than the whales, seals, etc. hurry splashing into the water and return to the accustomed places for the Greenlanders to hunt. Everything accomplished, the wizard and his *tornaq* set out on the homeward journey along the same road as they came, but by now smooth and without any obstacles. (P. Egede 1971: 45ff; 1939: 36–37, tr. BS)[13]

Obviously this text calls for some comments. First, the Devil's great-grandmother belongs to Nordic folklore, not to contemporary Christian theology. She is introduced due to the identification made by the first missionaries of the Devil with a particular kind of helping spirit, *Toornaarsuk* (Sonne 1986b). Second, wheels were not part of Greenlandic material culture at that point in history. Usually slippery, rotating stones or opening and closing objects (stones, icebergs, Symplegades effects in folklore) lead across a big river in this place (Sonne 2005: ID 29, 1196, 1354, 1649). Third, Sea Woman sits on her platform inside her house into which the intruders enter at the end of their tightrope walking through the entrance tunnel. In most variants a river flows beneath the rope (thin as a knife edge) in the tunnel, facilitating the return of sea mammals, "splashing into the water" and back to the sea of This World (ID 340, 349, 420, 891, 1354, 1445, 1649, 1882, 2070). Fourth, the *allerutut* stem from breaking the rules, *allerutit*, to be observed at menstruation, births, and, in particular, abortions. The unobserved events cause coagulated blood to drop as sticky impurities onto Sea Woman. Finally, the good life of the deceased below may have been mentioned in response to the new bad tidings of life in Hell.

A shaman's route to the heavenly realm of death was described by a Southerner passing by Nuuk in July 1735:

> The first time you [as a new shaman] want to go to heaven, it has to be at *Solstitium Autumnale*, because at that time the nearest heaven, namely the rainbow, is close to the horizon. Then you must let yourself be tied with a thick thong (like the one used for harpoons), with your head between your legs, hands behind the back, and then the entire body. A drum must be laid at your side. Thereupon, as soon as the light has been put out and the windows tightly covered up, leaving the room in complete darkness, and you have started singing the second song composed by our ancestors, you are suddenly released of the thong, and fly up through the roof and on through the air till you arrive at the first heaven. In this place is a big river flowing downwards from the uppermost heaven and alongside a flat and leveled mountain, across which you shall proceed to the uppermost heaven. And up there you shall see lots of animals and birds, as also

---

13. At only a few points did I make use of the translation of the slightly cut quotation in the Perlustration (H. Egede 1818: 102ff). I simply do not agree with the interpretation the translator brings to light. H. Egede's notes are worth quoting, though, especially one about the guard, said by some to be a fierce dog, which occasionally falls asleep for a short while, leaving a moment for the shaman to slip through. Another useful note refers to the hand of Sea Woman, said to be the size of whale's tail.

Angekut Poglik [*angakkut puullit*], i.e. *angakkut* with bags, their souls. (P. Egede 1971: 12–13; 1939: 14; tr. BS)

The commentaries on this text are fewer. The binding with thongs was the ritual prerequisite for traveling by flying, *ilimmarneq*, in Greenland as among the Iglulingmiut. The first part of the route leads across the sea, by far the easiest one compared to the spiraling one of the sun that would take at least a day and a night (P. Egede 1971: 134–35; 1939: 91; Rasmussen 1921–25: 82; Rüttel 1917: 39; Victor & Robert-Lamblin 1989–93, II: 246). *Solstitium Autumnale* must be either *aequinoctium autumnale* (see p. 70, note 36) or, stressing the low rainbow, which could mean the smallest distance between heaven and earth, winter solstice, *Solstitium Hibernale*. The "flat" mountain is my reading of a printer's error: "*flod*" as "*flad*" ("flat"). "*Flod*" literally means "river," but grammatically and in a position next to the river from above it appears awkward. The *angakkut puullit* will be dealt with extensively in chapter 5.

Among the recognizable difficult shamanic passages occurring worldwide (Eliade 1964: 482ff), the river to be overcome twice by the shaman on his journey to Sea Woman (*Sassuma Arnaa* or *Immap Ukuua*) evokes particular interest. First, the slimy stepping-stones of most variants lead across the river, and next, the bridge as sharp as the edge of a knife hovers lengthwise above the (same?) river running with garbage and dirt in the entrance tunnel of Sea Woman's house. The direction of its course is into the house until the shaman has succeeded in cleaning the giant woman, after which (in some variants) the river, similarly cleaned and attractive, runs outwards for the transformation of humanlike bodies into seabirds and sea mammals heading for the visible world. Another river, or perhaps the same one, originating in the uppermost heaven is followed by the shaman from the horizon of the sea via the rainbow to the upper parts of heaven, offering a life of riches. Up there the shaman may encounter a big lake: "The shamans tell about a big lake in heaven fenced in by a weir, which runs over at intervals and rains on earth. If the weir were to break, the entire heaven would fall down. Around the water the souls of deceased humans dwell in a great number of tents, and they are well off due to the prevalence of caribou, bird and fish in sufficient numbers" (P. Egede 1971: 51; 1939: 39; tr. BS). Granted that those rivers form a single course and thus connect the upper with the lower realms, the World River of ancient Siberian cosmography shows a parallel idea. In Napolskikh's construction of the Proto-Uralian worldview, this river runs from its origin in either a lake or from beneath the roots of a birch tree in heaven (in the south) downwards towards the world below (in the north). The lake revives the souls of seabirds and humans, and the river permits the shaman to travel between the three layers of cosmography (Napolskikh 1992). Yet the Proto-Uralian distinction between the lower realm as a cold and evil place and the upper one as both lovely and life-renewing (*ibid.*)—which fits Lakoff and Johnson's phenomenological assumption about the positive value of upwards and negative one of downwards (1980)—does not parallel the ideas of most Greenlanders in the early days of colonial history. At that time, the afterlife used to be fine in either realm (Sonne 2000a).

Exploring the Realms of Death

The Greenlanders' consciousness of their cosmography was certainly raised by the preaching of the Christian ideas of salvation versus perdition. The shamans turned their focus to the realms of death, the travels to which were less explicated in myth than those to Moon and Sea Woman. Evidently, it was no easy task to reconcile the afterlives in the Other Worlds of Christianity with the traditional ones. The preaching of eternal life, of burning in Hell, of no food in heaven—all of this was disturbing news. Evidently, the shamans had to go and see for themselves. As discussed by Sonne (2000a), the West Greenlandic sources reveal an ongoing dialogue between tradition and Christianity that ends in complete acceptance of the latter's ideas of Heaven and Hell. In short, from the very beginning the lives in the two realms were compared by the missionaries, who of course greatly preferred heaven, while the Greenlanders at times put a much higher value on the lower realm. In general, the Danes have found the latter preference funny to a degree that it has been adopted as the only true one. But the sources are far from clear. The earliest sources unambiguously underline that life is fine in either realm without any suffering, wants, or hardships. Animals and birds are plentiful above as below. The usually selected sources, which emphasize the downgrading of a rotating heaven that made one dizzy and offered no other food but ravens and slimy water to drink, differ greatly from these former statements and appear molded in opposition to the missionaries' polarization of heaven and hell. The results of the shamans' investigations are the statements that show the gradual development from sheer opposition to a final acceptance of the Christian notions. Most probably, as my thesis goes, the Greenlanders used to be less occupied with the afterlife than with the recycling of their names among the descendants in real life (Sonne 2000a).[14]

The East Greenlandic sources follow a similar, if less easily expounded, course, because unlike the West Greenlandic ones, they are not contextualized (in diaries) to any great extent. Nevertheless, Kaarali Andreassen expressed that: "They [the shamans] visited the 'Land of the Dead' in the sky and under the sea, in order to procure knowledge of what awaits man after his life on earth" (Rasmussen 1938: 94). Kaarali, who no doubt was well informed about the stories told about the historical shamans Akku, Maratsi, and Kukkujooq, had good reasons for his generalization (Sonne 2005: ID 1324, 1818, 1697, 1698, 1287). They belonged to the last generation of shamans, and they did undertake travels to the realms of death; conversely, stories on record about the former generations, including great shamans like Aqqi, Naaja, and Karraq, do not mention any travels destined for either realm of death. Both Aqqi and Naaja, who were said to have traveled to Sea Woman's place, merely observed the camp of the deceased close to her house (ID 29, 1196). Karraq/Uitsaleqanngitseq did not see any deceased humans, because in that text their camp is situated at the end of a side road passed by en route to Sea Woman (ID 1354). Within the same cosmography, both Akku and Kukkujooq of the last generation of shamans deliberately chose the shorter route to the nether realm of death, although they thereby precluded any later attempt on their own at reaching Sea Woman. In Kukkujooq's vision, the way was marked by three huge rolls of fog with two spaces in between, of which the first led to the realm of death below and the other farther out to Sea Woman (Sonne 2005: ID 1287; Victor & Robert-Lamblin 1989–93, II: 246).[15] Ajaqqisaaq, a helping spirit inherited by Akku, tried in vain to persuade Akku to go to Sea Woman first, whereafter he would be free to travel the shorter distance

14. The importance of naming and relations to deceased relatives has been particularly stressed by, e.g., Kublu and Oosten (1999); Blaisel and Oosten (1997); and Oosten and Laugrand (2004/05). For Inuit/Yupiit rites of death in general, see Sonne (1978, 1980), Morrow (1984), and Fienup-Riordan (1994).

15. According to Victor and Robert-Lamblin, three mountainlike boxes offer three ways, the first to the realm of death and the other two to Sea Woman (1989–93, II: 246).

to the realm of death (Sonne 2005: ID 1324).[16] The preclusion also worried the helping spirits of Kukkujooq with the same discouraging result.[17] So, investigating travels to the realms of death were undertaken by the last generation of East Greenlandic shamans, and apparently not by the previous generation, who still operated in the pre-Christian cosmology.

The East Greenlandic shaman's travels to heaven used to go to either Moon or to *Asiaq*, the *inua* of precipitation. He might be stopped on the way to Moon by the dangerous *Qulummiin* spirits, the Northern Lights, as proposed earlier. The way to *Asiaq* appears less dangerous, and the house of deceased humans engaged in nonstop cheerful song duels is sometimes placed next to her house (ID 1200). Detailed reports on the afterlife stem above all from the youngest generation of shamans. They were under impact by rumors from the south, as will be shown in the following.

Akku (ca. 1843–1891, not baptized) visited both realms, first the upper one, then the lower one, enabling him to compare and make his choice. In heaven he came to see his deceased father, who was momentarily saddened by the news that some of his relatives had ended up in the lower realm, barring any reunion. The depression was transient, though. He soon took to singing happily and had to explain to his wondering son: "Oh, you will come to realize that up here we do not live like on earth loaded down with sorrow; we sing a lot and we love being here." Akku also meets with people in foreign clothes that he had never seen before. He is informed of the diet of berries and young ravens and—more important than any other news—that the drinking water is icy cold (ID 1818). When going to the realm of death below, Akku is reproached by his idol down there, the great shaman Karraq, for breaking with tradition by having opted out of visiting Sea Woman. Otherwise Akku remains in fairly good correspondence with tradition, which banned the bad effects of prolonged mourning and granted the hunter drowned by a sea mammal an afterlife below.[18]

Again, the most interesting news concerns the temperature of the drinking water: it is lukewarm. Consequently, when asked about his priorities, Akku prefers heaven, meaning that he should be buried on the land, not in the sea (ID 1324). According to a note taken down by Rasmussen and his ending of the published story,[19] however, the choice is fortunately not all that decisive. It can be circumvented by being buried just above the mark of high tide for three days and nights and then thrown into the sea. In that case the deceased can henceforth travel from one realm to the other at will (1921–25, I: 81; KRH 52, 2, booklet 405: between 4 and 5; 1938: 79).[20]

---

16. By stopping short en route to the Other World the shaman set an impassable limit for himself (e.g., Sonne 2005: ID 1193, 1196, 1287, 1324).

17. When Kukkujooq told the minister Sandgreen about the visit, he added that it also made him give up his upcoming *saqqummerneq*, his public initiation (Sonne 2005: ID 1287). At that point in history the majority of the Ammassalimmiut had become baptized, and the alleged lack of an initiation did not prevent Kukkujooq from practicing, even after baptism (Sara Helms pers. comm.; Jens Rosing pers. comm.).

18. The effects vary, such as delaying the travel of the deceased to the realm of death, or that the tears shall freeze on his body when he arrives (Sonne 2005: ID 2283; H. Egede 1971, 2: 83; 1925: 375–76; 1818: 151).

19. The handwritten original of the story does not offer this choice. It is possible that Rasmussen added it from his note.

20. According to archaeologists, the Thule graves on land in East Greenland are too numerous for burial in the sea to have been common practice (Gulløv pers. comm.; Jensen et al. 2011). The distinction between the two practices may thus be of a more recent date. On the other hand, although the idea of combined burial on land and in the sea may be an even more recent solution to eternal separation from relatives in either realm of death, it tallies with central position of the foreshore combining not only land with sea but also heaven with underworld. See below and ch. 6, "Conclusion."

The decisive temperature of the drinking water tallies with the earthly fact that upwards is colder and downwards is warmer, as witnessed by the ice covering the uppermost inland areas and the comforting temperature of the sea that rarely freezes solid. A kayaker can warm his hands in the open sea when they are freezing cold. The preference also supports the Christian ideas, as does the entire discourse of these reports. First, the happiness in heaven dispelling all earthly worries and sorrows was a strong issue in missionizing (trust the providence of God). The ongoing singing in heaven was apparently a shared idea, though accentuated by the mission. The foreigners Akku met in heaven are without a doubt baptized Qallunaat. In the lower realm, the rotting of bodies may mean that they will be prevented from resurrection in the flesh. This issue is urgent in some acculturated stories, such as a variant of Akamalik, the Southerner who was taken to heaven by Jesus in a dream. Jesus showed him the burning abyss of hell and told him to stop his sinful way of life. Slowly waking up, Akamalik observes his body totter around like some lunatic, infested with crawling maggots. However disgusting it feels, he has to return into his body in order to improve his way of life and then become baptized (Sonne 2005: ID 491). Probably along the same line of thought, and in contrast to the traditional belief that deceased humans lived on in spirit (*tarneq*) alone, the lovely lake in heaven has in Christian times (Ammassalik in the 1930s) turned into a black abyss swarming with maggots on its banks. The maggots are deceased human bodies that also creep about in the entrance tunnel of the small house on the lake (ID 1991).

The eternal afterlife in separation from some of one's dear relatives appears to have caused some concern, and the solution—the special burial at the limits of sea and land—is not only brilliant but also in fine consonance with tradition; this is evoked in a spell, a *serrat* for resuming hunting after a period of mourning:

> I steam with corpse vapor.
> The great up there alone are without corpse vapor.
> I steam with corpse vapor.
> The great down there (in the sea) are alone without corpse vapor.
> I am hidden (?)
> At both ebb and flood of the tide,
> At its boundary I am hidden.
> (Thalbitzer 1923: 262)

The informant Keersagaq explains that the vapor surrounding the person under taboo scares away the game. The big ones above and below are the deceased humans in heaven and beneath the sea, respectively, and the boundary, the hiding place, where the *serrat* is to be recited, is both the place where and the time when the tide changes from high to low. Following that instruction, this *serrat* means protection against the punishment of the deceased in either place. This creative potential or liminality of the tide is continuously demonstrated by its transformation of land and sea, the marked Inuit oppositions, into one and the other.

Maratsi's (ca. 1854–1923, baptized 1912) journeys to both realms are less impressive, although he is visibly eager to prove his great abilities. Accordingly, one of his auxiliary spirits that stays with the audience enthusiastically reports the ongoing events of the journey. In the realm below, where summer reigns with seals splashing in the sea, Maratsi encounters persons in pain due to the breaking of the rules of mourning relatives above. "These are the ones you must release," he is told, and (in my interpretation) he plays the role of savior by simply blowing on them. A man, for instance, regains his sight when the blowing removes from his eyes some pieces of rose root caused by his brother's untimely consumption of such food. In severe cases Maratsi leaves the curing to a helping spirit (Sonne 2005: ID 1697, 1983). Christian influence is most probably also the reason why Maratsi has no similar liberating deeds to perform in heaven. He meets some of his younger sisters and brothers, who died at a young age and, contrary to tradition, have grown into adults up there. But he follows (the new?) tradition in stressing the agreement between the way of burial and the place of afterlife: if buried on land you will end up in heaven, if at sea, the lower world (ID 1698).

From inside tradition the Christian discourse peeps through, especially in the realm below, where Maratsi and his familiar cure and thereby liberate the sick to the effect of eventually permitting the cured ones to join the company of merry singing persons. The latter "custom" of singing Maratsi has borrowed from the realm above (Sonne 2005: ID 1200, 1818; Rasmussen 1929: 94–95). This joyous singing even makes another deceased person look out of her tent, exclaiming with delight: "Now I have been reunited with my dear relatives!" (Sonne 2005: ID 1697) All of this looks like a Christian message translated into a stubborn Greenlandic perspective. On the condition that life hereafter goes on eternally, the preferred prospect is a reunion with the beloved ones in the glory and festivities of singing. Also, the pains in hell, as I understand the message ironically, can easily be remedied by cures that hardly surpass the abilities of a great shaman like Maratsi.

The shaman Kukkujooq (1885–1962, baptized Apulu 1917), whose father was killed, visited the realm below in order to learn if the ideal of revenge was still in force. At that point in history, the mission had become fairly successful in banning murders of any kind. As mentioned above, Kukkujooq preferred this visit to his father to any future ones to Sea Woman, and he met his father, who looked the way he died, the same age with a big wound in his back, but lacking flesh all the same. He was not particularly talkative and to Kukkujooq's relief he did not mention a single word about revenge (ID 1287).

In conclusion about the last East Greenlandic shamans' journeys to the lower realm of death, it presumably came to take precedence over the one to Sea Woman, because the new prospects of the afterlife below were alarming and had to be ameliorated. As will be shown next, the eternity of afterlife in itself was a matter that made some East Greenlanders worry and try to find out more.

Temporal Aspects of Otherworldly Life

Time—in terms of reproduction, growing, aging, and death—yields the game animals a status on par with humans, in that they reproduce themselves, grow, and, provided they are treated properly upon being killed, will have their life renewed. As a rule, they visit This World in their manifest forms alone. At home in the Other World, some appear human in some way or other, particularly polar bear, fox, and birds. Deceased humans (preferably) live, as we know, in either the realm of death beneath the sea, hunting like live humans on earth, or the realm above, singing and producing the Northern Lights by playing ball with a walrus skull.[21] Their heavenly diet has been

21. East Greenlandic notions on record deviate from this pan-Inuit one of the walrus skull. One has just "skulls" (Rasmussen 1921–25, I: 71–72); another has stillborn and killed babies dancing and playing ball with their placenta (Holm 1972: 121; 1914: 82). See the discourse on young ravens above (pp. 84f).

negotiated throughout Christian mission in reaction to both the latter's identification of hell with the realm below and its promise (read: threat) of an eternal life above without any food (Sonne 2000a). Names of deceased relatives were (and are still, see Tróndheim [2010]) recycled, transforming human babies into genuine social beings. But in their realms both above and below, deceased humans remained the age they had been at death (aside from the deviation made by Maratsi above) and do not reproduce.[22] The figures of Sea Woman, Moon, and Sun take up a position in between, in that sea mammal and seabird are figuratively "reborn" at the house ("womb") of Sea Woman whereas Moon, attracted by his sister, Sun, guarantees the fertility on earth of humans and animals alike. They make the world go round. They often occupy the same platform but not as a married couple and not reproducing themselves (see also Sonne 2000b). Most spirits, especially those of the land and beneath the shore, are said to reproduce themselves and live like humans in families (e.g., Sonne 2005: ID 1205, 1218; Thalbitzer 1923: 485), but they differ in clothing, hunting techniques, and some bodily peculiarities from humans as well as mutually by species. On other issues neither informants nor stories agree. Thus, quoting Teemiartissaq: "They have, it is said... sons and daughters, which cannot grow, and since they don't fall ill, they cannot age... When their assistant spirits become ill..." (Thalbitzer 1923: 485). Actually, spirits may be killed, be robbed of their souls by a human shaman, get sick, be cured by a human shaman, or become the object of sorcery, in that spirits called upon human shamans for healing, witch finding, and difficult births (Sonne 2005: ID 55, 206, 1304, 1853). Some spirits were able to change size, and at times spirits were credited with eternal lives. "For how long do you live?" Missuarniannga asks Nakkalia, one of his helping spirits. "*Atanigte/atanitti naggatat nalunarpoq*" ("one does not know the end of affiliation to life"), meaning, as Rasmussen explains, that "we (the spirits) know nothing about dying" (Sonne 2005: ID 2283). Right before, however, Nakkalia told about the loss of his five sons. They were killed (*ibid.*). So, maybe the spirits could get killed, exterminated, but not die from accident or old age? The mother of Kaakaaq's first helping spirit, Papeqqia, used to have a husband, she told visiting Kaakaaq. But "his exit was blocked, so he died" (J. Rosing 1963: 287; Sonne 2005: ID 1243). Blocked by sickness or killed? one might ask. Out of context, the idea of immortality seemed strange to some Greenlanders when Poul Egede told them that God could not die. What an "exceptionally strong *toornaarsuk*" [particular helping spirit] he had to be (P. Egede 1971: 26; 1939: 23; Sonne 1986b)! Nevertheless, a *toornaarsuk* could be killed by flatulence during a shaman's performance (P. Egede 1971: 160; 1939: 106). For another example, a medium-size giant, one of Naaja's helping spirits and a shaman itself, was killed in a fight by another helping spirit. This deceased spirit shaman, *Uppiinnguaq* (Little Owl), was buried but then gradually revived by his father by singing *serratit* (spells) at his grave morning and evening for an entire month. Thus initiated by death and revival, *Uppiinnguaq* became a *great* shaman among his distant relatives, the biggest inland giants (Sonne 2005: ID 1198). In contrast, no second life was granted to the boulder threatening the longhouse in spring when it was fought and annihilated by the helping spirit *Equngasoq*. The remains were harmless small stones (ID 1192). And as we know, some species of dwarves possessed the ability to rejuvenate, five times in all. They were resilient but not everlasting, except as mythic figures whose

22. In one instance the Northern Lights is said to derive from miscarriages of the deceased (Victor & Robert-Lamblin 1989–93, II: 254)!

lives are frozen like those of comic strip characters. Otherwise the degree of temporality changed with context, and as far as I can discern, spirits are never encountered in the human realms of death. Only game animals were available, as food for souls.[23]

In summary, no afterlife is granted to the spirits. They can live eternally, become revived within their own Other World, or simply be annihilated. Some spirits have an origin story, though most tend to remain unaltered like comic strip or fairy tale characters, or like helping spirits taken over by younger generations of shamans who recurrently put them to action during performances. In these ways they meet the expectation of being timeless mythic figures, but in others eternity is a concept difficult to honor (Gessain 1984; Sonne 2005: ID 1247, 1312; see also R. Petersen 2003b).

Oosten and Laugrand (2004/5) emphasize the aspects by which these beings differ from earthly humans. The former observe no rules, are invisible, and have no names in recirculation, and thus temporally and spatially they remain outside human society. In contrast, human names are essentially social and even overrule the bonds of kinship. "They structure a society that is organized in terms of time and space and at the same time transcend that structure" (117). Observing no rules, the nonhumans should instead be called nonsocial beings. This latter argument rests on Iglulik and Nattilik origin myths about the rules observed by humans that supposedly do not apply to beings of the Other Worlds (*ibid.*). Variants of these myths are not on record from Greenland, nor does any statement make explicit that "rules" did not apply to the (nonhuman) "Others" (*allanat*). To reiterate, in Greenland several species among these "Others" are definitely portrayed as living in extended households of relatives just like humans. Also, strictly speaking, they *do* observe rules, however awkward or turned around. Raven observes no human taboos on eating, but he is never permitted indoors. The *innersuit* are said in one story to mourn a dying fellow man, but stop mourning at his death (Sonne 2005: ID 1598), whereas the relatives of killed *Uppiinnguaq*, one of Naaja's helping spirits, follow ordinary human rules. He is dressed for burial and buried, and the grave is circled in accordance with the movement of the sun (ID 1198). Every species of spirits had its habits and superhuman abilities transcending space and time, as pointed out by Oosten and Laugrand. But still, in Greenland they also had their limits. As mentioned above, the giants of the inland ice did not know how to use a kayak, as they did not possess the right bodily balance. In contrast, the *innersuit*, who were the size of humans, surpassed humans in kayaking and hunting at sea, because they were extremely clean (ID 50, 339, 394, 445, 1849, 2283), whereas the *filthy* tiny coastal dwarves were fine kayakers but unable to kill the smallest young of a seal (ID 1364). The light of cleanliness attracts game, the main purpose for observing the taboos among humans, and seemingly also for spirits. Apart from limits in movement, both spatial and temporal distinctions prevail insofar as the *innersuit* fear everything from the land and lead their lives in a reversal of seasons compared with those of the earth. Overall some definition of "rules" would make clear the discussion of differences in temporal and spatial conditions between humans and nonhumans; some superordinate rules which did apply may help clarification.

23. Many East Greenlandic spirits did have names; most were descriptive, some were personal, but apparently not in use for recycling between death and life (Sonne 2005: ID 1216, 1290).

Dyadic Relations

In my view one superordinate rule concerns the relationships between humans and helping spirits. Except in situations of offering future service to a solitary human or being called upon by their shaman (Sonne 2005: ID 1179, 984), the spirits generally keep away from ordinary humans in daylight and remain outside human social relations. As discussed by Sonne (1996), and mentioned also by Oosten and Laugrand in regard to their field (2004/05: 114f), alliances like marriage and adoption between humans and nonhumans do not work. Or, to be more specific, in Greenland they work as long as the alliance remains *dyadic* but dissolve or are ruined at the moment the allied Other is asked to meet human social demands like sharing and wife exchange (*ibid.*).[24] It works the other way round as well. A human becoming a member of a spirit family in the Other World has either to stay forever, visiting home only once (for the story to be told), or to flee, killing or leaving behind both spirit spouse and kids. The relations are similarly dyadic between the human shaman and his familiars. He cannot share a familiar with any other human, nor can he make use of any of the spirit's relatives unless an individual agreement has been made. In short, the two kinds of societies could not become mutually integrated (Sonne 1996), because alliance with the "Others" were either dyadic or the human had to go native among spirits.[25] Widening the focus, the rule of dyadic relations worked in asymmetrical ways. First, the shaman owned several helping spirits, who could not serve more than one human master. Shamans among spirits had helping spirits of the same species as humans, but, in contrast to the human shaman, never a deceased human. The consequences of these apparent "rules" for relations between the shaman and his helping spirits will be discussed in chapter 4, on shamans.

Remaking Cosmology on Christian Terms

Returning to the question of the promised eternity of Christian afterlife, the thoughts evoked appear to have required some remaking of cosmology. After some three years of mission, Hans Egede concluded that the Christian messages that made the greatest impression were the following: the end of the world, Christ's second coming on the Day of Judgment, and the resurrection from the dead (H. Egede 1971, 1: 133; 1925: 115). The promise of resurrection met with the problem that unbaptized deceased relatives would end up in the dreadful realm of Hell. Thus, to take one example, a

---

24. Three stories contradict this assertion: an East Greenlandic one about the marrying-in of a fox, the cunning animal who time and again saves his in-laws from starvation (Sonne 2005: ID 1323); a West Greenlandic one about having an *alliaruseq/innersuaq*, a magnificent provider, as a son-in-law; and the third (mentioned previously) about a historical person (Peter Ranthol), originally the son of a dwarf but purchased by a human shaman. The fox story might have referred to the East Greenlanders' new profitable trade in fox skins to Southwest Greenlanders about 1700 (H. Egede 1971, 1: 49, 50, 342–43; 1971, 2: 21; 1818: 38; 1925: 23, 24, 267, 324; Jensen et al. 2011), whereas at a closer look neither the second nor the third story disprove the assertion of keeping the societies of humans and "Others" mutually apart. Thus the family that gets the *innersuaq* for a son-in law has chosen to live *in isolation* apart from occasional visits to and from other human families (Sonne 2005: ID 214), and the purchased dwarf creeps into his adoptive human mother's womb. He remains there throughout babyhood, and when born and grown he has informative stories to tell about the *history* of his former ancestors (ID 1323, 214, 163).

25. All of which would contradict a main point in the theory of animism awarded by Descola (1994), whose "animists" permit human domestication of persons from the Other World (cf. T. Turner 2009: 16–17). Dyadic relationship is the Greenlandic prerequisite of such domestication. Only the domesticated dog took up a particular position in myth (Dog Husband).

dying baptized elder in doubt whether he would ever see his deceased wife and children again was hard put to understand Hans Egede's words of consolation in imperfect Greenlandic (1971, 1: 155; 1925: 149). Other dying persons responded with great joy as if the promise of eternal life in company with recently deceased relatives was new (1971, 1: 86, 116, 291; 1925: 69, 101, but on p. 238 the statement in 1971, 1: 291 is eliminated). In the South, Nicoline, a recently baptized immigrant from Southeast Greenland, is relieved. She explicitly expresses her pleasure at the prospect of coming together with her beloved ones after death, *because* she has been baptized (Rasmussen 1906: 191); her story reminds us of the happy woman in the lower realm of death who eventually reunites with her relatives due to the redeeming effects of Maratsi's visit. Similarly brilliant is the solution to the problem of separation forever and ever: the temporary burial just above the line of high tide. Akku, moreover, is credited a song about a new way of life in heaven. In a dream he received this song from one of his helping spirits, a deceased human, and he passed it on to his son, Eiriki, who shared it with Victor in 1935:

> *Je vais raconter*
> *la première fois que je suis allé là-haut*
> *là-haut dans le vaste ciel.*
> *Je me rappelle*
> *la première fois que je suis allé au ciel*
> *les marches était inclinées dans le mauvais sens.*
> *Les gens ne meurent plus*
> *là-haut, là-haut, là-haut, là-haut.*[26]

Waking up from his dream, Akku raced ecstatically across the floor as if it were covered with ice, showing his joy (Victor & Robert-Lamblin 1989–93, II: 338; Victor 1991: 213; Sonne 2005: ID 1992). In 1905–6 Thalbitzer (1923: 289; 1931: 88–89) took down a similar song from Missuarniannga, Akku's son-in-law:

> Up there when I had the fortune to come
> The people had ceased to die.[27]

The last line in East Greenlandic, "*ewin toquca.rput,*" does not differ in essence from that of Victor's rendering, "*iivit torutsaarsit.*" This song, Missuarniannga stated, was composed by an old Ammassalimmiu at the time the old people of his contemporaries were born (i.e., ca. 1830–1840). At that time, he continued, a smaller number of humans peopled the world, while too many babies crowded the realm in heaven (*ibid.*). The meaning of this explanation is far from clear, as it seemingly refers to the babies fetched by shamans in heaven for curing infertile women. But who had stopped

---

26. "I am going to tell about the first time I went upwards, up there in the extensive heaven. I remember that the steps were turned the wrong way. People do not die anymore up there, up there, up there, up there" (tr. BS).

27. The song was known also by the Southeast Greenlander Kuannia, who was interviewed by Thalbitzer in 1914 (1923: 407).

dying, the small number of people on earth or the babies in heaven? Whatever the answer, proportions had become imbalanced between numbers of heavenly babies and people living on earth, a conversion in a way of the traditional beginning in bygone times when death was absent and the earth tipped by overpopulation.

Thalbitzer took down the same song also from Aleqaajik. Its narrative frame concerns an imbalance as well, but of too many babies on earth, and Thalbitzer translates "*toquca.rpun*'" into the diametrically opposed meaning: "now they die at intervals in due time." Aleqaajik's complete story-song runs as follows:

> (In the beginning people could not die.) The children became far too numerous. Therefore he began to think: "the descendants become far too numerous. How shall I bring about depletion?" In the morning when he went into the house, he began to recite a magic formula over them: "Become scum!" While they dreamed in deep sleep, he caused them to become scum. Then some of them died, he who was first dead, when he awoke to consciousness he rose up to heaven. The dead must creep off. The way leads up a steep mountain-side with constant impediments, especially because the steps are turned "backwards." Through the small *aterqat* (?) they fight [their way?], they complain over the way (as they crawl up the steps). They fight [struggle?] much. The first dead reached heaven, just as the next moon appeared. (Weeping) he arrived to heaven, but his horror was soon turned to joy over all that he saw up there, and the first dead was surprised and sang from joy. This is said to be his song (drum song).
>
> Song of the first dead
> People have begun a new custom.
> People now die at intervals (in time) [*toquca.rpun*']
> Chopping out a little step,
> People die at intervals,
> After they have stepped through their heavy troubles.
> (Thalbitzer 1923: 407; Sonne 2005: ID 1015)

Evidently the imbalance of babies and adults is the opposite of Missuarniannga's vision. The children who become too numerous on earth constitute the problem in Aleqaajik's version in correspondence with the traditional origin of choosing light and death in exchange for eternal life on earth in darkness (e.g., P. Egede 1971: 80; 1939: 57–58; Sonne 2005: ID 1517; see below). The difficult passage and the heavenly joy of singing belong in tradition as well. But who is that person, the "he," who introduces death by transforming everybody into scum (rabble or foam?), and why does the transformation not cause the death of everyone at once? Because the scum, whatever it means, signifies mortality, I suppose. But again, why do people die at intervals *after* their arrival in heaven? Because, I dare say, Thalbitzer's translation of *toquca.rpun* is wrong. Literally it can be parsed as the following: die (*toqu-*) stop (*-tsaar*) they have (*-pun*), as also confirmed by the late linguist Jørgen Rischel (pers. comm.). So, following that translation, people up there have received a new custom: they have stopped dying. How come?

An answer could be the provenience of that story and/or song, which both Aleqaajik and Eirik *located in the South* (Thalbitzer 1923: 407; Victor 1991: 213). Christian influence received at places of assembly to the south can thus be assumed, which would explain not only "he" as God, and "scum" in the meaning of rabble viz. sinners. It would also explain Akku's racing joy at the news of eternal life in heaven as well as *the complete absence in the text of the realm of death below; the focus is on heaven alone.* While Missuarniannga's version remains unclear, the perspective in Aleqaajik's version appears to be a Christian-tinted interpretation of the Inuit origin myth of death.[28]

The Times of Mythic Events

Considering eternity, can the endless course of changeless time be identified with the so-called timelessness of origin myths? The timelessness of an origin myth does not refer to its narrative, a sequence of events in time that ultimately sets an order of the present day. The lack of time concerns its actuality, its eternal truth.

The earliest Inuit origin myths on record, quoted below, will be my point of departure for further discussions.[29]

The Earliest Recordings of Inuit Origin Myths

Fortunately, missionary Poul Egede, the son of Hans Egede, wrote summaries of several origin myths in his diaries from 1735 to 1741 as told by both local and passing Greenlanders. He became fluent in Greenlandic during his adolescence at his father's mission, then got his degree in theology in Copenhagen and returned to Nuuk as an ordained missionary in the summer of 1735. From June 1736 to August 4, 1740, Poul was the first and most northernmost missionary at Christianshåb/Qasigiannguit. He traveled the region and frequently had visitors from near today's Ilulissat and farther north, once from as far north as the Upernavik district. He did not literally "collect" stories. He put his own stamp on the reproductions, which thus call for discourse analysis. People either told a myth in polite response to his Christian myths, or in order to have their own stories accepted as true. Poul, of course, rarely complied. Convinced he possessed the ultimate truth, Poul used to mock their stories, foolhearted as he took them to be. In Poul's opinion, their most opposing idea in contrast to God's Creation stands out to be the Greenlanders' consistent idea that any important mythic figure derived from a human being. So, in addition to offering the date and provenience of the story, the diary often points to the reasons why the storyteller felt inclined to narrate. Some texts, however, are editorial insertions, meaning that no precise date can be set. Continuously calling attention to these reservations, I shall quote (and currently comment on) these very first recordings of Inuit myths at length (in my translation) because most summaries made by Hans Egede of the same texts for his "Perlustration" (1971, 2; 1925: 305–404; 1818) and translated into English (1818) are summaries of summaries.

---

28. Another piece of news delivered by Missuarniannga in the form of a song and a story tells about a woman's delight at having received the gift of singing upon her exhausted arrival in heaven. On earth she could not sing a note. A shaman received the story on a visit to heaven, and back home he had the story confirmed by another shaman in general terms, namely, that anyone who cannot sing a note will be able to sing in heaven. Hearing such news the widower twirled in a joyous dance (Thalbitzer 1923: 290). So the heavenly singing in the Christian heaven may have added power to that of tradition.

29. My discussion makes inroads to the ideas of some contemporary Inuit, who deny Qallunaat any right to interfere with Inuit cultural heritage. But because Greenlanders are less sensitive to this problem, I take the risk.

Poul received the first variant of the Inuit flood story in response to his story about the deluge, which in his own explicit understanding was sent by God as a punishment. The local Greenlanders knew that story very well, they said, and said that the flood left shells still to be seen high up in the mountains (1939: 27; 1971: 32).[30] Another short "story" on the flood points to the shells as well:

> July 12 (1738). A foreign Greenlander, having listened to my telling about the creation, told what he knew from hearsay: that the heaven in bygone times rested on the top of the mountains, but that it later was raised to its present altitude above the earth. That happened, he added, at the time when the big flood swelled up over the entire earth, an event which he, like his compatriots, concluded from the small shells and other things from the sea that were found in regular heaps far up in the inland region. (P. Egede 1971: 89; 1939: 63)

A more complete version is told some four months later, on November 7, 1738:

> While we stayed among the savages, who lived a [Danish] mile [7.5 km] to the north [of Christianshåb/Qasigiannguit], they talked about a person who had been lost in his kayak and that neither he nor the kayak had been found. The shamans have decided that he was stolen by the Ingnersoit [*innersuit*], i.e.: the "big fire trolls"; that's how they call the people and in-dwellers of the shore and sea. They used to live on earth, so they say, before the big flood swelled up all over the world, and when the earth capsized, it turned bottom up. In evidence of the explanation, that the kayaker had been robbed by these *innersuit*, the newly arrived shaman told about the fire that appeared right before his eyes whenever he practiced witchcraft [performed as a shaman]. Having responded to that [correctingly] I asked them how the earth had become populated since Antedeluviani became *innersuit*. One among the Greenlanders answered: After the flood, a man (from where he came, the Greenlander did not know) walked about alone without a wife. He copulated with a hummock that swelled, became pregnant and eventually bore a baby girl. At a later point he married that girl, and they had children who married one another, because they were the only people in the world. That ancestor, they went on, had trees instead of hair for a beard. (P. Egede 1971: 96–97; 1939: 67)

The association with trees was most probably to driftwood, in line perhaps with the Nattilik idea that driftwood stemmed from the bottom of the sea (Rasmussen 1931: 208–9). In that case he ascended from below the earth. Anyway, like trees (I presume), that very first man enjoyed a very long life: "In the old days a big man having trees[31] on the chin instead of a beard lived for so long that his wives, whom he had survived one after another, and had been buried next to each other, were so numerous, that he could not throw a stone all the way across the graves. Since in the end, our man said, he was not seen any more, could he be God?" (P. Egede 1971: 158; 1939: 105; tr. BS)

The flood appears in still a fourth version, which I take to be one of the earliest acculturated Inuit origin myths on record. Although presented at an early date in the diary, the story is an editorial

30. A storm surge.
31. Trees do grow in sheltered places and shrubs all over in Southwest Greenland.

insertion because, as explicitly stated by Poul, he received it at later date. The story is a millennial myth repeating the flood story and apparently stimulated by Doomsday:

> Having told him about the resurrection of the deceased, he told me from hearsay that: When all humans have died, a great flood shall swamp the earth, clean the blood of the deceased, and when mountains, earth and stones are all separated and split up, and everything has cooled down, a wind shall blow all over and beautify everything. The high mountains shall become transformed into a lovely plain with numerous caribou. All the bones of seals shall be revived. He up there shall blow on the dead humans, twice on the men and once on the women, and they too shall be revived. But he had no other explanation to offer about the identity of 'the one up there' but that he had heard that from others. (P. Egede 1971: 79; 1939: 57, tr. BS)[32]

As we know from "Kaassassuk," the one up there, *pinnga*, must be *Sila* in the aspect of stormy weather kicking around mountains and eroding boulders into pebbles. So traditional myth fit perfectly for identifying God's breath with *Sila*'s wind, and for imagining Paradise as the flat original world underneath that is recovered not by another capsizing of the earth but by this leveling and reanimating wind.

Returning to the long-living man with trees for a beard, another old man associated with wood can still be met with at a big (otherworldly) river that leads to the land of the birds. At this place salmon, or fish in general, are continuously fathered by an old man chopping wood. Poul Egede received the story to which this creative episode belongs on December 15, 1735, at the Nuuk mission before his move to Qasigiannguit/Christianshåb. The story in question is a variant of the widely extended swan maiden myth and it enters the scene at the "difficult passage" to be overcome by the main character in search of his escaped wife, a swan maiden.[33]

> On the way he arrived at a big stream, where an old man chopped shavings from a piece of wood, mopped every shaving between his legs, and threw them into the water, whereupon they turned into fishes.[34] The other [the main character] looked at him hiding behind a mountain. Eventually he decided to approach, but at the moment the old man saw him, he asked: Where did you come from? If you came from behind me you shall live. If you came from the front you shall die. He felt ashamed that the other might have seen him coating the shavings *sudore testiculorum*, for making them into fishes. The other answered: I arrived from behind you and did not see you until at close quarters. I have been walking for a long while looking for my wife and my son who have left me, and I do not know where to find them. The old man immediately seized his axe

32. "Every valley shall be lifted up, and every mountain and hill be made low; the uneven ground shall become level, and the rough places a plain" (Isaiah 40, 4). Händel's *Messiah* was not yet composed, but Poul of course preached the prophesies of the Old Testament.

33. Instead of the swan, a wild goose or merganser maiden appears in the Greenlandic variants. See Kleivan (1962) for analysis and complete translations of published Inuit/Yupiit variants. Search also "swan maiden" in Sonne (2005) for the Greenlandic variants.

34. Another parallel to the Proto-Uralian World River, which besides being the way of the shamans is called the (migrating) way of the waterbirds (Napolskikh 1992).

> and wood and chopped off a big piece, treated it his usual way, and placed it in the water, where it became a salmon. He then instructed the wanderer: Do sit on the back of this salmon, back to front, and close your eyes, and although you shall hear roaring and people talking, don't open them until you sense that the salmon has stopped. He dared not object and placed himself with fear on the back of the salmon and closed his eyes, whereupon the salmon rushed off. On the way he did hear whizzing and roaring, and at the point when he could hear the noise of people, he started opening one eye a little and almost dropped off the salmon. Quickly he shut the eye and did not open it until he clearly could hear people talking, and the salmon had stopped at the dry bank. Stepping ashore he immediately caught sight of his son playing with other boys. He went up to him and caressed him. The son, recognizing his father, ran into the tent telling his mother: Father is out there! I do not believe that, the mother answered, how could he ever get across the sea to me? But the man went into the tent and saw another man sitting next to his wife. She blushed and the man sitting next to her took his chest and went out.[35] This is the story about the origin of fish we used to believe in before you arrived in our country, he [the storyteller] said. Such fools and stupid people we are, right? But now we despise it. That characterization I could not deny but added that I hoped that they preferred to believe in my lessons. (P. Egede 1971: 19ff; 1939: 18–19)

Besides semen, both urine and wind have transformative effects. Combined, they turn a piece of skin into another kind of fish; as told by a boy accompanying Poul on a trip, a woman "once washed her hair in urine, but because a strong wind blew away the skin she used for drying her hair, that skin was transformed into the shark. That's why this fish smells like urine" (P. Egede 1971: 60; 1939: 45).

Like most peoples in the world, Inuit told myths about the origin of death. Poul Egede received *three differing short stories* about the end of eternal life on earth. The first, an editorial insertion placed in continuation of the first "flood" story, goes like this: "It is odd, but they blame a woman for the evil that people must suffer in this life and which for, eventually, they shall die. She said: *Toqorsarlutiq okko pilit Sillarsuak tettulissoat*: 'Let them die one after another, or there will not be enough room left in the world,' because, from the first beginning humans lived forever" (P. Egede 1971: 32; 1939: 27; 1988: 63, tr. BS).[36]

The second myth about death is dated to about a year later, some ten days after Poul had preached the Gospel to some visitors from the north and thereby caused them to question their own myths.[37]

> One among them told me another reason why people must die, different from the one already recorded, namely, that a serpent and a louse decided to compete to see who could come first to

35. At that time (December 1735), numerous West Greenlanders had bought wooden chests from the Dutch whalers.

36. *Toqusarlutik uku pilit, silarsuaq tattulisavaat*: let it be a rule that they die, or the world cannot hold them all (P. Egede 1939: 279, note by Ostermann, the editor).

37. One was terribly shocked at hearing about that horrifying God and his hell, and another popped up the following day just to tell Poul something about the world that he probably would not know, namely, that far up north the stars, Orion's belt in particular, were that much closer to earth that you should arm yourself with a whip for keeping them at a distance.

> the human beings. In case the serpent was first, people should go on living, whereas they were to die if the louse should win. They started out at once, and the serpent, as could be expected, quickly got far ahead. But then he unexpectedly tumbled down a mountain, and the louse won. That is why people must die. Is that so? He asked. Or do humans, i.e. the Inuit, as is their habit, also lie about that? (P. Egede 1971: 60; 1939: 45; 1988: 81)

Preaching the Gospel, Poul most probably translated the serpent of Eden into "the big worm" as, for example, he did three days later, when the myth of the Fall called forth a dispute among still another group of Northerners on a visit: "one among them asked me if our first parents had serpents instead of the lice we have now? An old woman quickly took the floor: 'nothing but lies: if their ancestors had serpents their descendants would have had the same. Humans [Inuit] are big liars: We believe you when you tell us, that God at the very beginning made two humans; that sounds reasonable as also that all of us are their children and descendants, because our faces, hands and feet are identical'" (*ibid.*). Poul won the day, as there was no fuss about ethnic identity; according to this woman Inuit and Qallunaat do not differ in being humans. Regarding the association of worms to death and lice to life, the myth appears reasonable in that worms belong within the earth and eat up dead, cold bodies, in contrast to lice, which die with their human hosts turning cold. The myth was told all over Greenland (search "lusen" in Sonne 2005), but the more interesting part of that particular variant is, in my view, the serpent's tumbling over and then falling down from a mountain. I recognize in that movement both the biblical fall of the disobedient angel (who developed into the Devil) and the idea of the Fall of Man caused by the serpent (alias the Devil) of paradise in a contemporary Inuit cultural translation. Consequently, I consider it an acculturated myth, which was told in variants without this serpent in the later Christianized regions (Sonne 2005: ID 433, 582, 602, 1408, 1515, 1538).

The third story about the origin of death, received in March 1738, is a variant of the first quoted, but its form as a rhyme points to it being an ancient myth. That evidence is important because it eliminates obvious considerations on Christian influence: "Two persons among the first humans quarreled. One said: Kausartlune unnutlartlune, Innuit tokorsarlutik (*Qaasarluni unullarluni, inuit toqorsarlutik*): Let it be day and be night, and people die. The other said: Unnuinnartlune, Kausunane, Innuit tokysinnartik (*Unuinnarluni, qaasunani inuit toqusinnartik*): Let night continue without any days, and people go on living. After a prolonged dispute, the words of the former set the order. The only difference between the former and the latter's Greenlandic words consists in the inflections" (P. Egede 1971: 80; 1939: 57–58; tr. BS). Indeed, receiving light in exchange for death has metaphors in common with the Christian promise of salvation, but the Inuit lights play other important roles in their spheres of life, death, and shamanism, of which much more will be discussed later.

No story or statement discuss how far light, generally speaking, differs from that offered by the heavenly bodies, sun and moon in particular. The origin myth of Sun and Moon was as popular in Greenland as anywhere in the Inuit world. Variants were told right through the centuries of mission, the first on record to Poul Egede in September 1735 on a visit some 200 km to the north of Nuuk, where he encountered people apparently ignorant of Christianity. From the horse's mouth they then heard about the Creation and the Fall of Man, the resurrection by Christ, and about Doomsday, heaven, and hell. One of the listeners politely responded by relating the origin of Sun and Moon, a remarkably long and detailed variant completely in line with those told by other Inuit. Consequently, a summary will suffice: An elder brother, Moon, falls in love and commits incest with his younger sister, Sun, in the playhouse of adolescents during a "putting out of the lamps." He is smeared with soot by the suspicious sister and afterwards easily identified by the black patches on his white caribou-skin clothing. She runs off, circling the house with Moon at her heels until, deeply ashamed, she stops, cuts off her breast with her *ulu* (crescent-shaped women's knife), and throws it at Moon with the words, "You seem to find only me tasty, eat this one as well!" She then lights a tuft of moss and rises into the air, pursued by Moon, who is holding another lighted tuft. But his flame is put out, leaving only a glow. He still follows her, and his glow shines with less luminosity than the burning light of the sun. Sun rose higher than Moon, who still has to hunt on earth and at sea, catching the seals he is wont to eat. Whenever he is not seen in heaven, he is down hunting. "In this way, he said, our ancestors told the story, but now I do not believe that story anymore" (P. Egede 1971: 16–17; 1939: 16–17).

Variants of the origin myth of the other important *inua*, the mother of the sea mammals, *Sassuma Arnaa*, or Sea Woman, are, as you may remember, extremely scarce in Greenland (Avanersuaq excepted). Among the four on record (Sonne 2005: ID 547, 1882, 2070, 2304), the earliest one, told to Poul Egede by a passing Southerner, consists of little more than an inserted note to another story relating some imagined relocation of Disko Island from the Nuuk area to its present location farther north. The man who did that trick is identified with the father of Sea Woman: "that giant woman far down in earth beneath the sea . . . because when he wanted her to marry some man, and she could not bring herself to do it, he [the father] threw her into the sea; but while she still held on to the gunwale, he chopped off her fingers, after which she sank to her lasting place and became a big Devil without fingers" (ID 2304). The usual transformation of her fingers into various species of sea mammals is not included—the fingerless Devil has stolen the scene.

Poul Egede's "Dog Husband" variant stands out as another early acculturated Inuit myth (Sonne 2005: ID 2306; P. Egede 1988: 69–70; 1971: 47; 1939: 37).[38] Like most eastern Inuit variants it relates the origin of Qallunaat (Euro-Americans), but not only is this one said to have happened in southernmost Greenland, one of the regions where the Norse used to live, but it also includes another story about the origin of enmity between the Inuit and the Qallunaat. (Since Hans Egede in his Perlustration copied the story almost verbatim in a note, its 1818 translation into English will do.)

> The Greenlanders relate a very ridiculous story, as well concerning the origin of our colonies (whom they call by the name of Kablunæt) as of their total overthrow, as follows: a Greenlandic woman, in her child-bearing, was once delivered of Kablunæt and dogs' whelps, of which the parents were highly ashamed, and for that reason withdrew from their neighbours and countrymen. This monstrous breed being grown up became so troublesome to their father, that he was not able to endure them; wherefore he retired yet farther away to some distant place. Meanwhile this inhuman race came to this horrible agreement amongst them, to devour their own father,

38. Poul declares that his father already communicated that story. It is found not in Hans's diaries but in his "Perlustration" (H. Egede 1971, 2: 7; 1925: 316; 1818: 12), that is, as an almost identical copy of the text recorded by Poul.

> whenever he should happen to come among them; which after a little while came to pass, when he visited them with a present of some part of a seal, which he had taken, according to custom. Kablunæt immediately went down to him, to whom the father delivered the piece of seal's flesh he had brought them. But he was no sooner got ashore, than the doggish race seized and devoured him, and then ate the seal's flesh given them. Whilst the Kablunæt dwelled there, one of the Innuits (or mankind), for so they call themselves, came rowing along the shore, and throwing the dart at some sea fowl, missed what he aimed at; which one of the Kablunæt, who stood observing on a point of land running out into the sea, mocked and ridiculed him and, laying himself down upon the ground, told him that as he saw he was so dexterous in shooting, he would be the bird; he might throw the dart at him, and take care not to miss him: whereupon the Innuit shot and killed him. This death caused continuous strife between the Kablunæts and the Innuits, who in the end became masters and overthrew the former. (H. Egede 1818: 12–13; copied from the Hubert Wenger Eskimo Database)

This variant differs in two respects from most other Inuit variants of Dog Husband: In all other variants the father is a dog, and the girl's father moves the family to another place to where the dog travels with meat to feed them. And the girl usually sends the children away in various directions. In doing so she confers their racial characteristics in future exchanges with the Inuit. The Qallunaat are most often sent across the sea on a boot sole and gifted with a talent for making nice things (with which they shall return on trading visits).[39] Evidently, in the P. Egede version the children are *not* given racial characteristics and *not* sent off by their mother in various directions. Instead, the children remain in Greenland until, due to their foolishness, they are exterminated by the Greenlanders. A differing version has the girl's father send the Qallunaat children away before he is devoured by the remaining doglike grandchildren (Sonne 2005: ID 610), meaning that the enmity was caused not by that crime but, as emphasized by the attached story, by Qallunaat belittling the skill at which the Greenlanders far surpassed them: hitting the mark in hunting. These variations bring forth the question: did the Greenlanders actually exterminate the Norse, as was the contemporary understanding among educated Danes, including the Egedes? The aforementioned earliest version about the origin and extermination of the Norse confirmed the presumption. On the other hand, from the moment Hans Egede arrived and as he came to know sufficient Greenlandic, he asked the Greenlanders about possible surviving Norse. His intention was to discover these Catholics and convert them into Lutherans. And since he and his son Poul did not hesitate to accuse the forefathers of the Greenlanders of having exterminated the Norse, they were the actual "planters" of this idea.[40]

A very early recounting of the story about the superb Inuit archer challenged by the foolish Qallunaaq supports the former proposal. It is dated to February 17, 1723, in Hans Egede's own publication of his diaries (1971, 1 [1738]: 80). Yet in comparison with Bobé's 1925 edition of the *original*

39. For the Greenlandic versions, see Sonne (2005: ID 125, 1083, 1084, 1132, 1317, 1550, 1606, 628, 629).

40. Kleivan (1982, 1984) put forth this hypothesis, which was further substantiated by Arneborg (1991, 1996). Thisted (2001) discusses the effect on Greenlandic national identity of Greenlanders clinging to the idea that the Norse were exterminated by them. A recent examination by Sonne in Danish, "Holdningsændringer: relationer til 'andre' mennesker," is available online at: http://sonne.arktiskleksikon.dk/index.php?id=50.

notes to that day (H. Egede 1925: 65), this early summary is absent and thus turns out to be Hans Egede's editorial insertion into his 1738 [1979, 1] publication.[41] This may support the latter proposal that the Egedes' accusation was accepted by the Greenlanders but not in the role of being the offenders. The Norse had only themselves to blame. Furthermore, the extermination also eliminated the Greenlanders' usual mythic connection with the Qallunaat, who were destined to come back for trade, not for taking vengeance.

Another variant of the Dog Husband story, told in the far south to Knud Rasmussen in 1904, takes even greater precautions by removing the guilt not only from the Greenlanders but also from the Qallunaat. To that end the girl's *father* sends off the Qallunaat children in the boot sole, *before* he is eaten up by the doglike children, and these are later to become split into two "races": the dangerous dog spirits of the inland region and the domesticated dogs of the Inuit (Sonne 2005: ID 610; 1990; 1996).

Sad to realize, but although the earliest Inuit variants on record were retold/resumed by Poul Egede, a missionary who knew Greenlandic and was the first to communicate with Greenlanders in a "virgin" area, they are influenced by the mission and/or colonialism. Hans Egede's journals from 1738, his Perlustration from 1741, and Poul Egede's Continuation the same year are to be read with caution, colored as they are by cultural biases, by considerations on the target group of the published editions, as well as by editorial afterthought. Furthermore, since, as widely read as they were, they came to affect writers of later texts, they are useful to consult when dealing with younger sources.

Timeless Myths of Origin in Chronological Sequences

Obviously this heading is a contradiction in terms. But in practice as well, the combination of events of origin may run into chronological difficulties. One eloquent example is Urulu being at a loss for an answer to the question Knud Rasmussen posed at the end of her version of the origin of the sea mammals from the chopped-off fingers of Nuliayuk, the Sea Woman. How could it be, Rasmussen asked, that the husband of Nuliayuk, a fulmar, was a fine hunter who lived exclusively on young fjord seals, before the seals were created?[42] Realizing the crux of the matter, Urulu laughed, and said: "Too much thought only leads to trouble. All this that we are talking about now *happened in a time so far back that there was no time at all.* We Eskimos do not concern ourselves with solving all riddles. And if there should then seem to be a lack of reason in the story as a whole, there is yet enough remaining in the way of incomprehensible happening, which our thought cannot grasp... Where did all the living creatures on earth come from in the beginning? Can anyone explain that?" Urulu next offers another example of chronological disorder in myth, and ends as follows: "You always want these supernatural things to make sense, but we do not bother about that. We are content not to understand" (Rasmussen 1929: 68, emphasis BS).[43] As to how far Rasmussen quotes his informant to the letter one

41. Remember that the Hans Egede (1971) publication is a facsimile of the edited 1741 publication, whereas the 1925 publication was made by Bobé using (what remains of) the original handwritings.

42. A variant told to Knud Rasmussen among the Nattilingmiut the following year did not lead to the origin of either Nuliayuk nor the sea mammals: The girl has children with the fulmar, who, when bereaved, ends up raising a storm that drowns the wife, her children, and her biological relatives (Rasmussen 1931: 405–6).

43. Yup'ik folklorist Elsie Mather talks about the Yup'ik belief that things just happen with no explanation. She suggests that explication is a particularly Qallunaaq (or, in the Yup'ik equivalent, Kass'aq) preoccupation. It is problematic,

may never really know, but undoubtedly they did talk about the problems of mythic chronology with Urulu who testified to the timelessness of myth or rather its lack of a position *in the past.*

Carpenter (1968), who did fieldwork among the Aiviliit in the 1960s, emphasized their way of making mythic events topical. Mythic events were not of the past but of a "timeless *present*." The former population of Tunrit (Dorset people), for instance, who in myth taught the arriving Thule culture Inuit how to use the land, are still there, in their ruins and cairns. The mythic past is not just a bygone thing. Just like highlights in one's life story, memorized as they are in leaps and grammatical present, myths are timeless and rarely told in chronological sequence. Dramatic highlights are the points of departure as in modern literary genres, Carpenter declares in reference to James Joyce. The same holds true for mythic events, he continues. No creator made the world, and to talk about myths of origin is pure nonsense, because time is not there, whether before or after. Events happen of their own accord and are in force still and forever (*ibid.*). Although Mircea Eliade's "eternal return" (1971) could be brought to bear, some comments on Inuit mythology and more recent research are appropriate.

Admittedly, a creator is missing, and some figures bring about changes unintentionally, such as Nuliayuk by her refusal to marry and the incest that turns brother and sister into Moon and Sun. On the other hand, the Alaska Raven appears completely conscious of the changes he causes, as are the quarrelling couple, be they two old women who introduce light and death or in Arctic Canada Raven and Fox, who made day change into night on a regular basis. They have an explicit purpose; thus not all creative acts happen of their own accord. Nor did any "before" and "after" prevail. Darkness ruled before light came into the world. People did not reproduce, babies were collected like plants (or eggs?), etc. Myths or stories are never told exactly the same way from one telling to another whether by the same person or others. Depending on the situation and the teller's intention the story varies as does the listener's understanding or interpretation of it (e.g., Narayan 1989; Basso 1990). Readers similarly vary in understanding and interpreting a text, by their knowledge, references, and repeated readings. Finally, to remember in leaps is no Inuit prerogative. For instance, one of my favorite mnemonic techniques for falling asleep is to recollect the course of events of a recently seen film, yet the dramatic highlights incessantly disturb chronology. The concentration it takes to keep the story on track is quite effective, and sleep comes gently. We too are in the centers of past events ("it all comes back to me now!") evoked by stories, by suggestions, by the taste of madeleines. This is the past-present-future time of lived life according to the theory of biocultural time as delineated above; writing keeps track. Like the Inuit we also perceive environment, even "nature," with the eyes of either theory, or history, or myth: Darwin, intelligent design, or Genesis.[44] What remains is Carpenter's insistence on the lack of chronology in mythic events, as in the story pointed out by Rasmussen and agreed to by Urulu. *It is said that it is so, and therefore it is so.*

---

she thinks, to question stories or try to resolve their apparent inconsistencies, because this analytical view diminishes the mystery in the world and prevents people from finding their own meanings as they reflect on familiar stories over a lifetime (Morrow pers. comm.)

44. Roland Barthes's theory of myth is not our topic here.

The lack of chronology is directly circumvented by arrangements of mythic stories in precisely chronological sequences. The much-quoted Polar Inuit story about the origin of the earth, to be analyzed below, is one outstanding example (Rasmussen 1908); it is a Polar Inuit genesis in a way, which reminds one of another put together by Saladin d'Anglure. He arranged Iglulik origin myths in a chronological order of events that we might call a genesis (1991). The result is structurally quite satisfying, but my objection is that the Inuit did not combine their separate myths in that consistent way. In continuation of the above objections, several myths each told their story about the same big event: Raven brought light into the world, as did Sun and Moon by committing incest, and as did human beings when they chose death instead of eternal life in darkness. Each origin myth has its message to communicate about the fate of human beings. Added episodes may certainly enrich and emphasize the message. Thus, a main character may attract numerous episodes, like Kivioq for instance (see above; Sonne 1990; Thisted 1994), or Two Little Birds (Southwest Alaska, Lantis 1946: 293–96, 315). This capacity for variation points to the timelessness of myth, ever ready for new messages. Nevertheless, sometimes rough contradictions will unveil a fresh combination in the making (Sonne 2005: ID 610; 1990; 1996). It takes some talent of an illiterate storyteller to combine event myths into a flawless course of events.

In his writings, Rasmussen turns out another maker of Inuit genesis when he quotes Naalungiaq, a Nattilik woman (Rasmussen 1931: 207), when he retells the much-quoted Polar Inuit myth of Creation, and again in his attempt to make sense out of some stray notions and short origin myths of the East Greenlanders. To wit: Naalungiaq told Rasmussen some five stories in a row about events that changed the world into its present state, each in its own way. But Rasmussen, as Remie (1998) pointed out, did not just let Naalungiaq follow her own course. He "guided" her with clever questions, with the fine result of connecting one story with another into a complete account. On her side, Naalungiaq did object to his silly questions that made her forget what she wanted to tell him (Remie 1988: 119). Furthermore, since Rasmussen did not take down the stories while listening but transcribed them from memory afterwards, in Danish, one is left wondering how to evaluate the very sequence of Naalungiaq's stories. Who, one may ask, made the following causal connections and time settings of the seals coming into being from Nuliayuk's chopped-off fingers, and then the thinking-out of rules by the ancestors?

> Everything came from the ground, and people themselves lived on the ground *at the times* [*taamani*?] *when* there were no animals to hunt. And they knew nothing of all the strict taboo that we have to observe *now* [*maannakut*?]. For no dangers threatened them; but on the other hand no pleasures awaited them after a *long day's* toil. *Then* it happened that a little orphan girl was thrown out into the sea... and for her sake people had *afterwards* [*kingorna*?] to think out all the taboo that makes it hard to live. For now they *no longer* [*-runnaarput*?] lived on the ground but on shy and live game. (Rasmussen 1931: 212–13, emphases and insertions BS)

I am unsure how to appreciate the obvious time setting of "before," "then," "now," and "afterwards" in this story as retold by Rasmussen in the shadow of afterthought.

We run into the same problem of time sequence in a much-quoted Polar Inuit origin myth about the first humans on earth. It is frequently quoted as an amazing example of a complete mythic text, and the problem concerns the conversion of oral stories into a literary flow like the Christian Genesis. The combination of the story's events was not due to Rasmussen alone. He was greatly helped by the storyteller herself, Arnaaluk. She told the myth as a sequence of events in her attempt to match the ideal of Qallunaaq literacy. This appears from the introduction to the story as quoted or reproduced by Rasmussen:

> Our forefathers talked much of the making of the world and of men—at that time so very long ago. They did not understand how to hide words in strokes, like you do; they only told things by word of mouth, the people who lived before us; they told of many things, and that is why we are not ignorant of these things, which we have heard repeated time after time, ever since we were children. Old women do not fling their words about without meaning, and we believe them. There are no lies with age. (1908: 99)

Immediately upon the introduction follows the story:

> *The Creation*
> That time, very long ago, when the earth was made, it dropped down from above—the soil, the hills and the stones—down from the heavens; and that is how the world came into existence. When the world was made, people came. They say that they came up out of the earth. Babies came out of the earth. They came out among the willow bushes, covered with willow leaves. And they lay there among the dwarf willows with closed eyes and sprawled. They could not even crawl about. They got their food from the earth.
>
> Then there is a story of a man and a woman but how can it be? It is a riddle—when did they find each other, when did they grow up? I do not know. But the woman made babies' clothes and wandered about. She found the babies, dressed them, and brought them home. That is how there came to be so many people.
>
> When there were so many of them, they wanted dogs. And a man went out with dog's harness in his hand, and began to stamp on the ground, calling "Hoc, hoc, hoc!" Then the dogs sprang out of little tiny mounds. And they shook themselves well, for they were covered with sand. That is how men got dogs.
>
> But men increased; they grew more and more numerous. They did not know Death, at that time so very long ago, and they grew very old; at length they could not walk, they grew blind and had to lie down. Nor did they know the Sun; they lived in the dark; the daylight never dawned. It was only inside the houses that there was light; they burnt water in the lamps; at that time water would burn.
>
> But the people who did not know how to die grew too many; they overfilled the earth—and then there came a mighty flood. Many men were drowned, and men grew fewer. The traces of this flood are to be found on the tops of the high hills, where you often find shells.
>
> Then when men had grown fewer, two old women began one day to talk to each other. "Let us do without the daylight, if at the same time we can be without Death!" said the one; doubtless she was afraid of death. "Nay!" said the other, "we will have both Light and Death." And as the old woman said those words, it was so—Light came and with it Death.

> It is said that when the first man died, they covered up the corpse with stones. But the body came back; it did not properly understand how to die. It stuck its head up from the stone sleeping-place and tried to get up. But an old woman pushed it back. "We have enough to drag about with us and our sledges are small!" They were, you must know, just about to start on a seal-catching expedition. And so the corpse had to return to its stone grave.
>
> As men by this had light, they could go on long seal-hunting expeditions, and no longer needed to eat the soil. And with Death came the Sun, the Moon, and the Stars. For when people die, they go up to Heaven and grow luminous. That is what our forefathers used to tell us, and their tales gave us knowledge.
>
> Another old woman, Aisivak, gave me a variation of this account when I asked her about the origin of man. In the beginning, she said, the world was inhabited only by two men, who were both great magicians. As they wished to grow more in number, one of them altered his body, so that he might give birth to children, and after that they had many children.
>
> How the first two men were created, Aisivak did not know, however. And where? Nor did she know that! "The world is so great, and we know so little," she explained. (Rasmussen 1908: 99–102)

Evidently, the stories put together repeatedly violate the "chronologic" of cause and effect. Arnaaluk herself wonders at how the first babies who lie helpless kicking on the ground could be collected by an adult woman who had met an adult man, because how did they grow up? The next striking flaw is the drowning of persons that tipped the balance of the earth before the introduction of death. Later death gives cause to the light, but it arrives before the first deceased person has died properly and ascended to heaven as light. Finally, clothing and harnesses for the earthborn children and dogs are made long before people got the light that enabled them to leave their plant life and go hunting. So how did they get hold of the material, the skins (Sonne 2005: ID 1517)? In other words, who came first, the chicken or the egg? Indeed, paying heed to chronology in putting together origin myths is no easy matter. Why did Adam need a helper at a point when no expulsion from paradise was mentioned?

One reason why Arnaaluk's construction works, despite its repeated flaws, is in my view revealed by its common theme: still life gives way to willed movement by means of the introduction of death and light (still life without death involuntarily leads to overpopulation that endangers the balance of *sila*). Indeed, Arnaaluk brings out the topic of movement herself at an early point: how did the first couple grow, walk around, and meet? This is the only flaw that puzzles her. Babies and old people cannot move, they are chained to the ground, the latter rise to heaven as light after death, and at the same time buried persons ought to stay in their graves, immobile. It is light alone that permits humans to leave their former life as plants. Thus the message of movement outshines the chronological drawbacks of the composition.

Did Rasmussen add some final touches? The archives do not really tell. Comparison of his first recording in pencil of Arnaaluk's story with a fair copy of a later date (see references in Sonne 2005: ID 1517) leaves several questions unanswered. His first (handwritten) recording in Greenlandic is no story. It consists of mere cues to these events: children emerge from the interior of the earth; a woman finds them and makes clothing for them; her husband kicks up dogs and procures harnesses. People multiply and become too numerous. A storm surge diminishes their number and leaves shells, still visible, far up in the mountains. People grow old. They do not know death. Two old women quarrel about having light and death instead of darkness and endless life with built-in aging. With the coming of light, people start to die. But there is still no sun, only the light of stars. After this, Arnaaluk tells the origin myth of the sun and moon.

Turning then to the fair copy, this is bilingually divided into two columns, one with the text in Greenlandic, the other in Danish. The latter is literally the one that was published in Rasmussen (1905 [1908 in translation] and 1921–25, vol. III). The text in Greenlandic contains a few more barely readable episodes, but every cue event is expanded into prose and connected into a continuous course of events. The origin myth of the sun and the moon has been separated out by Rasmussen, who may have found that ending too disturbing chronologically. In the end, the process of converting a set of short notes into a full story cannot be checked except for the separation of the last story about sun and moon. Furthermore, Arnaaluk knew about Christianity as discussed with Rasmussen prior to the telling of the Creation, and she must have known something about Genesis as preached to her parents and grandparents by Hans Hendrik in the 1850s (see Appendix; Rink 1878a: 287; 1878b; Lidegaard 1986: 49).

Suspicions raised, we may as well scrutinize the way Rasmussen presented East Greenlandic origin myths. As far as the sources go, East Greenlandic myths evoke no pronounced symbolism of an original plant life. Quite on the contrary, the first humans fell down from heaven (Sonne 2005: ID 959, see above). Nor is the turning around of the earth mentioned until 1961, when Jens Rosing collected the *Uniagaq* story in the Ammassalik district (see above pp. 72–80, and Sonne 2005: ID 1678).

In the 1921 first edition of East Greenlandic myths and legends, Rasmussen combines various short myths or sayings about the beginning of life on earth (ID 959). But the notes used and taken during his very short stay in Ammassalik in 1919 were not of his own collection (KRH 52, 2, booklet 405; Rasmussen 1938: 79). They stem in part from his reading of *Tunuamiut* by Christian Rosing (1906; Østgrønlænderne 1946: 13–14), whom he thanks for the permission. Other notes summarize some statements taken from Holm (1888) and the report of the expedition by catechist and steersman Hanseeraq put to print in *Atuagagdliutit* (1891–92). Finally, a slip of pen reveals insertions from the first publication of Hans Egede's Perlustration: "tum" (thumb) for "tue" (hummock),[45] as also the current opinion chosen by the Danes among the early statements by West Greenlanders that heaven used to be a nasty place to dwell. The myths referred to in the notes from Ammassalik are extremely short, and their lack of internal coherency noted: some say, others say, etc. Nevertheless Rasmussen combines them into a story:

> The first human being fell down from heaven where people used to live without death. He begot a daughter with the earth, they had children together and they multiplied excessively. Next an earthquake made the earth split with deep cracks and numerous humans fell down into the

45. H. Egede (1971, 2: 117; 1818: 199; 1925: 397 [here corrected by the editor, Bobé]). Rasmussen himself leaves out this thumb origin from his published essay (1921–25, I: 71–72), but it is preserved in print by Ostermann in his published English translation of Rasmussen's notes (Rasmussen 1938: 72).

> lovely land on the underside of the earth as *innersuit*, excellent hunters and useful as helping spirits. Then a storm surge came that flooded the earth until only the highest mountain tops stood out. Very few people saved their lives by climbing the only high mountain which had a flat surface on top for tenting. These became the ancestors of the East Greenlanders, counting very few families. After death "... many humans return to heaven ..." where they play ball with skulls and produce the Northern Lights. (Rasmussen 1921–25, I: 71–72; Sonne 2005: ID 959)

The combination of these two myths, one about the earthquake, which creates the subshore land of the *innersuit*, and the other about the flood, is mediated by a lengthy explanatory description of the pleasant land and culture of the *innersuit* and their exchanges with human beings. Continuity with the heavenly origin of human life is guaranteed, because explicitly, not *all* human beings plummet through the cracks, nor are *all* human beings wiped out by the flood; however, then only some human beings return to heaven after death. So, where do the remaining deceased humans end up? No answer is offered, apparently because the traditionally lovely submarine realm of death is passed by in silence and its pleasures conferred on the *innersuit* alone. This replacement is likely due to the missionaries' identification of the submarine realm with hell. The heavenly dead who played ball with skulls and thereby produce the Northern Lights is a pan-Inuit notion confirmed by the West Greenlanders. But it is not mentioned in Rasmussen's East Greenlandic notes, as also it runs counter to the information received by Holm, namely, that killed babies and miscarriages produce the light by playing ball with their placentas. Regarding the rescue on the flat mountain after the flood, the sparse inhabitants of Ammassalik and their marked intermarriage seems explained within the framework of Noah's rescue on Ararat during the deluge.

Another version recorded by Hanseeraq similarly combines two beginnings: "The first land was completely flat without either sea or mountains, but when *He up there* did not like the humans living on it he destroyed the earth, and the humans were transformed into fire trolls, from which descend the fire trolls (*innersuit*) of today. Later the earth came about anew but was completely covered by a glacier. When later, little by little, the ice disappeared, two humans fell down from heaven and from them the earth became populated" (Thalbitzer ed. 1933: 93–94; used by Holm 1972: 139; 1914: 106–7, emphasis BS). Rasmussen made a comment in his notes stating that this myth is a "reminiscence from the travellers to the south" (KRH, 52, 2 booklet 405, p. 1). Such travelers had regularly been on trading expeditions south to Aluk and Pamialluk, where Christian myths probably circulated. For his own published construction Rasmussen left out the discontented person up there, *pinnga* or *pissuma*, mentioned in his notes as a probable "supreme being," but about whom he could get no information other than that this designation was used by people under taboo for both the moon (male) and the sun (female). Furthermore, since *pinnga* is genderless the male sex of the translation cannot be ascertained. So Rasmussen, contrary to Hanseeraq, does not connect the destruction of the earth with *pinnga*. Instead, in a statement among the notes and left out of the published construction, the flooding was due to people becoming wicked and murdering one another. They killed fellow beings who had done no harm. This conviction was confirmed by everybody, Rasmussen comments in his notes, and it reflects the contemporary accusation (allegation) by the missionaries that the East Greenlanders would have exterminated each other had they not been saved by Christianity.[46] As pointed out in the analysis of "Kaassassuk" above, Rasmussen became decidedly more enthusiastic about *pinnga* during the Fifth Thule Expedition (1921–24), that is, right after he finished the manuscript to his publication on East Greenland (Rasmussen 1921–25, I). All in all, Rasmussen's presentation of East Greenlandic origins, called "*De første mennesker* (*The First Humans*)," looks plausible but consists of a chronologically ordered course of dispersed and selected bits of myths supplied with explanatory insertions and loans from sources on West Greenland.

Hanseeraq took down his version some weeks after he—supported by illustrations—had told people about Adam, Eve, and God and had preached about the end of the world. Christian impact from the south can be counted on as well, in that Hanseeraq's hellfire sermon was met with no misunderstandings: "they repeated their habitual remark about not being able to sleep at night for the fear of thinking of the end of the world, because we are pagans" (Thalbitzer ed. 1933: 84–86). Rüttel, the first missionary to Ammassalik/Tasiilaq from 1894 to 1904, was repeatedly told about that very fear and wondered about it, because he deliberately never mentioned Doomsday (1917: 112). Although the idea of a punitive being up there, e.g., Moon, was no novelty, he was not traditionally angered by the same "sins" as God. Women's violations of birth taboos was Moon's primary concern. Nor can Moon be identified with the person who transformed people into "scum" in order to decimate their number, as Thalbitzer was told in 1905–6.

Hanseeraq's version did not place the coming down of the first genuine humans at the very beginning. The origin of the first humanlike people on the flat earth remains unknown, as in the early West Greenlandic version by Poul Egede, which has the earth capsize due to the flood and place all the (prehuman) *innersuit* and their equally flat earth in a reversed position below. They left no descendants on the new surface to become mixed up with genuine humans, whether they derived from the earth or came down from above. The *innersuit* thus belong in the Other World in correspondence with the rule of dyadic relations. Rasmussen's construction does not follow that rule by its recurrent "not all," which means that some prehuman *innersuit* survived on earth and became mixed up with genuine humans. Returning to Hanseeraq's version, the way the earth was destroyed by "him up there" is not revealed by Hanseeraq, but the inland ice covering the new world implies a flooded land. Actually, the gradual withdrawal is rooted in actual observations: "Every single year, the East Greenlanders said, did they observe a diminution of the glaciers. Utuaq used to live at Sermiligaaq when the glaciers went right down to the sea shore, and by now they end high up in the mountains" (Thalbitzer ed. 1933: 94). So, at the time of the arrivals of Thule culture in Ammassalik—the first around Cape Farewell and the second from the north—the inland ice was still under the spell of the Little Ice Age, giving way to warmer temperatures with the following centuries. The second beginning of This World was not of a very distant past. In mythic time, it more or less coincided with these first newcomers to the environment.

46. In a variant recorded by C. Rosing (1946: 13), the earth cracked because people excelled at murdering each other. The cracking of the earth, but for no particular reason, was also told about in Avanersuaq (Sonne 2005: ID 1722).

Main Conclusions

Boundaries between This and the Other Worlds were set by sight, light, spatially, temporally, and socially. One boundary—the change in sight between them—was split into layers. Others were blurred, such as dusk and dawn, and so were the times for traveling between them and, in a way, also the shore, a place for leaving and returning, which changed continuously between land and sea by the tide. In the wilderness, beginning right beyond the range of sight from human habitation, a lonely person, preferably an upset child, could attract some being of the Other World who proposed a lasting relationship. Yet upon agreement such relations remained strictly dyadic. No mix of human and nonhuman societies could work. They were not on equal terms either. Unlike human shamans, the spirit shamans did not attract and "hire" deceased humans as helping spirits. In many cases such a ghost came out the winner of a showdown between a human and a spirit shaman. A human shaman went on visits among his helping spirits at will. They, on their side, had to respect the boundary of human habitation, and unless invited into the darkened room of their shaman's dwelling, a visiting spirit or a ghost usually arrived with evil intentions. So, considering such inequalities between the humans and nonhumans, the former ranked higher and were better off as go-betweens. Similarly, animals and spirits, however superior in one way or other, did not possess the human balance in body for moving about at sea as on land. You may call these notions ethnocentric pride.

The Christian preaching of Doomsday seems to have moved the realms of death into focus. Several among the last generation of shamans went to check and thus they first opposed and then made way, little by little, for the Christian ideas to take over. When both Akku and Kukkujooq/Apulu preferred a visit to the realm of death below to ever being able to get to Sea Woman, their helping spirits objected, but in vain. A new order had forced her into neglect. The explicit creed of Christianity, eternal life above or below, caused problems. They concerned the questions of lack of food in heaven, how the pains of deceased relatives already placed in the lower realm could be removed, and how the eternal separation from beloved relatives in either realm could be overcome. An intelligent solution to the latter was found at the shore, the coinciding point of This and the Other World. In Inuit pre-Christian theory, eternal life was also accorded the beings of the Other World. In practice, however, it did not work. Similarly the timelessness of myth seems to work on limited terms. Attempts at chronological orderings of origin myths may satisfy structural demands and Western academics, but due to the nature of oral myths telling each its own story, and because most Inuit did not care about this way of logical thinking, such attempts easily involve contradictions. Knud Rasmussen took his own liberties, and throughout this section I've tried to warn readers about blindly trusting such constructions. They inspire biased interpretations.

Inuat *and Perspectivism*

The Nattilingmiut told about a shaman who, starting from the top of the highest mountain, visited the full circle of related "others": the deceased humans above of more than one place, others below in two places, and finally the Indians, first the Chipewyan and then the Cree (Rasmussen 1931: 300–1, 391ff). Since none of the demanding *inuat* like Moon and Sea Woman were encountered, I take all these "Others" to be "related Others," to whom the Nattilingmiut were bound by kinship and/or interest of some kind—friendly, hostile, or both. Indians were considered in myth as being hostile, but because they were never encountered by the Nattilingmiut in real life they apparently belonged in the world of myth.

The Polar Inuit brought this story along from their Nattilik/Kitlinermiut/Copper Inuit origin (Sonne 2005: ID 1555, 662), but to my knowledge no similar tale of visiting the entire circle of the Other Worlds is on record in the other parts of Greenland. Here shamans would go visiting *either* above *or* below *or* abroad, and ordinary story people would only venture to foreign countries abroad—that is, except for the acculturated "obstinate" type visiting Moon (as previously discussed on pp. 129–33).

While called "nonhumans" in contrast to humans in scientific literature, a great number of the persons peopling the Inuit Other World(s) are nevertheless imagined to look like human beings of various kinds. The common term *inuat* (plural of *inua*) similarly reveals a common source with *Inuit* (plural of *Inuk*)—i.e., the root *inu-* in the verb *inuuvoq*, he/she/it lives. The theory of perspectivism offers a tool for analysis.

Inua, *Tarneq*, and Perspectivism

Among the large number of persons peopling This and the Other World(s), the main ones of the sea, heaven, and land have been presented in context above as *inuat*, (live) beings who differ by species or individuality in consonance with the part of the worlds they occupy.

Inua, "its person"—be that of animals, spirits, mountains, rivers, etc.—are called *inue* (*inui*) in the plural by Hans Egede (1971, 2: 110; 1925: 393; 1818: 186–87). Grammatically the possessive form asks you to choose between *Inuat*, "their person," or *Inui*, "its persons." Artificially I treat *inua* as a concept on its own, and thus *inua* will be *inuat* in the plural.[47]

Following all writers on the Greenlandic *inuat* since Glahn, it is important to add the *inuat* of concepts like laughter and sleep—as with Morpheus in Western animism. I never came upon sleep or laughter as persons in Inuit myth, but I encountered *inuat* affecting sleep, such as the medium-size dwarves, and several figures provoking laughter, such as the falcon in ritual play, the dangerous "tickler" in myth that can tickle you to death, or the Entrails Snatcher, who cuts out your lungs at the slightest smile on your face. One *inua*, however, surprised me, namely the *inua* of the ringing sound of a cracking iceberg. It has a story, because the sound once became manifest in a man with wrinkles and furrows all over his face. He married a human girl, whose mother mocked him beyond endurance. He left for good. But the son born by his ex-wife became an unparalleled hunter of polar bears (Sonne 2005: ID 1546). Clearly some association of iceberg to polar bear, its "land" so to speak, lies behind this. The sound of its cracking or "dying" transforms into a humanlike person with a wrinkled face, or "mask." In vain I looked for such a masked figure in ritual. So, let it suffice to say that in sum, apart from the well-established *inuat* like the heavenly bodies, faunal species, parts of environment, salient objects, also sound, smell, sleep, or laughter—whatever affects your mind and senses—may be or become an *inua*, a somebody, whether visualized in body or not.

Ever since Hans and Poul Egede posed the question, translations and explanations of *inua* have followed one after the other, such as "its owner," "its master," "its in-dweller," "its person" (e.g.,

47. As for Southwest Alaska, Fienup-Riordan states *yuit* to be the plural of *yua*. Grammatically *yuut* is *yuk*, "human" in the plural form, whereas the term of self-reference is *Yup'ik* (genuine human).

H. Egede 1971, 2: 110; 1925: 393; 1818: 186–87; Glahn 1921: 56; Merkur 1985; Oosten 1993). I prefer "person" because etymologically *inua* translates to "its live being" and semantically it means a being with recognizable habits and a characteristic way of life, individually or by species. In my understanding "person" thus involves "personality" in the meanings of look and habitus. As a Nattilik storyteller remarked about the big-bellied spirits, they are "a kind of half humanlike humans using habits (*ilerq-*)" (Rasmussen 1931: 387–88). In other words they, like humans, have their particular habits, their characteristic way of life. The Yupiit statements about ritually imitating the behavior of some animal *yua* (= *inua*) when dancing with its mask note that the more lifelike the copying, the happier and more flattered the animal (Sonne 1988a: 46, 214).[48] Or to quote a Greenlandic storyteller about a man (human) who became paralyzed but eventually recovered: "*nammineq... ileqquni ativaa*: Himself in his habits he dressed (again)" (H. Lynge 1955: 87), which is the common Greenlandic phrase for having recovered from a disturbing illness. This literal translation of "putting on" one's habits (= habit?) again leads us directly to the perspectivism of Viveiros de Castro, prominent in the renewed research on "animism," summarized this way by Fausto:

> From the pioneering work of Hallowell (1960) on Ojibwa ontology to Ingold's ecological phenomenology (1986; 2000), Philippe Descola's socialized nature and schemes of practice (1986, 2005), and Viveiros de Castro's perspectivism (2002), a new way of looking at the relationship between humans and nonhumans has emerged. The fundamental premise shared by these approaches is that, in Amerindian (and North Eurasian) ontologies, intentionality and reflexive consciousness are not exclusive attributes of humanity but potentially available to all beings of the cosmos. In other words, animals, plants, gods, and spirits are also potentially persons and can occupy a subject position in their dealings with humans. (Fausto 2007: 497)

Though not mentioned, Inuit/Yupiit ontology is not left isolated from this society of revised animism (M. A. Pedersen 2001; Hastrup 2007: Introduction).

Focusing on Viveiros de Castro, he forwards the theory that—among the natives of South America and in the subarctic—there is no ontological difference between humans, animals, and other beings. In "spirit" or "soul" every live being is a humanlike being, seeing itself and others of its own kind as humans. But they (animals) differ (by species) in body. They differ particularly in their "clothing," the privileged means for transformation, the very cover that—as Tim Ingold puts it—"identifies the capabilities, skills, dispositions that serve the being who can thereby *carry on a particular kind of life in the world.* The metamorphosis affected by that cover is an opening up of the person to the world: a new perspective" (Ingold 2000: 94, emphasis BS). This perspective means that any nonhuman being is a subject, a person, who sees the world with the same intentions (i.e., to get hold of something, food for instance), but, according to Viveiros de Castro, *it sees another world.* Jaguars see human blood as beer, vultures see maggots as grilled fish, and so on. Calling these differing world perspectives "multinaturalism," Viveiros de Castro states that these nonhumans look and live like human beings at home in their own world.

48. Similarly the Upper Kolyma Yukaghir hunter dresses like and empathetically imitates the prey's way of being (Willerslev 2001).

Whereas Ingold widens the scope of Viveiros de Castro's perspectivism, Terence Turner (2009) is strongly opposed. Turner (1935–2015), a lifelong anthropologist among the Amazonian Indians, finds no support among the latter for this theory, which he demonstrates to be a branching-off of Lévi-Strauss's theory of the savage mind. Subject to Turner's scrutiny, even this latter theory turns out contradictory in getting "culture" mixed up with or reduced to "nature" despite the claimed binary polarity between the two. Defining (like Ingold and Viveiros de Castro for that matter) the spiritual essence shared by all beings as constituting their natural intentions to subsist and reproduce, Turner leans on the first theory of animism as proposed by E. B. Tylor, who did not define this essence (soul, anima) as human, nor claim that the nonhumans received it from humans. Concerning the differing perspectives, although they see the world with the same intentions as humans of seeking food, shelter, etc., they do not, Turner objects, see differing worlds. They just recognize the ways of other beings' intentional behaviors as both basically identical to and differing from their own ways. The human eating his sandwich for lunch does not in essence differ in his behavior from the anteater eating ants at whichever time of the day. Both parties recognize the similarity in eating habits. I can easily follow this point of view without discarding that of the changing perspectives, that is, in the way set out by Ingold above.

Turner also attacks Viveiros de Castro's maintenance that animals do not differentiate between species by their differing bodies, because physiologically Amerindians recognize a basic uniformity of bodies. Turner never came across that idea among "his" Amerindians. I will try to mediate in this dispute. To hunters, wont as they are to flay, pluck, and cut up their game, the undressed creatures look basically similar and not all that different from the naked human body. Furthermore those thought to look more similar than others, e.g., bears, are specially noted (Morrow pers. comm.).[49] So do the interior organs. Viveiros de Castro, however, does not bring out that argument. The animal, he asserts, recognizes a different species from observing its unique affective behavior and abilities, its dispositions, the latter some "level in between" and likened to Bourdieu's habitus (2002: 316). But classical habitus also means cognitive abilities, Turner objects without touching upon this peculiar "intermediate level." His only focus is on the contrast Viveiros de Castro made between the interior essence and the body, the latter characterized as nothing but an (empty) envelope, which nevertheless decides the habitus and perspective of the being. Admittedly this is a paradox that Turner acknowledges but can't resolve. I choose to see two bodies, the basics of anatomy and the body on the "intermediate plane" (as a kind of "body in between"), which includes the cognitive abilities. Still, whose perspective is at the fore? Those of the animals observing other species, or of humans (Amerindians) focusing on a common basic physiological similarity? Or of humans observing animals observing their own and other kinds?

Unacquainted in any detail with the Amerindians, I shall turn to the Inuit, among whom, the Nattilik Naalungiaq had been told, in the dark times, before light came into the world, there were humans and all kinds of (land) animals (wolves, bears, and foxes), but they could change from animal to human—and vice versa—at will, and in human figure they were all alike. That is "*they may have*

49. As for me, my parents went hunting every weekend during autumn and winter. From my early years I watched my mother flay, pluck, and remove viscera and then cut up deer, hare, and various birds. Sometimes I was allowed for a short while to play dolls with a plucked fowl on the table.

had different habits, but they all spoke the same tongue, lived at the same kind of house, and spoke and hunted in the same way" (Rasmussen 1931: 208, emphasis BS). This storyteller, Naalungiaq, obviously did have a problem of complete identification between species in their human forms, which otherwise fits Viveiros de Castro's thesis about identical human bodies. Their differing habits cling to their name as differing species, it seems. How differentiation came into the world is not told explicitly, but implicitly with light coming to dispel the darkness in which "all cats are gray" (my phrase), and all beings either speaking *taartaq*, the language of darkness (the Other World), or Inuktitut, the language of This World. This question is not raised.

The Inuit absolutely accorded several faunal species a human body inside their manifest body, their cover. *Pooq/puuq* means a cover of all sorts: the skin and slough of an animal or bird, or a bag, such as the bag you buy in the supermarket, an envelope, the church tower enveloping the bell, a condom, a caul, etc. It is the same word, with multiple "appearances." But problems arise in our attempts at identifying by the correct term the ontological essence defined as the way a species sees its own kind as human beings when at home. In Inuit cosmology this shape is in many instances an *inua*. In myth the *inuat* of sun, moon, the air (*sila*), and the sea appear in human shapes. So do, for good reasons, humans imitating both these figures and the differing behaviors of animals in ritual disguised in matching covers. Even more to the point, the Southwest Alaska *yua* (= *inua* W. Grl.) of Yup'ik masks representing animals, birds, fishes, and mythic beings is most often carved as a human face at the center of the mask's animal body. In stories about human visits to faunal species that live and look like humans, no particular term is used for this shape except for its being human (e.g., Fienup-Riordan 1994; Rasmussen 1929: 269–70, 271–73, 276; Sonne 2005: ID 100, 138, 161, search: menneskeskikkelse). Provided these human shapes are *inuat*, however, one has to face the problem that they differ as much as do the *puuat* (*pooq* in the plural). The *inua* of the sun, the moon, the sea, *sila*, several stars, and the Northern Lights, who according to their mythic origin used to be ordinary humans, differ in their human look, size, gender, age, and habits. Among the *yua* faces of the masks some look neutral, some happy, some sour, some—with the set of teeth uncovered—aggressive. In case both the animal and the human side of the figure represented are equally stressed, the face may be divided longitudinally between the half face of the aggressive animal and the other half the neutral (or friendly?) human. Of the attached limbs two will be human and two animal, painted red and white, respectively (e.g., Sonne 1988a; Fienup-Riordan 1996).

Not every mask is given a human face. Some have none, and a pair of flounder masks have the *yua* of a seal (Sonne 1988a: 252), which may mean that their personalities, character, or abilities are like those of a seal. Another mask of a spirit called "three-in-one" represents a being that can change from fox when hunting small game into polar bear when hunting big game, and into a human being when hunting both whales and humans. The latter is feared as its most dangerous "manifestation" (248, 334–35). By chance this mask is reproduced not by a carving but by a drawing depicting the lengthy body of the bear wearing on its body the bipartite face of the fox-man. Both sets of its teeth are uncovered, that of the fox pointing upwards, that of the man turned even more dangerously downwards. Also, the latter shows his human personality by wearing labrets, the sign of an adult man in that part of the Inuit/Yupiit area. So, using the term coined by Turner, this *yua*'s human "essence" is depicted by its "social skin" (T. Turner 2009: 33). Actually, labrets and tattoo marks (female) not uncommonly signify the gender of the mask's *yua* (e.g., Sonne 1988a: 86–87, 122, 202).

Since a rapid development in the carving of masks during the 18th and 19th centuries prevents thorough analysis, the only safe conclusion is as follows: as represented in Yup'ik masks, the humanlike *yuit* do not look identical. The same holds true not only for Naalungiaq's little doubt about original identity in habits but also for several Inuit/Yupiit myths about animals in human form, as in the following ones from Greenland:

A human out alone comes upon and enters a house with two women (in human figures), a lightly colored one and the other completely black. The black woman serves him inedible food, some dried capelins that really (in human perspective) are willow twigs, and then some feces said to be the loin part of a woman. Next the light woman brings in some grayfish, delicious food that the visitor eats with pleasure. Then, bidding them good-bye, he realizes that the light woman is a gull and the black one a raven. His vision has changed. He now sees them in their clothing of This World (Sonne 2005: ID 1392).

Apparently, this story fits Viveiros de Castro's theory in all regards. In their home the birds look like humans, and the food they consider proper differs from that of the humans. Raven sees twigs as dried fish and excrement as the juicy meat of a woman. Gull sees grayfish as, well, grayfish, I suppose. Which raises the question: regarding food, does Gull's bird perspective differ less from that of genuine humans than that of Raven? And why should Raven see twigs, used for building her nest, or by humans for campfires, as dried fish for food? I have to leave both perspectives in the mix, and turn to my main point, namely: why is the humanlike body of the gull so light, and why is that of the raven pitch-black? This image contradicts Viveiros de Castro's theory, which demands that there should be no ontological difference between these birds in their human forms. The difference in species, in clothing, seems to affect the humanlike being when visualized.[50] Do they differ in their imagined *spiritual bodies*, their body on "the mediate plane"?[51] This leads to still more questions: how do Raven and Gull see each other without clothing, without their *puuat*? As naked human figures, differing in color, but still in human shapes? That is, do they recognize not only their own but also other kinds as humans? What is the difference? It may still be worthwhile to remember that the perspectives of the "Others" (at least as represented in stories and masks) are human perspectives of the perspectives of the Others.

The same story in another version depicts the transformation from human into bird in steps. Walking outside Raven puts on a dark overcoat, Gull a white one. They disappear from the view of the human visitor, who, looking up, sees them take off and disappear in their manifest forms (Sonne 2005: ID 603). Another instance of animal transformation from undressed or nude into dressed appears in versions of the ritual myth about the shaman who succeeds in liberating the seabirds and marine animals trapped in Sea Woman's house. From a dark corner in her house, they appear in their human forms. First come the very small ones, who let out the shrieks of guillemots and terns upon leaving the room through the tunnel. Next come some bigger humans with curved noses and others with straight noses. They are transformed into species of seals at the moment they jump into the river that takes them through the tunnel to the sea of This World. Finally some men with very big faces,

50. Differentiation by species of the humanlike *yuit* is clearly exposed by Fienup-Riordan (1994: 59–61); see also Willerslev (1991; 2007: 83, 87) regarding the Upper Kolyma Yukaghirs.

51. Willerslev makes the same comment on Yukaghir transformations (2001; 2007: 84).

big heads, and moustaches jump into the river and transform into walrus (Sonne 2005: ID 1445, 1468, 1882). In other words, the characteristics of species are inborn according to the perspective of the Greenlanders, who know this fact from their recurrent cutting up of killed pregnant animals. Indeed, in Greenlandic stories you will encounter differentiations in visualized humanlike bodies time and again.

Still another fine example of the human perspective on perspectives of the Others is a story resumed above that relates the deal made by a woman with a big family of polar bears about the exchange of bear's meat for skin soles. The bears look more or less like oversize humans, while their son-in-law, the walrus, looks heavier, clumsier, practically without any visible neck. Another son-in-law, the Arctic fox, is easily recognized in the human figure of a small, dark, supple, and cowardly man (ID 1806). Apparently then they see each other in slightly different human forms and not by affects alone. Or do they? In the perspective of the human visitor (with whom the teller identifies) they do, in that the equally unnatural and unenviable affinal position of the walrus in a household of several bear brothers reflects the Inuit preference of identifying with humanlike polar bear in contrast to charmless, clumsy walrus.[52] The perspective is human also regarding bears' need of skins for soles. These are made of the skin of bearded seal prepared and cut by the woman, because humans alone possess the cognitive capacity to produce, as pointed out by Turner in his shrewd interpretation of the origin myths of culture as told by the Bororo (T. Turner 2009). In other words, the bear father, whose intention is to see to the renewal of his family's soles, sees humans in the same perspective as anthropologist Turner as the only makers of prepared skin for soles. As for the humanlike bodies, they obviously differ in consonance with their manifest bodies as do their characters. But again, how do they see each other? To reiterate, they view each other in a human perspective as humans, differing the same ways as humans, ranked according to affiliation.

All of which goes to say that animals in their human home bodies not only differ according to their envelopes (*puuat*) in appearance, but they also recognize each other when at home as (differing) humanlike beings. In an Inuit worldview this home is in The Other World (*silam aappaa*), in contrast to This World, the visible one. In that case Viveiros de Castro's hypothesis awarded about animals recognizing only their own kind as humans and other kinds by their affects is problematic. Furthermore, applied to the Inuit worldview, it would—without the slightest notice—imply a decisive change in perspective from This to the Other World. In an Inuit perspective, the two worlds look different and so do their beings.

Take Kukkujooq, who, while still an apprentice, had a strong desire to visit his father in the submarine realm of death. He was out kayaking when he heard the song of a spirit from the top of a high cliff facing the sea. He climbed the cliff and met with the spirit, which changed his vision with a stroke across his eyes. The ordinary scenery slowly gave way to a view of a row of three fogbanks with dark spaces in between. The first dark space led to the realm of death, the spirit explained, the second to *Immap Ukuua* (Sea Woman). Kukkujooq had to make up his mind, because a visit to the realm of death would exclude any attempt at visiting Sea Woman (Sonne 2005: ID 1287). We can

52. Generally Arctic fox is seen as the small, younger cousin of polar bear who feeds on the bears' leftovers; in marriage with a human man, fox in human form is characterized by its foul smell when in heat. The disgusting odor prevents wife exchange—i.e., her social integration among humans.

also take the example of his mother, Kaakaaq, who once as a child experienced a change of vision by the usual way of having her view split into layers and reunited in a cleared view of the opposite world. A snow bunting she had just seen in its manifest form revealed its human form and asked her to assist his wife in labor. Kaakaaq succeeded and went away with two gifts, the shortest tent pole of the couple's house and some skin for soles. But as soon as her vision changed back into the ordinary one, the gifts turned out to be nothing but a straw of grass and some leaves of roseroot (Sonne 2005: ID 1702, 1290).

With *Gulliver's Travels* in mind, this story presents the reasonable idea that snow buntings live in other dimensions of the same world as humans. Snow buntings do use plant stems and straw to support their nests like tent poles, but I have no certain answers as to why roseroot are used for soles, except that the leaves do look similar in form. And then my (Greenlandic-colored) associations illuminate the following: roseroot used to be a delicacy in summer; preserved in blubber it became a relish in winter. This reminds me that the "speed effect" attributed to eating roseroot in Western herbal medicine may have been a realized experience by the Greenlanders as well. In that case it would fit the idea of soles closely associated with mobility (e.g., Sonne 2005: ID 1362). Still, this is guesswork. My reason for considering these meanings is the shamanic context of the gifts received by Kaakaaq, who developed into a shaman of great skills. The snow bunting is the first to realize these powers. "I am no shaman," Kaakaaq objects at being asked to assist at the birth. "Sure you are," the snow bunting declares. "Otherwise you would not have seen us (as human beings)." Next, enabling her to perform, the snow bunting man teaches her the ordinary *ritual technique* of a change in vision while she lies on the platform covered by a skin. Kaakaaq's ensuing vision is an even more intimate one of not only seeing the birds as humans but also of looking into the inside of the snow bunting woman in labor. She can see and remove an object barring the child's exit through the vagina. So, in consonance with other stories about Kaakaaq, I take the symbolism of gifts connoting summer to announce her future search of helping spirits, which all East Greenlandic pupils practiced predominantly in summer, as also her usual method of going into ecstasy by lying on the platform covered up.

Leaving this interpretation with such loose ends (if less in the lurch than the perspectives of Gull and Raven), I nevertheless wish to point to the meanings of the changing perspectives in an Inuit human perspective. The latter never gets lost in the translation of perspectives. It directs the ways of the "multinatural" *cultures*, making them reasonable by widening the knowledge of the world. Imagination, empathy, familiarizing oneself with the ways of "Others"—these are the means for "cultural translation," of coming to know the ways of the Other World on human cultural premises. There is more to be said, though, in an Inuit perspective, where cultural solutions to environmental challenges have a say.

In the Arctic cultures of the Inuit there used to be an even greater correspondence between human and animal dress codes than among the tropical ones of Amazonian Indians, who dress, it seems, predominantly for rituals. Posing the question of how the animals living at home like humans in humanlike bodies transform between these and their manifest bodies, an answer is had in the above example of Raven and Gull, who put on their outer garments when leaving the house, disappear from view, and then are seen flying. A closer look at the transformations is presented in a Polar Inuit story (among others) about a human woman who happens to visit a polar bear mother with two young in their human shapes. Passing through the entrance tunnel the visitor comes upon the skin of the bear mother. The skin's head sneers at her, but from inside the house the bear mother asks her in a calm voice to enter. Having seated her guest, Bear mother asks permission to leave for an errand, descends into the tunnel, puts on her skin, and disappears. She returns with a big freshly caught seal (in order to feed her guest) and again leaves her skin in the tunnel. So her skin is the sine qua non, not only for going outside into the cold but also for realizing her intentions of catching a seal.

Indeed, on reflection the bear in her behavior differs in no way from the Inuit hunter. Returning from the hunt in winter, he used to leave his outer garment outside, crawl through the tunnel, and enter the room where he stripped except for boots and the briefs (*naatsit*) worn by adult men. Women similarly wore only briefs and boots indoors, and both men and women slipped off their boots when sitting themselves on the platform. Children remained naked and barefoot indoors until puberty.[53] In fact, in Greenlandic stone and turf houses the heat from the lighted lamps was almost tropical. Naturally everybody dressed when going outside in winter, but the women were also expected to do so in summer for leaving the tent. Consequently, photos taken of women outside the tent in house dress (i.e., in briefs, boots, and ornaments) were considered indecent by some (see photos in Holm 1972: 98, 141, 162, 167; 1914: fig. 22, 23; Thalbitzer 1923: 189).[54] All of which goes to say that the similarity between humans and animals used to be striking in this way, as well: both parties live undressed indoors; and both dress in *animal skins* for going outdoors—animals in skins, humans in artfully sewn skin clothing. The only marked difference, because there is a difference, is the briefs, the *naatsit* worn by adolescent and adult humans.

This difference is emphasized in a variant of Paalineq. He left his unfaithful wife completely naked in spirit and took refuge among some giants, who were uncertain about his identity: was he a dog or a human being? When on request he was handed *naatsit* by his chosen giant maiden and put them on, he was recognized as a human being (Sonne 2005: ID 1359). The *naatsit* seems to have been the visible cultural mark of (Greenlandic) humans, or their "social skin." I shall take up the meanings of *naatsit* versus nudity in the end of chapter 4, on shamanism, *angakkuuneq*, and by now temporarily conclude that by accepting Viveiros de Castro's assertion that all the human bodies of the Other World are identical, we have to refer to their basically common anatomical build when "undressed," rather than the differing looks of this common build.

The Transmigrating Essence of Life

Looking for the common spiritual essence inside all bodies as defined by Viveiros de Castro, the Inuit would most probably point either to *tarneq* ("soul"), the so-called free-soul, or *anersaaq* (breath) (Sonne 2005: ID 631, 1089), rather than the *inua*.[55] The *tarneq* is generally said to leave the expiring

53. For the sexual symbolism of boots, especially men's boots, see Sonne (2001b).

54. The parallel with human ways falters when applied to the Canadian Inuit, who imagined mammals in human shape as well (e.g., Rasmussen 1929: 171–77). These Inuit used to live in less-heated igloos on the sea ice during winter and probably wore some clothing indoors but not at night. The stories in question, however, may reach back in time to the common Thule culture with houses built the same way as those of the Greenlanders.

55. *Tarnik* (W. Grl.) in the dual—i.e., one in the loin or the groin and one in the throat (Thalbitzer 1930: 92, 94, 96; P. Egede 1750: 179); or *tarnik* (Inuktitut), combining one in the loin and one in a small bubble filled with air, *pudlaq*, somewhere inside the body (Saladin d'Anglure 1986; Schneider 1985: 397); or *tarnit* in the plural (W. Grl.) in case the soul of every joint is referred to (Thalbitzer ed. 1933). Final conclusions on the definitions of spiritual essences of whatever kind—*tarneq*, *ateq* (name), *tarraq* (shadow), *inua*, *anerneq* (breath)—cannot be reached. See Oosten (1990) for a brave and clever attempt.

body, linger for some days, and then depart for one of the realms of death. In this figure, it mirrors the deceased person lacking flesh and bones. Breath, of course, leaves as well, disappearing into the air. Either may be active in the Inuit myth about a human being who takes up temporary residence in one faunal species after another. He or she is called an *arnattattoq/arnattaktoq*, etymologically a "seeker of mothers," translated by the late Apollo Lynge into "The person who dreamed about the dead or who took up residence in one female being after another" (Sonne 2005: 1059). "The transmigration" or "wandering soul" is the common translation by Westerners. The message of most versions is to clarify the differing habits of the species, experienced by the soul (or breath). At the time the reborn baby, turned human by being named, has come to master speech, he can report that whenever the soul finds a new mother it has to learn how to survive, as well as integrate socially. It is taught the ways of movement of caribou, walrus, and wolf by kicking at salient points in heaven (horizon, center, navel, respectively) in order to get food, or it has to endure somatic inconveniences like sweat or headache (blade of grass), being thrashed (dog), as well as to cope with troublesome mating (bladdernose seal), constant quarreling (speckled seal), and relax among the inoffensive elder bearded seals (e.g., Sonne 2005: ID 1059, 1833). Stressing such inconveniences, the way of humans comes out the winner, intellectually as well in that some variants implicitly praise the cognitive ability of humans to produce amulets for tricking the animals into getting killed. And so humans are the clever ones, as they possess the most imagination and creative minds. The soul or breath (Viveiros de Castro's "essence," I presume) either travels of its own accord or by being eaten by the next link in an Inuit food chain before entering a human woman. Either method demands that the penultimate "mother" sought by this mythic soul, a seal or a caribou, is killed by a human hunter.

Greenlandic versions (search Navagiaq in Sonne 2005) follow the former method. Killed and dragged home by the hunter, the seal is cut up by his currently barren wife. When she straddles the body while doing the cutting up, the "soul" or breath sees its chance to slip into her womb, where it is fed at intervals by her husband's visiting "dog." Birth gives some trouble, which can be overcome by an amulet. As for the consecutive naming, the baby cries incessantly until he is given the right name; that is, he cries for the one he used to have in his former incarnation as a human being. In case the traveler is a woman, her (soul's) fertility effects on the various "mothers" may be clearly stressed (Boas 1901–7: 321–23).[56] But this does not permit the conclusion that the essence is essentially human. Naming alone, by the name of a deceased human relative—in this story being the mother-seeker him- or herself—transforms the baby into a genuine human—i.e., a related social being.

So, we have *inuat* who are imagined to see their own kind as human beings and other, though basically similar kinds, as differing human beings. And we have the conscious soul or breathing of a human being seeking one mother after another. It takes possession of the "mother" like an embryo and causes her death on leaving her and then moves to another "mother." By trial and error and being taught, it learns the *inua* habits of each species. They are not automatically transferred on

56. Going into the particular discourse of every version would take us too far. Motivations, if any, for traveling differ, and some are told in little more than references to the well-known story; one teller, Amos Daniel, usually inserts bits and pieces of irrelevant episodes. Conversely, a Polar Inuit version told by Pualorsuaq requires an analysis of greater psychological depth. He starts out with the end and ends up with the transmigration into a polar bear who could hardly have communicated the story (Sonne 2005: ID 388, 289, 631).

the soul or breathing by the body. This is perhaps converse to Ingold's statement, namely that the metamorphosis caused by the cover is an *opening up* of the person to the world that creates a new perspective. It is contrary because, as observed by the Inuit, animal young learn like Inuit children. In a way, then, the Inuit essence of soul or breath, killing differing bodies by leaving them behind, suits the thesis put forth by Viveiros de Castro. Still, the human representations of the persons, the *inuat,* do not.

Apart from information on the habits of the faunal species, there is another lesson (for us) to learn from this story: the Greenlandic versions draw a clear distinction between a body left by the spiritual essence, and a body killed by a hunter.[57] The body left behind dies, whereas the killed animal does not lose its soul. It stays conscious and sensitive as long as it remains in the slain body. It feels a short-lived stitch when killed and a funny tickling when dragged along over rough ground by the hunter. During the cutting up it escapes the *ulu* (woman's lunar knife) by fleeing between parts of the body until eventually it succeeds in entering the woman. This distinction further explains why the corpse of a murdered human is cut up and the parts spread all over the environment, some placed in clefts, some in the sea, etc., in order to prevent the soul from entering the murderer (seeking him as a mother) for revenge (e.g., Sonne 2005: ID 372).

Arnanneq is not limited to the story about the transmigrating soul. It exposes the common idea of dreaming about deceased people, whom Hans Lynge identified with *arnartarneq,* "wont to seek a mother." He had heard about a couple of instances in Northwest Greenland. A woman named Peqquk became possessed by the deceased child of the informant's father's brother. Since the child had died within its first year, Peqquk became like an infant in her dreams who longed excessively for her parents. Being an elderly woman, Peqquk felt embarrassed (because she was past menopause, I suppose). She kept this a secret until one day, sick to the point of dying, she told her old mother. The latter informed the baby's parents, who were perfectly aware of what to do and quickly arrived with drinking water and some of their own food. Peqquk drank and ate with great pleasure; having also received several gifts from her "parents," she slowly recovered (ID 768). In other words, the soul of the dead baby, when satisfactorily cared for by its loving parents, disappeared from the body and mind of Peqquk. In this way her own life was saved. Similarly, Amalie, the mother of another informant, once observed how a recently deceased young girl first encircled her following the way of the sun, and then entered her in a blast of wind. Hit by the same stomach trouble that had caused the death of the intruder, Amalie not only lost her appetite. She also started relating some events from that girl's life. The parents took Amalie to the settlement of the deceased girl's family, who offered her food, for which she became so happy that she could not eat a single bite (because of the stomach trouble, I suppose). Soon, however, she regained her appetite and recovered (ID 769). All of which goes to say that, as far as Inuit are concerned, neutral souls are difficult to find. They do not immaculately meet the definition made by Viveiros de Castro of a common ontological essence. In many cases some identity sticks to the soul of a human "mother finder," no matter the species or gender of the mother body. The identity is personal, not particularly human except for the name.[58] Nor is it, as

57. In Inuktitut versions the "soul" clings to the harpoon head wishing for a transfer into the house (as ritual demands), enabling its final transmigration.

58. I have to leave further considerations on this aspect to people better trained in philosophy than me.

already stated, identified with an *inua*, in the meaning of a person of somebody or something. And confusing the issue further, distinction may—in the context of asserting one's identity—be made between souls of differing human categories as well. Thus, discussing the Qallunaat (Europeans), one East Greenlander would not appoint them genuine human souls. They had the souls of dogs at most, in consonance with their mythic origin as the progeny of a (domesticated) dog and an Inuit mother (Holm 1972: 122; 1914: 84).

Whereas stories about humans transformed into animals and vice versa abound, fewer are on record about animals said to transform between species, such as belugas into wolves (Fienup-Riordan 1994: 111; Lantis 1946: 199), a threateningly huge bear into geese by the mere calling out of the word "geese" by a woman (Boas 1901–7: 256–57), or the "Three-in-One" spirit mentioned above, whose human shape is particularly fearsome. I cannot attend to these stories here in regard to the interpretation of perspectives.

Mythic examples of marriage between differing kinds of faunal species, however, are frequent and they make sense in pointing out differences. Basically the perspective is human, as in a very popular Inuit story about the raven that marries a woman among the wild geese: When the raven dangerously lags behind in their migration, he is tricked into drowning. Imagination plays a bigger part in this instance, insofar as a raven has hardly ever been seen flying in company with migrating wild geese as visualized in the story. Only the well-known differing ways in mobility of the two species, wintering raven and migrating geese, are in focus, and no mention is made of their probable human bodies.[59] Differing habits are similarly the only issue of (human) interest in other stories about birds, such as the short one about the sparrow who mourns the death of her husband. Offered marriage by a raven, she rejects him by mocking his ugly feathers and rough beard. Raven returns the insult by taunting the deceased sparrow's poor abilities as a provider. The latter could get hold of nothing but petty worms, he sneers, implying his own superior scavenging habits. Rhymes are included in this story for children to learn by heart (e.g., Sonne 2005: ID 1330), following other short stories on the model of song duels between differing species of birds. Here, implicit learning and entertainment go hand in hand.

Returning finally to the species of spirits most frequently acquired by shamans for helping spirits in East Greenland—those dwelling in their own part of the land as also below the shore—they reveal themselves in different-looking humanlike bodies and as diverse in habits as the faunal species. Focus is less on the similarities than on deviations from the ordinary build of humans, bodily capabilities, the relative distance of the dwelling place from the coast, and hunting habits, as already described in various contexts above.

So in ritual as in myth the *inuat* are, as a rule, recognized as humanlike figures of the Other World, while far from similar in anything but the basics of a figure with head, torso, limbs, viscera, senses, and mind. Animals and birds encountered in human shapes may or may not be *inuat*. The outsider is not told. Masters/owners (*inuat/yuit*) of each species, common among the Yupiit, are not explicitly met with in Greenlandic sources, except, of course, for the huge *inua* of the moon, and Sea

---

59. Actually, most ravens move from the northern to the southern parts of Greenland in winter, traveling overland along the coast. Muus et al. prefer the term "wandering" to "sedentary" bird (1981: 330–31). Other species also winter in Greenland, but they are less eye-catching and not as close to humans.

Woman, the giant female *inua* of the sea: *Sassuma Arnaa* or *Immap Ukuua*. In her house (womb), transmigrating seabirds and sea mammals are reborn annually. She reacts to breaks of taboo towards game, as does *Qaammatip Inua*, the man of the moon, who is the cause of tides and thus the engenderer of life on earth.

The question of how animals see each other in their *manifest* forms in This World calls for stories much closer to real life, such as reports of Inuit observations of the (clever) polar bear's hunting habits (Muus et al. 1981; Born & Rosing-Asvid 1989), as well as the story about polar bear gnawing a big piece of ice into a ball for use as a weapon to knock a walrus unconscious and an easy prey (Sonne 2005: ID 1362). Animal young are taken into the house for pets (and at some point killed by their owners on the parents' command [e.g., Briggs 1974a]); furthermore, the domestication of dogs offers intimate knowledge of psychology and habits of dogs. Realism comes first—in my down-to-earth perspective, admittedly. So let me connect these points with Inuit ways of gaining empathic knowledge, by presenting an experience from Northwest Greenland in the 1970s: A mature hunter, who returned with a polar bear (killed by help of his dogs, as is the usual local way of hunting polar bear), put on the flayed skin of the bear. He walked a circle, his dogs following, creeping in a row, and whining with fear at this apparent cognitive dissonance. Obviously, they recognized their master disguised as the bear he had recently made them attack, but which or whom they by now could not possibly attack, only follow. The "play" was a funny one. People laughed, and if it had any other purpose I failed to receive the right answer to my questioning.[60]

As Viveiros de Castro, among others, states, shamans are the only humans able to return from transformations into other beings and from visits to the other worlds without losing human identity. Willerslev makes it one of his main points that ordinary Yukaghir men, who identify with their prey while hunting, do so only in part, and that they have to work hard on their reintegration as social humans upon their return to society (2007). Would this perspective make sense when applied to the event staged by the bear hunter who tricked his dogs into confusion about his identity by putting on the skin of the killed bear? Who could know? Perhaps regaining full command over his dogs was the main object of his play. Regardless, people were greatly amused at the dogs being tricked.[61]

Ending this section on perspectives, however, let us hand over the floor to the Others, who seemingly show less interest in *puuat* than in the interior life of the world. Let them speak for themselves—in the perspective of the Inuit on the perspectives of the Others.

---

60. Transformational ritual by putting on other beings' clothing has been extensively discussed in anthropological literature (e.g., T. Turner 1991). Lacking competence I shall leave the latter's theorizing of tropes alone.

61. In contrast to the abrupt exclamations without any great coherence, as observed by Willerslev among the Yukaghirs, West Greenlanders telling about exciting hunts usually occurred coherently in the circle of men having their evening meal together. This may have been their way of both reintegrating and receiving appreciative response. The telling, a privilege of mature men, was especially accorded the young hunter during the celebration of his *pernarneq* (Dalager 1915: 4). In general the recollection was a fluent, chronological narrative about the where, when, and how of the hunt, emphasized by habitual, culturally recognized gestures marking the movements of kayak, prey, harpoon, and lance. Glahn saw the value in these eloquent performances for boys' upbringing (Glahn 1921: 174).

The Language of the Others

Taartaq (E. Grl. "belong to darkness")[62] is the language of the Other Worlds, spoken by all its beings, be they helping spirits (*taartat*), spirits in general, animals, or deceased humans.[63] *Taartaq* is not a language on its own; in grammar, syntax, and prosody it does not deviate from the local dialect (Robert-Lamblin 1996: 122). The vocabulary is intelligible, in that the words are neither foreign nor artificial, although quite a few words are metaphors, archaisms, and paraphrases when compared to the language of This World. The scholarly allegation that the spirit language was a secret matter is not tenable. Through the generations the shaman pupils have learned that language from their teachers, and this was a surprisingly orthodox transmission as evidenced by the identity of numerous words in the lists on record from Greenland and Arctic Canada. Did this transmission take place in secrecy? Hardly! No source supports the idea that the shamans, outside performance, used that language among themselves. Nor did they belong to any secret society (apropos Lantis 1946). Evidently they did share secrets about how to do the tricks in performing, for instance (Holm 1972: 130–31; 1914: 95–96), but *taartaq* was no shaman's language. However, the shamans were indeed the humans who most frequently spoke *taartaq* in conversing with spirits, both at outdoor encounters and during performances.[64] In the latter case the audience of ordinary people was free to pick up whatever spirit word they grasped. Only children were protected, with their ears and the anus (the way of the soul) being plugged (Robert-Lamblin 1996: 122ff).[65] Furthermore, no prescriptions obstructed the transmission of ritual paraphrases, or stories containing spirits' words, the meanings of which would most frequently be revealed in context. Secrecy guarded the effect of a *serrat* (a spell), consisting of one or more sentences that sometimes contained spirit words. But these words did not cause the demand for secrecy. A clear recitation of any *serrat* in public would squander its effect. In short, the use of *taartaq* was not reserved for shamans and spirits alone, a fact that both Michèle Therrien (1987) and Robert-Lamblin (1996) make perfectly clear. In addition, the latter did a good job in categorizing the 458 spirit words collected by Émile Victor in East Greenland (Victor & Robert-Lamblin 1989–93, II: 252–63). Therrien works with a selection of 132 words collected by Rasmussen among the Iglulingmiut (1930b), and hers is the only analysis that offers an explanation of the meanings of these words in relation to the ordinary language.

---

62. *Tarriumaq* means "shadow language" in Inuktitut (Oosten & Laugrand 1999: 101).

63. A solitary statement points to some peculiarities in vocabulary or pronunciation used by a particular spirit or class of spirits (Thalbitzer 1930: 78). But since this information is held in general terms, we have to be content with the fact that the spirit language did not reflect differing perspectives among the Others. Also, magic formulars in *taartaq* were understood by all kinds of animals (Thalbizer 1923: 257f, 261f).

64. Kitlinermiut women under taboo were obliged to speak *taartaq* (Rasmussen 1932: 108). So, being isolated from society, they temporarily belonged in the Other World.

65. Unfortunately, the spirit words are not translated into their literal sense. Only the corresponding words in ordinary language are translated into French. Also, the orthography wobbles in less transparent ways. Michéle Therrien has asked me to transcribe into the authorized orthography of Tersis (2008), but it does not cover spirit language and I am no linguist. An earlier collection of 272 words from Ammassalik, printed in O. Rosing (1957–61, I: 87–96), has the West Greenlandic orthography applied to East Greenlandic. Although O. Rosing's list is in Greenlandic without any translations, it leaves fewer unsolvable problems than the list by Victor and Robert-Lamblin. Consequently, where words are used from O. Rosing's list, his transcription into West Greenlandic is used. For the words chosen from Victor's list, an approximate spelling is used. Identical words in both lists are spelled the West Greenlandic way.

Robert-Lamblin's categorization of the 458 East Greenlandic spirit words gives some idea of the most important fields covered. The greatest number (92) concern space and time, including weather and land. Next come daily life, habitation, clothing, and the division of labor (79 words). The category of body and health is also quite numerous (62), like that of religion, which covers sorcery, death, and performances plus helping spirits of shamans (51). Animal and bird terms are fewer (34), as are those of humans—i.e., their "life," ages, and civil state (27). Yet in this latter category the predominance of words for women in relation to births is marked. Finally, the verbs (103) are neither categorized nor characterized. The much shorter list used by Therrien shows a similar distribution by percentage: man and its body 25% (R.-L. 20%); space, time, and weather 17% (R.-L. 20%). Only the animal terms differ in numbers: MT 19%, R-L. 7.5%.

Although the spirits are said to live ordinary lives, they are long-lived, and though a great number of species live in families of several generations, as a rule they do not reproduce—or at least the deceased humans never do. By this I mean to say that the spirit language concerns the life of humans, not that of the spirits themselves. Birth, death, and health of humans are prominent issues, as are hunting conditions. This reflects the life of humans in their relations to the Others, as well as the works of shamans from their unveiled point of view in dealing with spirits. Indeed, by its name *taartaq*, "of darkness," the basic perspective is human (on the imagined perspectives of nonhumans).

Comparing spirit language with human vernacular, Therrien labels the former sacred and the latter profane. I stick to spirit and ordinary language, respectively, because spirit words are sometimes used in stories without giving you the feeling of anything sacred in the Durkheimian meaning of "set apart."[66] Therrien makes clear that one complements the other, because the spirit language unveils elements of ordinary words—and vice versa—that you would not guess from their separate meanings. Focusing on the body parts and their functions, she thus convincingly shows that while the body terms in ordinary language are spatial, the corresponding spirit words stress movement, life, and action: the eye sees, the mouth chews, the lungs breathe, the heart beats, the guts digest, the legs walk, the feet rest on the earth, the legs support the body like tent poles. All in all, then, the body is experienced as a synthesis of spirit with ordinary language, as something that moves around in space. They function in symbiosis, not separated in body and mind (Therrien 1987: 78–81, 113–42). Like *sila* and *silam aappaa*, I would add This and the Other World as a couple.

Ignoring the human body for a while, let us take a look at the animals. They appear less specified by age and species than in ordinary language. The majority are recognizable by their seasonal movement in space, and others by their way of life, and only one, the general species of seal called *puisi* (the emerging one), by its utility value (as boiled meat for humans, *qajivaq*). Generally birds, *timmiat*, are constantly on the move, flying about (*angataat/angitat*). Of the four species singled out, one is a seabird, the fulmar, called *angitajaa*, an "early flyer about" (arrives in April; Muus et al. 1981: 172), and three are birds of the land. Owl is simply *angadiwarti*, "the big one flying about." Raven is the bird to be seen moving about in winter, *angidaanerip angataajaa*, and the migrating snow bunting, *nunara angita'*, "the land's moving lively about," implies, like the fulmar at sea, the onset of spring on land. *Naaja*, gull (general term), is mentioned among spirit words, not because *naaja* is an

66. In recent personal communication, Therrien agrees.

original spirit word but because spirits are not subject to the prescription on mentioning the name of a recently deceased human. In ordinary East Greenlandic *naaja* became replaced by *qusiiq* (glaucous gull, *Larus hyperboreus*) at the death of a person named Naaja, and it remained *qusiiq*. In the same way, I assume, did several other ordinary words end up as East Greenlandic "spirit" words, insofar as they turn out to be ordinary words in West Greenlandic.[67]

The mammals are associated less with seasons than with their way of moving. Among the land animals mentioned, the polar bear walks by his hands' support, *ajappattoq*, and fox lazes spitefully around, *tarfiluttoq*. *Aqitsup* (what is soft, the sea's) *allannguarsua*, the "big one traveling a little at sea," is beluga or narwhal, and probably also a full-grown harp seal, *qaangilinngaaq*, "the passerby." The nonmigrating ringed seal, which bites holes through the thick ice for breathing and also makes use of its numerous teeth for getting hold of its prey (Muus et al. 1981: 411), is sensibly called *kikkalivatsiaq*, "the one with quite some teeth." The meaning of *matsaaq*, the spirit word for bearded seal, remains obscure to me. Nor are *punngoq*, literally "little bag" and, in the spirit language, "little mother," easily explained. It denotes a dog, and *aqitsup punngua*, a shark, is consequently the dog of the "soft," the sea. The walrus, however, is surprisingly characterized, as the term denotes neither its way of swimming or feeding but its way of walking sideways, *sisaangasoq*, alluding I suppose to its use of both sets of flippers as feet for walking the shore. By this it differs from other sea mammals (405).

To summarize, the animals and birds of the East Greenlandic language of the "Others" remain recognizable beings in their manifest forms, characterized as they are by their movements in space and time of This World. Apart from seals generally, which feed both humans and spirits, sharks, polar bears, and scavengers, the relations between animals and humans is not an issue, meaning that spirit language reveals little about the debate in the 1990s of whether Inuit and Yupiit relations to the "Others" are animalized (Fienup-Riordan 1994), gendered (Saladin d'Anglure 1986; 1990a; 1994), or both (Bodenhorn 1990). However, focusing on gender per se, another big issue in Inuit/Yupiit research, it seems that Saladin D'Anglure's gendered cosmology applies to *taartaq*.

In relation to one another, the men and women are the Haves and the Have Nots, respectively. The man, or rather a male being, is a person with a willie ("urethra"), *qorlualik* (W. Grl), and the woman or female being is a person without, or *qorluaqanngitsoq* (W. Grl). According to O. Rosing's list this distinction carries great weight among the spirits, who discriminate along the same lines between spouses, widow and widower, cousins, and, in space, between not only the two strong lights, Moon (*qaammaqivaaq qorlualik*) and Sun (*qaammaqivaaq qorluaqanngitsoq*), but also the prevailing winds, *nigeq* (*suttuarneq qortualik* [*sic*]) and *piteraq* (*suttuaneq qorluaqanngitsoq*).[68] Time is, as mentioned above, gendered as well, with *ukioq* (ordinary language), or winter, being the time of men, *angutaaneq* (spirit language), and summer, *aasaq* (ordinary language), the season of women, *arnaavoq* (spirit language). The connotational meanings, however, are not revealed, except, as mentioned above, for the explanation received by Thalbitzer of "summer" as being the season "when (the

67. The reason why the replacement words for prescribed names survived in East Greenland but not in West Greenland is explained by the lively traveling along the west coast in contrast to the lesser one in the east. In the west the local group under some name taboo would soon meet with people with whom it did not apply, and who in conversations thus reintroduced the temporarily forbidden word.

68. But not to Victor and Robert-Lamblin (1989–93, II: 253–63), where males and females alone are the Haves and Have Nots.

men) [males] have to do with the women [females], or are much occupied with them" (Thalbitzer 1923: 488). That is the way of all gendered beings including humans, I suppose, and not necessarily a claim on male dominance, although the man is, according to Therrien (1987: 131), the one to safely lean on. The female offshore hurricane *piteraq*, for instance, cannot be subdued. Whether female temper or the inland source of *piteraq*, or both, or some other aspect lurk behind the female character of this devastating storm, I cannot tell. Also, what does it mean that winter (*ukioq*) and a full year (*ukioq*) are homonyms? Following "movement," the red thread of Inuit life, one answer could be that men go out hunting, outdoors in *sila*, all the year round, while women stay indoors, especially in winter. Practically, they sew, feed the lamp, and cook most of the time sitting on the platform. But this idea of the active man on the move outdoors versus the sedentary woman indoors is such a Western cliché that one becomes suspicious, as it is also contradicted by examples of women brought up as kayakers or providing for themselves or their families in other ways of hunting and fishing (e.g., Keld Hansen 1986; Bodenhorn 1990). Indeed, apart from periods of taboo—at menstruation, miscarriages, giving birth, and the death of a close relative—no religious sanctions prevented women from being out hunting as their main activity. Myth alone will not agree. The mythic type of a female provider is in Greenland the lesbian mother-in-law who confuses hunting skill with sexual rights and therefore is killed by her son (see p. 249). In Baffin Island and on Nunivak, the mythic female provider is either a beggar or she does the hunting and thus leaves the man idle or merely tending the lamp indoors. This used to be the primordial (dis)order. The reversal was effected by a mythic event that at the same time made biological reproduction possible (Boas 1901–7: 178–79; Lantis 1946: 270–72).[69] The language of the spirits stresses difference in biology alone and to repeat, as regards the basic structure of the worldview, the Greenlanders' *taartaq* has its focus on generalizing gender.

Outside versus inside is another recurrent aspect of *taartaq*, and perhaps the most important for the obvious reason that spirits can see the hidden worlds, of which the interior of humans is of particular interest to the shamans in their job of curing the sick. Not only do they see the beating of the heart and the breathing of the lungs; conversations with spirits in biographical stories show that they also "read" your mind as an open book. "Now she wants to leave!" declared the mother of a new helping spirit-to-be who had persuaded the small pupil, Kaakaaq, to visit his home in the wilderness. The mother was right, but Kaakaaq, who had not uttered a word, had just come to think of leaving (Sonne 2005: ID 1243). "Why are you so irritated?" ask the first spirits met by resentful Naaja. "I am not!" he declares stubbornly. "But it shines out of your whole figure," the spirits object. Indeed, the spirit word for anger is "fire" (Sonne 2005: ID 1233; O. Rosing 1957–61, I: 89). In this context, there are overtones that Naaja, by means of a birth rite, was already inculcated with the first glow of the interior light that would grow into his "second sight" and attract helping spirits-to-be. "How shining you look, how attractive! Would not I be the one coming to you [at your future performances]?" "Yes, please be my helping spirit-to-be," the pupil answers, and both are speaking *taartaq* (Sonne 2005: ID 1270). But in the case of little Kaakaaq, since she does not understand that language in her first encounter with spirits, they fortunately know how to translate into the ordinary speech of humans (ID 1240). Correspondingly, at the onset of a performance the shaman talked to his spirits in ordinary

69. Simultaneously, the Nunivak myth establishes the duty of sharing children between brothers and sisters.

human language right up to the point when the spirit entered his body. From then on all speech was conducted in *taartaq*, if sometimes with insertions of words from ordinary language to help the audience to understand (J. Rosing 1963: 192; O. Rosing 1957–61, I: 86).[70] In short, in practice both humans and spirits had the opportunity to learn each other's languages during performances.

Looking next into the interior of a pregnant woman, the ordinary movements of her menstrual blood have come to a standstill—to a frozen state, as it were. The Iglulik spirits see the fetus as blood in transition, *quassaq*, "what will get frozen/coagulated," understood in opposition to flowing menstrual blood, as Therrien underlines (1987: 128), but only in that particular context (pers. comm.). In East Greenland the fetus is already viscid, *keerpia*, according to the spirits. What is freezing/coagulating is *kanik*, meaning blood (*aak* in ordinary language), as is the case in the spirit languages of the Kitlinermiut, Nattilingmiut, and Polar Inuit, and pronounced *kanuk* in their u-dialects.[71] All parties are thus in consonance with the proto-Inuit/Yupiit *kanuy*, meaning blood as well (Fortescue et al. 1994: 156–57; 2010: 171). The other way round (i.e., from a human point of view) ordinary visible snow was by some Greenlanders called the blood of the deceased (P. Egede 1971: 51; 1939: 39). Still, the freezing of the fetus sounds awkward considering the interior warmth of the human body, the Greenlandic helping spirit's source of revival or staying alive. On the other hand, blood coagulates at heating, as was experienced by the East Greenlanders in heating up blood for stored food (Sonne 2005: ID 1207). But again, *ice* was the matter to be removed from the uterus by the ritual performed at the onset of delivery (Victor & Robert-Lamblin 1989–93, II: 309, 320). Also the "soul," who "found a mother" in one animal species after another and ended up in a human woman, would in one version work hard at making room for himself by sending out the ice. Thereafter the woman became pregnant (e.g., Sonne 2005: ID 272, search "Navagiaq").[72] Menstrual blood presupposes fertility in the latter case, an unimpeded birth in the former—i.e., its outlet after being kept back during pregnancy. Blood at a standstill will coagulate, or freeze, in the context of nonmovement.

Although straightforward reversals frequently characterize the ordinary change between This and the Other World, that logic is not always at work. It works when "to die" is to "go in," *iserpoq* in *taartaq*, corresponding to *anivoq*, "to go out" in ordinary language (see also Sonne 2005: ID 1260). Going out of This World means to go into the Other World, a fact hard to deny from an Inuit perspective. Going inside, *iserpoq* in ordinary language, however, does not mean "to be born" in the spirit language, but to seek warmth, *oqqippoq*, in the inside of either a house or a live body, as the helping spirits do in the body of the shaman during performances. Indeed, the ways ordinary and spirit language may get mixed up depending on context can be inscrutable to the outsider. Folk etymology may play its part as well, as in the case of *aak*, blood in *ordinary language*, which seems to be the root of ordinary bleeding (*aanaarneq*), melting (*aanneq*), and rotting (*aaneq*). They are not

70. In short, the spirits were well versed in human language and knew how to heighten the spirits of the performance by their differing personalities. They were easily recognizable by their habitual way of speaking: quickly, slowly, if chewing some food, stammering, etc. This added to the value of entertainment (J. Rosing 1963: 192; O. Rosing 1957–61, I: 86).

71. East Greenlandic is a so-called i-dialect, substituting the phoneme /i/ for /u/ in a number of contexts.

72. Usually Moon is the one who in Greenlandic myth calls forth the first menstruation of a young woman. He soaks a feather in blood and lets some drops of blood fall on her abdomen. As a deliverer of snow he blows it out through a tube put in his mouth. Ejaculation is the obvious association. Men do not bleed from the inside. They emit something white (search "måne" in Sonne 2005).

identical, though, *aðuɣ* being the prototype for "blood," *aʀu* for "rot," and *auk* for "melt" (Fortescue et al. 1994: 5, 44; 2010: 5, 48). But in the 19th century the "semiotically" talented Kleinschmidt, who had no way of discriminating between such roots, either made up his own philosophy or perhaps relied on folk etymology, by taking *auk* as the root of both blood and rotting as well as melting. Anyway, he feels confident enough to state "auk [*aak*], blood. As can be seen from the many words formed from this root, its basic meaning is another, more comprehensive, something like: released, dissolved in its interior coherence; flowing, fading away; and extended: losing one's exterior connection with something else. So blood should thus be defined as the constituent part of the dissolved body" (Kleinschmidt 1871: 55, tr. BS). Judging from the above examples of identifying bleeding with melting regarding the flow of menstrual blood, and with freezing when it comes to a halt and then either prevents pregnancy or coagulates into a fetus, I am inclined to think that folk etymology has played its trick on both Greenlanders and Kleinschmidt. Being no linguist I cannot definitively decide on the interplay of the spirit word *kanuk/kanik* (snow) with ordinary *aak* in the meaning of blood, but apparently the melting in spring is the ruling metaphor. The spirits who see the fetus as stiffened liquid seem to agree with Kleinschmidt in the same way as they see drinking water, *imeq*, as *erngi*, as the resources of water inside the earth, bound in winter and let loose in spring. *Erngi*, or better the reinforced *erngaaq*, recurs in spirit words associated with drinking, e.g., in *erngaaq* (lake), *erngaartorpoq* (to drink), *erngaartorfia* (bucket), and *erngaartiitaa* (mug) (all spelled in W. Grl.; O. Rosing 1957–61, I: 88). In other words, the source of life stems from the Other (invisible) World. In her comment on this interpretation, Therrien mentions the preference of Inuit elders in Nunavut and Nunavik, who "are always grateful if they can drink spring water they find near the mountains at the end of winter. Doing so they regenerate their body" (pers. comm. and Therrien & Laugrand 2001: 168f). So, the problem of contradicting interior temperatures seems solved by merely referring to differing contexts, that of winter versus spring or that of flowing versus stiffening. In the end, movement versus nonmovement (like life versus death) come out the overriding or source metaphors.

Returning to Viveiros de Castro's proposed "multinaturalism," the spirits do not agree insofar that they distinguish between the human being of a human called either *sinaa* (coastal) or *taataa/taaq* and that of spirits named *titarti*. Only humans call either *ii* (W. Grl. *inuk*; Victor & Robert-Lamblin 1989–93, II: 255: Fortescue et al. 1994: 334; 2010: 363).[73] The covers of animals and birds are not an issue in *taartaq*, which means that their possible differentiation cannot be tracked down on that premise. It is differentiation in ways of movement that counts. Only spatial things like the land and the sea have covers, or warmth/shelter, *akissip oquuvaajat*, "the warmth/shelter of 'the soft' (sea)"—i.e., seaweed—and *nunarngaap oquuvaajat*, "the warmth/shelter of the land"—i.e., plants. The root of the spirit word for dehaired, scratched skin for clothing, *oquwarangici*, "for getting warm," is recognized in these covers, as in the above *oqqippoq*, corresponding to Victor's spellings *oqizaarpo* ("enters the [warm] house") and the helping spirit *oqizarderpo* ("enters little by little the shaman's body"). Even space as a whole, as we know, *sila*, is seen by the spirits as one big belly, *naaq*, at liminal points between day and night. Interior life certainly rules the invisible worlds of spirits. Does the Arctic cold play its trick against tropical Amerindians again?

73. Fortescue et al. refer to Rasmussen (1938: 205), who defines *taaq* as a person whose name has left him after death, and to Holm (1888: 55; 1914: 26), as a "human being."

Perspectivism Summarized

In testing Viveiros de Castro's theory of perspective, the ideas of Inuit and Yupiit do not apply. The ontological essence "breath" or "soul" giving life to any being among the faunal and floral species is not marked as being particularly human, nor as completely neutral. The spirits' human shapes at home in the Other World differ in the same ways as do their *puuat*, or "envelopes." Like humans, the *inuat*, be they human or like seals, need their *puuat* in order to move about for procuring food, the main focus of their intentions; the *puuat* determine both perspective and ways of procurement. In the Other World, the species may see each other as humans differing in appearance.

Apart from the sorry fact that I am unable to unravel the meaning of most words in the East Greenlandic spirit language, some tendencies can be made out. One is obviously its focus on the interior life of the whole bodylike world. Another, as already pointed out by Therrien, is to notice movement, as for instance the spirits' preferred means of differentiating between faunal species. This exists in contrast to the standstill of blood or water let loose at either menstruation as the sign of fertility and delivery, or in spring from the interior of the earth, actually the very source of life.[74]

Finally, concerning symbolism by returning to the proposal of *taartaq* being a sacred language, it was not even kept watertight apart from ordinary speech (e.g., J. Rosing 1963: 192; O. Rosing 1957–61, I: 86). As chapter 5 will illustrate, they can merge in mythopoeic ways, interacting in meanings, as do denotations with connotations and words with metaphors. They create cosmological coherences by their common source that in most cultures, including our own, are the bodily parts, functions, and senses.[75]

74. About movement as a prerequisite for "life" among the Yukaghirs, see also Willerslev (2007).

75. See Ortner (1973), Biesele (1986), Fernandez (1991), T. Turner (1991), Aitchison (2000).

CHAPTER FOUR

■ ■ ■

Angakkut (Shamans)

Introduction

The term "shamanism" refers to the practice of religious specialists who have acquired knowledge and mastery of ecstatic techniques for restoring the health of humans and the order of their perceived conditions of life. Shamanism does not refer to a noncontradictory system of ideas, let alone a theology. Consequently, in case a definition of the term "religion" involves such a systematization, shamanism is no religion. This demand was formerly discussed and similarly, as an alleged early step on the ladder of evolutionism, shamanism was relegated to a place away from science a long time ago. However, prominent in the "shamanistic complex"—a term coined by Hultkrantz (1973; 1989)—shamans were religious experts who used to function as mediators between This and the Other World within corresponding cosmologies in northern Asia and the indigenous Americas (*ibid.*). By their emphasis on the strong symbolism of animals in this complex, the widespread notions of animal masters, and the social function of shamans, Hultkrantz and others looked to cognate, egalitarian societies of hunters to find the earliest practitioners (Hultkrantz 1989; Siikala 1978; Viveiros de Castro 2002; Fausto 2007). The when and where of the origin of the shaman may still be debated, but archaeology and ethnology raise no doubt about the relations through millennia across the Bering Strait between (proto-) Inuit/Yupiit living on either side of the strait and their neighbors (e.g., Krauss 1988). Cultural similarities aside, the social position of a shaman has varied over time and from one society to another, as have ideas about the prerequisites of becoming a shaman, expectations of his/her abilities, initiation rites and myths, the course of performances, etc.

I shall treat such issues in a Greenlandic context and limit comparisons to salient differences and similarities. In general, premodern shamanism now remains a thing of the past. Epidemics, Christian missions, political ideologies (for example, Soviet communism), and modern health care all took their toll. In a few areas shamanic rituals have continued on a small scale, in secrecy, up to the present when revivals, either of "tradition" and/or inspired by New Age philosophies, have taken root in various places, with some appeal to the Inuit as well (for Greenland, see Thisted 2008;

Petterson 2008; Lyberth 2016).[1] Anyway, if premodern shamanism is ruled out only because it does not fit some scholars' definition of "a religion," a vast amount of documented ways of life would be thrown out with the bathwater.[2]

As for Greenland, sorcery, *ilisiinneq* (W. Grl.), an issue rarely dealt with in depth in relation to Eurasian shamanism, needs attention for several reasons. One is the curious demand on the East Greenlandic pupil that he had to acquire means of sorcery and helping spirits (*toornat*) in equal numbers. Second, not only was a Greenlandic shaman—like most shamans everywhere—liable to be accused of using his powers (helping spirits, spells, secret knowledge) for evil ends, but in the Greenlandic context, sorcery was considered an art or a subject on its own. *Ilisiitsoq*, sorcerer, was frequently a derogatory term, in that accusations might lead to killing the assumed sorcerer. In other contexts, however, the *ilisiitsoq* was an expert to be called upon for various beneficent ends. And finally, since Western (and consequently Christian West Greenlandic) ideas about pre-Christian sorcerers wrongly categorized them all as women, *ilisiinneq* is a gender issue as well.

To start, I provide a very short outline of Greenlandic apprenticeship, performances, and key symbols to put us on track to understanding shamans in this context. Next follows evaluation of general issues in Western research history in relation to Greenlandic statements about the definitions of shaman, both etic as well as emic; social criteria; and Western prejudices still haunting the internet. In general terms, the ordinary performances and jobs of shamans (as healer; diviner; finder of paths, witches, and objects; defeater of angry and evil spirits; master of ceremonies; and entertainer) are treated cursorily, whereas other social issues are given more attention due to their prominence in research on the Inuit. Finally, on their own terms, apprenticeship and the initiations involve considerations on theory, history, and the meanings of their key symbols.

Short Outline of East Greenlandic Apprenticeship and Initiations

Conclusions about fixed rules of apprenticeship are doomed to failure, because descriptions that generalize sequences of events and their connotations vary. Nevertheless, chronologically the following three stages remain manifest:

1. An introductory meeting with a spirit either in solitude or accompanied by a teacher.
2. An extended period of some five to twelve years of lonely and secret "searching" and "recruiting" of helping spirits in *Asia*, the Other World.[3]
3. The *saqqummerneq*, the ritual disclosure in public of being an *angakkoq*.

1. Juaaka Lyberth, who in 2015 collected a great number of interesting stories among his own countrymen, hypothesizes that many Greenlanders nourish parallel beliefs, one of Christianity and another of pre-Christian ideas. Although Christianity has apparently made a great impact on the pre-Christian ideas but not vice versa, the believers keep them apart.

2. Here I am hinting at the (in my view odd) tendency of Rane Willerslev, in his otherwise theoretically thorough defense of the term "animism," to compare shamanism of oral cultures with holy writ religions of literate ones (2007).

3. *Asia*: "the neighboring World of Others to whom we are attached by relationships" (Thalbitzer 1930: 85). Two apprentices were allowed to do the seeking together and exchange experiences (Sonne 2005: ID 1179, 1180, 1675; Holm 1972: 125; 1914: 88).

Introductory meeting: The first encounter was either due to an inborn talent for seeing "supernatural" matters or was provoked in some way. The possession of *qaamaneq*, the interior light for seeing the Other World(s), was a sine qua non, whether inborn, artificially engrafted, or acquired and strengthened by various means throughout apprenticeship. Children showing talent were urged by their parents or teacher to be constantly alert and aware of even the tiniest movement in nature.[4] Variations are treated under the heading "Motivations," below.

Apprenticeship: A satisfying examination of teaching cannot be done, absent as it is from most biographies. Tuition definitely seems to have been less interesting to the tellers and their audiences than the more exciting encounters with spirits. Among the teachers actually mentioned, the majority taught only a limited bit of knowledge; for instance, they might provide advice combined with a spell of either *angakkuuneq* (shamanism) or *ilisiinneq* (sorcery). Among the encounters with spirits, the "solitary" initiation by a "freshwater" monster bear, dog, or other devouring creature stands out as the richest in meaning. *By solitary I mean in solitude and secrecy in contrast to initiations in public.* Besides apprenticeship, the demand on secrecy covered a wide range of relations between This and the Other World: spells, sorcery, any secret activity that would lose its effect if revealed, breaks of taboo included. For better or worse, then, secrecy guarded the boundary between the invisible interior and This, the visible ordinary World.

Public initiation: On the other hand, keeping apprenticeship secret throughout life without breaking one's relations to the helping spirits was not recommended. This was a risky affair both socially, due to severe accusations of sorcery, and individually, due to punishing acts of revenge on part of the helping spirits. Presentation in public fulfilled the latter's wishes and secured their complete service. As a prelude to the presentation in public, *saqqummerneq*, the apprentice might go through the *ueerineq*, which Jens Rosing translated into Danish as "release" or "delivery" (1963: 175–76; O. Rosing 1957–61, I: 72). The approaching helping spirits would either make the pupil lose consciousness and call forth bleeding from the soft parts of his face or press him into a fit of rage. Whereas "ordinary" outbreaks of insanity were feared and treated roughly, *ueerineq* was eagerly anticipated. The well-guarded public secret of a person's apprenticeship and the staging of the event made all the difference in treatment.

The acquisition of powers for traveling the Other World(s) cannot be fixed to any particular event in this chronological sequence. Most shamans managed without such ability; some were taught by a helping spirit; and others went through a particular ritual after *saqqummerneq*.

The First and Consecutive Performances

The farther back in history the biographic story of an apprentice, the more impressive the initiating performance testifies to the abilities and spirits he obtained. The candidate called forth his "light," *qaamaneq*, by means of a trick with the drum if he was skilled in this art; helping spirits were sometimes visibly presented in a dim light, sometimes by a mediating spirit, but most often by their voices alone, making noises in common, or talking through the shaman whom they possessed in turns. Some, the so-called frightening spirits, arrived in body, armed with sticks, chasing people around,

4. This was a general Inuit admonition in upbringing, but of particular relevance for spotting manifestations of the Others.

and imposing blows at random. Not every shaman mastered a genuine, staged, thrilling, and beloved performance. To lie covered up on the platform and become possessed would suffice, especially for diagnoses of "soul loss" (partly or in toto), the common explanation of either illness, bad luck in hunting, or infertility (the East Greenlanders counted several souls). Post-*saqqummerneq* initiations or performances drawing on the symbolism of initiations would enhance the reputation of a shaman. Among these the initiation to an *angakkoq puulik*, shaman with *pooq* (bag, envelope), reveals an esteemed, if extremely difficult, one.

Terms and Key Symbols of Shamanism

Shaman, initially a Tungusic term, was not in use among the Inuit and Yupiit, who employed phonological equivalents of *angakkoq*, *toornralik* (with *-lik*, *toornat-* helping spirits), and, rarely, *kalalik* (with helping spirits) (Fortescue et al. 1994; 2010; Lantis 1946: 200). Etymology and semantics of *angakkoq* (pl. *angakkut*) coincide, in that the root *anga-la* refers to traveling in correspondence with the common Inuit/Yupiit epithet: (s)he who travels to places beyond the reach of ordinary humans (Fortescue et al. 1994: 31; 2010: 34; Fienup-Riordan 1994: 305; 1997: 238; Sonne 2005: ID 85).[5] Such destinations could be the heaven above, the world below, or, on the middle level, invisible parts of the earthly world at any distance from human habitation. Most frequently, however, the performance either implied no traveling or the shaman could send one of his helping spirits. The necessary and sufficient prerequisite of the Greenland shaman, and the most often quoted epithet, was his/her ability to *see* things, places, etc. invisible to ordinary humans (e.g., Sonne 2005: ID 312, 968, 2088). This second sight, or the "light" (Greenlandic *qaamaneq*, Inuktitut *qaumaniq*), and simultaneously the perspective of the "Others" connecting This with the Other World serves as a key metaphor of the worldview. Consequently *qaamaneq* constitutes a central issue of my analysis of the Greenlandic *angakkut* (sing. *angakkoq*), which for the historical reasons mentioned above I shall henceforth refer to as shamans.[6]

Pooq is another prominent polysemous symbol of Greenlandic shamanism that connects the coupled worlds *sila* and *silam aappaa*, as evidenced in particular by the initiation of a shaman to the title of an *angakkoq puulik*. Because the analysis is both comprehensive and demands further investigation of the polysemy of *pooq*, it forms a subsequent chapter on its own. Furthermore, *qaamaneq* and *pooq* are in several ways both mutually linked and associated with other symbols to be followed in various directions, neither without ends nor constituting a single coherent system. Nonetheless, as recurring aspects of the perceived world they not only offer meaning to a great number of rituals and stories, they also serve as suitable vehicles for communicating acculturated changes in worldview.

---

5. Another meaning of *angala-*, swinging to and fro (Fortescue et al. 1994: 31; 2010: 34; J. Rosing 1963: 304), also makes sense, namely as a technique of ecstasy. The waking up from ecstasy sometimes shows the same pattern of movement (Sonne 2005: ID 1313). The interpretation of *angakkoq* suggested by Thalbitzer—"leftover part of mother's brother," *angaa-* + *-koq* (1926: 79; 1928: 423–24)—has no foundation in linguistics (Fortescue pers. comm.).

6. For related issues in research history, see Sonne (1985; 1986b; 1988b); Thuesen & Sonne (2005).

Discourses in Research on Shamanism[7]

Combining two mutually colliding definitions in treating Greenlandic shamanism, one taking the culture historical view (Hultkrantz) and the other a structural functional one (Lewis), I shall try to make clear the divergences in these two approaches.

Some Definitions

Scholars apply the Tungusic term "shaman" to similar ritual experts throughout Eurasia, no matter their ethnic names. So, due to the development of Inuit and Yupiit cultures, one after another, in continuous exchanges between Eurasia and North America across the Bering Strait, I do the same for their Inuit/Yupiit counterparts. I thus come closer to the definition of a shaman offered by Åke Hultkrantz than that of Ioan Lewis; Hultkrantz looks to a common cultural stratum, Lewis to social structures. In my analyses, however, I look to both.[8] Lewis frankly turns down any hypothesis about cultural diffusion in prehistory (1975: 50; 1981). Ethics, not emics, should be in focus, he declares in line with his structural functionalism, whereafter he nevertheless picks out the term "shaman" from the Tungusic vocabulary and advocates its universal use. Well aware of the cultural biases that lurk behind both emic terms (like taboo, mana, etc.) and Western etic definitions of such concepts, he feels safe to apply "shaman" to healers and prophets alike wherever in the world they practice. The aim of his argument is to pull the carpet out from under the scholarly tradition of distinguishing between various types and depths of possessions and trances, or altered states of consciousness (ASC in the terminology established by Bourguignon). In research history, Lewis shows, these states have, in distinction from one another, been put to diverse uses: morally evaluated on Western premises by de Heuss (1971) and correlated to presumed antiquity by Eliade (1964: 94, 499–500), to types of society on scales of complexity by Bourguignon (1973), and to presumed cultural attitudes by Mary Douglas (1970). Yet via a close reading of Shirokogoroff, Lewis demonstrates how the Tungusic shamans, who distinguish between the same states, used to practice all types of possessions and trances (ASCs) not only on different occasions or in succession but also by the same shaman during the same performance. Furthermore, with regard to the scholars' frequent moral distinction between (bad) involuntary possession and (good) voluntary possession, Lewis calls attention to the succession of states, from involuntary to controlled possessions, experienced by healers and shamans alike. Both are "chosen" by a spirit, become ill, recover, and thereby come in control of the spirit that they subsequently incarnate in voluntary possessions. Accordingly, Lewis's definition of a shaman goes as follows: "an inspired prophet and healer, a charismatic religious figure, with the power to control the spirits, usually by incarnating them. If the spirits speak through him, he is thus also likely to have the capacity to engage in mystical flight and other 'out of body experiences'" (Lewis 1981: 32). I certainly welcomed Lewis's sociological approach, especially his distinction between the shaman's performance as being part

7. For research history see Hultkrantz (1989), Langdon (1989), and Atkinson (1992). My selected issues for treatment are limited to the possibilities offered by the sources for comments.

8. At a symposium on shamanism in the 1980s, I got caught between two nails in my attempt at defending Lewis's sociological approach, namely between Hultkrantz, who was present, and Lewis, who was not. I did not succeed in my defense, though, because I had to admit the flaws of Lewis's analysis of Inuit shamans due to a poor selection of sources.

of the society's central cult or constituting only a peripheral ritual, because it permits analyses of wider geographical extension than that of Hultkrantz's "shamanic complex." Nevertheless, I look to cultural-historical matters as well.

Hultkrantz not only reproached Lewis for rejecting the relevance of history and cultural settings but also for putting all kinds of professional ecstatics like healers and prophets on par with shamans, no matter the social engagement of the inspired specialist.[9,10] In his definition, Hultkrantz emphasizes both the shaman's social functions and the (emic) cosmology of his society: "A social functionary who, with the help of guardian spirits, attains ecstasy in order to create a rapport with the supernatural world on behalf of his group members" (Hultkrantz 1973: 35, or with similar words in 1978: 30; 1989: 46). Nor is this definition without problems, considering the general ambivalent position of a shaman, capable as he is of using his powers for social ends as well as to his personal antisocial advantage. I shall return to that ambivalence in due course.

However much devalued by late-20th-century social anthropology, the study of the culture-historical roots of Inuit/Yupiit and Unangan (Aleut people) shamanism has retained its attraction to both archaeologists and linguists.[11] According to their studies, the exchanges on the Asian side have been closest between the Yupiit of Chukotka and their neighbors, the Chukchi, despite differences in languages. More closely related in language are the Yukaghirs, if farther removed in time from a neighborhood with the proto-Inuit/Yupiit, as Fortescue concludes in a meticulously worked out hypothesis (1998). Fortescue traces the Yukaghirs back in time and place to the area of Lake Baikal (193), from where they moved north during the last millennium BC and came to occupy a territory stretching from the Lena River in the west to the Kolyma in the east, plus several pockets eastwards to the Anadyr River (Fortescue 1998; Jochelson 1910: 3–4; for contemporary Yukaghir territories see Willerslev 2007: 3–5). While long ago Siberian proto-Inuit/Yupiit and Yukaghirs were close neighbors, the situation changed due to the expanding Chukchi population, who then became the dominant neighbors of the proto-Inuit/Yupiit. So when, during the 13th century AD, the Tungus and Yakuts, arriving from the Baikal as well, made their great inroads to the Yukaghir land and impacted Yukaghir shamanism with their own (Jochelson 1910), the ancient connections between proto-Inuit/Yupiit and Yukaghirs became even more remote.[12] All of these details make it

9. By his numerous examples from Africa, Lewis also implicitly attacked the historical thesis developed by Hultkrantz, who saw no shamanism according to his own definition in either Australia or, with some reservations due to a possible European impact, in Africa (Hultkrantz 1989).

10. The critique was not completely just with regard to "Ecstatic Religion," where Lewis set apart the term "shaman" with the following definition: "Those who practice controlled possession, 'mastering' spirits, are in the Arctic context known as 'shamans'. I retain this term for men or women who play a wide repertoire of social roles on this basis" (Lewis 1971: 64). In the later article of 1981, however, Lewis employs the term "shaman" universally (1981).

11. Regarding a significant pre-Thule culture impact of shamanic objects from Siberia, supposedly of Scythian derivation, see Larsen and Rainey's report of their excavation of the Ipiutak (about 100 AD) remains in Northwest Alaska (1948).

12. The shamanism of the Tungus, considered by some to be the "classical" one, differed from more ancient complexes by its impact from Tibetan Buddhism (Eliade 1964; Hultkrantz 1989). Also Thalbitzer, most probably based on both Jochelson (1910) and Czaplizka (1914: 22), traced Inuit/Yupiit shamanism way back in time to the Baikal area, but he lost his way in untenable linguistic and evolutionary speculations (Thalbitzer 1926; 1928; 1941; see Sonne 1985; 1986b; 1988b; Thuesen & Sonne 2005). Michael Fortescue did far better tracing by linguistic analysis relations of proto-Inuit/Yupiit with Yukaghirs (1998). According to Rane Willerslev, Stalinism in cooperation with modern (effective) health care did away with shamanism among the Yukaghirs of the Upper Kolyma. But Willerslev's theory about

inappropriate for scholars to compare Inuit/Yupiit with, for example, Yukaghir cosmology. On the other hand, I would never have considered some geographical peculiarities of the Greenlandic Other Worlds in a new rewarding light (pp. 163–65) had it not been for inspiration from a drawing made by Napolskikh of the (hypothesized) proto-Yukaghir spatial worldview (1992). Similarly, the World Tree combining the tripartite worlds of Siberian cosmologies made me take a closer look at the contexts of the pillar(s) upholding heaven according to Greenlandic statements and stories.[13] And finally, a Tlingit myth about the tide as brought into balance by Raven made me realize my hypothesis on balance as a Greenlandic key concept in a wider context. In other words, comparisons along variations sometimes inspire me to become aware of hitherto neglected statements in the Greenlandic texts leading to more far-sighted ways of interpretation.

While old-fashioned, I am nevertheless not alone in looking across the northern continents for comparisons. Apart from the continued research in "cultural history" (e.g., Fitzhugh & Crowell 1988), certain contemporary anthropologists rethinking "animism" do so in comparing ontologies of Amerindians and hunting cultures of northeastern Siberia.[14] Their shamans are broadly defined from the angle of perspectivism, namely as the only humans who can safely pass between the two worlds of humans and nonhumans (Viveiros de Castro 2002: 310).

The East Greenlandic Shaman, Emically Defined

A list collected by Robert-Lamblin among the East Greenlanders, who in *public opinion were considered* to have been shamans (1997), offers a welcome possibility of clarifying the emic criteria of being a shaman in that region. Robert-Lamblin adds to the familiar publications notes she took down in the 1960s and '70s, and her list presents data on 44 shamans, including several who died before Holm arrived (in 1884) but survived in memory through stories and kinship ties. Robert-Lamblin discusses the following issues: the demographic rate of shamans, motivations for becoming a shaman, "dynasties" of shamans, ranking of shamans, and finally, their courses of life (age, marriages, sexual prerogatives, internal conflicts, ways of death, burial). Her rate of 20% of all adult males being shamans appears far below the 50% in the Iglulik region according to Saladin d'Anglure (1986: 97); however, Oosten and Remie (1997: 91) put the Iglulik rate at 20% instead. Yet her count of 2% of the Ammassalik female population being shamans compared to 10% among the Iglulingmiut (Saladin d'Anglure) poses a question.[15] Since Robert-Lamblin discusses the low percentage but offers no decisive answer, I shall continue the discussion further below. Concerning Robert-Lamblin's findings as to "dynasties and biographical data of shamans," I have nothing to add, but the issue of motivation is worth further considerations. It concerns both the emic definition and the ranking of shamans: Exactly on which criterion (or criteria) was a person named a shaman in public opinion? Although

---

its continuation through the hunter's partial identification with his prey as a sort of "do-it-yourself" shamanism is of relevance for studying Inuit shamans on the ontological level (Willerslev 2001; 2007).

13. Here I must confess I once thoroughly denied the existence of Inuit/Yupiit "world trees," as Rolf Gilberg, a specialist on Siberian shamans, asked me that question in public many years ago.

14. The Amerindians arrived across the Bering Strait at various points in prehistory before the proto-Inuit/Yupiit. See, for archaeology, Dumond (1977: 32–46), and Vajda's decisive findings based on linguistics, Kari & Potter (2010).

15. I cannot tell how Saladin d'Anglure arrived at the percentages of male and female shamans among the Iglulingmiut. Robert-Lamblin conducted diligent and transparent demographic investigations among the Ammassalimmiut and among their relatives at Ittoqqortoormiut/Scoresbysund.

they approximately did live up to Hultkrantz's definition—"a social functionary who, with the help of guardian spirits, attains ecstasy in order to create a rapport with the supernatural world on behalf of his group members"—borderline cases require a further division of criteria into (1) a fully served apprenticeship, initiation, and continued practice in public; (2) a sufficient number of helping spirits; (3) a cultural definition of ecstasy; and (4) the demand of serving one's fellow men.

The fully served apprenticeship can easily be ruled out as a necessary premise insofar as among the total of 44 shamans listed, nine had their apprenticeship cut off. Of these, three were women. Evidently, we cannot trust Holm on that point, as he had gotten the impression that the unsuccessful apprentice would give up shamanizing and turn to the art of sorcery exclusively (1914: 89; 1972: 127). The nine half-educated shamans did practice as shamans, three among whom (Aallaaq, Kunitsi, and Teemiartissaq) owned but a single spirit each.[16] Some scholars leave out from the category of Inuit shamans the practitioner of the *qilaneq* method, the *qilalik*, because they maintain that it did not demand a helping spirit (Merkur 1985: 67, 271 notes 30–32).[17] The average description has the *qilalik* just fasten a thong to a person's head or one of her limbs, hold on to the "rod" in the other end, and start "fishing" for the spirit who either had caused some pressing problem or knew the way out of it. The *qilalik* asked the arrived spirit successive questions while alternately raising and lowering the thong fastened to a stick. The spirit knew no answers but yes or no, and could not speak audibly. The negation or affirmation of the question was revealed by a change of the weight of the body part to which the thong was fastened (e.g., H. Egede 1971, 1: 123; 1925: 107; Kleivan & Sonne 1985: 26, plate XXVI). Apparently some spirit, although mute, is involved as partly affirmed by the example of Teemiartissaq. She figures on the list of shamans as a borderline case because she was cut off from her apprenticeship but given a *qilaneq* spirit by her aunt (Thalbitzer 1923: 464; Sonne 2005: ID 1109). She started out "fishing" the ordinary way, but having called her personal *qila* into the body of the patient, it (seemingly) did answer questions audibly.[18] On her request it would even go fetch a lost soul and have it lured into the patient correctly through the anus (Thalbitzer 1923: 464–68; 1930: 90; Sonne 2005: ID 1109).[19] The Nattilik Aupilarjuk ended up in a similar situation. He too was an apprentice when his father eliminated his son's shaman power by ritual in order to prolong his life. Like Teemiartissaq, Aupilarjuk was left with the possibility of doing *qilaneq* and he may have used a particular spirit "for asking questions," an *apigsaq* (Oosten et al. 1999: 20–21), as did other practitioners among the Nattilingmiut.[20] How another East Greenlandic woman, Aviitsuk, performed is not described. She was also in possession of a spirit, a sand hopper, by means of which she once dragged

16. In defining a shaman, Gilberg mentions that a single helping spirit will suffice (1978: 15).

17. The *qilaamasoq* is a person who practices *qilaneq* (W. Grl.), *qilalik*, a person provided with a *qila* (E. and W. Grl.), and *qilaqarter* a person who owns a *qila* (E. Grl.).

18. This according to the published notes (Thalbitzer 1923: 465). In a Danish retelling of Teemiartissaq's narrative, Thalbitzer at this point inserts a (or her?) description of the common *qilaneq* as the weight oracle of mute answers (Thalbitzer 1932).

19. Robert-Lamblin generalizes this solitary statement without references (1997: 282).

20. *Apigsaq* seems related to the East Greenlandic *apeqqiteq* ("invited for being asked questions"), mentioned by Teemiartissaq to be the superior of her *qila* spirit. Her brother, a full-flegded shaman, also had an *apeqqiteq* who told him (and the audience) the identities of his entering helping spirits during his first performance (Thalbitzer 1923: 464–65; Sonne 2005: ID 1017). Holm's (1914: 89; 1972: 127) generalization about the *apeqqiteq* as a middle spirit between the shaman and his particular helping spirit, *toornaarsuk*, is difficult to evaluate. Tradition and Christianity became in many ways mixed up due to the missionaries' early use of the term "Toornaarsuk" for the Devil (see Sonne 1986b).

a polar bear into accessible range by *qilaneq* during a famine (Sonne 2005: ID 1200). Aviitsuk does *not* figure on the list of shamans, nor does the wife of the shaman Akku. The latter practiced *qilaneq* on a child in order to reveal the identity of some terrifying spirit who was sneaking around. She did not own a helping spirit, though. Nevertheless, while "fishing" she invited or ordered the frightening spirit to *become* her helping spirit, possess the child, and reveal its identity. But this spirit answered every question in the negative, mute, and for good reason: the "spirit" was the shaman Akku, who had returned from hunting unseen and made fun by sneaking around the house (Bak 1979: 27). Granted, Robert-Lamblin's list is fairly complete; the possession of a single spirit, the sand hopper of Aviitsuk for instance, is a necessary but not sufficient criterion of being named a shaman. Greater importance was seemingly attached to apprenticeship, whether served or cut off. But again, this alone was not enough either, unless the half-educated shaman practiced in public. Peqqitissaq never did. He "became a sworn enemy of the *angakkut* and lost no opportunity of holding them up to ridicule" (Holm 1914: 102; 1972: 135). Nevertheless, Peqqitissaq figures on the list (Robert-Lamblin 1997: 276).

Teemiartissaq's *qila* spirit and her way of using it made Thalbitzer assume an early stage of shamanism prior to the more spectacular performance using the *drum* for invoking several helping spirits.[21] Being old-fashioned, perhaps, the East Greenlanders used the root *qila* for still another technique, *qila'cucercer* in Thalbitzer's spelling (1941: 710, fig. 224) and in Jens Rosing's *qilaaqutserneq* (Sonne 2005: ID 1702; or *qilaaqqutserneq*, to call in [*-qqut*] one's *qila*?). As pictured by Kaarali Andreassen in 1906, the *qilaaqutsertoq* lies covered up on his back on the rear part of the platform and the person to be cured is seated upright in the adjacent "loose box," facing the back wall (Thalbitzer 1941: 710, fig. 224). This method was called *nerfallarneq* in West Greenland, equivalent to *qilaneq* (Glahn 1921: 64; Rink 1866–71, II: 199; 1975: 57; Sonne 2005: ID 312). In East Greenlandic *qilaaqutserneq* was practiced by all shamans in summer (when darkness was difficult to obtain in other ways), with the effect being described as follows by Holm: "As they thus recline, they fall into a trance, in which their spirits speak through them and in which they are able to see visions" (1914: 90; 1972: 127). Obviously this was a technique of ecstasy, probably the one most commonly employed in East Greenland. Holm's eyewitness report of the *qilaaqutserneq* practiced by Aappaluttoq on Sanimuinnaq had a tripartite sequence. During the first "ecstasy" Aappaluttoq "saw" a loss of soul. Sitting up next to Sanimuinnaq, Aappaluttoq then "cross-examined him as to all the evil he had done. Sanimuinnaq answered partly in delirium and behaved quite as if he was mad…" The answers were confessions of murders by means of sorcery, hitting relatives and nonrelatives alike. Then "Aappaluttoq threw himself back again on the platform and communed with his spirits. He now ascertained that the infamous Maratuk [Maratsi],[22] Sanimuinnaq's cousin, had robbed Sanimuinnaq's soul. Aappaluttoq sent off his *tarajuatsiaq* [shadow spirit] to fetch it, but was obliged to return home himself before the spirit came back with the soul" (Holm 1914: 104; 1972: 136). Another description of a *qilaaqut-*

21. Thalbitzer could be right, insofar as *q/ə/la* is a proto-Inuit/Yupiit word that means both helping spirit and shamanistic divination, whereas only speakers of the Inuit dialects (of the later developed Thule culture) name the drum *qilaut/qilaat*, or "a means (*-ut*) for *qila*^" (Fortescue et al. 1994: 295; 2010: 322). But Thalbitzer's arguments are biased and linguistically strained (see Sonne 1986b).

22. See biography by Robert-Lamblin (1988).

serneq, but from the shaman's point of view, was told to Kukkujooq/Apulu by his mother, Kaakaaq; it concerned her being taught this method by her first helping spirit, a male snow bunting.[23] As described previously, the snow bunting man needed her help for his wife's difficult delivery. Kaakaaq declared herself incompetent, but the male snow bunting stated that she was a predestined shaman, or she would never have been able to see him as a human being. In agreement, Kaakaaq undressed and placed herself covered up on the platform. By his *eeq, eeq, eeq* the snow bunting man inspired her to rub her palms and puff between them. Her cover began flapping, and her breath left her body through the anus, making room for the snow bunting man to enter in spirit. At that point Kaakaaq's vision changed (a second time). She could clearly see and remove the thing obstructing the delivery.[24] "In this way mother tried *qilaaqutserneq for the first time*—i.e., spirit possession under the cover of a skin, permitting her to see whatever was concealed for ordinary people" (Sonne 2005: ID 1702 emphasis, BS; another variant ID 1260). Apparently then *qilaaqutserneq* became the technique of ecstasy preferred by Kaakaaq, although in possession of multiple helping spirits (Sonne 2005: ID 1239–1241, 1243–1244, 1246–1247, 1261, 1276, 1290, 1701–1703, 1706, 1708).

In theory Kaakaaq could have made no serious use of her various helping spirits unless she became initiated in public (ID 1205); trusting the informants of the minister Otto Sandgreen, she never did, and for this reason her helping spirits eventually made her blind (ID 1261, 1276). She did practice, though (Sara Helms and Jens Rosing pers. comm.; Gessain 1975a: 324), by *qilaaqutserneq* I presume. Kaakaaq's daughter, Elisabeth, offered a different explanation for her blindness: namely, the resentment felt by her familiars at her deciding on baptism, which meant their dismissal. But Kaakaaq did not let all of them go. The remaining ones continued attacking her with seizures that scared the wits out of her close relatives until finally the last spirit revealed itself by name to her daughter in a dream. When Elisabeth told her about that dream, Kaakaaq became furious. Elisabeth had stolen her last familiar in whom she still confided. But the spirit had left Kaakaaq for good in preference of her daughter, a true Christian, who let it go. Kaakaaq eventually calmed down (Sonne 2005: ID 1708).[25]

After all, *qilaneq* is difficult to define. In his caption to a reproduction of Kaarali's drawing, Ove Bak, fluent in the related dialect of South Greenland, translated *qilaaqutserneq* into *qilaneq* but defined it as a practice that differed from the divinatory one of weight (1979: 38). If so, the term *qilaneq* evinces several meanings: "fishing" a spirit without assistance from a familiar, conversing with a helping spirit (mute, rarely eloquent) for both diagnosis and curing, and the practice of becoming possessed by

23. As Robert-Lamblin proposed without specification, Kaakaaq practiced in a way different from the ordinary one (1997: 274).

24. Using a method, *kilummoorsorneq*, the shaman retires to the rear of the platform (*kilu*) facing the wall; this was a similar or perhaps the same technique used by lesser shamans for invoking their helping spirits (Rasmussen 1921–25, I: 20). Still another kind of shaman in control of only a single spirit, a "cuddling song" spirit, was the *aqartivinnalik* (Sonne 2005: ID 561, 813, 814, 1161). In contrast to the *qilaamasoq* the latter was held in high regard due to his spirit's skill in exterminating *tupilaks*. He acted out his performance in a peculiar way by swinging his body from side to side, circling around bent backwards, and then leaving his body on spirit travels. Petty songs, usually composed by the mother for her newborn baby (Thalbitzer 1923), were considered powerful means for calling back dying or lost persons (Sonne 2005: ID 14, 1742), as they were closely connected with both birth and mother. Furthermore, the petty song spirits were indigenous to This World in that ordinary speech was their language in contrast to the spirit language of the Other World. Since no named person, historical or mythic, is accorded the title of *aqartivinnalik* in any story on record, I shall interpolate the symbolism in a later course.

25. So, Schjødt's assertion that the acquired objects of the initiation are irreversible (1986: 104) cannot be maintained.

an eloquent helping spirit. Were they all techniques of ecstasy? Judging from Kaakaaq's experience above, ecstasy meant "seeing," changing sight, or coming to see the wished-for part of the Other World in focus, that is by means of the "interior light," the *qaamaneq* of shamans. Missuarniannga offered a similar explanation: "All shamans experiencing trances know these instances of interior clarity felt like a light filling one's soul" (Thalbitzer 1930: 77, tr. BS). During performances, the vision or clarity is attained at the moment the shaman's soul has left This World and is arriving in the Other World (Thalbitzer 1930: 95; 1910: 458–59). Although the vision might take in the entire Other World (Rasmussen 1929: 120–21; Sonne 2005: ID 1017), often in practice a more limited place is in focus. Ilinngivaki, for instance, who would hit either his *makkortaq* (a piece of skin for boot soles stretched in the palm) or his drum for letting his mind open up to the world of the spirits, also made use of a very simple *qilaneq*-like technique. Tying a thong tightly around his own head and lying down on the platform, he saw the platform's end open up and he could have a clear vision of some departed relatives whose well-being he wanted to verify. A person missing from his vision made him repeat the practice, which brought into focus the very person who had moved to another place (Thalbitzer ed. 1933: 50–51). In another case, Aadaarutaa, by his initiation in solitude, was enabled to follow the events going on at his distant settlement by merely closing his eyes (Sonne 2005: ID 2032). But did the *qilalik* lacking a personal helping spirit get visions while practicing? The answer remains open. On an even wider scale, however, the experience of "seeing" was recurrently brought about in isolation by stone rubbing and similar repetitive movements during apprenticeship. So, in memory of Eliade (1964), to master a technique of ecstasy was a necessary but far from sufficient criterion of being named a shaman.

Shamans were asked to practice in cases of illness, for finding lost objects, prophesying about the weather and having it changed, procuring good hunting, getting children for childless women, celebrating seasonal transitions (at least in Arctic Canada), for entertainment (their most frequent job, according to Holm), and, when set up on their own accord, most frequently in order to rise in recognition. They practiced for the benefit of others and were with few exceptions (entertainment being one?) paid, or rather, their helping spirits were. The shaman received and made use of the payment, the spirits got the honor. In these ways the East Greenlandic shaman fits Hultkrantz's definition. Serving somebody by extraordinary means, however, did not automatically give one the name of a shaman. Kunnak/Eqeeqqoq, for instance, a famous sorcerer/*ilisiitsoq* "of highest degree" (Sonne 2005: ID 1990) but not on the list of shamans, was called upon time and again to cure diseases. He tried, if in vain, to cure the madness of Nalakaaq (ID 1238) and once he treated an attack of shingles, openly and with success. At this point he went into ecstasy, breathing heavily to the effect that his dress, a gutskin anorak (*ikiaq*) fluttered (ID 1664). To put it another way, Kunnak represented a sorcerer who went into ecstasy for the benefit of society. Did he possess a helping spirit? Not on record. Would Hultkrantz or Eliade name him a shaman? Ammassalimmiut (apparently) did not. In short, the East Greenlandic emic definition of "a shaman" appears clouded by negotiations of posterity.[26]

26. Certain "liminal" persons—the *imaannaangitsut*, the "not just-so ones"—were not nonhumans, nor were they recognized shamans. They were humans with extraordinary (religious/magic) capabilities, whether inborn or obtained by ritual means. More or less abnormal and thus sensitive to otherworldly events and causes, they were of great use unless considered too deviant—i.e., a danger to communal life (Rink 1866–71, II: 187; 1975: 44). The line between

Research into Greenlandic Shamans

While conducting fieldwork in Ammassalik from 1905 to 1906, William Thalbitzer obtained a sure grip on both the main lines of the culture of the East Greenlandic shamans and the respects in which it differed from the prevalent interpretations of shamanism (1909; 1930). Only his hypotheses on its origin and history present a muddled story (see Sonne 1985; 1986b; Thuesen & Sonne 2005).

Based on years of fieldwork in East Greenland, Joëlle Robert-Lamblin has published several relevant articles. Among these the listing of shamans, put to use above, is especially valuable. It goes back to around 1800 and stops at the last baptism in the Ammassalik district in 1921 (Robert-Lamblin 1997). Her editing of the collections made by Émile Victor (Victor & Robert-Lamblin 1989–93) is of great import. As a stepping-stone for further consideration, I am indebted to M-L. Grandorf, who completed a fine analysis based on theories of liminality of most East Greenlandic texts about the main solitary initiation of shamans. In some regards the thesis by Merete Demant Jakobsen (1999) has also been useful. She takes her point of departure in the West Greenlandic sources showing enlightening correspondences with shaman practices in general, and she offers a fine comment on sorcery.

Testing Main Issues of Western Research in Shamanism on East Greenlandic Sources

The shaman's mental equipment and behavior have been points of fascination throughout the history of research. Is he mentally divergent?[27] Is he forced to practice again and again in order to cure himself? Is he "called" by the spirits and does he risk death if he does not comply, or is he free to decide for himself? Are his altered states genuine, or is he playing with the audience? Does he become possessed by his helping spirits, do they merely act on his behalf, or does he leave This World in an out-of-body experience? The question of which kind of trance, possession or journey, would be the "original" one in the (pre-) history of shamanism, remains open (see Lewis 1981).

The drug-culture breakthrough of the 1970s made exploration of Bourguignon's theory of altered states of consciousness (ASC) evolve into a comprehensive discipline in both "Classic" and New Age shamanism (Atkinson 1992). Thus Siikala (1978), quick off the mark in her analysis of the former Siberian shamans' ASC during performances, defines the shaman's role as the one he assumes and masters for communication between This and the Other World. The depth of trance, she concludes, depends on the size of the audience, the structure of society, and its way of production. Small hunting societies appear to favor the deepest trances (Siikala 1978). Later, the discovery of the production of endorphins and their effects under intense physical pressure offered new perspectives on the classic shamanic texts (Atkinson 1992; Hoppál 1992), and most recently, research in brain neurology presents interesting new angles (references in Christensen 2007). I shall not immerse myself in details of neurology of which I am ignorant, nor in testing the theory of ASCs in any correlation to either size or structure of society; like the Tungus shaman, shamans of the small, bilateral Inuit hunting societies mastered all states, some only one, but others several. What strikes me, though, is the joy

---

humans of extraordinary capacities and shamans appears to be thin. In myth, intelligent and knowledgeable heroes like Uiartoq, Qilaasuaq, and the Greenlandic Kivioq are not shamans either. Taking a second look at the West Greenlandic Akilinermiut across the sea (in Canada), they belonged there in myth but remained only mythic in part when knowledge was received about their Inuit roots. Thus the one-eyed Akilinermiu giant in-law, known by Hendrik in about 1860 to be a related *inuk* of the past, is caught betwixt and between being human and nonhuman (see pp. 92f)

27. Since the majority of Greenlandic shamans were men, I shall henceforward stick to "he" in general statements.

and experiences of light associated with a great number of helping spirits of an extended list received by Reverend Peck (Laugrand, Oosten, Trudel 2000; 2002). Were shamans liable to become addicted to their ecstatic encounters with some of their helping spirits?

Possession and Trance

Associated with devil possessions of Catholicism, shamans' possession by helping spirits used to be looked down upon in Western research. In contrast, Eliade, among others, elevated travels in spirit, a misleading attitude since some shamans, as we know, exceled in changing between the two states. Although traveling was held in higher esteem than possession alone, traveling *plus* possession was at a premium in East Greenland (e.g., Sonne 2005: ID 1818, 1108, 1683; J. Rosing 1963: 191; O. Rosing 1957–61, I: 84–85).[28] The chain of reasoning about possession and traveling, most clearly explicated by the East Greenlanders, and already referred to several times in passing, was as follows: during performances the helping spirits took turns entering their master's body as soon as he had opened the way by pressing his own breath down and out through his anus to a position on hold beneath the floor (Sonne 2005: ID 1203, 1205, 1311, 1312, 1313, 1667, 1673, 1674, 1696).[29] The spirits claimed their lives depended on repeated stays in his warm interior, to which they had access only during his performances. Consequently they persuaded their apprentice not to postpone his *saqqummerneq*, and thereafter to practice frequently. They might even turn nervous and aggressive in case their shaman was out of play or died (ID 1198, 1247). A single statement bespeaks a similar idea in Canada of the shaman being a *puuq* (W. Grl. *pooq*), a cover or—in the spirit language—a "mother" for his familiars (Williamson 1974: 48).

The succession of altered states are described in stories about historical East Greenlandic shamans who could either serve as the mouthpiece of the spirit, take on its figure, or, after a series of "possessions," take off in spirit escorted (but not possessed) by one or several of his helping spirits. A single spirit might be left behind with the audience in order to report on the travelogue (e.g., Sonne 2005: ID 1818). At other times, most spirits remained behind and, if their shaman ended up in danger of death, they sought shelter whimpering beneath the floor. But no sooner was the danger blown over than they did their utmost to call him back to life. They took turns in possessing his unconscious body while the audience repeatedly called *kiakkaaka*, the ritual way of giving support (e.g., ID 1203). Plainly, then, the discourse of possession versus traveling appears absurd in the light of Eastern Inuit shamans, unless the issue in focus is the esteem accorded the multitasking shaman.

Mentally Deviant?

Although sources for Inuit shamans offer some reported bouts of "hysteria," the large number of shamans—approximately 20% of all adults—does not suggest that psychological misfits were in the majority (Robert-Lamblin 1997: 286; Oosten & Remie 1997: 91; Saladin d'Anglure 1986: 97).[30] In

28. Lewis called attention to a similar mixing of states among the Iglulingmiut in his *Ecstatic Religion* (1971: 165).

29. This is why Jakobsen prefers the term "replacement" to "possession" (1999: 7) in line with the translation offered by Thalbitzer of the East Greenlandic *taartoq*, helping spirit, into the "substituting or exchanged one" (1909: 97; 1930: 95).

30. Kaakaaq, whose fits were a plague to her family, is the only—though very strong—case in point. As far as the sources go, however, shamans led ordinary lives as hunters and housewives.

consequence, generalized statements about shamans' mental imbalances that still haunt the internet cannot be applied to the Eastern Inuit.[31]

Inuit shamans knew plenty of tricks to perform (e.g., Holm 1972: 130; 1914: 88) before, during, and after trances of varying depth.[32] But the latter issue cannot be addressed the Western psychological way, partly because the few actual descriptions are made by coolly observing Westerners, and partly because the trance depth accorded a shaman in oral transmission tends to grow with distance in time (the ancient shamans far surpassed contemporary ones in tricks and trance technique). What the sources do offer, though, are insights on the Inuit ideas of the psychology of the shaman in his relations with his helping spirits.

According to Georg Quppersimaan, "fear"—an excited fear of the unknown—was an explicit prerequisite for seeing and communicating with spirits on their conditions (Sonne 2005: ID 1170).[33] Thus when Georg in a sad mood had been taken for a walk by his mother intending to cheer him up, he was taught a long lesson: Go look for the young of the sparrows! So he did, found some, forgot his gloom, and brought back a dead and featherless young. "I wish it would be alive again," he said. "But how?" Mother asked. "Yes, how?" Georg replied, convinced of the impossibility of realizing his wish. "Did you ever become frightened at some experience from the time you started to have sensations?" "No..." But suddenly he did remember something and said: "Yes, I was [constantly] very afraid from the moment I began to sense my surroundings." His mother then tells him how to revive the naked young with the purpose of simultaneously fighting that fear and acquiring the power of attraction to strange matters. Eventually Georg succeeds, the parents of the revived young become his first helping spirits, and they pay him back with a piece of grass as his means for the revival of deceased humans (ID 1152). Much later, in search of a giant spirit, he similarly had to concentrate *on getting sufficiently scared* in order to have an extended stretch of burrowed earth transformed into the very giant, which, still scaring him, made him come closer and agreed to become his "future helping spirit." So, fear made one become sensitive to seeing and hearing exceptional things (ID 1165). Not only pupils but also spirits of the friendlier type could be uptight upon their first meeting with a human, shivering all over to the extent that the pointed end of the anorak cracked (ID 1289). Paradoxically, as it were, among fear's many faces, the acquisition of helping spirits was at the same time motivated by the desire to fight or control fear. Nobody can verify the authenticity of Georg's stories—this one actually looks similar to one treated above as told about Kaakaaq (ID 1290)—but the conscious approach to the handling of fear fits in with other statements. At a later point in Sandgreen's arrangement of

31. Andreas Lommel: "Shamanism: The Beginnings of Art, draws a distinction between a medicine person and a shaman, noting that the future shaman acts under an inner compulsion... a psychosis that is emerging for some reason or other is so strong that the only way out open to the individual attacked by it is to escape from it into shamanistic activity, that is to say essentially by means of artistic productivity, such as dancing or singing, which always involves a state of trance" (1967: 9–10). See: http://www.cabrillo.edu/~crsmith/shaman.html.

32. See Jakobsen (1999) for West Greenlandic examples. My preference is a source of early extraction communicated by the liberal-minded, rational merchant Dalager, who became close friends with a distinguished shaman in mid-18th-century Southwest Greenland: "he [the shaman] has told me that he often has felt like being beside himself, seeing figures and pictures that, after recovering, seem like a dream. I too have frequently observed when present at sorcery [shaman's performances] that the shaman immediately upon the act looks completely confused and replies bewildered to one's questions, owing to his strong imagination it seems" (Dalager 1915: 32, tr. BS).

33. *Tamakkuat tamarnik ujarniarnerat naammattoorniarnerallu aatsaat piviusunngorsinnaasarpoq ersinikkut* [*ersineq* + *kut*: through fear] (Qupersimaan 1972: 140).

Georg's autobiography, the awakening of his senses is revealed to have occurred in early childhood at the sight of his mother's bleeding wounds. Georg's evil stepfather stabbed her time and again. The repeated shocks made him oversensitive for the rest of his life to a degree that fear of death became an obsession right until a most terrifying experience did away with it (ID 1170, 1167). Naaja got rid of his fear after a second solitary initiation of death and revival (by the giant of the inland ice, quoted concerning *naar*-times in a previous section) to a degree that he became indifferent to fear of death in later meetings with spirits (ID 1213).[34] Missuarniannga lost consciousness in most encounters with a new future helping spirit (ID 2283), as did any pupil when going through the decisive East Greenlandic initiation of being eaten and thrown up again by a particular spirit. Some felt pain, others apparently not.

Finally, fear also worked the other way round, in that the ambition of becoming feared (in this case, respected) among humans was said to be a strong motivation. Not only Sandgreen, a minister, presented that point in contrast to the Christian commandments of trust in God and loving one's neighbors (Sandgreen 1987: 224–25, 437; 1967, II: 15–16, 197), but Dalager, the rationalist colonial manager of the mid-18th-century South-Southwest Greenland, also put it bluntly: "Most future shamans start out studying the art of doing both good and harm in order to become feared and admired, but not least to improve their living by means of the costly payments they ask... [whereas] the honest ones, the genuine shamans receive nothing outside pure, dry compliments and the consolation that they can live in relative peace and quiet, in contrast to the cheating ones, who often have to flee from one place to another and nevertheless run the risk of ending up a martyr" (Dalager 1915: 33). This moral evaluation cannot be generalized without further ado, of course. On the other hand, there is no smoke without fire, as I shall take up in a further discussion of the art of sorcery.

As regards a pupil's mental state, occasional outbursts of rage are not on record. He is sometimes told to become gloomy when approaching his public initiation for the explicit reason that his spirits put pressures on him for allowing them to perform. This gloomy fear might find an outlet in the *ueerineq* ("delivery") ritual when the candidate, losing consciousness, had blood trickling out from the soft parts of the face. Some, falling victim to a fit of rage, rushed furiously around as a danger of death to his surroundings by his streaming blood splashing in all directions. An alternative way named *niilerneq*, wolfing down, concerns Akku (died 1891), who did not bleed but dashed around blindly and ended up swallowing inedible dry skins (Sonne 2005: ID 1211, 1311, 1312). During performances the shaman was generally said to be *sila-ittoq*, deprived of his *sila*, reason, according to Fabricius (1804), while, paradoxically, at the same time he obtained *sila*, *silanippoq*, "all the knowledge in the world" (Sonne 2005: ID 1312, 1206, 1666, 1695).[35] *Silanippoq* signifies the change in sight that opened up the Other World to the shaman by means of his *qaamaneq*, the interior "light." Usually, however, the performing shaman's varying states of consciousness were less dangerous to the audience than were some particular helping spirits who played the thrilling part: the so-called

34. The fame of Naaja, who lived in the first half of the 19th century, grew with an accumulation of stories that tell more about ideology—of decisive importance for the analysis of symbolism—than of "reality." But see Birgit K. Petersen (2006–7) for similar ideas about getting rid of fright among young children by reading them stories about thrilling, fear-provoking experiences.

35. Fabricius, a missionary to Paamiut from 1768 to 1773, managed to learn Greenlandic fluently and completed a dictionary (1804).

qimarratit (sing. *qimarrat*), the frightening spirits, literally made one flee. The shaman might start his performance calling in such a spirit to help promote an atmosphere of excitement (O. Rosing 1957–61, I: 84; J. Rosing 1963: 182–83).[36] Evidently, thrilling entertainment was a main function of the shaman, in that ordinary people, for want of anything better to do, would on a boring winter evening themselves play a shaman's performance with masks and surprising skill (J. Rosing 1963: 301–2; Sonne 2005: ID 2070). Later, when the mission put a ban on performances of any kind, they went on in secrecy until replaced by the exchange of stories about *qivittut* (see above pp. 162f) and ghosts, an exciting entertainment still. Named *qivittulersaarutit* and *aliortukkat*, they are currently published in print and particularly popular among young people for the bodily pleasure of shivering thrill (Pedersen 2002; 2006–7).

So, ritualized insanity during both "delivery" and, to a lesser degree, performances was not only expected but customary. Various "techniques of ecstasy" were used, like singing, hitting a piece of skin (*makkortaq*) stretched out in the palm, rubbing one's hands, closing one's eyes, pressing down and out one's breath through the anus, drumming, or, rarely, swaying to and fro (Sonne 2005 ID 561; see also Saladin d'Anglure 2001: 174). By contrast, nonritualized fits of rage, *perlerorneq* (starvation illness), caused tremendous fear. The symptoms were aggressive behavior and insatiable eating that allegedly would make the sick person attempt to devour his relatives. The afflicted person was struggled with, and in case it did not suffice, he was choked or restrained until death arrived, and in some instances, at the sick person's own request, killed or buried alive (Sonne 1984; R. Petersen 1990: 96; Sonne 2005: ID 1238, 1986, 849; Holm 1972: 114, 134; 1914: 74, 102; Rasmussen 1938: 168–69; Glahn 1921: 18; Bertelsen 1914: 48; Mylius-Erichsen & Moltke 1906: 573; Gad 1974: 166). The cause of going mad, especially in East Greenland, was the alleged boomerang effect of *ilisiinneq*, sorcery, due to the stronger means of defense possessed by the recipient such as helping spirits and/or amulets (Holm 1972: 133–36; 1914: 100–7; Sonne 2005: ID 1257, 1254, 980). An apprentice, if hit by illness, would recover by confessing either an attempt to do sorcery or the very fact that he was an apprentice, a secret matter until public initiation. Regrettably, however, by confession he might lose most of his powers and sometimes give up his future career as a shaman (Holm 1972: 132ff; 1914: 98, 102–3). Even senility, another kind of losing one's *sila*, was not always accepted as a harmless stage in life. Aged shamans who became unreliable risked accusations for all sorts of mishaps (Sonne 2005: ID 1191). The absentminded elder with a tendency to mumble also did not inspire confidence; mumbling was looked upon with suspicion because *serratit* (spells)—to whatever end, sorcery included—lost their power if spoken aloud (ID 757, 863).

Still another cause of mental disturbances was the demand of cutting the bonds to one's spirits at baptism, when either spirits or master did not seriously want to give up the relationship. Missuarniannga sometimes relapsed, it was reported (Bak 1979: 88), and Kaakaaq, when possessed by her spirits at intervals, became endowed with the gigantic strength of a lunatic. Her son had to fight her for long hours until eventually he got the upper hand by slapping her cheek (Sonne 2005: ID 1708). No wonder then that her continued attacks of insanity brewed an unusual number of stories about her attempts at sorcery (ID 1261, 1268, 1251, 1275, 1700, 1927).

36. During the performances described below of having Moon and *Nalaarsik* arrive for punishment, those two *inuat* were in fact playing the part of *qimarratit*.

Summing up the above examples of fears and mental deviance, the "fear" was not considered all that diffuse as propagated by Aua (Rasmussen 1929: 54–55), the statement unavoidably quoted in any representation of Inuit/Yupiit religion. The discourse of Aua's impressive oration on fear, I assume, was due to the Christian influence present in the new religious movement he had recently joined. Trust in God was its main dogma, an idea running counter to the unending number of precautions taken in hunting and other ways of life that time and again would prove inadequate (Kleivan & Sonne 1985: 32–33).[37] In East Greenlandic psychology or philosophy, fear was both feared and handled. Fear was the precondition of getting in touch with the Others, and it had to be overcome with the experiences of mortal dreads. Staged in public, the rage of the shaman-to-be might be a cause of fear to the audience, as was the arrival of helping spirits, especially a *qimarrat* at an ordinary performance. But the boundary between serious fear and thrill was a narrow one when staged by the shaman and then enjoyed by the audience like some thrillers of today. Insanity outside ritual, on the contrary, caused fear of insanity leading, as mentioned above, to the final killing of the afflicted person, unless (s)he, in lucid moments, would confess apprenticeship or the usual alleged cause, an unsuccessful attempt of sorcery.

Not being a trained psychologist and basically unable to distinguish between angst, fright, fear, etc. in the recounted examples, I shall leave the topic by resuming the considerations of Merkur and Oosten on the genuineness of the trances. Merkur, who offers a thorough survey of the history of research on altered states of consciousness, treats a good number of Inuit texts about trances on derived premises.[38] One attractive point that he presents concerns the demanding activities of the shaman. These alone, he suggests, would change the shaman's state of consciousness (Merkur 1985). Oosten, who justly challenges Merkur's lack of source criticism, decides the matter in another more sensible way. The whole question of genuineness of trance, he underlines, is completely irrelevant in the ritual frame of a performance, dominated as it is by representations and the active part taken by the audience. Furthermore, in case the shaman undertakes a journey in spirit that he relates on return, his account will meet the ideological expectations of the audience (Oosten 1989; Sonne 2005: ID 1983).[39]

Unavoidable Calling?

In Siberia and some places in Alaska, spirits would choose the person to become a shaman. The calling was unavoidable insofar that if the person did not oblige they would become sick and eventually die. If the person submitted, they would recover and come to control the spirit, as emphasized by Lewis (see above; Czaplizka 1914: 172–78; Eliade 1964: 376; Siikala 1978: 16; Sokolova 1989: 162; Mousalimas 1989). Among the Eastern Inuit, callings did occur (e.g., Sonne 2005: ID 1290, 1702,

37. And, by the way, this also runs counter to the trust in the all-round conditions of a hunting life as proposed by Ingold (2000).

38. Of late the confusion brought about by treating ASCs on their dubious premises seems overcome by research in possessions correlated with social, political, and cultural issues (Boddy 1994), a trend for which Ioan Lewis broke the ground (1971).

39. Regarding the shaman's own conviction, reference is made to Lévi-Strauss's *The Sorcerer and His Magic* (1953/1963), which has been discussed by Crépau (1997) and Neu (1975), among others. The term "representation" has been convincingly attacked by Ingold (2000: 56–57, 282–83), but I do not feel obliged to take up the challenge in the context of Oosten.

1152, 836), but they were either positively received or avoidable without bad consequences (Sonne 1982a). Moreover, whenever an author describes an early event in a person's apprenticeship as a "calling," one should consider the impact from Christian or Western ideas about vocation and the genius of Romanticism.

Besides the "calling," in Greenland capacities for becoming a shaman were considered either inborn or acquired by chance or artificially. In Eliade's judgment, both unavoidable calling and inborn abilities rated far above artificially acquired abilities (Eliade 1964: 13–14; 33ff). Not so in Greenland. Some children were "made" into shamans-to-be by ritual or teaching, as exemplified below. Inborn abilities were granted to a baby born in its caul, as well as to (trusting a single text) a child whose older sisters and brothers had all died (J. Rosing 1963: 173; O. Rosing 1957–61, I: 71; Sonne 2005: ID 1311). These potentialities, however, were not commands. Nor were other symbolically outstanding signs of predestination in childhood, such as the apparent death, burial, and reemergence of Akku (Sonne 2005: ID 967, 1312). Perhaps this was because no spirit was involved? I would say this is unlikely, because when a married couple of snow buntings in human form gave the girl, Kaakaaq, the seal of approval, this was seen as a positive recognition, not as a fatal, unavoidable calling (ID 1290). Closest to a "calling" would be the experience of being knocked down by light (Rasmussen 1929: 120–23), and the shocking experience of the death of a parent (J. Rosing 1963: 173; O. Rosing 1957–61, I: 71), whereas an event labeled a "calling" by Hans Lynge, namely the encounter of Ineqinnavaat with a family of spirits in the wilderness, was in no way unavoidable. She was invited by the spirits to become a shaman, but, as explicated, nothing would happen if she did not accept; however, she did. By becoming a shaman her sorry status as a poor and fatherless girl would most certainly rise (Sonne 2005: ID 836). Another example of romanticizing an event into a calling occurs in Jens Rosing's translation (1963: 173) of the story about the ritual that *artificially* made the newborn Naaja into a potential shaman (O. Rosing 1957–61, I: 71). Rasmussen makes the same general claim on the vocation of shamans among the Polar Inuit (1921–25, III: 28). Yet the only text about an apprenticeship from Avanersuaq has Uutuaq go in search of helping spirits of his own accord. He stays overnight far inland and happens to hear two giants singing song duels. He neither met nor exchanged words with them, but the listening alone made him "a little bit of a shaman" (Sonne 2005: ID 2142).

There were other ways of dropping out then choosing not to accept an invitation by the spirits. First, despite a strongly felt desire to become a shaman, the effort was not necessarily crowned with success. Some who tried did not experience anything and just gave up (Keld Hansen pers. comm.; Holm 1972: 172; 1914: left out in translation). Orlavaarsuk, who called up a spirit on his own accord, became scared and fled, but then regretted and repeated the calling; however, the offended spirit was above reappearing (Sonne 2005: ID 488, 1072). Others, although "called" or, better, invited, accidentally became seriously ill during apprenticeship and, in order to be cured, had to spoil their endeavors by revealing their project, a secret matter until public initiation, *saqqummerneq*. Teemiartissaq similarly was cut off from her carrier when her stepfather, a shaman himself, revealed her apprenticeship before *saqqummerneq*. The helping spirits took offense and withdrew, but without (further) punishing effects. The whole matter simply vanished (Sonne 2005: ID 1108, 1109, 1152; Holm 1972: 132; 1914: 102; Thalbitzer 1909: 95).

So, the assumed demand on either mental deviance or an unavoidable calling as the precondition for apprenticeship is not supported by the Greenlandic sources. Rather fear, which could be experienced by anybody, was indeed necessary, as was the courage to withstand the fear and continue. Without fear nothing extraordinary would happen to you. In a wider sense the thrill of fear also had an elementary social function, a genuine functionalist one of creating a fellow feeling among people for the time being.

"Artificial" Start

The very common ritual engrafting of "material" (*-ssaq*) for becoming a shaman, *angakkussaq*, resulted in skills as splendid as those developed by inborn talents. Several Ammassalik shamans of great renown got their start by some ritual with the aim of inculcating the first spark of *qaamaneq*, for seeing and attracting helping spirits. Newborn babies could, like Naaja, be treated with a piece of dry, burning moss propped down into the throat. This ritual was to be repeated at all ritual firsts, like getting one's first anorak, boots, tooth, kayak, etc. (Sonne 2005: ID 967, 1108, 1228, 1229, 1230, 1231; J. Rosing 1963: 173; O. Rosing 1957–61, I: 71). Alternatively, glowing blueberry sprigs were used, Apulu insists, for no obvious reason (Sonne 2005: ID 1257, 1289; Victor & Robert-Lamblin 1989–93, II: 242 [same informant]). Some were given "the shit of the sun," *seqernup anaa* (*Xanthoria elegans*, "sunburst lichen"), as an amulet, supposedly with the same attracting effect on the spirits as the "glowing" plants (Holm 1972: 124; 1914: 86–87; Victor & Robert-Lamblin 1989–93, II: 242).[40] Alternatively plants of the foreshore were used. Missuarniannga was told to wash his entire naked body with seaweed and was promised the effect of seeing the light, which at the same time would attract his first helping spirit-to-be (Sonne 2005: ID 2283). Maratsi similarly received his incipient *qaamaneq* in an artificial way from the sea, in company with his teacher, and not by means of plants but through a wing snail washed ashore (ID 1686). Other small children were placed naked on the lap of a performing shaman who in this way let his visiting spirits get used to the child, or vice versa (Sonne 2005: ID 1907; Rink 1866–71, II: 200; 1975: 58; J. Rosing 1963: 173).

Artificial start or not, people were liberal in making requests. Mature shamans looking for a pupil would ask the parents, as did Maratsi's teacher (Thalbitzer 1909: 94; Sonne 2005: ID 1686, 972, 984). A close relative would of his own accord stimulate interest in a young boy by teaching him some beginner's knowledge (Sonne 2005: ID 1257, 1144). An elder, in gratitude for some help offered by a young person, would offer to teach him in return (ID 984, 2031). Another, hoping to be paid back, would on her own accord offer the pupil some magic means for some end, evil or beneficent (ID 1242, 1258). Every piece of acquired "knowledge" had its prize and would work the same social way as the giving of some outfit to a kayaker, who would then pay back the giver with a suitable share of his prey.

So, to get started of one's own accord was fairly common (Sonne 2005: ID 1180, 2142; Cranz 1765–70, I: 268–69; see also Birket-Smith 1953: 126; Boas 1901–7: 509–10), together with invitations from the spirits among whom some types were very eager to create lifelong bonds with a human being. They saw their chance upon certain conditions that I shall disclose in the following.

---

40. Analogically, shooting stars were understood to be "the shit of stars" (P. Egede 1971: 59; 1939: 45; Thalbitzer 1923: 270–71; Rasmussen 1932: 24).

Motivations

"A man *chose* to be a shaman for various reasons. Some because they longed for those who were dead [a parent], others because they wished to be revenged, others because they were afraid of their fellow-settlers, and others again because he wished to be able to do better in the struggle for food" (Rasmussen 1938: 110, emphasis BS). The focus of these generalizations is on the individual in society, pointing to losses suffered, the ideal obligation of avenging the murder of a close relative, social insecurity, and survival within rough conditions. Checking the autobiographies, we see that these motivations are all richly represented, either on part of the apprentice, his parents, some close relative, an elderly shaman wanting a pupil, or even on the part of a spirit. Becoming a shaman meant a high if ambivalent reputation (Sonne 1978), and some income, though insufficient for making a living (Sonne 1982a; Oosten 1989). To treat the latter point first, no calculations can be made. As a rule shamans lived like anybody else. Men were hunters, providing for their families to the best of their abilities, while women were mothers and housewives. Mentions of exact payments are few. In return for having restored the soul of a man, one shaman is reported to have received an impressive amount of purchased goods: a big brass kettle, a shirt, and a piece of narwhal tooth and a knife (iron) (P. Egede 1971: 30; 1939: 26). Another shaman, being paid the skin of a caribou for the same treatment, tried to sell the skin to the colonial trader. The latter refused due to the high price asked by the shaman. Accused by Poul Egede of overcharging, compared with the ease with which it had been earned (namely by merely blowing on the patient), the shaman replied in defense that bringing back a lost soul from beneath the earth was no easy task (P. Egede 1971: 90; 1939: 64). Dalager's generalizing distinction between good and bad shamans on the criterion of payment is hardly reliable, considering that payment for services to individual nonrelatives was a must. Neglect was offensive, whether by an ordinary nonrelative in everyday transactions or the helping spirits of the shaman. A frequent proposal in research—that the shaman was paid only for treating individuals but performed for free in cases of common crises—does not apply to Greenlandic tradition. Trusting the legends, the shaman's travel to Sea Woman might be paid first by gifts of meat to be consumed by the shaman on his return from a successful trip, and afterwards by the first catch made from the procured animals by every hunter. The latter payment was sanctioned as limited in amount, in that each hunter was permitted to catch only one seal (or bird) on the first day of the released game's arrival. This "first fruit" went to the shaman. Catching more than one would either make the animals disappear or set a narrow limit to the guilty person's future catches. While the obedient hunters were afterwards free to catch as many as they managed at a time, the "sinner" had to make do with no more than two on any trip. Also, Sea Woman's release of seabirds and sea mammals was explicitly understood as a payback in gratitude for the cleaning she received from the shaman. She might even ask the shaman to mark a particular seal as a personal belonging to be delivered when caught by another hunter. If reluctant, the latter would lose his luck in hunting (e.g., Sonne 2005: ID 29, 340, 349).

The promise of making material profit by becoming a shaman is not mentioned in the autobiographies. Georg Quppersimaan, encouraged by his mother, looked for protection and means of revenge, as did Apulu/Kukkujooq, whose mother's brother tried to put him on the track of apprenticeship; Teemiartissaq looked for the ability to fly—i.e., for traveling to the invisible worlds. She missed her deceased brother, a shaman, whom she once in a dream met just outside the boundary of the lower realm of death. Together they deplored her poor fate, her spoiled apprenticeship. If she had carried out the rest of her training, she could have visited him at will (ID 1108). Otherwise the range of motivations in retrospective biographies for setting out on an apprenticeship is too wide for picking out a single, decisive one, let alone choosing between several listed for the famous (legendary) shamans of the past. As many as three or even four causes are attributed to Naaja, born at the end of the 18th century, for his beginnings. First, at his birth his father made him a shaman-to-be (through the ritual with the glowing moss), motivated by a desire to protect the child against the same kind of sorcery that allegedly killed his first children, a pair of twins. Second, Naaja's mother died in his very young years, and third, he took offense at a very mild reprimand by his father. In the latter case he ran away from home in a glowing rage—i.e., in a mood that attracts spirits. And so it did. An additional cause would be the death of Naaja's older brothers, the twins, a situation stressed in one text to have a similar effect (ID 1311). Kaakaaq, who was two generations younger, received her decisive shock when her father went insane, became fastened to two heavy stones, and, on the point of death, started to eat his own flesh. She also became peevish at some maternal reprimand and ran away from home; finally, her mother died an early death (ID 1238, 1239, 1246). Sanimuinnaq was likewise scolded as a small child and ran away into the wilderness (ID 575), and Akku, who in the first place was asked by his father to get tuition from his grandfather, a great shaman, encountered and received his "light" from a ghost atop a mountain. Later, when he apparently died, was buried, but woke up in the grave and found his way out, this event was considered an extraordinarily promising "initiation" (ID 967).

Among the various motivations, the death of a parent stands out as a common incentive in East Greenland (Robert-Lamblin 1997: 271–74) but for differing reasons.[41] Like Teemiartissaq, Missuarniannga was motivated by the possibility of visiting the realm of death and seeing his deceased father again (Robert-Lamblin 1997; Sonne 2005: ID 2283). Friendship with resolute spirits replacing the lost parent is a common explanation (J. Rosing 1963: 173; Thalbitzer 1941: 609). Several species, the tiny dwarves in particular, were not only eager to make contacts but also, in the function of a so-called "waking-up spirit" mentioned above (e.g., p. 83), served as a life-saving ally of the small pupil when in danger of getting lost to the Other World (J. Rosing 1963: 173; Sonne 2005: ID 1236, 1222, 1215, 1241, 2283). For boys made fatherless by murder, like Georg and Apulu, the means of attack and defense gained by obtaining helping spirits and knowledge of sorcery were attractive. Revenge, an ideal demand, was a risky undertaking, which also put the young future avenger's own life in danger.

Like children bereaved of a parent, offended children were easy targets. The offended child's radiating anger attracted spirits who did their best to soothe them. Thus, the spirit turning up close to Kaakaaq asking to be her teacher made these promises: the fear she would feel at first would disappear and in the end she would be an object of fear herself, an effective means of defense in the risky surroundings of a poor, fatherless girl (Sonne 2005: ID 1239). Offended Naaja, who would not admit his anger, was easily seen through and invited by his two dwarves on a first visit to their home (ID 1233). The reprimand that made Sanimuinnaq decide to start out on his own was a serious

41. A curious example is the legendary Nappajannguaq. He is an orphan providing well for his mother's sister and uncle, but he obviously departs in order to acquire powers for the revival of his deceased parents. He travels across the ocean to a place where a giant living atop a mountain of earth upon a huge iceberg sees to his death and revival, which enables him to revive and bring back his parents (Sonne 2005: ID 2074).

one; during a scolding his mother hit him with the stanchion of the small sledge of his own making (ID 575). Children are sensitive; even a light reprimand may feel like a refusal of family love, which invites spirits. Serious loss of *nallinneq*, of "loving care" or "empathy," on part of one's parents in particular opened up the boundary to the spirits. Besides the death of a parent or being scolded, other defects in family relations were similarly inviting. Aadaarutaa was attacked by some evil *innersuit* once he had left his wife in anger, asserting his intention never to return. The *innersuit* came to fetch him, not due to his lack of morals but because he apparently did not want to stay with his family. In that position he was easy prey. Fortunately then, he was saved by some of his strongest helping spirits (ID 2032). Nanngajak was not that lucky. The *innersuit* caught and kept him forever by cutting off his nose, making him noseless like them. The kidnappers were his own helping spirit and its relatives, his supporters, so why did they do that? A likely cause would be that his father, Kunnak, had put obstacles in the way of Nanngajak's apprenticeship in the first place; he did so by forcing him to join the family on a summer's travel, with the sarcastic remark that Nanngajak had no other reason for staying at home than a desire to go in search of helping spirits. This lack of *nallinneq* (empathy, love) from his own father, a shamanlike *ilisiitsoq* himself, put Nanngajak in danger of being stolen by evil spirits. Consequently he was in fact *saved* by his own resolute *innersuaq*, who cared for him. But Nanngajak would have preferred to stay on earth. This was how Georg explained the loss of his friend Nanngajak, who never returned from a kayak trip, and who (in a vision) told Georg the whole story during a later encounter at sea (ID 1180, 1996).[42]

Although the spirits may appear to be the keepers of social morality among humans, in most cases their intentions turn out to be self-serving. They want to take advantage of a defect in human family relations regardless of the (im)morality of the forsaken person's doings. A human who feels rejected, or bereaved of *nallinneq* (empathy), or is *isolating* herself, if only temporarily, from her closest of kin makes inroads for spirits, be they friendly, supportive, evil, or just greedy. The raised finger of the Nanngajak story points to his father, Kunnak, who later was punished by unrelenting sorrow at his son's death. Longing for a reunion, he attempted suicide by drowning, and eventually he drowned by accident (ID 1180).

It was important for parents to be supportive, and they would show this support by their silence. They did not ask questions like "How was your day at school?" (in search of helping spirits). Nor did they tell anybody else, of course. Secrecy was essential. Nor did nonrelatives, suspecting somebody's apprenticeship, feel inclined to spoil the endeavor by revealing the secrecy.[43] Instead, pupils were, as mentioned above, offered bits of knowledge by unrelated persons of the latters' own accord. Kukkujooq paid for such an offer with sex; Kaakaaq did similarly and perhaps with spiritual protection at a later point (ID 1258, 1249). Aadaarutaa, who had been helpful to an old half-educated shaman, was offered instruction out of gratitude, because one good turn deserves another (Sonne 2005: ID 1229, 1230; Thalbitzer 1941: 609–10).

---

42. Kayakers who did not return were said to have been kidnapped by the *innersuit*; this was also documented in West Greenland (N. Egede 1943: 55; Rasmussen 1981, I: 178–85: H. Egede 1971, 1: 236–37; 1925: 207).

43. For the special case of Teemiartissaq, see pp. 228, 397.

Conclusion about Greenlandic Attitudes to Becoming a Shaman

Altogether, ideas about becoming a shaman in pre-Christian Greenland differed from the common ones of Siberia and Yup'ik Alaska. Inborn talents were highly valued; they were associated not with mental deviance but rather with great sensitivity and brightness. Fear of the unknown promoted sensitivity together with reminders to always be alert. Talent-inculcating rituals were common and they did not produce shamans of lesser capacities. "Called" pupils were free to accept or refuse the calling. The spirit did not make the unwilling person sick, let alone take vengeance on "dropouts." A few known exceptions are Kaakaaq and Missuarniannga, who apparently did not manage (or want) to let their spirits go after baptism (Bak 1979; Sonne 2005: ID 1708). Several kinds of spirits were apparently eager to become attached to a human person. They were attracted to a child, who, due to a reprimand, felt neglected by a parent.

Social Aspects of Ranking and Gender of Shamans

In theory anyone could embark on a career as a shaman in pre-Christian Greenland, both young people of either sex as well as mature and older people. In practice, most apprentices were boys and young men, while a few were girls; some served a full apprenticeship, while others had to stop but might practice anyway, unintentionally disturbing the accepted definitions found in many academic writings.

Ranking

In agreement with the etymology of *angakkoq* (the traveler), shamans who traveled the Other Worlds were ranked highly among the Inuit in general. Greenlandic ranking of shamans appears in affixes like *-suaq* in *angakkorsuaq*, "great shaman," and *-vissuaq* (*angakkuvissuaq*), "a genuinely great shaman" (e.g., Sonne 2005: ID 1203). These "grades" are not explicitly defined, and most new shamans were to meet additional expectations in order to be named a great or really great shaman. Enumerating points of ranking, Robert-Lamblin places diagnosis by "spirit fishing," *qilaneq*, on the lowest step, with "lying covered up on one's back" a step higher, and the reputation growing with the number of helping spirits and impressive tricks to be carried out. At the top of the hierarchy hovers the shaman with the ability to fly, *ilimmarneq* (Robert-Lamblin 1997: 283), a capacity ranked by some East Greenlanders on par with another of wrapping up oneself, *poorsinnaaleq*, or *puulik*, "with a bag" (J. Rosing 1963: 191; O. Rosing 1957–61, I: 84–95).[44] Apparently this shaman *puulik* traveled by gliding. Gliding was also known by the Canadian Inuit (Rasmussen 1929: 126; 1931: 317, associated with traveling both horizontally and downwards) and by the West Greenlanders (to Sea Woman, N. Egede 1971: 38; 1939: 150; Sonne 2005: ID 1649).[45]

Though predominantly used for traveling to the lower abodes, the gliding method worked for traveling upwards as well, that is, by way of the sea via the horizon. Floating, *puttaannarneq*, like an ice floe across the surface of the sea, was a gliding method used in South Greenland but, trusting a solitary statement, used only by the lesser shamans incapable of flying (Sonne 2005: ID 2035). Not so in East Greenland, where, granted that he did employ gliding, the powers of an *angakkoq*

44. Not mentioned by Robert-Lamblin.
45. Most wading birds actually do glide upon the surface for taking off and landing.

puulik either matched those of an *ilimmartartoq* or were said by others to be hard at the latter's heels (J. Rosing 1963: 191; O. Rosing 1957–61: 85). Although in theory an East Greenlandic "flyer," *ilimmartartoq*, could be a *puulik* as well, the only example on record appears as a negation.[46] Naaja, a flyer in several stories, failed in his attempt to become a *puulik*. Upon failing, the storyteller's comment goes, Naaja did not raise from being an *angakkorsuaq*, a great shaman, to the higher position of an *angakkuvissuaq*, a genuinely great *angakkoq* (Sonne 2005: ID 1203). This statement would in theory support the idea that the shaman who mastered both ways of traveling achieves the highest possible rank. No matter who comes out the winner, the *ilimmartartoq* or the *poorsinnaaleq* or both, the interesting point is the very comparison that proposes only these two traveling abilities as a main criterion of highest rank. More ways were practiced in obtaining the ability to fly: some in public, others in solitude. The title of a *poorsinnaaleq/puulik*, however, demanded an impressive public ritual, which will be dealt with in the following chapter.

Male Shamans as Hunters

The frequent allegation that male shamans were bad hunters is not generally supported by the sources. Maratsi may have been one (Jens Rosing pers. comm.), the legendary Kanak another. The latter had his paddle stolen by his brothers, became deeply distressed, followed the way of the dead towards heaven, became initiated by Moon, and ended up a great shaman. Otherwise the majority of able-bodied men, whether shamans or not, went hunting, and disability does not appear as a common cause for becoming a shaman.

Female Shamans

Among the four individual female shamans on Robert-Lamblin's list, only Kaakaaq was considered a shaman of great powers, but probably due to her less-than-spectacular performances she was not named an *angakkorsuaq*. None of the remaining three—Teemiartissaq, who ended up a *qilalik/qilaamasoq* with only a single helping spirit; Putsutoq, who was baptized in 1911; or Pitaqqinia, who was baptized in 1917—served their apprenticeships (Robert-Lamblin 1997). I never came upon additional information about Putsutoq, but Pitaqqinia was mentioned by her big brother, Kukkujooq/Apulu (a shaman), to be in search of helping spirits; once, when accompanying him in sealing at breathing holes, she seemed to scare away the seals by means of her frightening spirit. She did not bother to drag home his killed seals, he maintained (Sonne 2005: ID 1284). Yet preferring to remain on good terms with his sister he did not let on his suspicion (which might have deprived her of continuing her search). The same Kukkujooq took no vengeance either when at a later point he was ordered by their mother, Kaakaaq, to assist Pitaqqinia in her first, difficult delivery. Obeying, he sent off all inhabitants, blew on her, and out came the baby (*ibid.*).[47]

Looking west, a few historical examples from South, West, and Northwest Greenland put one on a track worth considering, especially in comparison with stories about anonymous shamans. Sahra, of Southeast Greenlandic origin, was trained by her mother's brother, but to no avail, since she was

46. A mistake made by Rasmussen is discussed on p. 303.

47. Facing the minister Sandgreen, Kukkujooq insisted on never having performed in public. Yet, by assisting his sister he did, and by telling Sandgreen about the event he revealed the truth.

baptized at the age of sixteen (ID 1783). The ranking of Ineqinnavaat, from north of Upernavik, is impossible. Only a single report of one of her performances was recorded (ID 791), but she owned at least three helping spirits. That much is clear from biography. The first one(s) to appear were a spirit family who had named their baby after their former master, her deceased father.[48] As to how far the namesake boy and/or his parents became her familiars remains uncertain (ID 836). Another, a raven of hers, was involved in an accusation of sorcery (ID 860) and the third, her European helping spirit, was accused of having killed her husband, who refused to let her spend five days and nights in a cave with that spirit. His explicit argument was that she was still nursing their five-year-old son. With that stay in the cave, Ineqinnavaat would have fulfilled her apprenticeship, empowering her with untold capabilities (ID 841). A semi-educated shaman she remained, I suppose.

Moving south and back in time to the two female shamans presented above in the context of shamans' journeys to Sea Woman, the one married to two male shamans was childless, while the other lost her great powers at marriage (N. Egede 1971: 3–4; 1939: 129; P. Egede 1971: 67; 1939: 50). Farther south, marriage did not deprive the famous wife of Tuttu, a Southerner known from legend alone, of any powers.[49] Nothing is mentioned about her having children, but she far exceeded her husband in shamanic powers. Thus, when once she deserted him, he had to increase his abilities to an extent that permitted him to follow her deep into (or through?) the earth and persuade her to return. She, not he, was the shaman asked to visit Sea Woman in order to have the seals released. Her means of traveling, using a polar bear and a walrus in cooperation, implies her title of an *angakkoq puulik* (shaman with a bag), ranking on par with that of an *ilimmartartoq*, a flying shaman (Sonne 2005: ID 340, 1445, 1468, 2070). In other stories we encounter the stock character of an anonymous young girl of low social standing, orphaned or fatherless, who surprises everybody by traveling to Sea Woman, fighting her, and having the sea mammals released, etc. In these stories, all the (male) shamans present declare their incompetence due to their insufficient trainings (in traveling it seems). In contrast, the heroine, who has trained in secrecy and eventually performs in public for the first time, is met with Sea Woman's disdainful words: "The day before yesterday Utakkaaraq removed my dirt, but how on earth should you be able to do so? Such a baby like you! All the great shamans have tried to handle my oddities" (ID 349).[50] Thus the young maiden's age, not her sex, is emphasized. As in most stories about orphans, the contrasts are moving. The poor girl (and, in the above variant, her poor mother) get (temporarily) rich by the payment (in food) she receives from both the settlement and Sea Woman. The latter asks her to put a mark on a particular fine seal later to be rightfully claimed by her from the hunter who happens to catch it; the hunter shall never catch another seal

48. To fatherless Ineqinnavaat this was a welcome circumvention of the rule against mixing spirit and human societies. Deceased relatives commonly served as helping spirits, but usually their names were not inherited among their spirits. Ineqinnavaat did not know her father's name, and when she asked her mother she burst into tears and revealed his identity. Ineqinnavaat carved a relief of the spirit friends of her father at a much later point in life, after baptism.

49. For variants of "Tuttu's Wife," see Sonne (2005: ID 258, 1445, 1882, 2070), of which the first variant names the female part of the married couple Tuttutsiaq ("Lesser Tuttu"). In still another variant Tuttutsiaq is a poor boy without relatives who performs the same task as Tuttu's Wife (ID 1468).

50. Two years ago? The storyteller cannot be identified, nor the heroine, nor the point in history. The story starts out the mythic way: "Once, in the old days." In contrast, Utakkaaraq figures as a historical shaman in a variant listing previous successful travelers to Sea Woman. He performed several years earlier than Tuttu's Wife (Sonne 2005: ID 1882).

if he does not comply. Fame and transient riches, not a rich "prince" in marriage, are awarded this female stock character (*ibid.*). A variant about two orphans, a sister and her little brother, who visit Sea Woman together with success adds a subsequent episode about a shamans' contest between "Northerners" and "Southerners" at the latter's settlement.[51] This is the time for the little brother to show his powers, while the big sister is not involved. The great shaman from the north challenges the bashful young boy. The former knows both how to beat the drum (as a technique of ecstasy) and perform various tricks in public. The young boy hardly knows how to drum, but his powers come to the fore anyway, far exceeding those of the great shaman from the north, who is about to drown in an attempt at imitating the young man's power of gliding across the surface of the sea, a shaman's technique of traveling (ID 467, 1649).[52]

So, when it comes to tricks and competition in the stories, male shamans steal the scene. Furthermore, comparing both legends and stories about female shamans who succeed in traveling to Sea Woman, they appear in need of support and encouragement. In myth the orphan girl is either followed by her little brother or she travels on his behalf (he shall receive the prize offered, a much-needed paddle [ID 412], or his share of the priceless food offered [ID 420]). In one case a mother, who is also a shaman, supports her by dressing her in a new set of clothes for the journey (ID 349). But in still a third variant, the situation changes with a reversed relationship of the siblings, a big brother and his little sister. The girl remains at home and does not ask him to go. He is offered no price, only threats to his life, and he carries out the task without human accompaniment (ID 1468) as do male shamans generally when visiting Sea Woman (ID 29, 511, 807, 891, 1354, 1359, 1882). Among the historical female shamans, the legendary wife of Tuttu travels alone but is encouraged and ritually supported by her husband of lesser powers. The historical childless female shaman who was promised ten children by Sea Woman was married to two shamans, who may or may not have assisted her ritually (see pp. 137f). No information is had on the spouse of the other female shaman, who used to visit Sea Woman before she got married and lost her helping spirit (see above). Neither Kaakaaq nor Ineqinnavaat visited above or below as far as the sources go, whereas Teemiartissaq, depressed by her broken career, went to visit her drowned brother in a dream (ID 1108). Apparently against "the rules" she went in company with her two helping spirits, who ought to have left her for good at the disclosure of her apprenticeship. So, the ability to travel downwards, given to her by a voice she heard through her solitary initiation by a bleeding butterfly, remained fairly intact. The promise given by another voice, that she would soon acquire the power of flying through the air (*ibid.*), came to nothing. Indeed, no Greenlandic example of a flying *female* shaman was found.

Female Shamans and the Moon

Judging from legend, no live woman used to travel upwards on her own, flying or by other means, neither to Moon nor to the realm of the deceased above. Accidentally or not, the absence of information

51. It was not uncommon to find two young people training together. Ajijak apparently did so with his big sister (Sonne 2005: ID 1675), and Georg with his cousin, Nanngajaq. The two pupils were permitted to tell each other their experiences that otherwise were to be kept secret (ID 1179).

52. Three versions told in the north (Ilulissat and Uummannaq) have the young boy and his sister living in the north and the boy winning the contest with a shaman arriving from the south (Sonne 2005: ID 1005, 1649, 2024).

on that particular matter tallies with myth insofar as women visiting Moon are not shamans but maltreated wives who are fetched by Moon, made pregnant, and returned to their husbands (see above). Exceptions are mythic *ordinary* women, one involuntarily sent flying to human bears and walruses in a faraway country beyond the horizon, and the other the historical Kallaq, said to have flown by means of her amulet, a whip cord (ID 1134, 839, 879). Considering the differences in gender, there is a symbolic equivalence between the child fathered by Moon and the *qaamaneq* acquired by a male pupil on visits to Moon. This, however, does not prevent a female apprentice from achieving *qaamaneq*. Kaakaaq did so, as did Teemiartissaq, both long before marriage, that is (ID 1703, 1108). But neither went flying, and this ability is not said to have been achieved by initiation to *qaamaneq*. Also, a story told about the sister of the great shaman Ajijak reveals the connection between the light of female shamans and Moon to be particularly tricky. Ajijak and his big sister were training together, when the latter was asked to take care of an old lamp. By her neglect it caught fire, and her soul was taken by the angered Moon, who came down on a punishing expedition, but as we know (see p. 112) was fought back by the great shaman of that time, Uitsaleqanngitseq/Karraq (ID 1675). The structuring correspondence between the lamp (the female symbol par excellence), the "light," *qaamaneq*, and the moon, *qaammat*, is as close as you may wish for.

Several historical female shamans were obviously set back in their career by marriage and motherhood. The excuse made by Teemiartissaq's stepfather, a shaman himself, of disclosing her apprenticeship was that her little son was mortally ill. Indeed, this was a bad excuse in Teemiartissaq's view (ID 1108), but it was supported by her son's recovery, and consequently valid in public opinion. Ineqinnavaat lost her chance at becoming a great shaman due to sexual matters, in this case the jealousy of her husband, who came up with that silly, if workable, excuse of her five-year-old suckling child. And marriage alone made the helping spirit leave the anonymous female shaman who used to enjoy a great reputation. The other, married to two shamans, prompted Sea Woman to remedy her barrenness. We do not know such details about Tuttu's Wife. However, Kaakaaq was not so easily typecast. She lost her engagement in apprenticeship at marriage and childbirths (ID 1249) but got it back later. One story has it that she had been prepared for public initiation by a bird she had torn into parts, put back together, and reanimated with her breath (ID 1261). No report exists of her *saqqummerneq*, but she did practice in public, and the fame she won made her biographers stress her tomboy habits of preferring boys as playmates and wandering alone in the wilderness. At the same time, her female beauty is emphasized, a fact that is said to have spoiled her chance of becoming a great shaman, a shaman *puulik*. On the verge of becoming one, she was interrupted by her sister's husband, who suddenly turned up for a proposition, attracted by her solitude. She turned him down, of course, deeply annoyed (ID 1245). Thus, in public opinion, Kaakaaq's beauty deprived her of becoming a great shaman. At the same time, the emphasis on her masculine inclinations explains how she preserved her powers throughout married life, which was rich in as many as eight children. She was no traveler, though. Actually, the traveling powers of female shamans seem confined to visits to the realms below; that is, provided support was had from either a brother or a mother, in the case of an unmarried girl, or a husband, preferably a shaman. This will, in a short while, take us to Saladin d'Anglure's hypothesis of an Inuit "third sex."

To sum up, the majority of Greenlandic shamans were male, and with limited abilities. But some were great—i.e., able to travel by flying or gliding. They went on visits above and below. Female shamans went exclusively below, gliding or walking, according to the sources. Like ordinary women they have an ambiguous relation to Moon. The East Greenland Moon punished breaks of women's taboos at birth and death of a child, while he felt compassion with the ordinary woman maltreated by her husband. Moon then came down in person to fetch her, bring her to his home, make her pregnant, and bring her back to her husband. The son she bore, however, did not survive. In this line of thought, I suppose, marriage and/or childbirth meant obstacles to either becoming or remaining a great female shaman (almost the same conclusion reached by Haase 1987; see also Oosten 1989). In another line, there is a symbolic equivalence between a child fathered by Moon and the *qaamaneq* ("light") acquired by a male pupil on visits to Moon. This, however, did not prevent a female apprentice from achieving *qaamaneq*. In practice, I would add, the prerequisite of acquiring helping spirits, namely by roaming the wilderness alone in summer, was also a male inclination, greatly supported by their daily kayak travels along the coast. As a rule, girls went together to collect wood and berries or remained close to home. One actual female shaman, Kaakaaq, who was depicted as a tomboy and whose attractive beauty obstructed her chance of becoming "great," crosses or combines the categories. No Greenlandic statement has a female shaman use the drum at performances. The techniques left to most female shamans who became mothers and/or married were thus the art of *qilaneq*, or of performing lying on the platform beneath a skin cover (*qilaaqutserneq*), and/or of sorcery, all in the service of others. If accorded the degree of *-suaq*, great, that honorary title appears associated exclusively with travels to the lower abode. Unlike male shamans, she is supported in some way by another shaman close of kin, male or female. Public competition in shamanic tricks appears reserved to male shamans.

A Third Sex?

Bernard Saladin d'Anglure developed a hypothesis that Inuit shamans belong to a third, mixed gender (1986, 1994). Through structural analysis, Saladin d'Anglure reached the conclusion that male versus female is the basic binary opposition in Inuit culture of which all other oppositions (sea versus land, living versus deceased, This versus the Other World, etc.) are reflections. Since structural theory has it that mediation makes the worlds go round, and since shamans mediate between This and the Other World, they should, according to expectations, be androgynous in some way or other. Saladin d'Anglure points to four Inuit ways of mixing sex or gender: a change of sex at birth called *sipiniq* (W. Grl. *sipineq*); naming from a deceased person of the opposite sex; the acquisition of at least one helping spirit of the opposite sex; marriage between a male and a female shaman. Both *sipineq* and cross-sex naming can cause a child to be reared and dressed in the work and clothing of the opposite sex, but at puberty (first menstruation for women and first catch for men), biology takes over in that marriage brings together a man and a woman by sex, not (social) gender. Reproduction comes first, and the division of labor second, in that women reared as boys may continue to go hunting and the female men rarely become great hunters.

Several scholars have opposed this thesis. Trott has argued that differential upbringing leads to ambiguities in the context of kinship references, "and that the significance of this lies in the fact that it creates a structurally ordered set of on-going relations between people and their land rather than creating an intermediary gender" (Trott 2006). Oosten, who used to consider virility to be at the center of Inuit cosmology, was convinced by Saladin d'Anglure's assertion of the shaman's ability to cross both sexual and other marked borders, but he doubts the real existence of a third gender among the Iglulingmiut. Furthermore, he sticks to his former thesis of central virility by applying Dumont's encompassment theory, which asserts: "In a pair of contrasting terms one of the terms encompasses the other at higher level" (Oosten 1989: 334). By contrasting shamanic abilities with female fertility, as proposed by Haase (1987), male hunting abilities come out the winner, Oosten argues; he first points to the shaman's "male" jobs of fighting and killing off obstinate and evil spirits, and next to the fact that women who hunt use men's weapons (Oosten 1989). Finally, Fienup-Riordan has opposed the thesis that male versus female is the base of Yup'ik cosmology. By following the Yup'ik point of view through their entire complex of rituals, she argues that the opposition of humans versus non-humans (animals in particular) is the basic position (Fienup-Riordan 1994: 48–49). Their world is animalized, not gendered, she insists, whereas Bodenhorn, when analyzing the Iñupiat ideas and practices of North Alaska, finds both oppositions at work: "Her [Fineup-Riordan's] general thesis is valid for the North Slope as well, although, as this paper will argue, gender continues in the latter case, to be an important vehicle for marking not only relations between women and men, but also between humans and animals" (Bodenhorn 1990). The relevant Greenland sources do not permit a comparatively thorough analysis. But they at least reflect situations prior to the time when the Christian ban on polygamy and women's particular severe taboos came in force.

In the following treatment, a possible third sex of Greenlandic shamans comes first, then *sipineq* (a change in sex at birth), and cross-gendered upbringing. These subjects lead on to *piaaqqusiat*, or children dressed in odd clothing; next, in a further attempt to understand the positions of female shamans, I discuss the issue of male dominance as proposed by Saladin d'Anglure and Oosten. However, I shall exclude further discussion of an animalized versus a gendered worldview because, as evidenced above, the gender issue takes absolute priority in *taartaq*. This emphasis, of course, does not render invalid Fienup-Riordan's findings regarding the Yupiit.

Shamans and the "Third Sex"

The Greenlandic sources on shamans offer few opportunities for testing Saladin d'Anglure's four criteria. No shaman biography, be it legendary or historical, mentions either *sipineq* or cross-gendered upbringing. Both were Greenlandic phenomena on par with the Canadian Inuit ones, as was the way of naming (e.g., Robbe 1994: 350). An Inuit baby was given several names from deceased persons, usually relatives. Since Greenlandic personal names were gender-neutral except in Avanersuaq (Gilberg pers. comm.), the gender of the deceased namesakes is not stated for the names of the East Greenlandic shamans listed by Robert-Lamblin (1997). Worth mentioning is the way Kaakaaq identified herself in encounters with spirits: "I am called Aseriit" is her answer to (some of) her first helping spirits-to-be, who present themselves by names as well (Sonne 2005: ID 1240). From whom Kaakaaq got that name, a deceased man or woman, or a male or female shaman, is not disclosed. Similarly Georg had a name of unknown descent, Qipinngi, applied by his uncle during his (secret) apprenticeship (ID 1141). So however fascinating in context the bearings of these spirit-related names during apprenticeship are, they come to a dead end. Only the marriage issue offers some food for thought. Kaakaaq was twice married to a shaman (both of lesser reputation than her, it seems), Tuttu's Wife similarly to her less competent Tuttu, and the childless female shaman encountered by Poul Egede to two shamans, both apparently inferior. Neither Teemiartissaq nor Ineqinnavaat were married to shamans, and as for the female shaman who lost her helping spirit at marriage, we do not know. Among the male shamans of great renown, only Naaja and Akku are credited a wife with the powers of a *qilaamasoq* (a practicing *qilalik*) (ID 1200, see above). Of greater interest is the tomboy character accentuated in the case of Kaakaaq, as well as the frequent occurrence in myth of another cross-gendered relationship, namely that of an elder sister and a younger brother, both unmarried at the point in time of the story's concern. As already stated, the presence or support of some relative (a little brother or a shaman mother) turns out to be a successful constellation when we take a closer look, as in the following myth of ritually getting food from below: a widow and her only child, a daughter (or adoptive daughter, or granddaughter), are left behind by their fellow men. The widow digs a hole inside the house. It is filled with emerging water and every day a still-bigger animal appears for the girl to kill and for both to eat (ID 76, 1458, 1747, 1871). So in stories about female shamans procuring food, her need of support and/or encouragement, preferably by another shaman, is a recurrent issue.

Sipineq

The "splitting" of a newborn boy into a girl, *sipineq*, was an Eastern Inuit phenomenon, pointed out by Dufour (1975), and further discussed and belabored by Saladin d'Anglure since 1977 (see also 1986; 1994; Oosten & Laugrand 1999: 37). Pierre Robbe (1981) took up this belief as a matter of some concern also among the East Greenlanders. Four women told Robbe about their *sipineq* at birth—i.e., their transformations from boy into girl. Common knowledge had it that every human fetus has a penis. On its way out, the baby boy would take a firm hold of his penis in case he chose to be born as a boy, but leave it be if he preferred the life of a girl. In the latter case the penis would transform into a vulva at birth and probably split, as is the etymological meaning of *sipineq* (Robbe 1981: 74). These ideas align, as called to attention by Saladin d'Anglure (1986: 48ff), with the Canadian Inuit myth about the first human beings, two men living as man and wife. When the latter became pregnant, the husband uttered a saying that made the "wife" split and allow the child to be born (Saladin d'Anglure 1986). A transformation the opposite way, from girl to boy, was an additional notion held by the Iglulingmiut (Saladin d'Anglure 1986: 58; cf. Dufour 1975: 67) but not by the Canadian Inuit among whom Briggs (1974b) and Trott (2006: 95) did their fieldwork, and is not on record from Greenland. Furthermore, all Greenlandic *sipineq* cases were given other causes for the split rather than the baby's choice, such as a mother's fall during pregnancy or some break of taboo by either mother or midwife (Robbe 1981: 74; P. Egede 1971: 82; 1939: 58–59; N. Egede 1971: 70; 1939: 169–70; Holm 1972: 133; 1914: 99). The problem was a general one, according to a question Poul Egede was asked by a woman: "how come [she asks] that [some] boys at birth become girls? I responded that in my view... No, she said, last summer I had this girl, who came out a boy but split and became a girl, no doubt the air (Sila) was angry at some offence of mine. However much I tried to refute her argument, she insisted by saying: It was a boy, but it split" (P. Egede 1971: 82; 1939: 58–59). Thus, the Greenlandic cases all *point to a preference for boys* as do those of cross-gendered upbringing, below.

Cross-Gendered Upbringing

The rearing of boys as girls and vice versa is rarely mentioned in Greenlandic oral tradition. One instance, a probable historical one, was told to Sandgreen by Apulu/Kukkujooq. Apulu had his youngest child, a girl, initiated by magic songs into becoming a hunter. He built her a beautiful kayak in order to increase not only the family's standard of living but particularly their defense against enemies (Sonne 2005: ID 1279). Actual life might bring forth a great number of instances. Keld Hansen offers several examples of girls raised as boys (1986), and long ago Cranz happened to meet a strong man on the island of Kangeq who did no hunting but was very skilled in women's work. His mother, having lost first her husband and then a son out at sea, had forbidden him to practice kayaking (Cranz 1765–70, I: 215). The reason why the eldest son of a family in the settlement of my short fieldwork was not taught hunting and left a "female" of low standing was not revealed. Thalbitzer does not comment on a man who did women's work and preferred the company of women (2014: 111). More recently, Robert-Lamblin carried out a survey in Tasiilaq/Ammassalik during the 1970s (1981; 1986); she mentions *sipineq* in reference to the Iglulingmiut but not among the causes for cross-gendered upbringing in East Greenland. Parents repeatedly gave as their answer the unfulfilled desire to have a child of the opposite sex. Robert-Lamblin heard about twenty-seven cases of girls reared as boys in a total population of 2,300, and only seven boys reared as girls, which suggests a familial preference for boys. Together the number makes 1.3% of the population, hardly comparable to the ca. 20% for Canada (Saladin d'Anglure 1986). But, as Robert-Lamblin emphasizes, the number may have been higher in Ammassalik, because nobody considered such cross-gendered upbringing remarkable (1986: 42–43). A deeper motivation, she speculates, would be the loss of a child, especially a single girl among brothers or the other way round, whose name and gender was then given to the newborn child. But, Robert-Lamblin concludes, utility appears to have been the ultimate cause, because cross-gendered upbringing was more often than not practiced in families with a strong imbalance in the numbers of sons and daughters. A strong predominance of daughters created difficulties for the father, who needed helpers in the hunt, and in a family of mostly sons the mother would be hard up for nurses permitting her to do her time-consuming job of preparing the skins and sewing the clothing for all members of her family. Her work was as important as his, although ultimately dependent on the success of his hunt. Explicitly the Greenlandic sources do not state that the hunter was as conscious about being dependent on the behavior of his wife for this success in ways that made Barbara Bodenhorn's Iñupiaq informant state, "I am not a great hunter, my wife is" (1990). Nevertheless, the Greenlandic hunter was as dependent, of course, on the good quality of his clothing and the burden of prescriptions on his wife to be observed in relation to the animals. The equal value put on either sex in the division of labor may be seen also in cross-gendered upbringing, in that the gender of the eldest child, be that a daughter or a son, rarely was "*changed*" or "*sacrificed*," respectively (Robert-Lamblin 1981: 120; my emphasis, and please mind the difference in values!). As a rule, not the first but either the second, third, or fourth child was reared cross-gendered, especially when the older siblings were of the same biological sex (Robert-Lamblin 1981; 1986: 42–43).

The above conclusion, however sensible, is much too functional for Saladin d'Anglure's structural leanings. He relates the numerous cases of Inuit practices that constitute his "third sex"—*sipineq*, cross-gendered naming, and upbringing—to the Inuit ideal of a nuclear family with at least one son and one daughter. "Third sex" practices help Inuit realize this ideal, Saladin d'Anglure contends. He further compares this ideal with the basic prerequisite of a society to form and continue through exchanges of women, "*l'atome de parenté*" as defined by Lévi-Strauss (Saladin d'Anglure 1985; 1986:

64f; 1990a; 2007).[53] Saladin d'Anglure argues against the claim for utility, positing that because these children turn to the activities of their biological sex at puberty the cross-gendered upbringing is of limited value. In traditional Inuit society, mechanisms such as adoption or polygyny could make up for the lack of balance. Robert-Lamblin seemingly takes up the challenge when she underlines the difficulties met as adults by boys reared as girls, due to their insufficient education in hunting. In postcolonial times they take low-ranking jobs in the service sector, and some commit suicide. The comparatively less numerous girls reared as boys do much better (Robert-Lamblin 1986: 43).

Loose ends remain in this discussion, I would add, namely the effects of colonial trade and mission on the division of labor and social security. Colonial trade offered women a great relief in their sewing duties by introducing woolen sweaters and fabrics for clothing and, later, for boat covers (Bujis 2004). The mission brought relief by its ban on the manifold taboos and, not least, the feuds. In my view, a preference for sons shines through many of the Greenlandic examples of "third sex" practices. This is particularly true of the *sipineq* data of Robbe, Poul Egede, and Niels Egede. They all concern boys split into girls understood as bad luck owing to failures on part of mother or midwife. Below I shall elaborate on the proposed preference for boys, and right now turn to a Greenlandic peculiarity: *piaqqusiat* (sing. *piaqqusiaq*). They were children reared in odd clothing, which did *not* signify cross-gendered birth or naming.

Piaaqqusiat, Children Raised in Odd Clothing

A child whose older sibling had died was sometimes dressed in odd clothing. This child was considered to be an *angerlartoq*, a person "returned home" from an untimely death, and the newborn baby was named for the deceased sibling. As told by a *piaaqqusiaq* to Hans Lynge: "My mother's child, who died, rose again in me because I had come home [and had been named for her/him]. They said to me: 'You live against the rules/in a backward way [*killoq*],' meaning that all sorts of evil were to go wrong [*killoq*]" (H. Lynge 1955: 155–56). "To cheat death: was another saying about the ways of odd clothing" (C. Rosing 1946: 101–2). *Piaaqqusiat* were not raised cross-gendered, nor was their clothing like those of either a boy or a girl,[54,55] nor was there any dress code apart from an awkward look. Patterns differed in arbitrary ways. Seams were avoided in making the simplest clothing. It consisted of nothing but a piece of skin without cutting, except for a hole cut out for the head. The missing hood was no loss, in that *piaaqqusiat*, contrary to persons under prescriptions, were to go bareheaded outdoors

53. Can the common cherished wish of a married couple in Denmark, and probably most of the modern West, to have "one of each kind" (a son and a daughter) also be explained by the structural necessity of *l'atome familial*? The disappointed couple may go on trying until they accept their lot, usually after the birth of the third child of the same sex. In today's Denmark children are not a necessary labor force and a "third sex" upbringing is rarely resorted to. The tomboy girl and the soft boy are usually permitted to develop the way biology made them. I have chosen to exclude from my discussion the relatively recent, at present highly debated, issue of transsexual children, who in modern countries are addressed with growing sympathy and tolerance and offered legal gender reassignment surgery.

54. The proveniences of the *piaaqqusiaq* sources are East, South, and Northwest Greenland. None are on record from Avanersuaq.

55. In vehemence at observing girls dressed and raised as boys, Christian Rosing got them mixed up with the *piaaqqusiat* (1946: 101–2). His error was corrected by Robert-Lamblin (1981: 122) by referring to Thalbitzer (1941: 601–4), and her own data plus those received by Victor (Victor & Robert-Lamblin 1989–93, II: 322). See also Rasmussen (1921–25, I: 39; 1938: 189, 191; 1979: No. 49, 293, 316, 343, 386, 399, 404, 461, 469); F. Lynge (1981: No. 37, 78, 344); Dalager (1915: 62–63).

but to sleep in their anoraks. The anorak might be split open vertically in either front or back and provided with buttons or laces. The boots could have square toes and heels instead of rounded ones, or be made of differing skins, or the skin of one sleeve might have the wrong side out. The most impressive example is a thorough composition of contrarieties, in that the haired skin used for the anorak was turned at 90 degrees, and the trousers made up of two halves, of which the pelt of the right leg was turned opposite to that of the left leg. In addition, individual pre- and proscriptions of eating, etc., were associated with skins and patterns (Rasmussen 1921–25, I: 37; 1938: 189, 191; 1979: No. 49, 293, 316, 404, 461; F. Lynge 1981: No. 37, 344). Besides being ridiculous and thus cheating death, *killoq*, or "wrong, contrary, backwards," was in East Greenland also used to refer to the left side or hand (Fortescue et al. 1994: 170; 2010: 186) and turns out to have gender-transcending potentials. Thus in the case that the *male* northern storm blows persistently, a half-naked woman doing sexual movements outdoors will make it stop. Similarly a half-naked man can calm down the *female* southwestern storm. A *piaaqqusiaq*, however, can make *either* storm subside, not—being a child—by imitating sexual movements but by letting the wind inflate the urinary bladder of a seal or some other bag, and bringing the tightly closed bag indoors (F. Lynge 1981: No. 73, 74, 78). If the trick does not work, the child is asked to make use of its backward powers by first striking at the storm with the left clenched fist and second by putting its naked bottom up against the storm—i.e., showing the anus, the "door" between the Worlds, the outside and the invisible, interior one (No. 78). To wit, *killoq* does the trick of transcending the boundary between the genders of the winds, not the idea of a "third sex."

The *piaaqqusiaq* custom is linked with shamanism only once, in reference to a married couple who decided on the future career of a shaman for their newborn son (Dalager 1915: 62–63). Dressing a child in odd clothing can thus be added to the long series of means for an artificial start.[56] Indeed, the mere fact of being an *angerlartoqut* (named after a deceased brother or sister) could point to inborn powers of becoming a shaman, as in the case of Ajijak, born about 1800 in East Greenland (Robert-Lamblin 1997: 275; Sonne 2005: ID 1311). The logic of this idea, I assume, is the death and rebirth recently experienced by the returned child on par with the solitary initiation via death and revival of the pupil. Turning to the sex of the child made into a *piaaqqusiaq*, this can rarely be decided on, due to the gender neutrality of names and because most bits of information on this issue are generalizations. Yet judging from the translations into Danish by Greenlanders and Danes alike, the majority were boys. If this is the case, the *piaaqqusiaq* custom, like distribution in sex rates of cross-gendered upbringing, suggests a preference of boys over girls.

Preferring Boys to Girls

As we know, in Robert-Lamblin's survey the ratio of girls to boys reared cross-gendered was 27 to 7, and judging from the statement that the boys were "sacrificed" when reared as girls their small number may be close to correct. Also, the fact that the splitting of a boy into a girl was considered the effect of a mishap or punishment for some transgression adds to the conviction that sons were generally preferred to daughters in traditional Greenland. They were preferred not only as future providers, as discussed by Robert-Lamblin and Saladin d'Anglure, but also—before Christian mission put

56. Thalbitzer, who refers this case to Cranz (1765–70, III: 269), who obviously has used Dalager, speculates the same way as Saladin d'Anglure in further references to Alaska, Siberia, and the Aleuts (Thalbitzer 1941: 603).

an effective ban on feuding—as future allies in feuds, as was the explicit cause mentioned by Apulu above and supported by other sources (R. Petersen 1993; 1996). By virilocality, a rule with notified exceptions, a family of many brothers, *anguterpaat*, constituted a strong body in reality as in legend and myth. In actual life, a family rich in viable children, sons and daughters, would automatically give rise to envy according to Apulu (Sonne 2005: ID 1271). And in oral lore, a family of *anguterpaat* was a common obstacle to be overcome by the hero. Quite often such a body of brothers have only one sister whom they do not want to let go in marriage. Consequently she is married to a nobody who agrees to move to their place. Being the story's hero he turns out to be a traitor, a supposed fiend, or a covert superior (e.g., ID 77).

Piinngitsoq, "a good for nothing," was a common name for a newborn girl (Schultz-Lorentzen 1967: 232).[57] In support of the apparent preference for boys, the following quotations are of relevance: "As soon as his wife is enceinte her husband already regards her as the mother of the future hunter, and she is therefore treated with greater consideration... When a birth is impending, all the men and big children go out of the house, if the weather permits of it. Those who remain in the house put on their old garments, 'in order that the child may be a boy'" (Holm 1914: 61–62; 1972: 106); "the colony manager asked me why people cried in the house where a woman had just given birth. I knew no answer and asked Angusinaq, who replied that it was out of contempt because the baby was a girl" (P. Egede 1971: 149; 1939: 100). Dalager's writings illustrate the same preference: "in case a married woman is fortunate to give birth to one baby-boy after another, she braids some hairs presented as a horn of her forehead, also blamed by the missionaries, although it is nothing but a sign of rejoicing" (Dalager 1915: 59).[58] And for good reason! Her marriage was stabilized, her prospect of being provided for when aging was brighter, and her standing in society at large was higher. Divorce was a constant threat as long as she, generally about sixteen years old at marriage, remained barren, but by having children, especially sons, the threat usually evaporated, because the children belonged to her and in divorce she took them along (Dalager 1915: 6, 25–26; Holm 1972: 110; 1914: 65; Glahn 1771: 239; Sonne 2005: ID 1253). The preference for boys also showed up in cases of adopting orphaned children (Dalager 1915: 25) as did a widow's increased chances of a favorable remarriage by giving birth to a son. When asked why they continued bearing children, the widows told Dalager that the pleasure of having them was irresistible (49–50). The preference for sons might even overrun the strict ranking of age within the family, permitting the little brother to boss his elder sister (Holm 1972: 105; 1914: 59).[59] Such "spoiled" boys brought up as future hunters suffered when hunting gave way to wage labor and unemployment (Arnfred 1991; McElroy 1975). So however much spouses were mutually dependent on the work of one another, a provider, *nakkivik* (supporter) or *angutitartoq* (hunter for somebody; *angut* = man) or *piniartitoq* (hunter for somebody), was, with few exceptions, a man. Furthermore, due to a high death rate of able-bodied men lost at sea, a surplus of women had to be content with a position of either a second wife subordinated to the first wife, or

57. *Piúngitsoq* in the 1860 orthography.

58. Perhaps not a horn but the beak of a bird (a raven) is my qualified guess.

59. Exposure of girl babies is rarely mentioned in the Greenlandic sources. On record is predominantly the exposure of a baby (of either sex) whose mother died in childbed. The diet offered no substitute for breast milk (e.g., P. Egede 1939: 46; 1971: 61; Sonne 2005: ID 1265).

that of a mere *kiffaq*, a "handmaid" in the household of, preferably, some relatives (Dalager 1915: 8, 22–25).[60] In Dalager's words, the men could pick and choose (*ibid.*). No wonder that boys were at a premium.

Preferring Children

However much Greenlanders would prefer their first children to be sons, the beings of the Other World did not care. On par with a young man's first catch, *pernarneq*, a woman's bearing of her first child was also a *pernarneq* in the spirit language (Victor & Robert-Lamblin 1989–93, II: 256). It signified her passage into adulthood, both socially and, of greater import, in relation to game. As worded by Thalbitzer concerning the East Greenlanders: "The wife's independence is strengthened by her bearing children. As long as she has no children she dares not cut up and distribute the meat of the man's catch." In consequence only mothers among her in-laws, married or not, were to do the cutting up (Thalbitzer 1941: 650, 648; Robbe 1994: 341). Also the husband, I presume, gained independence to go visiting with his wife or set up a neolocal residence. In a patrilocal residence, authority was given to a young wife's mother-in-law regarding matters of handling the catch and seeing to its distribution according to set obligations. The daughter-in-law, childless or not, was still subordinate in her decisions. As long as she managed, mother-in-law did the cutting up, probably assisted by daughter-in-law. The former saw to the distribution, and disposed of the skin. I say "probably," because Robbe appears not too clear on that point. In a marriage of two wives, Kunnak explained to Thalbitzer, the second would assist the first in cutting up but not in distributing the meat (Thalbitzer 1941: 650). Other rules of further sharing that were in force for the division of big game killed by more than one hunter gave priority to kin relations among members of the bilateral family. But again, this piece of meat was cut up and the parts distributed by either the hunter's mother or his first wife (if a mother), or some close relative who was a mother (Thalbitzer 1941: 643–47; Robbe 1994: 336, 348–49, 354). Furthermore, the same woman was responsible for handing out a piece of meat with some blubber, however small, to every resident in the village from a big animal caught by her husband alone. Neglect would scare away the animals from that hunter (Robbe 1994: 356). In East Greenland small seals belonged to the household alone and sharing followed the naming. Right until his or her becoming a parent a child would receive the same piece of every small (ringed) seal (*natseq*) that the deceased namesake used to be given (Thalbitzer 1941: 643–48; Robbe 1994: 335ff). The mother decided which (gender-neutral) name among several given to the child came in force and, coupled with other considerations as well, she could manipulate the rules "in elegant ways" (Robbe 1994: 350). But it was cause for great concern if the presiding mother (i.e., the mother-in-law) was overworked and let her son hand over (some of) his seals to be cut up and distributed by his wife, and she showed too much generosity towards her own children (341–42). Negotiable or not, the rules of family shares were not to be overlooked once decided upon. Which takes us directly to Dalager, who wondered why most young married men did not oppose the insufficient pieces of meat apportioned to his wife and children by his mother. Some did oppose, but they were few, and

60. Phonological equivalent to *kevgaq*, "messenger," of the Alaska messenger feasts. In Greenland it refers to a low-ranking servant belonging to a household and, in colonial times, also Greenlanders (usually of mixed blood) working at the trade.

on which premises they had the nerve and succeeded was unknown to the indignant Dalager, who asked no further questions (1915: 23–24). Perhaps obligations of sharing played its part as much in Southwest as in East Greenland.[61] In other words, sharing was as crucial in relation to game and deceased relatives in East Greenland as among the other Inuit. Just like the animals, both shunned being cut up by a childless woman and treated as an object of greed, the deceased relative felt hurt in case his/her living namesake did not receive its share: "if he is badly dressed or goes hungry, the specter of the deceased namesake shall show up disturbing the dreams of the parents. In order to restore peace the latter are obliged to immediately [*pingitsoornani*] relieve the namesake of the deceased" (Robbe 1994: 356).[62] So, neglect of sharing obligations settled by naming and kinship ties was offensive to game and deceased relatives alike, and caused worry indeed on part of the superior woman of the household (*ningiu*). My proposal that similar rules caused the ignorant Dalager's indignation is pure guesswork, because few rules of sharing are available from early colonial West Greenland.

Male Dominance?

Among the reasons why far more men than women practiced shamanism, male dominance might be one. Its presence in cosmology is emphasized by both Saladin d'Anglure (1978) and Oosten (1989). Taken at face value, the Greenlandic sources on social life in early colonial Greenland leave no one in doubt about the fact of an ideal male dominance. To treat these sources in depth, however, is difficult for at least two reasons. One is the pattern of matrimony and sexual liaisons (polygamy, wife exchange, ritual wife exchange) that differ from the subsequent one governed by Christian morals. Consequently, comparisons become oblique with the solid analyses made regarding Canada (Briggs 1974b) and Alaska (Bodenhorn 1990; Fienup-Riordan 1994) all *in the Christian era*. The other well-known problem is the biases of most authors on early colonial Greenland. These Christian Danish/Norwegian men of the 18th century rarely took up residence in a Greenlandic household for any length of time, and the majority of their individual examples concern married life of polygamous families. I shall return to them below.

A hunter who was knowledgeable in a particular field of hunting was called for and led the hunting group as long the hunt lasted. This temporary leader was the only accepted type of leadership beyond the household (Nooter 1976; 1978; R. Petersen 1993). Within the household of early colonial Greenland the eldest able-minded man, *ittoq*, was in charge of domestic peace and making decisions about hunting and movement (P. Egede 1971: 136; 1939: 91–92; Holm 1972: 91, 105; 1914: 57, 59; Robbe 1994: 324), whereas the leader of the longhouse of several households was the hunter ranking highest due to his own and/or his sons' hunting abilities (Cranz 1765–70, I: 233; Holm & Petersen 1921: 612, 614; J. Rosing 1963: 125; 1970: 53). He did not interfere with the other men's dispositions in hunting affairs. Nor was his position dependent on being a shaman (Holm 1972: 91; 1914: 57–58; Sandgreen pers. comm.; Thalbitzer 1930: 75) as some generalizations will have it (as for instance

61. A recycling of names and matching "pieces" over two generations was the effect as Robbe underlines with reference also to Fienup-Riordan (Robbe 1983), who reached a similar conclusion about naming among the Nelson Islanders.

62. "*S'il a de mauvais vêtements ou s'il a faim, le spectre du défunt va apparaître, menaçant dans les rêves des apparentés. Pour retrouver la paix ces derniers devront obligatoirement* [*pingitsoornani*] *et le plus vite possible soulager l'homonyme vivant du défunt.*"

Kaarali in O. Rosing 1957–61, I: 75; J. Rosing 1963: 179; and H. Rink in particular).[63] In religious matters, the eldest couple of the longhouse was in charge of reintegrating mourning parents into both the natural and social environments (see above), whereas shamans predominantly took care of crises, whether asked to do so or by their own initiative. Also, the entertainment value of their séances was high. Yet, like ordinary men and women, they were cautious about interfering in social matters beyond their own narrow interests. In support of the overwhelming authority accorded *the* shaman by Rink in retrospect (e.g., 1866–71, II; 1975), you will have to pick one among the 20% of the adult population who were shamans. Public accusations outside the song duels were rare, as were the matrimonial conflicts, which were nobody's business except the involved spouses.

An important generalization offered by Dalager contradicts the unlimited authority enjoyed by men in relation to women. He illustrates the unparalleled authority enjoyed by a widow with adult sons. As a true *ningiu* (female elder of the household) subordinated to no *ittoq* (male authority) in any disposition (Dalager 1915: 23–24), she made decisions about not only all domestic matters but also, I assume, of the storages, of movements in the annual cycle, and in the entertainment of guests—all of which used to be rights of the *ittoq*. Data collected by Steenhoven among Canadian Inuit are consistent with this summary (1962: 55–56), as are responses in the mid-19th century to a questionnaire about which relations of authority people would like to have reintroduced as a remedy for those disturbed by colonization. A male leader of a household of an extended family (*ittoq*) is the preferred one, but in case no married man or widower is reckoned with, a widow with children will do. Like a male head, she will be entitled to decide on the admission of new members into the household; the relatives are to respect their head, be it a man or a woman (Rink 1881: 6).

A frequent remark in the early Danish sources, "Generally the men treat their wives gently," points to the Danes' unilateral focus, namely wife battering. Niels Egede takes the opposite stand and mentions how the wives' sharp tongues made up for the violence sometimes resorted to by the men. He is echoed by Rasmussen and Freuchen on both pre-Christian Canada and Avanersuaq (cf. Briggs 1974b: 190). Wife beating did occur, but the degree to which men beat their wives cannot be ascertained, because the generalized evaluations offered by the authors differ. Some consider it low (Dalager 1915: 6, 48–49; Glahn 1771: 244; Thalbitzer 1941: 650, apart from a few bad-tempered men), others high (H. Egede 1971, 2: 80; 1925: 374; 1818: 145; Poul Egede 1971: 77; 1939: 56; Holm 1972: 111; 1914: 68; Rüttel 1917: 43).

In a lampoon collected by Thalbitzer in 1905, the singer refuses the accusation made by his opponent of having maltreated his own wife. That is not true, he insists. He has hit her only for good reasons (Thalbitzer 1923: 319). Besides, another man justifies himself, the beating does the woman no harm (Rüttel 1917: 43). And which were the good reasons? Gluttony, particularly in times of

63. The common assumption, first awarded by Rink, that the Greenlandic shaman used to be the authority in society is hard to put down. But considering the great number of shamans, some 20% of the adult population, who among them had authority over which social unit, and in which situations? Without any question or analysis, Rink is taken at face value by Jakobsen (1999: 124–26) and Jørgensen et al. (2012). My attempt at an analysis pointing to witch finding as the only domain of the shaman's authority (Sonne 1982a) has apparently had no effect except on Hazel, who bluntly refuses it. Nonetheless, Thalbitzer (1930: 75) denies shamans as just shamans the position of leaders of the longhouse. Oosten reaches the same conclusion with regard to Canadian Inuit (1989: 331–41), as do Oosten et al. (1999: 128) and Saladin d'Anglure (2001: 73). Collective crisis used to call for the advice or performance of a shaman, as in Canada as ceremonial leaders of some annual collective rituals.

want; child neglect; childlessness; neglect of domestic work; and adultery behind the husband's back are all mentioned.

As mentioned above, early Greenlandic examples on record of conflicts between spouses concern polygamous marriages that jeopardized the husband's authority. They were worth reporting to Danish authorities as good causes for continuing financial support, striking as they were to contemporary Danish morals. Consequently their prevalence in the journals may be lopsided. Be this as it may, although the examples do not fit statistic demands, they reveal both pros and cons. Holm, for instance, mentions a fight between the two wives of a man who was violently thrashed by his meddling (1972: 111; 1914: 68). Another polygamous man, who had given a black eye to his first wife because she objected to him taking a secondary wife, was told by Poul Egede how a married Dane would be beaten out of the house by his wife in case of polygamy or adultery. Annoyed, this husband exclaimed, "The women in your country must be foolish wanting their men for themselves and making themselves the mistresses of their men. We reproach jealous women. They are despicable and bad. When I [P. Egede] had talked back and blamed them for their ways, and the women began to prick up their ears, he said: You spoil our women with your words. Then, when I left the house his wife came out offering me a piece of the [delicious] skin of beluga" (P. Egede 1971: 77–78; 1939: 56, tr. BS). Certainly, the monogamy preached by the missionaries attacked the pattern of authority as exemplified also by Niels Egede: "to a man... having three wives... I ended my talk by claiming that only one wife was legal, which made his first, right [legal] wife quite pleased saying that, indeed, I suffer a lot because of those two, to which the husband remarked, so that's the husband you would like, and he told me not to talk like that in front of her, evidently making her haughty" (N. Egede 1971: 26; 1939: 143, tr. BS).[64] Similarly sarcastic is another response to Niels Egede's teachings: "my goodness, how pleasing to our wives to hear that a man cannot chuck his wife out despite her naughtiness. In that case they can grumble as long as they like" (1971: 30; 1939: 145, tr. BS). Niels Egede gets an even clearer look into the difficulties haunting a polygamous man:

> [I]n the evening two sledges arrived... one [driver] had some days ago lost his secondary wife and thought out that she might have come to our place. The reason for her flight was the order given her by his first wife to dress some skins, but she did not want to and stormed and raged, for which reason he had given her black eyes... [When] I told him that having more than one wife never works, he said: You have corrupted them with your readings [written sermons read loud], and now they are jealous, and because she has left I do not want her back. [When] I asked him not to, nor to take any other [secondary wife], because it would lead to nothing good, he said: right so, but I fear that the one [the first wife] shall remain my mistress, although I beat her. (1971: 39; 1939: 150, tr. BS)

In sum, jealousy and the rights of the first wife to decide in domestic matters appear to have been the most frequent reasons for quarreling in polygamous households that the intermingling of the missionaries brought to the surface.

64. Competence in Danish literacy was no virtue of Niels Egede.

Poul Egede could come to think of only one henpecked man (1971: 136; 1939: 91–92), but he was in fact also visited by another, who wore clothes torn to shreds. The poor fellow had objected to his wife's adultery, but she simply moved to her lover, who then offered the husband that they could share. The latter accepted by showing up, but was immediately assaulted by the enraged wife and then gave up all further attempts (P. Egede 1979: 158–9; 1939: 105).

The last example is a grotesque story about a mother-in-law who, due to her superiority in hunting, feels entitled to rob and marry her daughter-in-law. Her son is a poor hunter in comparison, she sings while flying around supported by the steam of the boiling meat in the pot, and thereupon she orders her daughter-in-law to have sex with her. Her penis is the end of a kayak, a well-known Inuit symbol of exactly that. In the end she and sometimes also her daughter-in-law are killed by the rejected hunter (Sonne 2005: ID 228, 324, 436, 442, 581, 591, 1584). Obviously, this story sides with the man, whose sexual rights go with hunting. Women are free to hunt, but in sexual matters they better remain women.

The symbolic identification of male sex with male hunting, which is clearly documented for the Canadian Inuit (Saladin d'Anglure 1984: 496; Blaisel & Oosten; Therrien 1987), was also prominent among the Greenlanders as shown in chapter 2 in treating the public recognition of young man's (symbolic?) debut at his the first catch, *pernarneq*, and in discussing his ritual wife robbery when acknowledged as an able provider.

Women and Men at the Margin of Society: Accusations of Sorcery

In Greenland possessing knowledge of sorcery was valued on par with other useful knowledge, as will be dealt with below. Being a secret art of harmful effects, however, the appreciation was ambiguous, and the number of accusations appears to have increased with colonization and been nourished by Western ideas of the 1700s. Thus, a Greenlandic conviction still met with today about sorcerers (*ilisiitsut*)—that they used to be women exclusively—made Hans Lynge (1906–1988), who was educated as a catechist, feel inclined to add the following comment on a male sorcerer north of Upernavik: "The common conviction that only a woman could be an *ilisiitsoq* is consequently not correct" (H. Lynge 1955: 98; 1967: 64). Lynge may have been taught the incorrect assumption at the Teachers' College, since another catechist and missionary to Ammassalik, Christian Rosing, felt like correcting the same conviction (C. Rosing 1946: 50).[65] On the other hand, among the early instances on record, the majority of accused sorcerers were women, of whom six were killed, two were lynched, and one was saved by the missionary from being lynched.[66] Widows without support were the majority of potential scapegoats. But again, similar accusations against unreliable or destitute men did occur.[67] Also shamans, among whom one was lynched and two killed, formed part of the risk group. Taught means for doing both good and harm, shamans of either sex, especially upon growing old

65. Most college teachers were Danes, whose ideas about sorcerers shine through the problem of translation met with by the Greenlandic author Mâliâraq Vebæk when writing in Danish some twenty-odd years ago: "The term *ilisiitsut* (sing. *ilisiitsoq*) is difficult to translate into Danish, because *ilisiitsut* could be men as well. The majority were, however, women, and in this connection the term can be translated into 'hekse' (witches)" (Vebæk 1990: 39, tr. BS).

66. H. Egede (1925: 256–57, 271; 1971, 1: 324, 348); P. Egede (1939: 47, 49, 69–70, 81; 1971: 63, 67, 100, 119–20); N. Egede (1939: 137, 142, 152 [three cases]; 1971: 17, 24, 41); Saabye (1942: 20–21, 93).

67. P. Egede (1939: 38, 65, 95, 106; 1971: 48, 92, 141); N. Egede (1939: 137; 1971: 17); Saabye (1942: 56).

and weak, were liable scapegoats.[68] A single accusation, however, did not turn an *angakkoq* into an *ilisiitsoq*, Glahn underlines at a later point in history (Glahn 1771: 357), when a distinction between the two arts had dawned upon the missionaries. Nevertheless, the allegation that sorcerers used to be women exclusively got the upper hand and may still be encountered today.

"Third Sex" Summarized

Greenlandic statements do not support the assumption of a recognized "third sex," either among shamans or ordinary people. Instead, cases of *sipineq* (change in sex at birth), adoption, cross-gendered upbringing, and the joy and social benefits of bearing boy babies (firstborn sons in particular) all point to a general preference for boys. Male authority reigned in sexual matters, and his age in household matters of hunting, order, and hosting guests. But irrespective of the child's sex, the first-born child decided the wife's relation to killed animals. By this *pernarneq* (usually a young man's first catch but, in the spirit language, a woman's first becoming a mother) a woman was allowed to cut up and manage the sharing of the meat, provided that no mother-in-law presided in these matters in the household. Among the "initiated" women of the household (i.e., mothers) age similarly reigned. The widow with adult sons living with their families in the household was accorded an authority on par with an *ittoq* (the male leader of a household). Both women and men were accused of sorcery. The surplus of elder widows figures with greater frequency among the accusations, although poor elderly men and shamans growing unreliable and prone to dementia (regardless of sex) were similarly in danger of becoming scapegoats. Wife battering was not uncommon, and nobody had the authority to interfere (except the missionaries). Actually, a parallel can be drawn between the man's license to kill game and to beat his wife as demonstrated regarding the ritual bride robbery in the previous chapter. Again, motherhood comes out as a woman's best card in defense, with the sex of her first child being unimportant in relation to game. However, socially boys ranked highest.

The Art of Ilisiinneq

As much as *angakkuuneq* (practicing shamanism) demanded knowledge and skill, so did *ilisiinneq*, the practice of sorcery. Thalbitzer, who became fully aware of this fact during his Ammassalik fieldwork in 1905–6, did not hesitate to name *ilisiinneq* an art in line with the art of *angakkuuneq* (Thalbitzer 1930; 1941). Going against the Western idea of sorcery as an evil, devilish practice beyond any context, Thalbitzer preceded Evans-Pritchard by some seven years (if unnoticed in academia). In far wider circles of contemporary anthropology, the latter succeeded in dispelling the Western magic of sorcery by his famous analysis of Azande logic. The Azande made a clear distinction between witchcraft (unintended attacks) and sorcery (intended attacks). *Witchcraft* served as an explanation for inexplicable events, like bad luck and injuries. Anyone but nobility could be accused and proved either guilty or innocent by ritual tests. Of less frequent occurrence, *sorcery* was practiced by specialists in the art (Evans-Pritchard 1937). In Greenland *ilisiinneq* meant sorcery exclusively. Subsequent research has offered several suggestions of causes of sorcery globally, including the European witch hunts from the 14th to the 18th century. One conclusion points to a high frequency of sorcery in

68. Dalager (1915: 33); P. Egede (1939: 95, 106; 1971: 92, 141).

small-scale leaderless societies lacking common councils and short on institutions for solving conflicts and exercising social control. But in societies with leaders and political bodies, sorcery may be ascribed explanatory force and used for political ends. Also contributing is a worldview of reward and punishment in this earthly life and not in the hereafter, as are limited resources promoting jealousy and individual desires of retaliation. Finally, the demand for scapegoats during epidemics, famine, and heavy social changes is conducive to accusations of sorcery. Despite the most frequent identification with black magic, sorcery can also be used for beneficial ends, such as preventing other sorcery. Used to denote the gods' way of punishing, sorcery becomes a legitimized moral act (Ioan M. Lewis in *Encyclopedia Britannica* 1994–2002). In fact, the common practice of sorcery in small-scale societies made Hylland Eriksen create a humorous supposition. Imagine an anthropologist, belonging to a culture where explanations due to sorcery are the habitual order, doing fieldwork in a culture like ours and then trying to explain why no sorcery is practiced and mishaps are blindly explained by natural causes. In case he happens to be a structural functionalist, he would conclude that the (unavoidably ongoing) sorcery is kept secret for the benefit of social solidarity, in that secrecy prevents open conflicts between the families (Eriksen 1997: 275).

The pre-Christian Greenlandic society fit most of the above definitions. They were small, leaderless communities that maintained a level of politeness among their citizens, as their members were sensitive to a controlling and socializing public opinion. This was expressed among adults in funny teasing, in public satire, and in the famous song duels following strict rules of avoiding immediate subsequent brawl and murder (Kleivan 1971a; J. Rosing 1970). Only a few instances of breaking those rules are on record (J. Rosing 1970: 89).[69] Murder occurred and blood revenge was considered a family's duty, an ideal sometimes met by force of weapons, sometimes by sorcery, but in practice rarely exceeding a single (just) retaliation (Sonne 1982b). Punishment and reward did not await the deceased person in either realm of death. They would suffer if the surviving relatives overdid their sorrow or ignored the prescriptions, but these did not concern social morality (Sonne 2000a). Resources were limited, with marked and religiously sanctioned requirements for sharing—the main boon of pre-Christian society in the Greenlanders' own eyes—and causing an ambivalent ideology of equality. This ambience allocated the talented, lucky (and generous) hunters and their family high prestige, a prestige to be managed with care. Excess hunting beyond the needs of the family and permitting overwhelming giving were considered bad.[70] First, it would put receivers of such gifts into an uncomfortable state of gratitude. Second, since less game would be left for the others to hunt, both behaviors would arouse envy (R. Petersen 1963: 279; Sonne 2005: ID 72). And third, overhunting ruined one's own future due to the widespread notion that each hunter had a life quota of seals to be spent with care. Too much luck in hunting was considered a sign of impending death.[71] This quota,

69. A person in the audience stabbed one of the dueling partners in the back. Two instances are told of sorcery practiced by one of the partners during the duel (J. Rosing 1970: 108–10; Sonne 2005: ID 1684).

70. In Roepstorff's (2003) recent study of differing ontologies, he was told by Greenlandic hunters that the highest amount to be caught should match the need of the individual and his family. Exceeding was *-piluk*, really bad. The issue was the ethic of halibut fishing in contrast to statistics gathered by the biologists. The same Greenlandic ideal is reported in detail by Robbe in discussing East Greenlandic sealing and sharing in the 1970s (Robbe 1994: 316–18).

71. Birket-Smith (1924: 449); F. Lynge (1981: No. 408, 409, p. 155); Rasmussen (1979: No. 26, 27, 357, 362, 497); Robbe (1994: 316); J. Rosing (1970: 81).

however, seems not to have concerned a personal relationship between a hunter and "his" animals insofar as by murdering a hunter the murderer would appropriate the leftover number of his victim's seals. Be this a general idea or not, according to Rasmussen the murderer will be a hunter whose declining success shows that his quota has come to its end (Rasmussen 1921–25, I: 51). All things considered, they point to limited resources, diminished especially in East Greenland during the 18th and 19th centuries. A deteriorating climate, in combination with overhunting by Europeans—first whalers, then Norwegian sealers—took its toll.

Leaving theory behind, I ought to emphasize that the discussion of witchcraft versus sorcery in anthropology (e.g., Eriksen 1997: 254) makes little sense in Greenlandic traditions. *Ilisiinneq* was practiced by shamans and ordinary people alike. In Greenland *ilisiinneq* were invariably intentioned acts, sorcery, and they were meant to do harm, be that for individual or social ends. This issue will be elaborated upon in its actual settings below.

Early Statements on Sorcery in Context

In Labrador female and male shamans were generally called *ilisiitsut* (sing. *ilisiitsoq*) and *angakkut*, respectively, according to the earliest Moravian diaries studied by Garth Taylor (1989). The criterion used for a shaman is his/her ability to go into ecstasy. The diaries offer only a single example of an *ilisiitsoq*, a female shaman of minor capacity in the technique of ecstasy and whose prophesies proved fatally wrong. Foolish as she appears, she hardly meant to harm anybody. Another category, the *qilaamasut*, who used to practice the divinatory technique of *qilaneq*, did not go into ecstasy. These meager bits of information make Taylor look to Greenland for comparison.[72] So shall I, beginning with considerations on the cultural biases of the Danes and Germans (Moravians) who took down the earliest bits of information. The latter supplied the first Labrador Moravian mission of about 1765 with missionaries, due to their knowledge of the related dialect of the Southwest Greenlanders.

Heksemester ("master of sorcery") or *Heksekælling* ("female sorcerer") were the common derogatory terms used by Hans Egede for *angakkut* and *ilisiitsut* alike. If not necessarily accused of being allied to the Devil, both parties made use of devilish means, he declared, and consequently they opposed the progress of the mission (H. Egede 1971, 2: 114; 1925: 395; 1818: 194). Actually, in Denmark the last burning of a witch (convicted of being allied to the Devil) had taken place only three decades earlier, in 1693.[73] In his opposition to any Greenlandic religious specialist, Hans Egede made no distinction in his diaries. Not until writing the "Perlustration" did he introduce the term *ilisiitsoq*, that is, in an obvious copy of a passage from a rare use of this term by his son Poul (H. Egede 1971, 2: 113; 1925: 395; 1818: 192). As a rule Poul applied the term *heks*, sorcerer, indiscriminately. But in his fifth year of service, 1740, in hearing about a shaman who had turned into an *ilisiitsoq* he felt inclined to offer a comment. The *angakkoq*, he explains, "is a wise man, a doctor, a prophet, indeed their priest, who is said to consult Toornaarsuk like any pagan priest his oracle.[74] The other

72. Here I must confess a wrong etymological translation of *ilisiitsoq* that Taylor got from me and quoted in his article. It means a person who has lost his/her wits (not bereaved of his/her ignorance as I told Taylor).

73. The death sentence was not abolished in Denmark until 1930.

74. *Toornaarsuk* is literally "a particular helping spirit" but Hans Egede identified it with the Devil (see Sonne 1986b).

again, the *ilisiitsoq*, is a 'troldmand' [male sorcerer, mind the gender] who by sorcery commits evil deeds and kills people; such accusations of course are unfounded and usually hit people who have grown too old" (P. Egede: 1971: 141; 1939: 95, tr. BS).[75] At a much earlier point, in fact, Poul also had had to differentiate in passing on an event that involved both a shaman and a sorcerer. The former, named an *angakkoq* by Poul, had accused the latter, called *troldkælling* (sorceress), of sorcery. The latter was lynched in public (P. Egede 1971: 100; 1939: 69). Discussions naturally arose among the first missionaries and Greenlanders about the right to pass sentence and have it executed. Both Poul and Niels Egede gained some authority in prohibiting murders as a result of accusations of sorcery. Consequently they were asked by the Greenlanders to help people to get rid of some dangerous person accused of sorcery (P. Egede 1971: 159; 1939: 106; N. Egede 1971: 105; 1939: 191). Bit by bit, however, the mission's ban on murder in general, maintained by threats of hell, as well as the mission's refusal of any raison d'être of sorcery, had its effects. Sorcery lost ground insofar that accusations stopped being public affairs leading to executions.

Westerners usually consider sorcery entirely bad. Good versus evil is thus the basic opposition governing the distinction Poul eventually made between shamans and sorcerers, and in seeming correspondence with the attitude of the Greenlanders. Dalager distinguished between good and bad shamans on the criteria of honesty and being paid or not (Dalager 1915: 33), but regarding sorcery he added the important statement that shamans were to learn both arts and that sorcerers not only did harm but also knew how to prevent sorcery (53). All of which goes to say that the statements appear self-contradictory by, first, undermining the assumed clear-cut boundary between shamans and sorcerers on the criteria of good versus evil; second, by the conviction that sorcerers were women exclusively; and third, that the sorcerers invariably used their knowledge for harmful ends. Nor does another generalization made by Hans Egede in the "Perlustration" hold water, namely that any sorcerer, when spotted, was killed without compassion (H. Egede 1971, 2: 113; 1925: 395; 1818: 192–93).[76]

Moving on to East Greenland, the first ethnographic explorer, Commander G. Holm, who led the Women's Boat Expedition (1884–85), had no difficulty in taking a rational stand. He was neither religiously scared nor particularly impressed by the tricks performed by the shaman, Sanimuinnaq, who quickly lost his zeal at Holm's cold bearing. Nevertheless, the description of this séance, as the one revealing the most details by a European observer, is quoted time and again, whereas the equally interesting tricks communicated by Sanimuinnaq under pledge of secrecy (in Greenland) are not (Holm 1972: 127–30; 1914: 90–95). Holm was also told about several instances of persons, men and women, practicing both *angakkuuneq* and *ilisiinneq*. He underlines the hate and fear of those practicing *ilisiinneq*, and he is the first to mention the conviction that *ilisiinneq* may hit back on the

75. According to a much later second edition of his diaries, Poul remembers his great surprise at the application of both terms to the same person (P. Egede 1988: 123).

76. At a greater distance in time and mind, evolutionary ideas took over in considerations on Inuit sorcery. H. J. Rink, whose early political ideas made him accuse the mission of having robbed the Greenlanders of their former (alleged) authorities, the shamans, speculated that *ilisiinneq* represented an original art of shamanism, older than the successful *angakkuuneq*, which relegated *ilisiinneq* to the sphere of evil. Rink then identified this process with the Christian mission's total ban on paganism with the consequence that *ilisiinneq* lived on in secrecy (Rink 1866–71, II: 185; 1975: 49f). When discussing *ilisiinneq*, Rink writes in the past. Accusations hardly ever reached his ears. Still, no legal precedent existed for treating criminal cases among the Greenlanders until 1925.

sorcerer with an attack of insanity, which could be cured by confession alone (Holm 1972: 127, 136; 1914: 90, 103–4). Next in chronology, F.C.P. Rüttel, the first missionary to Ammassalik (1894–1904), yields only few statements on sorcery. His poor command of Greenlandic was the main cause of this, but he confirms Holm's statement about curing mental illness by confessions of *ilisiinneq*, whether or not actually practiced by the patient (Rüttel 1917: 113, 251 n. 113, 6). With his Greenlandic successor, Christian Rosing (1904–1921), educated a catechist at the Teachers' College in Nuuk, we are sent back in time to the ideas of Hans Egede. Rosing maintains that both *angakkut* and *ilisiitsut* are allied to the Devil, even if unbeknownst to either. The former are men, clever and sly, and the latter are predominantly women, but also sometimes men. This in contrast to the ideas about sorcerers held in contemporary (Christianized) West Greenland. But men alone can be both *angakkoq* and *ilisiitsoq*, Rosing declares (C. Rosing 1946: 18, 46–48, 50). Due to his being a native Greenlander and having a strong will and complete trust in the legitimacy of his vocation, Rosing made quick progress. Moreover, since he demanded that every person preparing for baptism must confess any pagan deed they had "committed" in the past, he had a good number of stories to tell when after only a year's service he composed his *Tunuamiut* (1906). His general condemnatory attitudes marking this publication were later to be tempered, according to Thalbitzer's comment on the Danish translation (C. Rosing 1946: 143). Actually, if Rosing had made a new description a few years later, he could have told of two female shamans, Teemiartissaq and Kaakaaq, of which the latter (baptized in 1917) was also a sorcerer. Still later, collections made by Thalbitzer, Knud Rasmussen, Otto Rosing, Jens Rosing, and Sandgreen offer rich sources testifying to the "contradictions" mentioned above: a shaman, male or female, was also an *ilisiitsoq*, and the art of *ilisiinneq* was useful in neutralizing other attacks of *ilisiinneq*. Killing sorcerers by force appears not to have been the order of the day. In fact, although murders occurred with some frequency, cases of lynching are not on record from East Greenland, and although accusations made against Kaakaaq abound, she was not openly attacked. Her alleged victims were either her own relatives or persons whose attempts at hitting her close relatives by *ilisiinneq* had their attacks returned to sender by Kaakaaq herself (Sonne 2005: ID 1251, 1264, 1268, 1261, 1275, 1282, 1283, 1700).

The Balancing of Shamanic and Sorcerous Means

Acquiring means for *ilisiinneq* formed part of the shaman's apprenticeship in East as in South Greenland. Missuarniannga made a list of his teachers and the kinds of knowledge they communicated. The majority concerned *ilisiinneq* (Thalbitzer 1941: 609–10), a fact he explained as follows: "Many of our people are considered unreliable and full of scandal [*sic*] and evil, and their wicked words and thoughts can harm my soul. *Iliseeneq* is, therefore, essentially the doctrine of how I can take care of my spiritual hygiene by magic means (observances). These partly protect me against the plots of my enemies (their evil thoughts), and are partly used by me to persecute and hurt them" (612). The Greenlandic word meaning "spiritual hygiene" is lost in translation, but the personal responsibility shines through of being careful in a society of tacit conflicts. Whereas Thalbitzer takes a sympathetic view, the missionaries emphasized the lack of mutual confidence and love, which may, I presume, have given rise to a peculiar rule, limited to East Greenland: that the pupil was required to balance his number of helping spirits with an equal number of means for sorcery. Otherwise, he would perish and die. The statement occurs in several mutually independent (?) statements.[77] Only Victor offers some explanatory details:

> The apprentice is to acquire one means of sorcery for every new helping spirit, who frequently is the one who also communicates the knowledge. If not, the pupil must buy one from a person with that knowledge (*ilisiitsoq*). In case the pupil makes use of the helping spirit without having balanced it with a means of sorcery, he shall die. The other way round he becomes insane, that is, if he makes use of a means of sorcery, received or bought, but still not balanced by the acquisition of a new helping spirit. Yet the same demand does not apply to *ilisiitsut*, sorcerers, who possess only knowledge about sorcery but no helping spirits. (Victor & Robert-Lamblin 1989–93, II: 247, tr. BS)

The balancing thus remains the responsibility of the shaman, who will be the only one to suffer any imbalance. To my knowledge, however, no example is to be found of a shaman who actually did suffer from a violation of this rule. All the shamans in question met the demand, it seems, and every one of them belonged to the last generation who gave in to Christianity. Checking the older sources, neither Thalbitzer nor Holm mentions the demand on balancing. Both accentuate that shamans usually possess a solid knowledge of sorcery, bought from *ilisiitsut*. Thalbitzer adds, as we know, that they are means of both defense and attack (Thalbitzer 1909: 95; 1930: 78; 1941: 609ff), and Holm notes that a shaman making use of sorcery risks becoming insane. In that case he has to confess whatever act of sorcery he has committed and he must stop that activity for good. However, he can still practice as a shaman (Holm 1972: 133–36; 1914: 100–7). This latter license sounds risky as well in case the demand on balancing is simultaneously in force. Consequently I take the idea of balancing to be fairly new, most probably in silent defense of the ban put on sorcery by the condemnatory missionaries. Added to the general ban could also be the latters' opposition to nonmarital sex because, according to one of Rasmussen's informants, the prerequisite of obtaining/buying some means of sorcery from a person of the opposite sex required intercourse for a start.[78] The mission did not succeed in eliminating sorcery, though, as I was told by Pierre Robbe: "sorcery can still (in the 1990s) be studied in East Greenland." And, as regards the recurring statements about the equal numbers, he stated, "All of us questioned the same informants."

Assuming that the demand on balancing helping spirits with means of sorcery was felt to legalize sorcery in the context of the Christian teachings, why would balance serve that end? Because balance was an ideal of life, I suppose, as emphasized in discussion of *sila* above. Balance apart, however,

77. Sonne (2005: ID 1239, 1242, 1244, 1686); O. Rosing (1957–61, I: 71); J. Rosing (1963: 174); Victor & Robert-Lamblin (1989–93, II: 247).

78. "When a person wished to learn evil practices of another, if it were a man approaching an old woman he had first to give his body to her, no matter if she were very old and he quite young, or vice versa. If it were a woman approaching a shaman, she had first to give her body to the shaman, before any kind of teaching could begin. It was said that coitus had always to precede a lesson in this mysterious and evil art. Only then could one begin to explain what it was one wanted to obtain or to learn to do against another. It was almost always a case of wanting revenge on account of anger born of envy" (Rasmussen 1938: 153, no informant credited). This demand on sex was met by Kaakaaq learning means for sorcery from Kunnak, as also by her son when offered a means by an elderly woman for defending his rich future catches against attacks due to envy (Sonne 2005: ID 1249, 1258).

Thalbitzer's informants left no doubt that means for *ilisiinneq* formed part of the bits of knowledge passed on through the generations. Most people, the elders in particular, would know some means of *ilisiinneq*, to be bought or inherited and used for appropriate ends (Thalbitzer 1930; 1941). Of a list of sixty-five amulets collected by Christian Rosing, sixteen (about 25%) were meant to protect the owner from early childhood and on against sorcery (E. Rosing 1994).

Plenty of examples testify to my above proposition that *ilisiinneq* was not necessarily an immoral act. Getting rid of a dangerous person by sorcery was a relief to all and was highly appreciated (e.g., Sonne 2005: ID 352, 1191), and to meet the ideal duty of revenge by sorcery was considered just (e.g., ID 33; Sonne 1982b; 2003). Besides, the term *ilisiinneq* also covered rituals performed by a sorcerer in returning the effect of sorcery to the offender (Sonne 2005: ID 1148, 1257), and a sorcerer could use his or her knowledge for other beneficent ends: decide on the right name for a newborn baby; cure bad luck in hunting; stop an attack of insanity (due to rebounding *ilisiinneq*), kayak dizziness, or shingles; calm down a storm; and ingeniously remove a severe taboo on eating during starvation (Rasmussen 1921–25, III: 17; 1979: No. 266; Sonne 2005: ID 1238, 1990, 1664, 1940). The general statement by Dalager, quoted above, supports these examples, whereas Cranz, the historian of the Moravians, who mentions cures by sucking out swelled limbs as the method preferred by *ilisiitsut*, names them "old hags who have no other chance of supporting themselves" (Cranz 1820: 198). Jakobsen, discussing Cranz, defines *ilisiitsut* in this context as wise old women or men on the model of the European witch: "a wise person, who might be seen as in contact with the Devil, although he also practices healing" (Jakobsen 1999: 99–100).

In the long run I agree, but however helpful these old hags might be, there were two sides to the coin. A person known to be a clever *ilisiitsoq* or in possession of sorcery means/knowledge was appealed to and paid for their service or "commodity." On the other hand, such people were also feared and handled politely with care—as were shamans—for their ambiguous capacities of doing both good and harm. By comparison, shamans were better off. They did, as a rule, reveal themselves as shamans and perform in public. They also had a great say in pointing out *ilisiitsut*, whereas the act of *ilisiinneq* demanded secrecy in order to work (e.g., Thalbitzer in C. Rosing 1946: 131; Sonne 1982b; 2003). Kunnak, for instance, had to give up his newly made and almost enlivened *tupilak* when caught in the act by two young boys: his own son, Nanngajak, and Georg Quppersimaan. Nanngajak called in his helping spirit to destroy the *tupilak*, and recommended that his father save his own life by leaving the scene (Sonne 2005: ID 1156). The advice was clever in fact (or fiction). Thus an elderly, impaired man, who was similarly caught making a *tupilak* by two young men, had his testicles ruined when they harpooned the still-sucking monster: "How clear the heaven looks," he exclaimed, dying (ID 793).[79] Cures performed by an *ilisiitsoq* could be done in public, as did for instance the notorious Kunnak, a sorcerer "of highest rank" (ID 1990). No performance was staged, but he was sent for and those who happened to be present witnessed his careful removal of a cervical vertebra placed in a suspicious way. The culprit soon would reveal himself, Kunnak promised the onlookers afterward. Certainly, in a short time the shaman, Taqqisima, became mentally ill (ID 1148, 1257). In curing Maratsi's sister of shingles, Kunnak

79. Neither story leaves the reader in doubt about the fact that masturbation was the way to feed a *tupilak*. A woman would let the *tupilak* suck her genitals. See Sonne (2005: ID 1261, 1275) and illustration in N.-K. Petersen (2013) in reference to Eigil Knuth about the tradition of carving figures of this act in East Greenland.

went into ecstasy for whomever present to follow in all details (ID 1664). He did not, however, let anybody grasp the words of the *serrat* (spell) he kept murmuring over and over. If they had been heard, the *serrat* would have lost its effect forever after (*ibid.*).

So, curing attacks of sorcery did not necessarily demand secrecy. The effect of practicing *ilisiinneq*, however, worked on the basic opposition of secrecy versus publicity, and not on the social moral of good versus evil. The effects of a *serrat* (spell) similarly demanded secrecy. Each spell (*serrat*) worked for its own end, be it "good" or "evil": some for transitions in life cycles and seasons, some for defense, some for success in hunting, for getting children, and some for the practice of sorcery or shamanism. Every adult owned one or more *serratit* and ownership was individual. When sold, the transfer of the words took place in secret and the seller could no longer use it. Put to use, the *serrat* was to be murmured, and the effect was worn out if used in and out of season (Kleivan & Sonne 1985). To use a spell audibly in public might have a strong effect, such as the calming of a gale by Ikerpaq, but the release in public similarly spoiled its effect forever after (e.g., ID 863). Conversely, the bad effects of a break of prescription or rebounding *ilisiinneq* were also neutralized by public confession. The secrecy guarding apprenticeship was a must and had to be respected, not only because shamans were useful and entertaining, but also because they were feared due to their intact knowledge of *ilisiinneq*. Allaallaq ruined his apprenticeship all by himself. Two years before initiation he revealed his secret in public, a confession that cured his sore feet. All but one helping spirit left him, but his petty performances were enjoyed and trusted all the same (Holm 1972: 132; 1914: 98). On the one hand the idea of rebounding *ilisiinneq* exercised some social control, while on the other it widened the field of explaining mishaps, illnesses, untimely deaths, etc. Wider bearings of secrecy, such as the reluctance to reveal personal problems, may still be in force as long as accusations of sorcery are considered. In an attempt to reach some understanding of this reluctance, speculated by modern Greenlanders to be the main cause of suicide, murders, and abuses of any kind, I picked the principle of secrecy, sanctifying as it were the "Other World" of one's interior self (Sonne 2003). Sacred and secret are not related etymologically, only in ways of thinking.[80]

Summary

Anybody could embark on a shaman's career, but most shamans were men, comprising 20% of the adult population in East Greenland. In the same measures as other men they were able-bodied hunters and mentally sane. Few shamans were great—i.e., able to travel the Other Worlds above and below,

80. The healing circles rapidly forming at present in Nunavut and Nunavik cope with the problem (Laugrand & Oosten 2008a). Making use of "confessions," less of immoral or clandestine acts than of the mental wounds received since childhood, healing is gained through outbursts of crying and screaming in a circle of confidentiality. The leaders do not claim to be prophets or neo-shamans. Quite on the contrary, as deeply convinced Christians they refuse any connection with shamanism, although, as Laugrand and Oosten point out, implicitly they have one. The use of public confessions, as well as the giving of presents to the leader for making the healing work, are rooted in the past, as is the protection and consolation to be gained by the increasing mutual love and empathy between the participants against evil spirits. Deceased relatives mourned too long still turn into evil spirits in that extended sorrow invites the missed relative to come down from heaven and take possession of the mourner's body, causing disease and an unhappy mind (*ibid.*). I am not aware of similar circles being formed in Greenland, nor are the sociopsychological effects of confessions led by shamans in the past mentioned in the sources. Furthermore, since confessions do not form a conventional part of the Lutheran church of Greenland, the impetus for a continuation has probably been less evident.

Fig. 12. *Qilaneq* by Teemiartissaq for a sick child. Photo by W. Thalbitzer, 1906. *Danish Arctic Institute, Copenhagen. ID 23548.*

and to stage impressive performances. Lesser shamans performed on a smaller scale. They made their helping spirits enter the darkened room, or they resorted to *qilaneq*, "spirit fishing" as did also most of the female shamans, who comprised a mere 1.3% of the adult population. One famous female shaman, Kaakaaq, practiced *qilaaqutserneq*, lying on the platform, covered by a skin for getting into trance and calling on her helping spirits. This was the common technique for all shamans in summer when a darkened room for a proper séance could not be had.

Legendary female shamans, who did travel, seem to have been either childless or unmarried. They went to visit Sea Woman supported by some shaman, usually male, but, as far as the sources go, they never went to Moon. As will be explained later, Moon held, in ritual as in myth, an ambiguous position in relation to women and marital matters. Still trusting legend, only male shamans competed in public on tricks. Saladin d'Anglure's hypothesis that shamans represented a "third sex" cannot be verified for Greenlandic shamans. Two of his criteria, a transformation in gender at birth (*sipineq*) and cross-gendered upbringing, which were common in Greenland society, were given differing explanations. They point to a clear preference for bearing and adopting boys. Continuing analysis of gender aspects in the pre-Christian society of polygamy and the many taboos on women, there is no doubt about men's authority as leaders of households and as owners of their wives' sexuality. Wife battering did occur in some indefinable measure, divorce was frequent in the early years, but since children were the desired outcome of any marriage, and divorced young mothers took their children along, marriages tended to become stabilized at par-

Fig. 13. *Qilaaqutserneq*/divination covered by a skin carpet. The sick person is sitting in the partition next to the shaman. This was Kaakaaq's common way of performing. Drawing by Kaarali Andreassen. *Danish Royal Library, Thalbitzer's Archive: NKS 2357 folio, unit 12, drawing 142.*

enthood. Women became adult in relation to game at the birth of their first child, but a woman's mother in-law presided over the rules of sharing. Elder widows with adult sons were respected as household leaders on par with men. At the opposite end of the scale were widows without support. They were liable to be accused of sorcery and, at times of crisis, sometimes lynched. Destitute men and male shamans growing demented were in danger as well. The art of sorcery, an integral part of both shamanism and social relations generally, was performed in secret with the intention of hurting or killing its victim. In case the latter was too strong, mentally or in magic/religious means, the sorcery hit back, usually with insanity. Public confession to a shaman was the common cure. Sorcery employed in "just revenge" or for getting rid of a person dangerous to society was considered a beneficial, not immoral, act. Means for sorcery, be they formulas or bits of knowledge, were, also in secret, traded at astonishing high prices. Actually, the ongoing trade in religious, magic, or secret means formed a considerable part of the "economy."

Apprenticeship (Angakkussarneq)

To state at the outset: very little is known about apprenticeship in West Greenland and Avanersuaq, such as duration, the number and kinds of helping spirits required, and how they were obtained, and almost nothing is known about public initiation. Consequently I shall primarily stick to East Greenland.

The purposes of apprenticeship were to obtain *qaamaneq* (vision), *toornat* (helping spirits), and at best, one or more capacities for traveling the Other Worlds, above, below, and abroad.[81] *Qaamaneq*, interior light, vision, or second sight, enabled the shaman to see the Other Worlds and, because it was visible to only spirits and other shamans, to attract helpers among the spirits. The apprentice was to keep his experiences secret until initiation in public, or the helping spirits would withdraw in offense. Sometimes, however, some of the spirits remained.

When engaged by a pupil, spirits (*inuat* or *allanat*, "aliens," may have served as a general term) were called *toornat* (sing. *toornaq*, W. Grl.) or *taartat* (sing. *taartaq* E. Grl.).[82] Some were old-timers, inherited from deceased shamans through the generations, most representing well-known "species" living at various parts of the land, including the *innersuit* beneath the foreshore, and a few at sea or brought to the foreshore by the tide (e.g., Sonne 2005: ID 2283). A lesser number were individual mythic figures having particular names and functions, either as initiators during apprenticeship or, during performances, as frightening spirits. As stated above (p. 44), the most plausible distinction between an *inua* and a *toornaq* is simple: the *toornaq* is an *inua* attached to a shaman.[83]

Generalizations on East Greenlandic Apprenticeship in Research

No invariable sequence can be laid down for the recommended practices and their bearings. Some scholars assign decisive importance to particular events, such as an unprovoked early "supernatural" experience in childhood (inborn talent), and others to being invited by a teacher, or to the experience of death and revival by being devoured by a monster and thrown up again. The latter event is sometimes placed at the end of apprenticeship (Robert-Lamblin 1997; Holm 1972: 126; 1914: 90; Rasmussen 1938: 107–8); in one instance it is stated to empower the apprentice with the ability to fly (Robert-Lamblin 1997). The biographies rarely live up to such generalizations. Naaja was given an artificial start, and no teacher is mentioned. He had his experience of being devoured as a very small child, an event that was said to have implanted the interior light, *qaamaneq*, although his father had already done so right after birth (Sonne 2005: ID 1230, 1236). How he acquired the ability to fly is not mentioned. Kaakaaq, who was offered instruction by the first among her future helping spirits, was later taught bits of knowledge by humans. She did not follow any program, and when devoured by the "freshwater bear" at an early age, she received *qaamaneq* (ID 1239, 1703, 1241). Apparently she never went traveling in spirit. Kaakaaq's son, Kukkujooq, followed no strict method either. The instruction given to him uninvited by his mother's brother made no sense to him. He never told researchers about having been devoured by the monster, but he obtained the ability to fly from a goose (ID 1257, 1271). Ajukutooq, who was devoured by a monster water beetle, said that he did not know how to fly like his father, Akku (ID 987). Yet Akku probably did not possess that ability either,

81. Among the Canadian Inuit *qaamaneq* is called *qaumaniq* or *angakua* (Boas 1901–7: 33; Rasmussen 1929: 112–13, 199, 122; 1932: 28, 36; Weyer 1932: 431; Saladin d'Anglure 1990a).

82. *Allajuartassat* translates to "very strange beings—to become" (as helping spirits mentioned below). Today: *anersaaq*, pl. *anersaat*, spirit, etymologically from "breath," *anerneq*, or "he goes outside," *anivoq*; *anersaapiluk*, evil spirit, *Anersaaq Iluartoq*, Holy Spirit. The *imaanaanngitsut*, the "just not so ones" or "simpletons," sometimes also means an unknown human person suspected of being an "alien" (Sonne 2005: ID 247).

83. *Toornaq* may etymologically mean a frightening being (Fortescue et al. 1994: 346; 2010: 378). The E. Grl. equivalent *taartoq* is translated etymologically by Thalbitzer as "the substituting or exchanged one" in consonance with the ideas of possession during performances (1909: 97; 1930: 95).

Fig. 14. Shaman's séance with assistants. Drawing by Kaarali Andreassen. *Danish Royal Library, Thalbitzer's Archive: NKS 2357 folio, unit 12, drawing 143.*

as I shall discuss in contexts of initiation symbolism. Actually, by comparison, whether including West Greenlandic stories or not, generalizations about "syllabus" do not work, nor do fixed meanings ascribed to fixed events. However, theories of environment, body, perception, and initiation do work, as does the method of analyzing key symbols, as will be done in the following section with *qaamaneq*, the shaman's link to the Other World(s).

Instruction and Syllabus

Previously I discussed the prerequisite for getting started—that is, a talent for seeing the Others, whether inborn, artificially implanted, or acquired through effort—along with the social aspects of motivations. Further comments are appropriate given that teachers and instruction receive very little attention in biographies or in general descriptions. Had it not been for the impressive list of Missuarniannga's total of sixteen teachers recorded and published by Thalbitzer (1941: 609–10), the few actual instances of instruction in the biographies would appear arbitrary and unimportant, and would thus not invite examination. My unreflected idea (probably like that of other Westerners) of Inuit shamanic tuition used to be the fixed one of one pupil having a single teacher throughout apprenticeship. The reason may be the term "education" used in translations, in the meaning of a craft's apprenticeship. Thalbitzer's list speaks to the contrary. Most teachers taught very short "lessons." They were paid and that was all. Nevertheless, Kaarali Andreassen's drawing of a performance showing two young assistants sitting on either side of the shaman evokes more enduring relations between pupil and (some) teachers (Thalbitzer 1941: 606–17, 710). The case of a first instructor who took the initiative by asking permission to teach a boy would fit into this relationship.

Apprentices paid nonrelatives for their instruction. Actually, all kinds of knowledge was paid for, sometimes at a high cost, depending on both the value accorded the piece of information and the capacity of the buyer. Knowledge of shamanism, as of sorcery and other magical means, differed only by being communicated in secrecy and, to some degree, practiced in secrecy as well.

The appreciation of knowledge, no matter which category, is borne out by the level of abstraction employed by Umeerineq, Thalbitzer's main informant on instruction. Umeerineq categorized knowledge and skills into seven subjects for teaching or giving advice: the use of kayaks; trials of strength (exercises) by wrestling, running races, or lifting stones; drum-contest singing; magic prayers; sorcery (spells and instructions for doing harm or repelling sorcery); hunting; and the *angakkoq* art of performances (Thalbitzer 1941: 608). Hunting was subdivided into hunting seal (regardless of subspecies), polar bear, walrus, beluga, and large whale (*ibid.*). The commonly held view that children in nonliterate societies are not literally trained but learn in practice *by imitation alone* proves wrong when it comes to kayak paddling and hunting. The tiny boy sitting on the floor with a toy paddle and moving his arms in the proper way was encouraged by appreciating endearments. As they grew, boys were taught the primary skill of paddling in a real kayak, at the outset frequently in a lake, later at sea, kept upright and supervised in a way quite similar to Westerners' of being taught to ride a bike. On the sea, beginners were not allowed to go kayaking alone nor to put out to sea. Surveillance was a must. Fathers or other close kin took care, but particular skills like that of turning around in a kayak, or hunting some species of animal, could be taught by other men known to be specialists. Instruction went on in practice, of course, but also orally, by demonstration and under guidance. Umeerineq had instructed a total of five adolescents in the art of turning around in a kayak. He had built a kayak for one and "himself received instruction in kayaking and all sorts of hunting, viz., in bear-hunting from Qilertaanalik's father, in walrus hunting from Kookiaat, and in beluga hunting from his father's cousin Qaasiaarter, who also instructed him in the catching of ringed seal and bearded seal ('for he was very conversant with this')" (Thalbitzer 1941: 607). Payment took the form of goods or a fixed share, sometimes lifelong, in one's catches. Statistics cannot be created for this "commerce" of payment for knowledge and training going on outside ordinary obligations of sharing, which was in no way insignificant.[84] Examples must suffice, such as the list of considerable payments made by Missuarniannga to his teachers in the secret arts ending with a sledge plus a dog (Thalbitzer 1941: 610). Another instance is the legendary amount of skins Naaja's grateful father paid to an old widow throughout her lifetime for a small bit of advice (Sonne 2005: ID 1229, 1230). Sexual favors as a form of payment were mentioned above and add another item to the fictional questionnaire.

Teaching shamanism took place both orally and in practice, according to the very few cases described. Imitation was one way of learning; oral instruction combined with practice and verbal

84. For sharing, see Robbe (1994).

encouragement was another. The teaching of *serratit* (spells) and similar knowledge had to be oral.[85] Wordless tuition was given to one pupil whose first teacher brought him to a lake, turned him invisible, and fastened his feet firmly to the ground by means of the sucking disk of a lumpsucker. Using a rubbing stone the teacher then called forth the monster bear, was devoured, and reappeared whole and hale (ID 985). Trusting Aadaarutaa's personal narrative, taken down by Rasmussen, his teacher, who was an old stiff-legged man, took him to a cave at the head of a fjord. The old man went inside, undressed, returned, and, plainly observed by Aadaarutaa, had a monster bear devour and then vomit up his entire body. Aadaarutaa was later to go through the same fearful experience on his own (ID 984). Since according to versions told by his descendants, the instruction was nothing but oral (ID 2031, 2088), imagination may have played its part in Aadaarutaa's own recollection. All the same, when Nicoline was offered this very first piece of instruction by an elderly shaman, he promised to join her in going through the same experience, which he described in detail. Young Nicoline returned the offer silently by fleeing in panic (ID 972). On a more modest scale the old Kilimersertoq demonstrated to Maratsi in practice how to get started by the rubbing of stones. Together they went to the seashore, filled a mitten with water, and brought it inland. They poured water into the deep hole of a flat rock, placed another stone on top, and then Kilimersertoq started rubbing a smaller stone in circles on the lid. The rubbing called forth a wing snail in the water. Teacher and pupil returned to the shore, where the wing snail had arrived, grown into the size of an anorak's sleeve and luminous. Looking at the two humans with big eyes, it showed itself (in my interpretation, BS) to be ready to become the first "light-giving" helping spirit of Maratsi; that is, provided that he repeated the entire procedure three times in solitude (ID 1686). Admittedly, the only words spoken may have been the demand on repetitions. Three was the "holy number" of repetitions in East Greenland, five along the west coast.[86] This teacher seemingly made no demonstration of the solitary initiation of becoming devoured.

Similarly, Missuarniannga's first teacher instructed him orally in where to go for the rubbing, how to rub, and what to do if it did not work—i.e., if light did not come upon him. Later he followed Missuarniannga right onto the lake for calling up the monster animal but left Missuarniannga to cope with the ritual himself (Thalbitzer 1941: 609; Sonne 2005: ID 2283).[87] The instructions Teemiartissaq received from her first teacher, her father, and from her next, Pikkinor, remained her secret. For teaching "the mysteries of angakokism," Pikkinor and Teemiartissaq stayed away together one or two days in the mountains. At another point he taught her some spells, and at a third about stories, *oqalualaat* (narratives, fairly new) and *oqaluttoqat* (old stories, myths) (Thalbitzer 1941: 208). Which stories and which spells were used for which ends are regrettably not specified. As we know, spells, *serratit,* were used for various ends and only one restricted end for each spell. All-round talisman effects were rare, such as the protection offered by a caul (see chapter 5 on *pooq*).

---

85. Teemiartissaq, for instance, taught her sons the use of certain amulets and *serratit* (magic songs) (Thalbitzer 2014: 122f).

86. The number three could be due to Western impact. Four or five are the common Inuit/Yupiit "holy numbers."

87. According to the original manuscript taken down mainly in Danish (Sonne 2005: ID 2283) and most probably dictated by Missuarniannga's son Kaarali in West Greenlandic, Missuarniannga's first teacher is Akku. The right man is Qatik Imaalikutsuk, as told by Missuarniannga himself to Thalbitzer (1941: 609–10).

As for the transmission of stories, the common opinion states that it was a public matter. Stories of all kinds were told, some for children in particular, but most for everybody during winter evenings. No Greenlandic source other than Teemiartissaq mentions ritual precautions or secrecy in storytelling. Perhaps the following experience related by Teemiartissaq was an enlivening of a teacher's story communicated in secrecy: in *asia* she encounters two foxes in human figures, one atop a mountain and the other at the shore, who in an antiphonal singing tell each other about the things to be seen on the land and at sea. The former are plants, nothing but species of plants, with the majority specified as to their uses. The latter have utility value as well: species of fish, shellfish, and in the end, all sorts and ages of sea mammals (Thalbitzer 1932; 1923: 455). In my understanding of this narrative, its level of abstraction and simultaneous categorization reveal an all-round kind of knowledge easy to learn, remember, and thus employ for persons like great shamans who were supposed "to know everything without exception" (Thalbitzer 1923: 467). This is a nonliterate worldview consciously categorized, I dare add. Prescriptions, especially in force at the death of a close relative, were still another subject taught by both parents and teachers and not in silence (Thalbitzer 1941: 608). But the sources allow for no listing or detailed insight into the sub-issues of *angakkuuneq* knowledge. Solitary training in the practice of performances and its tricks are mentioned superficially, whereas specifications of *ilisiinneq* abound. Furthermore, an outsider (me) has difficulty in separating *angakkuuneq* from *ilisiinneq*. Kukkujooq/Apulu, for instance, whose first uninvited tutor was his mother's brother, got the advice to supply his first kayak cover with two pieces of sealskin, one cut from the eyes to the fore flippers placed in front and another astern cut from above the tail to the hind flippers. The advice concerned the security of the kayak when left on the shore during his search for helping spirits in the inland. In addition, the vessel was to be filled with stones, preventing its flight during the loss of consciousness usually befalling its owner, the pupil, while in search of familiars. No explanation followed the first advice, and Kukkujooq did not dare tell his mother at the time she made the covering of his first kayak. She used her own knowledge about defense against sorcery by placing the fore flippers of an adult fjord seal inside the front part and some teeth astern. Maybe the uncle's first advice was accorded a similar effect on a kayak left behind for any passerby to attack with *ilisiinneq*, but this remains unknown. However, to be on the safe side, Kukkujooq always brought the recommended pieces of skin along when out kayaking (Sonne 2005: ID 1257, 1259).

In addition to human teachers, the spirits are said to have offered knowledge of all sorts. When Kaakaaq was taught the beginnings of apprenticeship by the first spirit attracted to her glowing shame (due to her mother's reprimand), she received three bits of knowledge. Obviously they were about sorcery, because under the penalty of death, she was to get them counterbalanced by achieving three *allajuartassat* (very strange-looking beings, "Others," helping spirits) (Sonne 2005: ID 1239; Sandgreen 1967, II: 16). Kaakaaq did not succeed in her first attempt. She knew about the rubbing of stones for invoking spirits, presumably from stories. Stumbling across a pair of the right colors, black and white, she tried them out in a suitable place, but to no effect. Too young for endurance in rubbing, she gave up and later declared that such stones were of no use (Sonne 2005: ID 1239). How provocative! Nearly all sources of the pupil's beginnings point out the rubbing of a small stone (white and/or black) on a bigger flat one in circles following the course of the sun as the requirement for deliberately attracting a spirit.

Specific examples of apprenticeship from the west coast of Greenland are less numerous. No teacher is mentioned in Ineqinnavaat's biography, except for her European helping spirit, who, had he got the chance for five days and nights on end, would have made her into "a great shaman" (ID 841). Not by devouring her! For all their vices (and virtues) Europeans were not considered cannibals. Sex, on the other hand, may have been on the helping spirit's agenda.

Another former apprentice, Sahra, from the far south, told her own story about how she was painstakingly trained by her mother's brother. She was placed on his lap during séances and time and again taken along into the cave, where his rubbing of stones called forth a faint whirring that grew into a deafening and paralyzing chorus of sounds. Sometimes, when blood poured out from his mouth and ears, Sahra fled and hid, but he always found her. When he regained consciousness, he cleaned himself in a lake (ID 1783). A notable person being taught *angakkuuneq* was, in fact, Poul Egede. Offering payment he asked for instruction from a Southern shaman passing by Nuuk on his return from wintering at Disko Bay. The latter agreed and gave his instruction orally on both beginnings and the method of *ilimmarneq* (flying) during performances. Egede then demanded a demonstration of the effects, a flight to heaven in clear daylight on a sunny day. The shaman made excuses and, not unexpected by the reader, he received no payment (P. Egede 1971: 13–14; 1939: 14–15).

This Southern shaman recommended a way of rubbing stones for invoking the first spirit in consonance with the East Greenlandic one: walk far away to a desolate place in the inland, find a big flat stone and start rubbing it in circles with a smaller one (*ibid.*). Thalbitzer received more exact information, learning that the place should be close to a lake, a stream, a high cliff at the sea, an old grave, or a cave (Thalbitzer 1909: 94). Such places would facilitate a spirit's access from the world below and, in the case of the grave, from above. In West Greenland the *angakkussarfik*, or "training place for becoming an *angakkoq*," is sometimes inside a rock cave, preferably a deep cave in a steep rock facing the sea (P. Egede 1971: 28; 1939: 24; N. Egede 1971: 68; 1939: 168), in order to facilitate the access of an undershore *innersuaq*, most probably. To an outsider there would be no difference, but the Moravian storyteller, Hendrik, of East Greenlandic derivation, had the two methods, outside in the open and inside a cave, compared in his variant to two competing apprentices, a Southerner (like Hendrik) and a Northerner. The Southerner, following the East Greenlandic method at a dried-up lake, loses his flesh to a water beetle and, naturally, comes out the winner in shamanic powers, far surpassing the Northerner, who sticks to his cave (Sonne 2005: ID 1803).[88]

In Search of Future Helping Spirits

Ujarlerneq, "seeking," was the term for getting in touch with future helping spirits or, in spirit language, "hunting" (*saqilerpoq*, "kayaking" in ordinary East Greenlandic) in the wilderness, *asia* (e.g., Sandgreen 1967, II: 28; Sonne 2005: ID 1243). The great majority of *toornat* belonged to the land, inside its surface or underneath the shore and skerries. Being out alone was a must, as clearly

88. Two old fishermen, a Southerner and a Northerner, bet on who will be first to have a son, then on whose son will become the greater hunter and then the greatest shaman. The Southerner asks his son not to train in a cave but at the more empowering dry lake, where he is "sucked" by a water beetle. He immediately acquires *qaamaq*, and sees by this light his competitor training in a rock cave; when he visits the Northerner by flight, the poor rival is too weak in powers to even sense the arrival of his Southern opponent (Sonne 2005: ID 1803).

illustrated by the story about Kaakaaq, who was asked to serve as a midwife to the wife of a snow bunting. In company with her mother, she sees an ordinary snow bunting outside its nest. When her mother wants to go home, Kaakaaq asks to be left alone due to her desire to catch the bird in its nest. Mom leaves the scene, as does the bird, but the latter reappears in the figure of a beautiful man, who asks Kaakaaq for her help (Sonne 2005: ID 1702). Dyadic relations work, whereas two or more people seeing or hearing some nonhuman being together are rarely said to communicate more closely, that is, to converse with or touch (or be touched by) the spiritual being. Exceptions are West Greenlandic *qivittoq* stories about encounters with well-known persons having left society for good (search in Sonne 2005: Vebæk qivittoq). In the rare cases of two apprentices going in search together—Georg Quppersimaan and his friend is a case in point (Sonne 2005: ID 966, 1179)—the one seeing a spirit first got the exclusive right to it. A similar individual ownership befell the ordinary person who caught sight of a polar bear, no matter who then killed it. Only in the darkness of performances could the shaman permit people to touch his spirits (ID 1677).

Generally, familiars were sought in *asia* of the inland and at the shore, to which the majority of potential helping spirits, dwarves and giants of various size, belonged. Either *innersuit* were encountered in coastal waters or they approached the pupil on the coast (e.g., ID 2283). Spirits belonging in distant lands of the Other World, such as deceased humans, specimens of the migrating animals, and particular mythic figures, turned up when summoned, or on their own, or, in the case of mollusks and shellfish, when brought in by the tide. A spirit's access from the worlds below to some place in the inland was had from the underside of the earth through clefts and lakes. Spirits from heaven descended through the air to a mountaintop or a grave. Summer was the season for seeking spirits, permitting as it did the possibility of roaming the land free from snow and ice. The family's tenting at streams and inside fjords similarly facilitated the "hunt" as did kayaking, the privilege of male pupils, who could then seek out desolate places without being observed. In short, apart from a kayaking pupil's encounter with *innersuit* in coastal waters, future helping spirits were searched out on the land (as among the Baffin Islanders; see Laugrand et al. 2000). The borderlines between the visible and invisible worlds, presented in chapter 3, "The Other World(s) and Its Beings," determined where to go and when to return.

Many spirits were attracted to the pupil of their own accord. Others were rubbed forth by circling stone upon stone, were called upon by a hard voice, or were met by chance. A few drew the pupil to their place in order to have him cure a fellow spirit. A good-natured spirit would start a conversation, identify itself by name, ask for the pupil's name (Kaakaaq using her particular shaman's name; Sonne 2005: ID 1240), and then ask the pupil to touch it in order to seal the alliance. Some asked the pupil to visit its place, whereas the more frightening ones made the pupil lose consciousness by the mere sight of it or by a touch of the hand or breath. While a few spirits became close friends and helpers throughout apprenticeship, the remaining ones did not return until called upon during *saqqummerneq*, public initiation. Until this event a spirit was termed "future helping spirit" ("to be," *-ssaq*), corresponding to the explicit desire of spirits to become those who were "to come to you in the future"—i.e., to turn up during the shaman's public performances. This focus on the future role of helping spirits underlines the pupil's moral duty to reveal his apprenticeship by *saqqummerneq*. As stated by one of Sandgreen's informants, helping spirits were of minor use to the shaman if he did not employ them in public—i.e., for the benefit of society (ID 1205). Or, in other words, social recognition granted the shaman's ownership to his spirits.

The number of helping spirits a pupil acquired varied considerably. The most complete list on record, that of Missuarniannga's familiars, counts some twenty-odd spirits, representing dwarves, giants of both the medium and greatest sizes, several *innersuit*, a *toornaarsuk* (special *toornaq*), a "lower means of rubbing"—i.e., a spirit for divination by rubbing the floor with the drum (see J. Rosing 1963: 179–80; O. Rosing 1957–61: 76), a couple of *qimarratit* (frightening spirits), one or two deceased humans, an *uersaq*, and a baby (Sonne 2005: ID 2283). In a few instances the spirit's type of support or instruction is mentioned, such as the protection given by a *toornaarsuk* in encounters with dangerous spirits; the ability to fly taught by a medium-size giant, or the said divinatory function of a spirit (*ibid.*). Though incomplete in the sense of general criteria, the systematization of helping spirits made by Missuarniannga's son Kaarali offers supplementary bits of information for comparison (J. Rosing 1963: 179ff; O. Rosing 1957–61: 76ff; see above pp. 79, 160). It allows for an identification of some of Missuarniannga's frightening spirits as being *qimarratit* (i.e., to be used at the opening of a performance) and reveals an initiating role of others, among which I shall return to *uersaq* in a while. The more amiable spirits seem to have followed their shaman on travels abroad and recurrently turn up at his performances for both entertainment and in order to receive reenlivening warmth in his body. As for species of spirits living like humans in families, they were of the land, inside the surface and right beneath the foreshore and skerries. As outlined above (*ibid.*), each species' place in relation to humans, "the people of the coast," decided its way of life (hunting) and relative size. They all looked like humans, but by their balance in body and ways of moving about, they were more like birds.

Social Conditions for Pupils' and Shamans' Relations with Spirits

The dyadic relations reigning between humans and nonhumans were outlined in the previous chapter. In the following section, mutual obligations between shamans and helping spirits will be the issue. On his part the apprentice was to observe certain extraordinary prescriptions, like keeping the apprenticeship secret, never being out of doors half-naked (not to mention naked), abstaining from using iron and other sharp instruments, and abiding to the prominent proscription of always being alert (e.g., Sonne 2005: ID 1220, 575). Regarding the helping spirits, a difference is seen between most *toornat* and the frightening *qimarratit*, in that the latter did not expect repeated visits during apprenticeship, and they did not as a rule possess their master. They acted on their own during performances. In possessing their master's body, the *toornat* took turns (simultaneous possession by two or more spirits would hardly make sense in any culture). Outside of his body, a shaman's helping spirits went beyond the rule of bilateral relations insofar as they cooperated as a group not only at his command but also on their own by urging him to overcome any fear of hindrances. One such fear might be the pupil's reluctance to go through his public initiation, to be followed by recurrent performances, upon which these helping spirits depended for their well-being (Sonne 2005: ID 1162, 1165, 1261, 1276, 1211, 1212). Since this very *saqqummerneq* also conditioned the shaman's full use of the spirits' abilities (ID 1205), the self-interest of the spirits ended up serving human society as well, that is, in consonance with the definition put forth by Hultkrantz. The same common self-interest similarly directed one rare (though extremely entertaining) case of a fight between a shaman's helping spirits, to be presented below.

Returning to the subject of no rules obtaining for spirits by Oosten and Laugrand (2004/5: 117), which I commented on in the previous chapter, I drew attention to the spirits' demand for a darkened room like that of their own world—their interior *naar*-world (in a human perspective)—for showing up at performances. I also noted the overruling obligation met by both spirits and humans in returning home at the *naar*-time of dawn from visits to the opposite World. An additional limit on the spirits in East Greenland dictated that *the spirit shamans* got their familiars among other spirit species alone, never among humans, living or deceased, whereas human shamans got theirs from both the spirit species and from among deceased humans (*ibid.*). Thus, this asymmetry, together with the spirits' dependence for their lives on their shaman's performances, but not vice versa, leads to the conclusion that, among the East Greenlanders, the often-advanced thesis of complete equality between Inuit and nonhumans did not apply without marked exceptions (e.g., Dorais 1988).

Toornat living in families liked to invite the pupil home for visits.[89] Did he intend to stay? This was the frequent question asked by *ningiu*, the term for the female elder of the household, be it human or nonhuman. If not, he was not allowed to eat, the means of becoming intimately related among the Inuit as well. Lore had it that during the first visit some member of the spirit family would be an aggressive person from whom the pupil was to be saved, either by his newly acquired helping spirit or another one previously acquired. The averted attack served as an initiation of sorts, in that the pupil subsequently became a beloved guest with the obligation to maintain friendship by paying recurring visits. Neglect might give rise to resentment leading to a dramatic attack either during a spectacular performance or in a less exciting fashion during an ordinary evening in the longhouse. Dramatic or not, made up or not, the defeat of the spirit testified to the shaman's great capabilities (Sonne 2005: ID 1690, 1691).

The opposite case—a too-intimate friendship—could inspire the helping spirit to look for closer contacts by intermarriage or adoption. While still a bachelor, Naaja was offered a nice girl among the *innersuit*. He was really tempted but had to reject the proposal because she, being of another "culture" (my term), did not know how to sew human clothes correctly (ID 1218). Uppiinnguaq, the little owl, was one of the medium-size giants attached to Naaja; jealous of Naaja's big and cozy family, he similarly tried his best to acquire a new relation. He almost succeeded, stealing not a relative but an orphan belonging to Naaja's household. Uppiinnguaq gave the young man to his own daughter, a big lump of a young girl. The boy was scared, but he became used to her, and they had sex eagerly for a long, long while. Eventually the orphan had enough. Prevented from getting away he told his not-too-clever wife that he wanted to go see his deceased cousin. She followed him to a cliff, whereupon he jumped into the sea, leaving the girl waiting fruitlessly for his return. Upon her arrival home she dissolved in tears. Uppiinnguaq did not blame her but rather himself to a degree; this prevented him from showing up at Naaja's performances and led to his attempt to kill Naaja. The attack resulted in an intense war between Naaja's helping spirits, because killing Naaja meant the loss of their source of reenlivening warmth. Uppiinnguaq was justly killed and buried, but his father had him revived by

89. Rasmussen's statement that only spirit shamans made invitations (1938: 105) is not supported by the biographies.

singing *serratit* at his grave every morning and evening for a whole month. Having lost his attachment to Naaja, Uppiinnguaq, himself a shaman, moved away to be with his ancestors, the biggest giants in the farthest-away inland region. He not only became their shaman, but since—implicitly—he had been initiated once more through death and revival, he turned into an *angakkuvissuaq*, a genuine great shaman (ID 1199, 1198). This is quite a story about the ranking of shamans' emotional relationships with helping spirits, and its apparent lack of episodes known from other stories is also surprising.[90] Nevertheless, it adheres to the rule of dyadic human relations with individual "Others" as presented above, and definitely not to the demand that the "Others" follow no rules (as proposed by Oosten & Laugrand).

So, as dependent as the spirits attached to a shaman were upon the reenlivening warmth of his interior body, they might cooperate mutually, irrespective of their own family bonds, or end up in a fight. To the best of my knowledge, these cooperations were the only way to go beyond the demand on the dyadic relationship (no example can be found as to how cooperating shamans kept their helping spirits apart).

Sexual Relations with Spirits

The ideology of dyadic relations takes us to the subject of nonhumans' sexual desire for humans, and vice versa, a constant threat to hunters among the Yukaghirs as discussed by Willerslev (2007) and a complicated matter among Canadian Inuit shamans as exemplified by Saladin d'Anglure (Saladin d'Anglure & Morin 1998). Problems arose with Christianity, the latter authors conclude, a view hard to contest by means of Greenlandic personal statements on that issue. Pre-Christian Greenland ideology demanded boundaries between This and the Other Worlds to be respected by both ordinary humans and shamans alike. Ordinary humans who engaged in sex with a deceased human or a spirit risked bringing forth a monstrosity (P. Egede 1971: 82, 87; 1939: 59, 62; N. Egede 1971: 6; 1939: 130),[91] and although shamans apparently were permitted to have sex with spirits, no children (creating blood relations between humans and spirits) were to survive from such contacts, a rule quite similar to that found among some Siberian shamans by Hamayon (1990: 450–51 and note p. 773; cf. Saladin d'Anglure & Morin 1998). Sexual overtones may certainly be inferred in the effect of the interior light of a pupil on the spirits: "How attractive you look, how luminous," an approaching spirit declares. "Could I be the one to come to you in the future [e.g., enter your body at your future performances]? You are so attractive, so luminous!" The pupil agrees, the two parties tell each other their names, and the spirit asks the pupil to touch it (Sandgreen 1987: 317, 348; 1967, II: 92, 119; Sonne 2005: ID 1270, 1275, 1162, 2283). Between "the big fires," *innersuit*, and a pupil, the attraction was mutual, as Naaja experienced when he was approached by two *innersuit* while catching gulls (Naaja means gull): "it felt like they drew him automatically" (Sonne 2005: ID 1219). Did such mutual

90. The record of Missuarniannga's apprenticeship suggests spirit shamans did not become attached to a human shaman (Sonne 2005: ID 2283). The Uupinnguaq story speaks to the contrary, as does another about how Naaja happened to be saved by one of his helping spirits' helping spirit, a *toornaarsuk* (ID 1218).

91. Old East Greenlandic Idisi, an ordinary woman who for several years met with her *innersuaq* husband outdoors at intervals, is the only historical example I could find. No bad consequences are mentioned, but a visit of the *innersuaq* indoors, which was not respected by the residents, made the spirit disappear and apparently give up the relationship (Sonne 2005: ID 1997).

attraction lead to sex? Not always. First, in most contexts the shamans' attracting light concerns the shaman's reenlivening interior. And second, since the majority of helping spirits were male and few hints to homosexuality can be detected (except symbolically in initiations, see below) female rather than male shamans (and spirits) would be tempted. In consonance, female shamans figure in nearly all of the few cases on record about sex with spirits. One case is Ineqinnavaat, whose jealous husband would not permit her to stay in a cave for five days and nights alone with her Qallunaat spirit. The offense led to the husband being mortally hit by a rock slide caused by the spirit, people said. A less clear statement has a monstrous spirit tell Teemiartissaq how to kill off her future human husband at marriage (Sonne 2005: ID 1108), whereas Kaakaaq was given the unmistakable advice by a beautiful female spirit, Saddiniarit, to abstain from *any* sexual liaisons during apprenticeship. Kaakaaq did not follow her advice. Still unmarried, she paid her teacher in sorcery, Kunnak, with sex (ID 1244, 1249) and fell deeply in love with one of her first helping spirits, Aanilaat (ID 1247). No mention is made of their probable sexual relations, or in connection with a spirit baby that Kaakaaq happened to find at the foot of a slope. Delighted, she tried time and again to carry the baby home, but because it grew much too heavy at the range of vision from the tents she never succeeded. It returned on its own to the slope, and hearing the voice of her recently deceased mother at that place Kaakaaq became greatly consoled. Sandgreen, the collector and editor of these recollections, speculates that Kaakaaq had an illegitimate baby stored away. He may be right, but this is hardly the main idea of the story. Besides abiding to the boundary of ordinary human view, the text identifies the baby as being the *inua* of lamp moss and thus closely related to the comforting warmth of her mother's lamp (ID 1248). Much later, at some point past her menopause it seems, an informant stated that Kaakaaq (attracting stories about sex) has an awkward spirit child created.[92] She went far away into the inland region in search of an evil spirit for making a *tupilak* instead of making one on her own (for killing her own son!). Hearing a depressed spirit singing about his sorrow over not having a child with a human being, she approached, became inflamed with desire, and agreed to his wish. The ensuing child was a *tupilak* made by the spirit from the head of a seal Kaakaaq brought along from one of her son's catches. The evil spirit changed the head into the figure of a seal with the ritual cry of a newborn baby, *ungaa*, and the spirit then urged her to make it alive (*uummarsarniaruk*!).[93] She let it suck her genitals; coming to life, the *tupilak* was ordered by the spirit to attack somebody out at sea, and off it went (ID 1275).

The hair-raising intentions of Kaakaaq killing her own son substantiate the use of "evil spirit," a rare term in Greenlandic pre-Christian contexts. Spirits differed by degrees as to their characters and powers, between the extremities of being aggressive and forthcoming, but on the whole they seldom interfered with the social morality of humans. They served their human master, no matter the social moral of his intentions, unless he treated them impolitely. In that case a helping spirit turned aggressive against him or his close kin. Some spirits, like the *qimarratit* used at the beginning of a séance to

92. Kaakaaq's son, Kukkujooq, was one of Sandgreen's chief informants. He suspected his mother of having tried to kill him with a *tupilak* in the figure of either a huge trout or a seal (Sonne 2005: ID 1278, 1282). Her occasional paroxysms took their toll on the family and were not particularly reassuring (ID 1708).

93. Apparently the distinction of "to be or not to be" goes between a newborn nonhuman being belonging to nobody and, after being suckled, to its human "mother."

heighten the thrill, were dangerous and difficult to obtain, and certain spirits of prey would devour and thereby initiate the pupil (see below). Still, being "killed" and regaining consciousness was not unusual during a pupil's first encounter with a spirit. Repeated twice, the spirit became his future helping spirit, as richly exemplified by Missuarniannga's biography (ID 2283).

Individual Property of Spirits and Catches

Since sexual affairs with spirits do not take a prominent position in East Greenlandic shaman biographies and legendary stories (except those about Kaakaaq), which kind of bodily alliances do the shaman's relations with their spirits represent? The fetus-mother relation prevails, being in line with both the idea of actual motherhood as an obstacle to becoming a shaman and that of "seeking a mother" (see above). As an aspect of the dyadic relationship, individual ownership on the part of the shaman prevailed.[94] The aforementioned significant example, drawn from the onset of Christianity and thus speaking to its durability, is the fit of rage befalling Kaakaaq at the news that her last helping spirit has left her by turning to her daughter, Elisabeth (ID 1708). Individual ownership prevailed in the same way that catches made singlehandedly by one hunter were his individual property (encumbered with obligations of sharing [Robbe 1994]), as also ownership was granted to the first pupil to see a spirit in the same way as being first in seeing a polar bear. Spirits could, like personal belongings, be inherited, or given to somebody or taken over by another person. Teemiartissaq received a *qilaneq* spirit from her aunt. Kaakaaq, when humiliated in her youth by proposals from an elder married hunter, attracted a stray helping spirit; upset at the death of its former master, this spirit was immediately ready to defend its new master, Kaakaaq. She had to prevent him from killing the offender (ID 1247). Maratsi tried to get hold of the spirits of the late Ajijak. He summoned Ajijak at his grave but, much to Maratsi's annoyance, he had been anticipated by his own brother, Puukaarteq (ID 1692). So, owing to the idea of individual ownership and inheritance, several helping spirits became old-timers when they, inherited, reappeared at performances of new shamans (Gessain 1975a). They acted like stock characters of plays. Akku, for instance, was clever in having his main helping spirit announce its delight at both being back at the settlement of its former, now-deceased master, a mighty shaman, and pointing to Akku as his worthy successor (Sonne 2005: ID 1312).

In continuance of individual ownership, the pupil made a deal with one helping spirit at a time, and it would not come to his assistance unless called upon (or merely thought of).[95] In this way, the spirits were in a servantlike relationship with their shaman. Turning aggressive due to being neglected, a temperamental spirit was defeated by its shaman in public (e.g., ID 1691, 1690). They did not seemingly attack in cooperation, nor did they have their way without the shaman's consent. If the shaman refrained from performing his *saqqummerneq*, the relations simply weakened. When siding with their master in his personal insults, the spirits proposed to take revenge, but nothing came of it without his consent. As noted above, social morality among humans was really none of their concern. Although

94. The ban on getting human and nonhuman societies mixed up agrees with the Christian edict that "Humans should stay humans and animals stay animals," as a headline by Rasmussen goes (Sonne 2005: ID 612). But all indications point to its validity among the pre-Christian Inuit as well.

95. Sometimes there were two, either a father and son, two brothers, or a nephew and uncle. The pupil was to touch both at the first encounter, and they invariably arrived together (Sonne 2005: ID 1198, 1216, 2283), but hardly possessed him, I suppose.

the pressure for *saqqummerneq* might work and thus have a desired social effect, the spirits' longing for the warmth of their master's interior, and most probably also the human applause had at séances, emerge as the real motivations. When Kaakaaq's spirits at long last obtained their mistress's permission to kill her mother, they paid no heed to social morals. She died from a swollen hand caused by spirits, who were upset that the beautiful Kaakaaq had been handled too strictly by her less-courted widowed mother out of jealousy (ID 1246). As they were true servants, the helping spirits provided for their shaman so long as he fulfilled his social obligations towards them.

Summary

A helping spirit was called a *toornaq* (pl. *toornat*)—i.e., an *inua* or merely an "alien" attached to a shaman either by mutual agreement or by some violent attack on the pupil by the spirit. Other attempts at distinguishing *inuat* from *toornat* have proven futile. Most *toornat* were spirits of the land, inside the surface or beneath the shore and skerries. Some were stranded by the tide. Not much is to be found on instruction, but the knowledge acquired in bits and pieces from various "teachers" constituted only one category among several of knowledge and skills taught and learned. Against common theory about learning in small-scale societies, not all teaching consisted of mute demonstrations. To several examples mentioned above (see p. 262) one can add that spells, for instance, and most probably prescriptions, were taught orally among both ordinary people and shamans. As for the pupil he could be taught how to go in search of helping spirits by demonstration or orally. Some children were offered unprompted advice by some relative—orally.[96]

The pupil acquired most of his *toornat* by going in search of them across uninhabited land. Most often, a spirit was summoned by long hours of rubbing a smaller stone in circles following the way of the sun on a bigger one. The relationship was, as we know, dyadic, but not bilateral insofar as a shaman's helping spirits could join forces in persuasion of their own wishes, such as encouraging their human master's *saqqummerneq*, public initiation. Humans and helping spirits were not equal. Spirits were dependent on the heat of their shaman's interior, by which they—like embryos—became reenlivened during performances, and not the other way round. Their shamans did not, like human shamans, own deceased humans as superior helping spirits. Provided their shaman treated them politely, helping spirits served him irrespective of human social morals. Attempts on the part of a spirit to become related to its master's family, were, of course, unsuccessful. Not much is known regarding shamans' sexual relations with spirits in Greenland. It seems that the pupil/shaman was free to have sex with his spirits, as long as no children came of it. Like a hunter's relation to his prey, private ownership ruled in a shaman's relation to his spirits. However, this ownership did not work unless the spirits were presented in public.

Initiations

Shamans went through initiations in *solitude* during apprenticeship (being secret) and at its end in *public*. By the latter the candidate earned his recognition as a shaman, and he could choose to go through more demanding public initiations at later points for the enhancement of his reputation

---

96. Also Fienup-Riordan and Rearden question the theory about mute learning and emphasize oral teaching among the Yupiit of Southwest Alaska (2013: 29 and the entire paragraph about *qanruyun*: wise words).

and abilities. The solitary initiations lived up to mythic expectations, sometimes demonstrated or told beforehand by a tutor, sometimes known from stories or hearsay, sometimes merely added to the biography of a shaman. The myths served the pupil as a frame of reference for his frightening experiences.

Biographical stories told about the East Greenlandic apprentices' acquisitions of helping spirits and/or particular abilities range from peaceful to frightening encounters, of which the latter clearly follow the tripartite sequence of initiation rituals. They transfer the pupil into a situation of mortal danger, a liminal phase that, from the pupil's point of view, either passes uneventfully in a state of unconsciousness or takes on a series of exciting events framed by well-known myths. Recovery may similarly either occur without much ado or constitute an extended narrative of its own. The outcome or "gain" of the process is usually the "light," *qaamaneq*, or its increase, and/or a future helping spirit. Stories about some initiations *in public* (the *saqqummerneq*) stick to ritual exclusively, whereas others take in descriptions from myth. During his *saqqummerneq* the ideal candidate would make *qaamaneq* ascend by a ritual technique, present his helping spirits, and be accorded the title of a shaman. So *qaamaneq* was in focus as the "gain" of the ideal shamanic rite of solitary initiation to be demonstrated at *saqqummerneq* for future use in public performances.

In Theory

J. P. Schjødt stresses the "gain" as the particular outcome of *initiation rites* in contrast to other tripartite *rites des passage*, the rituals of crises and seasons as categorized by Lauri Honko (1975). In defining the initiation rites, Schjødt first focuses on the symbolic interpretation by Eliade (1975) as a process of death and revival that confers qualities of sacred knowledge. Next he takes in Victor Turner's (1967) contribution about the importance of the liminal phase as the fertile chaos of transition, and finally he turns to Terence Turner (1977) for a useful insight in the structure of the process. T. Turner argues that the three phases of the horizontal course of events in all (tripartite) rites of transition are not on the same level because, as described by Schjødt (see fig. 16): "The horizontal axis differentiates the status and position in the pre- and post-liminal phases, while the vertical signifies the contrast between these and the liminal phase, which regulates the transition between them. The semantic content of the liminal phase is therefore defined as a cultural variable in that it is dependent on the two non-liminal phases" (Schjødt 1986: 97–98). Furthermore, whatever the cultural content, semantic oppositions appear to characterize the transitional entrance to and exit from the liminal phase. In his graphic representations of the sequences within the coordination of the horizontal and vertical axes, Schjødt puts the liminal phase of mixed oppositions on a lower, negative level in relation to both the first and the third sections (my students named this phase "the liminal bucket"). The participants in *the seasonal rites* accordingly descend from the level of ordinary life into the reforming chaos of the liminal phase, and ascend with both their own selves and the world restored to the level of ordinary life. During the *ritual of crisis* the participant(s) start(s) out at a level beyond zero (a lack), continues downwards into and through the liminal bucket, and ascends to the level of ordinary life. During the latter two rituals, neither party has gained anything *new* but merely restored themselves and the world to the level of ordinary life. The outcome of the initiation ritual, however—be it any rise in status such as adulthood, coronation, or, as was said about the initiation in solitude of an Inuit pupil, a new ability—is a gain. *Qaamaneq* is the gain mentioned in most cases, and any acquisition

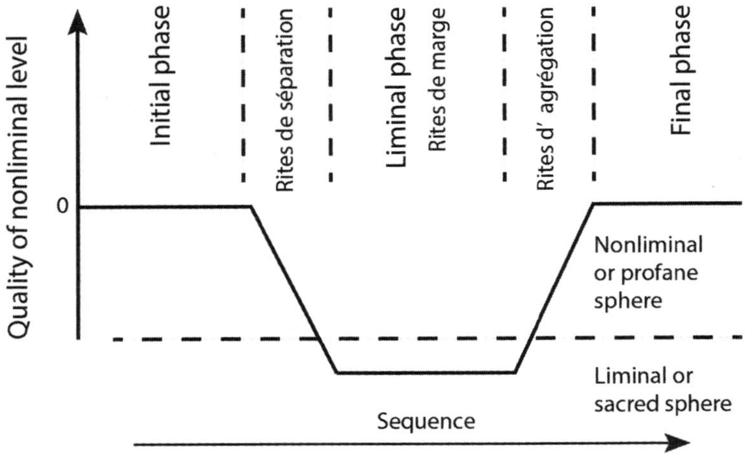

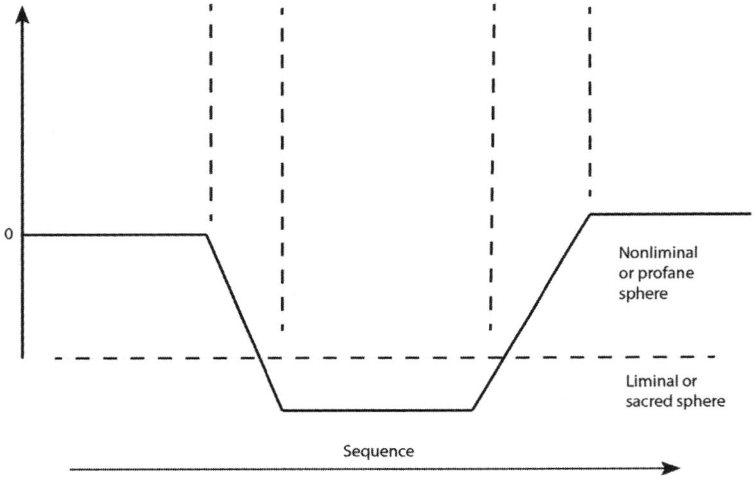

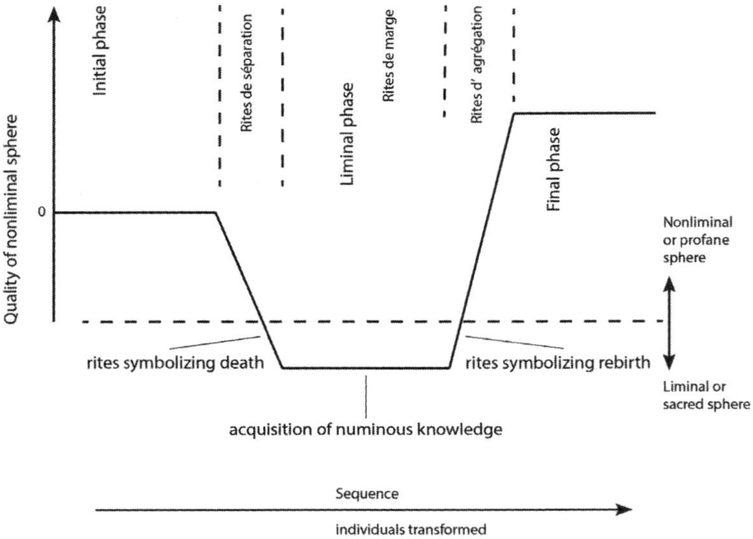

Figs. 15, 16, 17.
Rites of passage: Both calendrical and crisis rites bring the participant(s) from disorder through the liminal sphere back to normal. The initiation rite of death and rebirth brings about something extra, a "gift" of numinous knowledge. *Schjødt (1986), courtesy of J.P. Schjødt.*

of a helping spirit meant further support and a share of its particular powers. For gaining *qaamaneq*, some animal spirits "of prey" stood out as particularly fruitful.[97] To these I shall turn after first highlighting salient cultural semantics of "light" in myth, ritual, and ordinary life.

Shaman's Light (Qaamaneq)

"Every shaman, who experiences moments of trance, knows the instants of interior clarity or a light which seems to fill his soul."[98] Connotative identifications between light, sight, and insight may be universal; at least they are sufficiently numerous between Greenlandic and Western languages to call for careful handling because, in spite of significant overlapping, they do not evoke identical associations all the way round. "Culture," or "worldview," or whichever term for differing frames of interpretation comes into play. The pupil's ways of obtaining the interior light, for instance, hardly seem natural to any native speaker of a Western language. Why should the mythic experience of being devoured and thrown up again by a monstrous predator produce the *qaamaneq* for seeing the Other World(s)? Evoking Christian ideas of God's light created at the beginning of time will only muddle the understanding. The Greenlandic myths of light are a better point of departure.

Light, Movement, Attraction, and Heat

As quoted from Poul Egede's diaries above, "light" in sheer opposition to "darkness" was created by a woman, who expressed the stronger words in a discussion with another woman about death. The latter preferred continuous darkness without death, but the former victoriously chose light and death in exchange for eternal life in darkness (P. Egede 1971: 80; 1939: 57–58). According to Arnaaluk, this event made possible a life of moving about hunting animals in exchange for living from the earth (i.e., immovably, like plants). Still trusting Arnaaluk, we learn that deceased humans rise to heaven as lights, and indeed, the heavenly lights have a great say in understanding *qaamaneq*. Moon (*Qaammat*) and his neighboring star, the Entrails Snatcher (*Nalikkatteeq*), used to be givers of *qaamaneq* (e.g., Sonne 2005: ID 1676). Beneath Moon's house, the heavenly *qulummiin* (W. Grl. *qulummiut*) spirits, to be identified with the ball-playing deceased humans producing the Northern Lights, may see to another initiation.[99] The Sun, too hot to approach, offered pupils "light" only by its "shit," *seqernup anaa* (*Xanthoria elegans*); when placed between the kamik sole and its cover, this orange-colored lichen would attract spirits, the *innersuit* in particular (Victor & Robert-Lamblin 1989–93, II: 242; Holm 1972: 124; 1914: 89). Like the heavenly lights at night, the *innersuit* underneath the foreshore also looked into the dark interior night stomach of *sila*—the *naaq*—as phosphorescence at full moons (Rasmussen 1979: No. 166; H. Egede 1971, 1: 236–37; 1925: 207; P. Egede 1988: 105; Thalbitzer ed. 1933: 192; C. Rosing 1946: 98–99). Lit up by Moon on a regular basis, no wonder the *innersuit* were considered unparalleled hunters at sea. By structural logic, these prehumans ended

97. Considering Morrow and Toby's (1975) interpretation of the figure of a diver with ivory eyes among the Ipiutak shaman objects excavated by Larsen and Rainey as a bird associated with the shaman's "seeing," one may wonder why the diver does not appear among the Greenland givers of *qaamaneq*. Several Greenland variants of "The Blind Boy" who regained his sight by the help of a diver are on record (search "blind" and "Tutigaq" in Sonne 2005).

98. "*Tout angakkok, qui a eu des moments de transe, connaît de clarité intérieure où une lumière semble emplir son âme*" (Missuarniannga in Thalbitzer 1930: 77).

99. *Qulumiq*: hold athletic or song festival + *-miut* (Fortescue et al. 1994: 316; 2010: 344).

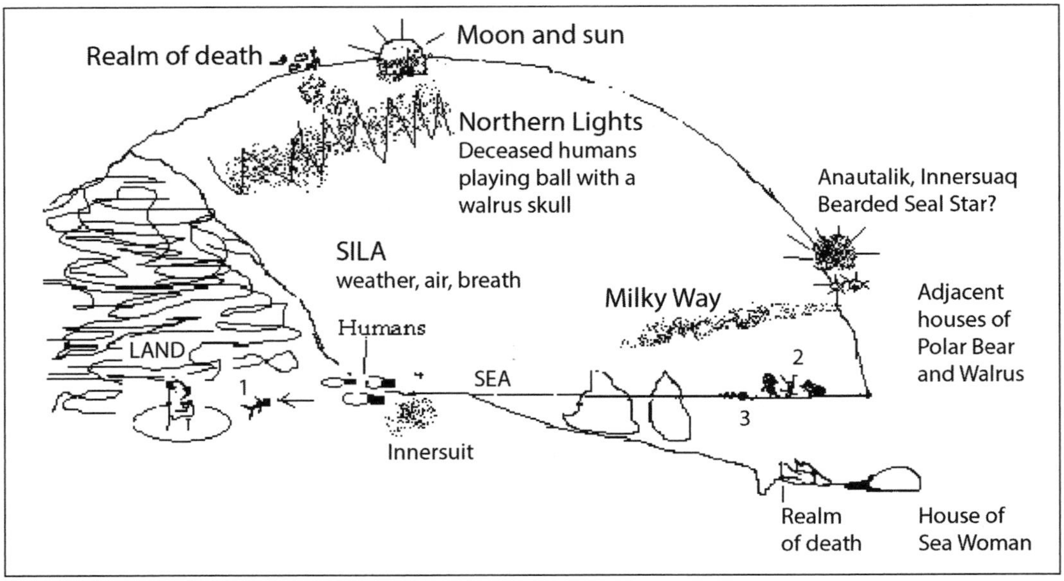

Fig. 18. The two main East Greenlandic shaman initiations: (1) as a pupil on the land by the "freshwater bear," and as a recognized shaman (2) across the sea (3) and back as a skeleton reincarnated en route into an *angakkoq puulik* according to the East Greenlandic worldview. *As imagined and drawn by the author, BS.*

up as light underneath at the turning around of the earth—i.e., in spatial opposition to Arnaaluk's ordinary humans who rose to the sky as heavenly light givers. In short, the heavenly lights and the reflecting *innersuit* looked into the night the same way that the pupil was enabled by his obtained *qaamaneq* to see the Other World(s) of darkness, including the dark interior of ordinary humans as well as the enlightened one of other shamans.

Movement, the other prominent association with "light," tallies with the heavenly bodies; apart from fixed stars, they are themselves constantly on the move. The origin of several heavenly bodies consequently highlights this issue of quick movement. Prominent are conflicts ending in one party pursuing another right unto heaven into an orbit of continued pursuit. The boy of one star myth, for instance, was provoked by an old woman into returning her recurring insults. He had to flee, and was pursued by the old woman. Both rose to the sky, where the old woman holding a stick is still in pursuit of that boy in the constellation of the twin stars announcing the New Year, *Aassuutit* (W. Grl., Holtved 1951, cf. MacDonald 1998: 284). Another *Aassuutit* myth from the Noatak River does not refer to a conflict. Quite on the contrary, it relates the joy caused by this twin star's appearance that predicts the return of the sun: it makes a boy dance ecstatically right into heaven followed by his grandmother, who knows no way to stop him. At New Year you can see them dancing, one star smaller than the other, grandmother and grandson, respectively (MacDonald 1998: 283–84). Still a third idea about *Aassuk* (W. Grl. *Aassuutit*), alias *Aagjuuk* (in the dual) among the Nattilingmiut, identifies its *inua* with the Entrails Snatcher robbing a guest to Moon of his lungs as he cannot resist smiling at her awkward dancing (Rasmussen 1931: 238; Oosten et al. 1999: 59–60). Actually, the only heavenly body explicitly seen to stop temporarily in orbit (by Inuit expression, to "sit," like a woman on the platform) for several days (at latitudes below the Arctic Circle) is the sun at winter solstice (atop its sine curve; see also Fienup-Riordan and Rearden 2013: 62).

Since by comparison the stories and names of stars overlap (MacDonald 1998) in less translucent ways, I better stick to the mutually similar versions of the pan-Inuit origin myth of Moon and Sun, the incestuous story of a big brother and his younger sister recounted above. In addition to the key symbolic aspect of movement being created by light (or vice versa), it points to light's outspoken attraction and heat (a bodily experience by movement as well). The flaming Sun attracts the cooler Moon into continuous pursuit. He in turn attracts the sea in tidal movements, which in turn attract the sea animals and leave a variety of edibles on the shore at low tide. He further enlightens the *innersuit* into visibility, and they also attract game to the coast, as well as a lone kayaker, the common explanation for a young man being lost at sea. The latter is said to feel the attraction of the *innersuit* as a strong current drawing him towards the coast, which raises and lowers itself as during the tide, but at a much faster pace because the sea opens and closes like a mouth (Rasmussen 1979: No. 167). Cultivated mythopoesis![100] Similarly, the deceased humans constituting the Northern Lights were, in their continuous motions between heaven and earth, inclined to attract and catch live humans. Some Greenlanders liked the idea of being caught at the point of dying in exchange for the strenuous walk through bogs to the realm of death (Dalager 1915: 60–61). However, most people feared an untimely death on that account and were warned not to call upon the lights by whistling (MacDonald 1998). We have met with similar opposing ideas about shamans' visit to the Northern Lights. The Iglulik shaman who flew on his own accord to the Northern Lights had great fun, whereas his East Greenlandic colleague was strongly warned against the tempting call of the *Qulummiin* spirits. The slightest look in their direction and he was *drawn* into their midst for an extremely rough handling. And to repeat: a pupil having obtained *qaamaneq* can then attract spirits to volunteer as his future helping spirits.[101]

All four notions—of movement, heat, attraction, and light—are the perceived effects of rubbing a flat stone with a small stone in circular movements, *sila malillugu* (the way of heavenly bodies). In most parts of Greenland this was the common way to attract helping spirits-to-be. Even "rubbing" the surface of a lake by skipping flat stones could have the effect of making a spirit emerge (e.g., Sonne 2005: ID 1241). Rubbing produces heat, and hard stones like quartz, flint, and granite emit sparks when thrown against other hard stones. Correspondingly, lightning was produced by the mythic *Ingnirtoq* by knocking together two stones in heaven above the Baffin Islanders (Boas 1901–7: 498). In Arctic Canada the return of the sun used to be celebrated with a ritual of lights: in analogy with the sun, lamps were extinguished in every igloo, after which fresh dried moss for lamps was lighted by sparks from striking a piece of flint, and the lamps were rekindled. At the same time, this "new light" meant a renewal of life to the participants (cf. MacDonald 1998: 109).

Picking up again the polysemy of stones treated above in the contexts of "Kaassassuk," the additional ideas of fertility and luck in hunting have entered the scene. All in all, since on a higher level stones were means for mediating between the lives of *sila* and its partner *silam aappaa*, the ritual act of attracting spirit helpers-to-be by rubbing stones makes perfect sense. Also, from a Western

---

100. Indeed, the strength of the tidal wave can be greater than the force with which the kayaker can paddle.

101. Among the 347 helping spirits listed by Reverend G. Peck, a great number are said to emit light and give joy to the conjuror (Laugrand, Oosten & Trudel 2000).

psychological point of view, the repetitive rubbing for hours on end was liable to alter the pupil's state of consciousness into having visions by the production of dopamine. With training merely rubbing one's palms produced the same effect (e.g., Sonne 2005: 1696, 1699, 1702).[102]

The Experience of Change in Vision

According to an Inuit "theory of complementarity" (my phrase), no human person can see both This and the Other World clearly at the same time. Like in the common experience of "seeing pictures" at the point of falling asleep as well as upon waking up from a dream, the shaman's vision becomes blurred between the two states of seeing. Either way, the transition may effect a splitting up in layers, or a stratification, of one's vision, which makes way for a clear sight of the opposite world (Sonne 2005: ID 1668, 1688, 1695, 1701; Victor & Robert-Lamblin 1989–93, II: 245; Boas 1901–7: 133).[103]

The change, which by various techniques is called forth during *saqqummerneq* and consecutive performances, was experienced acutely during apprenticeship. Kaakaaq, for instance, when invited to visit a future helping spirit, suddenly felt her vision split in the middle of nowhere. A few moments later the hidden entrance to the spirit's home stood out clearly before her eyes (Sonne 2005: ID 1701). Later, returning from her visit to her sparrow spirit, the same transition in view made Kaakaaq realize that the gifts she received for being a midwife to the sparrow's wife were of no use in the ordinary world (ID 1702). Her son, Kukkujooq, had his vision changed into a very wide view on top of a towering cliff at the sea by a helping spirit striking his eyes. The change came gradually: "At the second stroke I felt the object of my view [the reduced icebergs in the sea far below] change and mist over but disperse with small dark spots. All of a sudden, without noticing his third stroke my recent view changed completely. The sea with its marked icebergs had disappeared. In front of me were three things like fog banks in a row, and they spread out to the sides with some distance apart, the first gap being wider than the second. And darkness reigned between them." The spirit then explains how the first gap leads to the realm of death below and the second farther out to Sea Woman. Kuukujooq, who wants to see his deceased father, chooses the first (ID 1287, tr. BS).

102. Less obvious to read is the placing of a crab or a crayfish between the small rubbing stone and the bigger flat one (Thalbitzer 1930: 178; Sonne 2005: ID 988). Both belong in the liminal, shallow waters of the sea, and both were used as amulets for assisting a difficult birth (Sonne 2005: ID 1059, 1523, 339); the crab is noticed for both its claws (like hands, *assagiaq*, in W. Grl.), its legs (for walking, *pisuutilik*, see ID 1457), and its eyes (ID 211, 1457, 1458). In the same vein Missuarnianga was asked to wash his entire naked body with a stone covered with seaweed from just beyond the limit of low tide. Next he was to use this stone for rubbing in order to promote the coming of his "light" (ID 2283). Maybe because the rubbing took place on land (Thalbitzer 1909: 94), some being or object belonging to the sea—but found on the mediating foreshore—was felt to be appropriate for a completion. Most spirits summoned by rubbing, whether or not they belonged below, arrived from below through the earth via deep caves, streams, or lakes—i.e., the recommended places for rubbing.

103. Mind the reference to Boas concerning Inuit in Canada. The light of the transition can be likened to the dizzying glare reflected by snow and ice, provoking snow blindness. Teemiartissaq's brother obtained his *qaamaneq* by such light on the inland ice (Sonne 2005: ID 1110); Ajijak had it demonstrated by permitting the audience to see his helping spirits lined up for a first presentation. People could not stand to look, as the light made one dizzy (J. Rosing 1963: 228; Sonne 2005: ID 1676).

Initiations through Death and Revival

The common idea that an experience of death and revival mediates access to the Other World(s) must rest with the equally common mythic fact that death brings one to a world beyond and by rebirth—in a culturally specific way—back into This One.[104] To the Inuit, ordinary rebirth was secured through the naming of a newborn baby, whose deceased namesake(s) supported the growth of the child. In case a sister or brother had recently died, the baby was received as an *angerlartoqut*, that is, a "home comer," and thus given back its own name (see p. 396). Similarly a live hunter was a "home comer" upon his delayed return from some mishap at sea, and demanded a particular ritual of revival performed, preferably by his mother (Sonne 2005: ID 506, 14, 19; Victor & Robert-Lamblin 1989–93, II: 338–39; see fig. 26, p. 395). As analysis will show, the "home comer," like the pupil initiated on his own accord, was "reborn" outside an ordinary mother's womb, from the womb of the Other World, and both were credited abilities for becoming a shaman.

Initiations in solitude supplied the apprentice with means for "seeing" and attracting future helping spirits. The accounts of the particular experience of being devoured and thrown up again are in fact (or fiction) very similar. The eater, the "freshwater bear," was a monstrous bear, dog, water beetle, or *Sermersuup Inua*, a giant of the inland ice, whereas the Entrails Snatcher never came to eat the cut out entrails of the visitor to Moon as the latter saw to their rescue. Nor did deceased humans like the *qaamaneq*-giving Northern Lights or a ghost summoned to its grave or a mountaintop devour the pupil. The former might handle the pupil very roughly and the latter might make him lose consciousness for a while, but, faithful to their human origin, neither committed cannibalism. Beyond the question of reality versus myth, Akku had an experience of a real "death" and revival, and this memorable event got its story in revealing consonance with the ideas about the shaman's bodily exercises with breathing during performances:

At age six Akku apparently died from a nosebleed. He was buried but came back to life within the grave, where he had to struggle to reunite his soul with his body. One variant has him (his soul) observe his anus widen and shrink, showing the body's desire to get back its soul. The body is placed on top of three big stones, forming a staircase that he has to climb. Surmounting the first step he immediately starts to yell "*hajee, hajee, hajee*"; this is the ritual cry of a performing shaman who returns to his lifeless body (Thalbitzer 1923: 489). This cry facilitates both his climbing the two remaining steps and the slipping into his body through the anus. He screams until people remove the cover stone for a happy reunion with his mourning parents (Sonne 2005: ID 967).

The other variant gives way to a more dramatic ascent of the soul, which fails during the first attempt because the soul can only inhale but not exhale his breath. This is to be understood as the shaman's opposite ritual technique of pressing out his soul through the anus by exhaling without inhaling. In this way, the performing shaman's interior light could ascend to see the Other World and make room for a helping spirit to enter. Also, the soul of Akku's attempt at simply joining his parents mourning at the grave is deemed a failure (because he is no ghost, who in that case would only scare them and not come back to earthly life). Eventually, having managed to climb all three steps, he slips into his body with sparks flashing before his eyes (ID 1312). Since at this point Akku, according to

104. This of course excludes the anti-reincarnation creeds of Christianity, Islam, and Judaism. Nontheless, *angerlartussiaq* naming is still practiced. See Trondheim (2009).

both variants, had already been taught some shamanism by his grandfather, his death and revival is seen as a sign of a glorious career. Thus "light," the true follower of transitions between *sila* and *silam aappaa*, also marked the reunion of Akku's recovered soul with his live body.

At a later point Akku had to go through the solitary initiation of becoming devoured and thrown up again by "the freshwater bear," an experience mentioned only in passing (ID 967).[105] Perhaps his burial and revival, an event that everybody could observe, overshadowed the imagined one of secret initiation in solitude.

Initiation by Individual Deceased Humans

Heavenly light used to be the source of *qaamaneq* (or knowledge, *sila*), also in the case that the giver is a single deceased human. Shamans, as we know, could ask advice from a mountaintop (N. Egede 1971: 87; 1939: 180), the place where Akku received his first pat on the back from a descending ghost. And when by rubbing the cover stone of a grave, the pupil invited its deceased person to appear, it made its descent by a rainbow, a lightning at twilight, or a streak of light; it might return as the Northern Lights, connecting earth with the upper realm of death (Sonne 2005: ID 370, 1907, 1764, 187, 1254, 2283).[106] The performing shaman who placed a small child on his lap or directly on a grave might similarly invite an initiating ghost from above (ID 187, 370, 1907). Thus, one unknown man succeeded in making his son into an apprentice (or shaman). He took him to a fairly new grave, made a hole in the grave clothes at the body's abdomen, and then asked his son to put in his finger. The son obeyed, and the father withdrew; the son wanted to follow but was stopped by the father and ordered to stay put until twilight,[107] and then, as soon as fire (the dead person) came down (to the body), to flee. The light struck, and the father took to his heels, but the boy could not get loose. He stayed away for a long while and then returned—smiling—in the middle of the night. The satisfied father had completed his job, and the story ends (ID 187).

The Northern Lights, Moon, and *Nalikkatteeq*

Qaammatip Inua, the *inua* of the moon (Moon), his neighboring star, *Nalikkatteeq* (the Entrails Snatcher), and the Northern Lights were prominent among the sources of the shaman's *qaamaneq*. A rare example from West Greenland, taken down after half a century of mission at Aasiaaq, relates

105. Missuarniannga offers an objection to some new idea voiced by Akku about the relations between water beetle (*minngua*) and the freshwater bear. It remains a mystery (Thalbitzer 2014: 72).

106. Although light shines in the lower realm of death (P. Egede 1971: 71–72, 67; 1939: 52, 50; N. Egede 1971: 36–37; 1939: 149; Sonne 2005: ID 592, 1196, 1697), the inhabitants are not on record as light givers—quite on the contrary, as in the case of Missuarniannga, who against custom achieved ghosts as his *last* helping spirits. On a visit to the lower realm, he made his own interior light revive the deceased humans for an ascent to heaven with the Northern Lights (Sonne 2005: ID 2283). In my understanding, he is likened to a resurrecting Christ of pagan ancestors by the storyteller, his son, the catechist Kaarali Andreassen. In West Greenland, *innersuit* were the common light-giving initiators, whether inside a deep cave or below the shore. In one variant they apparently cut up the pupil, after which his deceased grandparents ascend from below, heal him, and return him home with the promise that his helping spirits (a walrus and three *innersuit*) will bring back his clothes—an *angerlartussiaq* type of story (ID 1078). Another version merely returns the novice naked back to earth, whereupon his clothes appear, flying toward him (ID 392). The Moravian Hendrik's version presented above (note 88) has another, clear agenda by his ranking (E. Grl.) initiation by being sucked out in a dried-up lake far above the initiation inside a cave (ID 1803).

107. *Naar*-time in fact.

the solitary initiation of Kanak, who may have been a historical person. Depressed because his elder brothers exclude him from their kayak hunts by stealing his paddle, he turns his back on society and follows the swampy way of the deceased. He encounters and shakes hands with a great number of singing people, who take him along toward heaven. Looking back he realizes that his helping spirit, a lamp stick (for trimming the burning moss of the lamp), follows him with a blazing flame. Close to heaven he hears a voice, telling him to change direction. This is Moon inviting him for a meal served by Moon's sister, the Sun, and a demonstration of his powers: one of taking in the entire world below, another of provoking the first menstruation of a young unmarried girl. Next *Nalikkatteeq* enters the room ready to cut out Kanak's entrails at the slightest smile on his face at her extremely funny dancing. But Kanak, advised by Moon to rub the nails of his little fingers in the hollow of his knee, passes through this ordeal unhurt. Overpowered by this trick, *Nalikkatteeq* falls backwards into the entrance tunnel. She has her servants ask in vain for the dish she left behind, but eventually, by her threat of making the pillars supporting heaven give way, Moon gives in. He returns the dish, cutting nasty notches along the edge. The time has come for Kanak to return, says Moon, who slips him out through the hatch at the window. Losing consciousness he feels nothing until received by his grandmother on earth. As stated in the end, he has by now become a great shaman (Sonne 2005: ID 159).

Apart from the European custom of shaking hands with the people receiving him en route to heaven, this story follows tradition. These deceased humans of the Northern Lights who welcome Kanak in their midst have to let go of him at Moon's calling. This means that Kanak is neither dead nor going to die, as also repeated by Moon's advice for how to avoid smiling at *Nalikkatteeq*.[108] Kanak is placed in a female position, because he is bereaved of the male symbol, his paddle, a necessity for kayaking, and left with a female symbol, the lamp stick, for his means of transport to heaven; this evokes the wrong idea that male shamans generally were poor hunters in real life. Simultaneously, however, he is apparently accorded great shamanic powers due to his mix of male and female symbols of light (Moon and lamp stick). This mythic initiation not unexpectedly follows the sequence of any initiation rite as defined above: Kanak is made to remove himself from society and subsequently enters the Other World along the route of the dead for a liminal threatening stay, returning with the "gain" of great shamanic powers. The reintegration into society on earth is emphasized by the reception given him by his grandmother.

Another mythic example, described in detail above, of the close association between woman, lamp, and Moon, takes a less successful course in spoiling the promising career of a female pupil. She, who trains together with her little brother, Ajijak, neglects an old lamp in her care. When it takes fire, the angered Moon takes away her soul (like Kanak's blazing lamp stick, the lamp on fire sends Ajijak's sister off towards Moon. However, the latter's is a journey of no return). As you may remember, in this event Moon arrives on a punishing expedition causing a splendid series of séances led by the famous Uitsaleqanngitseq/Karraq. Among the audience is Ajijak, still a child and later to become a

108. A Baffin Island variant has Moon guide a woman who is to encounter *Ululirnang* (much like *Nalikkatteeq*) in exactly the same way: "If you cannot help laughing, put your left hand under your knees, and then raise it with all the fingers bent down from the second joint except the middle finger, which you must extend." This woman not only avoids smiling but also scares *Ululirnang* by removing her hand and pointing the outstretched finger at her. Terrified, *Ululirnang* takes it for a bear and flees (Boas 1901–7: 198–99). A mythic reflection of some ritual or children's play, I propose.

great shaman. Three versions are on record about his *saqqummerneq*, one by Kaarali Andreassen, one by Sandgreen, and the most recent by Saajooq (Sonne 2005: ID 1311, 1271, 1674 + 1675 + 1676). They agree in that both have Ajijak visit the *Qulummiin* spirits (Northern Lights) and return for the only reason that his father had made him into an *angerlartussiaq* (potential home comer). Kaarali names this ritual Ajijak's *saqqummerneq*. Sandgreen's informant merely narrates the course of events. Saajooq's version, however, not only adds the introductory story about the sister's poor fate, he also has Ajijak's father decide to postpone the his *saqqummerneq* because Ajijak needs supplementary helping spirits for becoming a great shaman. These he receives through a consecutive visit to Moon after the return from the Northern Lights. The reason for both the introductory and latter additions seems to be a lack of stories about Ajijak's apprenticeship: as Kaarali was told a generation earlier than Saajooq, it was because his older sister had died that Ajijak was destined to become a shaman. In consequence he passed quietly through and acquired his helping spirit without any exceptional events (ID 1311). Apparently then, Saajooq, Ajijak's great-grandson, fills out the account by adding additional moonlight stories about Ajijak.

Being Devoured by Moon's "Freshwater Bear"

Missing in the biography of the otherwise famous Ajijak is the myth attached to any East Greenlandic shaman of some greatness. It describes the transformative event of being devoured by a monstrous being emerging from a stream or a lake. Called the "freshwater bear" or "freshwater dog," this is either an oversize, slim polar bear with a thick neck, a monstrous dog (known also among the Northwest Greenlanders [Sonne 2005: ID 864]), or a water beetle monster. By structural categories the ordinary species of both polar bear and dog were transitional beings, the former the animal of both land and sea par excellence, and the dog a wild predator living with, fed by, and domesticated by humans. So, in consonance with theories of the liminal phase, they were perfectly qualified for mediating transformations. In addition, these particular freshwater monsters belonged to Moon as part of his identity and could act as substitutes on his behalf. Like Moon, the "freshwater bear" would punish the breaking of taboo with hail, snow, earthquakes, thunder, and lightning (Rüttel 1917: 216; Sonne 1990: 15; Victor & Robert-Lamblin 1989–93, II: 334, 387); like Moon, the bear might also threaten to ruin or even to flood the house (Victor & Robert-Lamblin 1989–93, II: 387; Sonne 2005: ID 1343). During the notorious performance of driving away the punishing Moon in person by Karraq and his colleagues, Moon's dogs were heard barking in the air and his bear growling beneath the ice. Called "the one dressed (from top to toe) in polar bear skin," you could take Moon for a bear (Gessain 1978).[109] His dog, lacking skin on its forehead (Sonne 2005: ID 1347), emphasizes the phallic character it shares with numerous other mythic dogs among the Inuit (Sonne 2005: ID 1523, 1597, 588, 1059; Sonne 1990; Saladin d'Anglure 1990a). Both bear and dog symbolize, or, better, connote, Moon's phallic power, by which he engenders life on earth in spring and calls forth the menstruation of young girls (e.g., Thalbitzer 1928). You might call the two animals his extended potency. In its manifestations, recognized by the Inuit and dealt with above, the moon sets the waters of the earth in motion daily by the tides, increasing in level at new and full moons, particularly at spring tide when

109. The West Greenlandic Moon was dressed in white caribou skins, an animal of the land not extant in East Greenland since the 15th century.

Fig. 19. "The freshwater bear" ready to consume the unconscious pupil. Drawing by Kaarali Andreassen. *Owned by Oli Madsen, public domain.*

it forces water to penetrate the ice of lakes and shores. Perhaps you may observe, as did the little boy Naaja, a small waterfall in a stream suddenly start to run upwards. It takes imagination, however, to witness an oversize reddish dog being formed in the rising water and approach, as in Naaja's case. Naaja took flight, but stumbled and was devoured (Sonne 2005: ID 1222, 1221, 1236). Kaakaaq called forth her initiating polar bear by skipping stones on a lake. A column of water rose at the center of the lake, broke down, rose again and broke down, and when it reached its third peak the column made Kaakaaq break down. A monstrous bear then emerged with its back to Kaakaaq. It turned around, lay down, and started swimming towards her. She was about to run home to announce her "catch" (being the first to see a polar bear meant ownership of the killed bear), when she felt immovably glued to the ground. Like Naaja, she lost consciousness before being devoured. And, like Naaja, she was woken up at the last minute by a helping spirit at sunset, stark naked and freezing but whole and hale. Both were met by their clothes while running home (ID 1241, 1703). This myth of initiation in solitude, told about several pupils in slight variations (ID 575, 966, 967, 971, 972, 984, 985, 988, 1017, 2031, 2088, 2283), points to Moon's freshwater monsters of *rising waters* as the initiating beings. The pupil's "gain," if stated, is most frequently either explicitly *qaamaneq* (ID 971, 1222, 1703, 1803, 2032,

2088) or implicitly the identical ability of seeing and/or attracting helping spirits (ID 575, 966, 984, 1108, 2031).[110]

Another devouring spirit, said to equal the freshwater bear in powers conferred on the pupil (Thalbitzer 1930: 78), is the *inua* of the inland ice, *Sermersuup Inua.* Regaining consciousness from this ritual death, Aadaarutaa merely had to close his eyes to see things happening at a distance, at his settlement or at sea among the seals (Sonne 2005: ID 2032, 2088). Obviously his "gain" was *qaamaneq*. Naaja, who hunted up this being for a second initiation of being devoured, and then had to pass through a pitch-dark tunnel in the obvious symbolism of birth into the light of This World, was already supplied with "light," but "he felt greatly enriched in capabilities and skills" (ID 1215). In the composition of Naaja stories, these abilities soon lead him to commit the first in a series of murders (ID 1214).

Teemiartisssaq's brother went through a similar process. He got two giants belonging to the (nunataks of the) inland ice for his helping spirits and was enabled to return home by flying. The intermediate episodes are barely transparent in the record (ID 1110), but read with the above story about Naaja in mind, the story reveals itself as just another version, though following an opposite course of events. While Naaja is eaten first and then led by two dwarves through a pitch-dark tunnel of the inland ice, shunning the light at the end and then returning into darkness, Teemiartissaq's brother encounters the two giants as a start. Since neither party can stand the dizzying light on the ice, the giants invite him inside the ice, where terrible darkness reigns but fortunately no cracks lurk to swallow the wanderer. They ask him to go look for the aggressive polar bear with the peculiar face that is twice the size of a normal one, and they help him (as did the dwarves for Naaja) pass by some hindrances; after this they leave him and disappear toward the dark north (inside the ice). The confrontation with the monstrous bear is, for untold reasons, missing. Supposedly he was devoured and thrown up again for a fresh reincarnated "birth." His "gain," the ability to fly, may have been earned either from this supposed process or from the giants (as did Missuarniannga from the medium-size giants [ID 2283]). As we know, they were famous for traveling by the bridges of fog formed from their frozen breath between the mountaintops.

The term "freshwater dog" is further applied to the oversize figure of a water beetle, *minngua*, which devoured Ajukutooq (ID 988). No effect is mentioned, such as the acquisition of *qaamaneq*. Nor is light the obvious association to *minngua*! Rather, its transformations and ways of movement come to the fore. In its manifest form this beetle is, on its own scale, as predatory as any bear or dog. In transformations, *minngua* beats them all by changing from grub to pupa to beetle, and also surpasses them in ways of movement. The polar bear walks on ice and land, swims on the surface of the sea, and dives to some extent. The dog can run, dig holes, hop, and swim. But the water beetle can fly, dive, and even "skate" over the surface of the lake (Brehm 1907, III: 296ff). Traveling abilities such as gliding (like skating) may have been the "gain" insofar as Ajukutooq denied being able to fly.

110. In no visible association to Moon, other heavenly bodies, or the *innersuit*, have, in a singular statement, the *unconscious* pupil attract a great number of helping spirits of all kinds, who appear to him by telling him their (secret?) names. Afterwards he can call on any of them by name for support (Thalbitzer 1930: 78).

Being Sucked Out

In a story told by the Moravian Hendrik of East Greenlandic heritage, the *minngua* is involved in another way of initiating the pupil. It literally sucks the pupil to death (for a new revival),[111] and then the pupil gains *qaamaneq* to the full. The place is a dried-up lake or bog, it seems, perhaps where the swampy route taken by ordinary deceased humans begins (Sonne 2005: ID 1803). One obvious association is the mythic larva *qullugiaq*, which sucks blood from its adoptive mother. She becomes completely emaciated while it grows to immense size instead of transforming into an ordinary flying insect. When the *qullugiaq* is killed by her family or neighbors, the entrance tunnel fills with blood, an Inuit symbolic analogy with menstruation and birth (ID 77, 608, 1296, 1297, 1604, 2229).[112] In an elaborated Baffin Island version, the story starts at the beginning of time when babies were to be found on the ground. Baby boys were scarce, nor did they grow into adulthood at same speed as girls insofar as the only boy found was still very young when married to his adoptive mother's sister. She had never succeeded in finding any babies, and although married, she continued to go in search of babies. Finding none, she found and adopted a chrysalis, which sucked blood from various parts of her body and became still more demanding. Lacking blood, the emaciated woman had to go begging for food, because her young husband was still no seal hunter. He sat immovable on the platform like a woman, naked to the hip and tending the lamp. However, at the moment the monster—left by the outgoing mother in its bed (pupa), a stocking in a leg of her trousers—leaped out and started to suck blood from the young man's sides, he had enough. Tearing off the creature, he flung it into the entrance tunnel to the dogs. Whining loudly, they made short work of it, devouring the beast. "Its blood was spattered all over the porch and over their pelts." The returning adoptive mother died of grief (Boas 1901–7: 178–79).

Evidently the development of larva through pupa to a flying, biting, bloodsucking insect is the outer frame of reference within which the very beginning of natural reproduction takes its course; it is embedded as in the Inuit symbolism of gender, menstruation, sex, house, and movement. To wit: trusting Saladin d'Anglure's informants, the father builds up the embryo's skeleton by feeding it with his semen, the mother builds its blood by her blood, and both create its flesh by the animals they eat (Saladin d'Anglure 1986: 39; Sonne 2005: ID 343, 588). The tunnel and interior of the house are likened to a woman's vagina and uterus (*ibid.*), and movement is an Inuit key symbol (see above). Thus, fed by the blood of its "mother" the pupa is likened to a fetus with a growing appetite. She has to eat out (with sexual overtones), because her husband, immature with regard to sealing and, consequently, also sexually, procures neither food for his wife nor semen for feeding the fetus. So the couple has still not consummated their marriage. But at the moment the creature, out of hunger, leaves its "bed" (the parts of its mother's clothing for moving about), it is "born" from its pupa. Thus enabled to move on its own as an insect, it bites the young man as if he were a nursing woman performing his female role of tending the lamp. Its painful bite wakes the boy up along with his (phallic) dogs, who know how to fulfill the consumption. Menstrual blood fills the tunnel.

111. See *milluarpaa* (Thisted & Thorning 1996: 180, 182, note 1).

112. Shocking? Most probably.

Now, considering the role accorded to this creature in myth, its transformative power may explain its presence in a passage of a very unclear text told by Teemiartissaq.[113] She relates her initiation by a butterfly, perhaps a bloody being. Puzzled, Thalbitzer asked Aadaarutaa for a translation some eight years later, but, still confused, Thalbitzer proposed one himself; in my view, his is in better keeping with the above symbolism (not expounded by Thalbitzer): the initiating creature, an *isarqatäta*, is no full-fledged butterfly (*isaqqiiq*) but still a pupa at the point of bursting. A chrysalis is called a *puulinngortoq* in West Greenlandic, "somebody having become supplied with a bag" or, in the spirit language, with a "mother."[114] Teemiartissaq envelops herself into and/or loses her flesh to it. Reincarnated, she sees the creature lick up all the blood (Thalbitzer 1923: 455, 460 notes 4–7; resumed in Sonne 2005: ID 1108). So, choosing Thalbitzer's interpretation, the course of events comes close to that of being sucked out by a *minngua*, a water beetle. Georg called this particular "dog" by its name in the spirit language, *puunnguatsiaq*, the disgusting (*-tsiaq*) dog (*puunnguaq*) or little (*-nnguaq*) mother (*pooq*) (Qúpersimân 1972: 62).[115] Taken together, all these transformative (i.e., border-transcending) freshwater beings combine male and female symbols of engendering, eating, feeding, and birth.

We still have to consider a slimy creature that assaulted Maratsi. It is hard to identify except for its association to "light." Like the dog devouring Naaja, it became visible in a small waterfall of an inland stream running upwards (caused by the powers of Moon, I presume). The creature took the form of a big blue tent, which crept slimily over Maratsi's body. The tent, or better the central tent pole, sometimes bears phallic meanings (Holm 1972: 124; 1914: passage left out!), as might the slimy track, which nevertheless more directly would refer to Maratsi's first, luminous initiating wing snail. As you may remember, this snail was attracted to the inland region by its teacher's stone rubbing and returned to the sea on its own; and Maratsi, having lost consciousness due to the creepy blue tent, unwittingly follows the same trail. At the point he regains consciousness he finds himself lying at the shore (Sonne 2005: ID 1686). With fewer details, Teemiartissaq, lying down at a stream calling on whichever spirit it pleased to arrive, obtained her first initiation by a similarly colored creature emerging in a stream. In consonance with myth, she lost consciousness and clothing and then regained both in the ordinary mythic way (ID 1109).

Symbolism of Being Devoured and Regurgitated

Structurally, on an etic level the process of being devoured by an animal may simply recall the opposite one of a hunter killing and eating the flesh of an animal, which is believed to become reincarnated through rites and prescriptions. But neither the hunter nor his family members throw up the meat and blubber, unless they get sick. They keep up their bodies, get rid of the ingestible matter the other way out, and, according to the symbolism mentioned above, they produce children by the fluids created by the food they eat. In continuation of this body symbolism, I take the father's ejaculation as an act of vomiting in the same way as his "dog" spits semen for the fetus to eat and the *inua* (person) of the moon sends out snow through a tube put to his mouth (Sonne 2005: ID 588, 1059, 1597, 440;

---

113. On the continuing fear of transformational insects, see Laugrand and Oosten (2010; 2015: 113–47).

114. Somebody who (*-toq*) has become (*-nngor*) supplied with (*-lik*) a bag (*pooq*).

115. According to Peter Irniq (Nunavut), *punnguq*, the spirit dog, served the shaman as a helping spirit in finding animals, finding one's way home in a blizzard, and threatening spirits to be chased away (Tester 2010: 132).

Rink 1866–71, I: No 15; see also drawing in Saladin d'Anglure 1986: 46).[116] The phallic connotations of this engendering *inua*'s freshwater animals, the oversize polar bear and dog, appear spectacularly emphasized by the rising waters announcing their emergence. Yet the analogy I see between eating and having sex is such a Western idea (of consumption) that it asks for Greenlandic examples. The origin myth of Sun and Moon is an obvious one. Discovering that her brother, the Moon, was her secret lover in the cover of darkness, Sun cuts off a breast and throws it to his feet like feeding a dog with the words, "I seem to be to your taste, eat this as well!" (e.g., Sonne 2005: ID 180, 1086, 1087, 1088, 1123, 1519, 1595; Rasmussen 1929: 81; Boas 1964: 189–90; 1901–7: 173). In the same line of thought, among the Inuit in Canada, stealing meat was identified with adultery (Saladin d'Anglure 2001: 119). In short, Moon's polar bear or dog satisfies its appetite on the pupil and ejaculates his flesh, a quick conception that has the pupil wake up naked as a newborn baby. The same interpretation does not work for the carnivorous or sucking water beetle and the bloody pupa. Rather, their transformational powers seem to work in association with a female symbolism of procreation (see also Oosten & Laugrand 2010; Laugrand & Oosten 2015: 113–47).

Entering and Leaving the Liminal Phase

Movement characterizes the first, removal phase of the solitary initiation. As a prelude, the pupil leaves the inhabited environment of humans, heading solo for the hinterland. The small child Naaja was out berry picking with his grandmother when suddenly he felt an irresistible urge to rove about the surroundings. His grandmother complied, suspecting that he might be pulled at by somebody (from *asia*). He came upon a small stream and started to jump repeatedly from one edge to the other, when the conspicuous small waterfall running upwards made him stop. He saw the monster take form, and then he fled, stumbled, and lost consciousness (Sonne 2005: ID 1236). Tomboy Kaakaaq was skipping stones when she saw the water column rise three times at the center of the lake, and then the bear emerged and approached. She felt glued to the ground, lost consciousness, and was devoured (ID 1241). Sanimuinnaq and Georg Quppersimaan did likewise without this particular effect of the foreboding rising of a water column (ID 575, 966). Alternatively, some anonymous informant was himself thrown twice around by the bear before being devoured. He rubbed forth the monster from the lake with stones the ordinary way (ID 985), as did Missuarniannga, bringing forth a maelstrom that made the lake rise and fall towards the shore (like the tide) and thus provoked the emergence of the bear. It looked much like a dog (ID 2283).

Regardless of whether the monster of prey announces its arrival by raising columns of water or strong tidal movements, its emergence brings the pupil to a sudden halt. Glued to the ground, he soon finds himself paralyzed. He mercifully loses consciousness as well as his clothes, pointing to nakedness as a prerequisite for transformation. One variant has it that the clothes were as scared as their owner, but unlike him were able to flee at the sight of the monstrous predator (ID 1221). Waking up shivering cold at the liminal point of the setting sun, the pupil starts running homewards for reintegration, still frightened, and en route becoming dressed by his own clothes returning in two

116. When the moon makes snow, it is alternatively said to pee some muddy fluid (like semen) (Sonne 2005: ID 350).

parts: anorak first, trousers with kamiks last. Not until fully dressed did Kaakaaq eventually feel safe and confidently returned to her true self (ID 1241).

So, in entering and leaving the liminal phase, entering means immobility, a loss of clothing (that is, identity), as well as consciousness (*sila* and balance), giving way to the loss of one's flesh. For leaving the liminal phase the neophyte lying immobile on its back, naked like a newborn baby, is brought back to consciousness by his waking-up spirit (a tiny dwarf, see *ijaajavatsiaq* above), shivering cold and on the transitional *naar*-point in time of getting lost forever after. Recovery occurs through movement, by getting to one's feet, running for warmth, and becoming dressed in one's own familiar clothing. The pivotal point of transformation—nakedness—plays the decisive part in the symbolism of initiations in solitude. However reasonable this hypothesis of nakedness sounds, it does not fit in all cases of transformation, as will be shown below.

Louise Grandorf (2004; 2005) has the entire process fit the theory about "prey into hunter" proposed by Maurice Bloch (1992).[117] Being tortured and devoured, the prey—i.e., the apprentice—becomes one with the predator, an identification that turns him into a hunter himself. By violence he has to recapture his daily life in order not to lose the benefits gained from the initiation, defined by Bloch as the overcoming of the transitoriness of life. In Grandorf's analysis the recapture of the clothing becomes the prey. I do not quite agree. The recapturing is actually done by the clothing of the still-terrified pupil while he is fleeing home. They insist, sometimes barring his way, sometimes dressing him on their own accord. But neither they nor the redressed pupil are exactly violent. Only Naaja can be credited with a violent behavior in imitation of his predator, the "freshwater dog." Upon returning to the camp, he begins playing with the other boys while he, ravenously hungry, *tears* mouthfuls of meat from the shank of a seal. Cutting the meat off with a knife was the civilized way (Sonne 2005: ID 1221). Later, when grown into an able hunter, Naaja certainly turns violent after his second initiation by the *inua* of the inland ice, *Sermersuup Inua*. Already experienced and resistant, he remains conscious while being eaten right until the giant cuts into his heart (this is some kind of civilized predator by the way, using an iron knife for cutting the meat from the bones). Regaining consciousness, Naaja finds himself inside the mouth of the tunnel, but no mention is made of his clothing. He is led through the tunnel by his two dwarves for a symbolic rebirth into the light of the setting sun. You cannot help feeling that something is missing (nakedness and clothing). Is this on purpose? At closer inspection a substitute is placed in the aftermath. Descending in the setting sun from the tunnel to his kayak, he discovers that his catch, a bearded seal, has been stolen. This meant not only a personal insult but also the possibility of becoming a target of sorcery. Turning a part of one's adversary's catch against its owner by magical means was a common way of practicing sorcery, because the catch made single-handedly by a hunter belonged to him as a (metonymous) part of himself. Naaja sets out to recapture this missing part of his "self." He catches up with and succeeds in killing the thief right before the calving of an iceberg, which makes the crime look like an accident. The waves will send both body and smashed kayak ashore for the relatives to mourn (ID 1214). In the narrative, this recapture then serves as compensation for the lack of losing and being recaptured

117. Grandorf (2004), remaining faithful to the text, which lacks any explicit analogy between sex and eating, refused my interpretation. She found a suitable explanation in mouth metaphors, a fine analysis that, nevertheless, has to take in other texts for substantiation. So, each in our own way, we find support in departures from the very text.

by the clothing. Otherwise, as we shall see, violence is less characteristic of the initiation in solitude than of the "delivery," the ritual prelude to the *saqqummerneq* performed in public.[118]

Uersaq, as the Spirit of Public Initiation

Ready for *saqqummerneq*, Kukkujooq was practicing tricks with the drum in an old grave when the hermaphrodite *Uersaq* attacked him, threateningly ordered him to perform in public, and then raped him (Sonne 2005: ID 1286). He woke up naked, and put on his clothes. Later, in the middle of winter the same spirit arrived on its own, encountering him in the entrance tunnel. The request was repeated but Kukkujooq returned to the room, deathly pale, and did not dare obey (*ibid.*). Anyway, Kukkujooq's first encounter with the bisexual *Uersaq* was an initiation. He lost consciousness during the act and woke up as naked as the pupils who were devoured by a freshwater being. Plainly this is another correspondence in myth of sex with eating.[119]

Uersaq was studied by Robert Gessain. He compared figurines collected, along with stories told to Victor in the mid-1930s, and some additional points later verified by Pierre Robbe and Robert-Lamblin (Gessain 1975a). *Uersaq* (future husband) meant either a carved puppet, a figurine, a frightening carving on the wooden support of the gun on the kayak, a *tupilak* (see p. 79, note 52), or a spirit. Most figurines are provided with the tuft of hair and breasts of a female and the penis of a male. Some have very big mouths and some an extra penis, either at the navel or between the breasts.[120] In addition, some have a mix of animal and human limbs. Sent out as a *tupilak*, it tries to copulate with the victim. In case the latter happens to see it before penetration, it withdraws and, as is the habit of a repelled *tupilak*, it turns against its maker. Female *tupilak* makers dared not go out alone owing to that effect, but after a while they lost their fear, left the house, and were raped to death by the monster. For unclear reasons the victim is invariably a woman, be she the person against whom the *tupilak* is sent in the first place or the unsuccessful *tupilak* maker hit by the boomerang effect (Sonne 2005: ID 1928, 2001). Regardless, copulation with *Uersaq* means death to the ordinary human. The apprentice may lose consciousness, but ultimately survives and thus obtains *Uersaq* for a helping spirit. What remains an open question is the method for giving life to the *Uersaq tupilak*. Usually a freshly made *tupilak* was fed by sucking the genitals of its maker, man or woman (e.g., ID 428, 1275), which I speculate was a perilous method in the case of a deadly copulating *Uersaq tupilak*.

As a helping spirit, *Uersaq* is accorded various functions that defy straight interpretation (ID 2283): The place where *Uersaq* belongs cannot be determined. Kukkujooq was initiated to *saqqummerneq* by *Uersaq* in an old grave (on the land) and later visited by the figure in the entrance tunnel of the longhouse (Sonne 2005: ID 1286 [Sandgreen]; Gessain 1975a: 327). The variant received by Gessain also has Kukkujooq meet *Uersaq* twice, first inland and then at sea. In consequence the spirit belongs everywhere, on the land and at sea; Gessain generalizes this in consonance with the structuralist equation of man :: woman : sea :: land (Gessain 1975a). Having sex with a woman it

118. I am indebted to Ingrid Müller, retired from the University of Aarhus, for this insight.

119. No mention is made of the gain (or threat) received by Teemiartissaq when she lay down beside a stream, saw a blue-black monster appear, lost consciousness, and awoke naked (Sonne 2005: ID 1109).

120. Fig. 22 in Kaalund (1990) looks like an *Uersaq* figure with enlarged vulva and a penis between the breast of a female figure.

shows its male side, with a man its female look (Gessain 1975a, referred to by Saladin d'Anglure & Morin 1998). Yet the *Uersaq* acquired by Missuarniannga emerged from a rock cleft stark naked with no female traits. Meaning, I assume, that it emerged from the underground sea into the land as did other spirits from below. Missuarniannga also lost consciousness from fear and woke up naked, apparently from a sexual affair that appears to be a homosexual one. His *Uersaq* did not ask him to *saqqummerneq*, but served him as a protector against attacks from *tupilaks* and for revival from death caused by touching deceased humans (Sonne 2005: ID 2283). In addition to these variations in *Uersaq*'s looks, places, and functions, Rasmussen, in editing his imperfect record (*ibid.*), appoints *Uersaq* the title of the Master (*inua*) of *uersat* (pl.), "the illegitimate children" (Rasmussen 1921–25, I: 31). In pre-Christian terms, such children would primarily be fathered by spirits. The informant, the catechist Kaarali, understands the term to reflect the Christian opposition to children born out of wedlock and perhaps homosexuality. Association of bisexuality with the diabolic sphere apparently happened with the advent of the Christian mission. Thus, Kuannia, an immigrant Southerner, compared the story about the lesbian *Ukuamaaq* to original sin. *Ukuamaaq* steals her daughter-in-law, does all the hunting, and uses the point of a kayak for a penis (treated on p. 249). Sahra, another Southerner baptized as an adult, declared that in contrast to the multitude of helping spirits, *toornat*, there existed only one *toornaarsuk* (the Devil in Christian terms). This particular spirit was both male and female and could not be acquired as a helping spirit (ID 1783). Frightening or not, in pre-Christian ritual *Uersaq* and other bisexual spirits had their counterparts. During *uaajeertoq*, the festival of masked persons at New Year in East Greenland (see above), various bisexual *uaajeertut* were invariably played by men dressed in women's clothes, sometimes heavily pregnant, and often sexually aggressive (Thalbitzer 1923; 2014: 173; Victor 1991).[121] Neither *Ukuamaaq* nor *Uersaq* are recognized among them, but *Nalikkatteeq*, the Entrails Snatcher with male accessories, is (J. Rosing 1957). Like other ambiguous events in a joyous atmosphere, these figures caused a lot of thrilling fun. Yet exactly how traditional *Uersaq* changed into the *inua* of illegitimate children escapes my understanding.

Summary

Schjødt's theory of ritual initiation makes good sense when applied to the myth about the East Greenlandic pupil's transformation into a future shaman. He enters a liminal state (is killed and loses consciousness), the entrance and exit of which are semantically opposed (upright body fully dressed versus naked lying on the back), and he has gained something extra. Most frequently the East Greenlandic pupil gains *qaumaneq*, the "light" or "vision," an interior light, visible only to other shamans and the beings of the Other World. Ultimately it derived from the heavenly lights, the moon, some stars, and the Northern Lights, whose *inuat* look into the dark night of This World the same way as the shaman by his *qaamaneq* looks into the ordinarily hidden *naaq*, the night or stomach of the Other World. The "big fires," the *innersuit* reflecting the light of the moon, were another source as was the "glowing" lichen, called the shit of the sun. Seemingly it connoted the glow of the rising and setting sun, which could be directly faced. The shaman's light did not permit him to see both worlds at the same time. As mentioned above, the change in view meant a transition of blurred

121. Wearing women's clothes is felt to be degrading to a man. A (business) woman in men's clothing is no fun.

sight either way. By this light the pupil attracted spirits to become his helpers, found his way in the Other Worlds, and "saw" the cause of sickness inside his patients.

The common process of death and rebirth of initiation rites resounds in the Greenland naming rites and the idea of the *angerlartoq*, a deceased child returned in the next baby born to its mother. *Angerlartut* (pl.) were considered potential shamans, as was Akku, who actually died, was buried, and came back to life. The stories told about his striving inside the grave for a reunion of soul with body illuminate stages in the performing shaman's recovery from his trance.

The Inuit are far from alone in connecting light and sight with insight, but their origin myths of light stress the condition of life, namely death, which they preferred to an eternal, immobile, plantlike life in darkness. Light, movement, and attraction similarly caused another beginning of earthly life by the ascension of Sun and her incestuous brother, Moon, from earth into orbit. Here the bright, traveling Sun still attracts the less shining, pursuing Moon, who by his light causes the movements of the life-giving tide. Frequently the beings that provided the pupil with "light" were themselves liminal animals, such as polar bear and dog. Called the Moon's "freshwater bear" or "dog," they devoured and regurgitated the pupil. The polar bear, connoting both land and sea, and the dog, living at the threshold of human habitation, bore strong phallic connotations, as did the *inua* of the inland ice, some kind of a polar bear as well. The water beetle, *minngua*, transformed from larva via pupa into a flying insect with the ability to skate open waters, dive, and fly, is in one variant said to suck out the pupil like a suckling baby—suckling blood. Considering that in Inuit symbolism the father feeds the fetus with semen and the mother with blood, this suckling *minngua* evokes female symbols of procreation. So does a similar suckling creature in myth, a chrysalis, which causes the conversion from the primordial collecting of babies from earth into orderly sexual reproduction. A pupa transformed into a butterfly and a couple of other initiating spirits, which may be wing snails, elude identification. Finally, *Uersaq*, a particular dangerous, androgynous spirit, neither devours nor sucks out the pupil. It rapes him into unconsciousness and a naked rebirth in order to promote his public initiation. Christian morals may have renamed this dangerous bisexual spirit into "the *inua* of illegitimate children."

Additional Research in Greenlandic Initiating Spirits

Apart from Gessain's meticulous analysis of *Uersaq* and a continuous interest in the particular helping spirit *toornaarsuk*, which is sometimes accorded an initiating function, little research has been devoted to the initiating spirits in Greenlandic shamanism. Grandorf was the first to analyze aspects of the "freshwater monster," and I did the above follow up, but otherwise only its consecutive function has been considered. C. Rosing makes the general statement that this monster did not become a helping spirit (1946: 42). Nonetheless it served Sanimuinnaq as an ally for defense (Sonne 2005: ID 575), and an anonymous informant (most probably Georg Quppersimaan) as defense against a *tupilak*-like being (ID 966). And so I call upon the reader to make her own choice.

Toornaarsuk

The research history of *toornaarsuk* is a lengthy, rather complicated matter, but those hooked on acculturative processes may find the story—to which I shall add a fresh ending—stimulating.

A helping spirit named *Toornaarsuk* haunts the earliest West Greenlandic sources as the one and only spirit, not only for the very first initiation in solitude but also for serving all other functions of the shaman. *Toornaarsuk*, meaning literally—and perhaps ironically—nice, dear, little, special (*-arsuk*) helping spirit (*toornaq*), was identified with the Devil by the first missionaries, causing misunderstandings and centuries of debate in academia (Sonne 1986b). My conclusions reached about the West Greenlandic *toornaarsuk*, or better *toornaarsuit* in the plural, were the following: *toornaarsuk* used to be no proper noun (as, e.g., the Devil) but rather served as a qualifying denotation and, in wider geographical perspective (including the Iglulingmiut), it may have denoted a decisive initiating spirit (*ibid.*).[122] My additional conclusion in 1986, however, about the East Greenlandic *toornaarsuk* as a figure introduced with its Christian connotations from the West Coast (*ibid.*), may have been premature, because back then the publication of Victor and Robert-Lamblin (1989–93) had yet to appear. Victor and Robert-Lamblin's second volume enumerates five "classes" of *toornat*, helping spirits, of which the first and the fifth are named *toornaarsuk aquda* and *toornaarsuk*, respectively. Both are classified as wing snails: one black, the other white (II: 374). The latter—or maybe both—seem represented by carvings made of *toornaarsuit* fastened to wooden objects bought by Gustav Holm in 1885.[123] Indeed, the kind of *toornaarsuk* owned by three shamans, Immaakutsuluk (Thalbitzer ed. 1933: 87–88), Sanimuinnaq (Sonne 2005: ID 575), and Georg Quppersimaan (ID 1163), are wing snails, the latter of the black kind, the former two of the white. The *toornaarsuk* belonging to Naaja, Missuarniannga, Teemiartissaq, her brother, and her stepfather, Taqqisima (ID 1666, 2283, 1017, 1109) is not specified, but the latter is characterized by its call, a trembling *o-o-o* (ID 1017, 1109). Finally, both Kaakaaq and Maratsi came to possess a wing snail, which are not named *toornaarsuit*, but the former is of the black kind, the latter being either black or white. This was the very first helping spirit obtained by Maratsi, as described above (pp. 263, 286), and it may have assisted Maratsi in getting hold of other helping spirits from the sea, which was one function of a *toornaarsuk* according to both Teemiartissaq and Georg Quppersimaan (ID 1017, 1163). Thalbitzer's other informants distinguished between two kinds of *toornaarsuit*, of which Thalbitzer received a description of only one: a big creature measuring about 2 meters in length and 60 centimeters in breadth across the breast. Thalbitzer states that the upper half of the body looks like a human being with face and arms, the lower like a seal, just like the carved *toornaarsuk* figures (Thalbitzer 1919: 99). Yet Kaarali's drawing of the *toornaarsuk* owned and described by his father, Missuarniannga, looks more like a smiling bear from top to toe, but with the very long arms of the carved figures (Rasmussen

---

122. Although Jakobsen refers to this conclusion in Sonne (1986b), she trusts the early missionaries and accords *Toornaarsuk* an independent position on par with Moon and Sea Woman in a sort of pantheon (Jakobsen 1999: 65–72) not unlike that thought out by Thalbitzer. He, however, had *Sila* as the third *inua* in the position taken up by Jakobsen's *Toornaarsuk* (1926; 1928).

123. The wing snail also appears in a lower category of minor (*-tsiat*) *toornaarsuit*—i.e., *toornaarsuatsiat*, listed by Kaarali (O. Rosing 1957–61, I: 76; J. Rosing 1963: 180). Most shamans, he comments, have to be content with such lesser *toornaarsuit*, because the real or superior *toornaarsuit*, redfish (*Sebastes marinus*) and grenadier (*Macrouridae*), are extremely difficult to obtain (*ibid.*). They both live at great depths (Muus et al. 1981: 63, 110–11), in contrast to surface-swimming wing snails. Uncertain spelling by Jens Rosing complicates matters. Thus, since the spelling of *toornaarsuk* in the plural, *toornaarsuit*, is hardly distinguishable from *toornar-suit* (great *toornat*, helping spirits, mind the second short a), he sometimes gets them mixed up. To take one example: Kaarali distinguishes between *toornaarsuit* and *toornaarsua-tsiat*—i.e., "lesser" (*-tsiat*) *toornaarsuit* (O. Rosing (1957–61, I: 76), while Jens Rosing mistakes the former for *toornarsuit*, "great" *toornat*, but copies the latter correctly (1963: 180).

1921–25, I: 56). A shaman's *toornaarsuk* guides his travels through the sea to Sea Woman, Thalbitzer continues, and during performances it answers his questions mediated by his *apeqqiteq*; this oracle or "questioning" spirit is situated at the equally structurally mediating shore (Thalbitzer 1909: 99). In 1941 Thalbitzer accorded *Toornaarsuk* a high position as a demigod (Sonne 1986b), but his speculations on the mediating role of the spirit were most probably inspired by Missuarniannga's biography as told by Kaarali and published in Danish by Knud Rasmussen in 1921 (Sonne 2205: ID 2283). To this we shall return later, as well as to the ritual call "*ululoo, ululoo*" (*ooloolo-o*) which is accorded *toornaarsuk* in some stories, or the "*o-o-o*" mentioned by Teemiartissaq.

Let's treat the wing snails first: in their manifest forms as plankton mollusks, both species are tiny creatures that, in the perspective of the Other World, take on much bigger, even monstrous forms. In their spirit forms they are still recognizable by their zoological characteristics, but for unknown reasons Victor and/or his informants mixed some of them up (Victor & Robert Lamblin 1989–93, II: 244, 374). Call me a positivist, but I shall stick to zoology regarding the linguistic meanings of the names and then let the remaining sources have the greatest say. The black wing snail, *Limacina retroversa*, is called *qaartulaajik* (the little bursting one) in East Greenland and *tulukaasaq* (ravenlike) in West Greenland.[124] Georg Quppersimaan called the white stripe along the spiral of its shell "its finery" (Qúpersimân 1972: 113; 1982: 107–8); Victor's informant considered it to be amulet straps (Victor & Robert Lamblin 1989–93, II: 374). Such straps are clearly seen on Kaarali Andreassen's bearlike drawing, while its prolonged arms would refer to the wings of the white wing snail. The latter species is called *aaquda´* (W.Grl. *arrusaq*), meaning "formed like a harp seal" (Latin: *Clione limacina* or *Limacina helicina*); its long "arms" are means for moving vertically. Appearing translucent whitish but with visible red "entrails," you may call it white or red as you please, or even orange when they swarm the surface in pursuit of their favorite food, the black wing snails.[125] Of the bone carvings, the white wing snail is easily recognized by "prolonged" arms, no neck, and marked "ears" (wings) on top whereas two small chubby *toornaarsuit*-like cubes may represent the black species (e.g., Holm 1972: 216–17; 1914: 121; Kaalund 1990: No 152).

In addition to answering the shaman's questions mediated by *apeqqiteq*, many very useful abilities and habits are accorded these East Greenlandic *toornaarsuit*. They can catch and devour *tupilaks*, travel through hard rock, serve as guides to unknown countries, and save their human shaman when caught in the ice. But the peculiar call "*ululoo, ululoo*" attributed to a *toornaarsuk* in three stories as well as in a summary of its characteristics is felt to be strange. Jens Rosing has had a hand in them all. He did the summary along with the Danish translations of two stories he recorded in 1961 and one Kaarali wrote down at some earlier date (Sonne 2005: ID 599, 1683, 1695, 1677; J. Rosing 1963: 180). Only the latter can be checked in its Greenlandic wording (in typescript in West Greenlandic; the

124. From *qaarpoq* (explodes)—i.e., identical in meaning with the Norwegian name *kruttåta*, "powder snail," because it produces gas that makes fishes who feed on them burst from explosion. Seals feeding on these snails have to lie down for some time for the acid of the stomach to do its job (see *Polarfronten* 1:12 [2001], at http://polarfronten.dk/wp-content/uploads/2012/08/PF011.pdf). Also I suppose they become unpleasantly filled with air. Would they also fart? The name *qaartulaajik* points to such facts observed by Greenlandic hunters rather than to Norwegian impact.

125. See photo: http://www.marinbi.com/nudibranchia/clione_limacina.htm. The red color comes to the fore in presentation of this spirit with the bloody mouth it gets from devouring tupilaks (Thalbitzer ed. 1933: 89). Sometimes its excellent hearing is stressed due to its big flapping "ears" (Sonne 2005: ID 1666). http://polarfronten.dk/wp-content/uploads/2012/08/PF011.pdf

handwritten original is not available).[126] It describes Akku's initiation into an *angakkoq puulik* (see below), an impressive performance ending with the audible arrival of his only companion throughout the initiation, *toornarsua* (his great *toornaq*, helping spirit) named *ulutoortortoq* (*ululoortortoq*? the one wont to call *ululoo*) (O. Rosing 1957–61, I: 115). Jens Rosing translates *toornarsua* into "*the* great *toornaardik*" (the great *toornaarsuk* [W. Grl.], my emphasis BS)—i.e., mistaking a great *toornaq* for *Toornaarsuk* (1963: 247).[127] So the identification of the *ululoo*-calling spirit with notorious *Toornaarsuk* is in this case due to Jens Rosing. With regard to the remaining two stories making the same identification, nothing certain can be said, except that Kaarali hardly ever made this identification. His listing of fishes and mollusks to be obtained as *toornaarsuit* and *toornaarsuatsiat* (mentioned above) reveal nothing about the sounds they make. Of greater import, in 1933, the year of Kaarali's death, his description of a spirit was published; the spirit, while not identified as a *toornaarsuk*, calls out *ululoo*: "Ululoq is a helping spirit, a particular spirit, usually named *ululortartoq* [the one who keeps saying *ululoq*]. Its appearance is never described like that of 'Amo' or 'Ajumaaq' [two well-known frightening spirits used at the beginning of performances]. Its sound alone is heard and even when emerging right beside the *umiaq*, there is no mention of seeing him" (Andreassen 1961, tr. BS). This is a commentary on the use of an *ululoo*-calling spirit summoned by the shaman of a traveling party in distress. They are helplessly caught in the drift ice at a great distance from land. The *ululoo*-calling spirit arrives with a thundering sound, cleaving a channel in front of the shaman in his kayak at the head of the *umiaq*. By and by the lead opens right onto shore (*ibid.*). The difference between the clearly visible bearlike *toornaarsuk* as drawn by Kaarali and the invisible *ululoo*-calling *toornaq* catches one's eye. No identification can be made.

Returning now to Rosing's summary of ideas about *toornaarsuit*, he obviously partially quotes Rasmussen, who took down (primarily in Danish) Kaarali's account of his father Missuarnianngâ's apprenticeship.[128] Edited for print, Kaarali's comments on *toornaarsuk* run as follows: "The name [*toornaarsuk*] sounds like a pet name, 'the nice little helping spirit,' but he is in reality '*tôrnat nâlagait*,' *the* master of *the* helping spirits, and is put to use more frequently than any other spirit. In the case that nobody else can solve a problem, *Tôrnârssuk* is called upon. But it is very difficult to achieve. You will have to search in vain for a very long time in the mountains in solitude until it eventually turns up" (Rasmussen 1921–25, I: 25, tr., emphasis BS). All the same, this quotation is not an exact copy of Rasmussen's notes, which read: "*Tôrnârssuk* is the one among all helping spirits that most frequently approaches the shamans and they consider him usually to be *Tôrnat nalagait* [*toornat nalagaat*, master of helping spirits]. In case the other helping spirits cannot clear up a matter, the shaman calls on *Tôrnârssuk*. *Equngasoq*[129] alone is considered a greater spirit than *Tôrnârssuk*, but only rarely does

126. Jens Rosing once encouraged me to study his entire collection of tape recordings from Ammassalik in the archives of the Danish Folkore Institute. Regrettably I had to decline his offer, as I am not well versed in spoken Greenlandic, not to mention East Greenlandic.

127. Surprisingly, however, Rosing correctly translates the *ululoo*-calling *toornardivin* (pl. E. Grl.) into "great helping spirits" in a story told by his main informant, Saajooq (Odin Maratsi), in 1961 (Sonne 2005: ID 1677; J. Rosing 1963: 230).

128. Rosing: "The name *tôrnârdik* (sing.) is a euphemism: 'the dear little spirit'—'The dear little spirits' are altogether the shaman's most powerful spirits. In case the other helping spirits cannot solve a matter, the shaman calls on *tôrnârdik* [*toornaarsuk*, W. Grl.]" (J. Rosing 1963: 180, tr. BS).

129. *Equngasoq*: the fulmar spirit that connotes spring and overpowers the descended Moon, who threatens to smash the longhouse; see pp. 104, 133.

a shaman manage to get this one as a helping spirit" (KRH 52, 2, booklet 418: 10–11, tr. BS; Sonne 2005: ID 2283 copying the original notes).

Rasmussen's changes may be slight, but are of no small effect. First, Greenlandic has no definite articles that justify a translation of "master of helping spirits" into "*the* master of *the* helping spirits." Second, the wording "*klare op*" (clear up, detect) has been edited into "*klare*" (to solve, manage). A change from diagnosis into healing! With regard to mastery, some East Greenlandic spirits were shamans—i.e., themselves masters of helping spirits, and naturally greatly favored by human shamans for helping spirits. Such a master belonged, for instance, to Naaja. It had a *toornaarsuk* for a helping spirit, indeed a very strong one, and was sent by its master to save Naaja when in danger on a visit to other spirits (Sonne 2005: ID 1218). Nevertheless, the *toornaarsuk* of another story, also taken down in Danish by Rasmussen, was owned by the "Great Shaman from Sermiligaaq." Degraded here into "the master of *many* helping spirits" (my emphasis), it is of no help against the giants of the far inland. They are themselves richly supplied with *toornaarsuit* (plural). Though the shaman's ghost spirit and the hairband of his deceased grandmother both have some effect, his falcons are the spirits who eventually get the upper hand and he is saved (ID 1368). And finally, in strict keeping with the manuscript, the spirit most difficult to obtain is not *Toornaarsuk* but *Equngasoq*, who even surpasses *Toornaarsuk* in strength. My advice follows as ever: in using Rasmussen, do be on guard. In this case the conviction sowed by the early missionaries to West Greenland about the preeminence of *Toornaarsuk* steers his exegesis.

Neither Holm nor Thalbitzer, who both explicitly tried to find out more about the mastery of *Toornaarsuk* in East Greenland, received answers in the affirmative (Holm 1972: 240 n. 44; Thalbitzer 1926: 22–25). Not until his publication in 1941 did Thalbitzer, most probably inspired by Rasmussen's description above, place *Toornaarsuk* in a position of a demigod, a mediator between shamans and the "Olympic" triumvirate of *Sila*, the Moon, and Sea Woman (Sonne 1986b).[130] However, no source, including those published by Thalbitzer himself, permits any decisive conclusion about the antiquity or novelty of the East Greenlandic *toornaarsuit*. In favor of the latter, old Teemiartissaq is the first on record. In 1905–6 she told Thalbitzer that every shaman owned a *toornaarsuk* guiding him in the acquisition of helping spirits from the sea—i.e., a higher-ranging spirit as far as the spirits of the sea are concerned (Sonne 2005: ID 1017). Thus left out are the majority of helping spirits, which belonged to the land. Kaarali made his list of *toornaarsuit* and *toornaarsuatsiat* before 1933. It was published by Otto Rosing in 1957 and Victor received his information in 1936–37. Catechist Hansêraq, Holm's steersman, got his in 1885 from Immaalukutsuk, who spoke to the opposite point of view of slightly older Teemiartissaq: "Immaalukutsuk did not consider (a) *toornaarsuk* to be a benevolent being, because the *toornaarsuit* of the East Greenlanders were related to the *toornaarsuk* called the Devil by the Christians, and although they served the East Greenlandic shamans well they also used them for getting rid of their enemies" (Thalbitzer ed. 1933: 87–88, tr. BS). The statement evidently reveals impact from Christian West Greenland. In my view, then, although immigrants to East Greenland from West Greenland in the 16th century brought ideas of particular helping spirits, *toornaarsuit*, similar to those (diffuse) beliefs held by their West Greenlandic descendants

130. The first speculations appeared in Thalbitzer (1928).

at the beginning of colonization, Christian impact no doubt sharpened the focus on *toornaarsuit*. *Toornaarsuk* as the Devil was preached first by Hansêraq 1884–85, and consecutively by the West Greenlandic missionaries to Ammassalik from 1904 onward. A remarkable history of *Toornaarsuk*, as told in Ammassalik, probably in 1919 (by whom?) to Rasmussen points to this fact. It relates a development in *Toornaarsuk*'s powers:

> In the bosom of the earth live a multitude of evil trolls. The most powerful among them was called *Toornaarsuk*. The story told about this spirit goes like this: "Once upon a time there was a shaman who had a helping spirit—an *aorrussaq* [*aarrussaq*/*arrussaq*], an *autaussánguaq* [W. Grl. *aataasannguaq*, white wing snail]—a little animal that lives in the sea. It was a shaman's *tôrnârssuk* and became a mighty spirit. It was spoken of with great awe; it seems to have been regarded as more powerful than all other forces on earth. Not even the Mother of Sea Beasts—*savssuma arnarssua* [*sassuma arnarsua*]—could match herself against it. (Rasmussen 1938: 73)

Indeed, in 1884–85 Sanimuinnaq, when asked about *Toornaarsuk*, was the first to name his *aorrussaq* a *toornaarsuk*. I am inclined to credit this wing snail with the above development.[131]

Contradictions abound in any attempt to define an East Greenlandic *toornaarsuk*. For instance, against the statement on the difficulty of obtaining a *toornaarsuk* we may quote Teemiartissaq again: "Every pupil has to acquire a *toornaarsuk*." Consequently, a *toornaarsuk* cannot be all that difficult to acquire!

Mastery and *strength* turn out to be the criteria mixed up in Western attempts to define the notorious *Toornaarsuk*. Although a spirit of great power and abilities, no East Greenlandic source has any spirit subordinated to a *toornaarsuk*, apart from *apeqqiteq*, the asking spirit, and unless the former's guidance to other spirits of the sea means mastery.[132]

Apropos the function accorded a *toornaarsuk* by Teemiartissaq of supplying a pupil with other helping spirits, this makes a *toornaarsuk* an initiating spirit in correspondence with early West Greenlandic statements as well as with both her own and Maratsi's biographies (Sonne 1986b; 2005: ID 1109). Yet the "light" that attracted spirits, *qaamaneq*, was more frequently conveyed by the "freshwater animal," as also most East Greenlandic historical shamans obtained their *toornaarsuk* at a later point in apprenticeship. Missuarniannga, for instance, who received a dwarf for his first helping spirit, had both been devoured and acquired two other spirits prior to getting hold of a *toornaarsuk* (ID 2283). Also Sanimuinnaq, in possession of a wing snail *toornaarsuk*, happened to see the animal or human figure of a (masturbating) *toornaarsuk* at a very late point in his apprenticeship (ID 575).

---

131. Gulløv awards a particular hypothesis about the *toornaarsuit* that decorate several wooden objects bought by Holm. Some few made by shamans were decorated with wing snail figures: a throwing board, a water bucket, and a urine bucket. Gulløv argues that these reflect the catching and ritual treatment of a seal, caught by means of a throwing board, then smeared with urine and offered a drink of water. And so they reflect a situation of crisis, the severe decline in resources, to which the shamans responded by their symbolic decorations (Jensen et al. 2011). Gulløv may be perfectly right.

132. Kaarali (Sonne 2005: ID 1666) and his wife, Johanne (ID 806), and the much younger Apulu (ID 1673) have *toornaarsuk* guide the spirit team going with their master, the shaman, to West Greenland. His extraordinary fine sense of hearing due to his big ears (the snail's wings?) puts him in front. He shows which direction to go by waving one or the other of his big ears.

And Kaakaaq, who obtained her first helping spirits long before marriage, was married and a mother of three children when she came upon a black wing snail at the shore. In her own interpretation this snail was a guarantee for her next child to become the son much wanted by her husband. The very wing snail became the boy's amulet with the power to transform him into such a snail when attacked by enemies (ID 1255). These examples all contradict the notion of *toornaarsuk* as an initiating spirit necessary for the acquisition helping spirits.

Concluding Remarks on the East Greenlandic *Toornaarsuit*

In short, variation is staggering. A *toornaarsuk* could be a pupil's initial spirit, but more often than not it was obtained at a later point of apprenticeship. Similarly, no one invariable function is accorded an East Greenlandic *toornaarsuk* besides its appetite for *tupilat*, the adeptness to cause the *tupilat* of the souls of its shaman's enemies to ricochet, and the ability to save its master from danger in situations sometimes better managed by other helping spirits. But a frequently mentioned idea (for instance, by Saajooq), namely that a *toornaarsuk* is never allowed to enter the room of the shaman's performance, fits its ritual role in West as in East Greenland (J. Rosing 1963: 180; Thalbitzer 1926: 22–23; Graah 1932: 134; Victor & Robert Lamblin 1989–93, II: 244; H. Egede 1971, 1: 70–71; 1925: 57, Glahn 1771: 345; Kleinschmidt 1871: 370–71; Sonne 1986b).

The *Ululoo*-Calling *Toornaq*

Returning to the great *toornaq*, or *toornardik* (E. Grl.), calling *ululooq*—what kind of a being was it? Is Teemiartissaq's "*o-o-o*," the call of her stepfather's *toornaarsuk* at his public initiation, identical with the *ululoo* call? Thalbitzer described the first as music, a continuous repetition of only two notes, a higher and then a lower, producing a trembling sound (Thalbitzer 1923: 478). With an eye to myth, stories, ritual, and real animals, the call could be one of two, namely, either the "*ulurra*" or "*ulukka*" (my *ulu*) of the narwhal (Sonne 2005: ID 23) or the hunter's decoy signal, "oo-h, oo-h, oo-h" otherwise known as the mating sound of the male bearded seal (Thalbitzer 1923: No. 119, 295–96). The former proposal would refer to the origin of the narwhal taken down in numerous versions among the Eastern Inuit (Mishler 2013). In most Inuit variants, an evil mother or grandmother blinds the young hero by sorcery in a dispute about the use of the skin of a bearded seal. She next lies about a polar bear he kills from the window, supported in aiming by his little sister. Given no part in the meat, the blind young man is handed only mussels for food. So, when his vision is restored by a seabird, he takes revenge using his (grand)mother as a hunting bladder in catching beluga. By the harpoon line fastened around her waist she is drawn by a big harpooned beluga into the sea, where she, riding the beluga, calls repeatedly for her *ulu* (for cutting the line). She becomes a narwhal, and (sometimes) her braided hair forms its peculiar tooth.[133] Said Johanne at the end of Kaakaaq's version to Victor: "Seeing a narwhal having a woman on its back calling: 'my ulu, my ulu' [*ulurraa, ulurraa*] you will know that the narwhals will arrive in big numbers" (Sonne 2005: ID 23). So does the great *toornaq* call *ulurra* or "ooh, ooh, ooh"? The choice among the two *ulu*-calling animals, narwhal and

133. Among the Iglulingmiut and Nattilingmiut alone, the story forms the prelude to the origin myth of Sun and Moon (Mishler 2013). The link could be *Ululirnang* (the *ulu* woman alias *Nalikkatteeq*) who threats visitors to the moon, but no reference occurs to this figure in the texts.

bearded seal, is greatly facilitated by recordings of their differing sounds on the web. The narwhal utters an extended series of creaking sounds interrupted at intervals by a single "OO"! The bearded seal lets out a high, long-drawn whistling drowned in a series of "ooh," changing pitch. I am in for the latter variant, which tallies better with Thalbitzer's description of the bearded seal decoy signal demonstrated by Kuannia: "o-o-o . . . e in a falling chromatic scale" (Thalbitzer 1923: 295), as opposed to the repetitive two notes "O O" of Taqqisima's *toornaarsuk*. Following the sound of bearded seal, its mating aspect comes to the fore in the *uaajeertoq* dance, performed by a man acting out the enticing and harpooning of a bearded seal. After the kill he exclaims, "Ha, I shall repair (the skin) of my *umiaq*!" After which he sings, dancing, "Here is a great barb" [for a covetous woman to accept]; that is, he asks whomever it would please among the women to offer him a piece of bearded seal skin. And, as explained by Thalbitzer, the great barb is "literally the upright bone peg of the throwing board which fits the corresponding groove in the dart (*qaquiseq*), but also generally used of any upright peg or barb; very commonly of the *membrum erectum*" (Thalbitzer 1923: 296). In other words, this *uaajeertoq* dancer, who by the decoy signal entices a female bearded seal and has it killed, secures for himself the skin needed for repairing his *umiaq*. Simultaneously, with the big barb he invites whomever it pleases among the women to play the part of the booty. The woman who then hands him the wished-for skin has agreed to lie with him during the following putting out of the lamps (Georg Quppersimaan's description of the *uaajeertoq* dances above fits in with this scenario).

A story told in the same humorous spirit supports a proposed connection between the spirit calling *ululooq* and the decoy signal for bearded seal. A kayaker, attracted by the lovely women of the household of Iaqqa's father, is forced to stop over in the tunnel of an empty house by the new ice closing in upon his kayak. Disturbed in his sleep by some frightening spirit or ghost, he calls on his *toornaq*, which makes the ghost disappear by its call: "*ululooq, ululooq*."[134] At the house of Iaqqa's father, however, the kayaker turns out to be of no use when another frightening ghost arrives in the tunnel. Iaqqa's father has to step in, and courageously fights the ghost with a burning lamp, because the guest has taken refuge among the women, rubbing his bare buttocks on their (naked) bodies. He has, as stressed in the story, lowered his trousers at sitting down, the "dress code" demanded of a male guest in showing his inoffensive intentions. So—implicitly—already well situated among the women, the mating signal of his *ululooq*-calling spirit has lost its momentum (Sonne 2005: ID 559). In line with the emphasis on the sexual aspects of male bearded seal, Josias Amosen thinks that the kayaker seen one afternoon passing by the summer camp was an *innersuaq*. It towed a big bearded seal with an impressive erect penis (ID 2027).

In the remaining examples of the *ululooq*-calling helping spirit, long-distance travels at sea rather than sexual hints are at play. We already met with Kaarali's story about the invisible, ice-cleaving, thundering specimen above summoned from afar. In ritual, the *ululooq* call ends the initiation into an *angakkoq puulik*, by which the spirit announces the candidate's successful endeavor at his returning from the horizon across the sea. One was Akku, the other apparently Missuarniannga (ID 1683, 1313). Still a third story relates Maratsi's eventual success in eliminating the revengeful soul of his murdered victim, Quarrajeeq. He has one of his helping spirits do the job and bids the *ululoo*-calling

134. Similarly, they are in one story said to serve as attendants to the biggest giants of the inland ice (Sonne 2005: ID 1677).

spirit to announce the victorious feat: "My master has nothing more to fear... Out there, at the end of heaven, he is forever dead, burst into a blob of blood!" (ID 1695). The end of the world at sea, the horizon, is the point in space often associated with *ululortartoq*. About this *ululoo*-calling, libidinous, and long-distance-traveling spirit, which I take to be a bearded seal, much more will be said in the next chapter on the *angakkoq puulik*. For now it suffices to say that although the great *toornaq* that sounds like a male bearded seal is sometimes called a *toornaarsuk*, *toornaarsuk* seems to be the white wing snail that happened to be the first to become identified as an East Greenlandic *toornaarsuk* in colonial literature. Consequently, "spoken of with great awe" it came to be "regarded as more powerful than all other forces on earth. Not even the Mother of Sea Beasts—*savssuma arnarssua* [*sassuma arnarsua*]—could match herself against it" (Rasmussen 1938: 73). The Devil *Toornaarsuk* certainly had his way.

Achieving Travel Powers

Whereas initiations to *qaamaneq* are richly and explicitly documented, stories are scarce about initiations to flying and gliding, the main ways of traveling the Other World, apart from walking. In transmission or more likely in translation, the distinctions between the ways of traveling have become muddled, because visits to heaven are in a Western perspective associated exclusively with flying. Besides, as it strongly appeals to the imagination, the flying shaman has come to preside in anthologies of republished stories, theater, and pictorial presentations right on to the present.

Ilimmarneq

The sources do not agree on the acquisition of the ability to fly. The experience of being devoured and reincarnated would empower the art of flying as well as the other abilities of a great shaman (Gessain 1978; Victor & Robert-Lamblin 1989–93: 230–33; Robert-Lamblin 1997: 263). Going through the same experience, one of Christian Rosing's informants obtained the ability to travel downwards to the interior of the earth (a place more in consonance with the Christian than the pre-Christian spatial view: hell, to where shamans belonged). Kukkujooq, however, plainly learned to fly by a goose, which he "thought in" out of season and without going through any ordeals of being attacked or losing consciousness (Sonne 2005: ID 1271).[135] Similarly, Missuarniannga suffered no pains when a medium-size giant communicated its ability to fly by demonstrating how to glide between the mountaintops along the bridge of frozen fog formed by its breath. Missuarniannga merely had to touch the spirit for a transmission (ID 2283), whereas Teemiartissaq's brother apparently received this ability either because he had been devoured by the enormous bear with the odd face, an uncertain point of the story, or passed on to him by the giants that led him through the inland ice (see above p. 284). He traveled home by flying, whereas Naaja, in the comparable version, did not. He was evidently devoured by the giant of the inland ice, and he had his kayak lying on the shore, ready for the next story about his violent recapture of his stolen catch. Naaja seems to have obtained his ability to fly long after his public initiation, when, after a prolonged winter without means for coping with the masses of snow that hid the breathing holes, he resumed his "search," *ujarlerneq*, and got hold of

135. Intense concentration could make your wishes come true.

some unspecified means. In this way he, well prepared for the next time of threatening snow masses, flew to *Asiaq*, the *inua* of precipitation, in order to persuade her to let it rain (ID 1200). Later, when visiting Sea Woman in demand for seals, he neither flew nor glided. He simply walked along the bottom of the sea (ID 1196).[136] Maratsi got access to either world, above and below, by means of a magic cord he attracted from Uviak, the alleged murderer (by sorcery) of Maratsi's father (ID 2292). Did Maratsi fly or glide? Approximate answers from other parts of his biography are presented below.

In two texts, acquiring the ability to fly is associated with bleeding during *ueerineq*, the "delivery" leading to *saqqummerneq*. Both were taken down by Kaarali, and one dealt with Akku, who did not bleed during his "delivery" and admitted his inability to fly for this very reason (ID 1312).[137] Ajijak, who did bleed due to the possession of the spirit of a black guillemot called Oortortoq/Oordortoq, is bound with thongs for flying during his first performance. Supplied with wings from a black guillemot fastened into his armpits, he is ready for takeoff (ID 1311, 1676; J. Rosing 1963: 175, 181; O. Rosing 1957–61, I: 72). Naaja also bled, but without any noticeable effect in the record edited by Sandgreen (Sonne 2005: ID 1211). Maybe Kaarali, by his own reasoning of two examples, one affirmative of Ajijak, the other negative of Akku, connected bleeding with flying. More likely Oortortoq, the black guillemot spirit possessing Ajijak and represented by the wings inserted into his armpits, made the difference. Thus, as Jens Rosing was also told in 1961: "Many shamans never manage to get hold of a black guillemot spirit, which is extremely difficult to obtain. They shall never be capable of flying and are consequently called weaker shamans. During *ueerineq* ['delivery'] they become possessed by a seal, and they bleed from the soles of their feet" (J. Rosing 1963: 181, tr. BS).[138] Apparently, then, bleeding during *ueerineq* tends to be associated with the obtainment of all travel abilities. Not only the *ilimmartartut*, as stated above, but also nonflyers may bleed during *ueerineq*; the latter do from the soles of their feet, the former, as will be shown later, from soft spots on their faces (Sonne 2005: ID 1211, 1311). Still, by generalizing you end up on shaky ground, in that Oortortoq also figures as the devouring spirit on par with the "freshwater bear" in a poorly recorded story about an anonymous shaman. His mother spoiled the unspecified effect by washing his clothes in urine afterwards. The ability to fly, however, was offered to this pupil by a couple of ravens, if also to no avail. He lacked the courage to try (ID 986). In short, the stories are not all that helpful in deciding on a unanimous way of achieving the ability to fly: by being devoured by the freshwater bear, by bleeding during *ueerineq*, by medium-size giants, the biggest giants, ravens, a black guillemot, and a goose. In reference to space, the latter bird covered long distances in its migrations, while the black guillemot was a diving and flying seabird reborn annually in Sea Woman's house (ID 468); ravens were associated with the coast; and flying giants belonged in the uppermost inland. The "freshwater bear" signified the powers of Moon. Any choice among them meets with associative contradictions.

136. Ideologically a great Inuit shaman was able to visit both heaven and the underworld. Naaja, the great shaman whose fame hardly faded in posterity, could not be imagined defective in such powers. Neither story about his travels to *Asiaq* and to Sea Woman offer any variations to the mythic stereotypes except for added information on his encounters with deceased humans in either realm.

137. In contrast, bleeding characterized Akku's life from his first apparent death from nosebleed to his death due to suffocation while vomiting blood (tuberculosis it seems) (Sonne 2005: ID 32).

138. An insertion made by Jens Rosing into his translation of Otto Rosing's *Angákortaligssuit* (1957–61).

Flying (in public) demanded the tying up of the shaman according to Rasmussen: "Some held seances without being bound, others were bound; it was the latter, who were to make the spirit flight" (Rasmussen 1938: 125). Weyer makes the same point in collecting examples from the Diomede Islands, East Greenland, Iglulik, and Hamilton Inlet (Weyer 1932: 437–39). Apparently, however, it did not work the other way round, insofar as the bound shaman did not always go by flying. Sanimuinnaq was laced up without any apparent flight to follow when observed by Holm (Holm 1972: 127–30; 1914: 90–95). Both Naaja and Missuarniannga each started out their *saqqummerneq* by being tied up, not for flying but in order to make the drum dance on the back and obtain *sila, silanippoq* (Sonne 2005: ID 1206, 2283). On the other hand, the moon was implied, because, as will be elaborated below, the drum danced due to Moon's power (Gessain 1978: 212), and the worldwide view obtained by *silaninneq* was like the one shown to the shaman who visited Moon. Confusingly, however, Maratsi is said to have been tied up for his travel to the realm of death, although he walked (or glided) and wore his boots out (ID 1983). Statements on the tying up of the Inuit shaman of Canada are also contradictory. The Iglulik shaman who went to visit the Northern Lights was laced by thongs, stripped to the waist, in short trousers and without boots (Rasmussen 1929: 129–31; Saladin d'Anglure 2001: 156ff; photo: Boas 1901–7: 512). Reverend Peck, however, has the shaman laced up for visiting Sea Woman but freeing himself from the thongs before he *ascended* (Laugrand & Oosten 2008b: 63–64)! So, although the lacing up was a prerequisite of flying, it did not invariably demand flying. It may also have served as a technique of ecstasy due to the pain the trammels caused.

Returning to the black guillemot, it steals the picture of the East Greenlandic ritual takeoff for flying in public: in preparation the shaman would be laced up, his hands tied behind his back, his forehead bent down and tied between his knees, and supplied with the wings of a black guillemot fastened in his armpits. Tipped over on his side he set his drum dancing in order to be raised into a sitting position and next up onto his feet for hobbling around on the floor in circles with difficulty. Soon he was heard circling above the floor for some time, pausing on the clothes dryer above the lamp before resuming circling, and finally, slipping out through a hole that opened up in a corner between ceiling and wall (Thalbitzer ed. 1933: 84; Holm 1972: 240, note 47). Taking off, he disappeared, escorted by his helping spirits in a shower of sparks (Sonne 2005: ID 1666, 1665, 1677, 1312). Like drilling, my association goes, in that the circling movements produce both the exit hole and the sparks sent out. Apropos the flying direction, this is always towards the inland according to Thalbitzer (1909: 97) or the realms of heaven and foreign lands (Thalbitzer ed. 1933: 84).

As for the paraphernalia of the bound shaman, he did not put on any extra clothing. The East Greenlandic shaman wore nothing but his indoor briefs (*naatsit*), the thongs, and the wings of a black guillemot stuck into his armpits. The Iglulik shaman wore indoor clothing as well, short trousers and perhaps a shirt along with the thongs (Rasmussen 1929: 129–31; Boas 1901–7: 512). Except for the thongs, Weyer does not mention the outfit of the Diomede Island and Hamilton Inlet flying shamans. Maratsi, who flew without being laced up but in new female boots and his hair tied into a tail, will be discussed shortly.

Gliding

As mentioned above in the discussion of ranking, in Greenland gliding was predominantly associated with travels to the nether realms. Similarly among the Canadian Inuit, a Nattilik shaman who was seen gliding across a strait later went to the lower realms by falling backwards into the sea (Rasmussen 1931: 317–18). Among the Iglulik, a shaman of highest rank managed to glide impeded as within a slippery tube right down to Sea Woman. He wore nothing but kamiks (skin boots) and mittens (Rasmussen 1929: 126). Gliding must also have been the way of traveling to Sea Woman by a West Greenlandic shaman, who went along like a flying fish, taking turns above and beneath the surface of the sea (N. Egede 1971: 38; 1939: 150). Legendary Tuttu's Wife, a Southern shaman, was sent halfway to Sea Woman by being thrown like a ball across the frozen sea by a collaborating polar bear and walrus, and the remaining way at the breakup of the ice by the lopsided kayaker or "twistmouth," *Equngasoq*, a fulmar in human form (Sonne 2005: ID 1445). Since this *Equngasoq* (E. Grl. *Eqingalik*) was identified with *gliding* by Jens Rosing's informants in 1961 (pers. comm.), the way of traveling by Tuttu's Wife most probably connoted gliding as well.[139] "Floating," or *puttaannarneq* (like an ice floe), was a term used in Southeast Greenland, in characterizing a shaman ranking below a genuine shaman, whatever this would mean. The source is late, and the term points to gliding, but nothing more is said (ID 2035). Gliders similarly ranked below the flyers in Ammassalik. Nevertheless, they could travel to Sea Woman, to Moon, and to either realms of death below and above. Unlike *ilimmarneq*, no particular term was used for gliding (except the identification with lopsided *Eqingalik*/*Equngasoq*, "Wry Mouth" [Jens Rosing pers. comm.]). Instead an ordinary suffix for traveling, the ending *-liarneq* or *–mukarneq* added to the place-name of destination would do, and they did fine: "They glide along on their heels as swiftly as the flying shamans. The route to the lower realm leads through the sea, but it is not felt that way they say. You suffer no lack of breathing. It feels just like gliding over the mountains" (J. Rosing 1963: 181–82, tr. BS). No route to heaven is mentioned in this context. But although going downwards, *alliarneq* (*ibid.*), was the predominate association to gliding the nonflying shaman could glide across the sea right unto the horizon from where access was had to the land of heaven. The same route in low height above the surface was available to the flying shaman as well (P. Egede 1971: 134–35; 1939: 91; Rasmussen 1921–25: 82; Rüttel 1917: 39; Victor & Robert-Lamblin 1989–93, II: 246).

Two historical shamans were evidently "gliders": Akku and Maratsi. Both traveled to the realm of death below in *ikiaq* (gutskin anorak) and some type of footwear, Akku in stockings and Maratsi in boots. The wear and tear on Maratsi's boots is described in two versions on record, one told by Kaakaaq in 1937 to Victor, the other by Saajooq in 1961 to Jens Rosing. In the latter, a short retelling, the soles merely need repair on the way (Sonne 2005: ID 1697), whereas in Kaakaaq's more detailed description the boots are brand-new at the outset but completely worn out, wet, and sandy on his return. Presumably Kaakaaq was present at the performance, which at the outset has Maratsi tied up as for flying. But Maratsi certainly *does not fly*. No further comment is made on his thongs either. During his prolonged trip he goes through the earth together with his helping spirits, proceeds with difficulty a long way through very soft sand, wades through a dam of blood run off the deceased humans on their way to their realm of death, continues around a cliff, and then downward into the

139. The association of gliding with the fulmar would point to fulmar's extreme speed of flight (J. Rosing 1963: 189; O. Rosing 1957–61, I: 81) as well as to the way it keeps very close to the crests in stormy weather (Muus et al. 1981: 172). In my view other "gliders" could be seabirds that take off from and land on the surface of a lake or the sea.

valley of the dead.[140] Among the deceased he relieves, one by one, several who suffer pains caused by the breaking of taboos by their relatives on earth, whereafter he returns with the wet and sandy old-looking boots—"and this was in the middle of winter!" (ID 1983). Evidently Kaakaaq (or Victor) does not automatically associate being laced up with flying, as Knud Rasmussen was told in some other context. Rasmussen, on the other hand, automatically associates the journey to heaven with flying: in his published translation of the story about Akku's visit to heaven, Akku is said to take off flying across the sea and via the horizon climb the steps to heaven. In Rasmussen's handwritten original, however, Akku put on stockings that he needed for his *walk* (ID 1818).[141] Most probably Akku did glide. This shortcoming fits in with the story about Akku's first performance, when he asked not to be bound due to his inability to fly (ID 1312). Nor was he laced up for subsequent performances; in people's memory he sat cross-legged like a woman on the floor hitting his *makkortaq* (Rasmussen 1938: 124).[142] Ajukutooq, Akku's son, however, ascribed to his father the ability to fly because the wings of a black guillemot were fastened in his armpits (Sonne 2005: ID 987). Be this as it may, another bird used by Akku during his *ueerineq* (see below) points directly to gliding. This is no black guillemot (*serfaq*) but explicitly a guillemot (*appa*). He swallows the dried skin of this bird together with a piece of dried bearded-seal skin, cut into shape for soles. Soles allude to gliding, as does—in my interpretation—the departure of the migrating guillemot towards the south in September. The adults have lost their flight feathers and the young still have not learned to fly. Consequently they leave Greenland along the coast, riding the waves towards the south (Muus et al. 1981: 314)—i.e., in the mythic direction for a fresh rebirth in the house of Sea Woman. Furthermore, once Akku woke up from a dreamed visit to heaven with the happy news in a song that people up there shall no longer die, he raced ecstatically across the floor as if it was covered with ice (Victor & Robert-Lamblin 1989–93, II: 338; Sonne 2005: ID 1992; Victor 1991: 213). Time and again gliding recurs as the epithet of Akku. In short, apart from Ajukutooq's conviction about his father's ability to fly, and Rasmussen's blunder (cultural bias?) in changing "walk" into "fly," all evidence points to gliding and/ or walking as the travel methods used by Akku.

A More Direct Way Upwards?

Taken together, the stories about Maratsi's travels to the realms of death are puzzling. As we know, in Kaakaaq's version Maratsi is said to be laced up at the outset for his travel downwards. However, he travels unbound, wearing out his boots. For going upwards he is explicitly *not* laced up and he *flies directly upwards* to heaven in a peculiar outfit: beautifully decorated female boots, *ikiaq* (gutskin anorak), *naatsit* (briefs), and his long hair tied into a tail. Upon his arrival up there he encounters two relatives, a younger sister with ears like a seal who was killed and thrown out *on the land* at birth, and a younger brother who died in early age and was *buried on the land* (these are the reasons they ended

140. They were to get rid of their earthly "juices" en route to the realm of death (Rasmussen 1921–25, I: 13).

141. "Avgo [Akku] was a shaman but he still had to go visit the deceased humans in the live world up there. In preparation only stockings were brought out. These he needed for his *walk*" (KRH 52, 2: booklet 418: 72–77, tr. and emphasis BS; Sonne 2005: ID 1818).

142. Holm was told that Akku could fly to the moon in order to get children, but Akku directly denied this (Holm 1914: 98; 1972: 132). Either statement defies analysis. *Makkortaq*: piece of skin for boot soles tapped or blown on by the East Greenlandic shaman as a technique of ecstasy.

up in heaven). Both have grown into adults, which is another and completely inexplicable peculiarity breaking with the rule of timelessness in the Other World. Furthermore, unlike his relatives in the realm below, those in heaven suffer no pains. Consequently Maratsi does not have to remind the audience of the taboos at death on his return. Instead he is told in heaven to tell his fellow men to remove the complete skin (used for inner boots) when flaying their dogs, because dogs that arrive in heaven with pelt left on their snout and feet frighten the small children (Sonne 2005: ID 1983). This unusual trip to heaven took place shortly before Maratsi enrolled in the preparatory teachings for baptism in 1910, that is, when the already-baptized East Greenlanders put on their finery for service and, relieved of their traditional taboos, looked forward to a blessed afterlife in heaven (Thalbitzer 1946: 96). This knowledge can hardly explain the children's coming of age in heaven, which is neither a traditional nor a Christian belief. But it may explain the beauty of Maratsi's outfit—the boots, the *ikiaq*, his hairdo—and perhaps also his direct vertical flight to heaven.

Having tried in vain to explain every part of his outfit and flight on its own, a common point of view made sense to me. Although speckled with traditional meanings, Maratsi took the festive dress of the churchgoing West Greenlander as his model: the decorated female boots point to contemporary West Greenlandic fashion; the *ikiaq*, more relevant for trips downwards through the sea, to the festive white anorak of West Greenland men; and the hairdo to the missionaries' disapproval of the long, loose hair of the pagan men, who had it cut at baptism.[143] The flight directly upwards is likely the way opened to deceased Christians and used by angels who went up and down without circumventions. On the other hand, there is a supplementary explanation as to why Maratsi chose neither the usual way taken across the sea via the horizon, nor the protracted swampy way walked by the ordinary dead, and nor, for that matter, the spiraling way of the sun (Thalbitzer 1930: 83).[144] Maratsi apparently rose the same way as people caught by the Northern Lights: directly without detours. In that case his conquered magic cord did the trick, because it was explicitly said to have given him access to both realms, below and above. Indeed, for his journey downwards a crack "*like a whiplash*" had opened a passage for him through the ice at the shore and passing directly through the dwelling of a sand hopper, the somersaulting being of the shore (Sonne 2005: ID 1697, emphasis BS). No mention is made about the way the same cord might have sent Maratsi upwards. The only hint is from the story about his conquest of the cord out at sea, where its owner, Uviak, being unaware of Maratsi's apprenticeship, let loose his magic cord by rubbing his palms. When Maratsi saw the animated cord tearing around on the surface, he caught hold of it. The alarmed Uviak continued rubbing his palms in order to have it return. Too late! It remained in the greater power of Maratsi (Sonne 2005: ID 2292). At closer inspection, this cord behaves exactly like the first of Ajijak's thongs lost when he was caught by the *Qulummiin* spirits (Northern Lights). Dropping down from heaven, it tore around on its own like a live scourge (ID 1674), as did the thongs of both the Iglulik and Labrador Inuit shaman

143. "These frocks [*ikiat*] are either clear and transparent, or white and dull. In order to render the guts white and dull, they are put out to freeze, so that they are dried by the cold before they are prepared" (Holm 1914: 30–31; cf. Buijs 2004: 48). The white anorak with stiches resembling the *ikiaq* of the past became the chosen ethnopolitical East Greenlandic festive male dress in the 1990s. Without stitchings, the West Greenlandic white linen anoraks gained a footing after ca. 1910 (*ibid.* 116, 195, 205).

144. The spiraling way of the sun was considered too time-consuming by some, while for others a day and a night would do (Victor & Robert Lamblin 1989–93, II: 246).

upon return from their *ilimmarneq*. Most likely Maratsi's cord had been used in a similar performance referring indirectly to the Northern Lights. If so, Maratsi's cord, as much as his "Christian" outfit, took him along. Still, why did he wear *naatsit*, briefs, for his ascension? Baptized men did not attend services in briefs! I presume that this is because Greenlandic shamans always traveled to the Other (interior) Worlds in indoor briefs; they added boots or inner boots for going downwards but went to heaven in nothing but briefs and thongs. So, all in all, Maratsi's outfit for one of his last performances before (officially) giving up his shamanic career demonstrates his inventive way of mixing old with new: the traditional *naatsit* and *ikiaq*, the latter as much Christian as traditional, Christian female festive boots (cross-gender ideas?), and a hairdo in compliance with mission. Years later, when baptized, Maratsi played the part of *Nalikkatteeq* portending Judgment Day by the disappearance of her star (see above pp. 122f), he demonstrated the very same inventiveness in mixing old with new. No wonder Maratsi was a beloved storyteller considering how elegantly he could introduce new ways by old keys.

Dress Codes for Flying versus Gliding

In readily accessible statements from all over the Inuit/Yupiit world, there is a tendency for traveling shamans to perform in nothing but briefs or breeches, in case the room is very warm. But there is no general rule. One Kitlinermiut shaman, for instance, walked half-naked outdoors in a snowstorm for extended periods of time in order to get inspiration. The interior of the igloo was not particularly warm (Rasmussen 1931: 30), nor was the igloo of the Iglulik shaman who performed his *ilimmarneq* in bare legs, breeches, and mittens—i.e., stripped to the waist. As for Alaska and Chukotka, the sources tell us that performing shamans wore a gutskin parka (Merkur 1985: 3, 259)—and to this we shall return in the following chapter on *pooq* (meaning cover). Yet exceptions occur: the séances observed by Nelson along the Bering Strait and Bering Sea all have the shaman perform indoors (in warm houses), *naked* in one case when curing a child but dressed in the gutskin parka for curing the weather (Nelson 1899: 432). More recently, in a performance witnessed by a Nelson Islander (Bering Sea), the Yup'ik shaman, who succeeded in procuring rain, took off from inside the house, stark naked except for boots, and laced up. The lacing up meant explicitly—as in Canada and Greenland—that he was going to fly (*elumar-* equivalent to W. Grl. *ilimmar-*). But in Greenland boots were for gliding, not for flying. In addition to the Yup'ik shaman's boots, however, two objects were tied to each corner at the floor, an inflated sealskin float and a gutskin parka (*imarnitek/qasperek* in Yup'ik). These two pieces, first the float, later the parka, were set in violent motion at certain points of the shaman's flight. I imagine that they reflected their owner's (the shaman's) movements in space, and the waterproof gutskin parka also his eventual success in having the rain come down (Orr & Orr 1995: 307–17).

Apparently, then, generalizations are hard to make. Comparing Canadian Inuit with East Greenlandic statements on flying and gliding, the same outfits were used in both places (except for the inventive Maratsi): tied up with ropes and bare legged for flying in contrast to being dressed with kamiks or socks and unbound (when leaving) for gliding and/or walking. In East Greenland, for both flying and gliding, shamans' torsos were naked except for *naatsit*, that is, some wore an *ikiaq* for traveling below. The Yup'ik rainmaker fits in part. He was laced up for flying. Apart from the (disturbing) boots he wore no clothing, and the usual dress of the Alaska shaman, the gutskin parka, was part of the performance in some role of representation as was most probably the inflated float. Maybe the Alaska shaman dressed in the gutskin parka only for travels through the sea. To my knowledge, there are no Alaska statements on gliding. But my first supposition in regard to Greenland and Canada—that gliding was used exclusively for travels to the lower realms—is contradicted in East Greenland, where gliding could take the shaman to heaven as well, across the sea via the horizon and from there up the heavenly steps turning backwards.

So, maybe the only lesson to be learned about traveling East Greenlandic shamans is the variation in capabilities of flying, gliding, and walking, achieved by differing means, at differing points of apprenticeship, and differing demands on dress codes. Generally, however, flying demanded being laced up and there is a tendency that gliding asked for boots or socks. *Naatsit* alone appears to have been the common outfit of all practicing East Greenland shamans, and sometimes an *ikiaq*, the gutskin anorak of travelers to the lower realms.

Public Initiations

The famous historical shamans presented their competence in public by a series of performances, starting with a *ueerineq*, "delivery," followed by a *saqqummerneq*, "coming forward" or "disclosure." A presentation of helping spirits, *naasaaleq*, either ended the *saqqummerneq* or took place at a later performance. In the capacity of a genuine initiation, the *ueerineq* can be seen as a recapturing of oneself, as proposed by Bloch concerning initiations in general (Bloch 1992).[145] In East Greenland it put an end to the apprentice's numerous initiations in solitude, established ownership to his helping spirits, and enabled him to perform without risking his life on ordinary visits to the Other World.

Prelude to Disclosure: *Ueerineq* ("Delivery") and *Niilerneq* ("Wolfing Down")

The great and famous shamans Naaja, Ajijak, and Akku were all credited with a spectacular prelude to *saqqummerneq*. The preferred time was winter solstice, marked on the latitude of Ammassalik by the sun resting shortly just above the horizon. Naaja's *ueerineq* is—either by storyteller, editor (Sandgreen), or both—closely tied to this event, followed by a clear sky gleaming with myriad sparkling stars and magnificent Northern Lights. Naaja had been approached time and again by his helping spirits, pressing him to reveal himself as a shaman in consideration of his father's impending death. His father, who had gotten Naaja started as a future shaman, hoped for a sign of success.

On a fine evening, Naaja peacefully lost consciousness. He remained unconscious for three days, interrupted by short partial recoveries at sunrise. But on the third day the sign was had. Naaja began to bleed from the corners of his mouth, eyes, hairline, and other soft spots. So, in joyous anticipation of his son's becoming a shaman, his father invited people for a feast, which ended in a competitive race across the frozen sea in which, the story goes, the soul of the unconscious Naaja took part. Upon awakening the third day Naaja went straight to the bowl of cooked meat with a ravenous appetite (Sonne 2005: ID 1212, 1211). Prey into hunter, according to Bloch's theory? If so, it coincided with an accumulated appetite that testified to a complete and healthy recovery.

---

145. As described above p. 288: Being tortured and devoured, the prey (i.e., the apprentice) becomes one with the predator, an identification that turns him into a hunter himself. By violence he has to recapture his daily life in order not to lose the benefits gained from the initiation, defined by Bloch as overcoming the transitoriness of life.

Fig. 20. Shaman's séance. Laced up, the shaman is elevated by his drum in front of the entrance hole, which is covered by a loose hanging skin. Drawing by Kaarali Andreassen. *Courtesy of the National Museum of Denmark, Copenhagen.*

Although meant to follow right upon *ueerineq*, Naaja's *saqqummerneq* is placed at a much later point, if still in the middle of some winter (ID 1206). Inserted between the two events are stories about Naaja's marriage and several about his young wife, the logic for which would be the untimeliness of his *ueerineq* caused by the helping spirits in gratitude to his father. The demand on the candidate to be married is explicated by Kaarali (O. Rosing 1957–61, I: 71) and indirectly confirmed by the married state of the other historical *saqqummerneq* candidates. Durable or not in reality, marriage was the condition of well-run alliances with beings of the Other Worlds, be they game animals, deceased relatives, or helping spirits.

Two variants are on record about Ajijak's *ueerineq*, one told by Kaarali (Sonne 2005: ID 1311) and another, a generation later, by Saajooq (Odin Maratsi) (ID 1676). Again, the event was tied to winter solstice, that is, in addition to the previous one of midsummer; according to Kaarali, it was during the latter when Ajijak was told by his helping spirits to get ready for his coming *saqqummerneq* by catching two particular kinds of seals. His wife was to prepare the skins as curtains to cover the entrance (from the tunnel into the room). Saajooq does not mention the skins. He dates the *saqqummerneq* right upon Ajijak's *ueerineq*, which happened shortly after he married. Like Naaja's *ueerineq*, Ajijak's was also combined with midwinter festivities and called forth bleeding, but Ajijak lost his senses in another, more spectacular way. He became possessed by his black guillemot spirit, Oortortoq, lost his *naatsit*, and raced across the floor stark naked, the blood streaming from the corners of his mouth, sprinkling in all directions with the power to kill anyone it hit. Everybody raced around avoiding the drops. Ajijak ended up by puffing away every drop of blood. This was repeated for another two evenings, the last one demanding complete darkness because Ajijak had started to strip off the skin of his head. At the moment the mouth crept to his forehead the light was extinguished and dreadful plops were heard when the skin slipped off. He had the skin pulled on again.

Evidently, the staging emerges more into the open in the description of Ajijak's *ueerineq*. Both Naaja and Ajijak knew the trick of bleeding, and Ajijak had this other skill, of first removing and then pulling on the skin of his head (by means of some prepared skin mask?). Furthermore, the statement that by his bleeding Ajijak obtained some "gain" (the power to *ilimmarneq*, to travel by flying) turns out to catalyze the course of his *saqqummerneq* immediately after this last trick, as we shall see below.

Naaja and Ajijak's bleeding prelude was called *ueerineq*, "delivery," whereas Akku's trick of swallowing dried pieces of black guillemot skin and prepared skin for soles was termed *niilerneq*, or "wolfing down." Akku "happens" to become possessed while the people present are playing blind man's bluff (Sonne 2005: ID 1312). Blinded with rage, Akku takes on playing the part at the center. He shouts "*Massaasammoo*," then the oldest man present repeats it back into his face, he immediately returns the shout to another, receives it back, etc.[146] This ritual game is called *akiversaarineq*, to tease somebody into answering. It was repeated for another two nights. As argued above, Akku's voracious swallowing of the dried skins could point to his nonflying way of traveling. In that case he also seems to have "gained" something new: gliding as a travel method.

Outside ritual, the rage befalling both Ajijak and Akku would have put them in peril. The treatment given to attacks of *perlerorneq*, an insanity characterized by a frightening appetite directed against one's closest of kin, was rough and might end in a painful death. The possibility of transforming prey into hunter lurked. Though ritually true, no such mistake was made in the cases of Ajijak and Akku. Their madness, however seriously lived through, was obviously meticulously prepared and carried out by familiar ritual procedures. Akku, for a start, kept telling his wife that he was about to be hit by madness, and Ajijak tried in vain to make Oortortoq, the spirit possessing him, go away. Naaja's helping spirits repeatedly fluttered along his chin in order to make him come forward. But his completely peaceful bleeding was not a big deal. Ajijak and Akku went mad but played the frightening parts in a game. Only the moving description of the "delivery" of Missuarniannga, as told by his son Kaarali, lives up to the idea of the shaman as a suffering psychotic who cures himself by performing. In the compassionate wording of Rasmussen, the incident is as follows: "He woke up one morning with shooting pains in his head. His brain grew and swelled and the labor pains of mighty thoughts pressed to become delivered. He had to speak, to bode, to foretell and pass judgment in order to keep madness at bay. Consequently he, in the way of shamans, called together the people of his settlement for celebrating the practicing of his art in the darkness of extinguished lamps, pinioned as a helpless bundle" (Rasmussen 1921–25, I: 34, tr. BS, summarized in Sonne 2005: ID 2283). Why Missuarniannga is accorded no "delivery" in public remains an open question. Leaving out any transition of prey into hunter, his pains lead directly to his *saqqummerneq* (below).

Saqqummerneq, Coming Forward

Apart from a first presentation of helping spirits, most shamans' *saqqummerneq* did not noticeably differ from his ordinary performances, which varied according to individual competences. Skilled or

146. According to the spelling by O. Rosing (1957–61, I: 108), *masassammoo* by Jens Rosing (1963: 241), this is a shout reminding one of the tempting shout of the Qulummiin spirits: *Massa, massa* (here, here)!

not, however, they all mastered some method for making the *qaamaneq* ascend (from one's interior, Thalbitzer 1930: 77)—i.e., for "seeing," and the most impressive technique was practiced by shamans mastering the ritual of getting *sila*, *silanippoq*, "he gets all the knowledge of the world." Ajijak, Naaja, Akku, Maratsi, Missuarniannga, and Teemiartissaq's brother—i.e., all great (male) shamans, except Maratsi—demonstrated this skill during *saqqummerneq*. They made the drum dance on its handle, jump onto their back, and go hammering along the spinal cord right on to the neck, at which point the interior light wiped out the ordinary limits of sight (Sonne 2005: ID 1017, 1206, 1312, 1695, 2283). In fact, Moon was the *inua* said to make the drum dance (Gessain 1978: 212), a belief fitting perfectly with the moon symbolism of *qaamaneq*: it was transmitted by his freshwater animal, the worldwide view was enjoyed by Moon in the darkness of night, and a striking correspondence occurs in the spirit language: *jajaq* for Moon (Gessain & Victor 1973: 130) and *jaja* for the drum (*jaajaatsaaq* according to J. Rosing 1963: 255).[147,148] Indeed, the same worldwide view was demonstrated by Moon to his visitor from earth. So in both solitary and public ritual, Moon was a recognized and recurring source for the acquisition of *qaamaneq*.

The experience of *silanippoq* differed, it seems. Naaja had some difficulties, first because he got a shock when the handle hit his neck and sent him back into the ordinary state of mind, and next in the following attempt because he saw two big mountains obstructing his vision. This, however, became revealed when, at the audience's request, he moved his feet each to one side (Sonne 2005: 1206).[149] In contrast, the recollection of Missuarniannga's reception of *sila* during his *saqqummerneq* went all out in poetics of "light":

> [W]hen the drum touched his heel, it felt like the early white dawn ascended from night; he could see dimly in the dark.[150] Later, when it touched his hips, the very day arrived. Darkness no longer existed for him in the night, his eyes cut through everything. But eventually, at the coming of night, the drum stood quivering and reverberating on his shoulder as if led by invisible hands; the sun's light in all its might gushed into his face, and all the countries of the earth assembled in a circle in front of him. Distances however remote no longer existed. Missuarniannga had become omniscient and had gathered *the entire world inside him*. (Rasmussen 1921–25: 34; Sonne 2005: ID 2283; tr. and emphasis BS)[151]

Evidently this was a literal identification of the Other World with one's own interior world.

---

147. It is *jajak* in the spirit language of the West Greenlanders according to Thalbitzer (1914: 21; 1926: 21).

148. Both O. Rosing (1957–61, I: 96) and Victor and Robert-Lamblin (1989–93, II: 261) have *jaajaatsiaq*/*jaajaacila* ("almost jaajaa"). Referring to Vasilevic (1968: 340), Gessain and Victor presume a correspondence with jaja, the drum among Koryak and the Chukchi (1973: 130), quoted also by Robert-Lamblin (1996: 126–27) and Victor and Robert-Lamblin (1989–93, II: 255). Furthermore, the name of the drum among the Yukaghirs is *ya'lgil*, and even identified with the lake through which one could gain access to the world below (Jochelson 1910: 195, 197).

149. Sandgreen, the collector, told me that the storyteller and some listeners chuckled when relating that event.

150. Or, stated in other words: "The light of his interior vision is . . . characterized literally as his dawn: 'his soul passes with his dawn into 'the Other World' (*asia*) crying . . ." (Thalbitzer 1930: 96).

151. This identification of *qaamaneq* with the light of the sun appears as the exception to prove the rule of *qaamaneq* associated with either the moon or the other nightly lights.

Among the other "ecstatic techniques" employed, a swaying to and fro was used by a rare type of shaman having only one helping spirit (Sonne 2005: ID 561); others rubbed the drum with the drumstick while seated on the platform (J. Rosing 1963: 179–80; O. Rosing 1957–61, I: 76) or drummed like an ordinary drum dancer (Gessain & Victor 1973). Aappaluttoq, Allallaq, and Kaakaaq lay covered up on the platform either hitting the *makkortaq* or rubbing their palms (Holm 1914: 98, 104; 1972: 132, 136; Sonne 2005: ID 316, 968, 1017, 1312). Holm, who happened to witness Aappaluttoq diagnose and cure the mentally stricken Sanimuinnaq, made the following report:

> The angakok *Augpalugtok* [Aappaluttoq, portrayed in Holm (1914: fig. 52; 1972: 175)] arrived. He threw himself back on the platform, was covered with a skin, performed incantations over the sick man, and saw that his soul had departed. He sat down on the platform by the sick man's side and cross-examined him as to all the evil he had done. *Sanimuinak* (Sanimuinnaq) answered partly in delirium and behaved quite as if he was mad. Everyone was convinced that he was bound to die, but after *Augpalugtok* had plagued him for some time by trying to worm out all his secrets, they left him in peace, his head began to feel lighter, and he felt better altogether. He had, however, confessed that he was an *ilisitsok* [*ilisiitsoq*] and had killed many persons, among them his foster-daughter's father, with the help of spectres. *Augpalugtok* threw himself back again on the platform and communed with his spirits. He now ascertained that the infamous *Maratuk* [Maratsi], who was Sanimuinnaq's cousin and former accomplice in a real murder, had robbed his soul. *Augpalugtok* sent off one of his *Tarajuatsiaks* [*tarajuatsiat*, shades] to fetch it, but was obliged to return home himself, before the *Tarajuatsiak* [*tarajuatsiaq*, shade] came back with the soul. (Holm 1914: 104; 1972: 134)[152]

So, trusting this description, Aappaluttoq used singing incantations as his technique of ecstasy—of coming to see.

The presentation of helping spirits meant to follow upon the ritual of *silaninneq* is not on record for Naaja or Missuarniannga. Akku's *saqqummerneq* ends this way. Maratsi limited his *saqqummerneq* to a mere presentation of spirits, but famous Ajijak incorporated a flight, an *ilimmarneq*, for his. As proposed above, this spirit flight could represent a former, traditional journey to the Northern Lights like that of Iglulik shamans, but as part of a *saqqummerneq* it asks for further treatment. It followed immediately upon the third repetition of the delivery, when Ajijak, apologizing to his wife for having scared her out of her wits, asked for the skins she had prepared for the curtains to be hung in front of the entrance opening. A dialogue ensued between Ajijak and his supportive father, weighing the advantages of a great career against the risk of undertaking an *ilimmarneq* instead of a mere presentation of spirits. Ajijak left the room in order to make a decision in solitude. He returned with a long harpoon line. He sat down on the skin placed in front of the entrance and began to lace up his hands by blowing, apparently a sign for his father to complete the operation, which called forth piercing shrieks of pain from Ajijak. During this torture his father called to the helping spirits, "Look, we are mocking him, are you ready down there?" "Haj, haj," the spirits

152. The aforementioned drawing by Kaarali in 1906 of the practicing *qilaaqutsertoq* (Thalbitzer 1941: 710, fig. 224) tallies with this observation by Holm in 1885. See fig. 13, p. 259.

responded, "we are ready." Tightly laced up, with his forehead on his knees and hands tied behind his back, Ajijak had a pair of wings from an adult black guillemot inserted into his armpits from behind. Tipped over by his father, he was lying on his side with his back to the drum. The lamp was extinguished. In complete darkness he made the curtains rattle furiously and set the drum roaring and afloat, pitching over his shoulder until possession took over. He sat up, and uttered a deafening shriek; while the drum continued its wild pitching, Ajijak's father suddenly interrupted the entire noisy affair by asking his son about his destination. "Where I feel tempted to go," was the answer. His father said, "If that will be southward, don't cast any glance at the *Qulummiin* spirits. From them no human returns safe and alive." Ajijak promised not to, and with a penetrating whizz he started all over again with rattling curtains and the drum going, soon easing off the volume. Then, suddenly, the room filled with roaring voices of all sorts (the entrance of his spirits). The drum began bouncing on its handle (the movement called *kaluartertoq*, Jens Rosing adds). It was heard getting hold of Ajijak's big toe, by which it raised him into flying in slanting circles with the sound and speed of a flying black guillemot. During the third round, a shower of sparks above the window and a loud shriek announced his takeoff through the wall. The drum continued its movement while the giant among his helping spirits, *Ipak*—supported by the scared (and frightening) comments by the father on the possible insufficiency of Ajijak's *angerlartussiaq* powers—kept the audience informed about the unfortunate capture by the *Qulummiin* spirits. The report about their rough ball playing with Ajijak was accompanied by the continued movements of the drum from floor to platform back to the floor and around. When eventually Ajijak was saved by his (grand)mother's ghost and announced to have slipped out, Ipak left the relieved audience. The other helping spirits then took the floor one after another, placing themselves on Ajijak's sitting skin asking whomever to touch its body. Some were very big, some small, but all had human figures. People were allowed to touch one or two of them. Ajijak's return was of course just as noisy as his departure, supplied in the end with the trick of his two thongs. The one lacing his hands was untied by one among the audience, who hardly had returned to the platform before the cord snapped the wall skins on the sidewall as if it were alive. By blowing, Ajijak let loose the bigger one lacing his forehead to the knees, yelling "Ajaa, ajaa." The rattling of the curtains and sounding of the drum ebbed. At the rekindling of lights, Ajijak was seen sitting on his skin, the thongs at his side, neatly folded with the wings of the black guillemot on top. His body was blue all over with big bruises. Some days later an old shaman, a relative, had Ajijak perform at his place and afterwards accorded him the title of a shaman (Sonne 2005: ID 1674).[153]

In my interpretation, Kaarali's reproduction of an orally transmitted narrative, published in Greenlandic and translated into Danish by Jens Rosing, makes completely clear both the prepared staging and the audience's understanding of all the sounds.[154] In comparison, the frequently quoted performance by Sanimuinnaq as observed by Holm in 1885 (1914: 91–93; 1972: 128–29) is nowhere near as explicit about the cultural frame of reference. Similarly, the disclosure of shaman's tricks as

---

153. In his general description of *saqqummerneq*, Kaarali places the appointment immediately upon its ending by the oldest shaman of the audience. He gets tied up, performs shortly by making his helping spirits almost arrive, loosens his ties, and then exclaims, "You are now a shaman and provided you zealously continue, you shall become very attractive (to the spirits)" (J. Rosing 1963: 179; O Rosing 1957–61, I: 75).

154. Original is not available. Partly translated, partly summarized into English by BS.

confided to Holm by Sanimuinnaq fits our Western frame to the minute.[155] If we remain within the East Greenlandic frame, however, Kaarali's reconstructed narrative of Ajijak's *ueerineq* and consecutive *saqqummerneq* forms a clear course of staged events, creating a perfect illusion from the bleeding start to the bruises in the end. The "master of ceremony" turns out to be Ajijak's father, whose part appears well known and prepared. So also is Ajijak's bleeding *ueerineq*, staged at the right time of the year and understood to presage his father's questioning about the possibility of an *ilimmarneq* at the outset of the *saqqummerneq*. His father's explication of the splendid powers to be gained by a successful flight is addressed as much to the audience as to Ajijak. Similarly instrumental is his father's interruption of all the heavy noise, first by calling in the supporting spirits and second by his question about the destination of the flight. Apparently lacking any idea about a definite place, Ajijak declares his intentions to follow any temptation en route; this is a clear allusion to the *Qulummiin* spirits' tempting call of "*massa, massa*" or "here, here." For good reasons, then, his father warns him against the *Qulummiin* spirits, implied to be dangerous, thereby presaging the thrilling events. Here, his worries serve to heighten the suspense. Ajijak's skill in handling the drum and making all the different sounds are convincing in calling up possession (vision), of producing a cacophony of voices at the arrival of his spirits, as of imitating the recognizable flight of a black guillemot at the moment of his takeoff. Apparently Ajijak himself made the report, that is, through Ipak in possession of Ajijak's abandoned body accompanied by the sounds and movements of the drum in sympathy with his pains. The production of the cacophony of spirit voices is less clear to me, but obviously one or two assistants must have played the parts of some of the tangible helping spirits in human figures. The final tricks, with the thongs in darkness and then in full light the bruises testifying to the rough handling by the *Qulummiin* spirits, impressively end the performance.

Whatever Kaarali intended to communicate, he seems to be a loyal reteller of the account. Although he was an educated and practicing catechist, he wished to improve the reputation of his father's religion among his fellow Christians. There is no point in discussing belief versus disbelief. My way of paraphrasing from some "haughty" distance is meant to emphasize the ritual character of the performance, a play of theater involving everybody present, humans and nonhumans alike. I take theater seriously. Provided the illusion works, it tells you some truths of life, and the illusion works provided it is based on a common frame of reference. In this same way the narrative taken down by

155. "The angakok performance depends on the angakok's power of making so much noise and to-do as possible, and on his ventriloquial skill. Whereas, when the lamps are lit, the drum is always beaten by striking the drum-stick on the edge of the wooden rim, during the angakok performance the drumming sometimes is performed by rocking the drum on the flat stone, which can be done with the elbow or leg, when the hands cannot be used, and it sounds just as if the drum-stick were being used with extraordinary quickness. When the angakok strikes the loose, flat stone on which the drum lies, it gives a very hollow and mystical sound. By speaking and singing down between the hollow spaces under large stones and driving the sound along the drum-stick, voices from the nether world are produced. Sanimuinak one evening gave in our house, with the lamps lighted, an exhibition of his ventriloquial skill, making his tartok speak outside the house. The dry skins which hang before the entrance and the window can of course produce a very loud and weird noise. The thong for lacing up the shaman is tied in a kind of noose, which is certainly drawn uncommonly tight, but which can be loosened and slipped off by forcing the arms closer together, so that it becomes possible to get the hands free. As has been already mentioned, the prime object of the angakok in performing his arts is to produce a demoniacal, mystical impression on his audience and to work upon their nerves. The following incident may serve to illustrate the impression which the angakut can make with their arts" (Holm 1914: 96; 1972: 130).

Kaarali regarding Akku's "blind man's bluff" prelude summarized above, and his *saqqummerneq* to follow below, live up to expectations.

There are two versions of Akku's *saqqummerneq*, one by Kaarali in his own writing and a less detailed one taken down by Rasmussen (original not available, informant unknown; Sonne 2005: ID 968). Both speak to the splendor of Akku's powers and thus contradict the information had by Holm from the horse's mouth: No, Akku protested, the rumors were wrong. He was no great shaman. He did not know how to make the drum dance. He had never stolen any souls; never, in fact, had he been able to see any of the spirits, did not know how to get babies from the moon, etc. Holm had no confidence in Akku, who apparently had no other intention but to please the ignorant Qallunaaq (Holm 1972: 132–33; 1914: 98–99). We, however, by reading the story as heard, recollected, and taken down by Kaarali, are convinced of Akku's talents in staging the ideal of a splendid performance, e.g., his *saqqummerneq*, as follows.[156]

Abiding by tradition, this initiation took place right after the third repetition of his "wolfing down." Fatherless Akku was assisted by the oldest man of the longhouse, Kaattuarnaaq (not listed as a shaman or apprentice—here, age counts), who asked Akku at the opening if he wanted to be tied up (hands on the back and forehead on the knees). No, he answered, because he had not been "delivered" by *ueerineq* (bleeding). Seated on a skin in front of the entrance from the tunnel (hung with skin curtains to produce an accompaniment of flapping and stillness), Akku asked to have a lamp kept burning.[157] He remained quiet for a long while, collecting his thoughts. Eventually, by blowing on his *makkortaq*, he made the skin curtains rustle slightly. Kaattuarnaaq, still on the floor, called into the tunnel: "We have eased him off; we have mocked and humiliated him. Has he got anybody to help him out?" Akku hit the *makkortaq* thrice, and the answer came from underneath the floor in spirit language: "Yes, here we are, arriving before *naar* (space, *sila*, light, or the sun) has risen."[158] Visibly embarrassed, Akku started hitting his *makkortaq* in time with the increased roars of the curtain skins and his drum, until suddenly he called out, "Put out the lamp!" Immediately the drum started dancing independently on its handle, jumping onto Akku's back, hammering away, then down to the floor, up and down, etc. Arriving in ecstasy (*silanippoq*, he gets vision), Akku stopped drumming. "Did you see anything?" Kaattuarnaaq asked. "Yes, they [the spirits] are coming." After some more hefty drumming and making the curtains rattle, Akku began to press down his breath and out through the anus, calling "haj haj haajh!" Time and again he managed this, encouraged by Kaattuarnaaq's appreciative comments. The sixth time Akku made his breath disappear into the deep abyss with a terrifying shriek (*nillerujussamik*).[159] (Akku had by now cleared the way for the spirits to enter.) The first to arrive were frightening spirits, *qimmaratit*, beginning with *Amoo*, the floating spirit exclaiming "*amoo, amoo.*" Somebody in the audience then answered by imitating the call. *Amoo* came swiftly floating at close quarters when another listener turned its attention away by repeating the call, etc. Eventually *Amoo* left, audibly floating away. Accompanied by violent

156. Try to compare this transmitted description of Akku's performance with the repeatedly quoted one made by the uncomprehending Holm of Sanimuinnaq's performance (Holm 1972: 128–29; 1914: 90–93), and you will know what actually was supposed to be acted out.

157. He sits cross-legged and, like any performing shaman, wears nothing but *naatsit* (Rasmussen 1938: 122–23).

158. "*Uvaniippun narta makinginngmati nutiarsi tutivarpun.*"

159. This sounded like "*aatjiwitjiwitji ho-hooi-ho-hooi,*" according to Thalbitzer (1930: 96).

drumming and rattling, two more *qimmaratit* entered. They arrived one at a time, each with its characteristic voice and call: *Ajumaaq*, a ghost, and *Ungaa*, cry of a baby. They were also teased by the audience. The remaining spirits were supposed to be less aggressive. First among these was a spirit who, when asked its name by Kaattuarnaaq, turned out to be the familiar *Ajaqqisaaq*, a spirit inherited by Akku from an earlier (great) shaman. It arrived humming, and as all noises from drum and curtains stopped, it sat down on the end platform and spoke: "How pleased I am to be back in your settlement." Audibly sitting on the end platform, *Ajaqqissaq* apparently did not possess Akku's body, who arrived in breath from far below in order to encourage any nonbeliever to touch *Ajaqqisaaq*. The latter moved to the threshold and sat down, an impressively big figure it turned out. Its intentions, however, were not all that friendly. When Kaattuarnaaq asked it to tell its story, Akku again interfered, asking a certain Kukku among the audience to guard his wife with a circle of blubber (keeping spirits at bay). After this, Akku's voice returned below. "Oh, nothing escapes your vision," the annoyed *Ajaqqisaaq* exclaimed, being barred by the ring of blubber from attacking Kukku's wife (and thus giving in to the splendor of Akku). "So, why don't you tell your story, almost a human being as you are," Kaattuarnaaq urged *Ajaqqisaaq*. *Ajaqqisaaq*, implicitly glorifying Akku's powers, related how in the past he had left one master for another, literally much brighter one. But at some point when the latter was murdered by two persons, *Ajaqqisaaq* did not turn up in time to help. Enraged, *Ajaqqisaaq* killed the murderers and continued to plot against their descendants, to whom Kukku's wife belonged. Having thus emphasized Akku's saving feat (by warning Kukku) and also highlighted the power of Akku's vision and mastery over his helping spirits, *Ajaqqisaaq* disappeared and was followed, one after another, by a great number of entering spirits, presenting themselves (most probably by name at Kaattuarnaaq's request). Finally, Akku's breath returned to his body. He is said to have repeated this *saqqummerneq* another two times (Sonne 2005: ID 1312).

The staging and important role of the father replaced by the senior Kaattuarnaaq is quite clear, as is that of the audience in sending *Amoo* and the other *qimmaratit*, *Ajumaaq*, *Ungaa*, and a ghost floating around. This was obviously a ritual game that repeats the *akiversaarineq* of Akku's prelude, and was equally thrilling considering the darkness and because, as the saying goes, being touched by *Ajumaaq* meant certain death (ID 2283). The temporary return of Akku's breath in order to warn Kukku was not contrary to the rules, as recorded by Thalbitzer: "His [the shaman's] body is like a house with alternating occupants; now the helping spirits enter and leave, now the soul of the shaman" (Thalbitzer 1930: 93; Sonne 2005: ID 1017). Nothing is revealed about the person(s) who may have played the parts of the various spirits. (On a general level we can refer to Kaarali's drawing of a performance, which shows two assistants, pupils, on each side of the practicing shaman; see Thalbitzer [1914: 710] and fig. 15, p. 261.) Akku played most parts, no doubt, famous as he was for his skill in imitating voices (Sonne 2005: ID 967). Yet the oversize figure of touchable *Ajaqqisaaq* obviously required a stand-in of some dimensions. I take it that this spirit spoke ordinary human language intelligible to all, "almost a human" as he was. Except for the cacophony, Akku has only one spirit acting at a time, whereas Ajijak, according to Saajooq, staged several together for his presentation. They sat in a row on the side platform, visibly chatting away, but enveloped in some unbearable shimmering light (ID 1676).

The transmitted story about the *saqqummerneq* of Maratsi (ca. 1854–1923) is simply a summary. At the time he had happened to steal the magic whiplash from the shaman Uviak, and thus became able to travel wherever he wanted, his spirits told him to perform in public on the shortest days of the New Year. He practiced to make sure that drum, curtains, and spirits were at his beck and call. No delivery presaged the event. Maratsi simply invited people: "If you feel like attending a performance, I shall come forward to you. I shall play like a shaman. Don't hesitate. Do come and listen." People arranged the room for the performance, and then Maratsi came forward, sat down, quickly made the curtain flutter excessively while the light was still on, and, upon the putting out of the lamps, caused the drum to roar. One after another his helping spirits arrived, filling the room with distinct voices. In this way Maratsi had his cohabitants *sense* his helping spirits (Sonne 2005: ID 1688, emphasis BS) rather than touching or seeing them. Did he have his *qaamaneq* ascend? Or did his breath descend for his spirits to enter? A poor report or a poor performance? Or better, a cautious start? As will be shown presently, Maratsi improved his skills as the years passed.

Finally, a text taken down by Thalbitzer describing the *saqqummerneq* as told by Teemiartissaq lacks coherence. It feels like reading the two versions of the Creation in Genesis, the second following right upon the first. For a start, Teemiartissaq tells about the pupil's apprenticeship in general terms, but she ends with the feat of her brother who achieved the frightening spirit, the female *Niimilaa*, as a helping spirit.[160] Entering the shaman's *saqqummerneq* this spirit scares everybody outside, adults and children alike, tears down the skins from the walls, and presses the shaman down into the earth. By following behind, *Niimilaa* apparently makes room for the presentation of the shaman's other helping spirits, either outdoors or more likely to a returned audience inside: the shadows, the dwarves, two kinds of inland giants, the vagrants close by as well as the distant living ones. After this Teemiartissaq immediately starts all over again by having the shaman lose and regain consciousness, fasten the curtains in front of the entrance hole, start hitting the drum on its edge with his drumstick (as was usual), and simultaneously blow his *makkortaq* alternating with his rapping out "*aala-laa-laa-laa-auci-witci-witci-witci-wit*." At his first presentation of spirits he mumbles "*aataa-taa-taa*." Then they arrive, one after another, his falcon, his *toornaarsuk*, next his frightening spirit [not *Niimilaa*] trying to pull the people with its "*amoo...h, amoo...h!*" Because the shaman does not recognize his helping spirits he asks his *apeqqiteq* [asking spirit] about their names. But at the point the dwarves living closest to humans have entered, his drum starts dancing and jumps to his back. This is when he obtains his vision. With a "*håi, håi*," he sinks into (through?) the earth for a talk with

160. *Niimilaa*, as a cave dweller high up in some mountain busy making a big *ulu* due to her appetite for human lungs, reminds one of both *Nalikkatteeq* and the giant of the inland ice. The ambitious pupil is to entice her out of her cave by using her call, "*niimilaa*," then take flight around a lake into which *Niimilaa* sinks in her persuance. But she reemerges without seeing him and returns to her cave (Sonne 2005: ID 1017). A variant told about Naaja has this cave facing west, in contrast to the north-facing cave of the *Sermerssuup Inua*. Being devoured by the latter was empowering, while being eaten by *Niimilaa* of the cave facing the setting sun meant a certain death. While fleeing from *Niimilaa* Naaja happened to put one foot into the swamp surrounding the lake, a decisive act that turned Naaja invisible to *Niimilaa*. She ran swiftly passed him, continued for another couple of rounds, and then returned to her cave. *Niimilaa*, more than any of his spirits, insisted on his *ueerineq* (ID 1213, 1215, 1211), and as a genuine *qimmarat Niimilaa* is credited with an exciting performance directed by Naaja. Upon the announcement of her arrival, everybody fled outside the house except a poor woman under taboo. *Niimilaa* tears down the skins from the walls, finds and empties a stocking filled with blubber, and then turns her appetite to the poor woman who at the last moment is saved by the bucket filled with urine into which *Niimilaa* happens to put her one foot. Both urine and blubber are poison to spirits. She takes flight and, turned visible to the outside audience by the blubber she has devoured, is seen stopping at intervals and then disappearing. In daylight her tracks are clearly visible from the blubber that made her sick (ID 1195).

his helping spirits on the mountains of the underworld. Upon his return with another "*håi, håi*" he is questioned about the patient he was asked to diagnose and cure (ID 1017).

So seemingly Teemiartissaq got at least two performances mixed up: her brother's *saqqummerneq* beginning with Niimilaa followed by a presentation of his spirits, then another in general terms of a *saqqummerneq* that ends in an ordinary performance of curing, that is, a first demonstration of some shaman's particular skill.

Concluding Summary of *Ueerineq* and *Saqqummerneq*

The stories about historical deliveries and disclosures all tell that the occasion, winter solstice, and the social prerequisite of being married were unavoidable demands. Of further social significance, having a supportive father or, in substitute, a male elder was a great advantage (Qilertaanalik, the husband of Maratsi's stepdaughter, always hung up the curtains for his performances [J. Rosing 1963: 273]). He need not be a shaman, in fact apparently he never was.[161]

Stories about the great feats of contemporary shamans differ in certain ways from those about shamans of the more distant past, although transmitted by descendants in a direct line. Like most peoples, the East Greenlanders glorified their shamans of the past at the expense of contemporaries (Holm 1972: 132; 1914: 98). Saajooq's mythologization of his great-grandfather Ajijak's unknown apprenticeship and final visit to Moon (see above pp. 310ff) confirms this, as do the great accomplishments credited to certain former shamans of visits to Moon, or *Asiaq*, or Sea Woman. These stories appear contrived and detached, in contrast to detailed descriptions of the outstanding performances observed and transmitted by audience members. Whether reflecting firsthand observations or changed through oral transmission, they testify to a rich interplay between shaman, his probable assistants, the "master of ceremony" (be he a father or an elder), and the audience. In this art, Akku, who was still alive during the Women's Boat Expedition of 1884–85, no doubt matched his great predecessors Naaja, Ajijak, Aaqqi (about whom no stories are published), and Uitsaleqanngitseq or Karraq, who were among the first generation on record. Akku alone was considered a contemporary outstanding shaman by Holm's informants and for good reason (see also below).

Going into (pre)history, a midwinter celebration, including at minimum a ball game and better a *saqqummerneq* or at best an *ilimmarneq* to the ball-playing people (dead relatives) in heaven, turns out to have been part of the expanding Thule culture. In whichever form they were brought along from North Alaska, these particular New Year rituals allowed for changes or additions: some enigmatic, and others straightforward. To the former belongs the assumed falling into oblivion of the obvious identity of the *Qulummiin* spirits with the Northern Lights among the Ammassalimmiut. Nor did they, or at least Holm's select informants, hold the unfailing pan-Inuit recognition of their ball as being a walrus skull. Instead, stillborn and small children killed before naming danced hand in hand and played ball with their placentas (Holm 1972: 121; 1914: 82). The West Greenlanders shared the notion of a walrus skull, and in a way, the West Greenlandic shaman who managed to have the very spirit of this skull enter at his *saqqummerneq* as a prelude to an *ilimmarneq*, happened, consciously or not, to incorporate acculturative news. The date presented is winter 1739. Besides the

161. The appointment of Ajijak as a shaman by Karraq/Uitsaleqanngitseq happened at a later point at the latter's place.

skull grooving scores in the floor, another helping spirit is a wooden doll speaking Dutch. In plain interpretation, this doll was bought from the Dutch whalers, the long-distance seafaring people who arrived in spring and left in late autumn in company with the transmigrating mammals and birds of the sea. The distance was once covered by a shaman on an *ilimmarneq* to Holland. He observed how the Dutch brought their dolls to life by blowing. No wonder, he said, that Holland was so densely populated (N. Egede 1971: 22; 1939: 140).[162]

By his *saqqummerneq* the shaman earned his title in public. According to a solitary source, Kaarali, it was announced at the end of the third repetition by the greatest shaman among the audience who, being laced up and going into ecstasy afterwards, could confirm that the spirits (of the new shaman, I suppose) were visible if still a bit blurred (J. Rosing 1963: 179; O. Rosing 1957–61, I: 75).

Enhancing Reputation

The biographies of East Greenlandic shamans bring out some extraordinary performances that evidently raised the reputation of the shaman concerned. Some were true initiations endowing the shaman with new faculties whereas some served additional social purposes, but even failed performances, which put limits on further developmental experiments, added to publicity. One example, Ajijak's curing of his wife, is treated at the end of this section. Let's turn to Maratsi first.

Maratsi (born ca. 1854, baptized 1912), who was prominent among the youngest generation of shamans, made up for his poor *saqqummerneq* in his colorful career. First, he had success as a doctor in the figure of a polar bear. Asked to cure Iarqa/Iaqqa, daughter of Uumiitsuk, of a great abscess, he performed lying next to her on the platform, covered by a skin and rubbing his palms into ecstasy. Transforming little by little into a polar bear, he cut the abscess and sucked it out to the mixed disgust and fascination of the housemates. Refusing payment until Iaqqa proved cured, he was later rewarded with a fine white male dog, half a bearded seal skin prepared for making boot soles, and, still later, a small, most valuable iron saw (Sonne 2005: ID 1696). Iaqqa lived into old age in a childless but peaceful marriage (J. Rosing 1993: 110–12). Two other times Maratsi became gorily wounded by a helping spirit while lights were on in the midst of a peaceful evening. The event won him genuine reputation, although according to the eyewitness Usoqqu, people were used to such behavior from shamans. The idea of the double wounding was to enhance his powers as a shaman. Indeed, he had to remain in bed several days for the last wound to heal. It had let out his guts and he ended up removing some little knot from the scar (Sonne 2005: ID 1691). Maratsi also had his *toornaarsuk* perform a trick with stones in order to have it relieve its angry feelings against him. In they came sliding, four stones in a row, all meant to hit him but failing. The last one, a boulder leaving grooves in the wooden floor, was stopped by the audience on orders from Maratsi. Evidently this was a stone from shallow waters below the impenetrable ice with only a thin tidal split at the shore.[163] However Maratsi managed to have it enter the room, his reputation increased (Sonne 2005: ID 1690).[164] No less did his fights

162. Wooden dolls for magic ends were created in Greenland as well.

163. Making a helping spirit throw some big stones overgrown with seaweed into the house may have been a common trick, in that one newly fledged West Greenlandic shaman knew a similar trick. He had his *innersuaq* from the submerged skerries send in big stones in 1736 (P. Egede 1971: 28; 1939: 24–25).

164. Apart from being an imposing trick, some ritual function is likely like that of a down-rolling boulder (in myth) stopped from smashing the longhouse by the spirit *eqingaleq* (*equngasoq* W. Grl.) from the outermost skerries.

with human enemies contribute to his standing. As the ideal of revenge required, he had Uviak, the alleged murderer of his father, killed, not in actual confrontation but by soul robbery performed by his dwarf, Sorpik (ID 1689). The text does not describe any public performance in this case, or his attempt to gain possession of one of Ajijak's helping spirits. Appropriated, these spirits were meant to be employed in defense of threatening Iisimmardik, Maratsi's cousin and a mass murderer. When, at Ajijak's grave, Maratsi called him up by rubbing the gravestone, Ajijak came down like a black clotted cloud from above.[165] In return Ajijak was on request permitted to glide across Maratsi's legs. The latter's brother, however, had already taken possession of Ajijak's helping spirits. Nevertheless, by gliding over Maratsi's legs, Ajijak himself must have become a helping spirit of Maratsi—not a bad consolation, so to speak. Maratsi was never attacked by Iisimmardik (*ibid.*). A case of a far more serious character was closed during the performance mentioned above in treating the *ululoo*-calling spirit, namely, when Maratsi succeeded in having the revengeful soul of Quarrajeeq burst into a blob of blood out there at heaven's end beyond the horizon (ID 1695). Maratsi killed Quarrajeeq, who was married to Maratsi's man-eater of a mother, either because Akku, who wanted her for a second wife, had pressed him (ID 1693), or on Maratsi's own accord, because her bad housekeeping had earned her severe beatings from her young husband, Quarrajeeq (ID 1918). Although Sanimuinnaq, persuaded by his cousin Maratsi to assist, ended up being the one who gave Quarrajeeq the death-blow, Maratsi was a party to the murder (ID 1695). No matter who was guilty, Akku, by his desire for Maratsi's mother, or Quarrajeeq for beating her up, this demonstration of power is flat out shocking to our moral standards. Not only did Maratsi deny Quarrajeeq a just revenge, but he also discouraged Quarrajeeq's potential avengers. Well, a comparable outcome could be produced at a Western court by a clever lawyer bribed with sufficient money.

Naaja of the early 19th century was credited a journey to "The Land of High Tides," Tinitarseerpik (W. Grl. Tinitarsuarfik) on the West Coast, which may reflect some séance he actually performed. But the story most probably reflects rumors about both Southeast Greenlanders' emigration north and the Christian mission. "The Land of High Tides" could be at Qaquk (J. Rosing 1963: 198) in the fjord of Nipisat opposite Nuuk. It was inhabited by immigrated Southerners and visited by relatives en route to whaling and trade farther north (Sonne 2005: ID 1750, 1765). Naaja is the shaman of two versions, one taken down by Kaarali, the other told by Naaja's descendant Apulu/Kukkujooq to Jens Rosing. A third variant, taken down by Kaarali's wife, Johanne, has an anonymous shaman as its hero (Sonne 2005: ID 1666, 1667, 1673, 806). Christian impact is seen in the spirit, who is the only one to find its way, a very long distance, by means of its extremely long ears: *toornaarsuk.* As you may remember, he was considered closely related to *Toornaarsuk* of the Christians.[166] Furthermore, the people visited are spirits, who regret that no humans pick them for helping spirits anymore. Therefore they rejoice when right upon arrival the visiting shaman obtains two helping spirits among them. They take off in exchange—i.e., by paying a simultaneous entertaining visit to Naaja's audience

165. Baptized Saajooq, the storyteller may have considered his pagan great-grandfather Ajijak condemned, in that the soul usually arrived from the realm of death to its grave by emissions of light (see p. 280).

166. The long ears remind one of the white wing snail, whose wings, understood as ears, were prominent among the *toornaarsuit* owned by East Greenland shamans. In addition the *toornaarsuk* of the anonymous shaman calls *ulololo*—i.e., like a bearded seal spirit with the ability to travel very long distances.

at home.[167] Apparently then, one implicit goal is to form a glorious friendship with these spirits of the West Coast. The shaman does not participate in the notorious hunt at low tides. In Johanne's variant, the hero is told by his hosts; in Kaarali's, Naaja is informed by the visiting spirits to the audience in East Greenland. They further receive a (correct) description of the route along the coast. In the version told by Apulu, a mere explanation for the name Tinitarseerpik appears sufficient: "[the place] where narwhal and beluga are caught in pitfalls digged at low tide" (ID 1673, tr. BS).[168] Actually, Jens Rosing may have added this explanation because Apulu's mythic frame of reference is not an actual place on the West Coast but rather a visit to heaven on par with the *ilimmarneq* of Ajijak to the *Qulummiin* spirits (see above). According to Apulu, Naaja becomes uncomfortably anxious among the foreign spirits because they let his thongs come loose and *fall down* like swishing whiplashes among the audience in front of his father at home. By this allusion to impending death among the *Qulummiin* spirits, however, an episode present in all three versions makes perfect sense: an invitation to attend a game played among the spirits of hitting a small hole in a suspended piece of bone with a pointed awl.[169] This is a game of life and death as far as the visiting human shaman is concerned; missing the mark, he shall suffer an untimely death. Striking the mark earns him the predestined length of his life. Naturally, the earthly shaman succeeds. Naaja of Apulu's version reacts by stealing the souls of two spirits, two brothers whose father does not dare take revenge. Apulu claims that this is proof of his great-grandfather Naaja's unsurpassed powers (*ibid.*). The same mythologized rise in reputation comes to the fore in comparing the Naaja version recorded by Kaarali. The latter makes no hints to heaven, nor does Naaja show his superior powers by any mean tricks. So, while some core of truth can be substantiated, such as knowledge about the route to a place for tidal hunting like Qaquk, the version recorded by Kaarali, who had been to Nuuk for his education, comes closest to the point. Apulu, absorbed in raising his ancestor's reputation, could not care less.

Among actual successful attempts at enhancing one's reputation, Akku ingeniously had his inherited helping spirit's former master lend luster to his talent (see pp. 314, 334). Karraq/Uitsaleqanngitseq won praise by staging and playing the central parts of driving away Moon although in cooperation with two other shamans and an old man (see pp. 127f). Another cooperative feat bestows fame not on Karraq but on Ajijak, his younger relative and likely pupil. After *saqqummerneq* Karraq accorded him the title of a shaman. Later he invited Ajijak to a common *ilimmarneq* for attending a song duel among the giants of the inland ice. Both had a giant for a helping spirit among the hosts. Karraq suffered defeat from his spirit, Qujuk, whereas Ajijak, having no score to settle with his helping spirit Ikilerpik, let it shine in proving its marvelous strength. He had it kill with its bare hands a giant narwhal called in by another giant among the hosts.[170] In a last-minute return flight, when Ajijak arrived safely and Karraq barely made it before sunrise, the latter exclaimed: "Why were you not here in my young days. Such wonderful flights we could have made together!" (Sonne 2005: ID 1677).

---

167. Only the local spirits (*innersuit*) used that method, leaving the ordinary way of sealing to their human neighbors.

168. See Kivioq/Kiviuq, as treated above.

169. *Nordortaun*. The game was also played among the Nattilingmiut as demonstrated in the film *The Netsilik Eskimos* (1968), made by Balikci about the Pelly Bay Inuit.

170. Signifying or promoting success in the narwhal hunt in the year to come? Giants knew how to hunt narwhals at the bottom of ice fjords or through its cracks by turning the course of rivers and currents of the sea continuing beneath the earth disk backwards.

Ajijak nevertheless had his reputation attacked when his wife fell seriously ill and people began gossiping. Such a minor shaman, this Ajijak, who was unable to cure his own wife! But Ajijak planned his rehabilitation, it seems. The performance was a rare occurrence in that it took place outdoors in May at Qingu, the place of assembly at the bottom of the Ammaassalik fjord for fishing capelin. Ajijak's wife had been ill for a long time, but he knew her secret. She had been hit by the boomerang effect of a *tupilak* of her own making. If the person against whom it was sent was too strong in magical means, the *tupilak* returned to the sorcerer, who had to confess in order to be cured. Ajijak could not persuade his wife to confess. That particular summer, Ajijak's household arrived late, and no place was left to put up a tent. He went further on and pitched the family tent in isolation. In a short while he invited everybody to a shaman's performance, outdoors, with the sun high in the sky. Usually in summer the shaman would lie down, covered up, but Ajijak appeared from the tent carrying his wife in his arms and placed her on a piece of skin. Contrary to the dress code for women outdoors, she was completely naked. Ajijak placed another piece of skin a short distance away and a big knife between the skins. Then *he* stripped naked, lay down on his skin, and worked himself into ecstasy, sent his breath downwards and out through his anus, and relaxed. Then his flesh started to shrink until nothing but skin and bones were left. His wife lost consciousness from fear. When somebody pulled her hair, she came to. A helping spirit arrived with a humming sound from below, went into the body of Ajijak, who had made room for the spirit by pressing his breath down and away through the anus. His possessed body recovered in flesh and became the ordinary figure of Ajijak. But his soul had changed place with the now-incarnated spirit, who fetched his knife and addressed the audience, scolding them for having belittled Ajijak behind his back. Next the embodied spirit killed and cut up the naked wife, a bloody event, went back to the skin, and lay down. Once again Ajijak's body lost its flesh and recovered, this time in the figure of a roaring polar bear. Rising on its feet, the bear sneezed around the cut-up woman, licked a little blood, but finding nothing worth removing it just went back to the piece of skin, and again, the body lost and regained its flesh, making way for a new transformation. This time Ajijak returned in spirit, that is, by letting his breath return, but still in a sufficient ecstasy for putting together and reviving his wife. Alive but appalled, she finally asked to confess. Too late! Ajijak declared, and put on his outdoor clothing. He lifted up his wife, gave the audience a knowing look, and disappeared into the tent with his wife. He did not reappear for any applause, of course. Quite a few among the dead-silent audience had passed out, and Ajijak's wife died in a few days. So, Ajijak, apparently well aware before staging the performance that his wife was beyond hope, and having demonstrated his mastery of the entire bodily art of shamanism, stood his ground (Sonne 2005: ID 1674).[171]

A last example of a well-described raise in reputation, the actual initiation to an *angakkoq puulik* carried through by Akku, comes as close to both history and ideology as one can wish for. Interpretation, however, necessitates long, far-reaching analyses of the symbolism of *pooq* in general and the ritual in particular. To this we shall turn in chapter 5, which follows upon some considerations on nudity as provoked by the transformations of Ajijak and his wife.

---

171. A variant retold by Jens Rosing is far more compassionate, stressing Ajijak's sorrow (J. Rosing 1993: 38–40).

Degrees of Nakedness

Nudity turns out to be the prerequisite, the pivotal point of both the killing and revival of Ajijak's wife, as well as of Ajijak himself for the various transformations. Ajijak even loses his flesh. How he managed to give that impression in the clear light of day, I cannot say. But the difference in degree of nakedness between this and ordinary performances is worth considering. Usually the shaman managed to transform while keeping his *naatsit*, briefs, on, sometimes also boots if he was a glider and sometimes an additional gutskin anorak for travel to the marine realms. Provided he had pressed his breath down and out through the anus, he became possessed by his helping spirits, one after another. They took turns using the body as mouthpiece for people's entertainment, as well as for relating the fate of their master who was out there, traveling in spirit. But was not the anus blocked by the *naatsit*? Not in East Greenland and not as far as male shamans were concerned. Like all adolescent and adult men they wore their *naatsit* hanging low on the back as noted by Buijs (2004: 55). Kaarali, who created an impressive number of drawings, consistently has the shaman perform in *naatsit* pushed down in the back whether indoors or flying outside (Geertsen 1990: 46, 47, 48, 58, 61, 65, 66, 72, 90, 116 no. 236, 119, 140 no. 82).[172] The men of the audience in Kaarali's drawings also wear their *naatsit* hanging low in the back (see fig. 21). It appears as their "male social skin" in relation to adult women, who wear their *naatsit* pulled up completely. Kaarali makes this difference perfectly clear in his drawing of a married couple using a bow drill to make fire together, with the wife wearing her *naatsit* pulled up, and the husband's pushed down in the back (55 no. 108, 58 no. 113). Interviewed by Sandgreen, Georg Quppersimaan described the custom this way on the men's behalf: "when we sat down, because they [the *naatsit*] hang so low, we always sat on the bare skin.... For paying visits we always wore both long trousers and *naatsit*, and having come indoors we merely did up our trousers, let them fall to the heels, sat down, and on going out we pulled the trousers up again" (Sonne 2005: ID 1177, tr. BS). Since pulling down the long trousers was a request of courtesy showing one's friendliness, it can be understood as a laying down of arms by leaving the vulnerable anus, the way of the *tarneq*, open in public.[173] So, uncovering the anus was hardly meant to be an invitation to becoming possessed by spirits. No, it was the shaman's pressing of his breath down and out and/or his going into ecstasy that invited a spirit to enter.

Complete nakedness is a thing apart. Stories and statements point to connotations such as these: belonging in the Other World; representing some particular character at *uaajeertut*; a loss

---

172. Kaarali's drawing of a fully dressed person flying (said in the legend to be a shaman) is hardly a human shaman. See fig. 22 above. He looks like a dwarf and has a funny smile showing only two upper teeth (Geertsen 1990: 79). Ove Bak places this drawing opposite one of *Asiaq* as an illustration to the story about Ajak's (Ajijak's) visit to *Asiaq*. He flies in company with several helping spirits, among these a dwarf always ready to laugh. In the tale, he is asked not to laugh at the awkward-looking *Asiaq* (Bak 1977: 21–26). Bak's publication is a reprint of Rasmussen (1921–25: I: 99–104; Sonne 2005: ID 1355).

173. In West Greenland, at the onset of colonization, guests were asked to undress the moment they entered (H. Egede 1971, 2: 70; 1925: 368; 1818: 126). The men's *naatsit* is not mentioned; supposedly they kept them on. The women also kept their *naatsit* on at night (H. Egede 1971: 73; 1925: 370; 1818: 132), suggesting, I suppose, that the men slept stark naked under the family's common skin cover. A century later, at the time of Rink, a renowned Greenlander, baptized Hans Egede remarked in his autobiography about how one of the very old men always let his trousers down on visits (Sonne 2005: ID 399). So, either the custom had died out, or the old man had been raised the East Greenlandic way.

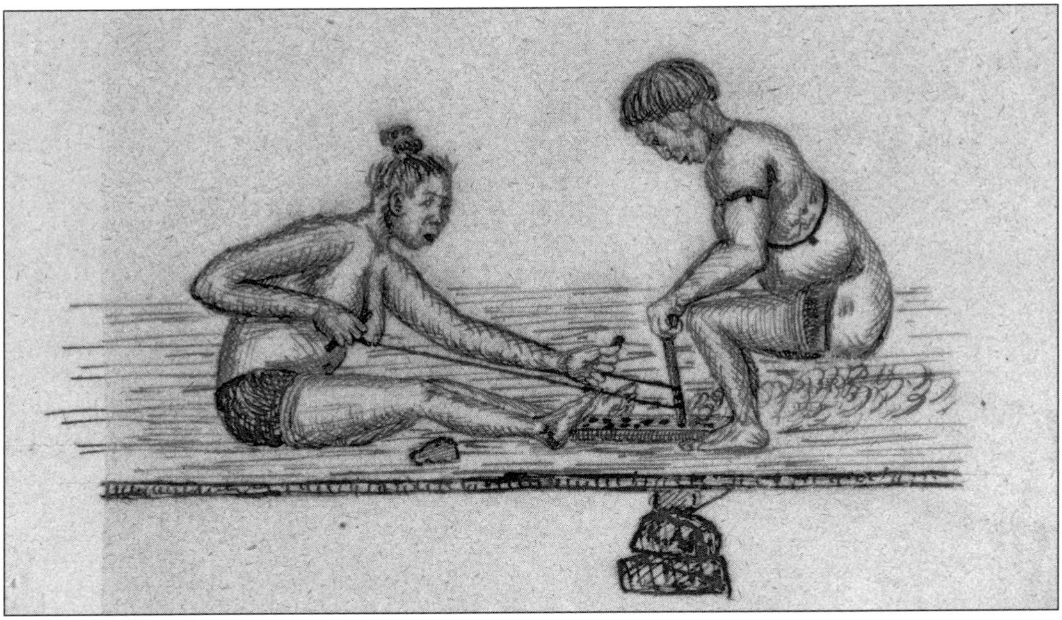

Fig. 21. Married couple drilling fire. Note the man's low-hanging *naatsit* (briefs). Drawing by Kaarali Andreassen. *The Royal Collection of Art, National Gallery of Denmark, Inv. No. KKS1977-474.*

and regaining of one's flesh; raped by a spirit; and going crazy beyond control. Let us go through the examples one by one.

A close look at Kaarali's drawings reveal that the spirits are completely naked on their visits to the shaman's performance indoors but fully dressed when moving about outdoors (Geertsen 1990). The shaman wears nothing but *naatsit* outdoors, either because the lifeless body remains lying on the floor or because he travels the Other World, understood as the interior of This World—or for both reasons. However, the meaning(s) of nudity at *uaajeertut* remain enigmatic: "*Uaajeertut* are men who appear either naked—often with sootspots on parts of the body—or dressed up. Women appear less often and then wear *naatseen* [*naatsit*]" (Thalbitzer 1923: 292). Only four examples of naked *uaajeertut* dancers are mentioned: the first one invented the *uaajeertut* by distending his cheeks with a bone from a seal's flipper, and then "seized the drum and 'danced' naked (in the Eskimo fashion) with his back towards the platform and his face toward the entrance" (*ibid.*).[174] The second naked dancer mocks a person in the audience who, when asked if the dancer is worth looking at, answers yes and is told, "I am not more worth looking at than you, you ass!—[You] who are always in the habit of lying" (297). The third naked dancer represents a visitor, an old man, so thin that his skin cracks and shows parts of his flesh. Wriggling and looking down his back he exclaims, "*Kike, kike, fie!*" (298–99). The fourth naked dancer wriggles as well, with a probable reference to a children's play of wriggling one's posteriors (like a twist dancer, I suppose) (301).

174. Ordinary drum dancing was not performed stark naked (e.g., photos in Gessain & Victor 1973; drawings by Kaarali in Geertsen 1990).

Fig. 22. Flying helping spirit. The smile on the face identifies the figure as the merry helping spirit who is warned by the shaman to stay serious during the visit to *Asiaq*, the akward-looking *inua* of precipitation. Drawing by Kaarali Andreassen. *Courtesy of The National Museum of Denmark, Copenhagen.* (See p. 321, note 172.)

Maybe more examples could point to a common definition of nudity in this context of the *uaajeertut.* If we leave the naked *uaajeertut* alone and turn to the account of Ajijak's attempt to cure his wife outdoors, the interpretation is more straightforward. Ajijak undresses twice completely in order to lose his flesh and transform into his helping spirits. The cutting up and reassembling of his wife's body demands nudity as well. The same process is true of the solitary initiation of the apprentice by the "freshwater bear." The monster did nothing to the pupil's clothes. They stripped his body by their own will, leaving his flesh to be devoured and regurgitated. The pupil did not go insane but rather lost and regained consciousness. And the clothes returned of their own accord. In the following chapter we shall see that the shaman who was initiated into an *angakkoq puulik* also lost and regained his flesh. He returned indoors with bruises all over his body. But in this case we cannot tell exactly whether he wore *naatsit* before and/or after. He hardly wore them en route, because the walrus and polar bear threw him along by his genitals (metaphorically, they raped him). In most versions, they did not eat his flesh, which might be temporarily lost in pieces to the icebergs, and in the case they ate him piecemeal, the pieces were recovered by the shaman as turds. Another case of being raped is Kukkujooq. He was directly raped by *Uersaq*, the androgynous spirit who thus prepared him for his *saqqummerneq*. Like the pupil devoured by the freshwater monster, he lost and regained consciousness and woke up stark naked lying on his back. So, the analogy of sex and eating tends to arise forcibly at initiations.

Turning to the examples of insanity in cases of nudity, they concern visible acts indoors. Thus, when Ajijak undressed completely during his *ueerineq*, the prelude to his *saqqummerneq*, he suddenly became possessed by rage. He lost his *naatsit*, started bleeding, and raced the floor, a mortal danger to his surroundings. Old Napartuku is another case in point. In actuality, he was hit by madness in a delirium. His sons tied him to a very large stone, but he broke loose, got outside, climbed a slope, and then fell down. He landed between his dogs and undressed while yelling that a certain woman (Aataaq's daughter) had arrived. Somewhat later, having announced her disappearance, he entered the house right through the window, tearing its gutskin, and then raced the floor stark naked with an erect penis. He threw an enormous heavy dish filled with meat against the platform, smashing both the platform and his wife's lamp. His sons got hold of him in order to tie him once again, but one son who accused him of having killed his (the son's) wife and son by sorcery broke his father's back and bones. After some days in bed, Napartuku died (Sonne 2005: ID 1922). In my interpretation, Aataaq's daughter was most probably a deceased woman, maybe in the figure of a dog (or a deceased dog?), arriving as she did among his dogs, and the attack on the wife's lamp, the prime symbol of a married woman's life, is plainly significant of whatever grudges Napartuku may have felt against her.[175]

Less intricate is acculturated Aron's story about the shaman Taatsiarsuaq, whose *innersuit* saved him from drowning. They dressed him in a fine shirt bought from the British whalers and brought him to their place, where they removed his clothing so that he was stark naked. At the moment he started to get warm, he went mad and raced the floor until fully warmed up (Sonne 2005: ID 1853).[176] Finally, as you may remember, the *naatsit* marks the difference between nonhumans and humans, as is emphasized in a variant of Paalineq. To quote from above p. 198: "He left his unfaithful wife completely naked in spirit and took refuge among some giants, who were uncertain about his identity: was he a dog or a human being? When on request he was handed *naatsit* by his chosen giant maiden and put them on, he was recognized as a human being" (Sonne 2005: ID 1359).

So, my proposal when analyzing Ajijak's outdoor performance—that nudity served the Greenlanders as the pivotal point of transformation—cannot be generalized as a matter of course. It holds true only as long as the uncovered anus of the shaman in ecstasy is read as nakedness in relation to the spirits. The correspondence in figures between naked faunal species "at home" and humans applies only to newborn human babies, humans ritually devoured and reborn, children at home, maniacs, and some enigmatic *uuajeertoq* figures. At home, adolescent and adult humans wore *naatsit*.

In a second look at the essence of humans, *tarneq*, we see it travels in spirit on temporary visits to the Other Worlds in dreams and to the land of no return (preferably) at death. The shaman traveled by his own will and returned alive. But did he really travel only in pure spirit? The stories make perfectly clear that he left neither memory nor senses behind, nor that of bodily pain. Ajijak, for instance, who was caught by the *Qulummiin* spirits on his way to Moon, was thrashed into bleeding right to the point of dying, when eventually he was saved by a particularly strong helping spirit, a

175. The story behind this affair with a deceased woman remains a secret.

176. An exception that perhaps proves the rule of *naatsit* connoting human sanity might be the *tivaleq* (W. Grl. *tivasoq*), the drum dancer. This particular spirit could appear, dressed in *naatsit*, to the apprentice when alone in a house or a tent. Remaining on the threshold the *tivaleq* started drumming, bending towards the floor and almost touching it with its nose, then let the drum go on its own, hammering the floor, and began dancing frenziedly on the threshold. Eventually, on letting its *naatsit* go, the *tivaleq* calmed down, picked up its *naatsit*, and disappeared. At that point the apprentice knew that he would be able to perform the shaman's tricks with the drum in public (J. Rosing 1963: 191; O. Rosing 1957–61, I: 83). I have to resort to the plain logic of reversals between This and the Other World in order to understand the opposite effect of the *naatsit* on the mental sanity of the spirit.

ghost. To repeat: spirits without body or senses are hard to imagine, to relate, or to communicate. I am not claiming that the Inuit did not distinguish between mental and somatic pain. You may know the famous statement by an East Greenlander about a physical wound that will heal fairly quickly, in contrast to the never-ending pain felt by words that hurt your feelings (J. Rosing 1970: 11). Nevertheless, "essences" are hard to imagine without some bodily appearance. Essence without flesh will work, but not without form (see R. Petersen 1990). Essences seem hard to visualize short of that particular "interface," the bunch of senses, habits, and dispositions, much like Bourdieu's *habitus*, as proposed by Viveiros de Castro (2002: 316) in characterizing the differences in bodies (in contrast to "identical" essences). Apparently, imagination tends to make peepholes through borders set by philosophy.

CHAPTER FIVE

■ ■ ■

Angakkoq Puulik (Shaman with a Bag)

The title *angakkoq puulik*—literally, "a shaman with a bag"—was confined to East, Southeast, and South Greenland, but it is based on common Inuit/Yupiit symbolic meanings of *pooq*.[1]

Pooq, *a Multitude of Meanings*

Pooq, "bag," refers to any kind of bag: a poke, a condom, a caul, a coat, or a bag bought at the supermarket. However, of wider import to our discussion, it can also indicate many types of covers, such as the complete skin of an animal—and consequently a hunting float—as well as a church tower covering the church bells, or the box in which the church organ was delivered (Kleinschmidt 1871: 300). In short, it can be any kind of a protective envelope.[2] But absolutely central to our issue, *pooq* also means "mother" in all spirit languages on record from East Greenland and Arctic Canada (O. Rosing 1957–61, I: 94; Kroeber 1899a: 323; P. Egede 1971: 54; 1939: 41; Boas: 1901–7: 353; Rasmussen 1930b: 78; 1931: 312; Therrien 1987: 129). Furthermore, in a metaphoric sense another meaning of *pooq* is "soul": "*Angakkut Puullit*—i.e., *angakkut* with bags, their souls," as Poul Egede was told by a southern shaman in 1735 (P. Egede 1971: 13; 1939: 14).[3] Two centuries later, an East Greenlander made use of the same metaphor in the plural *puuat* to define the difference between Inuit and Europeans. An Inuk was constituted of numerous bubbles (souls), he declared, in opposition to the Qallunaaq, who owned but a single soul (the soul so important to save according to the missionaries, I suppose) (C. Rosing 1946: 39).

---

1. My first attempt at an analysis was published in Sonne (1986a), the second in Sonne (2007), the third, written in 2008 (Sonne 2017), is still in press.

2. It is spelled *pooq* in Greenlandic and *puuq* in Inuktitut, Iñupiaq, and Sireniki. Of the same root, we have *pugi-*, to emerge, and Yup'ik has *pugtaun*, meaning a lung, hunting float, or life jacket (Fortescue et al. 1994; 2010: 291; Jacobson 1984).

3. "*Angekut Poglit, d.e. Angekut med Sække paa, deris Sjæle.*"

This soul meaning leads to an immediate comparison of *pooq* with *pullaq*, the soul bubble of the Iglulingmiut, reported by Rasmussen and later both corroborated and discussed by Saladin d'Anglure. *Pullaq* is described as a bubble filled with air surrounding the body soul, *tarniq* (W. Grl. *tarneq*), and situated in the lower part of the trunk. The *tarniq* is received at birth; the moment a newborn child draws its first breath, the bubble becomes inflated and the *tarniq* slips in. When breathing comes to an end and disappears into the air, the *tarniq* leaves the body for (one of) the realm(s) of death (Saladin d'Anglure 1986: 39; 1990a: 82–84, 88, 94, 96; Boas 1901–7: 353).

Though seemingly identical to *pullaq*, *pooq* differs etymologically in that the root of *pooq* is *pugi-* (emerge, surface) and that of *pullaq* is *puvi-* (swell) (Fortescue et al. 1994; 2010). In everyday usage, however, some mix-up has taken place in the meanings of words derived from the differing roots (M. Fortescue pers. comm.), though the basic difference in meaning appears to be maintained in the ideas of *pooq* and *pullaq*, respectively. When the fetus *emerges* into the world from its mother's womb, *pooq*, it draws its first breath and its *pullaq swells* like an inflated bubble.

Pooq and *pullaq* are definitely related, not only in ordinary speech but also semantically. Both belong to the field of birth as the newborn infant's "soul" or "life." The *tarniq* in its bubble resembles the fetus. Exclaiming, "*Pullalliuvunga* (I am *pullaq+ -lik*)," the Iglulik *angakkoq* identified himself as a live being filled with air when visiting Sea Woman or the deceased of heaven (Rasmussen 1929: 127, 130).[4] If he did not do this, neither would let him return to earth. Would *pullallik* compare also to *puulik* as a shaman's degree? I shall return to this question later.

Extending comparisons to the entire Inuit/Yupiit area, the most obvious parallel to both *pooq* and *pullaq* is that of the urine bladders (*nakasut*) of the Bladder Feast, the pre-Christian New Year ceremony celebrated in Southwest Alaska. The bladders of all the animals a hunter slayed that year, dried and preserved by his wife, were returned by the same women to their "owners." The hunter inflated and painted his bladders with his patrilineal symbols, and had them suspended in the *kazigi* (ceremonial and men's house, W. Grl. *qassi*), where they were feasted collectively for five days on end. Finally, the contained souls were given back to their proper milieu by thrusting the bladders, punctured, through holes made in the sea ice. Bubbles rising to the surface were considered a promising sign of return in new flesh to the hunter in the year to come (Lantis 1946: 197; Morrow 1984; Fienup-Riordan 1994: Index, Bladder Festival).

Inflated bladders also abound in other "Alaska Eskimo" ceremonies (Lantis 1947), inviting interpretations along the lines of *pooq* symbolism that I shall resist for the time being. In Arctic Canada, a killed polar bear was sent back for reincarnation with gifts signposted by its own urine bladder and sometimes accompanied by a spleen and gall bladder (for a female bear) or a penis (for a male) (Boas 1964: 188; 1901–7: 124). In Northwest Greenland, catching a polar bear, a walrus, or a bearded seal lacking a gall bladder foretold the hunter's imminent death (H. Lynge 1967: 88; Sonne 2005: ID 911). Indeed, the texts swarm with such *puuat* clearly connoting death and rebirth. Strikingly, even the sun or daylight was "born" from a *pooq* according to a MacKenzie Inuit myth, which you soon will realize bears strong similarities to the ritual initiation myth of an *angakkoq puulik*: darkness reigns in the world when raven and fox steal a bag (*pooq*) from some superbeing, with which they play ball

4. Knud Rasmussen's translation, "I am flesh and blood," is culturally off-key, since *pullallik* refers to breathing.

in a relay race for a very long time. Eventually irritated, they puncture the ball by biting and sticking it, and light pours out into the world (Rasmussen 1942: 71–73). Similarly, the initiation myth has the *puulik* candidate play the part of the ball, bitten and stuck by polar bear and walrus in a relay race across the sea. I take both as references to the Inuit ritual ball game, significant at winter festivals, as a renewal of the world. Taken together, the Inuit ball game episodes in stories evince a multitude of meanings among which the semantics of *pooq* are part of the play.

Pooq *Combining This with the Other World*

In the way of connotations turning into denotations by daily usage (T. Turner 1991: 123ff), the spirit meaning of *pooq* has become part of the ordinary human language as well (Eleonora Jacobsen, Louis-Jacques Dorais, both pers. comm.). Indeed, my favorite example of the key metaphoric import of *pooq* (Ortner 1973; Fernandez 1991) is the following clever advice: a hunter whose wife is pregnant should let the air out of his hunting float when a thunderstorm breaks, or her stomach shall explode (Rasmussen 1979: No. 476). The identification of space and/or weather (or in the spirit language *naar*, stomach) with both a wife's *pooq* and her husband's inflated hunting bladder takes in the very essential values of Inuit life. The inflated hunting float made from the complete flayed, uncut skin of a seal is a *pooq* as much as his wife's "live" womb. The inflated hunting bladder used to signify the hunter's life can be seen from another example: on a stormy day, August 28, 1738, while Poul Egede waited for calm on an island, he had a talk with people about death—our common destiny getting closer day by day. At some point a man offered this piece of philosophy: "The way of humans is like that of an inflated bag that little by little loses its air right unto the end when it is all gone" (P. Egede 1971: 93; 1939: 65; tr. BS). This statement instantly reminded me of the masked persons in the roles of spirits at the Sedna Feast, which drop dead at the point their hunting bladders are punctured by the men. However, the former statement identifying the hunting float with the pregnant womb brings another curious example to the fore. The hunting float has a dried newborn lemming fastened inside a hunting bladder for its protection against attacks from a harpooned walrus (Boas 1901–7: 152 and a note about a possible parallel in Alaska; Rasmussen 1929: 186, 235–37). To come to grips with this peculiar effect, three associations arise: first, the lemming, in contrast to most mammals, is born naked without pelt. It looks like a newborn human baby.[5] Second, lemmings are likened to humans by their ability to stand up straight "just like a sensible human" as exemplified previously in the discussion of *sila* in the meaning of balance, or standing erect. And finally, placed inside a *pooq*, it looks like a baby born in a caul, that is, one who possesses great potential. In East Greenland, this baby was said to have inborn talents for becoming a shaman (J. Rosing 1963: 173), and in Northwest Greenland it had its caul dried and used as an amulet (e.g., Hindsberger 1997: 70, 134). Thus the (historical) Kuungaseq, "going (mentally) into his caul," became invisible—not to his terrified little son at his side but to an upright polar bear about to attack. Suddenly the bear looked confused, then turned around and jogged away. According to the storyteller, the *pooq* made Kuungaseq invisible to the animal. Later, after he was baptized, he forgot about his *pooq*, which he also used for an amulet in his kayak. Consequently when the nonbaptized Nulooq borrowed this kayak, he was the one to

5. Apart from the ermine, no other land mammal is born that naked in the Arctic, or *almost* naked, as they are covered by a thin layer of very fine hair (Muus et al. 1981: 371, 389).

become confused (*puuppoq*). People said he paddled aimlessly around, as if he was caught in a closed bag. He lost his senses and fooled around blindly (Sonne 2005: 851, 852, 853). The particular effect of an amulet, a strictly personal thing, could not be employed by anybody else.[6] Consequently Nulooq was hit by the opposite effect of the caul. While Kuungaseq had become invisible to the polar bear, Nulooq lost his mind as the ordinary visible world became invisible to him. Resting on the symbolic identity of the hunting bladder with the fetus in its *pooq* (alias a caul), the newborn lemming baby in the "hunting bladder caul" has the same effect as the caul of Kuungaseq; it makes the bladder invisible to the aggressive walrus.

Certainly, *invisibility* in the meaning of being protected inside one's mother or caul is the main benefit to be gained from the initiation to *angakkoq puulik*. In particular, this invisibility extends to aggressive beings, as will be shown in due course.

Initiation to Angakkoq Puulik

On July 11, 1735, a passing southern shaman taught Poul Egede the ways of becoming first a shaman and then an *angakkoq puulik* (shaman with a bag):

> There are lots of shamans but few Angekut poglit [*angakkut puullit*], and the candidate must be a shaman already recognized in public. The light is to be put out, complete darkness must reign, but he is *not* to be laced up.[7] A polar bear arrives through the entrance opening, bites this wizard in his big toe, drags him to the sea, and throws him out into the water, where immediately a walrus is prepared to catch him by his testicles. It devours both him and the polar bear. A little later his bones are thrown in [the entrance tunnel] to his former position on the floor, and when they are all returned, his spirit ascends from the earth, unites with the bones and he revives. (P. Egede 1971: 13; 1939: 14, tr. and emphasis BS)

No ritual myth was told to Poul Egede for an explanation of this ritual witnessed by the audience. The audience obviously sees the shaman sitting unbound and waiting for the bear. When subsequently the light is put out, they only hear the bear enter and carry off the shaman, after which they are meant to wait in silence for the walrus waiting at the shore to have devoured both bear and shaman. They clearly hear the bones being thrown in and, by the relighted lamps, they see the shaman again, now whole, hale, and alive. The destiny of the polar bear remains enigmatic. But an important "gain" obtained from the initiation emerges from a note by Hans Egede—most probably also received from Poul's southern informant. It states that the *angakkoq puulik* was the only kind of shaman capable of passing by the watchdog at Sea Woman's house (H. Egede 1971, 2: 119; 1925: 398; 1818: 202), an aggressive beast as it were. A century later, Rink, having inquired but not obtained any

6. Anybody not baptized. Baptism eliminated the effect.

7. Poul repeated this in the later edition of his journals published in 1788 (P. Egede 1988: 51). Unfortunately Hans Egede got his son's information wrong by stating that the shaman *did* get laced up. Cranz wisely trusts Poul Egede (Cranz 1765–70, I: 271). But the error occurs in two translations of the "Perlustration," one into French (see Merkur 1991: 237; H. Egede 1763: 143f) and another into English (H. Egede 1818: 91–92). Apropos Merkur, I have chosen not to consider his treatment of the *angakkoq puulik* (*ibid.*) based on a restricted set of sources and combined with ideas of *toornaarsuk* refuted by me in Sonne (1986b).

affirmative answers about the *angakkoq puulik*, concluded that the tradition had fallen into oblivion (Rink 1866–71, II: 200, 202; 1975: 58–60). He seemingly did not ask people from farthest south around Cape Farewell, that is, people of Southeast Greenlandic heritage who certainly would have had something to tell. He did in fact receive one variant of the myth as recorded by Peter Motzfeldt about 1860 in the south (Sonne 2005: ID 1468), where, a century later, Mâliâraq Vebæk taped another variant (ID 2070).[8] Actually, as substantiated in my first publication about the *puulik* title, the tradition was confined to the east-southeast coast, and brought along with the immigrants to South Greenland (Sonne 1986a).[9]

The East Greenlandic *Puulik* Initiations in Ritual and Myth

In East Greenland the initiation to a shaman *puulik* or *poorsinnaaleq* (enabled to become enveloped) was as desirable as it was difficult to obtain. Naaja tried but failed in public (a most thrilling performance); Karraq was said to have lost an eye in an otherwise successful attempt, also in public; Akku earned his high renown by succeeding in public; Kaakaaq failed in solitude (disturbed by a fresh proposal from her brother in-law); and Georg claimed to have succeeded in solitude (Sonne 2005: ID 1203, 1984, 1245, 1170). Trusting the generalized record by Kaarali Andreassen, which you may choose not to, the solitary initiation to an *angakkoq puulik* was the prerequisite of *saqqummerneq*, of becoming an *angakkoq* in public. To quote:

---

8. At present, some elders of the south still know variants of this myth (Eleonora Jakobsen pers. comm.).

9. Back in the 1980s, when I looked for parallel *puulik* rituals and/or myths among the other Inuit and Yupiit, I did not encounter any Canadian Inuit story, but found two from Seward Peninsula and one from Nunivak Island (Sonne 1986a). The former two, variants of an Orpheus-type myth, have a shaman travel across the sea in search of a brother and sister in the land of no return. Needing his remaining three brothers for company as well as powers sufficient for carrying out the trip, the shaman kills and revives his brothers by cutting them up and rejoining the parts. His physical powers are those of the shoulder of a walrus and the arm of a polar bear (the same, if opposite, parts presented by the East Greenlandic moon to his son, see below p. 363). In the realm of death they first have to fight down its cruel master (guard). Next the shaman alone liberates the poor sister, who is laced up, emaciated, dressed in rags, and covered in filth with tangled hair. Having released, cleaned, and dressed her in new clothes, the shaman takes her and all his brothers home by *umiaq*, but because they forget to light a bonfire on the shore upon arrival, they all immediately die (Garber 1975: 242–55; Keithan 1976: 47–51). Obviously the realm of death below is in question. The "forbidding" guard of the entrance fulfills the "function" of Sea Woman's dog, and like her the buried and laced-up sister is liberated and cleaned for a renewal.

The Nunivak myth relates a journey across the sea by a cheated wife and her baby boy. They are supported en route by her mother's brother (avunculate), a shaman in the transformed figure of a walrus. The baby son on her back is held in place by her waist belt of polar bear skin, which transforms into a polar bear, warming both her back and baby during the trip lasting all winter. The boy grows polar bear hair on his hands and feet, and mother and son transform into a single polar bear when, attacked by five hostile polar bears, they come ashore on a desolate island. Having killed these "guards" of the polar bear island, they live on undisturbed, supplied with stranded sea mammal bodies sent by the walrus uncle. Coming of age, the boy is given an axe by the uncle and told how to build an *umiaq*. The uncle also points out the way home, after which he dies due to having transformed into a walrus so many times. The mother remarries and bears a daughter, who becomes a shaman with the ability to procure animals from the sea but not the land (Himmelheber 1951: 85–91; 2000: 63–67). The similarities are striking with the *angakkoq puulik* in the story about Tuttu's wife (Sonne 2005: ID 1445), who travels across the sea by means of polar bear and walrus in order to procure sea mammals by fighting and then cleans the Sea Woman. The joined forces of polar bear and walrus are decisive in both myths for getting across the sea, fighting aggressive guards, and, on Nunivak Island, for obtaining the shamanic power of procuring sea animals as well.

> The big polar bear and walrus are considered the most difficult to obtain as helping spirits. As the last endeavor of the young apprentice, he descends to the shore where he calls on the bear and the walrus by their names. This he repeats for three days on end—and, if failing, he has to give up incorporating the two spirits into his great entourage of helping spirits. In case he succeeds, the deeply resonant roar of the bear and the whistling nose sounds of the heavy-breathing walrus are heard approaching from beyond the horizon. Terrified, the young man tries to flee, but a sudden, overwhelming heaviness holds him back. Far out at sea, the polar bear and walrus come into view. Arching their backs, they dive, reemerge, then stare at each other, and their huge bodies, being close to one another, move along like a single animal. Their approach makes the pupil feel all his power dwindle. At close quarters the bear climbs ashore, bites the pupil nowhere else but into his genitals, and throws him to the giant walrus; the latter, rising out of the water, catches him above the surface. The bear throws itself with great force into the water and when the two animals start playing ball with the pupil, he loses consciousness. Upon recovery, he finds himself lying stark naked on the shore.... The pupil is from now on enabled to wrap himself up (*poorsinnaaleq*), meaning that when summoning the two animals they will take him along for the ride. It takes a good many public performances, which diminish his fear of the spirits, to master this way of becoming abducted. Another explanation has it that the other spirits are wrapped up, and thus prevented from disturbing this way of traveling. Mastering the performance of being abducted earns the shaman the greatest respect; according to some, this is greater than that credited the shamans who go through the *ueerineq* and are enabled to fly. Others place the former right below the latter in rank. (O. Rosing 1957–61, I: 84–85; J. Rosing 1963: 190–91; tr. BS)

Kaarali's statements about the abilities gained by this initiation in solitude are far from clear. The pupil is said to have obtained the two animals as helping spirits for transport, but, though protected from being attacked by other spirits en route, he is unable to make use of them until much later in his shamanic career. Only one story—of South (East) Greenlandic origin—substantiates this assertion by having the old wife of Tuttu travel partway to Sea Woman as the "ball" roughly handled by the polar bear–walrus couple, who throw her along by her genitals. Then, for no obvious reason, they leave her in the lurch far out at sea, where fortunately another spirit turns up to help complete the journey (see below). The East Greenlandic *puulik* stories do not tell of any travels by means of this brutal couple outside the public initiations to *puulik*. Nor can support be found for Kaarali's claim concerning a solitary initiation as a prerequisite for performing in public. Neither Akku nor Naaja nor Karraq (who all performed in public with differing success) are presented as having had any experience of the abduction in solitude—quite on the contrary, in that Naaja became too scared and Karraq lost an eye. All three were publicly recognized shamans (by *saqqummerneq*), the demand also stated by Poul Egede's informant, for carrying out the initiation to an *angakkoq puulik*. Furthermore, like Jens Rosing (1963: 190), I doubt Kaarali's statement about an acquisition of the two animals as helping spirits on par with the remaining ones obtained through apprenticeship. Perhaps Kaarali, inclined as he was to systematize and generalize, drew his conclusions too far. The religious gain obtained was, as indicated above, invisibility to and/or protection against aggressive spirits. The acquisition of the two animals as spirits for transportation remains a possibility, but appears to be of secondary importance.

As for the two pupils who attempted the initiation in solitude, Georg and Kaakaaq, the former claims to have succeeded but offers next to no details, except that the *amoo* spirit arrives while he is practicing in some ruins. It carries him to the waiting bear and walrus at the shore, from where he is taken far out to sea at a furious speed. He cries out of fear of death, dripping a trail of snot as he goes along; but, having survived, he feels resistant to any attack from his fiends (Sonne 2005: ID 1170). The *puulik* story about Kaakaaq follows another red thread, her sexual appeal to both polar bears and men. Standing on the shelf of a bird cliff at sea, she suddenly hears the polar bear's growling approach when the noise of her brother-in-law's footsteps drowns out the promising sound. Irretrievably it disappears. She knows how to turn down the in-law's offer, but her chances of becoming a *puulik* are ruined for now and ever (ID 1245). The event is placed (by the editor Sandgreen?) before her marriage and after she obtained a balanced number of helping spirits from the land, and no other source is on record in support. Similarly, Georg's own, very brief report of being abducted stands alone.

Akku's Successful *Puulik* Initiation

Speculations aside, the two stories on record about Akku's *puulik* initiation in public are as trustworthy as one can hope for, because they catalyze Akku's timely attempt at overcoming a failing recognition of his powers. People were comparing Maratsi's powers with Akku's, to the former's advantage. The event is dated to the winter of 1879–80, when rich stores and easy traveling over ice inspired people from all over to attend festive get-togethers spiced with thrilling entertainment (J. Rosing 1963: 245; O. Rosing 1957–61: 112–13).

Akku had a messenger invite his former settlement to be present at his abduction by the giant polar bear and walrus. People accepted: "Yes, we shall go see Akku play like a child." The offended messenger told Akku, who took his preparations seriously. Tent poles were dragged into the longhouse and raised in front of both the rear platform and the east side plank bed. Skins pierced with peepholes were then stretched between tent poles. The guests arrived. Women and children were seated behind the curtains; the men were placed there as well, but closer to the unshielded west side plank bed. Akku seated himself on his skin in front of the entrance and called in clear words to his spirits for support against these people who did not believe him capable of anything. Akku made the drum roar, ordered the lights off, and the clatter of violently shaking and cracking tent poles broke out. Abruptly a hush fell on the room. After some calling in vain, Akku apparently gave up, merely mumbling a few words at intervals. Suddenly a terrifying big bang brought the poles and skins to violent, brief life. Quiet followed. Then a second bang sounded, and again after another suitable interval the third bang had the audience severely shaken up. Eventually, in complete quiet, a deep growling was heard approaching through the entrance tunnel. The opening was, as usual during performances, shielded by two skins. Now the approaching being tore down the outer skin and made its appearance, a huge polar bear clearly seen in the light of the full moon shining through the uncovered gut windows. A foul stench of rotten seaweed filled the room while the growling and hissing bear nosed about for Akku, who had disappeared. Having found him behind the drum, the bear dragged the screeching Akku off backwards through the tunnel. The dying away of his scream was ghastly. Some of the men replaced the torn-up curtain with a new one. Returning to their seats, they realized that their feet were soaked in blood, seemingly testifying to the bear's rough handling of Akku. The subsequent quiet made the audience start singing to the helping spirits, who nevertheless remained silent throughout the entire night. At dawn, people's singing changed into desperate shouting and magic whistling, calling on Akku's special helping spirit, *Ajaqqisaaq*, by name: "*Ajaqqisaaq*, your master, albeit not sick, cannot come round. Do come, lend us your support!" And they called to the drum as well: "Drum, drum, recover, take power, please drum, take power!" The drum responded, its power increasing in summoning the helping spirits, which began to make themselves heard. At the moment *Ajaqqisaaq* emerged from beneath the floor at a dizzying speed, the drum fell silent. "Where is your master?" he was asked. *Ajaqqisaqq* took his time to breathe, three deep puffs, and then loudly exclaimed: "Just like in the old days. My master is on his way dressed in a shower of sparks. One would think it was my former master!" Akku was on his way from far away, the outermost gap of the sea. Once more *Ajaqqisaaq* compared Akku's arriving figure with that of his former master, after which the characteristic "*ululoo, ululoo*" (English: *ooloolo-o*) of Akku's great helping spirit, his only companion for this trip, was heard. *Ajaqqisaaq* left at the moment Akku, uttering one cry after another, arrived. He was heard circling for some time beneath the floor, then emerging, rushing around, and finally silencing both drum and skins. The recovered Akku sat dumb, head dropped for quite a while when eventually somebody broke the silence: "Did you get safely through?" "Yes, I managed. Whether in body or in spirit, I do not know!" Amazed, people looked at his body, bruised all over, except for the soles of his feet. They were intact. Forever after, nobody felt compelled to compare his performances to child's play, and his skills became known far and wide (J. Rosing 1963: 245–47; Sonne 2005: ID 1683; tr. BS).

Unfortunately we are never informed of the name of *Ajaqqisaaq*'s former master, with whose skills Akku was also glorified at his *saqqummerneq*—a useful heritage indeed. Regarding his only companion, the spirit calling *ululoo,* I take it to be a bearded seal spirit, as argued previously due to details presented above. Thus Akku's initiation involved three animals: polar bear, walrus, and bearded seal. Turning to the staging, I shall take the clear record at face value. Akku's competence in setting up movable tent poles and skins for making noise, protection, and partly concealing the scene matches his skill in imitating differing voices as also in timing the suspenseful elements. The three big bangs that announce the arrival of the polar bear are awful noises punctuated by periods of silence, and then, for a very long time, complete silence. No spirit makes the slightest report, but the audience keeps singing for countless hours when finally *Ajaqqisaaq* sets things going again. People are told that Akku is on his way from the outermost gap of the sea. Properly modest in affirming his success, this is convincingly demonstrated by his bruised body.

The *Puulik* Myth

What in fact, or better myth, happened to Akku in his absence? Holm briefly reports that "It is related that once during the performance of his arts he [Akku] was seized by a bear, who dragged him down to the shore, where a walrus fastened its teeth in him, dragged him out to the horizon, and devoured him there. The skeleton returned and met on its way the pieces of flesh, which little by little grew up around it, and finally the eyes, so that the man returned whole" (Holm 1914: 98; 1972: 132; Sonne 2005: ID 1683).

According to the teller of Naaja's ritual attempt in public, he imagined the course of events before getting started in far richer detail. At the moment the drum handle hit his neck and he heard the arriving polar bear growl, he became terrified at imagining the pain and danger of the trip he was about to embark on: the bear would enter, close its jaw around his testicles, and carry him down to the beach where the walrus lay waiting ready to thrust its tusk in beneath his collar bone. It would then throw him out over the sea to the polar bear, already in place to catch him, and they would continue on in a throwing relay right to the rim of heaven. All along the icebergs would grab his flesh, piece by piece, to be kept in store for his return. At the horizon, at *qilaap sillia*, called the Milky Way by Poul Egede (1988: 80), the two animals would disappear, leaving him to find his way home alone and get hold of every piece of meat. This was a solitary trip because none of his helping spirits could go that far.[10] Anticipating all this, Naaja burst into tears. His fear awakened some discarded trousers stuffed with lamp moss in the entrance tunnel, which set the arriving bear to flight. Immediately recovering from fear, Naaja set off in pursuit but was stopped dead by the trousers. A loud noise silenced the drum. Naaja's wife ordered the smallest lamp lighted, and then found him in the opening of the entrance way in an upright, reverse position. They eased him on to the floor, put out the lamp, and by repeatedly calling "*kiakkakaa, kiakkakaa*" they made his spirits take possession of him for a return to consciousness. Eventually, at the first dim light of dawn, he took to crying. He cried "*ungaa*," like a baby. So, Naaja, conversely reborn, never became a genuinely great shaman, an *angakkuvissuaq*, or an *angakkoq puulik* (Sandgreen 1967, I: 120; Sonne 2005: ID 1203).

Karraq, Missuarniannga, and Tuttu's Wife

Karraq/Uitsaleqannitseq did manage in his performance, but lost an eye. The version is a very short one, told by Kaakaaq, baptized Karen and called Kara by Victor, who took it down in 1936. Drawn by his helping spirits to the shore, Karraq encountered a huge walrus trailed by a polar bear. The walrus bit his throat then threw him along to the polar bear, who threw him further on. He lost a piece of flesh each time he was caught and passed forward until nothing but his skeleton remained. When the animals left him far out at sea, his flesh was spread along the route like lumps of shit, ready for his piecemeal reincarnation. However, his eyes had changed into icebergs. He did not realize their transformation until he had passed by one and then got hold of the other. Upon his return, the audience became aware of his missing eye (ID 1984). The loss earned him the name Uitsaleqanngitseq, "unable to open his eyes."

Finally Missuarniannga, shortly before beginning the preparations for baptism, arranged for a performance lasting three nights, which resembled a *puulik* initiation more than anything else. The first two nights he lost consciousness upon seeing a strong light approaching across the sea. Missuarniannga set out screaming on the third night, when the light arrived as the shadow of a huge polar bear. Entering with a rumble and thunder, it let in the light of the full moon by breaking

---

10. Naaja's failed attempt leads me to pose this question: Did Naaja not own an *ululoortortoq*, the only spirit accompanying Akku? The story states that none of Naaja's helping spirits were capable of going that far (right on to the horizon [Sonne 2005: ID 1203]). By chance or not, this spirit is exclusively mentioned in connection with shamans belonging to the lineage of the Sermiligaaq and Ammassalik fjords: Akku, Karraq, Maratsi, and Missuarniannga. In contrast, both Naaja and Kaakaaq, who failed, but also the not very reliable Georg, who claimed rank of a *puulik* obtained in solitude, belonged to the people of the Sermilik fjord. The difference between the peoples of the Sermilik and the two other fjords is felt to this day (Robert-Lamblin 1986: 55f), and they may represent each its immigration, one arriving from the south about 1500 and the other from the north a century later. Apparently the Sermiligaaq and Ammassalik fjord people have retained stronger similarities in symbolism with Alaska than the Sermilik people. Naturally this proposal asks for support by the archaeologists.

the thong of the curtain in front of the entrance. The turmoil also broke the new panes of glass to pieces, and when the bear left his body, Missuarniannga was lying unconscious halfway into the entrance tunnel. He cannot be dead, his wife declared, or he would have fallen right into the tunnel. People straightened him out and placed him on his skin on the floor. The thong of the curtain was replaced, whereupon darkness and silence reigned. The audience began calling on both Missuarniannga's helping spirits and the silent drum, but to no avail. Then his wife took action. She let in the light of the full moon by removing the curtain from the entrance, revealing the pale, cold Missuarniannga, who was checked and found lifeless. His eleven-year-old son, Kaarali, burst into tears. "Stop that," his mother said, "if you want your father to come back to life." After still another long time of silence, the curtain began slightly to rattle and the drum to sound, but only with three hard strokes. The ensuing silence was eventually broken by the voice of an approaching helping spirit. It asked for a piece of skin to be spread out close to the lifeless body, because Missuarniannga's breath was still too far away for the spirit to revive him by taking possession of his body. Emerged and seated next to the lifeless body, the spirit, an enormous figure, pitched into the body, while the drum and curtain resumed sounding. Asked about the whereabouts of Missuarniannga, the spirit told the audience that his faint voice could be heard getting nearer from far away below. The big spirit began blowing on the body. Then the sounds of *ululoo*-calling spirits were heard below the floor for quite some time, followed by renewed silence, and again broken by the big spirit shouting: "Listen, listen, listen!" In complete silence, the feeble voice of Missuarniannga was heard approaching from a great distance beyond the mouth of the fjord. Voices spoke all at once beneath the floor, and the big spirit declared, "That's it, now I am leaving," and so it did, leaving the floor to the laboriously awakening Missuarniannga. Slowly sitting up, he began swinging the upper part of his body to and fro; he then came to his feet and staggered to the platform where he remained for another three days of recovery. Shortly afterwards, he enrolled as a proselyte and was baptized Andreas in April 1901 (Sonne 2005: ID 1313).

The probable teller of this performance, Kaarali, an eleven-year-old witness, does not name his father's performance an initiation to an *angakkoq puulik*. This, however, speaks not only to the light seen approaching for two nights before the huge bear arrives but also the deportation of Missuarniannga('s breath) to some faraway place beyond the mouth of the fjord. The *ululoo*-calling spirits, which also ended Akku's initiation, enforce the impression of a *puulik* ritual. Like the ritual description of Akku's initiation, nothing is said about Missuarniannga's experiences while away from the room. Both reports remain with the audience's point of view. But unlike Akku, who armed the room with secured tent poles, Missuarniannga did nothing to prevent the damage made by the entering bear.

Gains

In summary, obtaining the powers of an *angakkoq puulik* primarily meant a cooperation of two animals arriving from the horizon, a giant polar bear and a walrus. Most often the former went ashore in order to fetch the candidate on land while the latter remained waiting at the shore. Being drawn to the shore by a helping spirit was another possibility (in the cases of Georg and Karraq). Losing and regaining one's flesh in painful ways seemed to characterize the public initiation. The initiation in solitude, which according to Kaarali meant no loss of flesh, only of consciousness and clothing, is a lonely source insofar as Kaakaaq missed abduction entirely and Georg had nothing else to report except his dread of death. Carried through in public, the initiation meant a marked rise in reputation. Karraq and Akku managed while Naaja lost his prospects of becoming a genuine big shaman. The gain of either initiation, whether solitary or in public—i.e., the ability of enveloping oneself for a safe travel—seems greatly valued. But to what end?

The statement recorded by Hans Egede, that only an *angakkoq puulik* managed to pass by Sea Woman's watchdog, does not fit the equally traditional East Greenlandic sources in any perfect way. Karraq, an *angakkoq puulik,* did visit her with success in company with his various helping spirits. Together they merely walked the way of the dead, overcoming various hindrances en route. The storyteller seemingly forgot the watchdog but had the helping spirits advise their master, who was told to enter Sea Woman's house and fight her on his own (Sonne 2005: ID 1354). Naaja, no *puulik* indeed, similarly walked the route in company with his spirits and cleaned Sea Woman (ID 1196). Finally, Aaqqii, about whom next to nothing is on record, made the same journey in company with one particular spirit called *Qadidika* (the bass voice), which followed him all the way and calmed down the angry woman by revealing that Aaqqii was a shaman of great recognition (ID 29).[11] The *angakkoq puulik* Akku preferred a visit to the submarine realm of death, which prevented any later visit to Sea Woman. No polar bear and walrus duo took him along to that place. Instead, he traveled in his gliding outfit, a gutskin anorak (*ikiaq*) and skin socks (ID 1324). The aforementioned Tuttu's Wife, however, most probably of Southeast Greenlandic heritage, did visit her by means of polar bear and walrus for part of the way:

Although advanced in years, Tuttu's Wife is persuaded by the great sealer Qujaavaarsuk and encouraged by her husband of lesser powers to try her hand in "removing the ice." The scene is set, the lamps put out; soon the polar bear enters.[12] It sends her sliding backwards and forwards across the floor due to its heavy breathing in and out. Having carried her outside and down to the waiting walrus, the latter seizes her by her genitals and throws her along for the relay race far out across the frozen sea. Suddenly, at the point a storm arrives and breaks up the ice, both animals disappear. She seeks refuge on an iceberg where a kayaker, the *Equngasoq* spirit (which possesses an intricate sense of balance), turns up and offers her a ride. It takes her farther out to sea close to a foreign land, the land of Sea Woman. She is to jump to this land from the top of a huge wave. Having managed the encounter with the giant fury and seen the seabirds and animals leave for the open sea, she returns home without any difficulties (and without comments on her way or travel means). At home, the ice is still not removed. Her scratches are to be healed, she declares. Then, one night, a storm opens up the sea. Every bit of ice is removed from view in the morning (ID 1445).[13] So, like her colleagues at Ammassalik, Tuttu's Wife is violated in a brutal way by both animals, but instead of losing and then getting back her flesh, she returns with severe scratches to be healed before her mission is accomplished.

---

11. Sea Woman tends to consider shamans visiting her for the first time to be inferior in powers—i.e., unable to fight and clean her (e.g., Sonne 2005: ID 349).

12. No mention is made of her being laced up. On the other hand, to my knowledge, female shamans never were.

13. The one resumed here; ID 1468 mistakes Tuttu *alias* Tuttutsiaq for his wife; ID 2070 was recorded in the 1960s.

The Puulik *Myth's Polar Bear and Walrus*

The story about Tuttu's Wife is unique in having the *puulik* animals serve as means of transport towards Sea Woman, which nevertheless supports Hans Egede's statement about the shaman *puulik* as the only one who could obtain access past her dog. What strikes one in this story, however, is the failure of the animals to bring her to her destination. Both animals of the sea, they might easily have continued their relay race across the reopened sea. Why and where do they leave her? I take this point in space to be the one from where the East Greenlandic *puulik* candidate was also entrusted to his lonely skeletal return. In the Naaja variant, this point is called *qilaap sillia*, the Milky Way, "as attractive as difficult to get to" (Sonne 2005: ID 1203). And what did the Milky Way represent? *Siblia*, in the spelling of Poul Egede, marked the border of heaven (P. Egede 1988: 80) or, in body symbolism, the longitudinal line along which the front of any slain animal was cut for skinning and then divided into symmetrical halves (Schultz-Lorentzen 1967: 263; 1927: sivdleq).[14] The same notion is recognized in a solitary transmitted description at Iglulik of the Milky Way as the "Divider," *Avigutaa*, and perceived "as a separator for the winds. It is here the winds collide... and where stronger winds prevail" (MacDonald 1998: 91–92). After all, then, the strong winds (of spring) breaking up the ice around Tuttu's Wife at the disappearance of the animals may have been no arbitrary episode. At Iglulik, situated at 69 degrees north latitude, the galaxy is not seen full length above the horizon (10). This is perhaps why information on it was scarce (*ibid.*). At the lower latitude of Ammassalik, however, polar bear and walrus were said in a couple of stories to live far away beyond the sea, and in another story beyond the cleavage of the Milky Way. They go as follows.

In both stories, a dreaming woman visits the two animals at their dwelling place beyond the sea, in some heavenly abode. The first, which I name "The Deal," concerns an arrangement made between humans and polar bears about an exchange of their skin and flesh for human-made boot soles. The other, "Dying Woman" (also my label), has the woman attacked by the two animals and returned towards her home like a shaman. The woman of "The Deal"—already summarized when discussing Viveiros de Castro previously (see pp. 154f, 196)—is under death taboo. In her dream, she walks easily across and far beyond the ice-covered sea to a brightly lit house of a big family of polar bears and two sons-in-law, a walrus and an Arctic fox. The walrus does nothing but sit there, a big mute, clumsy body. As a son-in-law among several brothers-in-law, he can be in no enviable position, because the Greenlanders prefer polar bear to walrus for identification (a supposition confirmed by Arctic zoologist Dr. E. W. Born, pers. comm.). The Arctic fox, with its more extensive knowledge of the foul ways of humans, tries to warn the bears, but in vain. The polar bear father makes the deal, and ever since polar bears have received readymade skin soles in exchange for their willingness to let themselves be killed. The dwelling place of this family of surprising composition, in a bright shining house far beyond the horizon in heaven, seems to point to a constellation of stars (Sonne 2005: ID 1806).

Dying Woman has been asleep for a full night and day when her husband moves her to a place at the window in an attempt to awaken her. She is still breathing, but suddenly her consciousness (*sila, anerneq* or *tarneq*—only the Danish translation exists) leaves her. In spirit she travels through her (outdoor) clothes kept safely inside the reversed *umiaq* placed on the scaffold, and then farther on

14. The statement not included in P. Egede (1971) or (1939).

across the sea. She arrives at the Milky Way, *sigdlia/qilaap sillia*, a steep cleft to be jumped. Fortunately she stoops when reaching the other side; if she had fallen backwards, she would have been lost in the awesome gap.[15] Continuing through the air, she arrives at the two houses of polar bear and walrus. She visits polar bear, who also receives another visitor, walrus, for buying a thong. Polar bear refuses, and when walrus, enraged, tears the thong to pieces, the woman takes flight to the walrus's house. Both animals follow, and inside the house they give chase in circles until eventually a passage opens for her in an upper corner of the house. Her return is difficult. Time and again she cannot find her way, but by singing magic songs, *serratit*, her family draws her back home step by step, where she regains consciousness at the moment her husband is about to drag her out for burial (ID 1134).

Analysis of "Dying Woman": When the dying woman's spirit takes leave through the gutskin window, she apparently needs the clothing, deposited inside the *umiaq*, for her travel. No woman used to wear clothing inside the house, but outdoors her dress code was strict. The cleft of no return is the first hindrance en route; the second is the aggressive confrontation with the two animal neighbors. Despite being mutual fiends they nevertheless cooperate in chasing her in circles for a difficult return to life. At this point the *puulik* myth presents itself for comparison with "The Deal" as well as the story about Ajijak's flight to the *qulummiin* spirits (which I take to be the Northern Lights, see above). The cooperation of the two animals comes to the fore in most variants of the *puulik* initiation myth. Polar bear and walrus arrive together, and they take their "ball" far out at sea in a common, torturous game. In "The Deal," a polar bear family live together in an asymmetrical relationship of in-laws, a walrus and an Arctic fox; in "Dying Woman," polar bear and walrus start out as mutual enemies, like in actual life. Also, here their relationship proves asymmetrical in that polar bear refuses to sell walrus a thong, whereafter walrus immediately tears the thong to pieces. Obviously you cannot make deals with a bad-tempered walrus the same way you can with a polar bear! Yet the two animals cooperate in chasing Dying Woman around in circles for her exit hole to be "drilled." As can be expected, in their short-lived cooperation the *puulik* animals see to her "breaking through" the "surface" of the house. Her difficult return may be due to the thong ruined by walrus, the only thong mentioned in "Dying Woman." Ajijak, as you may remember, was in danger of never returning from the *Qulummiin* spirits because he lost one of the two thongs with which he had been laced up. However, he managed to return because he still had one of his two thongs left. The *puulik* candidate was not laced up. He had an extremely difficult return, which at the same time meant a literal, piecemeal recovery in flesh. Similarly, Dying Woman only returns due to the spells sung by her close relatives. The story about Dying Woman stops at her revival. She is not said to start out as a shaman, or to have become a shaman, or an *angakkoq puulik*. On the other hand, her route is not the swampy way of ordinary deceased humans. Her route is that of the *puulik* candidate across the sea, but, flying on her own, she continues farther on by jumping the vast cleft of the Milky Way. Apparently she is attracted by polar bear and walrus, who live apart as unfriendly neighbors except for their short-lived cooperation in sending her off. The Milky Way, as stated in the version about Naaja, was also the attractive goal of the *puulik* candidate. He was thrown that far by the *puulik* animals, and left to a dangerous solitary return. Tuttu's Wife, however, on her way to Sea Woman, was left in the lurch at

15. In Cumberland Sound the same destiny of falling backwards befell the pupil in search of a helping spirit among the polar bears in their homeland situated on the other side of a cleft (Boas 1964: 183–84).

the breaking up of the ice by a furious storm. Where did they go? According to "Dying Woman" and the Naaja variant, they returned to their houses beyond the Milky Way.

A subsequent question arises as to what kind of *inuat* the heavenly polar bear and walrus are. Tuttu's Wife sees them approach from the horizon as two flames (Sonne 2005: ID 1445), as did the South Greenlandic shaman Pruutars: "A long time ago, in my prime, when shamans were still here, everything was tried. Once while performing I saw two flames approaching from the west. I could not force them back, nor make them go backwards. My only concern was being a shaman, this was my only incentive. At close quarters I realized that they were a polar bear and a walrus. And I heard the elders say: 'They must be the ones destined for becoming your bags' (*puuat*). I got scared and stopped performing" (ID 1850). Naaja shrank with fear at hearing the polar bear enter, Pruutars at the sheer prospect of the ordeal of getting the two flames for his bags.

Approaching as lights from beyond the Milky Way, the *puulik* animals can hardly be anything but star beings on a visit to This World, but no certain identification of these heavenly bodies can be made as several twin stars exist as possibilities (MacDonald 1998). A tempting choice, *Aassutit* (E. Grl. *aattik* or, in the dual *aagjik*), the twin stars of the New Year, seems to be contradicted by the stories of Tuttu's Wife where the time is definitely spring. Akku's initiation takes place at some indefinable full moon in winter. The editor Sandgreen depicts summer as the time for both unsuccessful attempts by Naaja and Kaakaaq, whereas Kaarali Andreassen sets no date or season for Karraq, nor does Georg for himself. On the other hand, the two animals are connected in some decisive instances. Taking a prolonged glance at Iglulik, the local women were under taboo from eating any part of a polar bear or walrus at winter solstice (Rasmussen 1929: 195). Together, the same animals used to block the entrance to the very fine house of *Nappayoq* (the upright standing one) or *Anautalik*, reported by Lyon in 1822–23 to be the father of Sea Woman and the master of the land animals. Very few if any shamans had the nerve or power to pass by this guard (Lyon 1824: 326). His informant on the matter, the shaman Toolemak, "acknowledged very candidly that he never dared to enter this mansion but by looking through the door he could see that it was good" (364). Taking hypothetically that this house corresponds in some way or other with a heavenly body of the starry *puulik* animals of the East Greenlanders, and trusting both myth and astronomy, I shall reveal my firm idea that the *puulik* animals must represent *Aassuutit*, the double star of the New Year, called *Aagjuuk*, in the dual, by the Nattilingmiut.[16] They marked not only the New Year by their appearance around winter solstice, but in East Greenland also the onset of spring, namely on the morning when the sun took over their point of rising on the horizon (Holm 1972: 137; 1914: 105). From New Year to spring[17] they are at some point(s) seen closely together (their short-lived cooperation in myth as in Kaarali's description: "being close to one another, move along like a single animal"), but most of the time they remain

16. The astronomer Ole J. Knudsen at Aarhus has willingly offered some options, and among these is my preference, the double star of the New Year, *Aassuutit* (the bright Altair and less bright Tarazed).They rise at about 5:15. a.m. January 1 at Ammassalik. They can still be seen due east at 6:50 a.m. and perhaps until 8:00 a.m. in the east-southeast, when dawn takes over. In the twilight Altair reappears at 3:00 p.m. in the southwest, both stars at 4:10 p.m. in SWS. At 10:00 p.m. they settle in west-northwest. At their highest visible point at 3:00 p.m. in southwest, they are 28 degrees above the horizon, a third of the arch to the top. When rising, Tarazed is seen right above Altair, but at their setting Tarazed has moved a bit upwards and to the right of Altair.

17. Above the Arctic Cirle the latter is seen also in autumn, but not recognized as the same star(s) (MacDonald 1998: 46). The latitude of Ammassalik/Tasiilaq is about one degree below the Arctic Circle.

at varying distances, one above the other (like polar bear above the surface or ice, and walrus below) (Sonne 2005: ID 2070). Their disappearance by the onset of spring is clearly marked in the variant about Tuttu's Wife by the sudden disappearance of *puulik* animals at the breaking up of the ice and leaving the scene to the kayaker called "Twistmouth," *Equngasoq*. Also known as the fulmar with its twisted beak, this is the first seabird to arrive in spring with reopened waters and thus another symbol of spring (Rasmussen 1938: 210). So, the movements of the *Aassuutit* covered the intricate period of the year when the days lengthen and temperatures grow more severe until the final coming of spring. Generally, at New Year the stores were rich. Feasts were held among all Inuit and Yupiit. In regions of limited resources as in Greenland, a delayed coming of spring could mean death by starvation. The disappearance of the *Aassuutit* was a promising sign of spring. But *sila* might lack behind.

Polar Bear and Walrus in Cosmology

Some difference in mode appears between West and East Greenlandic stories about polar bear and walrus. The popular "Katerfarsuk" of the west coast seems to reverse the ranking and sides with walrus against polar bear. The latter, alias an elderly man disguised in the skin of a polar bear, cannot resist the temptation to scare the wits out of an orphan boy, who is working hard on building a kayak with an insufficient tool. In vengeance, the boy puts on the skin of a walrus, allows himself to be harpooned by his opponent, disappears underwater, and later, while the housemates sit listening to the elderly man's sad story about the loss of his harpoon, the boy hands him this very thing (search Katerfarsuk in Sonne 2005). "Don't mock a poor boy!" the moral obviously goes, for he may get hold of dangerous powers. Although modified by comic relief in this story, the vengeance is just.[18] Ranked as valued characters, however, polar bear comes out the hero as shown in still another couple of East Greenlandic stories: the aforementioned "Qilaatuaq" (W. Grl. "Qilaasuaq"), who travels with his son(s) and an in-law across the sea on an ice floe to Akilineq, and "Aloruttaq" ("bootless"), a poor boy killed by a *tupilak* but reborn in the end as himself.

"Qilaatuaq"

Set adrift on an iceberg at the sudden breakup of the ice by a springtime off-shore storm, Qilaatuaq's family survives thanks to his intelligence, his authority in magic knowledge, and their amulets: polar bears in the patriline and walrus for the affinal member. As a first proof of his knowledge, Qilaatuaq cuts four dolls from the cross boards of the sledge when everybody is almost dying from thirst. They are two married couples, arranged for a nocturnal exchange of wives in a scooped-out little cave. This magic works, and water spurts forth, but the in-law spoils the effect by rushing to be the first to drink. The water immediately stops running, because—naturally (culturally)—Qilaatuaq was to be first. He has to repeat the magic, drink first, and then everyone, even the in-law, gets his fill. Impatient at the iceberg's slow pace, Qilaatuaq suddenly jumps into the sea. He emerges as a polar bear due to his amulet. His son(s) follow(s) suit. However, the in-law has to dive several times in order to transform into a walrus. They start swimming in the manner of their animal figures, the

18. The West Greenlandic stories in Sonne (2005) offer no mythic example of polar bear and walrus in any form of a mutual relationship. A story told by Esaias about a polar bear attacking a walrus, ending in the death of both, is as authentic as a transmitted account can be (ID 1448). See paraphrase in note 23 on p. 343.

bears climbing and walking the ice floes en route, and the walrus quickly swimming under the floes and waiting at the opposite site for the bears to pass. Arriving at the solid ice in front of Akilineq, the bears hurry to undress behind some block of ice in order not to be killed by the approaching Akilinermiut, whereas the walrus changes into its human figure without any effort the moment it gets a foothold. Led to the settlement by the hunters, the newcomers are asked to visit a sorcerer, who serves them a toxic food—human brain. The visitors can stand it, but the old sorcerer turns into a lunatic when Qilaatuaq forces her to have a taste. She leaves the room and dies on her way out through the tunnel. In a subsequent trial of strength by arm wrestling, the strong man among the guests, the in-law (walrus), stretches out his opponent's arm, but the latter snatches his testicles and swallows them up. The in-law's body is dragged outside, where the waiting Akilinermiut cut him up for food. The next to take a turn, Qilaatuaq, has learned the lesson. He allows his arm be stretched out but uses his free hand to tear out the testicles of his opponent. In one variant Qilaatuaq also gulps down the handful and orders the body taken out.[19] When the people out there recognize the body as one of their own, they bar the entrance. Time has come for Qilaatuaq to use his other amulets: a fox, which turns out to be of little value, and a raven kept in the collar of his coat.[20] Sent out through the tunnel, the hot-tempered raven finishes off the enemies one by one, except for a poor boy whom Qilaatuaq invites to steer the *umiaq* for the return journey in spring. The boy, however, is cheated.[21] Left behind sobbing, he tries to bewitch the boat by throwing a scapula, which Qilaatuaq naturally knows how to ward off, sending counter-magic out through his sleeve.[22] Back home, family life is resumed. Only the variant recorded by Rasmussen has the survivors deeply mourn their lost in-law (Sonne 2005: ID 565, 1099, 1326).

In all variants Qilaatuaq is portrayed as the ideal family head. Although he travels at sea in the figure of a polar bear at a slower speed than his walrus in-law, he possesses the sufficient knowledge, amulets, and ingenuity for a successful round-trip. Walrus, impatient and not too bright, shows himself to be inferior in every other way than sheer muscles and speed underwater. A similar highlighting of the father's virtues associated with polar bear amulets characterizes the West Greenlandic variants as well. They were taken down in the 1860s and around 1920, but here polar bears are not in thematic opposition to either walrus, or an in-law. A beloved adoptive son possessing an unimpressive snow bunting for an amulet serves as the means for comparison. He is killed in the arm wrestling and cut up, but later he is revived by his adoptive father. And on the return journey, the time of transformations into amulet animals in these variants, he lets the insignificant bird comfortably ride behind his polar bear ear (polar bear swims on the surface most of the time) (Sonne 2005: ID 292, 499, 528, 1434, 1623, 1864). However insignificant, the snow bunting signifies spring in West Greenland, which is the time of the party's return home.

19. Sonne (2005: ID 565).

20. The raven is a lemming in some Southwest Greenlandic variants.

21. Usually the lone surviving enemy is meant to warn everybody against trying to take revenge. In this story, which praises Qilaatuaq from beginning to end, his knowledge in warding off sorcery seemingly overshadows the usual bearing.

22. A single empowered sleeve appears quite often in East Greenlandic stories, as for instance Maratsi's first helping spirit, a wing snail transforming into a big-eyed luminous being in the form of a sleeve. Letting the sleeves hang empty while hiding one's arms inside the anorak signals one's peaceful intention. Maybe a direct connection, way back in time, is the single arm guard used by warriors in northeast Siberia in addition to the telescopic band armor sewn the same way as a protective gutskin parka (ill. in VanStone 1983: 15–16).

"Aloruttaq"

In "Aloruttaq" (bootless), the superior intelligence of polar bear, an old male, is emphasized in its human way of killing a big walrus. The episode, wonderfully reproduced in translation by Knud Rasmussen, starts off with the bear's cautious reluctance to attack the walrus despite the latter's inattentive, reclined position. Having thought it over for a while, the bear finds a big piece of ice and gnaws it into a ball, which, when tested, turns out to be too heavy for handling in an upright position; more must be gnawed off. Eventually the bear rolls the ball in front of him close to the walrus, seizes the ball, rises, swings the upper part of his body once, and smashes the ball into the head of the drowsy animal. The walrus, in a stupor from the impact, can offer no resistance against the bear's quick kill.[23] An eyewitness to this amazing planning, production, and use of a weapon by an animal is Aloruttaq. He himself is reluctant to attack the walrus and has been hiding throughout. But now he gets his chance. He loosens his dogs so they can surround the bear, which, now short of breath, offers an easy kill. With the meat of both animals Aloruttaq saves his own and neighboring settlements from starvation at a great feast, from which the guests return with grandiose gifts of meat. From this point onward the walrus keeps the story going, because Aloruttaq's former foster father, an evil-minded man, uses two ribs of his gift of walrus meat to make a *tupilak* against Aloruttaq. The two ribs, in fact, have been at play from the beginning of the story, as they are double the meager share appointed Aloruttaq at the time he still lived with the foster father who starved him. At mealtime, the foster father used to cut off and hand him only one meatless rib. Fortunately Aloruttaq is adopted by another man. Invited for a proper meal at the neighboring settlement, bootless Aloruttaq follows his (evil) foster family on his bare feet over ice and snow, and the host, a great hunter, takes pity on the boy. He adopts Aloruttaq by asking him for help in bringing in food and asks his wife to sew clothes and boots to dress the boy from head to toe. By now able to move around, the boy develops into the area's best hunter and later marries. His benevolent adoptive father even lends the boy his dog sledge for the magnificent double catch, which offers Aloruttaq the opportunity to serve the evil foster father, present among the feasted guests, the two-rib piece of the walrus. This is a mere teasing reminder in the light of the rich gifts of meat the foster father receives upon his departure. Nevertheless, the villain builds a *tupilak* around the two ribs and sends it off for Aloruttaq, who, when suddenly losing his luck in hunting, expects his impending death (implicitly: the great hunter has used up his quota of seals). But aware that he has once been made an *angerlartussiaq*, he asks his wife, in case he fails to return, to collect his kayak and gear when they wash ashore. He tells her that after a year he shall return from a travel around the world through the sea using only his *kapussivik* (a small stick placed at the point used for balancing off the kayak with the paddle) as both his kayak and tiller. Expecting a sudden death, Aloruttaq nevertheless harpoons the *tupilak*, because a *tupilak* usually looks like a seal when approached out at sea; upon being harpooned, it drags down the kayaker. But this *tupilak* has the power to glue his hunting bladder to the kayak (when thrown out, the bladder

23. Esaia of the former Moravian mission relates a similar event witnessed by the great hunter Qattaarsunnguaq of a settlement close to Paamiut. The bear hides by pushing a big lump of ice in front of it and hits the walrus with a force that smashes the ice. The two animals fight underwater, appearing on the surface once, dive again, and remain underwater until first walrus then polar bear emerge, and both cover their eyes, fall backwards, and expire (Sonne 2005: ID 1448). For similar experiences of bear killing walrus, see Hall ([1865] 1970: 534); Lyon (1824: 375); Olsen (2009).

detaches the line, which permits the wounded animal to swim along for a while, until exhausted and easy to kill). Aloruttaq gets a firm hold on the line, keeping up his balance against the *tupilak*'s attempts at making him capsize. Annoyed, it appears abovewater, an ugly red-colored beast with a dog's head, which suddenly starts to jump over and swim under the kayak. Repeating this movement several times, the *tupilak*, still harpooned, laces him up until it ends up close by and starts to devour the immovable captive. At the point when Aloruttaq has lost a good part of his flesh on one side, he loses his balance and drowns (in spirit), leaving the monster to eat up his remaining flesh. Upon Aloruttaq's return from a world tour through the sea, the *tupilak* is still there, barring him from getting ashore. Lost at sea, he is nevertheless revived through naming, because his pregnant wife bears a son who, called Aloruttaq, develops into a true copy of his father: he becomes a great and generous hunter, who marries his mother/wife, is attacked by the *tupilak*, is devoured, travels the world at sea, and returns after a year to the kayak and gear collected by his mother/wife. This time, however, he manages to slip ashore unseen by the *tupilak* monster, and although a thoughtless housemate places the tiller close to some blubber, which makes Aloruttaq lose consciousness, he slowly recovers and lives happily hereafter (Sonne 2005: ID 1362).

This story also ranks walrus below polar bear in regard to (human) intelligence and keeping alert. On the other hand, walrus performs perfectly cleverly when used by an evil-minded human for creation of an aggressive being, the *tupilak*. Its lacing up of Aloruttaq matches the ingenuity of the story's polar bear. Still, polar bear remains superior on the scale of moral values. With regard to the story's effect of naming—which comes fairly close to incest—it serves, upon closer inspection, to underline the *pooq* aspects of the story.[24] In fact, every element of the *pooq* initiation myth is present: polar bear, walrus, the candidate who loses his flesh, travels the sea in spirit, becomes reincarnated. But Aloruttaq does not become an *angakkoq puulik*. As an orphan who travels the way of *sila* due to his being an *angerlartussiaq*, he obtains *pooq*, a mother, in the form of the wife he himself made pregnant. This "gain" turns him, like the initiated *angakkoq puulik, invisible to aggressive spirits*, in this case the *tupilak*. Having obtained *pooq*, "mother," he eventually passes by the monster unseen.

Characteristics of Polar Bear and Walrus

Spatially, both polar bear and walrus are liminal beings. Both break through the surface of the sea, the boundary between This and the invisible Lower World. So does a *puisi*, "the emerging one," which designates any kind of seal, because its head appears into This World for breathing at necessary intervals. Being creatures of the sea they nevertheless depend on the air of This World for life. To emerge is literally "their way of life." *Puisi* derives like *pooq* from the same verbal stem, *pugi-*, emerge, surface. No wonder that walrus can serve as a *pooq* animal. Polar bear swims the surface and breaks it as well when diving for seaweed or for catching swimming birds from below. Polar bear and walrus not only dive and emerge. In the variant about Tuttu's Wife going to Sea Woman, they are associated with the breakup of the ice in spring, the idea of the shaman's visit to the giantess.[25] Yet the two animals do not

24. This is rarely encountered in Greenlandic lore but common in stories told by the Yupiit of Siberia (Dolitsky 2000). As he was an adopted orphan, Aloruttaq's lack of a mother may have set the agenda.

25. I am greatly indebted to Phyllis Morrow for this straightforward insight, which, embarrassed to admit, I was slow to see.

share their characteristics in even parts. Their breathing, a certain marker of one's position in space (see above and Sonne [1996]), differs. Conforming to reality, the Greenlandic epithet of polar bear is heavy breathing (Rasmussen 1921–25, II: 224–25; NKS 2488, II nr. 17; H. Lynge 1955: 24; Born & Rosing-Asvid 1989: 82) whereas walrus similarly breathes heavily but remains underwater for much longer. The polar bear's long nose evokes the breathing of surface beings, amusingly emphasized in the way Tuttu's Wife is sent to and fro across the floor by the inhaling and exhaling of the entered *puulik* bear (Sonne 2005: ID 1445). In contrast, the walrus's snub nose may resemble the almost nonexistent noses of the *innersuit*, who have no need to breath beneath the shore (Sonne 1996). These *innersuit* are strongly associated with walrus. They decorate kayak and gear with tusk objects from their own catches, and they are the only beings capable of hunting the giant walrus, *aaverpak* (O. Rosing 1957–61, I: 80; J. Rosing 1963: 188), spelled by Kleinschmidt as *auvfagfaq/aaffaffaq*: a huge walrus with short legs and a horn on its nose or back that is stronger than an old polar bear (Kleinschmidt 1871: 59). This creature might simply be inspired by a printed portrait of a rhinoceros, a likely possibility at that time in West Greenland. But all the same this monster (without the horn) is also encountered among the beings depicted in masks on the Bering Sea island of Nunivak. Their mythic *âsvarpaq*, a "giant walrus," is equivalent to *aaverpak* or *aaffaffaq*, phonologically as well as semantically. The most conspicuous feature of this Nunivak monster is its lack of breath; it seems not to breathe at all (Sonne 1988a: 11, 335 no. 27). Not surprisingly, the animals' emic characteristics are particularly accentuated or enlarged in their giant forms. Similarly, the breath of the Greenlandic peculiar "ice-grown" giant polar bear hits the opposite extreme. Dwelling on the deepest bottom of the ice-covered fjord, its inhalation through an immense hole is said to swallow up icebergs and *umiat* alike, and its exhalation to raise waters for icebergs to form (Sonne 2005: ID 1325).

Walrus and polar bear cover both land and sea, but in differing measures. Polar bear swims the surface, dives to some depth, but prefers walking on the floes and the ice, and roaming on the land. Walrus prefers swimming underwater, diving deep, and searching the bottom for food; he goes ashore on sand banks and sandy shores during the molting season and breeds on the solid ice. Their differing ways of moving in space are clearly reflected in "Qilaatuaq" above. Similarly, the *puulik* initiation myth has polar bear and walrus arrive together across the sea, with walrus waiting at the shore while polar bear walks over land to fetch the candidate and carry him down to shore, from which they take turns throwing him outwards the way they came. Polar bear, or *pisuttuartoq* ("the wanderer"), needs, as we know, skin prepared for soles in exchange with humans for its meat and skin (see also Søby 1969/70).[26] It is important to note, though, that the *puulik* bear travels the salt sea like an ordinary polar bear, not like "the freshwater bear" emerging in a lake for the pupil's first initiation. In its land aspects, the latter is closely associated with Moon as an extension of his body. Moon's relation with the *puulik* bear is of another kind, as will be shown below.

Walrus is primarily a creature of the sea. In diving and swimming underwater, walrus will outdo polar bear as clearly demonstrated in both "Katerfarsuk" and "Qilaatuaq." Their differing ways are even stressed by contrasts in "Qilaatuaq," in that the protracted transformation from human into

26. I am aware that Saladin d'Anglure accentuates the sea aspect more than the land aspect of the polar bear (1990b), but the land aspect becomes prominent when structurally compared to that of the walrus. As animals of the sea, the basic contrast seems to be in the way of movement: surface versus subsurface.

272–73). The West Greenlandic shaman, who right before January 1, 1737, secured for himself the skull of the Northern Lights as his helping spirit, similarly gained access to heaven (P. Egede 1939: 35; 1971: 44). At Iglulik during the time of Lyon (in 1822–23), hordes of polar bear and walrus guarded the house of *Anautalik*, and ordinary people killed by *either* a walrus *or* a polar bear would go to the realm of death in heaven (Lyon 1824: 372). The same destination was attributed to the Greenlandic *angakkut puullit* according to Poul Egede (in 1735). Initiated by polar bear-cum-walrus, they went to the uppermost realm, where they joined the council of *angakkut puullit* whom shamans on earth could ask for advice (P. Egede 1971: 13–14; 1939: 14; copied by H. Egede 1971, 2: 112–13; 1818: 91). Finally (only) the upper parts of the body of two giant, fierce walruses guard the house of Moon in a Baffin Island variant of the shaman's visit to this heavenly being. Due to his obviously stronger helping spirit, a polar bear, the shaman passes by unhurt (Boas 1964: 190).

Thus, in ritual as in myth, both polar bear and walrus appear as liminal creatures that converge at liminal points in both space and time. Apart from short-lived mythic cooperation, they are enemies in reality as in myth. Both cover aspects of land and sea in differing measures, together making up a full coverage. They meet and part at liminal points in space, the foreshore and beyond the horizon, the cleft between the Other Worlds of heaven and sea. Furthermore, at Iglulik, they mark the liminal time of the New Year. Contrasts are briefly amalgamated, passages made open, and both are associated with mother and birth metaphors in various senses. Still, in which particular meaning(s) is *pooq* the metaphor of the two animals' role in the *puulik* initiation in East Greenland? The first stepping-stone to an answer will be a survey of some *puulik*-like shamans among other Inuit, whereafter a series of such stones treat the connection between the "gain," its protective material, and the placing of its animals in cosmology and ritual.

Other Inuit Shamans with Angakkoq Puulik *Qualities*

Would *pullallik,* as exclaimed by the Canadian Inuit shaman on a visit to either Sea Woman or the realm of death in heaven, compare to *puulik* as a shaman's degree? The only hint appears in a text told by Amaunalik from the Thule area, who had inherited her entire repertoire from her immigrant Baffin Island grandmother (Sonne 1990; R. Petersen 2003a). The story, a version of the shaman's visit to *Nerrivik* ("place of food," Sea Woman), draws a distinction between great shamans and ordinary humans who practice as shamans. The latter are tickled into old age by her father, who is lying under his sleeping skin on the platform. Although returned to earth, their days are numbered. Only the great shamans recognized as *pullalliit,* sing. *pullalik* (filled with air, that is alive), like the Iglulik shamans (p. 328), are allowed to fix her hair and clean her house for the captured sea mammals to get out (Holtved 1951, I: 63). Regrettably, nothing is told about how Amaunalik's *pulalik* would earn his power for getting access to Sea Woman. Another distinction was made at Iglulik, not between shamans able or unable to visit and clean Sea Woman, but between ordinary and very great shamans. The former had a long and perilous way to go, whereas the latter traveled at great speed directly into her house. Without hindrances, he slipped gliding through a tubelike passage kept open by all his dead namesakes (Rasmussen 1929: 126). This is a gutlike passage, and most probably the quick glider would have been awarded the title of a *puulik* in East Greenland, as was—by his name—the mythic shaman Puulineq.[28] He traveled through an extended intestine inflated by a strong wind that blew behind him. In other words, he went along inside a *pooq* filled with air, hardly distinguishable from his speedy Iglulik colleague who moved through his slimy tube. In both cases, I take this tunnel to be a farting intestine! Puulineq, however, did not go down below. Leaving his unfaithful wife, he ended up with some giants living far away in the upper inland region. Apparently, then, this windy tube was his means for going anywhere beyond This World. His younger brother, who trained to become a shaman in order to find his disappeared brother, is called Ilim[m]ageeq. He does not travel in a tube; rather, his name most probably indicates his method of travel—i.e., Ilim[m]ageeq *ilimmarpoq*, goes flying (*ilimmarneq*: spirit flight) (Sonne 2005: ID 946). This means that the familiar East Greenlandic way of ranking shamans, by comparing flying with traveling covered up (*poorsinnaaleq*), structures the story. The East Greenlanders set no limits for the destinations to be reached by the latter, while the Iglulik shaman's tube went right to Sea Woman, as also, according to Hans Egede and the southern story about Tuttu's Wife, the *angakkoq puulik* alone had the power to slip by her guard. So, in this way the Iglulik easy glider could be named an *angakkoq puulik*.

A third possible Canadian Inuit candidate to the title of an *angakkoq puulik* could be, considering the cosmological setting, the shaman hit by the mythic double-clawed winter lemming living among the stars of heaven. In the case that such a creature falls right down on the back of a shaman, his powers will become considerably enriched (Rasmussen 1929: 113; 1932: 23). The name of a lemming, *avinngaq*, "the divider," must be due to its habit of digging furrows and tunnels through earth and snow.[29] In winter, the latter practice is facilitated by the extra claw it grows at its change into winter dress (Muus et al. 1981: 370–71). Did these winter lemmings dig the big furrow, the Divider (*Avigutaa*)—i.e., the cleft of the Milky Way? As mentioned above, this place is said to be both the meeting point of the winds and the attractive goal of the *angakkoq puulik* candidate, as well as the boundary separating his initiating stars, polar bear and walrus, from This World. The association is tempting indeed. The general association of the Other World with the interior of This World by body symbolism makes sense if we consider the idea of such a windy gut as *naaq*, the stomach of *sila*. Still, the specific powers received by the lemming-struck shaman remain obscure.

Now we shall set aside the connection of an *angakkoq puulik* with Sea Woman and turn to the one of invisibility to aggressive beings gained by initiation into an *angakkoq puulik* but inborn to a

---

28. This is spelled Paalineq or Paaleeq by Rasmussen and Rink (Rasmussen 1921–25, I: 210–18; Thisted & Thorning 1996, no. 44), but the editors of the translation into Danish and English, respectively, take the spelling to mean Puulineq (Rasmussen 1981, III: 26–30; 1939: 30). This reading structurally makes sense, as outlined above. In the Paaleeq story (Rasmussen 1921–25, I: 210–18) the younger brother is called Keligilik. Maybe Qiligilik would have been the correct spelling, thus meaning the one who was laced up (for *ilimmarneq*) in contrast to the unbound *angakkoq puulik*.

29. The epithets of the lemming as a collar amulet and a furrow-making animal recur in reality as in myth: it has a light-haired "collar" around its neck (collared lemming; *Dicrostonyx groenlandicus*). The heavenly lemming, which enriches the powers of a shaman, hits him on the neck. Similarly one Greenlandic hero, locked up in the house of enemies, has a dried lemming amulet in his collar, to be soaked alive in his mouth and used for *penetrating* his adversaries to death (Sonne 2005: ID 1434). Correspondingly, in the spirit language of the Nattilingmiut, lemming shares this epithet, "the penetrating one," with marmot and ermine: *puto .rte* (Rasmussen 1931: 312).

baby born in a caul. As will emerge, the caul is associated with interior skins forming bags of any size, and with the guts of the bearded seal in particular. Of wider extension is the dressing in gutskin for travels under the sea (see previous chapter) in contrast to the undressed shaman being laced up for his *ilimmarneq*. In either case, however, bearded seals provided humans with the material to be converted into the means for traveling the Other Worlds: guts for the gutskin anorak, *ikiaq*, and skin for thongs. The seal also provides for Maratsi's magic whiplash, which offered access to both the upper and lower realms. In sum, objects produced from skins of the bearded seal were the material prerequisites for traveling the Other Worlds, with the interior skins preferable for the submarine realms; this calls for an extended treatise on this animal as the main deliverer of protective clothing. The human caul, however, is our point of departure.

Protection by Invisibility

The invisibility associated with the caul (e.g., the one owned by Kuungaseq above) is, upon closer inspection, not complete—not to humans at least. Like opaque gutskin panes, both permit a blurred view both ways. Blindness is nevertheless stressed in the ritual myth of the *puulik* initiation, such as Akku receiving back his eyes as the last part of his body and Karraq losing one of his.[30] Still, when traveling inside the Other World, they appear able to find their pieces of flesh on the return route, though Karraq finds out too late that the first of his eyes is no turd but has been transformed into an iceberg like the other eye. This leads me to the conclusion that while inside his *pooq*, the shaman lacking his eyes is not blind as long as he travels the Other World. To its beings, however, he is as invisible (or inaccessible) as the fetus is to ordinary humans within its mother's womb. More striking is the blurred view in opposition to *qaamaneq* ("light," vision), the common gain of the pupil's main initiation in solitude, which made him both able to see the Other World and attractively radiant to the spirits. This *qaamaneq*, gained in close association with the light and sight of Moon, turns out to be structurally opposed in both sense and space to the *puulik* initiation. Invisibility to (aggressive) spirits is obtained by crossing the sea assisted by two star animals, in the South in an adjacent association to Sea Woman. The former initiation by the "freshwater" being was an initiation of the land (associated with Moon), the latter definitely of the salty sea, but still also of heaven due to the role played by the *puulik* animals as star beings. Something more than ordinary structuralism seems to be at stake insofar as a simple opposition of Moon versus Sea Woman does not suffice. I shall reopen this case in the Conclusion. For now, a change in focus to actual *puuat*, such as the caul, the mother *pooq* above all *puuat* and its associates, will prove to be more rewarding.

Caul, *Ikiaq*, First Clothing

Resuming the notions of a caul, protection, and invisibility, they also hold true for the *ikiaq*, the anorak made of gutskin. As a raincoat-cum-windbreaker, this attire offered protection in East Greenland as it did in the equally humid climates of Alaska, though in Greenland it served also as winter underwear for adults (Sonne 2005: ID 1177). As underwear for small children in East Greenland (Buijs 2003: 71, 73; 2004: 46–48), the prominent idea may have been that it provided

30. Foreshadowed (in narrative retrospect) in his prelude of playing blind man's bluff.

protection like a caul against hostile nonhuman beings. In myth, in case the first dress of a baby is an *ikiaq*, it has the same effect of turning the hero invisible to an aggressive animal (or bird, or foreign human) as did the polar bear-confusing caul amulet of Kuungaseq (Sonne 2005: ID 379, 517, 519, 1447). The same notion of protection is substantiated by the use of the gutskin parka by all participants in Yup'ik ceremonies (Fienup-Riordan 1994: 270, 280, 291, 294, 298, 303) as well as by the shaman in function all along the Alaska coast from the north down south to the Pacific (Fienup-Riordan 1994: 204; Lantis 1946: 203; Merkur 1985: 3, 259, note 17). For traveling the submarine world in order to procure seals, the shaman Kangciurluk put on five such parkas, whereas the shaman whom Billy Lincoln assisted wore female boots and a female parka underneath the same number of gut parkas for travels at sea (Fienup-Riordan 1994: 308–9, 312). The gut parka served, Fienup-Riordan concludes, as ritual protection against dangers implicit in the opening of passages from the Other World into This World (260). Surprisingly, some shamans at Ammassalik also performed occasionally in an *ikiaq*, which I take to be due to common heritage. Most Alaska gut parkas, called *kamleika* or *kamlieka* by the 18th-century Russian colonists, are sewn differently from the Greenlandic *ikiaq* in that the guts were stitched together horizontally (they were stitched vertically in Ammassalik). On St. Lawrence Island, however, both types were made, one stitched in horizontal bands using black sinew and considered to be a men's parka, the other in vertical bands, most likely a women's parka.[31] I speculate that the latter type alone was brought along by the Thule culture expansion in the 12th century, because the East Greenlandic *ikiaq*, although predominantly considered men's attire for hunting, was worn by both sexes. Regarding the Canadian Inuit, readily accessible information is scant, but a single Canadian Inuit specimen on exhibit is of the vertically stitched type.[32] In Alaska the southern type may have spread north to St. Lawrence Island at a later point in prehistory, when these islanders had become the famous makers and suppliers of gut parkas offered at the large Native cross-continental markets of the 19th century.[33] Among the buyers were the maritime Chukchi. They received their cultural know-how from the Siberian Yupiit but did not know how to sew the gutskin parkas, which every participant in their big annual *Keretkun* festival was liable to wear, small children included. The reason, they said, was that this *Keretkun*, the walrus master of the sea mammals, and his wife were both dressed in gutskin parkas (Bogoras 1907: 393).[34] Taking together the increased market opportunities (see Burch 1988a) and the high status of the southern type, a spread of the latter northward appears reasonable. So, having argued that the East Greenlandic gutskin anorak sewn in vertical bands formed part of the expanding Thule culture of the 12th century, I shall focus on the

31. The pattern resembles the *protective* telescopic banded armor skirt of North Alaska and Northeast Siberia (VanStone 1983). See also note 62 below.

32. See http://www.inuitcontact.ca/index.php/en/artifact/315. Merkur lists references (1985: 3, note 17) to the gutskin attire used by shamans from North Alaska to Kodiak and includes Labrador. The Labrador source is Hawkes (1916: 132, 137), where his observations in Alaska are mixed up with statements from Labrador in indistinguishable ways. See Fran Reed (2008) for a more comprehensive presentation of Alaska gutskin parkas.

33. See Reed (2008).

34. "All the members of the family, down to the smallest children, must put on light overcoats made of dried seal-guts. The reason given for this is that Kere'tkun and his wife are dressed in such overcoats. On the Pacific coast, overcoats of this kind are prepared only by the Eskimo, the best and prettiest of which come from St. Lawrence Island: therefore the Chukchee have to buy such overcoats from an 'alien' tribe, which may imply that the whole ceremonial is of Eskimo provenience" (Bogoras 1907: 393).

Fig. 23. East Greenlandic *ikiaq* (gutskin anorak). *Courtesy of National Museum of Worldcultures, Leiden, RV 1071, 2, ca. 1890.*

correspondence in ideas of protection against aggressive spirits offered by both the Yup'ik ceremonial gut parka and the "gain" obtained by becoming initiated an *angakkoq puulik* in East Greenland.

Performing in *Ikiaq*

As a rule, the performing Greenlandic shamans wore nothing but briefs, *naatsit.* However, as mentioned above, Maratsi was dressed in an *ikiaq* for his visit to the submarine realm of death, as was Akku for his. Akku was not laced up, but according to Victor's informant, Maratsi was. Nonetheless, both put on footwear and traveled by gliding: Akku wore a pair of skin stockings, and Maratsi his kamiks, which needed repair with new soles en route (Sonne 2005: ID 1697, 1324). For his visit to heaven, Maratsi also put on an *ikiaq* and kamiks, while Akku wore only kamiks (ID 1698, 1818). Akku went gliding, but Maratsi ascended directly upwards for reasons explicated above. When Kunnak, the famous sorcerer, dressed in *ikiaq* to cure Maratsi's sister of shingles, he succeeded by heavy blowing while the *ikiaq* went flapping around him (ID 1664). So did Akku's *ikiaq* on another occasion, a song duel outdoors that led to a murderous outcome justified by the storyteller. Usually the opponents wore nothing but *naatsit,* but Akku put on this special attire for reaching ecstasy and summoning his *Equngasoq* to have it kill his opponent's small child (ID 1684). *Equngasoq* brings to mind both its immediate East Greenlandic identification with gliding (see above), as well as the lopsided kayaker in the storm that brought Tuttu's Wife close to the coast of the land of Sea Woman.

walrus is opposed to its immediate transformation back into human the moment it gets ashore. Conversely, the quick transformations from humans into polar bears by jumping from land (ice) into the sea are opposed with their difficulty in changing back. Arriving on shore, they are to hide while removing their *puuat*, their clothing.

Like seals during their breeding period, walruses spend some time of the year ashore, to molt. But in distinction from other sea mammals, walrus alone uses its hind flippers for walking, or, more aptly, waddling (Muus et al. 1981: 405–7). These characteristics are reflected in several ways: one by the walrus waiting at the shore for the *puulik* candidate, another by emphasizing the short legs of the giant walrus, *âsvarpaq*, and a third by the spirit word for walrus, "the bandy-legged" one, *sissangasoq* (O. Rosing 1957–61, I: 94; Victor & Robert-Lamblin 1989–93, II: 255). Moreover, walrus enjoys an exceptional position among sea mammals, according to a Baffin Island rule of keeping the flesh of walrus apart not only from that of caribou but also from any kind of seal's meat (Boas 1901–7: 122).

So, both the polar bear and walrus are of both land and sea, though in differing measures; polar bear is land-based while walrus is more of sea dweller. This "more of" is also seen in their animal alter egos. If Iglulik women looked directly at a polar bear or a walrus, they became transformed into a fox (land) or a sea scorpion (water), respectively (Saladin d'Anglure 1990b: 91–92). In East Greenland they change into a grouse (land) and a long-tailed duck (shore and water), respectively (Victor & Robert-Lamblin 1989–93, II: 241).

Considering all the evidence, walrus has a certain affinity with the shore in both reality and myth. The sea scorpion comes in close to shore, the long-tailed duck breeds close to shore, and the walrus waits for the *puulik* candidate at the shore, while polar bear goes to fetch the candidate. So walrus and polar bear part and meet again at this point, the shore, the easiest approachable liminal part of space—i.e., the tidal part of land and sea, which offers access to both realms of death, above and below (see above pp. 167, 384). This point of parting and meeting has its counterpart in heaven.

Polar Bear and Walrus in Heaven

The East Greenlandic Moon, dressed from top to toe in polar bear skin and represented by his "fresh-water polar bear," is not the only heavenly figure associated with this animal. As a star on its own, polar bear is pursued by dogs in the constellation of Taurus (MacDonald 1998: 57–59, 68–71) and is a neighbor to walrus beyond the Milky Way in "Dying Woman." Walrus, in addition to this particular East Greenlandic placement, enjoys the widest possible extension as the ball of the Northern Lights—that is, in its form of a skull. This connection, common to all Inuit and Yupiit (except some East Greenlanders, see p. 316), was accentuated by the Nunivak Islanders, who had walrus play ball with a human skull and the animals themselves retire to heaven in winter.[27] Thus, a poor boy (orphaned and bootless like Aloruttaq) acquired complete shamanic knowledge about the winds during a stay in heaven, where he had been taken by the transmigrating walrus (Lantis 1946: 199,

27. In early summer and marking the end of the bearded seal spring rituals involving a prolonged particular treatment of the bearded seals' bladders, a walrus skull was the center of a feast celebrating the young children from about six to twelve years old. Fathers gave lavish gifts in their honor. The small girls danced one by one and the boys speared the skull together. "A young man brought in salt water in a little cup and poured it over the skull; then he took the skull out and placed it below the village, facing the village, all the little boys accompanying him" (Lantis 1946: 195).

This windy element brings up both the farting gut and the strong winds of the Milky Way. The *ikiaq* itself, however, points directly to the bearded seal, the primary supplier of the guts.[35]

Bearded Seal in Everyday Use, Ritual Practice, and as a Metaphor

Despite its central position in the subsistence economy, the bearded seal (*Erignathus barbatus*), the biggest seal in the Arctic, has not received as much attention to its importance in ritual and myth.[36] The meat, appreciated only in North Alaska, except dried or fermented, was used mostly as dog food. However, its skins—both the solid outer cover as well as the interior skins—were indispensable in Inuit/Yupiit technology. More hard-wearing and larger than those of the other seal species, skins of bearded seal were the preferred material for producing most skin objects (e.g., A. M. Jensen 1987. On both sides of the Bering Strait, only walrus could compete. Among articles of trade offered by coastal people at the annual markets, skin products of both animals were in particularly great demand among inland traders.

As I shall attempt to show in the following sections, the many uses of bearded seal as well as its position in ritual and myth add to the polysemy of *pooq* in connecting This and the Other Worlds, as well as keeping them apart.

The guts of bearded seal, when cleaned, split, washed, dried, and sewn together, were primarily used for anoraks/parkas, underwear, and window panes, the "eyes" of the house permitting daylight to get in and lamplight to go out in the dark. The exterior skin was cut in a spiral into one long thong for a multitude of purposes: bowstrings for drilling fire and hunting caribou; harpoon and tow lines connecting hunter with prey; ties for tightening clothing and bags; and all means of transport, such as whips for driving dogs as well as for their traces; thongs for lashing sleds and frameworks of *umiat* and kayaks; and bootlaces. For boot soles, bearded seal skin was preferred above any other, as were whole skins for *umiat* covers. Connection, protection, and movement are the driving factors for the multiple uses of bearded seal (see also Laugrand & Oosten 2006).

Movement/transport are further connoted by the various *ritual* uses of this animal's guts and skins, such as the *ikiaq* donned by some for obtaining ecstasy (or summoning a helping spirit), for traveling in spirit underwater, for boot soles for gliding shamans, and for lacing up the shaman for spirit flight—which sometimes ended in thongs dropping from heaven to the floor in ingenious figures or tearing about like some live whiplash. The effect of the magic cord giving Maratsi access to either realm, below and above, seems based on the same idea as the spirit of the whiplash owned by Kallaq of Northwest Greenland. As the only person who survived an epidemic at Qeqertaq, she was flown by this whiplash spirit across the sound to other survivors at Sarfaq (Sonne 2005: ID 839). The travel in spirit is further connoted by the *makkortaq*, a piece of skin for boot soles tapped or blown on by the East Greenlandic shaman as a technique of ecstasy. In short, objects produced from skins of bearded seal give access to see and travel the Other Worlds.

In a more restricted way, the rope fastened to the rod for divination, *qilaneq*, also provided a mode of access, which in one surprising instance is associated with the umbilical cord by Aupilaarjuk.

35. Walrus guts for *kamleika*s were just as common in Alaska, especially among the Siberian Yupiit (e.g., Hughes 1984: 252, fig. 11).

36. Except in regard to Nunivak by Margaret Lantis (1946) and Sonne (2007).

Practicing *qilaneq*, he would refer to his younger brother in the spirit language as his baby fellow because they were tied together by the umbilical cord to their common *pooq*—i.e., their mother (Saladin d'Anglure 2001: 15). With this association in mind, another image suddenly becomes intelligible: a vision of something like the extended intestines of bearded seal filled with water. The mythic traveler Kivioq comes upon them far out at the very center of the sea, in front of a whirlpool, which is the navel of the sea (Sonne 2005: ID 595, see also p. 113). Apparently, bearded seal guts could be identified with the umbilical mother cord of the sea. Returning to reality, the possible reason for this birth symbolism may be found in the bearded seal's way of life. It does not migrate south in winter like most species of seal; in Greenland it leaves the hard frozen fjords for the open sea beyond the ice edge, where it stays throughout winter, due to its difficulty in making breathing holes through very thick ice. As it bears its young on the ice out there sometime between March and June (most frequently in April or May), the hunter going out that far will encounter pregnant females or mothers with newborn babies "walking the water."[37] When new ice forms in September "within a radius of some hundred meters the bearded seal keeps open 3 to 4 breathing holes by using them in turns. In distinction from the breathing holes of the ringed seal, they are easily identified because they are both bigger and surrounded by a big cupola of ice which, reflecting the light of both moon and sun, are visible at a great distance" (Muus et al. 1981: 416–17). I immediately associate the glinting soul bubbles or *pullat* with these cupolas, or *puuat* for that matter. They mark the way of breathing—i.e., the exceptional position of the emerging bearded seal in cosmological space. During April, adult male bearded seals begin their underwater "singing," which I identified with the *ululoo*-calling helping spirit above. This spirit not only hails the successful initiated *angakkoq puulik* on his return, it is also the invisible icebreaker for its master, the shaman caught in the ice. At this point of my analysis I dare name the *ululoo*-calling bearded seal the third member of the *pooq* complex.[38]

The cosmological setting of the *pooq* complex can also be discerned among the Iglulingmiut. As already mentioned, near Iglulik the bearded seal can be hunted at a very early point of the year. The double star *Aagjuuk* (W. Grl. *Aassuutit*) marks not only the New Year but also the arrival of bearded seal from the open sea towards the land-fast ice (MacDonald 1998: 48). At the same time, women were forbidden to eat polar bear and walrus. These close connections between bearded seal, the twin stars of winter solstice, and polar bear and walrus are recognized in the *pooq* complex of East Greenland. It draws upon the same cosmological setting, that is, between the stars appearing at New Year, the polar bear, and the walrus. But the later arrival of bearded seal in East Greenland marks the opening of the waters in spring, the time for the *Aassuutit* to disappear.

Moving west to the coasts of Alaska, bearded seal is the first among the seals to arrive in spring. On Nunivak Island in the Bering Sea, bearded seal was appreciated in excess of all economic profits. The prestige accorded the hunter with the greatest number of bearded seals caught during the year was evident in the title of "best hunter" and eagerly sought by the Nunivak men. Bearded seals arrived first for the spring hunt, the big event opened with elaborate ritual for both launching the kayak and treating the first catch. Also, the bladders of bearded seal were handled with special care (Lantis 1946). Whaling was not possible on Nunivak as in many other places along the Alaska coast, but in

37. I associate this with the shamanic ability of gliding.
38. The mating call of the bearded seal: https://www.youtube.com/watch?v=sK5Sr7U-LpM

places where whaling took the lead, the hunt for the bearded seal came next.[39] At Ammassalik in East Greenland, the first bearded seal received a particular treatment, mentioned above among the spring rituals. People from all over the region came to cut their part (the three days of taboo before flensing permitted word to spread and people to arrive in time). It was literally plundered, apart from the head and breast, which belonged to the hunter (Holm 1914: 49; 1972: 86). This rough treatment can, by the regionwide competitive sharing of its meat, simultaneously be seen as an act of honoring this animal herald of spring.

Let us return to Nunivak where, as on the opposite mainland, a bearded seal in the figure of seal-man *Kunuuneq* (*Quniniq* is the correct spelling, as in Jacobson [1984: 340]) took on various meanings.[40] It would emerge in the same number of five gutskin coats like the seagoing shaman but transform into a two-year-old bearded seal if harpooned by a kayaker. The attempt was a daring one, because the moment of transformation foretold the hunter's lifespan (Fienup-Riordan 1994: 83; Lantis 1946: 199). Due to the figure's long hair, Lantis compared it with Sea Woman of Canada and Greenland (Lantis 1946: 199), while according to Himmelheber (1980: 30) it could influence both tide and waves, that is, like Moon in an eastern Inuit context. Finally, the person who commented on a drawing of *Kunuuneq* received by Knud Rasmussen during the Fifth Thule Expedition, which showed its long hair, boots, and mittens, pointed to the latter objects as symbolizing its relationship of exchange with humans. "[I]t is ordinary people ... he continues ... rather than shamans who meet the Sea Man. He should be treated in a special way: three times the hunter must pretend that he will harpoon the Sea Man, whereupon the latter transforms himself into a bearded seal, which the hunter can kill without risking his life" (Sonne 1988a: 109–10). Taken together, all statements agree on this merman as dressed in gutskin and transforming into a bearded seal if hunted with some caution. It neither serves as a helping spirit nor figures as the *yua* (master) of the bearded seals. Later, however, in chapter 6, it can be seen in a clearer light by comparison with other masters of the tide.

The Bogey of New Year Festivals

In person, the bearded seal man has a surprisingly wide extension in his ritual function of a bogey. In myth he is invariably attracted by noisy children playing alone in a house. He arrives from afar and, apart from the Nattilik children who climb some snow blocks, he kills them off with his weapon, a live bearded seal, in the form of either a club or a whip (the lash cut from a whole skin). The flayed body is a third, solitary possibility. The figure in a Mackenzie variant has a bag of a complete bearded seal skin filled with ice (Rasmussen 1942: 130–32). In most variants the bereaved adults make him return by making a lot of noise and then, at the moment he arrives at the threshold of the entrance tunnel, scald him to death by tipping boiling water or seal oil over him.

---

39. "After the completion of the spring whale hunt, the migratory bearded seal (or 'urgrug') were hunted from umiat. The skins of the bearded seal were eagerly sought as a source of harpoon lines, dog harnesses, and boot soles. Most importantly the toughness of the skin made them ideal for boat coverings—six full skins would cover an umiaq frame." See: http://collections.australianmuseum.net.au/amweb/pages/am/NarrativeDisplay.php?irn=17&QueryPage=./NarrativeQuery.php (accessed April 25, 2017).

40. "*Quniniq*, legendary person who lives in the sea and wears a gut rain-parka; mermaid." The root apparently connotes either stinginess or generosity.

Apart from the epithet of a bearded seal in one form or another, the name and identity of the bogey, like that of most mythic figures, vary with time and place. He has no name in the Nattilik version (Rasmussen 1931: 247). *Anautalik*, "the one with the club," is the name among both the Aivilingmiut in the late 19th century (Boas 1901–7: 497–98) and the Mackenzie in 1923 (Rasmussen 1942: 130–32). Way back in 1822–23, Lyon's informants at Iglulik named the father of Sea Woman *Anautalik*, a curious statement to be discussed below. A century later, in 1922–23, the bogey's name among the descendant Iglulingmiut was *Unatautilik*, the man with the whip (Rasmussen 1929: 217–18).[41] In Greenland, by the name *Innersuaq*, "The Big Fire," he is accordingly seen approaching like a strong light, usually from the horizon across the sea. If specified, his weapon can be a whip with a whole bearded seal as its lash (Sonne 2005: ID 1529, 1552, 660), an accompanying bearded seal (ID 661), or a piece of wood to which is fastened a skinned bearded seal (ID 1334); or he is himself a composite bearded seal with an indefinable animal as the lower part of the body (*ibid.*).[42] In West Greenland this punishing and threatening person is for very good reasons identified with the Devil by the acculturated Jens Kreutzmann who, accordingly, has the figure arrive as lightning among the coastal cliffs (ID 237).[43] Among the Yupiit the dialectic equivalent of *Innersuaq* is *Itqiirpak*, who has neither club nor whip but rather a big hand with a mouth on each finger to be guillotined by the adults (Fienup-Riordan 1994: 85, 146–47).

Taking a closer look, we see that several bogey variants disclose themselves as ritual and/or origin myths. One has a female *Anautalik*, who transforms into a benevolent divinatory spirit demanding a darkened room at every performance; this is obviously an origin myth of this common requirement (Boas 1901–7: 497). In most Greenlandic variants, the adults have gone *feasting* in another house, leaving the children alone (Sonne 2005: ID 121, 237, 660, 661, 1024, 1334, 1529, 1552, 1599, 1734). In East Greenland the children or adults play bogey without any shaman to protect them, but as they are armed with sticks, they will know how to defend themselves in case the play comes true (ID 1334). Perhaps the annual rough treatment befalling the first big bearded seal caught in spring also alludes to such bogey rituals. The Iglulik and Inuvialuit (MacKenzie) versions take place in the winter feast house, *qassi*. When *Unatautilik*'s live whip is killed by the Iglulik adults, he disappears and has never since been a disturbance to the winter festival.[44] The anonymous Nattilik bogey, having scared the noisy children into climbing out of reach inside an ordinary house, proceeds to the *qassi*, where it is scalded to death: "But the whip, which was crawling about the floor, the live bearded seal, was stabbed to death" (Rasmussen 1931: 247). Shamans and adults join forces against *Anautalik* among the MacKenzie Inuit, who afterwards demonstrate the skin bag with the melting ice left in the entrance tunnel. In cultural translation to Western lore, this action calls up some ritual overpowering of the "King of Winter." Yet the finest description of a bearded seal bogey ritual was taken down by Margaret Lantis. It used to form part of the (New Year) Bladder Festival on Nunivak Island. The small children were put away, covered up under their clothing in a

41. Rasmussen translates *anautaq* into a scourge (1942: 130ff), Boas into a knife (1964: 178), Fortescue et al. into a club or stick (1994; 2010).

42. One variant commented on by differing informants.

43. Placing *Toornaarsuk* (alias the Devil) in the underworld, he would, like the undershore *innersuit*, appear from coastal caves and clefts.

44. *Never* is a strong word in regard to ritual killing at annual ceremonies.

corner, before the old men started calling three bogies in a row by their singing. The first, a rare species of seal, appeared from the entrance tunnel with an object—usually a mitten—atop its head, to represent its young (like the devouring hand of the mythic figure?). The second bogey represented a male bearded seal pretending to rape the women sitting together in the tunnel; they yelled piercingly. The third was a female bearded seal with its young pretending to eat the small children, who at this point were being hustled down into the entrance tunnel. Thrilling indeed! It took the small children several Bladder Feasts to realize the cheating and true identity of the bearded seal figures (Lantis 1946: 186; 1960). Note that besides the strong association of gutskin parka with bearded seal, both characteristics of the East Greenlandic bearded seal figure, aggressive eating and libidinous behavior, were also emphasized on Nunivak.

Anautalik, the Father of Sea Woman?

Whereas there is no doubt about the importance of the bearded seal as an Inuit/Yupiit bogey in both ritual and myth, Lyon's identification of its namesake *Anautalik* with the father of Sea Woman in 1822–23 is puzzling.[45] To repeat: he is also called *Nappayoq*, he dwells apart from his daughter in a fine house guarded by hordes of fierce polar bear and walrus, and is the master of the land animals. The latter authority cannot be corroborated by other sources, but the father-daughter relation is confirmed independently (?) some fifty years later, in about 1890, by the related Aivilingmiut with whom Capt. Comer cooperated. His informants simultaneously also named their bearded seal bogey *Anautalik*, as did the MacKenzie Inuit in 1923 (Boas 1901–7: 146, 497–98; Rasmussen 1942: 130–32). Lyon may never have heard about this *Anautalik*, because he describes Sea Woman's father in utter contrast to a bogey. He is a nice and benevolent character, no bigger than a boy of ten years, with only one arm, wearing a huge mitten made of polar bear skin. Yet the latter body arouses suspicion. It must be the *anautaq* with which he is provided (*-lik*) and for which he is named. An *anautaq* means a club or stick, or in other contexts a scourge, a snow-beating stick, and once even a knife (Fortescue et al. 1994; 2010; Rasmussen 1942: 130ff; 1929: 241; Boas 1964: 178). So, Lyon's *Anautalik* may actually have been a bogey and the more so because the big mitten reminds one of the big hand of the Yup'ik bogey *Itqiirpak*. But still, why this appointment to the father of Sea Woman, the mother of sea mammals? Furthermore, because her watchdog is said to be her husband, *Anautalik* is also implicitly identified with the father of the girl who married a dog (Dog Husband). He was killed by his daughter's offspring, his grandchildren, who became the ancestors of Indians and whites.[46] Her dog husband was one of her "agents in punishing the wicked souls after death" (Lyon 1824: 363–64). Apparently, then, the two mythic mothers, Sea Woman and the mother of Indians and whites, were amalgamated into the prominent one of the two, *Nuliayuk* (Sea Woman). In later variants on record, however, the father has joined his daughter inside her house and is accorded the punitive measure.

45. Another quality accorded *Anautalik/Nappayoq*, that he requires no food, defies further substantiation (Lyon 1824: 364).

46. It took several clumsy attempts over the years to have these two origin myths combined into a noncontradictory *narrative* (Sonne 1990).

Comer's informants told such a variant in this way: "The souls of the dead go either to the lower world or to heaven. The former is the abode of *Nuliayuq* [Sea Woman], and of her father, *Anautalik*. It is very warm there. The souls of those who have transgressed taboos go to this country, where they are made unhappy by *Anautalik*" (Boas 1901–7: 146). Despite his move, the father of Sea Woman is still called *Anautalik* in his new role as a purgatorial "devil," reflecting the former role of Sea Woman's punitive dog at the time of Lyon.[47] The transformation causes some change in myth, in that the father moves in by means of suicide, lying down until the tide comes in and covers him up. This episode contrasts with most Dog Husband variants, which have the offspring bred by the dog kill their mother's father, who thus disappears from the story. Consequently, in order to "fix" the identification of the two "mothers," Comer's Aivilingmiut have the father *almost* killed by his grandchildren, the dogs in a variant of Dog Husband. Immobilized, he commits suicide on the shore, and then, without further explanation: "The woman [married to a dog] became *Nuliayuq* [Sea Woman]. Her father and her dog live with her under the sea" (Boas 1901–7: 327–28). At this point in history the latter's former name, *Anautalik*, seems to have lost its appeal. By then, however, the same Inuit still named their *bearded female seal bogey Anautalik*, as did the Mackenzie Inuit their male counterpart in 1923 (Boas 1901–7: 497; Rasmussen 1942: 130–32). Among the Aivilingmiut encountered by Rasmussen twenty-odd years later, in 1922–23, the figure was called *Unatautilik* ("with a whip") (Rasmussen 1929: 217–18). Nevertheless, whatever Lyon got right or wrong about *Anautalik*, the father's other name, *Nappayoq*, "the upright standing one," makes no sense in the context of his move from a separate splendid house to Sea Woman's submarine house. In contrast to being an upright figure, he, crippled by the offspring of the girl who married a dog, *lies down* at the shore for his suicide, and he remains *prone* forever on his daughter's platform, covered up by his sleeping skin. In this role of a torturing father, he pinches or tickles the poor victims with a knife (*savik*) or clawlike nails. The model for this punishing figure seems to have been the Christian Devil (Sonne 1990).

Moving to still-pagan Avanersuaq in Greenland about 1860, to the variant brought along by the immigrant Baffin Island ancestors of Amaunalik, the father is a torturer as well, but not of ordinary deceased humans. As you will remember, by tickling he reduces the lifespan only of visiting shamans who are not *pullalliit* (Sonne 2005: ID 626). A short variant recorded by Kroeber (1899b) accords the father no punitive role nor afterlife. He cuts his daughter's fingers and disappears out of the story. A third Polar Inuit variant, told by Aisivak of *no* Baffin Island heritage, mentions no father at all. The brothers throw Sea Woman overboard for a solitary life below (Sonne 2005: ID 1524). So in case Sea

47. An impact explicitly recognized by Knud Rasmussen during the Fifth Thule Expedition in comparing the fear of the entrance forbidding one (*Isarratsaitsoq*) with contemporary ideas among the proselytes of the Catholic mission at Chesterfield. Said Aua's wife Orulu: "[h]e is always in a bad temper and snaps and strikes at all who enter. We call him *Takannaaaluup angutialua*, the father of the sea spirit; the Netsilingmiut have a special name for him . . . and that is *Isarrataitsoq*. Everyone is very much afraid of him, and it is he who mercilessly punishes all those who have transgressed the old rules of life and more especially those who have been guilty of sinful love" (Rasmussen 1929: 66). And at Chesterfield: "Those whose offences against taboo are not wiped out by a violent death, and who have therefore to go to the Sea Spirit for *purification* before they can pass to the company of the '*blessed*' in the Narrow Land, have then to pass through a period of *purgatory*, under the guardianship of Isarrataitsoq ['the forbidding entrance one' (the needle eye?)], the length of time varying, according to the magnitude of the offences, from one to two years, or even several years. Exceptionally good people may, however, get off with less than a year" (97–98, emphasis and brackets, BS).

Woman's father was already inspired by the torturing Devil in Amaunalik's grandmother's variant, this idea was not kept alive in pre-Christian Avanersuaq.[48]

Variants from West and East Greenland are of little help. Sea Woman's father plays a minor role. He is in only one variant the person who cuts her fingers, which in Canadian Inuit variants become transformed into sea mammals (Sonne 2005: ID 2304).[49] However, he is once identified with the Devil, because he is said to be the Greenlander who moved Disko Island north to its present place, while another version has a *toornaarsuk* do the job. Combining the two variants, Poul Egede felt safe to identify Sea Woman's father with the one and only *Toornaarsuk*, the Devil of Christianity (Sonne 1986b: 201). But, apart from Amaunalik's (Canadian Inuit) version of the ritual myth about the shaman's visit to Sea Woman's abode, the Greenlandic shaman does not encounter any father residing in her house. Her only companion, if any, is the outdoor guard, most frequently her dog.[50] As far as the variants go, deceased humans going to the lower realm in Greenland were not tortured in her house, which was located some way beyond the realm of death. Her father was accorded no afterlife in any variant on record.[51] To summarize it in my view: in Greenland, hell became no purgatory because, for better or worse, the Lutheran and Moravian creeds allowed for no purification. The options were either blessed salvation into heaven or eternal perdition into burning hell.[52]

So, was Lyon, though confirmed by Comer seventy years later, wrong in identifying *Anautalik* with the father of Sea Woman in 1822–23? Did he once figure in ritual as a bogey using his big bear-skin mitten (suggesting a polar bear paw?) like his namesake in myth some seventy years later? *Anautalik,* who used to punish noisy children once a year, most probably became transformed through Christian impact into the purging Devil who tortures deceased adults for breaking the rules.[53] The Christian West Greenlander Jens Kreutzmann actually identifies the Greenland bogey *Innersuaq* with the Devil and consequently has him moved away from the horizon and placed in the underworld of the *innersuit.* But since the remaining Greenlandic sources are silent on the issue, the true answer to Lyon's *Anautalik* as Sea Woman's father remains hidden in the ethnohistory of the Inuit of Canada.

---

48. The immigrants, fugitives leaving Southeast Baffin Island in about 1840, settled among Iglulingmiut for almost twenty years before they moved on, stopping for some years on Devon Island, and finally arrived in Avanersuaq in 1863 (Mary-Rousselière 1980: 177; Rowly 1985: 10–11). Changes in ideas about Sea Woman's father may have formed during that interval.

49. Boas's statement on a Greenlandic variant sent him by Rink, which has the fingers transformed (Boas 1964: 179), cannot be verified.

50. In one variant, two sharks serve as her guards (Sonne 2005: ID 420), and in the oldest version, from 1737, a school of seals standing in an upright position fulfill the role (ID 2305).

51. That is, in an obviously acculturated version by Cecilie of Sisimiut about 1900, Sea Woman is named the *mother* of "the one down there"—i.e., the Devil (Sonne 2005: ID 1492); Poul Egede himself also identified Sea Woman with the great-grandmother of the Devil at a much earlier point (see above).

52. No variant of the origin of Sea Woman is found among the stories sent to Rink in the mid-19th century. Some were still told in the far south until recently (Sonne 2005: ID 547, 1882, 2070), but none were taken down in East Greenland.

53. In Sonne (1990) I focused on the revengeful Sea Woman exclusively, neglecting the torturing function of her father.

As far as my studies go, the purgatory Devil of myth did not trigger a counterpart in ritual. But other figures with "weapons" of both ritual and myth reveal interesting meanings. They seem to cluster around New Year and elicit other associations with bearded seal figures.

Armed Figures in Inuit and Yupiit Ritual and Myth

One armed figure is of course our bogey, which recurs at Inuit/Yupiit New Year festivities and owns a weapon (*anautaq*, scourge, flayed bearded seal, the skin filled with ice, etc.) for killing noisy children. The myth hints at a ritual rarely described except on Nunivak, where a female bearded seal pretended to eat the small children and a male counterpart pretended to rape the adult women, tickling and pawing them into screaming. Similarly, a Polar Inuit origin myth of the New Year stars, *Aassuutit*, has an old woman with a stick for hitting a small boy fleeing in front of her. In this case no connection with ritual is stated. Another *anautaq* was used in the Iglulik winter ceremony, *tivajuut*. In this context it means a snow-beating stick (Rasmussen 1929: 241), serving as the tool of the female part of the masked couple who pair off men and women for a subsequent temporary sexual intercourse. The male figure is supplied with a big artificial penis, a big artificial beard, and a little whip, *tiigaruti* ("for sexual stimulation"). They are notorious for mentally tickling one selected couple after another by their provoking sexual play, at which all onlookers except the couple laugh heartily. The couple is dismissed if they cannot withstand the laughing (Saladin d'Anglure 1993: 74–76, 82–83). Saladin d'Anglure speculates that the ritual *Anautalik* and her partner with the small whip once represented Sea Woman and Moon, respectively, and they might (80).

In ritual, *Nalikkatteeq* ("Big Crotch," the Entrails Snatcher) of the East Greenlandic *uaajeertut* has a stick but an *ulu* (women's knife) in myth, like *Ululiernang* who is encountered in a Southeast Baffin Island myth (Boas 1964: 100–1; 1901–7: 198–200). *Nalikkatteeq, Ululiernang*, and the *tivajuut* couple all try to make somebody laugh by their frivolous dancing. At the *tivajuut*, in case a couple gives in they are not hit but excluded. *Nalikkatteeq* of the *uaajeertut* hits wildly around with her stick at the first outbreak of laughter. In myth she, like *Ululiernang*, cuts out the entrails of the visitor to Moon with her *ulu* if he cannot resist smiling. By giving in to his opponent he has surrendered or lost the game.[54]

The inventive *Nalikkatteeq* dance, performed by baptized Maratsi as described above, identifies *Nalikkatteeq* with the star of the New Year, which forebodes the end of the world if it does not appear. In myth she is the star to be avoided en route to the bipartite house of Moon and Sun (Rüttel 1917: 39–40) and the figure threatening to let the world collapse in case she does not get back her emptied dish. The Nattilik *Nalikkatteeq* was actually identified with the New Year stars, *Aagjuuk* (W. Grl. *Aassuutit*), "who [stood] outside the house of the sun" (Rasmussen 1931: 238, cf. MacDonald 1989: 49). *Ululiernang* is in one version married to Moon, who like the Greenlandic *inua* of the moon also lives in a bipartite house with his sister, Sun. This house is guarded by the upper parts of two aggressive giant walruses, whom the visiting shaman, supported by his polar bear helping spirit, must overcome. *Ululiernang* is not present at the shaman's arrival indoors. Turning up at a later point, she immediately stoops and makes the oblong vessel containing her *ulu* spin like a whirligig.

---

54. The first Inuit/Yupiit example I found was the victorious effect of the mimicry of the lousy Indian as described by Hawkes (1913).

Next she starts to dance, showing her hollow back to the shaman, who realizes that only her heart and lungs are retained in place.[55] When finally Moon joins the dance, the couple looks so funny that the shaman can scarcely keep from laughing. Reminded by Moon to call on his polar bear helping spirit, the shaman escapes unhurt (Boas 1964: 190–91). So, although married to Moon, *Ululiernang* belongs in another place, which, in correspondence with the place of *Nalikkatteeq*, may be the New Year star.

The placing of the *Nalikkatteeq* star, either in front of the sun by the Nattilingmiut or to the left below the common house of Sun and Moon by the Ammassalimmiut, make perfect sense considering the position of the *Aassuutit* as morning stars from about the time of the winter solstice right on to their disappearance at the onset of spring (with the rising of the sun in their place). In myth the upholding of the world is at stake in the event that *Nalikkatteeq* is denied her emptied dish. Eventually she has her way due to her threat to overthrow the pillar upholding the heaven. The balance of *sila* is threatened. Perhaps Lyon's *Anautalik* made out a parallel by his other name, the upright standing one, *Nappayok*. A similar meaning could be attributed to the immediate stooping of *Ululiernang* and the subsequent spinning of her dish like a whirligig. Her balance seems to give way to a sloping ground; the spinning object may also be read as some divinatory ritual in the same way the downfall and spinning of the lampstand during Karraq's performance call Moon and Vega down (see above p. 127). This happening tells people of the impending ruin of their house and makes them flee in horror to another settlement. Their world, in analogy with their house, is actually ruined in their absence, calling on Karraq for a reordering of chaos—just as is many a religious specialist of New Year rituals all over the world.

As partially inconclusive as my analysis is, it points to common Inuit and Yupiit ideas of aggressive/punitive figures of ritual and myth appearing at the turning point of the New Year. Quite often they are star beings. The recurring issues are their aggressive behavior, inspiring sex among adults, or killing noisy children. Restraint is preached by the combined danger and fun of giving in. Tickling in particular, mentally or bodily, makes sense in differing contexts, in ritual as in myth. At the Nunivak Bladder Feast, the tickling of women and "eating" of children by a male and female bearded seal, respectively, take place in the tunnel, the liminal "vagina" (?) of the *qazigi*. Among several Baffin Island groups, the *tivajuut* ritual couple cooperate in playing the act and thereby "tickle the laughing muscles" (a Danish metaphor) at the Iglulik winter feast. In myth the moon and his wife, *Ululiernang*, perform a very similar dance in front of the visiting shaman. The Greenlandic androgynous *Nalikkatteeq* strikes a familiar chord in her frivolous dancing. In myth she cuts out the lungs, in ritual she hits out wildly. Most likely the participants ended up with an exchange of spouses. The same was undeniably true when, by singing the mating call of the bearded seal, the *uaajeertoq* player invited by his big teasing barb whomever it might please among the women to join him in the subsequent *qaminngaarneq*, the putting out of the lamps. A correspondence in outfit can be recognized in the male part of the *tivajuut* couple with his teasing stick, big false penis, and false beard. Sea Woman's father in Amaunalik's Baffin Island/Polar Inuit variant reduces the life of fake

55. *Ululiernang*'s hollow back, of whatever significance, characterizes the sun in the Greenlandic variants. This, of course, does not identify the wife of Moon, *Ululiernang*, with the sun since it would violate the Inuit mythic axiom of Moon and Sun being brother and sister.

shamans by tickling. No wonder that such figures asked for transformation into the torturing Devil by the Christian ban on sexual liaisons in Arctic Canada. In Greenland other transformations took place. This is demonstrated by several myths involving the *pooq* complex, and to these we shall turn at the end of this chapter.

Many epithets travel between imagined figures, lending each some important meaning, sometimes clear, sometimes obscure. Returning to *Anautalik* at the time of Lyon, he looks like some heavenly body living in a house guarded by fierce walrus and polar bear, and his *anautaq* may point to a ritual role on par with the other armed figures at Eastern Inuit New Year rituals. Personally, I cannot help but associate this figure and his guard with the *puulik* complex of bearded seal, polar bear, and walrus. As you will remember, at Iglulik winter solstice announced the arrival of bearded seal, and the meat of polar bear and walrus were taboo to the women. The kill of either destined the hunter to the realm of heaven at death. In Lyon's myth they belong in and outside the same house. In Ammassalik the three figures are not encountered inside or at the same house. But they are all situated right beyond or at the horizon, bearded seal alone or with young in reality, walrus and polar bear as co-dwellers or neighbors in myth. The bearded seal is hunted far away, beyond the ice edge in the midst of winter, and it breaks a lane in the ice in early spring as an *ululoo*-calling helping spirit. It annihilates Maratsi's fiend beyond the horizon and, as I have argued, it follows the recovering *angakkoq puulik* back home from the horizon as a helping spirit. All three—polar bear, walrus, and bearded seal—appear in myth as shining heavenly bodies arriving from the horizon, the bearded seal bogey as "big fire," *Innersuaq*, the other two as flames to the *puulik* candidate.[56] Nevertheless, the *angakkoq puulik* is accorded a particular connection with Sea Woman.

Angakkut Puullit and Sea Woman

Let us repeat: at the time of Hans Egede, some said that Sea Woman's dog prevented all shamans but *angakkut puullit* from entering her house because, I surmise, they pass unseen by the aggressive creature. In Amaunalik's version, of Baffin Island origin, Sea Woman permits only shamans with *pullaq* to do the cleaning job for the release of the sea mammals. The meaning of this *pullaq*, however, "alive" or "protective *pooq*," cannot be ascertained. Similarly, among the Iglulingmiut only great shamans possessed the courage to pass by the dog guarding Sea Woman's house (Rasmussen 1929: 126). But again, exactly what it meant to be great remains unclear apart from the statement that the very great shamans would glide unimpeded within a tube to her house, in contrast to great hindrances to be overcome by ordinary shamans (*ibid.*). This indicates, first, that the latter were not barred from the approach, and second, that the tube could be a *pooq*, a slimy, gutlike means of transport on par with the gutlike, flatulent *pooq* of Greenlandic Puulineq (see above p. 348).

On the premise of travel abilities, "greatness" of the *angakkut puullit* was in East Greenland measured in relation to that of the *ilimmartartut*, the "flyers," with whom they either matched or ranked immediately below. Most probably the former were "gliders," or, as reported by Niels Egede, traveled

56. I am struck also by the saying mentioned by the Northwest Greenlanders, that catching a polar bear, or walrus, or bearded seal, which lack a *gall bladder*, means impending death to the hunter. Both archaeology and linguistics point to former close relations with the East Greenlanders, as also the Northwest Greenlanders' ideas about the caul as an amulet fit the *pooq* complex to the letter.

like a flying fish breaking the surface now and again. Indeed, this breaking usually connotes a *pooq* movement. The "gliders" were, however, not excluded from any part of the Other Worlds, or from visiting Sea Woman, who could be reached by walking the bottom of the sea as well.

The only *explicit* association of the *angakkoq puulik* with travels to Sea Woman is confined to South-Southeast Greenland. The statement Hans Egede recorded came from some early 18th-century visitors of Southeast Greenlandic heritage. Of southern provenance are similarly all versions of the story about Tuttu's Wife, who was thrown across the sea by a polar bear and a walrus towards Sea Woman. The latest on record was taped in the 1960s (Sonne 2005: ID 258, 340, 1445, 2070). The south appears to have been (or remained) a stronghold of Sea Woman. Apart from the Avanersuaq stories of partly Baffin Island heritage, all Greenlandic versions on record of the myth of her origin and all statements on actual visits to her abode by shamans are of southern origin (see above note 52 and p. 140f). To this was added the *angakkoq puulik* tradition brought along by immigrant East Greenlanders. This transmission includes the disappearance of the polar bear and walrus (alias the *Aassuutit*) at the ice-breaking storm, which brings in the marker of spring, *Equngasoq*, the fulmar, in the figure of a kayaker with a delicate balance. It takes Tuttu's Wife along, but not all the way to Sea Woman. Tuttu's Wife is forced to jump into the land of Sea Woman from atop a high wave. Thus, the animals for her transportation, polar bear-cum-walrus and fulmar do not reside with Sea Woman. Neither did the *angakkut puullit* of the southern tradition end up near her place at death. According to Poul Egede they went to heaven, joining a council of colleagues. Iglulik hunters killed by either polar bear or walrus were granted the same destination. In short, the figures of the *puulik* traditions were *heavenly figures,* which could be associated with the travel to Sea Woman. The power of invisibility gained by the initiation apparently served the shaman *puulik* in passing by her dog unseen. But they were no integral part of her complex.

The same can be said about shamans on visits to the maritime world for whatever purpose protected by gutskin, a *pooq* named *ikiaq* in Greenland. This dress was brought along from the North Alaska/Northeast Siberian origin together, perhaps with some proto-Sea Woman figure. Actually, she may be recognized as "the woman who feeds people," *Ni-givik*, at Tigara, Northwest Alaska. Here, up to about 1900 the shaman hired by a whaling captain made a married couple of underwater spirits procure favorable conditions for the spring hunt: the man went to air for a change of wind to the north, his wife to the house of *Ni-givik*, who would make the sea calm (Rainey 1947: 258, and see above p. 140).[57] But the impressive Inuit traditions about Sea Woman seem to have formed in Canada and were then brought along to Greenland. Sometimes the idea of traveling by means of some *pooq* became part of these, such as the assumed gutlike tube of the great Iglulik shaman and the polar bear-cum-walrus of Tuttu's Wife in the south. Although both Akku and Maratsi of the family residing in the Sermiligaaq fjord dressed in *ikiaq* for travels below, the East Greenlanders did not, as far as the sources go, connect their *puulik* initiation with traveling to Sea Woman. As underlined above, only the southerners did. Some of the Ammassalik shamans credited this feat were not *angakkut puullit*, and the stories told about their endeavors do not deviate from the meager schema of the myth. In other words, they look contrived. Most probably the particularly humid climate turned the East

57. This is a phonological equivalent to *Nerrivik*, Sea Woman of the Polar Inuit.

Greenlanders' focus on both their *ikiaq* and the heavenly powers of *Asiaq* with her snowing and peeing baby-husband. Anyway, no sooner did the Christian message of eternal afterlife in either heaven or hell reach Ammassalik did first Akku and later Kukkujooq explicitly prefer to inspect the realm below to a visit to Sea Woman. More will be said about *ikiaq* and Sea Woman in the Conclusion.

Summary of Bearded Seal Issues

Connection, protection, and movement are the driving factors for the multiple uses of bearded seal skin for covers, lines, lashings, boot soles, *ikiat*, underwear, and raincoats. In actual life as in cosmology and ritual, the bearded seal is a marker of early spring. It arrives from beyond the ice edge calling *ululoo*, the male's actual mating call, which in myth (by its heat?) breaks a lane in the ice and, most probably, marks the success of becoming an *angakkoq puulik*. Further substantiation of its position as a surface-breaking *pooq* creature is seen in the ice cupolas that form over its breathing holes in the new ice in September. They reflect the light of sun and moon and thus the association of the bearded seal with heaven in ritual and myth. In ritual the bearded seal person is a common Inuit/Yupiit bogey. It arrives from the horizon, often as a strong light (*Innersuaq*/*Itqiirpaq*), "kills" noisy children with its weapon, is killed by their parents, and is sometimes associated with the origin of mussels from women's genitals. The sexual connotations are similarly marked by its tickling the women during the Nunivak Bladder Feast as in the *uaajeertut* plays at Ammassalik. Other armed New Year figures of ritual and myth "tickle" the laughing muscles by their frivolous dancing. In myth, death and/or chaos befall those who give in to laughter, in ritual exclusion from the game or a severe thrashing. Apparently these figures' punitive characters and weapons were conferred on the Devil of Christianity with its ban on sexual liaisons. In parts of Arctic Canada he thus came to reside with Sea Woman as her purgatory father, armed with a knife or pinching nails.

The Making of Cosmology: Acculturative Potential of the Puulik *Tradition*

Several myths and legends reflect the East Greenlandic symbolic meanings of the *puulik* ritual and myth in their ways of adapting to changed views of the world. Some were told by East Greenlanders and some by Moravian proselytes, among whom Aron, my last example, wins the prize in subtlety.

"The Child of the Moon"

In 1885, the commander of the Women's Boat Expedition, Gustav Holm, received a frightening story about a boy fathered by Moon with an earthly woman. As in other versions, he tries by various gifts to establish his legal right to fatherhood—i.e., as a provider. More often than not, however, the husband spoils the attempt by forcing his wife, against Moon's demand, to eat from his own catches. Spoiling the connection with Moon as the provider of the child, the husband causes Moon's son's death and at times also his wife's (e.g., Sonne 2005: ID 407, 1520; Boas 1901–7: 198–200; 555; Rasmussen 1929: 85–86, 87–88). Yet in "The Child of the Moon" of 1885 (Sonne 2005: ID 1128), Moon succeeds. His conspicuous gifts for provision and equipment are these: the flipper of a walrus, the shoulder of a polar bear, a whip, and a gutskin anorak made from the guts of bearded seal (an *ikiaq*). The day the son is born, a puppy is born to the formerly sterile dog of the household; that is, boy and puppy implicitly have the same engenderer, and by interpretation, the dog is his alter ego (see also Laugrand & Oosten 2002a; 2015: 151–78). The character of this son of Moon leaves much to be desired. Playing with his

Fig. 24. The giant falcon catches the son of Tunutoorajik and Ittuku. Drawing by Kaarali Andreassen. *Courtesy of Ilulissat Museum, Ilulissat, Greenland.*

whip, he kills first his own dog and then one of his playmate's. Fearing revenge, his mother moves the family to a rocky island that is difficult to climb. When the men of their former settlement approach for revenge, she dresses her son in his first suit, the *ikiaq*, and tells him to jump into the sea. Since this dress permits him to swim for long distances underwater, he lures the flotilla of kayaks far out to sea to a point from which the view of coastal mountains becomes blurred. Catching cold, the boy dives to the bottom, where he shouts from the roots of some seaweed (winged kelp, *Alaria esculenta*), calling forth a light wind; he next calls at the roots of another kind of seaweed, raising the northeastern storm from the highest mountaintop of the island of Kulusuk. The kayakers turn around but drown, some by capsizing, some by having their paddle grabbed away by the boy (Sonne 2005: ID 1128). The moral seems obvious: Moon's meddling in human affairs ought to have been stopped in time. The interesting parts of this version, however, are not only the annihilation of a whole community but also the complex of *pooq* elements for execution: polar bear (shoulder), walrus (flipper), whip, and gutskin anorak (both bearded seal) for long-distance travels underwater, and a strong northeastern wind.

"Tunutoorajik"

In 1919, after twenty-five years of successful mission in Ammassalik, Knud Rasmussen arrived and took down the story "Tunutoorajik." Like "The Child of the Moon," it tells about the son of a supernatural being and an earthly woman, but because Christian ideas and colonial relations have apparently got the upper hand it has called for some rearrangement. Nonetheless, "Tunutoorajik" is still completely embedded in the symbolism of the *pooq* complex.

Paraphrase of "Tunutoorajik"

Scared by a false threat, Tunutoorajik flees with his family to an island far to the south, which is opposite another smaller island. The family is welcomed by the owner of the island, a one-legged giant, Ittuku (*illuku*, W. Grl., half humanlike body cut lengthwise). Because Greenlandic star persons visiting humans frequently are such half bodies, I take Ittuku to be a star person (Sonne 2005: ID 103, 1782, 1977, 2329).[58] The southern migrations in autumn and winter all pass by the island of Ittuku: the Qallunaat in their trading ships, the birds, and hordes of first polar bear and then walrus. In case the Qallunaat show their mean disposition by ignoring his calling, Ittuku catches them by winding his huge whip around the mast. Having unloaded the cargo of iron, he stuffs the hold with a great number of polar bear skins in exchange. This "trade" explains his beautiful iron gear and impressive attire: he is dressed in iron from top to toe. In defense of the next migrations, Ittuku must prop the supports of his house. The feces of the seabirds, which buries both land and house, smashes Tunutoorajik's kayak, but Ittuku, although he is no kayaker, cleans and repairs the broken vessel in no time. Cleaning both land and house is no problem either, but because Ittuku loves and talks with the birds, he strongly objects to Tunutoorajik's hunting of them. Feeling guilty, Tunutoorajik begs his pardon. Ittuku forgives him magnanimously and then, persuaded to taste the meat when cooked, he immediately permits Tunutoorajik to hunt as many as he likes. The winter sets in, and grows extremely severe; Tunutoorajik's pee drops down in crystals, and no game is available. At its climax, however, one-legged Ittuku walks the sea ice alone for a long, long distance, which Tunutoorajik cannot think of matching. Ittuku returns with the intestines of a bearded seal, caught in the open water at the ice edge.[59]

A funny catch indeed, but significant: welcome to the *pooq* complex! The polar night arrives (at Ammassalik of short duration—i.e., identical with winter solstice, when the sun does not rise for a couple of "days"), and this is the time for polar bears to pass by in multitudes.[60] These are hunted by Ittuku, who alone possesses sufficient adroitness and strength. Tunutoorajik is only permitted to assist in the skinning. The following invasion of walrus, crawling all over both island and Ittuku's house, are easy prey because their skin cracks in the heavy frost. Tunutoorajik is allowed to take part in the hunt while Ittuku kills them with his whip alone.

Tunutoorajik's wife bears a son with one leg, and everybody rejoices in celebrating the birth because the father can be nobody else but Ittuku. Quickly growing and supplied with supernatural powers by Ittuku, the son fights two monsters threatening people on the mainland, accompanied by Tunutoorajik only as a bystander. The first one is a giant ice-grown polar bear, a monstrous creature

---

58. In two variants the visitors are identified not as stars but merely as living far away across the sea from humans (Sonne 2005: ID 1431, 1782; Danielsen 2006). However, all variants have the human hosts serve the visitor(s) some food, which make the latter flee saying, "But the dish tilts," referring—in my interpretation—to the sloping of the earth in the perspective of stars. See Fienup-Riordan and Rearden (2013: 111, The Earth is our bowl).

59. The extraordinary power needed to cover the enormous distance is demonstrated by an Askeladden hero who saves housemates or settlement from starving to death. He is an idle son-in-law who adds nothing to the hunting throughout most of the year, but in the end of a harsh winter with everybody skinny and in bed, he covers an enormous distance in the reopened sea and brings home a bearded seal (Sonne 2005: ID 1486, 39, 397, 224). Askeladden is a common type in Nordic folklore. He represents the small man who succeeds where all others fail. He always succeeds and often wins the princess and half the kingdom.

60. For a few minutes at midday the sun is seen just above the horizon.

living at the bottom of the fjord with a breathing hole through the ice in winter. The other is a giant falcon. Like his two-legged mythic colleagues among heroes in both Canada (Saladin d'Anglure 2001: 66–67) and Greenland, the one-legged son kills the polar bear monster. In "Tunutoorajik" he lures it to the surface by imitating the calls of a bearded seal (*ululoo*?) and hitting its armpits. But unlike other heroes who usually, if narrowly, escape the giant falcon, the one-legged son fails. The thickly feathered giant bird arrives with a polar bear in its claws, invulnerable to the young man's arrow. Dropping the bear, it claws the son up, and flies up and along. The young man tries to escape by slipping his clothes off. But the monster quickly lets the empty clothes go, falls upon the naked body, tears him to pieces, and takes them to its nestlings to tear into shreds and devour. Tunutoorajik, as a witness to this tragedy, despairs and remains forever with Ittuku (Sonne 2005: ID 1325).

Interpretation of "Tunutoorajik"

Pooq, in the meanings of cover, skin, and clothing, constitutes the main thread of the story. Between the contrasts of Ittuku's impenetrable armor made from iron and the final vulnerable nakedness of his son we find: the birds covering land and kayak with shit; the cold of winter covering the sea with ice; the intestines of the bearded seal fetched at the ice edge (to what end?); the skins flayed off the dangerous polar bears for trade into iron; the cracking skin of the walrus; and the ice covering the giant polar bear being as impenetrable as the plumage of the giant falcon. While polar bear has its sore armpits as an Achilles' heel, the falcon has none, contrasting—like Ittuku's armor—with the final nakedness of the latter's son. Besides the familiar elements of the *pooq* complex, namely whip, polar bear, walrus, and bearded seal (intestines), the newcomers are Europeans and their iron, birds, the giant polar bear, and falcon. Missing are the strong winds. Spatially, Ittuku's island with a smaller one close by is situated in the far, far south, a long distance and far beyond view from the mainland.[61] I take these islands to be stars, because, to repeat, star figures in Greenlandic lore are most often—like Ittuk—one-legged. One-legged figures possess a delicate sense of balance; thus from their perspective the surface of the earth slopes, and, despite the lack of half a body they travel, at high speed in space, covering the entire *qilak* in the course of a night (i.e., they travel like stars). These characteristics are emphasized by Ittuku's need to balance his house by strengthening the pillars, and the immense distance he covers from morning to night to the edge of the ice and back. According to seasonal time, the story runs from Tunutoorajik's departure in summer, through the passing of foreign merchant ships and birds southward in autumn, and on to midwinter, the time for fetching bearded seal intestines, which announces the hordes of polar bear followed by walrus. Socially, both the Qallunaat and the birds introduce disagreements, the first between Ittuku and the spiteful foreigners, overcome by Ittuku's whip, suit of armor, and authority, and the next between him and Tunutoorajik ending in peaceful agreement on the lovely taste of cooked birds. Everybody rejoices at the birth of the son. Ittuku cares for his supernatural outfit, whereas Tunutoorajik accompanies him on his heroic excursion to the mainland, from where, bereaved of his son, he returns and remains forever at Ittuku's house. The women involved in the implicit exchange of wives between Ittuku and Tunutoorajik are hardly mentioned. Regarding the power of the cooperating polar bear and walrus

61. Greenland's southernmost island is actually called Illukoq (E. Grl. Ittuku), but it is situated quite close to Cape Farewell (Jensen et al. 2012: 28, fig. 6).

in myth, it has been split, preventing at the same time their mutual enmity, because they never meet. Furthermore, they are killed in hordes, polar bears for trade, and walrus for no apparent use except food. Easily overcome by Ittuku's whip, the walrus are treated on par with the spiteful Qallunaat. Why? Furthermore, the way of walrus moving over land in the middle of winter and the frost cracking their otherwise extremely tough skin appear odd, against nature. The aggressive monster bear and giant falcon threatening ordinary people on the mainland are well known from other stories, as is also, if less often, a son fathered by a spirit through wife exchange with a human man (Sonne 2005: ID 1119). Recognizable or new to the *pooq* complex, every single figure and object (Tunutoorajik represented by his skin-covered kayak) is characterized by its *pooq*, be it clothing, pelt, cover, or lack of protective clothing. Only the bearded seal guts, marking midwinter at its hardest, are apparently hunted for no use at all. They allude more than any other skin to a protecting *pooq*. Maybe the allusion serves as well.

Nevertheless, the characteristic calling of bearded seal is the sound by which the young son lures the "ice-grown" giant polar bear to the surface from its place on the deepest bottom of the ice-covered fjord. Breathing through the immense hole, its inhale is said to swallow up icebergs and *umiat* alike, and its exhale to raise waters enough for icebergs to form (ID 1325). Among its favorite foods, however, bearded seal is obviously one. New to the episode of its killing is the bear's Achilles' heel, the armpits. Usually, if killed in other variants, its eyes are the sore point, unless the hero gets swallowed up by the bear's heavy breath and cuts his way out, either bald and scalded due to its interior heat or whole and hale due to the "armor" of skin thongs covering the hero's entire body (ID 144, 129, 350, 1071).[62] Intra-narratively, the sore armpits refer to the Inuit myth of two girls, one married to a whale and the other to either a falcon or an eagle. The bird is in the end killed by the arrows of its human brothers-in-law through its armpits (or by magic means), because arrows cannot—like in "Tunutoorajik"—penetrate its plumage *pooq* (e.g., ID 1187, 1126). By moving these sore parts to the monstrous bear overcome by Ittuku's son, what would then be the weak part of the falcon? His eyes? Not directly, but as we are told by other variants, its sight cannot penetrate a *pooq*. Thus in another story, the giant falcon of this episode is deceived by the hero's *pooq* clothing, his *ikiaq*. It hides his body from the falcon's view. The same is true of *ikiat* "blinding" aggressive animals of similar episodes (ID 379, 517, 519, 1447). In "Tunutoorajik" the young man's stupid act of letting his clothing slip off exposes him to the bird. By comparison, then, by actually killing the hero, the giant predatory bird of "Tunutoorajik" is raised to a position above that of the traditional hero.

Another reference to the *pooq* complex, or better the ritual initiation of an *angakkoq puulik*, is Ittuku's bracing the pillars of his house in expectation of the animal migrations. It can with little doubt be likened to former preparations made by East Greenlandic shamans for the arrival of a very strong helping spirit, which, though called upon by its master the shaman, was much too dangerous to let indoors. As you may remember, a particular resistant cultic house, the *ajangalisaq* (the "propped up"), which had hard rock for both floor and rear wall, was also buttressed with long tent poles, some sticking (horizontally) out through the entrance. According to baptized Saajooq, they

62. This is the way mythic Uniagaq and his brother who survived the turning around of the earth were dressed, as was Nunagsigaq, the spirit cleaning the land in Arctic Canada. It further brings to (my) mind the banded armor skirt of North Alaska and Northeast Siberian warriors (VanStone 1983).

were meant to keep the helping spirit, *toornaarsuk*, from getting inside when called upon, whereas an earlier statement refers to the very strong *napalariaq* (somersaulter)—i.e., a sand hopper (J. Rosing 1963: 180–81; O. Rosing 1957–61, I: 83, see above). Saajooq showed Jens Rosing the *ajangalisaq* of Ajijak and Maratsi, a very small house without windows, which was in ruins by 1961 (J. Rosing 1963: 180–81). Georg Quppersimaan informed Sandgreen about the *ajangaalisaq* (*sic*) as well. It was used, he said, by the very ambitious shamans for becoming *angakkut puullit* (Qúpersimân 1972: 46; left out in the 1982 translation). The latter statement of course appears closer to the *pooq* complex of "Tunutoorajik" than the others. Indeed, in preparation for his initiation to *puulik*, Akku had the room of the ordinary longhouse propped up with several tent poles. They served partly for fastening the skins in front of the main platform in order to shield women and children from the entering bear, partly for giving a convincing representation of a shaking house, and partly for making deafening noise at the arrival of the huge polar bear as well as at other suitable points.

Among the acculturative impacts, the superiority of the *pooq* made from iron is the first detail to catch one's eye. In comparison with old-fashioned Moon, dressed from top to toe in polar bear skin, Ittuku explicitly exchanges such skins for iron, the much-coveted article offered by the Qallunaat. Exactly how the armor of Ittuku appeared in the eyes of the anonymous storyteller is hard to know. In continued comparison of Ittuku with Moon, their offspring end up in complete contrast to one another. Ittuku's one-legged son comes out a heroic martyr in his attempt to save humans from a deadly threat, whereas Moon's child ends up an outcast murderer in his destruction of society. I certainly read "Tunutoorajik" as an implicit message of the crucified Savior, causing a conspicuous refurnishing of the cosmology current in "The Child of the Moon." Both myths operate within the *pooq* complex of bearded seal guts and skin (whip), polar bear, and walrus. Ittuku, the punishing superior of spiteful whites, begets a son with an earthly woman. So did Moon—the punishing superior of the taboo-breaching Inuit. Both fathers furnish their own sons with superhuman powers: unspecified by Ittuku, and the food and outfit representing the *pooq* complex by Moon. The effects are detrimental for both. The one-legged son tries (explicitly) to *save* people on the mainland from threatening monsters, killing one but becoming the prey of the other. Using his whip, Moon's son kills off first his dog or alter ego, next a member of society, after which, using his *ikiaq* for swimming underwater, he destroys every man in the storm he raises from the bottom of the far-out sea (the wind element of the *pooq* complex). He ends up socially and spatially outside society, demonstrating the traditional nonsocial character of Moon, who, having offered his paternal gifts, takes no part in the subsequent tragic course of events. In contrast, Ittuku is the active figure throughout "Tunutoorajik," right until the one-legged son's departure for the mainland, but then reintroduced in the end as Tunutoorajik's host forever after. Active from the beginning, Ittuku uses his whip in two ways, in catching but not killing mean foreigners and for killing the swarming walrus of equally obnoxious standing. He cleans the land of bird shit and repairs Tunutoorajik's kayak. He prepares for the arrival of birds and animals by strengthening the pillars of his house, travels an immense distance from morning to night, and kills dangerous polar bears for an honest exchange of pelts into iron. He sees to his son's superhuman upbringing by magical means. But why does Tunutoorajik, and not the mighty Ittuku, accompany the one-legged hero to the mainland? Why does Ittuku allow the one-legged son to end up as shreds of food for the young of his elevated murderer, thereby exposing the weakness of Tunutoorajik, the social father of the son? Why this lack of love on Ittuku's part, the young man's biological father who took care of his supernatural outfit? This is because the son, whose birth is joyously celebrated as being the unquestioned son of Ittuku (like the celebrated birth of Jesus at Christmas), is destined to become the savior by being sacrificed. The possibility that the son's flesh devoured in shreds by the nestlings is a translation of the Eucharist into Greenlandic is my second qualified guess. Also, considering the main thread being *pooq*, the undressing of Christ and his crucifixion outdoors atop a hill, wearing only a loincloth for his ascension, would bear a strong meaning in a culture imbued with ideas of *puuat*, which—as clothing—protected the naked body of humans when outdoors, and had the shaman *ilimmarpoq* (fly to heaven) in *naatsit.*

In tracking acculturative transformations, which kind of transformed traditional being could Ittuku be? He is most probably a star person, whom I liken to God. He shares his weapon of a killing whip with both heavenly bodies, Moon and the bearded seal bogey *Innersuaq*, and his habit of bracing the pillars of his house calls to mind not only the microcosmic *ajangalisaq* but also the Entrails Snatcher, the star being (Thalbitzer 1941: 713–14; Rüttel 1917: 39–40) in charge of the supporting pillar of heaven. Ittuku has a share in them all, a mythopoeic gathering of epithets put into play; this is a *bricolage* to which the new element, Ittuku's inaccessible cover (the iron of the Qallunaat), sets the agenda. He dominates the *pooq* complex, represented by his whip, the intestines of bearded seal "hunted" in midwinter, and polar bear and walrus arriving in turns at midwinter. However, it is important to repeat that, contrary to the *puulik* initiation myth, the latter two neither cooperate nor do they come to fetch anybody. And, instead of remaining at the shore, walrus moves across the land, swarming the roof of Ittuku's house while exposing its vulnerable skin to the extreme cold of winter. It is easily killed, even by human Tunutoorajik. Allusions abound, such as to the devils of Christianity, to the *puulik* stars passing over the heavenly vault (roof), and to death signified by the skull of a walrus used for a ball by the deceased humans in heaven. Yet if we stick to the main thread of the story, the *puuat*, at least the ranking of walrus below polar bear is strongly accentuated. Whatever the double entendre in meaning, the inferior quality of walrus skin reflects its invariable ranking below the polar bear in East Greenlandic lore: as a son-in-law in a family of polar bears, as bad-tempered neighbor of polar bear, or as prey killed by the clever polar bear. The ice-covered giant polar bear is a monster overcome by other heroes in myth, but differs from all other polar bear figures in size, with its habitation beneath the ice of the inlet and breathing like a sea mammal using a breathing hole. Perhaps it fits the new idea of a Devil, subdued by Jesus? In any regard, above them all ranks the giant falcon and Ittuku. Compared with tradition, the former only gets the upper hand because the young man lets go of his clothing. Ittuku remains undefeated throughout.

With all due respect to the Savior and God, the story is not all that serious. It has its touch of irony in presenting Ittuku as some colony manager setting the price of the load of the recalcitrant ships, and by putting a ban on hunting birds, his pets. Like God he talks with them, as does in fact the Greenlander Tunutoorajik, who is asked by the birds themselves to hunt them. Such is the traditional deal between Inuit and the animals to which Ittuku, having tasted the delicious meat, eventually gives in. Reflecting ongoing controversies between Greenlanders and Qallunaat officials about hunting restrictions, the Inuit view emerges the winner. Like the Qallunaat, Ittuku is no kayaker but an extremely clean and competent craftsman. As said by their mother in the origin myth of the Qallunaat: "be makers of lovely things [for trade]!" The power of *pooq* symbolism in the story's remake of cosmology is obvious. The image of naked Jesus, crucified despite the embodied powers given him by the father, may have set the story of *puuat* circulating in a framework of colonial presence.

Baptism in the Light of *Pooq*

In a few instances the initiation to an *angakkoq puulik* has been connected with transition to Christianity. As mentioned above, Pruutas in the south became very frightened at being told that the two approaching flames were to be his *puuat.* He stopped the performance, gave up being a shaman, and asked the missionary for baptism. Missuarniannga did not give up, however. Quite on the contrary! He had the huge bear approach on two days, and take him away on the third, and he required a convalescence of three days afterwards. But why did he go through this ordeal right before his conversion? Obviously as an impressive end-of-career performance, to which may be added a desire to obtain the protection gained by the initiation to *puulik.* Some helping spirits tended to become very aggressive at the point they were dismissed (e.g., Sonne 2005: ID 1708, 1288), an unavoidable consequence of their master's baptism.

The shaman who was unprovoked by his helping spirits but turned his back on them was a novelty that broke with tradition. However, the converse—the spirits leaving their careless master—was a constant concern both during and after apprenticeship. Easily offended helping spirits offered convenient opportunities for performing a serious attack, which was overcome in the end by the shaman (e.g., ID 1690, 1811, 1138, 1691). Apparently, bidding one's helping spirits farewell at baptism never became ritualized in the same way that the presentation of them at *saqqummerneq* was. Neither Missuarniannga nor Imaneq took leave of their individual spirits in public. Imaneq, a shaman of the 18th century, belonged to Pisuffik, a small settlement north of Nuuk/Godthåb on the west coast. In 1768, when he, moved by a convincing dream, decided to become baptized, he caused a revival movement that spread along the coast north and south of Pisuffik. Competition was rife between the two missions at Nuuk. Both parties took measures to get hold of the "souls," with the Royal Danish Mission establishing an annex in Pisuffik and the German Moravians persuading their proselytes to move to one of their places. Some Pisufimmiut chose the former and some the latter. Gulløv uses archaeological and historical data to analyze opposite preferences in the mixed population of northerners and southerners at Pisuffik. The northern locals chose the Danes, the southerners—as had other immigrants from the south until then—the Germans (Gulløv 1986b). Imaneq was the elder of the southern party, which consisted of some thirty-two or thirty-eight related people. Of these, some went back to Pisuffik after baptism, while Imaneq and his close kin settled among the southerners on the Moravian-dominated island Kangeq (*ibid.*).

Kristian, a Kangermiu who told Rink the story about Imaneq about 1860, was a descendant of a family that followed Imaneq and belonged to the Moravians (*ibid.*). Considering the Southeast Greenlandic heritage marking a great number of the stories told by Moravian followers, the story's use of *pooq* elements is no surprise.

The dream inspiring Imaneq to decide on baptism is a late event in the story. It was provoked by an experience that one would recognize as an initiation, but having an opposite effect: as a great successful shaman, Imaneq was a beloved person, who by and by came to consider himself immensely powerful. He arrogantly postponed the cure of a young woman who consequently died. He even forgot the taboo against wearing any part of the clothing used at the funeral on the following hunting trip. So, out at sea he is met and strongly reproached by his great helping spirit, the smiling giant of the sea, *Qungussutariaq*. The "smoke" of his kamiks ruins visibility and provokes contrary currents in the sea. The delayed attempt to cure the woman also infuriates the spirit, who cuts Imaneq and his kayak lengthwise, and then slices the two halves into smaller pieces, scolding each one of them and throwing them around. But Imaneq is an *angerlartussiaq*. Coming to his rescue from below, his dead grandparents put his body together and send him along gliding on the skin he sat on in his kayak. They return for a new reenlivening when he loses consciousness close to Pisuffik due to the smell of a woman's hair let down (a common break of taboo in situations of crisis in stories). He happens to get ashore at a neighboring settlement, where people know how to treat him for the following five days with minimal food and drink. Back home, Imaneq continues to practice as a shaman, but his powers have diminished. God did this, says the storyteller. God wanted Imaneq to convert, as evidenced by an intruding strong light from the east which increasingly impairs his powers. Time and again he loses consciousness for long hours and experiences the wonderful bliss of heaven. This light induces his desire for baptism for himself and his relatives (Sonne 2005: ID 506; see Aron's illustrations on the front cover and endsheets).

Strictly speaking, Imaneq did not go through an initiation to *angakkoq puulik*. The spirit cutting him up is no combined polar bear and walrus, which were rarely encountered in this part of Greenland. He is not healed by his own efforts; being an *angerlartussiaq* (one who can return after an untimely death) his body is reassembled by his dead grandparents. Nor does he come out a greater shaman. Quite on the contrary—he slowly loses his *qaamaneq* while his genuine "gain," the bliss of heavenly light, is won through subsequent initiations of "dying" and regaining consciousness. In opposition to the (starry) lights from beyond the sea in the west as seen by the southern *puulik* candidate (Pruutars and Tuttu's Wife), the glaring light of heaven comes to Imaneq from the east. Still, Imaneq is cut up, he returns gliding (on his sitting skin), and the illustrator, Aron, has him return as "blinded" as a returning *puulik* candidate. Aron has Imaneq's head wrapped up in his hunting bladder, in all meanings the *pooq* of a hunter at sea. Aron painted it just as luminously yellow as the light from heaven that hits the unconscious Imaneq on a subsequent illustration (see endsheets; Thisted 1999: 176–77; Thorning et al. 1999: 176–77). His executor is the smiling *Qungussutariaq*, defined above as a fertilizing *inua* of the deep sea.[63] This figure, as indicated above, bears a direct likeness to all those Inuit figures of ritual and myth, which provoke and at the same time punish smiling: helping spirits who with sticks hit wildly among the onlookers at East Greenlandic shamans' performances, *Nalikkatteeq*; *Ululiernang*, the copulating couple of shamans in disguise at the Iglulik *tivajuut*; and the comical giant merman who, when laughed at, falls backwards causing a tsunami to flood the land. Furthermore, the statement mentioned by Rink that *Qungussutariaq* is an enemy of noisy children (Rink 1868–71, II: 189) demands further investigation into probable *pooq* associations with this figure. This is my attempt in the following section.

63. In a younger version it is called *Avinngaq*, the "splitting one" or "lemming," obviously in reference to its way of cutting up Imaneq (Sonne 2005: ID 470).

A Prominent Accculturative Pooq*: Tricksteresque Qivaaqiarsuk*

In 1902, Knud Rasmussen's storyteller Aqajaq did not consider *Qungussutariaq* a dangerous being; nor was he the first to belittle this figure. By 1860 both the acculturated Jens Kreutzmann and Aron already did so, but Aron less explicitly in his version of "Qivaaqiarsuk" (Sonne 2005: ID 69). This story has been treated ethnolinguistically by Arnaq Grove (2000), and I shall refer to her shrewd interpretation pointing to the ambiguousness of Qivaaqiarsuk's appearance and character whenever there is the opportunity. My basic reason for choosing the story, however, is its particularly rich number of *pooq* elements employed by Aron in a contemporary, actual context.

Paraphrase of "Qivaaqiarsuk"

Qivaaqiarsuk ("the special sculpin") is a genuine fjord dweller, living in Kangersuneq close to the inland ice at the innermost (eastern) settlement of the extensive system of fjords behind Nuuk. Although a skinny weakling, he is an excellent hunter who provides single-handedly for a good number of women. Hearing about the rich hunting at the island Kangeq in the sea west of Nuuk, he sets off, travels for a long time through the fjords, and then arrives and settles on Kangeq. There, as the only kayaker to return from a gale, he soon finds himself once again the sole provider for many widows. He still does well, hunting in an exemplary manner by living up to the ideal of never catching more than necessary (Grove 2000). However, his longing for home works against this ideal way of living, especially in spring, when he used to hear the roar of calving inland ice at the bottom of Kangersuneq. So, when at the very low spring tide the widows have gratefully accepted his offer to ferry them to an emerged skerry for collecting red seaweed, he subsequently ignores their calling at flood tide. Quite satisfied at being let off the burden of provision, he for no explicit reason remains at Kangeq. When he comes across an iceberg trapped in a coastal cleft, he hits it hard with his tensely inflated hunting bladder so that it makes a sound like the roar of calving ice. Delighted, he continues beating the iceberg, and the sound calls up smiling *Qungussutariaq* with its head surrounded by a transparent bubble of water. Unlike Imaneq's helping spirit, this giant neither cuts up nor scolds Qivaaqiarsuk when he smiles back. He is merely reproached and then told the reason why his wife bears no children. She is a shaman in secrecy who ought to come forward and reveal her powers in public. But Qivaaqiarsuk, who returns home and becomes absorbed in distributing the rich catch he brings, forgets to tell his wife about the injunction.

So, due to his resumed beating of the iceberg, two *bubbles* announce two emerging kayakers in spotlessly clean kayaks—an epithet of *innersuit.* Polite Qivaaqiarsuk invites them to his place, but having realized their nonhuman identities he asks his wife not to serve them any food. Displeased with her look, they each hand her a small piece of *mattak*, one black (from narwhal) and one white (from beluga), for curing cradle cap. Grove associates these with the impurities of Sea Woman's hair, which prevent her from "bearing" the sea mammals pent up in her house. The pieces of *mattak* are thus apparently meant to be used by the infertile woman to remove her blocking impurities, alias the secrecy of her *angakkuuneq*. She, however, takes no notice, and since Qivaaqiarsuk does not interfere, she soon falls fatally ill. Qivaaqiarsuk cuts open her dead body, and he removes her stomach; when cleaned and dried, it is made into a chalk-white towing bladder. It increases his luck in hunting considerably, and, when used for beating the trapped iceberg, it brings about the most convincing, wonderful, far-traveling boom, which calls forth another giant kayaker from below.

Frightened and worried about the recurring noise, the submarine kayaker wants to know the source. Oh yes, Qivaaqiarsuk says, he has also heard it for some time! Relaxed, the giant invites him to his place, the island Uummannaq in the fjord that forms a continuation of the Pisissarfik fjord, parallel to Kangersuneq but closer to Nuuk.[64] The giant must be an undershore *innersuaq* because his gear is made from tusks (of walrus), the most common epithet of the *innersuit*. Furthermore, like *innersuit* he and his relatives hunt big animals never encountered by Qivaaqiarsuk, neither off Kangeq nor at his former place in Kangersuneq. But Qivaaqiarsuk proves his superior attraction to both women and animals. He is warmly welcomed into bed by the only sister of many (reluctant) brothers, he begets a son, and single-handedly he kills two impressive animals, an extremely aggressive red (male) walrus and a huge bowhead whale. When harpooned, the bowhead does not flee for the open sea. Instead, it moves unnaturally towards land and comes right ashore, where it dies like a thrashing capelin. For towing the whale, however troublesome, Qivaaqiarsuk needs no help (due to the power of his towing bladder *pooq*, I suppose). He even returns well ahead of his in-laws and immediately asks the women to quickly make him an *ikiaq* from the guts of a walrus caught on the same hunting trip.

So, there he sits outdoors, dressed in his new *ikiaq* and waiting for his in-laws, who spot his shining white figure from afar. By this sign of strength on top of his hunting and towing feat, they feel assured about winning their upcoming competition with enemies to the south. And so they do, thanks to Qivaaqiarsuk, this insignificant, meager "sculpin" with immense muscular strength. In revenge, the enemies steal Qivaaqiarsuk's son, as eventually revealed by another infertile, secret shaman, whom Qivaaqiarsuk directly orders to perform in public. She, in fact, is closely related to the child, because her husband, grieving his childless situation, came to love the boy and looked after his upbringing and hunting outfit. During the (familiar) episode of stealing the child back from the enemies, Qivaaqiarsuk kills every single one of them.

Next the in-laws, despite Qivaaqiarsuk's explicit warnings, beg to be presented for his trainee or opponent in youth, a giant *tuneq* dwelling in the mountains beyond Kangersuneq. The in-laws do not trust his statement on the strength of the *tuneq*; they insist on seeing it, according to the explanation. Arriving at the *tuneq*'s house up on a vast plain, Qivaaqiarsuk goes to the window and asks the giant to come outside. Both set off moving at great speed (implicitly like sculpins) and meet outside at the mouth of the entrance. But then the giant *tuneq* completely ignores Qivaaqiarsuk. Hands on knees and its back to the visitors it tacitly invites Qivaaqiarsuk and his in-laws to jump through a big hole in its crotch. Nobody gets hurt. But in the subsequent fight with Qivaaqiarsuk, the *tuneq* happens to kill one of the in-laws. Embarrassed, it scurries into its house "like a sculpin." Actually, as confided to the reader by Aron, Qivaaqiarsuk is the culprit who, when struggling with the giant, sees his chance to lift up the giant and hurl the body towards the in-laws. The youngest, not able to move backwards quickly enough, is killed by the giant's head (as also illustrated by Aron [Thisted 1999: 356; Thorning et al. 1999: 356]). All the same, Qivaaqiarsuk feels guilty. Mentioning his fears of having made the in-laws his enemies, the in-laws ask him to please not mind (they dare suggest nothing else). While paddling homewards, they ride the waves by an off-shore gale (tailwind in this case) sent by the *tuneq*.

64. In a note Thisted (1999: 346) identifies this Uummannaq as the place. The giant points to a place west of the trapped iceberg—i.e., west of Kangeq. I shall stick to Thisted's placement, because only this Uummanaq of the region has the small settlement mentioned in the story.

The story's last episode takes place just south of Nuuk, at the coastal mountain Kingittorsuaq (implicitly a "seamark" visible from up to 150 km away). Qivaaqiarsuk has brought his son to see the lovely sight of the land becoming green in spring. Suddenly, short of breath, he asks his son to go home and just leave him alone to enjoy the view. He then starts to pee, and continues peeing for a very long time. The glacier of Kingittorsuaq forms from Qivaaqiarsuk's pee, and he never returns (but his son, remaining with his nonhuman adoptive parents, can relate his last whereabouts) (Sonne 2005: ID 69).

Analysis

The great quantity of *puuat* in this story is really impressive. What immediately catches one's eye are the inflated hunting bladders used for producing sounds similar to that of the calving inland ice when hit against the iceberg. The excised female stomach, "fertile" with hidden shamanic powers (*angakkuuneq*), connotes "mother" (*pooq*), albeit in an awkward sense. Since shamanic powers used to be opposed to women's fertility (in theory, female shamans are childless) and hidden shaman powers to morals (e.g., *saqqummerneq*, making oneself known in public was a moral must), the grandiose effects of this *pooq* seem implicitly likened to sorcery. That is, unless the drying and bleaching of this *pooq* into a shining white towing bladder meant a transformation into less repulsive powers. I shall return to this possibility later. In any case, first his ordinary bladder and then his wife's cured stomach bladder, when hit against the iceberg, call forth creatures from below through the cleft in which the iceberg is trapped. *Qungussutariaq*, connected with *pooq* in Aron's illustration of the returning Imaneq blinded by his hunting bladder, is granted an even closer connection in "Qivaaqiarsuk." Thus, emerging in front of Qivaaqiarsuk the giant's head is covered up, not blinded but visibly smiling, within a *transparent bubble* of water. Aron hardly invented this idea of apparent southern origin, in that the Southeast Greenlander Aadaarutaa had a similar experience during his apprenticeship. He saw *Qungussutariaq*, identified as an *innersuaq*, emerge inside a translucent bubble between frozen cupolas on the ice (Sonne 2005: ID 971). The latter bring to mind the cupolas forming above breathing holes of bearded seal, glinting in the light of the sun or moon (see p. 353). So in this context of bubbles, the name *Innersuaq* of the bearded seal bogey falls into place as identified with *Qungussutariaq*. Actually, Rink was told that *Qungussutariaq* punished noisy children—i.e., like *Innersuaq*. In "Qivaaqiarsuk" the two *innersuit* bringing the *mattak* also emerge in such bubbles. Another recognizable *pooq* is the quickly sewn *ikiaq*, white and shining, which Qivaaqiarsuk can be seen wearing from a great distance by his in-laws. This serves as a parallel, of course, to the seamark, Kingittorsuaq, dressed in the frozen pee of the hero who dies by draining his urine bladder, a *pooq* of life. Still, who is this Qivaaqiarsuk?

It is critical to make clear at the outset that Qivaaqiarsuk's grotesquely enlarged powers give the narrative one of its very funny twists. Time and again he proves himself a better kayaker and hunter to whom women and game are far more attracted than to anybody else, be they ordinary humans or not. Physically, he overcomes any opponent, even the giant *tuneq* of the eastern gale, with its peculiar hole in the crotch. Socially he is an impressive, albeit unreliable, provider. He is a boaster nobody dare oppose, or they risk being killed. In (religious/magic) knowledge he cannot be beaten either. Taking neither admonition seriously, the explicit one of *Qungussutariaq* and the less explicit idea of the gifts brought by the two *innersuit*, he knows how to profit from his disobedience by securing for himself the most fantastic *pooq* in the world, his wife's stomach containing her shamanic power in place of an embryo. His name, the dear/peculiar (*-arsuk*) "sculpin" or, better, male Atlantic poacher (*Leptagonus decagonus*), connotes a phallic being according to Arnaq Grove (2000). Grove also underlines Aron's tricky characteristics: he looks skinny with a big (healthy) stomach and he *intentionally* lets his wife die because he prefers an effective means for sealing over having a son. The apparent role model of an unrivaled hunter thus hides a very ambiguous figure, whose original placement farthest east may support this character flaw, because in West Greenland "east," says Grove (2000), connotes (pagan) supernatural forces. And Aron, himself a Kangeq islander, stresses Qivaaqiarsuk's easternmost place of origin by causing the greatest part of his behavior to result from a homesick longing for the sound of calving ice. Reproduced by means of the inflated *puuat*, it calls up (traditional) underworld beings in the seas to the west. One cannot help thinking how, after all, did the Kangermiu Aron think of the innermost fjord dwellers? At the point of writing the story, they included his co-religionists who had moved from Noorliit into the innermost parts of the Nuuk fjord. In 1867, when Aron sent his recording of "Qivaaqiarsuk" to Rink, the Moravians had been running their new annex at Uummannaq for these easternmost fjord dwellers since 1861. The headquarters of Noorliit was founded in Nuuk in 1733 with the islanders of Kangeq and immigrant southerners, who were annexed at an early date. Aron has Qivaaqiarsuk move between exactly these places: from the easternmost habitation in Kangersuneq farthest west to Kangeq, back east to Uummannaq, down south to ill-natured enemies, return to Uummannaq, then east to the *tuneq* living inland behind Kangersuneq, back west to Uummannaq, and finally, west to the south of Nuuk to Kingittorsuaq, which guides seafaring people to Nuuk. With regard to some of the early immigrants to Kangeq, they did have enemies in the south, whom they had escaped by moving north (Sonne 2005: ID 50, 1450, 2147; Gulløv 1986b). Thus, by his moving about, Qivaaqiarsuk covers the spatial and social world of the Moravian proselytes centered at Nuuk.

The pivotal point of Qivaaqiarsuk's odyssey is the *pooq* of his wife's shamanic power. None of the other three versions on record has it: the most recent, a very short one, was told on the radio by catechist Simon Nielsen in the 1950s, another was told by Jaakuaraq (ca. 1920),[65] and a third was presented by catechist Eli Sivertsen (ca. 1867) about an anonymous bachelor.[66] Simon Nielsen's version comes closest to Aron's at one point, in terms of the effect of the dead wife's stomach. Used in beating ice floes, the sound attracts seals of various kinds in great numbers to the coast. But Aron alone has *shamanic power* hidden in her stomach. In Simon Nielsen's variant it contains a piece of black (devilish?) *mattak* offered by the two submarine visitors. Jaakuaraq and Eli Sivertsen have the hero cut out the stomach not from the wife but from one of the drowned widows at Kangeq. Sivertsen's bachelor chooses the naughtiest widow and Jaakuaraq's Qivaaqiarsuk the giddiest. So, the secret effect of this *pooq* is understood in a most diverse manner by the tellers. To Eli Sivertsen and Simon Nielsen, it is either something toxic (devilish?) or indecent (naughtiness). Jaakuaraq and Aron represent the

65. The version published posthumously in Rasmussen (1981, II) quotes verbatim Rink's summary of Aron's variant (1866–71, II: No. 54).

66. Here there are no movements between east and west, no killing of widows, and no *Qungussutariaq*. The two submarine kayakers bring only a black piece of *mattak*, which kills the wife as she eats from it. The story ends with Qivaaqiarsuk's successful use of her stomach to beat ice floes. Simon Nielsen from Kangeq, a catechist, told his version to KNR, Radio Greenland, in the 1950s.

extremes; Jaakuaraq, as was his habit, makes fun, while Aron employs a well-defined concept of the pre-Christian past, namely, ill-intentioned sorcery (alias concealed *angakkuuneq).* Furthermore, the hero's reaction to the sea mammals attracted from the high sea towards land by the stomach *pooq* varies. Sivertsen's bachelor asks them not to arrive in such great numbers so as to block his way, and Jaakuaraq's Qivaaqiarsuk demands that they not arrive in such great numbers inside the skerries. Both are punished for criticizing the animals' behavior; the bachelor dies from hunger, and Jaakuaraq's Qivaaqiarsuk loses his wife at the end of the story. Not until this late point in this variant do the two submarine kayakers bring her the toxic *mattak*, which she eats. Turning wild and insane, she dies shortly after; in pre-Christian times this is the boomerang effect of sorcery, closely associated with concealed *angakkuuneq*. Apparently then, Jaakuaraq transferred the effect of keeping one's sorcery a secret to the *mattak* stemming from below, which in Aron's version was supposed to remove the infertility caused by the concealed *angakkuuneq*.

Simon Nielsen identifies no guilty person in the story. Rather, he humorously emphasizes Qivaaqiarsuk's intelligence, but realistically his point of departure is a contemporary decline in the population of seals, and sympathetically he has Qivaaqiarsuk's longing for company attract the two *mattak* bringers for his first episode. At the point his wife dies from having had a taste, clever Qivaaqiarsuk cuts up her belly, etc. And when he asks the arriving seals never to hide again in case they happen to be together in such great numbers, they obey, "due to the power of his words" (Grove 2000: 236). Aron does not include this latter motif. The belly *pooq* merely increases Qivaaqiarsuk's individual attraction to game of any size while his "otherness" attracts and connects well-known episodes from contemporary lore: the drowning of widows, meeting *Qungussutariaq*, encounters with *innersuit* recognized by the epithets of cleanliness, the outsider marrying the only sister of many reluctant brothers, the harpooned whale going towards land, displaying one's swiftness by donning a quickly made *ikiaq*, winning the competition with enemies, and the recapture of the stolen child.[67] Only the encounter with the giant *tuneq* as well as the cascade of warm pee dressing the mountain in cold perpetual snow appear invented, albeit by meanings of bits and images from other stories. Training with the *tuneq*, for instance, reflects the popular story about Kaassassuk, who was trained by either an inland giant or a land predator (see earlier in the book), whereas the hole in the *tuneq*'s crotch points to *Nalikkatteeq*, as I shall show shortly. The frozen pee, perpetually glazing Kingittorsuaq, is associated with the ice cap towards the east, *pinngamut*. Its sound of calving ice, described as peals of thunder, sets Aron's variant in motion and brings the story full circle at Kingittorsuaq.

So, however the Kangermiut, including Aron, used to think of their eastern co-religionists, the "easternmost" Qivaaqiarsuk, with his supernatural powers, is *imaannanngitsoq*, or no ordinary human, as emphasized by Grove (2000: 240). His character is shrewd and morally ambiguous. Still, why is Aron's "Qivaaqiarsuk" imbued with all that many *puuat*? The peculiar *tuneq* offers a clue.

The *Tuneq* of Aron's "Qivaaqiarsuk"

Admittedly, not much of a clue is offered to the uninitiated regarding this giant *tuneq*. The "initiated" reader, however, would recognize an allusion to *Nalikkatteeq*, as the big hole in its crotch also

67. See "Qujaavaarsuk" supplied with the power of the worm of the deep sea, exchanged by *Qungussutariaq* by Aqajaq (Sonne 2005: ID 258, 1316).

points to this figure. *Nalikkatteeq*, meaning literally "big crotch," used to sing like this: "*por, por peja*" (*pooq, pooq, piaa* = "*pooq, pooq*, one's personal belonging"), as recorded by Poul Egede in 1738 (P. Egede 1971: 87–88; 1939: 62). Her jingle is understood by Niels Egede as a name: Pompajak (N. Egede 1971: 81–82; 1939: 176) or Pompeia, identified as the weather giant of the inland ice, blowing icy winds from his mouth and warm air (a southeastern fall wind) from his anus (N. Egede 1971: 65; 1939: 166). This is the wind with which the giant *tuneq* sends its visitors home to Uummannaq. The foul stench of this gale could easily be an implied joke. In other words, there is a likeness bordering on identity between the giant *tuneq* and Niels Egede's construction of Pompeia, an animation of the jingle sung by *Nalikkatteeq* about her *pooq*. In West Greenland in about 1860, this jingle was in no way a forgotten thing of the past. Thus, in his "Manguaraq" (about an obstinate visitor to Moon), Hendrik, Aron's contemporary, has *Nalikkatteeq* repeatedly sing to the meager sculpin dangling in her crotch, "My big crotch, poor, poor, poor" (Thisted & Thorning 1996: 292, tr. BS).[68] The "meager sculpin" is Rink's translation of *kanajukasik puukulleq*, etymologically "a dear/poor sculpin with quite some swollen belly (*pooq*)." Judging from Rink's notes, Hendrik, while telling the story, had explained to Rink the appearance of an Atlantic poacher, *Leptagonus decagonus*, with its extremely long and thin hind part and much shorter "swollen" forepart (Muus et al. 1981: 129). In a later variant of "Manguaraq" told by either the son of Hendrik, Esaja Martensen, or more likely the latter's contemporary, Jaakuaraq (see Sonne 2005: ID 1394), *Nalikkatteeq* sings: "Look at the crotch of my trousers, *ataneqanngitsut* [not hanging together, split open], and with dangling small/ugly sculpins (*kanajoraatsiat*). *Porporpoo!*" (K. Lynge 1978: 17; tr. BS). In Avanersuaq, *Nalikkatteeq* sings about feeding her little dogs, and in Ammassalik she instructs her dangling (phallic) dog's erect head covered by a red mask with two white spots over the eyes: "'Smile my lengthy crotch,' after which the mouth of the dog revealed a pipe contracting from laughter" (J. Rosing 1963: 227, tr. BS; Sonne 2005: ID 1676).[69] The Atlantic poacher is also without exception the dangling "object" in the southern versions of "Manguaraq" (Sonne 2005: ID 440, 1018, 2079), among which ID 2079 (taped in 1965) even quotes a complete song repeating *Nalikkaataak sapangall, sapangallin, qivaaqinngivani sapangall sapangallin*: "My crotch is decorated, it is decorated with sea scorpions, a bullhead is hanging from my crotch as decoration" (Vebæk 2006: 195, emphasis and important note BS).[70] At Sisimiut to the north, Albrecht Beck uses the local name: *kanioq puullasuaq* ("big swollen sculpin") or a *pooq* sculpin, as sung by *Nalikkatteeq* in his "Manguaraq": "My big crotch, *pooq, pooq, pooq*" (Sonne 2005: ID 1070).

Returning then to the *tuneq* as illustrated by Aron, this is a male giant in a European buttoned dress and pixie cap. It has nothing dangling in its crotch, but it is explicitly said to behave in the manner of a(n ordinary) sculpin (*kanajoq*); when hit by shame at having killed a man, it scurries into its house. Still, like *Nalikkatteeq*'s, its crotch has an immensely big hole through which first Qivaaqiarsuk and then all his in-laws jump, because the *tuneq* invites them to do so by placing itself with its hands

---

68. "*Illartukasiullumi pugutarsuani qissussuaq timumiarlugu, ulorsuaq iluanut ilillugu, kanajukasik, puukulleq nalikkaamminut pitullugu allamik nipeqanngitsoq: nalikkaassuaka, pooq, pooq, pooq.*"

69. Please make the explication yourself, whether in Latin or your own language.

70. This is an incorrect translation of *qivinngivanni* into English. "One's dear Atlantic poacher" is correct. Unfortunately I did not know this at the time of editing. The song can be heard on the CD-ROM included with Vebæk (2006).

on its knees, its back to them.[71] Something similar happens to Manguaraq who travels skiing (!) to Moon in the funny version recorded by Ole Petersen, Paamiut (?). Coming upon *Nalikkatteeq* standing with her back to Manguaraq, he glides in between her legs and sees the Atlantic poacher hanging there. He then has to stop, putting his arms around her, whereupon, of course, he loses his entrails; they are subsequently returned to him by Moon (ID 440). Nicolai of Narsarmijit/Frederiksdal similarly has the figure placed with its back to the visitor, even leaning forwards, hood overhead, and the visitor explicitly approaching from behind. He also loses consciousness and temporarily his entrails (ID 1827). *Some ritual play seems reflected in this act*, of whatever imagined effect, mixing as it does the danger of death with quick movement and fertilizing powers.[72] Consequently it appears safe to compare or even identify Qivaaqiarsuk, the Atlantic poacher, of Aron's version with the laughter-provoking *pooq* of *Nalikkatteeq*, herself an ambiguous, androgynous figure.[73] Another ambiguity may be seen in the combination of *Nalikkatteeq*, depicted either as an *inua* of some high inland mountain or a star being (living close to Moon) and the Atlantic poacher, a creature of the deep sea (Muus et al. 1981: 129–30). Thus Ilasiaq, who originated in the deep sea and was given an Atlantic poacher for his kayak amulet, was the first child of Juliane to survive, due to the rite performed for his conception. Advised by the shaman-*cum*-catechist Simon, Juliane picked up something washed ashore, placed it in the tip at the lower end of the front of her anorak, and, as previously arranged, the lovely "child" she had "found" was welcomed by the settlement as they came out to meet her. In addition, she was sensibly not allowed to drink freshwater and obliged to throw her son's worn-out clothes into the sea. This is sensible because freshwater connotes land. In the same line of thought, Ilasiaq ("foster child") was given this Atlantic poacher of the deep sea for his amulet (Sonne 2005: ID 855, 856).

Thus, I aim to reinforce the message that Qivaaqiarsuk is himself a *pooq*—a cross-gendered *pooq*, in fact, like the one dangling in the crotch of *Nalikkatteeq*.

Acculturative Trickster

In an attempt to sum up the *pooq* structure of Aron's Qivaaqiarsuk, the palimpsest effect of Qivaaqiarsuk's likely identification with the *pooq* of *Nalikkatteeq* leads one to find double entendre

---

71. In addition to mocking the Qallunaat, the European dress together with the "play" of jumping through the big crotch may point to the children's game "Bro, Bro, Brille" (bridge, bridge, ??), similar to "London Bridge Is Falling Down." The two persons playing "pillars" and forming a "black pot" with raised arms holding each other's hands used to be called Sun and Moon. While the "pillars" sing, the children hurry through the hole in a row, until one is caught at the end of the jingle. The captive is whispered a choice of either sun or moon (or apples and pears, or the like) and tacitly lines up behind the chosen "pillar." With everybody caught and lined up, a tug of war follows. Granted there is such an impact, instead of letting anybody get caught in the "black pit" of the *tuneq*, Aron has the youngest in-law killed due to his slow reaction. As mentioned in the following note, other figures like the Inuit salmon maker may be reflected in Aron's *tuneq*.

72. Usually the figure that must be approached the right way is the Inuit maker of salmon. He smears pieces of wood with his semen for the transformation. The demand in the Greenlandic versions is a frontal approach (Sonne 2005: ID 512, 1389, 1540) except for Poul Egede's 1738 version where, like two published by Boas, the approach should be from behind (Sonne 2005: ID 2297; Boas 1964: 209; 1901–7: 181). In any event, the wrong approach means death, whereas the right one ensures a swift river journey on the back of a salmon to the land of birds. Another Greenlandic figure, *Tissinaq*, the funny one, has, like *Nalikkatteeq*, a dangling sculpin in his/her crotch and an awful laugh. This *inua* of a falcon is called upon to cheer up low spirits at a party celebrating a human guest who is served more or less edible food by *inuat* of ravens and gulls (Sonne 2005: ID 1004, 351). The picture of some *uaajeertoq* dance pops up by itself.

73. This is also stressed by Saladin d'Anglure in one of his treatises on a third sex (1986: 47).

meanings all the way through. The various meanings of diverse *puuat* make the entendre threefold, and the ambiguous morality of Qivaaqiarsuk fourfold; the spatial thread combining supernatural east with "civilized" Christians of the west coast represents still another element woven into the weft of the story. Yet the plausible connection of Qivaaqiarsuk with the personal belonging of *Nalikkatteeq*, her *pooq*, would explain the astonishing great number of *pooq* elements employed by Aron in 1860. Obviously, as exemplified, *Nalikkatteeq* used to present herself by this image in Central and Southwest Greenland from the time of Poul Egede at the latest and onward, especially in the oral tradition of the Moravian-baptized Greenlanders and their descendants.

Besides the frequency of *pooq* elements, Aron's multifarious variant involves figures of plausible former ritual import: the giants *Qungussutariaq* and the *tuneq*, the former a being of the deep sea emerging inside a translucent *pooq* of water, the latter of the inland region and at the same time an alter ego of *Nalikkatteeq* or her *pooq*. Both are put down by the invincible Qivaaqiarsuk. Though *Qungussutariaq* (and *Nalikkatteeq*) should not be smiled at on the peril of death, Qivaaqiarsuk is only given a mild reproach for smiling back at *Qungussutariaq*, and thereupon also receives well-intentioned advice on how to cure his wife's barrenness. Not even his exploitation of this advice to the opposite end rebounds with sickness, bad luck, insanity, or death. Similarly, he exploits the giant *tuneq* to his own advantage. He explicitly warns his in-laws about the danger of meeting this giant, a danger then demonstrated by himself when—unobserved—he uses its body to kill the one who proves himself slow off the mark. The *tuneq*, unaware of the trick as well, assumes responsibility. Embarrassed, in a cowardly fashion it scurries back into its house. And so no punishment ever befalls Qivaaqiarsuk. Greatly superior, he always gets his way. In short, Aron gives an impression of him as a trickster who breaks the rules and lures dangerous figures by exploiting their powers with superior deceit.

Defining Qivaaqiarsuk as a trickster by going through the various theories would make an extended paper on its own. Suffice to say that Aron's Qivaaqiarsuk exhibits the most common trickster characteristics: humor, phallic connotations, and deceitful breaking of the rules, the latter pushed to extremes by his oscillation between following them and then grossly breaking them. He starts out providing for the widows in an exemplary manner, then later lets the tide swallow them.[74] Absorbed like a homesick child in bringing forth the lovely sound of calving ice, he unintentionally calls up several nonhumans that try to have him make his wife abide to the shamans' moral rules. He pays no heed or, perhaps even better, as proposed by Grove, he half-consciously seems to have sensed his own advantage in letting his wife die. He serves his Uummannaq in-laws in every perfect way. He attracts big game, vanquishes their enemies, makes an infertile sister-in-law reveal her *angakkuuneq* (thereby becoming fertile) for "seeing" his captive son, and then, by using the conquered *tuneq* as his undetected weapon, he kills the youngest brother-in-law. As for the question of why Aron has Qivaaqiarsuk feel guilty at only this immoral act and none of the others, I have no clear answer.

Actually, Qivaaqiarsuk differs from ordinary tricksters who are as often duped as victorious. Apart from the pang of guilt just mentioned, he seems invulnerable. In breaking the rules the heroic

---

74. Providing single-handedly for many women appears as an epithet of his character. The destiny of the women he leaves behind at Kangersuneq is uncertain, until one or more years later when, settled at Uummannaq, he resumes responsibility in bringing meat to their place.

Qivaaqiarsuk never plays with open cards. In this way he derides the perilous laughable figures of the pre-Christian past, the ritual tricksters like *Qungussutariaq* and *Nalikkatteeq*. He does so in his acculturative way of making a partial farewell to the pre-Christian, precolonial past. It is partial, because the mocking only works on the premise that the former meanings have retained some of their appeal. Semiotically, he operates in the clash of categories, in the meeting point between perception and creation, which C. V. Spinks defines his so-called "tricksteresque" T-point "where are nested the relations between the functional needs of older, but superseded order and those of a newer more inclusive order" (Spinks 1991: 15). Granted the identification of *Qivaaqiarsuk* with the *pooq* of *Nalikkatteeq*, Aron, a catechist and a gifted story writer, recounts the traditional stories in an entertaining mix of old and new keys.

With regard to the powers of Qivaaqiarsuk, he is no shaman. Although in possession of his wife's *angakkuuneq pooq*, he still needs a live initiated shaman in order to "see" his captive son. And although he "rubs" his hunting *pooq* on an iceberg trapped in a cleft with a similar effect of calling forth a spirit as the pupil's stone-rubbing at a cleft or a lake, he does not go through an initiation of death and revival. His smiling back to *Qungussutariaq* offers an unexploited opportunity. Also, instead of being cut up by *Qungussutariaq*, Qivaaqiarsuk is the one to do the cutting when he removes the shamanic stomach from his wife's body. His relation to the giant *tuneq* of the inland region echoes the training given to Kaassassuk (in Aron's repertoire as well) by the big fox or an inland giant. Nor does Kaassassuk become a shaman, but the episodes differ in that Qivaaqiarsuk, unlike Kaassassuk, has ended up stronger than his trainee. Qivaaqiarsuk also has not had any ill treatment to revenge or lack of hunting skills to overcome. From the outset, Qivaaqiarsuk is an able hunter at sea, an ability further improved upon by the shamanic mother *pooq*. It adds to his sound-producing powers by calling up still another giant of the sea, connected by epithets with the undershore *innersuit*, who live like humans with humanlike relatives, either at the coast or below the island of Uummannaq. Nor is Qivaaqiarsuk an ordinary human. He is a particularly ambiguous being, a mix of otherness and "thisness." Named after a fish from the deep sea, he belongs on earth at the coast as close as possible to the uppermost inland area. Appearing weak, he nevertheless matches the *tuneq*, the *inua* of the eastern gale, in strength. Like the Atlantic poacher dangling in the crotch of androgynous *Nalikkatteeq*, he is both phallic and female in body, with elongated hind parts and swollen in belly, as also in "soul"; this is represented symbolically by his hunting bladders, his own together with the more effective one of his wife. The immense, far-traveling roar of thunder produced by the bladders when banged on the iceberg reminds me unreservedly of the advice given a hunter with a pregnant wife, mentioned above: in case of gathering thunder, he should let the air out of his hunting bladder, or her stomach shall explode. In sum, Qivaaqiarsuk is cross-gendered in more than a single sense. By all means and meanings he personifies a tricksteresque, category-crossing *pooq*.

Pooq *in the Making of Cosmologies: Summary and Discussion*

How consciously Aron employed the various meanings of *pooq* will remain forever a secret. But one recurrent change in meaning is particularly striking. *Pooq* means protection, be it against nasty weather or aggressive otherworldly beings, the latter because the *pooq* renders its owner invisible to their sight. By contrast, Qivaaqiarsuk's processed shamanic *pooq*, as also his *ikiaq*, and snow-clad Kingittorsuaq, are significantly visible one and all. The cut-out stomach is dried and bleached into chalk white (*qaqungaarami*), and Qivaaqiarsuk waiting outdoors dressed in the *ikiaq* is spotted by his in-laws at a great distance, just as Kingittorsuaq is by sailors, dressed as he is in the frozen Inuit "soap" and "tan," the urine of the bladder *pooq*, turned white in the high altitude, Like a hunting bladder losing its air as a symbol of losing life, Qivaaqiarsuk has let himself be drained of his life by peeing amusingly vast amounts. His movement has come to a standstill, as has his running pee. Frozen in perpetuity, Kingittorsuaq guides people to Nuuk (or Noorliit) like some lodestar, an interpretation on par with the meanings of light in Kristian's contemporary version of "Imaneq." The light Imaneq received in return for his *qaumaneq* is explicitly of eastern (heavenly) origin, as is the glacier of Kingittorsuaq. Initiated by *Qungussutariaq* and his deceased grandparents from below, Imaneq gained the passage for baptism. Aron, in his illustration of the Imaneq story, implies this exchange by painting the hunting bladder enveloping the head of Imaneq in the same color as the heavenly light. Aron thus associates this transforming light with the individual life of the hunter, symbolized by his *pooq*, his buoy (see endsheets). Imaneq's exchange of lights is a simple one, caused as it is by his haughty character and breaking of pagan taboo. It is punished by the smiling giant of the sea and repaired by his deceased grandparents, both acting in traditional roles. Pagan Qivaaqiarsuk, however, is a superhuman of mixed morals, a trickster of the heathen past transforming its symbolic *puuat* into enlightening ones of the Christian present. Some national pride peeps through, I think, in this emphasis on an eastern (connoting supernatural) tricksteresque creation of a contemporary cosmology. And again, like trickster stories, the fun of "Qivaaqiarsuk" is unmistakable. The dangerous, tickling, laugh-provoking ritual figures of the past, *Qungussutariaq* and the giant *tuneq* of the eastern (farting) gale, are transformed into laughingstocks themselves. The giant *tuneq*, behaving like a sculpin, reflects both *Nalikkatteeq* and, in its dress, also the Qallunaat.

The acculturative way of using *pooq* in "Tunutoorajik" is much less complicated. All through the story it signifies "cover" differentiated by resistance, some according to animal species and others to space and time (land shit and sea ice). The plain acculturative meaning of the superior strength accorded European iron in exchange for traditional polar bear skins speaks for itself as does, on reflection, the undressed, mixed nonhuman/human one-legged son caught and killed by the giant falcon, and in the flesh distributed in morsels among its young. As could be expected, "Tunutoorajik," as told by an East Greenlander (Kaarali?) after twenty-five years of mission, echoes the initiation to an *angakkoq puulik* to a much greater extent than Aron's "Qivaaqiarsuk." The latter is composed in writing by a Christian descendant of third- or fourth-generation immigrant East Greenlanders. Polar bear and walrus, providing the *puulik* candidate with invisibility to aggressive others, arrive in hordes at midwinter in "Tunutoorajik." They demand a propping up of Ittuku's house just as they do the house used for an initiation to *angakkoq puulik*. In cosmological symbolism, the pillars of the world need support or repair at the turning of the year. Intestines of bearded seal, hunted at midwinter beyond the ice edge by Ittuku, who seems to move as quickly as a star, may reflect the *ululoo*-calling spirit announcing the success of the candidate in having become an *angakkoq puulik*. Less uncertainty remains with the interpretation of bearded seal as the common deliverer of material for the *ikiaq*, which offers a similar effect as the *puulik* initiation—invisibility to aggressive spirits. The undressing of Ittuku's son turns the traditional episode of a giant falcon deceived by the *ikiaq* of the murderer of its young on its head. This making of a Christian cosmology by means of *pooq* in the single sense of protective "cover" may be semiotically tricksteresque, but no trickster seems to mock a mythic authority of the past. Still, like "Qivaaqiarsuk," the Christian myth transformed into "Tunutoorajik" is not all that serious; I propose that it has been overshadowed by the Qallunaat manager as the storyteller's implied laughingstock. Nobody, however, would call Ittuku (alias God, alias a giant falcon) a trickster.

In comparison, Aron is farther removed from the *pooq* complex. There are no polar bears, only a single aggressive walrus (the common prey of a hero), but there may be a reflection of the bearded seal bogey, *Innersuaq*, in the figure of *Qungussutariaq* emerging in a bubble (and as an enemy of noisy children, according to Rink). Regarding ideas of visibility versus invisibility, they have been turned upside down in apparent service of the new creed. One might call the secret *angakkuuneq* of Qivaaqiarsuk's wife hidden in her *pooq* the power of a shamanic *puulik*. However, it is not revealed, and thus it bars inception and alludes to sorcery in a devilish understanding of the concept. Only by being cut out, dried, and transformed into a hunting bladder does it become as white and luminous as both the *ikiaq* and the ice-covered Kingittorsuaq. Its sound is heard a long way off, just as the shining whiteness of both *ikiaq* and Kingittorsuaq meet the eye from a long distance. Qivaaqiarsuk's warm pee stiffened into an eternal white standstill, and therefore connotes the opposite meanings of traditional *pooq*: visibility and attraction have replaced the invisibility and protection against aggressive beings of the past. Represented by *Qungussutariaq* and the giant *tuneq*, they may both have survived in thrilling games, perhaps mixed up with those introduced by the colonists. This could at least explain why Aron has dressed the *tuneq* in European clothing.

CHAPTER SIX

■ ■ ■

Conclusion

Undetected cultural biases are liable to sneak into any attempt to understand a worldview differing from one's own. Soul searching that leads to new revelations may be the result of being confronted with other attempts. In my overall attempt to align the cosmological ideas of the Greenlandic sources with those of the Canadian and Alaska Inuit and Yupiit, I met with no contradictions, only variations. Either they are basically comparable, which is the axiom of my method for analysis, or I have come to think along the lines of my colleagues abroad due to reading their accounts.

Some of my findings regarding Greenland, however, are new and call for comments on possible cultural biases. One is the movement of the earth and its apparent rocking, threat of capsizing, and turning around; this led to conclusions about the pervasive importance of balance in space as in body and mind. Raven's part in the Greenlandic symbolism—not only of light but also of balance—extends Oosten and Laugrand's (2006) findings regarding Nunavut, and an even more far-reaching understanding rolls up through a long look to Alaska. The ritual life of the East Greenlanders has, by including both traditional and acculturated stories, proved richer than it appears on the surface. Celebrations at New Year imply, like so many other New Year rituals, a renewal of the world on the tip of chaos. Several excellent eyewitness descriptions of shaman's performances give the impression of lively communication between shaman, the lay ritual leader, and the audience. The initiations of shamans in solitude as in public offer new insights to the sources of the shaman's light or vision, *qaamaneq*, for seeing the Other World (the normally invisible counterpart to This World). So does the initiation of an *angakkoq puulik* (shaman with a bag), which provides the shaman with the opposite ability, to become invisible to aggressive beings. Although this initiation was restricted to East and South Greenland, the polysemous symbolism of *pooq* (bag, in the spirit language "mother") applies to all Inuit and Yupiit but particularly to the Alaska groups and their Siberian neighbors. A last issue concerns the relations between humans and nonhumans, especially the dyadic relationships between shamans and their helping spirits, which touch upon ideas of boundaries between

This and the Other World as well. I shall treat these issues in the following sections and repeatedly draw attention to the potential of polysemous symbols for reorganizing worldviews.

Being at the Balancing Center of the World

The place, season, and weather at the time of one's birth identified the human individual as a rightful "inhabitant" of *sila* at its center, a situation revived by a ritual calling on the weather on one's birthday, in an emergency, and in seasonal rites. In everyday life the center of *sila* is at the point where you are, as explained by Kleinschmidt.[1] To be harmoniously in this center meant being sensible, or having *sila*. Thus, it seems obvious to add "balance" to the many meanings of *sila*. I have been inspired to select and treat balance per se by the scientists' news about climatic changes beginning in the 1960s. I was thoroughly alarmed, and still am, but what first triggered my focus on balance were statements in the Greenlandic sources of an apparent rocking of a tilting earth. Later I found support in Knud Rasmussen's translation into Danish of the Polar Inuit saying "*Sila najûmivdlugo* (*najuummillugu*)," "*opretholde balancen i verden*" (keeping up the balance of the world). The translation in the English publication is the literal one: "in order to hold the world up." Without this support gained by observing the rules, avalanches (coming down) or tsunamis (rising) will destroy the settlements (human life on earth). My acceptance of Rasmussen's translation of "support" into "balance" may thus have colored the analysis, but the testimonies pile up: the apparent bobbing of the earth in slow motion with the tide, the imagined probability of it either capsizing or becoming flooded at spring tide, a ritualized threat to the house pillars at the turning of the year, along with a multitude of body metaphors of falling, turning around, tilting, wobbling, getting dizzy, and becoming crazy. Parallel ideas of congruent "balance" in space-*cum*-mind are found among other small-scale premodern cultures, as pointed out by Anthony Cohen quoted above (p. 86).

In structural-spatial terms the foreshore was the mediating center of land versus sea, which changed continuously with the tide, turning from sea into land and vice versa. The foreshore thus served as a juncture between the Other Worlds, of the sea below and the heaven above. Localizers of "down in front of you" and "up there behind you," which denote sea and inland directions, respectively, reveal a sloping profile of the land and its continuation under the sea. The Baffin Island notion of a complete somersault of the earth at the equinoxes indicates a renewal of the land twice a year, the very idea of a ritual for cleaning the land in spring and autumn by the raven figure, *Nunagiqsaqtuq* ("the person who beautifies the land"). The cleaning consisted of his transmission of people's confessions to Sea Woman, by which the hunter secured good hunting in the season ahead. There is no trace of a similar figure in Greenland, except the mythic character *Uniagaq*, in a story about the primordial capsizing of the earth. Comparison and pursuit of the connotations of Raven in Greenland offer new insights.

Uniagaq shares with *Nunagiqsaqtuq* a peculiar clothing, bandaged, consisting of skin strips. Apparently he also shares the characteristics of the raven, described by Oosten and Laugrand (Oosten & Laugrand 2006: 196; Laugrand & Oosten 2015: 102–5) as the bringer of light, female fertility, human birth and death, and the rejuvenation of the land. *Uniagaq* and his younger brother

1. In Danish, it is illustrated by the wanderer who stops in an unfamiliar place in the countryside, saying, "Here am I, there is north, and where is my lunch pack?"

survive a primordial capsizing of the earth by fleeing towards the light. They end up on the outermost island, where, by *Uniagaq*'s mere wishful thinking they receive the means—and a woman—for (re)creating the Inuit way of living. Besides the well-known technology, the basics of this culture are clearly emphasized: light, balance in body for kayaking, the sexual division of labor, and successful sealing at the open sea as a condition for marriage. Thus the woman, who arrives to cover the kayak, is not given to the younger brother in marriage until he, trained in kayak balance by *Uniagaq*, has developed into a successful hunter. *Uniagaq*, who remains a mere hunter of eiders along the coast, courts her in vain. When he is refused, he casts a spell on her that rebounds and disables his hip (alluding to the way a raven walks?). So, the culture hero and trainer of balance for hunting at sea loses his own bodily balance. He fails in the end like a trickster, who, by breaking the rules of marriage, ends up outside "society."

Indeed, this is the actual social position of Raven, who is never permitted to enter the human dwelling. He belongs to the outdoors, to *sila*; indoors, he will suffocate people because he has too much air (*sila*) in him. It is in the context of *taqqama*, the outside of being inside and vice versa, that the Greenland Raven is structurally lopsided. His outdoor belonging explains why in another myth an awkwardly born, dumb mother receives the gift of human speech at the moment she is thrown out by her husband. Her children had died and been transformed into ravens because their names could not be uttered. They became humans again when she, enabled to pronounce the names, found them. The ritual of naming confirms this idea about human speech in that raven, by its cry, *qaut*, announces the transition of a nonhuman baby into a human being.

According to this train of thought, the peculiar notion among some East Greenlanders about the Northern Lights makes sense, namely, that the vivid lights were the outcome of miscarriages and killed unnamed babies who played ball with their placentas. Shamans went for fetuses in heaven, where a multitude of raven young were easily caught by deceased humans. Apparently then, the raven young can be identified with fetuses. In support of this proposed identity was an *angerlartoqut*, "homecomer," a child named after a dead sibling, identified with either a raven or a seal fetus. So, before such a newborn baby returned home for its human name, it had stayed in realms of death below and above.

Like humans, ravens are coastal beings, but unlike Inuit, the "people of the coast," ravens are unable to travel the sea at any great distance from the coast or the edge of the ice. Raven is a splendid performer of somersaults in the air. He brags that he is going to practice this art backwards all along the migration route of his in-laws, the geese. Quickly exhausted, he is left to drop out and drown. In some variants, he drowns in slow motion while listing body parts from the feet upwards being covered by the sea. It seems to be a nursery rhyme, both mocking Raven the trickster and serving as a lesson in body parts to remember by name.[2]

As a coastal being Raven impersonates the transformational boundary between sea and land. Like humans, it belongs to the land. But unlike humans, it is unable to hunt in the open sea. This appears to be a paradox as long as a young raven can alleviate the kayaker's dizziness; however, the cure is implemented at the cost of the young raven's life. Besides Raven's imagined suffocating effect

2. Oh my, suddenly I remember that once during fieldwork, a Greenlandic bachelor courted me by listing my body parts!

indoors, a life within human society is out of the question for at least one observable reason: unlike humans it is indifferent to eating rules. For instance, seeing its chance, it will eat from the kill of a big seal before the taboo dictates its age. Aqqasaaq took advantage of this liberty by performing a raven dance, which removed the taboo on a newly caught bladder nose seal during a period of starvation. Transitions in time at dawn and dusk are also announced by the raven's cry, and these are the times for both shamans and spirits to visit and return from their opposite worlds. Regarding the realms of death, Raven (or maybe only its young), belongs in either, although most frequently is associated with heaven. They serve as food for deceased humans and, as proposed above, as embryos to be fetched by shamans for infertile women on earth. As a *sila* being in This World, Raven is strongly associated with *sila*'s meanings of both weather and a mind in balance. To spoil a raven's nest causes storms, madness may be caused by a raven flying overhead at dusk, and recovery from the same when this happens in daylight. So, the polysemy of the Greenlandic Raven also covers the same aspects of life as "the bringer of light" among the Canadian Inuit (Oosten & Laugrand 2006; Laugrand & Oosten 2015: 83–112). Furthermore, by advertising dusk by its cry and connoting madness at that time, Raven is also a remover of light.

Raven's double role of a culture hero and a trickster, so prominent among Northwest Coast Indians, Yupiit, and Northeast Asian peoples, was—however implicit in sayings and disguised figures of ritual and myth—apparently brought eastwards by the Thule culture. Raven's trickster role of a clumsy fool has been emphasized as the only characteristic of the Thule culture legacy (Hultkrantz 1962; c.f. Kleivan 1971b: 42), but Thalbitzer (1930), Kleivan (1971b), and Oosten and Laugrand (2006; Laugrand & Oosten 2015: 83–112) have also pointed to its creative role. To the latter I shall add Raven's association with the coastal phenomenon of the tide. It implies balance, a key concept in the Greenland worldview. Balance also comes to the fore very clearly in a Tlingit myth about the devastating flood, which is transformed by Raven's attack on the "old woman below" into a beneficent balanced tide that brings accessible edibles to the coast. Among the Inuit of Baffin Island, the raven figure, *Nunagiqsaqtuq,* cleans the land at equinoxes, the times of highest tide, when the world is said to turn around. Similarly, mythic *Uniagaq* restores East Greenlandic culture after the capsizing of the earth. Here Moon is in charge of the tide, and in the event that he should be killed, there will be no tide leaving mussels, seaweed, etc. to be picked at low tide. Along the coast of Southwest Alaska *Qununiq*, a bearded seal figure, is said to influence the tide. This peculiar seal emerges dressed in five gutskin parkas (like the Yup'ik shaman on visits below). But since it changes into a two-year-old bearded seal when harpooned and foretells the lifespan of the hunter, not everybody dare make the kill. Besides this ominous connection with times of death, *Qununiq* also stands out as a being of exchange characterized by its long hair, boots, and mittens. The long hair made Margaret Lantis experimentally compare it with Sea Woman (Lantis 1946: 199). I would not exclude such a parallel in ideas but would rather emphasize the connections with the tide and relationship of exchange—i.e., the animals and other edibles brought to the coast by the tide. Considering the prominent position of bearded seal in that region, highly celebrated as the first to arrive in spring, and to be followed by the other species of seal, the connections make perfect sense. And since bearded seal was the first seal species to arrive in spring all along the coast, we can take a long leap back to the raven figures of *Nunagiqsaqtuq* and *Uniagaq*. *Nunagiqsaqtuq*'s bandage covering the entire body consists of strips of bearded seal skin, a *pooq* as it were, and *Uniagaq*'s of another *pooq*, an old emptied blubber poke, a complete skin shredded into one long band. Adding the prominent meanings of *pooq*, a protective mother bag (summarized below), I see in either case a raven figure dressed in a *pooq*. He thus connotes spring in agreement with his job of cleaning or balancing the land at spring tide. Sea Woman is part of this complex of cleaning the land of the Baffin Islanders, whereas Moon is the master of tides who may cause havoc with the down-rushing forces of spring in East Greenland. Here *pinnga*, a taboo word for Sun and Moon, reacted to human wrongdoings by sending the flood that capsized the land. Clever *Uniagaq* escaped by running towards the light for a re-creation of the Inuit culture of humans on the new land. So, no matter which *inua* (person, indweller, owner of a live being) gets too great a say, Moon or Sea Woman, the temporal superiority in rage of one or the other due to breaks of taboo disturbs the balance of the world. The shamans were to fight or calm down as tradition had it. Furthermore, for comparison, Tlingit mental balance is, like that of the Inuit, also referred to in terms of a balanced tide. Thus the Tlingit story about the flood turned into a balanced tide by Raven was told at funerals in order to restore balance to the disturbed minds of the mourning relatives (Swanton 1970: 377; cf. Tybjerg 2008).

All of these connotations of the tide, Raven, balance between the powers of above and below, and renewal of the world in spring point to the importance of the tide to coastal peoples at places where it runs high and thus is a decisive natural force to be addressed when analyzing the worldview of such cultures. People fear its potential flooding of the land as much as they enjoy the edibles it brings to the coast. Killing Moon in East Greenland would mean an end to this source of food.[3] The Tlingit Raven has to dive for his sea urchins due to the flood sent by "the old woman down there." Raven then forces her to re-create the balanced tide, leaving sea urchins easy to pick on the shore. *Qunuuniq* (Yup'ik bearded seal figure of exchange with humans) brings edibles to the coast, and the Eastern Inuit myth about Kivioq/Kiviuq has two lonely women, mother and daughter, doing perfectly well by the seals stranded at low tide. Easily harpooned, the catches are subsequently sent ashore by the ordinary flood of high tide. However, these things do not happen of their own accord. The condition is the sexual act of reproduction, carried out by the women by using male symbols like the supporting poles of the house or a penis emerging in a freshwater lake. In actual life the Greenlanders settled at Qaquk opposite Nuuk could practice a similar tidal sealing. Indeed, "the land of high tides" was the name given to West Greenland by the East Greenlanders, whose stories about shamans visiting over there thus emphasize the importance they gave to the tide.

In sum: a normal tide shows a regularly changing, favorable balance between the powers of above and below. The rising tide sends seals towards land, and when it recedes, it leaves food to be picked on the land laid bare. This makes sensible the access offered by the foreshore to either realm of death, one in heaven and the other beneath the sea. Breaking the rules disturbs the balance, which must be restored by the shaman (sometimes representing Raven) in ritual and by Raven in myth. Some woman below is frequently to be fought, or cleaned, or persuaded to abide: "the old woman down there" among the Tlingit, *Sedna* (*Senna*, the one down there in front) among the Baffin Islanders,

3. "In areas where there is a significant difference between low tide and high tide, storm surges are particularly damaging when they occur at the time of a high tide. In these cases, this increases the difficulty of predicting the magnitude of a storm surge since it requires weather forecasts to be accurate to within a few hours." See: http://en.wikipedia.org/w/index.php?title=Storm_tide.

Nerrivik (the place of food—i.e., Sea Woman) among the Polar Inuit, and *Sassuma Arnaa*, "the woman down there in front," in West Greenland. Less concerned about Sea Woman, the East Greenlandic shamans fought Moon, or persuaded *Asiaq* (the *inua* of precipitation) of the upper world to let her baby-husband pee so the snow cover would melt. The baby-husband has the characteristics of the giant baby *Naarjuk*, a personification of *Silap Inua* among the Iglulingmiut, while *Asiaq*, with her hook on a long line for getting food from humans in return, mirrors the Spider Woman. Folklorists commonly take this type to be another connective link between heaven and earth. The whale hunters at Tigara looked to both the woman *Ni-givik* (= *Nerrivik*) below and *Silap Inua* above for favorable whaling conditions in spring: the shaman hired by the *umelik* (leader of a whaling crew) first descended to the coastal spirits leading a mirror life of humans above (like the *innersuit*, the undershore "big fire spirits" of Greenland). Among these he looked in vain for a deceased human, but then he had a married couple do the job of procuring the right winds. The husband (with a dog's tail) rose to *Silap Inua* (the *inua* of *sila*) for the northern wind to break up the ice. His wife descended and visited *Ni-givik*, "the place of food," for her to calm down the ensuing waves. *Silap Inua*/*Ellam Yua* is a pan-Inuit/Yupiit being, whereas *Ni-givik* apparently had her phonological equivalent, *Nerrivik*, the Sea Woman among the Polar Inuit.

In short, to coastal people, at stretches of high running tide the balance of the medial world is a seesawing one, which brings the means for a living towards the land by the currents of the tide. This balance is due to the powers of beings of the Other Worlds above and below, who react to human behavior. Indeed, the breaks of taboo that bring the world out of balance by floods or avalanches among the Polar Inuit fall smoothly into place. Here the effect is even brought about by the offenses alone, and not by the intervention of a punishing *inua*.

If we restrict the focus to *balance in body*, it can be shown that neither the spirits nor the animals of the middle world were perceived to possess the balance of humans. Spirits and most animals had much faster ways of movement than humans, but not the balance of the kayaker for turning around. This ability, together with the bipedal flight of their upright bodies, set humans apart. Movement comes to the fore also in the spirits' language, *taartaq* (of darkness), in that the animal species were named by their different ways of moving about. The spirits identified humans by their belonging in space, as *sijaata ijivat* (W. Grl. *sinaata inuat*), "residents of the coast." Situated at this center in space, humans represented the yardstick in relation to the land and undershore spirits. The spirits differed in body size and/or length of the nose—i.e., in the depth of their breath, according to the distance of their dwelling in a diagonal line from the coast, both upwards and downwards. The Other World beneath foreshore and skerries of the *innersuit* was reversed vertically, and that of the inland spirits horizontally. The latter were oriented towards the inland ice; that is, they were positioned in the opposite direction to humans who faced the sea. Accordingly, these spirits had the power to reverse the direction of streams, which caused the sea mammals to go backwards upstream and to be caught with a lasso around the tail. The *innersuit* similarly attracted sea mammals. They drew them towards the coast by means of their light or "fire" (*inneq*), which reflected the light of Moon. And Moon caused the movements of the tide, bursting the ice cover of lakes in spring as in the initiation myth of pupils for its "freshwater bear" to emerge in a rising column of water or its dog in a reversed waterfall of a stream.

Indeed, the unique balance or distribution of weight of the human body in comparison with the other creatures of the Arctic, real or imagined, has proved to be a rewarding tool for analysis of the Greenlandic worldview.[4] A human's balance grows from the inability of an infant who can only lie on its back and kick into complete mastery in the younger and adult years; in the case that one lives into old age, it slowly decreases into an everlasting lying down, the immobilization of death. Arnaaluk's myth of origin takes us through the entire process, which even has the liberated soul take up movement in a much stronger sense as a star that travels the entire *qilak*, the arch of the sky during a winter's night. And then, the vivacity of dreams testifies to a life of still livelier movement in darkness (alias the Other World). Similarly, the states of being absentminded, of closing one's eyes in order to concentrate, or being absorbed in thought help imagination and memory to vitalize darkness. On the other hand, appearing absentminded in the company of others could arouse suspicion of either practicing sorcery or having leapt into dangerous insanity. The line between being in possession of one's *sila* and losing it could be very thin. Ritual helped to draw a thicker line, as in the case of any shamanic performance.

In its meaning of sanity, *sila* speaks as much to balance in mind as in body. Regarding its definition of "space outside the house," *sila* has in modern Greenland come to mean nature, and is defined this way in an up-to-date Greenlandic campaign called "Inuit Sila": "[a] Greenlandic concept for weather, the mind, consciousness—a universal order where man is in unity with nature. Sila is the shared life that the sea, wind, mountains, animals and humans possesses [*sic*]. When you share consciousness with nature you handle nature with respect."[5] The aim of the campaign is to make known the European Union's 2010 exception for Greenland from its general ban on the import of sealskin, because this clause had no effect at this point on encouraging trade. The market still shuns these skins and thus deprives Greenlandic seal hunters of their livelihood. If we step aside from the actual message, the identification of *sila* with nature in a Western sense is interesting. While explained on Greenlandic terms, it lacks any personifications of *sila*, thus differing from both the Christian and pre-Christian definitions. Nature, according to the missionaries, was *pinngortitarsuaq* (the big made world), which owed its existence to *Pingortitsisoq*, the Creator (God). The Christian creed saw to the demythologization of the *inuat*, such as the Greenlandic Entrails Snatcher (Big Crotch, *Nalikkatteeq*), who created space by raising the supporting pillar of heaven, and *Asiaq* with her snowing and peeing baby boy in East Greenland.[6] But by now God has been demythologized as well. He plays no part in the aforementioned identification of *sila* with nature. Respect towards *sila*, however, has been retained, as has the wish to live in harmony by sharing consciousness with nature. Psychologization

4. The hypothesis concerns the spirits of the land and the *inua* of the moon insofar as the latter apparently shares the lack in balance of the inland giants for kayaking. He travels by dog sledge and hunts at breathing holes. Sea Woman is never encountered outdoors in Greenland lore. She sits continually on her platform, but leaps to her feet when fighting the shaman. Animals and birds in human form change into their animal forms from the moment they flee or begin to pursue someone or something. However, more research is needed to test the hypothesis.

5. Quoted in part in Lauridsen (2015: 8), but added to the unity are the underground beings. "*Sila* is the *inua* of the air, it is sense and balance between everything. Between living and deceased, animals and humans, between the underground beings and the aboveground [in the abstract]. We aim at *sila*. In Greenlandic *sila* means weather, the sense or the order of the world, and the root [*sila*] is used in the vernacular for characterizing everything good, right and sensible" (78; tr. BS).

6. Greenlandic artists still look to personifications like *Nalikkatteeq* and Raven for inspiration (see, e.g., p. 16).

so characteristic of modern times has gained momentum. In a way, then, my addition of balance in *body and mind* to the meanings of *sila* tallies with the campaign's message of being in harmony with *sila*. An up-to-date study of the Greenlanders' ideas about their *sila* in mental terms might be revealing.

Rituals at Points of Transitions in Time

For all Inuit and Yupiit, a decisive transition in time, winter solstice, was announced by the appearance of the twin stars, *Aassuutit/aatit/aagjuuk*, while their disappearance—i.e., the sun taking over their rising point on the horizon—marked the beginning of spring in East Greenland. Spring was the other decisive time in the annual round, the season stressed in the spirit language, *taartaq*, but less regularly marked by collective rituals. Winter solstice occasioned regionwide festivities of abundant eating and drum dancing, among which the individual dances of the *uaajeertut* (masked dancers) in East Greenland are better described than interpreted. Women danced in their ordinary *naatsit* (breeches), but the men, who did most of the dancing, performed either stark naked with spots of soot indicating flesh, dressed in ordinary clothing, or disguised as pregnant women. Their faces were either soot-covered and distorted or (formerly) covered by masks. Violence, sex, and reproduction were the main themes (as among the Iglulingmiut) (Saladin d'Anglure 1993). Obviously the *uaajeertut* were meant to inspire the wife exchange that ended the night of dancing. In Greenland the pairing off of temporary couples was apparently not led by shamans representing mythic figures as in parts of Arctic Canada, but, negotiated ritually as described superficially by Hans Egede and in detail by Georg Quppersimaan. Georg (Qúpersimân 1972: 196–97) says that the men, one at a time, took the initiative in inviting, by ritual singing and gestures, any woman to accept. The agreeing woman similarly did her part by ritual phrases and gestures. The idea of this "putting out of the lamps," as stated by Georg, was to have fun and aid in reproduction. Violence came in with an *uaajeertoq* armed with a stick for hitting the participants, who either gave a wrong answer to some question or who burst into laughter at his awkward dancing. The *Nalikkatteeq* figure, "the big crotch" with male sexual accessories and considered to be in charge of the pillar upholding heaven, was a strong case in point.

A downfall of heaven was the threat most feared in addition to the dangers implied in a seesawing world, and it increased with the missionaries' sermons about the Day of Judgment. The signs were irregularities like eclipses in sun and moon, an apparent delay in the return of the sun in winter, and storms. In East Greenland *Nalikkatteeq* impersonated a star close to the moon, and she may, as was the case among the Nattilingmiut, have also been identified with the *Aassuutit*. She fed on the lungs of deceased humans and, due to her hilarious dance, she was in myth a threat to live visitors en route to the moon. At the slightest smile on the visitor's face, she cut out his lungs, let them cool off in her dish, and thus offered Moon the chance to fetch the dish and restore his guest to life. Time and again she came in vain to Moon's house for her emptied dish, but eventually she got it back by threatening to let go of the pillar supporting heaven. In ritual the first onlooker to let go a roar of laughter caused her to hit around wildly with her stick. Baptized Maratsi excelled at an inventive performance of the *Nalikkatteeq*, including a pretended disappearance of her star. It made people change to their best for the Second Coming and thus disclosed with all clarity the equality in meaning of a downfall of heaven with Judgment Day. On the other hand, although the Christian message of the last day means an end to death in a nonearthly realm, the mythic *Nalikkatteeq* remains true to the Inuit idea of death as the reason for life on earth: if deprived of her dish, from which she fed on the lungs of deceased humans, *Nalikkatteeq* would overturn the pillar supporting the world. Eventually, however, the Christian message won out, at least over the fear of *Nalikkatteeq*. Thus, in a late variant about the obstinate hunter's visit to Moon, she was in a brand-new attached episode attacked by the visitor. He smashed her dish into her face, broke her arm, and sent her weeping from the scene. Aron offered another interpretation in the light of Christianity. He composed a story about a particular sculpin, *Qivaaqiarsuk*, which he implicitly identified with the accessory of *Nalikkatteeq*, called her *pooq* in the mythic context of her ritual. I shall pick up in the conclusion on *pooq* below.

Various ideas were held about the upholding of heaven. Besides steady pillars and mountains, the air of changing winds also kept earth and heaven apart, as did *ayaγutaq*, the rainbow. The rainbow's changes in convexity had a direct impact on the mental states of the Kitlinermiut: the higher the arch, the higher their spirits. Called *neriussaq*, "cause for hope" in Greenland,[7] the rainbow similarly lightened one's spirit. Being closest to heaven in autumn it served the shaman as a direct route to the upper realm. North of the Arctic Circle in Canada, the change in distance between earth and *qilak* was explicated by the two games played during and after the period of the polar night, the string figures, *ayaRaRaR* (diminishing distention), and cup and ring, *ayagaq* (propping up/pushing away), respectively. Obviously both names share the root *ayaγ* (to prop up), as does the peculiar *ajangalisaq*, a cultic house of shamans of the Sermiligaaq fjord in the Ammassalik region. It had a solid rock for its rear wall, and two extra tent poles were put out in order to keep particularly dangerous but summoned spirits from entering the room. The somersaulting sand hopper was one, a *toornaarsuk* for consultation another, and perhaps also the polar bear for the initiation into an *angakkoq puulik*. In East Greenland *toornaarsuk*, chosen to designate the Devil by the missionaries but used by the West Greenlanders for several mutually differing spirits, *toornaarsuit*, meant—or maybe came to mean (due to Hanseeraq's questioning in 1884–85)—at least two kinds of wing snails: the white and the black species. The former is recognized as a distinct figure decorating some select wooden objects sold to Gustav Holm in 1885.

A reflection of the *ajangalisaq* may be recognized in a solitary myth depicting the house of one-legged Ittuku, most probably a star person. It needed a strengthening of its supports when the auks took leave in autumn and just past midwinter, when first polar bears and then walruses passed by in immense hordes. A strengthening of the *ajangalisaq* may have been made at similar points. Maybe this peculiar building also reflected some particular traditions of the latest, northern arrivals to the Ammassalik district. Apparently it was not used for public séances and thus it was no *qassi*, the round, windowless ceremonial house, which in Greenland went out of use at the transition from smaller houses into the longhouse of several families (Sørensen & Gulløv 2012). So, the shamans' performances took place in the longhouse, blacked out with skins in front of the windows.[8]

Winter solstice was also the ideal time for a shaman's public initiation, *saqqummerneq*. The complete course of events was a demanding task, which only the better-talented apprentices dared attempt. It started with the "delivery," continued with *silaninneq*, the ritual obtainment of enlightening by means of the drum, and ended with the presentation of spirits. Most shamans gave less-demanding

---

7. Perhaps colored by the Christian meaning of the rainbow as the promised hope of salvation?

8. Some descriptions of performances have the light of the full moon through the windows lighting up the room (see, e.g., p. 333). Why, I cannot tell.

Fig. 25. The threatening boulder figure, *Aqajarormiorsiorpua*, is surrounded by the shaman's helping spirits, but only *Equngasoq* ("Wry Mouth") has the power to annihilate the boulder. *Equngasoq* is in real life a fulmar, the symbol of spring in the figure of a flying kayaker. *Courtesy of the National Museum of Denmark, Copenhagen.*

proof of their abilities in some technique of ecstasy for summoning a spirit and "seeing" for a diagnosis to be made. On the surface the "delivery" was an unintended outbreak of ecstasy; in reality it was a well-prepared ritual play between the stricken candidate and the audience. The skill of having the drum dance on its own and up one's back in order to *silaninneq*, "achieve all the knowledge of the world," took quite some training in secrecy, and assistants were sometimes needed for the subsequent presentation of spirits. Ajijak, Akku, and Missuarniannga performed with great success. Maratsi did not put up a big show, and instead took his revenge later. Naaja started out with the delivery but postponed the *silaninneq* until married, and his presentation of spirits is missing among the sources. But they are listed and the main ones described in a separate text following right upon the record of the *silaninneq* performance: *tôrnat píkorigsut/De dygtige hjælpeånder* (the capable helping spirits) (Sandgreen 1967, I: 112–14; 1987: 152–54). This division of the phases supports Kaarali Andreassen's statement that bachelors were not allowed to go through this ritual of public recognition. Ideally, society did build on the married couple, no matter the frequent divorces in the early years of a marriage and the polygamy of competent hunters. Bachelors did not inspire confidence, especially not as masters of loyal (potentially immoral) spirits.

Travels to Moon by actual shamans are said to be events of the winter around New Year, whereas the time for a performance like the impressive one staged by Karraq of having Moon come down may have been early spring. This is my guess because the ritual myth of the giant boulder coming down in order to force its way into the house, but stopped at the last minute by the shaman's *Equngasoq*, the fulmar, is just another variant of the same story. And this is an event of spring with stones, pebbles, and water coming down the sloping mountains. Indeed, the helping spirit *Equngasoq* is the very sign of spring in East Greenland.[9] In any event, fighting the boulder or Moon reflects the widespread religious phenomenon of fighting down "the dragon" or challenging chaos at such a decisive point in the year.[10] Moon intended to smash the house with his black stick, and the boulder *inua*, *Aqajarormiorsiorpua*, literally, to force its way into the stomach (of the house). In short, hazardous, "wild," male sexual connotations cannot be overlooked. In the same line of thought, spring not only meant an increase in sexual activities of every adult male, human and animal, it was also the key season in the spirit language of the Other World, *taartaq*. Figuratively one might say that *silap ingerlasia*, the movement of the world, became sped up in spring, jeopardizing its balance.

No Greenlandic statement confirms that the onset of spring called for a collective confession of taboo breaks led by a shaman, as was the case among Baffin Islanders at the equinoxes, when *Nunagiqsaqtuq* cleaned the land by transmitting the confessions to Sea Woman. Instead the ritual myth of the shaman's travel to, fight with, and cleaning of Sea Woman (*Sassuma Arnaa*) takes place in spring in order to have the ice cover removed by a great storm. The removal of her dirt, the transformed breaks of taboo sticking to her hair and body, allowed the transmigrating mammals and birds of the sea to become reborn into the reopened sea of This World. Far from every shaman had the competence to visit Sea Woman, nor was the visit a prescribed annual event. In the context of myth the occasion is a prolonged winter. Similarly, a crisis was the recurrent cause among the Eastern Inuit of Canada, as settled by Laugrand and Oosten (2002b). Boas's description of the so-called Sedna cult, which begins with a ritual killing of Sedna (Sea Woman), has led research astray in considering it an annual must. In Greenland, in the early times of contact, Sea Woman seems to have had her stronghold in the south. Variants of her origin myth are all of southern provenance, as are the reports of *actual* visits by shamans. Of the more widespread variants of the shaman's journey to Sea Woman, the majority were told in West Greenland. My hypothesis—that she was particularly associated with whaling in the early contact times of southern travels to the whaling grounds of midwest Greenland—is inspired by the goal of the shaman's travel to her abode, namely to have the ice removed. Not only would the migrating animals and birds be released but the reopened sea would simultaneously make possible the travels to the whaling grounds and the trade with the Dutch whalers in the north. The development of her myth of origin in Arctic Canada shows a similar connection with whaling. Here Sea Woman's origin became combined with the origin myth of the Qallunaat as fathered by a dog; my thesis states that this combination of the two myths was mainly due to the wintering of the Euro-American whalers, who employed and cooperated with the Inuit. They attracted Inuit from afar and fathered quite a few children of mixed blood, who most probably were not excluded from ritual but were recognized as Inuit on par with their Inuit half-siblings (Sonne 1990).

In myth the big Sea Woman received the shaman as an exact copy of a woman under taboo. She sat locked up on the platform in a fit of rage, her hair hanging loose, filthy with coagulated blood due

9. *Equngasoq* is sometimes identified with a sculpin (*Micrenophrys lilljeborgi*, Norway bullhead), which alludes to *Nalikkatteeq*'s *pooq* dangling in her crotch (Sonne 2005: ID 1463).

10. E.g., Indra's killing the dragon Vrita for freeing the rivers at New Year in Vedic mythology; the transformation of the most dignified Zuni god, Putiwa, into a sorcerer god for ten days during the New Year ceremony, threatening to let the whole world lose its way in devastating earthquakes, storm, and sorcery (Prytz-Johansen in Asmussen & Læssøe 1968, I: 90–97).

to women breaking their taboos on earth, and with a complete lack of fingers for tending her lamp. The shaman had to fight and clean her and then put her hair up in the hairdo of the adult woman, which signified her harmless state with regard to hunting (Sonne 1975). In addition, the stream in her tunnel was cleaned and reversed to its right course for the "rebirth" of birds and animals to the reopened sea.

The myth of the shaman's journey to Sea Woman leaves a strong impression. Until recently she has survived more prominently than any other figure in Greenlandic art, theater, and Western research.[11] The incestuous origin myth of the moon and the sun comes in second, though the fighting down of the threatening, libidinous Moon or his effect on the tides seem absent. In pre-Christian East Greenland, Moon could be represented in a shamanic performance, whereas no trace can be seen of a human figure representing Sea Woman in ritual. This frightening woman remained in her house below until modern times. Thus, in the play "Inua" of the Tuukkaq Theater in the 1970s, she is transformed into a motherly figure who ascends to earth and saves the Inuit from the Qallunaat subjugation. The mother symbolism prevails in contemporary art as well, where it is significant that she is only very rarely depicted without fingers. The origin myth had them cut off by either her father or a brutish hunter, and in Canadian variants they were transformed into the sea mammals. But few contemporary Greenlandic artists have the heart to let this cruel act befall their beloved mother figure. In this modern Greenlandic understanding, she used to be a benevolent mother who was changed into a devilish witch by the missionaries. So I, a Dane, can anticipate my contrary interpretation in the neck!

The East Greenlanders, who, in contrast to the southerners, were dependent on sealing at breathing holes in early spring, were less concerned about the reopening of the sea, and thus about Sea Woman. Due to the humidity of their local climate, their recurring crisis was caused by the thick layer of snow covering the seals' breathing holes. Rain for melting the snow was obtained when *Asiaq* shook her baby-husband's diaper, an event caused by the (mythic) shaman's visit to her house above and the actual, reciprocate ritual of opening the pokes of food for her to help herself. This environmental condition shines through a couple of stories, one of them Aaqqii's travel to Sea Woman, the other Teemiartissaq's generalized *Asiaq* version. The latter does not stop with an apparently reopened sea but has Moon cover the surface with a fine layer of new ice (for the men to hunt at breathing holes). In the former version, the shaman Aaqqii succeeds in having the cleaning of Sea Woman reopen the sea, but when a greedy hunter's break of taboo effects a renewed close up, local nature apparently takes its preferred course. Indeed, instead of a flood, masses of snow were the main threat that *Uniagaq* told his master, the shaman Ajijak, about, in that only an extremely heavy snowfall would make the world capsize once again (Sonne 2005: ID 1678; J. Rosing 1963: 234). A heavy snowfall, that is, in spring. Finally, hearsay about Christian afterlife made some of the last shamans, although reproached by their helping spirits, choose to scout the realm of death below instead of ever visiting Sea Woman.

Christianity transformed Moon into a laughingstock in younger variants of "Visit to Moon." This is particularly conspicuous in the version of the obstinate hunter, who forces Moon into a human

11. At present, Greenlandic art, literature, and theater less often look back to traditional mythic figures and ways of life. International trends guide the fields and have done so for several decades.

Fig. 26. *Angerlartoq*, the homecomer's "rebirth": The *angerlartussiaq* (destined to return from an untimely death) is drawn backwards into the house. He whimpers like a baby. The mother wrenches the ice scraper out of his hand and places it beneath the burning lamp. He breaks down and, when nursed like a baby for three days, recovers completely. Drawing by Kaarali Andreassen. *Courtesy of the National Museum of Denmark, Copenhagen.*

relationship of balanced exchange. Literally, he is brought down to earth, and consequently he, like the human hero, needs five days of training for his return to heaven. On the other hand, not to let him return would mean absolute disaster. The tide would come to a halt, etc. He is only bereaved of his frightening and punishing role.

At the Center of Society: Naming

Shortly after birth, the ritual of naming (mediated by the raven's cry) transformed the baby into a genuine human—i.e., a social being, who, in addition to his/her biological relatives, inherited the kinship bonds of his/her deceased namesake: "The ways of addressing each other usually refer to the relationships of people to their deceased namesakes or to relationships between deceased namesakes in the past. Relations between people therefore derive meaning from the relationships between their ancestors" (Kublu & Oosten 1999: 69). This conclusion about naming and its social bearings among the Canadian Inuit applies in part to the present as well as to the Iñupiat and Yupiit. They also seem to have been in force in pre-Christian Greenland. Dalager (1915) of the 18th century testifies to people keeping track of their relatives up to ten generations back in time, Robbe (1981) to the ways in which naming was closely connected with sharing in East Greenland during the 1970s, and Leonard (2014) recently to its ongoing validity for Polar Inuit collective identity. In wider circles in Greenland naming rules are currently negotiated in line with the changes of modern times. Increasing stress on individual liberty is gaining ground, along with a tendency among some parents to avoid renaming; however, on the other hand, the reintroduction (by church legislation) of Greenlandic names for baptism is cherished by some as markers of cultural identity

(Tróndheim 2010).[12] In pre-Christian times, birth, in a way, presided over death, not only by the revival of the deceased relatives' name and network but also by the notion and rites of *angerlartoqut*, a baby named for a recently deceased child, and the *angerlartussiat*, people destined to return home. The sorrows caused by a high rate of infant mortality were soothed, and the name and kin relations of a beloved relative were saved. In East Greenland, the returning adult "homecomer," usually absent due to a prolonged stay at sea, was supposed to enter the entrance tunnel backwards upon return and become clasped in his mother's arms from behind: a reversed birth ritual, as it were. The practice of ritually turning a child into a future "homecomer," or *angerlartussiaq*, appears to have been common but is poorly described.

Relations of Sex and Gender

In the academic discussion about the kind of dominant relationship in Inuit/Yupiit worldviews—animalized or gendered—the Greenlanders seem to have been in favor of gender. The language of the Other World, *taartaq*, sides with the gendered view stressed by Saladin d'Anglure regarding the Eastern Canadian Inuit. The gendered ritual exchanges point in the same direction. At this point, it is necessary to comment on the symbolism of sex in pre-Christian Greenland; to conceal the multitude of sexual connotations prevalent in religious matters is to otherwise deprive them of their sense. Men and women are, in *taartaq*, characterized exclusively as the "haves" and "have-nots" of a penis. Moon's wild sexuality engenders life on earth. Cultivated or ritualized, the sexual act is represented in the drum dance with its orgasmic ending as a prelude to the ritual exchange of spouses. Considered to be useful in promoting reproduction and consequently a mixing of "genes," it is difficult to see any promiscuity in this.[13] Curiously, the birth symbolism of Sea Woman has never been all that suppressed in research. Western scholars (mostly men?) feel free to discuss female private parts and periods; Greenlanders were just as liberal about the male parts. Through the generations most Greenlanders have never let go of the pleasure they take (at least when talking among themselves) in this sphere of life. The double entendre of sexual fun and puns are particularly prominent in acculturated versions of traditional stories told by the excellent tellers. They can be sensed as implicit outlets of passive resistance to the clerical dominance of the Danes, who rarely knew how to appreciate the nuances of Greenlandic such as the meaning of the name Aron gave Kaassassuk's last opponent, *Ususarmiorsunnguaq* (the small penis with the ability to grow). At any rate, time and again I have asked myself: did the other Inuit and Yupiit never, besides the sexual analogies in ritual and myth, engage in the fun of such matters?

Nonetheless, warnings against sex, "wild" sex in particular, are prominent in myth (personified by, e.g., the *inua* of the moon and *Nalikkatteeq*), and rules about sex did obtain, of course, in Greenland. Common wife exchange was ritualized, wife exchange between partners was arranged, shamans got their share as deliverer of babies,[14] and the husband owned his wife sexually as much as he owned and could dispose of his catches. The young man's ritual rape of his bride, a violent affair,

12. Adoption, a very common way of "redistributing" children among the Inuit and Yupiit, often goes with naming: "Inuit attempt to recreate the social groups of previous generations, not only through the presence of names but by actually bringing the people together" (Trott 2005: 17; cf. Tróndheim 2010: 182).

13. An anthropologist, the late Margaret Lantis, told me several times that the Inuit (or "her" Yupiit?) were sufficiently experienced in dog breeding to know and appreciate the health-promoting effects of spouse exchange.

14. Apropos Saladin d'Anglure (1993).

bore a strong resemblance to his first catch of a seal, his *pernarneq*. He was not allowed to taste this seal, which was celebrated and consumed by the entire settlement. At the end of the *pernarneq* he was asked to touch a young girl in her private parts, and then he could eat freely from his subsequent catches. Years later, when able to provide for a family, and a marriage was arranged, the woman he raped (frequently after mutual consent) and brought to his family posed on the platform in a mourning position and let loose her hair. Ending this rite of transition and abstinence after a couple of days, marriage was consummated and interrupted only in her periods under taboo. Despite the husband's individual ownership, his (first) wife did have some say in sexual matters and definitely in deciding on and keeping check of the distribution of meat shares. Examples on record of her liberty in accepting a partner for the collective ritual of wife exchange should be stressed as well. Wife beating, the main concern of the Danish authorities in reports on the Greenlanders' married lives, turns out to be a matter of opinion. But by their insistence on lifelong monogamy, the same authorities provoked both some polygamous women to bring their discontent into the open, and some men to complain against attacks on their marital authority. In a myth clarifying their sexual rights, a woman, as competent in hunting as any man, and despite all symbolic equivalence between hunting and sex, was not allowed sexual ownership of another woman. Kuannia, when baptized, likened her misdeed, the rape of her daughter-in-law, to Eve's original sin in Paradise.

All things considered, in traditional Greenland, a level of male dominance cannot be talked away: boys were preferred to girls as firstborns, in adoption, in explanations of *sipineq* (the split of a boy into a girl at birth[15]), and in changing the gender of a child in clothing and upbringing. Nevertheless, to bear a child, no matter its sex, ranked highest of all. Motherhood was a woman's key to obtaining the identity, privileges, and social standing of an adult woman. This seems to be the reason why the number of female shamans was extremely low. Apart from practical hindrances, the restrictions put on women to embark on the career of a shaman were symbolized in two ways. One is the equivalence in myth of men getting *qaamaneq* (vision) by Moon, while women become dangerously pregnant on visits to Moon. The other is the idea of the performing shaman, male or female, as a "mother" to (some of) his or her helping spirits. The possibility of a human fetus already in place could hardly allow for a spirit to enter. Talented Kaakaaq may have temporarily quit her career until her last child was born. The sources are silent on that issue, but they do tell that she performed past baptism and was haunted by possessions in her old age. Teemiartissaq was a mother of one child when her stepfather disclosed her apprenticeship and thereby spoiled her career; he seems not to have been blamed by anybody except Teemiartissaq, who never stopped complaining that he cut her off from a future liberty to travel the Other Worlds by flying.

Men were better situated, in that hunting did not put up notable barriers to their training and practice as shamans. As a mother to his helping spirits, one might say that the male shaman represented a "third sex" (as Saladin d'Anglure proposed for shamans generally). But since female shamans of any competence also became possessed by their spirits, and most spirits in either case were male, a Greenlandic substantiation of the thesis becomes difficult. *Piaaqqusiat*—children dressed in awkward clothes, but not those of the opposite sex—were sometimes accorded the mixed powers

15. There are no examples on record of a girl changed into a boy at birth in Greenland.

of a man and a woman. Men disguised as pregnant women at the masked dances (*uaajeertut*), the androgynous *Uersaq* figures, and *Nalikkatteeq* with her phallic dog or sea scorpion in her big crotch gave, depending on context, rise to the entire spectrum from fright and thrill to laughter, all so characteristic of liminality.

Others, Foreigners, and Boundaries

Essentially animals, deceased humans, and spirits belonged in the Other Worlds. They could all be seen in dreams by ordinary people and summoned by shamans in solitude or protected by darkness. Other *allanat*, different humanlike beings, were humans of a different culture, language, and look. In between were strangely behaving Inuit of no danger to the community and not feared like lunatics. Evidently animals also appeared in their manifest forms to the ordinary eye, and let themselves be killed provided the rules of exchange were observed.

Social Obligations of Relations with Game Animals

Thalbitzer (1941) and Robbe (1994) asked the East Greenlanders questions of contemporary relevance about their relations with animals; Thalbitzer asked about the spirits as well. Otherwise nothing like the systematic interviewing of Alaska and Canadian Elders regarding "the rules" has been done in Greenland. Consequently, the moral of the human rules concerning the animals, which forms the red thread in both Fienup-Riordan's treatise and several reports by Oosten and Laugrand on the Nunavut Inuit,[16] is less explicit with regard to Greenland. Here, a good number of traditional taboos, which made little sense by Western cultural logic and thus were nullified by baptism, were gladly abandoned by the Greenlanders, particularly the women. However, the rules of sharing, the premise of social life, stood their ground, supported for a long time by the belief that neglect displeased the animals. The celebration of happy "ritual firsts" continued as well, and with similar imagined effects of strengthening both social bonds and exchange with the animals.

The pre-Christian Greenlanders were no doubt as responsible for the reincarnation of the animals' souls (*tarnit*) as the other Inuit and Yupiit. Taboos at birth, abortion, and death were (almost) as severe as anywhere else, and the obligations of ritual handling and sharing of killed animals were as strict on the individual hunter and his wife.[17] Taken together, the Eastern Inuit's collective rituals concerning the animals were not as elaborate as the whaling and annual hunting ceremonies in Alaska, where whaling captains and lineage heads took the lead. On the other hand, shamans were less prominent in these ceremonies than in the collective rituals among the Eastern Inuit. This may be one reason why, despite all ambivalence, shamanism was at a premium among the Eastern Inuit.

---

16. Put together, augmented, and commented on in Laugrand and Oosten (2015).

17. Isolation, whether in a solitary hut for women giving birth without assistance as among Canadian Inuit, or at puberty as in Southwest Alaska, was not practiced in Greenland. All inhabitants were asked to go outside in order to further a birth. Only the assisting midwife stayed behind, and the mother observed her isolating birth taboos by remaining on the platform with her back to the room, where she did not put up her hair or change her clothes for a long time.

Shamans—Socially

One-fifth of the adult population was considered to be shamans, of which the number of female shamans was extremely low. Childbearing turns out to be the most common hindrance, together with some contempt on the side of male shamans (see below for symbolic confirmations).

Becoming a shaman was as much a source of fame as of respect, and the element of entertainment was as prevalent as curing and restoring the balance with the Other World; the news of an approaching *saqqummerneq* or a supplementary ritual initiation attracted people from afar. And last but not least, the respect furnished the shaman with some social security, especially within the ideology of blood feuds, the dependency on kin relations, and the lack of an institutionalized judicial system. The song duels offered outlets without necessarily doing justice (Kleivan 1971a; J. Rosing 1970). Nevertheless, the great authority credited to Inuit shamans by most Western researchers is hardly tenable. A shaman did not decide in settlement matters, unless he also possessed knowledge in a particular field of hunting that called for a temporary leader, the only accepted type of leadership beyond the household (Nooter 1976; 1978). But when asked to perform in times of crisis, the shaman could have a great say in the matter, especially in detecting sorcerers and breaks of taboo. Shamanism as a source of material security has also been overvalued. Although payments (in skins, trade goods, and hunting implements) could, in certain circumstances, be large, hunters of medium skill seem to have been better off in the long run than invalid shamans. Relatives and nonrelatives, who on their own accord offered knowledge before and during apprenticeship, could hope to become included in the circle of security. On the other hand, close kin could be hit by sorcery intended for the shaman, whose defense in religious means turned out to be too strong. The shaman's public presentation of his abilities and spirits did not automatically eliminate the ambivalence. Greenlandic shamans often regretted the choice of their (part-time) trade, as they were often accused of either sorcery or using their spirits for evil ends. Generally the helping spirits were considered completely loyal to their shaman regardless of the social morality of his acts. If a helping spirit became angry with its shaman, the usual cause was neglect on his part of the alliance.

Motives for becoming a shaman were multifarious and voluntary. The spirits did not fatefully pick and choose. Before *saqqummerneq* (initiation in public), the deals made with spirits could be annulled without further consequences brought on by making the apprenticeship public. However, a shaman's sudden break with his helping spirits at baptism might cause the spirits to attack their former master.

Fear of a shaman did not prevent people from attending his séances, which followed a protective ritual procedure; the social demands on shamans also worked insofar as no really satisfactory fame was gained without practicing in public. Suspicion of undisplayed powers raised the level of public fear, which put the secret shaman in danger. Nor could a shaman who hid his talents entirely exploit the powers of his spirits, unless he made them publicly known. When a spirit offered its service on its own accord to a human apprentice in solitude, it would ask to be called on at his future performances, and by consent ask the apprentice to touch it. From then on it was called a "future helping spirit," which eagerly awaited his human master's *saqqummerneq*. In case the shaman hesitated, his spirits could by combined efforts bring pressure to bear on him, and when he gave in, the public presentation eliminated the suffix of "future." Eventually the helping spirits became his possessions—literally, as it were. The other claim on the shaman—to permit (some of) his spirits to "refuel" by entering his body during performances—recurs as the reason why a spirit offered its service: it was attracted by the radiance of his interior *qaamaneq*. So, although the shaman's helping spirits were neither caught nor killed like animals, he was as responsible for their lives by temporal "incarnations" (into his own body) as was the hunter for the reincarnation of his animals through other rites. And to repeat: bachelors were not accepted as candidates for the ritual cognition in public. Nor was another shaman required as ceremonial master of séances. A father, some other close relative, or maybe a friend did service.

Beyond Relative Boundaries

Human view marked the spatial boundaries of This World. While only the closest surroundings were known to the inexperienced mind, This World widened as an individual moved about collecting, hunting, and traveling long distances. Out of view from the house or tent, a child roaming the unfamiliar land alone was in the wilderness, the space where spirits dared approach with their offerings of future support. Being scared (on both sides) was a condition for such meetings to happen; a fright no less terrible when, in myth, the initiated pupil woke up naked and shivering in the setting sun. Not until the pupil was dressed and with human habitation back in view did the fright disappear—only to return in the middle of night with everybody asleep—and vanish again with the light of day. To the outsider (me), this children's psychology of recognition and light versus darkness is immediately intelligible. To adults, fear of *qivittut* (sing. *qivittoq*, a person who has left society for the wilderness in despair) can still be stimulated by stories exchanged during the dark evenings of winter, and fright increases with distance away from the coast. Families or small groups out caribou hunting in the inland regions still feel an impulse to entertain one another with frightening stories about spirits and *qivittut* (Grønnow 2009a). The threatening powers of the distant inland region and its heaven "up behind you," or *pinnga*, come strongly to the fore in the story about the orphan Kaassassuk. They are the land powers of spring, and his handling of stones appears as symbolic and significant as his eventual development into a balanced person in the most recent acculturated variants. Stones turn out to be polysemous, in that they, accorded fertile powers, are used in a multitude of ways, and as objects of sacrifice they connect This with the Other Worlds.

As seen from the point of orientation (the coast, facing the sea), *Sassuma Arnaa*—the woman "down there in front" (*sanna*), the main source of life—was personified in Sea Woman. Out at sea, a sudden unfavorable change in weather, sea, and ice conditions were expected events that called to mind whatever experience and communicated knowledge one possessed regarding how to manage the situation. Sea monsters were encountered by both Greenlanders and Qallunaat in the 18th century (e.g., H. Egede 1971, 2: 47; 1925: 349; 1818: 85–89); the smiling sea giant, *Qungussutariaq*, a weaker maritime counterpart to *Nalikkatteeq*, was primarily encountered in myth and probably in ritual, but an attack of kayak dizziness or being raped by *innersuit* appear to have been the most frequent sources of fear. K. G. Hansen's (1994) hypothesis of kayak dizziness as an outcome of the fear of sorcery places this kind of imbalance right in the center of social relations.

More or less realistic knowledge of other Inuit (Greenlanders) was gained from actual gatherings and rumors heard along the trade routes. Staying en route or wintering in a settlement of nonrelatives or partners required acceptance through gestures, with the inhabitants showing up outdoors. Myth does not reflect the animosity between West and East Greenlanders as expressed by the name given to the latter, Tunuamiut, the dwellers of the backside. But in myth, annual ball games with people living to the north or the south of one's own locale took on warlike dimensions.[18] In reality, fleeing from a feud left real enemies behind. The knowledge mediated by the Qallunaat of Inuit-like beings living in Akilineq, the opposite coast across the sea of West Greenland, grew out of myth into more realistic ideas. They stressed both likeness and differences between Greenlanders and the Akilinermiut, to the advantage of the former. The storyteller Hendrik even came up with an interesting conception (in the 1860s) of an alliance between the two parties against colonial administration.

The Greenlanders' attitudes towards the Danes and other Europeans—be they whalers, missionaries, trading directors, craftsmen, or sailors—during the early days of colonization have not been a separate object of my investigation.[19] Disagreements about colonial trade, hunting restrictions, and territorial hunting rights pop up in the earliest historical sources and later stories. Constant attention has been paid to explicated disagreements with the worldviews of Christianity and natural sciences.[20] Impacts from encounters with the Norse have been considered insignificant, as can be concluded from a recent article on differences between the Norse and the vanguard Thule Inuit in regard to worldview and attitudes to foreigners (Jørgensen et al. 2012; Gulløv 2008). However, these differences raise the question of rules about boundaries between This and the Other World and thus ask for some comments.

The Norse subsisted by farming, hunting, and long-distance trade from 986 to about 1450. At that point, due to both the climatic deterioration and the break in contact with Norway, they seem to have slowly trickled away, mostly to Iceland (Lynnerup in Arneborg et al. 2012). The Norse and the Inuit did trade, and they did fight—at least once. But they differed in spatial orientation, mobility, social organization, religious ideas, and practices, not to mention ways of dealing with foreigners. Norse social organization was hierarchic, centered on the farm of the chief where the church was placed, oriented towards the rising sun (east by convention), and supervised by a bishop appointed by the archbishop of Nidaros (Norway). The authors emphasize the institutional, settled character of the church, as well as the sharp boundary the Norse drew between cultivated land and the wilderness

---

18. Interestingly, this game was considered heathen and abandoned by the baptized Greenlanders on their own accord, which thus points to the game's former character of a ritual. The parties were always called the southern and northern people. The winning part was to throw the ball into the sea (Robert Petersen pers. comm.: *Atuagagdliutit* 1933/34: 123f). A ritual counterpart could very well be the New Year ball game in Arctic Canada, which as proposed by Blaisel and Oosten (1997) refers to the Northern Lights produced by deceased relatives playing ball. As a frequent event in Greenlandic *stories,* the ball game bears warlike connotations and the character of an annual event between two sites. When *Qivaaqiarsuk,* for instance, wins this game on the part of his in-laws against their southern enemies, the encounter appears scheduled in advance. Sometimes, as exemplified above, a gathering between the two sites included competitions between the two shamans, who each represent their site (see p. 236, note 52, and Sonne 2005: ID 467, 1649).

19. Apart from controversies about the rights to the subsurface (apparently settled in 2009, but recent decisions about uranium mining show that they are not), the Greenlanders' title to their island has never been in dispute. A common saying among Greenlanders—that they do as they have always done despite any rules set by the Danes (Naja Trondhjem pers. comm.)—must be taken with a grain of salt. From a historical point of view, impacts have been immense. Instead, the saying reflects the Greenlanders' nonaggressive way of guarding their "interior" life, which is protected in many aspects by their language; it has been officially recognized by the missions from their very beginning, but is generally difficult for Indo-European speakers to learn. *Grønlands indre liv* (*The Interior Life of Greenland*), as the title of the late Hans Lynge's memories of childhood and adolescence (H. Lynge 1981–88) goes, relates occurrences in which the Danes took no part. Nevertheless, Lynge wrote them and also had them published in Danish. A 2013 commission of reconciliation by the Greenlandic government demonstrates the still-smoldering feelings of resentment towards the Danes.

20. See Sejersen (2001) and Kjeld Hansen (2001; 2002) for current discussions.

of "outlaw" trolls. This supposedly included the Inuit, who could legally be killed without paying a fine, but with whom they nevertheless established trade partnerships (Jørgensen et al. 2012).

In contrast to this sun-oriented worldview, the authors continue, the Inuit worldview is anthropocentric.[21] As they expanded southward, the coastal Thule Inuit pioneers brought along no such institutions like a church: only portable, independent shamanism. Wherever they settled in winter and camped in summer, they observed the taboos and rituals demanded by game and spirits in order to make a living and maintain the balance of the world. The spirits inhabiting the land were always close by, and the Norse settlers, regarded as a resource like game, were exploited in trade. In sum, the settled Norse lived *with* their mental institutions whereas the mobile Inuit mentally lived in their world (Jørgensen et al. 2012).

Ingold's concept of "dwelling" is the inspiration to the latter emphasis, and however much I fancy his theory, I am less sure about the premise for comparison with the depicted world of the Norse, as also I have to object to the idea of close relations between humans and spirits in a world without boundaries. In all practices, boundaries did obtain between the Inuit, their game, and their "trolls"—i.e., the spirits of the land among whom the shamans found the majority of their helping spirits.

By definition alone, taboos set up boundaries; for instance, keeping human birth and death apart from the life cycles of game animals—rules acknowledged by Ingold, the Inuit, and the above authors. However, social life created another all-important boundary, a boundary of security. The socially rejected orphan (e.g., Kaassassuk) became extradited to threatening powers of the Other World, as did the *qivittoq* who left society in distress. This is also the recurrent theme in stories about the small vilified child who, when running away from home glowing with shame, attracts his first helping spirit-to-be. It took courage to cross *without company* the spatial boundary right beyond view from human habitation to *Asia*, the wilderness or hidden Other World of the earthly spirits.

The boundary of visibility separated the human or social world from the invisible ones of talking animals, *inuat*, and deceased humans. A change in view from one to the other in either direction demanded a short transition of blurred sight. On the other hand, by turning to the analogy of the relation of This to the Other World with that of the visible outside to the dark interior of the body, I agree that the two worlds are indeed intimately close to one another—like a couple. Correspondingly, events and occurrences in This World, *sila*, affect its "partner," *silap aappaa*, the Other World, and vice versa. Relations that served to keep human society apart from spirit societies simultaneously allowed for communicative exchanges; that is, provided that these relations remained dyadic and the spirits invited in public were received in the cultic replica of their world—in darkness, inside the house.[22]

---

21. As defined by Ingold: "in the strict sense of placing the human beings at the hub of a dwelt-in world, a centre of embodied awareness that reaches out, through the activity of the senses, into its surroundings" (2000: 218). According to Gulløv this meant "having no boundaries between inhabited and uninhabited land. ... Their social structure and technology were integrated parts of the Arctic environment and were made known through established social relationships and contracts" (Ingold 2000: 290; cf. Gulløv 2008: 22).

22. Some performances did take place outdoors, such as Ajijak's failed but impressive attempt to cure his wife (see pp. 320f). During this event he did not invite spirits but rather transformed into his bear spirit himself. Neither did the divination methods of *qilaneq* or *qilaaqutserneq*, practiced by shamans in summer, invite spirits to appear in their own bodies. Legends tell of shamans' contests in tricks at places of assembly in summer. A solitary source describes a hunt for an *anngiaq* (a transformed child born and killed in secrecy) at such a place. Three shamans cooperated, hiding their

Turning to *Asia*, it was just as uninhabited by humans as the uncultivated land of the Norse—and similarly inhabited by nonhuman beings. A useful place for finding helping spirits, it might be dangerous all the same. Giants of the distant inland were in the habit of stealing infants, and the prehuman *innersuit* living right beneath the foreshore were feared for their tendency to rob kayakers. Only shamans with strong helping spirits in their defense could escape them. However, when mediated by the shaman, they served society perfectly well as helping spirits. Raven was, as we know, particularly close to humans, remaining in visible space all year round but bounded nonetheless to the outside. Similarly, several outstanding helping spirits were, although summoned, never permitted to enter the house. Also spatially close was the foreshore right below the dwelling, the juncture between sea and land and the worlds below and above as shown by the movements of the tide. Passing between land and sea in This World called for no rituals except after the period of mourning. But as a point of departure for shamans to the realms above and below, as well as for the deceased for a free change between them, it always took ritual of one sort or another to exploit its possibilities. Furthermore, the sad outcome of stories about individual "Others" who trespass the boundaries of time, space, and social relations *demonstrates that the boundaries ruled on either side.* In short, ignoring the simultaneously separating and connecting boundaries, not to mention their transformative, —i.e., creative, liminal powers, would cause the pre-Christian Inuit world collapse.

Perhaps all these ritual keys to the Other Worlds and the other way round can just be subsumed under the above heading set by Ingold of the taboos and rituals observed as demanded by game and spirits? In my view, considering the importance given to boundaries among the Yupiit (e.g., Fienup-Riordan 1994), the spatial, temporal, and social boundaries between the worlds of the Greenlanders should be explicated as well.

In contrast to the proposition by Jørgensen et al. (2012) of close and apparently easygoing relations between humans and spirits including the game animals, Oosten and Laugrand (2004–5: 114ff) take the view of a particularly sharp boundary on social terms. Humans have names and rules; spirits have neither. Spirits exceed all boundaries, and observe no taboos. Outside time and space, they cover unimpeded immense distances in no time; unhindered by bodily limitations, they can change size and live forever while seeing and following the doings of humans and reading their thoughts. But because they do not follow rules, they cannot become allies of humans. I agree with the latter statement insofar as only dyadic relations reign between Inuit humans and nonhumans. Yet I find that some comments on the former generalizations are appropriate. Some appear in the following passage and some in reconsiderations on perspectivism farther below.

Asymmetrical Dyadic Relations

Individual ownership reigned in relation to both spirits and slain animals (R. Petersen [1984] and Robbe [1994] both make the latter very clear). The shaman abided by his *saqqummerneq* (initiation in public) and subsequent performances of either splendor or modesty, and the hunter by his treatment of the animal's head, the symbol of ownership and responsibility for the observance of proscriptions

---

eyes with skin soles in order to "see" the *anngiaq*. That is, one among them had made holes in his sole, while the other two went staggering. One got hold of the *anngiaq* and ate it up, piece by piece, in a profusion of blood (P. Egede 1939: 108; 1971: 163).

and prescriptions befalling both him and his wife. Individual ownership goes hand in hand with the rule of dyadic relations with the "Others." They were dyadic from a human point of view, but not symmetrical. While the human shaman could have a great number of helping spirits, a spirit could have but one human master at a time. Spirit shamans could engage the same kinds of helping spirits as humans, but never humans themselves, nor a deceased human nor a ghost. Stories about fights between a human shaman and aggressive spirits who possessed helping spirits themselves emphasize that the shaman would get the upper hand by means of his ghost spirit. No relatives on either side were part of the contract between an apprentice and a spirit. In agreement, they told each other their names and touched each other's body. At the shaman's death his helping spirits might seek a new master of their own accord or become sought out and acquired by another shaman. Generally, among the Canadian Inuit and Greenlanders alike, human relations such as marriage (producing offspring) and adoption across the boundary with "Others," be they animals or spirits, were out of the question.[23] Stories make it clear that no animal or spirit could live up to the social obligations of humans, and in case a man or woman came to live with "Others" he or she either had to remain in "exile," commit suicide, cut all bonds with humans after a single visit at home, or flee from the spirits. In the latter case, children born to the alien spouse were killed. Asymmetry reigned in mutual visits, in that the majority of the shaman's helping spirits were assembled at his performances, whereas he, the human shaman, could not visit a spirit and its cohabitants in the company of another human. The oft-claimed equality between the Inuit and their animals (and spirits) appears true only insofar as responsibility of keeping up beneficent relations was of highest priority for individual hunters and shamans. The "Others" were demanding, but human ancestors had intelligently thought out the rules of exchanges. All in all, ontologically humans presided at the center of their own worldview.

From the perspective of outside versus inside, some superhuman abilities of the "Others" can be said to make human sense when looked at from the inside, from one's invisible interior of thoughts and imaginations. Conversant with the dark interiors of worlds, the spirits could see humans' secret deeds and read their thoughts. The shaman had only to remember a spirit in order to summon it in no time. Suspense increases in the stories as long as the shaman does not remember the only one among his spirits with the ability to save him from mortal danger. Oosten and Laugrand stress the annulment of the limits of space and time in regard to the spirits as listed above (2004–5). I agree insofar as being on their own, the various spirit species are imagined to cover immense distances with extreme speed, but the distance is still there to be covered and speed is necessary for doing it. In the vision of the shaman, however, time and distance disappear. The very remembrance of a helping spirit makes it appear right before one's interior eyes. *Imaginative thought* belongs in the interior of the body, the world that the shaman shares with the "Others" by means of his *qaamaneq*.

23. This is according to Oosten and Laugrand (2004–5). Saladin d'Anglure passes on actual cases about shamans who were married to both a human and a spirit among the *ijeqqat* in the pleasant inland region of the caribou where the shaman would go after death. Keeping the two relationships going simultaneously led to problems, as did the choice after baptism between the two happy lands of the afterlife: one of the *ijiqqat* and the other of heaven. One clever solution was to stay with the *ijiqqat* until Judgment Day and then join Jesus (Saladin d'Anglure 1983; 2001).

Air, Drinking Water, and Light: The Basics of Life

Once upon a time heaven and earth were not separated. Heaven weighed heavily on the mountaintops. Only gradually did space come into being, as the saying goes (P. Egede 1971: 89; 1939: 63). The origins of *sila*, alias air or space, consist in such naked comments. As a personification of *sila*, *Nalikkatteeq* is said to have raised the pillar separating heaven from earth and is accorded the power to let it go. The Nattilik *inua* of storms similarly has the power to knock over the mountains upholding heaven. The Canadian origin myth of the unpredictable baby *Naarjuk* concerns weather, not space as such. Since air leaves the body at death and *Nalikkatteeq* feeds on the lungs, questions are sometimes asked as to the breath needed for the happy singing in heaven. No stories can be seen of *Silap Inua*'s human origin such as that of Sea Woman, Sun, and Moon. Nor is any origin myth on record about drinking water, another prerequisite of life. But it is recognized in ritual by being dripped into the mouth of the baby at the time of naming, as well as into the grateful mouth of the killed seal, which is said to suffer from thirst due to its life in the salty sea. Drinking water is of the land. In winter, water was fetched through holes made through the ice cover of lakes, ice cut out from old icebergs, and snow. Spring came with drinking water free to everybody, let loose from inside the land, the *erngaaq* in *taartaq* (*nunarsuup erngi* or *ermi*, the resources of the land in contemporary West Greenlandic). Following this line of thought, the ritual of wife exchange performed by Qilaatuaq by means of four wooden dolls makes sense: on his way with sons and a son-in-law on an iceberg across the sea, he overcame the threat of dying from thirst by the effect of this ritual. The heat called forth drinking water from the iceberg, an outcome that adds still another aspect, the spring melt, to the interpretation of wife exchange at winter feasts. Several mythic animals that saw to the solitary initiation of the shaman belonged to Moon and the land in terms of "freshwater animals." They initiated the pupil into seeing the Other Worlds by the light of Moon, *qaamaneq*.

Light as a prerequisite for human life on earth was granted in exchange for the introduction of death according to the clever, efficient argument of an old woman quarreling with another woman holding the opposite opinion. In line with the Canadian Inuit story that has Raven bring the light by its cry, *qaut*, the vocal women likely remind one of crying ravens. Together daylight and death brought movement to the world, according to Arnaaluk's myth. Daylight changed the life of humans from a plantlike immobility into one of mobility needed for following game, whereas death changed humans into stars on the move, covering the entire heaven during a night. Other stories had them turn into the quickly moving Northern Lights, and the pre-humans, the fire people, *innersuit*, who continued life beneath the foreshore, reflected the light of the moon. Sun and Moon had their own pan-Inuit/Yupiit myth of origin in explanation of changes in seasons as between day and night, and, north of the Arctic Circle, between the polar night and the times of light. But apart from the sun, all these heavenly lights looked into the darkness of this world at night, the same way as the shaman looked into the Other Worlds by his interior light, his *qaamaneq*. The shaman's public demonstration of his *qaamaneq*, the ritual of *silaninneq*, was realized by an ingenious trick with the drum brought to dance on one's back. The drum was called *jajaq* like Moon (in the spirit language, *taartaq*) and was said to communicate the light of Moon, as was the same worldwide view of *sila* shown to Moon's visitor through a hole in his house. Moon was a land being, dressed in white skins—polar bear in East Greenland, albino caribou in West Greenland. Larger than life and very manlike, he nevertheless possessed no kayak, the male ticket to human marriage in Greenland. He went by sledge and hunted at breathing holes and the ice edge, and he shunned the open sea. He connoted "wild" male sexuality in multiple ways: by his incestuous character at the outset of his "career," his carnivorous dog and polar bear as the extensions of his potency, and as the engenderer of life on earth. He caused the nonmigrating seals to multiply, while keeping the sea in regular motion (i.e., alive) by his tide, which sent sea mammals and other edibles towards the land. He called forth the menstruation of young girls (however necessary, a danger to human relations with the animals), and he was liable to rape women who exposed themselves to his light (Thalbitzer 1928). He often took pity on a woman asking him for support against a violent husband, but the ensuing child, always a boy, could not be adopted by the woman's earthly husband. The husband, by forcing his wife to eat from his own catches, cut off Moon as the provider and thereby caused the boy's death. By Moon's power, Kaassassuk in Canadian Inuit variants ended up a downright wife tormentor. So, apart from the Polar Inuit, who accorded his human offspring a splendid life as a magnificent bear hunter, Moon's attempts at becoming reintegrated in human society caused only tragedy.

The sun of course looked on with even greater light, transforming night into day. To the astonishment of the Qallunaat, the sun was not given much ritual attendance, because, as stated by the Greenlanders, summer meant the disappearance of all trouble.[24] Nor was the sun a common source of *qaamaneq*. She was too difficult to approach and (as we all know) to look at directly. Only the sunburst lichen, called the "shit of the sun," was a useful source of *qaamaneq*. The immediate association goes with the glowing of the setting and rising sun, which can be looked at more directly, and with pleasure. The glowing sun simultaneously marked the transitions in time, *naaq/sila*, dusk and dawn, the time of the raven's cry for transitions between This and the Other World. Apparently then, *silaninneq*, the worldwide view obtained by means of the drum at *saqqummerneq*, was not the view of the sun in full daylight, however illuminating it was felt.

The recurring mediator of *qaamaneq*, the "freshwater bear" in the figure of a giant polar bear or dog, was, as we know, directly associated with Moon. Other initiating creatures like the highly transformative *minngua* (water beetle) and the sucking worms of a dried-up lake or bog also belonged to freshwater, but without any obvious connection with Moon. Associations in myth point to the swampy way of the dead and female reproduction—i.e., menstruation and breast-feeding.

The breastless sun did not figure as a source of babies for infertile women. Fetched (in the form of young ravens?) by male shamans from Moon, the shamans had the privilege to add to the fertilizing effect themselves. This was not considered a female shaman's task, of course, and receiving babies from Moon was not the only remedy; small white stones from heaven would suffice. Nonetheless, the symbolic connections in Greenland shamanism between the connotations of Moon—i.e., light, fertile sexuality, drums, and drumming—also fit in with the ritualized sequence of the East Greenlandic drum dance performed by ordinary people. Both men and women went through an intercourse-like procedure in motions and facial expression ending in the imitation of an orgasm. The men did so by exclamations of joy, *qatewaarteq* (at its highest pitch), repeated thrice, and the women by trembling all through the body.

24. Saladin d'Anglure (1990a) has called attention to Iglulik sun rituals, especially the ritual extinction and relighting of lamps, symbolizing the reappearing sun ending the polar night.

So, while a man on a mythic visit to Moon might obtain the interior light of vision, an ordinary woman got a child, which, because it involved social relations with Moon, put her at mortal risk. No Greenlandic story is on record about a *female* shaman visiting Moon. As a pupil, she could obtain *qaamaneq* by being devoured by the freshwater bear like any male apprentice. This light of the interior (dark) body was of course seen only by the spirits (and other shamans). Its radiance attracted spirits, and the full-fledged shaman, male or female, became the "mother" of their spirits, their source of life, in apparent equivalence with a woman made pregnant by Moon. But obtaining *qaamaneq* from Moon, directly or indirectly, did not imply similar risks as bearing his child, nor unswerving obligations.

Qaamaneq obtained by female pupils tended to fade away at the moment they became ordinary mothers. Nevertheless, talented Kaakaaq, who stopped her training at that point, later resumed shamanizing, though not with the drum but rather by lying on the platform covered up. Actually, drumming seems to have been a technique of shamanic ecstasy employed in public by male shamans alone. I have not run into any description of a *female* shaman performing with the drum, as also the ordinary women's drum dancing was comparatively more subdued.

The Mediating Twilight of Outside versus Inside

The opposing metaphors of outside versus inside, which seem to dominate the relations between This and the Other World, are mediated in many ways. In ordinary language there is no difference between being outside or inside. When outside (in *sila*), everything inside the house is *taqqama*, just as from the inside point of view, everything outside is *taqqama*. Still, the entrance tunnel was to be passed either way by crawling; and in symbolic terms the tunnel was likened to the vagina, the room to the uterus, and light dawned upon the infant at the end of the "tunnel," as vividly described in the story about Naaja's "rebirth" after being devoured by the *inua* of the inland ice (see p. 328). The symbolism was reversed in *taartaq*, in which "going out" was swapped with "going in" to refer to "dying." By analogy and logic, then, death meant a return to the interior world. The light of the women's lamps—the prime female, uterine symbol of life—told a person standing outside at night that people were alive inside. But the view through the gutskin windows was blurred either way, as was the shaman's change in view between the Worlds, one excluding the other at the moment of clarification. The light of Christianity was in certain contexts contrasted to *qaamaneq* as recapitulated below.

Pooq

The common Inuit meaning of *pooq* is a "bag," but in the spirit language, *taartaq*, it means "mother." This meaning offers the key to the analysis of the particular initiation of a shaman into an *angakkoq puulik* (shaman with a bag) by a polar bear and a walrus. The two animals play ball with the candidate across the sea. They throw him along by impaling his genitals, he loses his flesh piece by piece en route, and, when left alone for the return, he has to find the pieces and recover on the way. Redressed and returned he is protected—like some embryo by its caul—from aggressive beings. He is invisible to them, and he himself is blind in This World but can see while inside the Other, interior World. The interpretation of this apparently unique East Greenlandic tradition (though hardly created from scratch) has been my obsession for some forty years. Only gradually has the combination of symbolic analysis with facts of Inuit/Yupiit culture and environment brought about some understanding of the entire complex of the *puulik* initiation. So, I hope my attempt at communicating the results resonates with others.

Comparing the main initiations of shamans in East Greenland—one to gain *qaamaneq* in solitude on the land, the other to gain *pooq* across the sea in public—the spatial oppositions are obvious, but they are not reflected in opposed *inuat*. The private initiation is closely connected with the moon and takes place in summer, but the public one, a New Year or spring ritual, is not so directly linked with Sea Woman. Both the "freshwater bear" called forth in summer on the land and the ritual obtainment of worldwide vision at *saqqummerneq* at winter solstice relate to Moon. Sea Woman plays no part in the initiation to an *angakkoq puulik*, but in a solitary statement from the southern tradition, passing by her dog unhurt is said to be a prerequisite. Perhaps it is more correct to say "unseen," because protection in the form of invisibility is the "gain" of this initiation. Still, the *puulik* animals, polar bear and walrus, did not live with Sea Woman. Trusting the East Greenlandic tradition, they lived in their own country beyond the Milky Way, and to this place they most probably return in the southern tradition about Tuttu's Wife, whom they for no explicit reason leave alone, abruptly, at the moment the sea ice breaks by the springtime storm. At this same point in the year, the *Aassuutit*, the twin stars of the New Year, also disappear from view. Along this train of thought, the two animals of the *puulik* initiation can be identified with the *Aassuutit*,[25] which mark the hardest time of the year. By their appearance around winter solstice and disappearance with the sun's takeover of their rising point on the horizon, they mark the period in which the starvation threat increases with a prolonged winter. Adding credence to this interpretation, the *puulik* candidate saw them approach as flames from the horizon, that is, as the *inuat* of stars. The spirit who calls out "*ululoo*" at the end of a successful *puulik* initiation can be added to these star animals. It arrives from beyond the horizon and can, to my best understanding, be recognized as the male mating call of the bearded seal. The impetus to seek support for this identification came from my analysis of "Tunutoorajik." This story, which is literally "dressed" in differing *puuat* (sing. *pooq*) covers, adds perfect sense to the import of this triumvirate for a reconstruction of the worldview under the impact of mission and colonial trade. It situates the bearded seal, the deliverer of material for the *pooq*-like gutskin anorak, the *ikiaq*, in the middle of winter beyond the distant ice edge, where it is hunted by Ittuku for its guts alone. Polar bears arrive next, followed by walrus, both passing by in hordes, which demand a propping up of Ittuku's house (alias the world). We are at the turn of the year now: winter solstice or New Year, or maybe at the dangerous time of spring, when, as stressed above, a too-heavy snowfall would turn the earth around.

The addition of the midwinter bearded seal to the *puulik* complex involves another "light": the New Year ritual bogey of this animal, called *Innersuaq*, the "big light," in both Greenland and Southwest Alaska. This figure either incorporates a bearded seal or is armed with a club or whip of a whole bearded seal. Among the 19th-century Iglulingmiut, this bogey's name was *Anautalik* ("with a club"). His namesake, mentioned by F. G. Lyon (1824), may have been a bogey as well, because he has a single arm with a big polar-bear-skin mitten, which seems to be his weapon (*anautaq*). Curiously, Lyon's informants positioned *Anautalik* as the father of Sea Woman. He dwells in a house guarded by

25. Their probable identification with *Nalikkatteeq* belongs in the context of the ritual punishment for smiling.

hordes of aggressive polar bears and walruses (*ibid.*), but in more recent sources he found himself in his daughter's house, guarded by her dog. Covered by his skin shroud, *Anautalik*, most likely inspired by the early Catholic mission, had become a purgatory devil. Apart from Polar Inuit Amaunalik's Baffin Island version of the myth, where he tickles fake shamans visiting Sea Woman to the point of dying, there is no parallel to this transformation to be found in Greenland. Here, a particular helping spirit, *toornaarsuk*, was chosen by the missionaries in translation for the Devil, *Toornaarsuk*, who came to preside in hell. Sexual connotations also cling to the pre-Christian bogey. At the Bladder Feast on Nunivak, one bearded seal bogey pretended to eat the small children, and then another tickled the women in the tunnel. Two Greenland variants have mussels originating from the genitals of a woman. She either slides them off on the back of the killed bogey lying in the tunnel in her attempt to get out, or she cuts them off after the kill, sliding her buttocks along the killed bogey (Sonne 2005: ID 1334, 660). Similarly, among the Eastern Inuit generally, other armed figures tickled the laughing muscles of adults by their frivolous acting. Those who gave in to laughter were killed in myth and either excluded or severely beaten in ritual.

Returning to Lyon's *Anautalik*, I take this figure's guard of polar bear and walrus to be as significant as was the taboo on Iglulik women against eating any meat from these animals at the appearance of the New Year twin stars, which in addition marked the arrival of the bearded seal to the island of Iglulik. The heavenly position of the polar bear-*cum*-walrus is further emphasized by the heavenly afterlife granted to not only the Iglulik hunters killed by either of the animals but also the *puulik* shamans in early-18th-century South Greenland. References to the realm below—i.e., to Sea Woman—are only made in Greenland by having Tuttu's Wife in the southern *puulik* tradition be taken most of the way across the sea to her land by the cooperating polar bear and walrus. But neither they nor the fulmar who takes her close to the land of Sea Woman belong in the latter's realm. So, "light" as the prerequisite for the shaman to see the Other World may be the reason why the two main initiations at Ammassalik—one of the land, the other across the sea—are both associated with lights of heaven, the former with Moon and the latter with *Aassuutit*. They are opposed, but not like heaven versus the realm below sea, or like Moon versus Sea Woman. They are opposed as enemies but act as mediators in temporary cooperation when (like the Northern Lights) they play ball with the *puulik* candidate across the sea. So, from a prehistorical point of view, a hypothetical explanation could be provided, in that *pooq* objects and ideas about (urine) bladders and gut clothing had a much wider extension than Sea Woman. Although her prototype may have been part of the early Thule culture, as recognized in the submarine provider of food, *Ni-givik* at Tigara (Northwest Alaska), and for that matter the mistress of the tide, "the old woman below" of the Tlingit, the development of her well-known complex apparently took place in Canada. From there it was brought to Greenland, where she kept her stronghold primarily in the south.

Gut clothing was pan-Inuit/Yupiit. It served as protection in daily life as in ritual; it was the festive dress, *kamleika*, of the Pacific Yupiit and the dress of the shaman all along the Alaska coast to the north. On Nunivak Island, the shaman dressed in several gutskin parkas for his travel downwards through the sea. In northeastern Asia it was the dress of the walrus master Keret'kun, his wife, and all participants in his annual feast, and the St. Lawrence Islanders produced it for sale in the heyday of Native intercontinental trade. A natural association obtains between gutskin and water, be it rain, the salty sea, or both combined when hunting at sea. The *puulik* initiation is also a ritual of traveling the sea. Thus, the similar waterproof *ikiaq* could have been the right outfit for shamans visiting the Other World(s) of the sea in Greenland and Inuit Canada, but it is only encountered on record for this use in East Greenland. Undoubtedly, the particularly humid climate of East Greenland promoted the use of the *ikiaq*. Nevertheless, the *pooq* connotations are clearly recognized in the gutlike tube through which the great Iglulik shaman glided at high speed right to Sea Woman's house. This tube calls to my mind the bearded seal guts encountered by Kivioq at the navel of the sea, which I understand to be the umbilical cord of the mother house (*pooq*) of the sea mammals. In relation to *sila*, *pooq* ("mother" in *taartaq*) applies to *silaluppoq*, meaning rainy or bad weather of low visibility, and the interior of the sea.

Bearded Seal as a Pooq *Animal*

In Greenland, babies born in cauls and who secure the caul as an amulet retained their *pooq* protection of invisibility to aggressive beings throughout their lives. Otherwise the predominant deliverer of *puuat*, the bearded seal, took up a prominent position among both Inuit and Yupiit. Walrus guts were preferred in some places, but the bearded seal is recognized as the first to arrive in spring (or at New Year at Iglulik) and is treated accordingly, in Southwest Alaska by an elaborate kayak launching ritual and at Ammassalik by attracting people from all over the region for the plundering of its meat. In all variants of the myth told from Southwest Alaska to Ammassalik, the bearded seal bogey is attracted by the noise made by children left alone and having fun. Most frequently, the children are killed, and the bogey is then killed in revenge by the adults, who know how to attract the figure by making noise. Mussels, as we know, owe their origin to the woman whose genitals touched the bearded seal bogey (I shall leave further grim associations to the reader). In the Nunivak Bladder Feast the male bearded seal figure tickled the women, and then the female pretended to eat the children; both events happened in the tunnel. Similarly, the (masked) *uaajeertoq* player at New Year who invited any woman who pleased to choose him for the wife exchange drew heavily on the sexual connotations of bearded seal (see p. 360). These agreements in the sexual connotations of bearded seal ritual and myth between Ammassalik and Nunivak have led me to identify the male part of the couple leading the Iglulik paring off for the wife exchange. Like the inviting *uaajeertoq* player he, besides his false *beard*, is fit out with a big false penis and "teaser."

On a more abstract level, both the bogey and the teasing couple belong to the broad type of armed ritual figures who are most frequently in action at Inuit/Yupiit New Year feasts; they inspire fear among children and (masochistic) sexual appetites among the adults.

Acculturating Puuat

The close connection between light and view/vision is not limited to the Inuit, and far from confined to cultures of small-scale societies. Christianity is bathed in life- and knowledge-giving symbolism of light, which came to outshine, or rather eclipse, *qaamaneq*. Many newly converted Greenlanders blankly accepted the missionaries' saying that they had lived in the darkness of complete ignorance until baptism. This may be one reason, I guess, why conversions of shamans were not associated with the *qaamaneq* of Moon, as Moon himself, bereaved by Christianity of his punitive aspects, became in more recent variants a laughingstock. Among the described examples of conversions, three historical stories point to the *puulik* ritual of becoming invisible to aggressive beings. Imaneq exchanged his *qaamaneq* for the light of Christianity by a *puulik*-like initiation performed by the smiling giant of the sea, who cut him up into pieces. He was then reassembled by his deceased grandparents and protected on the return trip by his *pooq*, the enlightened hunting bladder covering his head (see front cover and endsheets). Pruutas preferred conversion to the pains awaiting him in case he gave in to the approaching polar bear and walrus, and Missuarniannga, who most probably performed this ritual shortly before enrolling in the course for baptism, may thereby have armed himself against the anticipated attacks by his helping spirits.[26] Apparently no public ritual except baptism itself was created for quitting one's helping spirits, and in fact, some shamans continued to perform without the ministers' knowledge.

The most drastic acculturative change in the meaning of *pooq* is made by the splendid storyteller and catechist Aron, who takes the matter into his own hands. He turns the entire symbolism of *pooq* around in his story "Qivaaqiarsuk." Here, its meaning of invisibility transforms into the meaning of the Christian lodestar. By hitting the iceberg with the extremely white stomach *pooq* of his shamanic wife, Qivaaqiarsuk calls up and confronts various *innersuit*-like beings with his superiority. The long-range shining light of his invincible gutskin anorak leads the spirit people of Uummannaq back home to the island deep in the fjord, where the Moravians had established their last mission in the region. The third light, the shining Kingittorsuaq, dressed in eternal snow, leads the seafarers to Moravian Noorliit at Nuuk. Its snow stems from Qivaaqiarsuk's almost inexhaustible urine bladder, the traditional Inuit "soap" and tanning agent of an interior *pooq*. Urine was used to scare away spirits and added to the durability of skins; it is turned into the light of Christianity by Aron's trickster figure. It operates at the liminal tricksteresque T-point "where are nested the relations between the functional needs of older, but superseded order and those of a newer more inclusive order" (Spinks 1991: 15). Furthermore, unlike other tricksters, Qivaaqiarsuk never fails. Victoriously he sets the new order. Aron, in addition to his extraordinary talent in literacy, as greatly emphasized by Kirsten Thisted (1999), was also a genius in turning traditional symbols into new ones while retaining the meanings of both. His use of stones in the story about Kaassassuk similarly draws on the entire view of a rocking but supported world in his successful attempt to put the modern self-reflective human at the center of the new world.

Inuit/Yupiit Perspectivism Reconsidered

Cover

The multifaceted protective *puuat*, natural or manufactured (be they of objects, embryos, humans, animals, the land, the sea, breath, or some *inuat* and spirits), offer fascinating tools for analyzing Inuit ways of distinguishing differences by means of a common concept. Admittedly, I am the one who recognized *pooq* as a concept, or better metaphor, to be identified everywhere, not the Inuit. Numerous covers not called *pooq* in Greenlandic I recognized as *puuat*, either due to their equivalent spirit word or in the way they looked and functioned. On these premises, the Inuit can be seen to have employed *puuat* pervasively for making sense of their world, as expressed in their stories, masks,

---

26. Schjødt's hypothesis about initiations includes the maintenance that the transformation is in principle irreversible (1986: 92). If so, conversion by baptism in Greenland follows another principle.

rituals, clothing, and drawings. *Pooq* has also shown its usefulness ("Tunutoorajik," "Qivaaqiarsuk") in the remaking of cosmology. But do the "essences" follow suit? Are we still talking about multinaturalism by widening the restricted field of Viveiros de Castro's faunal species to include all the differentiating *puuat* of the entire world(s)? Apparently we are not. First, among the Eastern Inuit, not all "live interiors" of differing *puuat* were imagined as figures, let alone figures of a human shape.[27] They may have been so among the Yupiit, but their multitude of humanlike figures in masks, paintings, and stories differed mutually and were still nonhumans in relation to genuine humans as stressed by Fienup-Riordan (1994: chapter 2). Among the Greenlanders, the air of a sealer's hunting bladder, for instance, which by analogy is identified with the "lives" of both weather (e.g., thunder) and the pregnant uterus of his wife, constitutes a relationship between *puuat* among which the pregnant woman is *the very pooq* in *taartaq*. Her fetus is a real, invisible humanlike figure; in myth, thunder is visualized as two humanlike figures, stark naked according to Kaarali (Geertsen 1990: 67), but not active in this context. Nor so the other figures of *sila* in the meaning of weather. Air of the inflated bladder derives from the hunter's breath, *anerneq*, which, on par with the *tarneq* ("soul") in other variants of "the transmigrating soul" story, is the part of a deceased human who takes up residence in one natural species after another. First and foremost, however, in the case that essences appear in human shape, they differ in consonance with their respective *puuat*. Furthermore, they also differ from adult humans. Both humans and humanlike animals undress when entering their dwelling, but adult humans remain partly clothed. They keep their short *naatsit* (underwear) on, the men letting theirs hang low on the back, leaving the anus—the way of the soul (and spirits)—uncovered. According to Kaarali's drawings, the performing shaman also keeps his *naatsit* on.[28] He even travels the Other Worlds in *naatsit*. So why did Ajijak undress completely for his ritual of transformations, (pp. 320f) first into a reprimanding helping spirit and next into his polar bear? I propose that it is because these transformations demanded a loss and regaining of his flesh. Similarly, the dismembering and reassembling of his wife presupposed nudity. Comparable to the symbolism of the death and revival of the pupil who lost his flesh to the freshwater bear, the pupil woke up reincarnated but stark naked like a newborn baby. In other situations, apart from some enigmatic naked *uaajeertoq* figures, nudity of an adult human signaled loss of *sila* or insanity, and this was a dangerous state to be in outside of rituals. In regard to helping spirits present on indoor visits to humans, they all appear naked in Kaarali's drawings. But they differ by deviant body sizes and/or parts, because, of course, they were recognized by their individual powers, character, voice, and other characteristics during performances. In short, adult humans wear *naatsit*, human figures of animals, etc. do not.

So, although in Greenland the human figure is indeed the model of visualizing the otherworldly life of some animals (polar bear, walrus, fox, dog), birds (many species), some vermin, and spirits, they do not appear as congruent lookalikes.[29] They differ as much as do their covers or their *puuat*.

---

27. Weyer makes the same point in treating *inua* as the possessive form of *inuk*, meaning human being, despite the nonhuman figure of most *inuat*: "The everyday connotation of the word *inua*, however, is not to be taken too strictly from its literal meaning. Perhaps the root word might better be translated 'individual', rather than 'man' or 'person'" (Weyer 1932: 299).

28. As for female shamans lying covered up on the platform, I do not know. Kaarali's drawing of a covered-up shaman shows a man wearing only *naatsit* the men's way (Thalbitzer 1941: 711).

29. Birds frequently reveal their humanlike nature by the ability to speak (*taartaq*), and less often by a humanlike

They are distinguished by their habits, culture, and personalities, be they faunal or spirit species. And, as subjects, they need their *puuat* in order to realize their intentions of getting food, or simply for moving about outdoors.

Few land spirits are credited an origin story like the *innersuit*, the prehumans, who ended up beneath the foreshore and skerries at the primordial turning around of the earth. Nor do such spirits appear among the animals in human shape at the beginning of time, when, as phrased by Naalungiaq, animals and humans did not differ but spoke the same language and could change from one to the other at will. Still, "*they may have had different habits*." Perhaps it takes a scholarly trained philosopher to retain an idea of humanlike shape bereft of any differentiating connotations. Thus, for instance, why could the humans and animals change from one to the other at will, if they did not differ? An Alaska version of the myth offers a sensible answer:

> in early days all animate beings had a dual existence, becoming at will either like men or taking *the animal forms they now wear*. In those early days there were but few people; if an animal wished to assume its human form, the forearm, wing or other limb was raised, the muzzle or beak was pushed out as if it were a mask, and the creature became manlike in form and features. It is believed that many animals still possess this power. The manlike form thus appearing is called the *inua* and is supposed to represent the thinking part of the creature and at death becomes its shade. (Nelson 1899: 394, emphasis BS)

The focus of this recollection is exclusively on the animals, differentiated as they already are from the early days by their removable "masks" (put on by humans representing them at rituals), but all with the faculty to think as expressed by their humanlike bodies. Fienup-Riordan emphasizes this thinking part of animals, which demands the respect regulated by the rules of human conduct. At the same time, she also points to the differentiation by both species and individuals between the humanlike bodies of animals as figured out in myth and ritual. They turn out to differ individually as much as humans do, and by the same moral characters (Fienup-Riordan 1994: 59–61). My examination of their masks in the first chapter arrived at a similar conclusion.

In comparison, because they wore manufactured clothes, spirits were more humanlike than animals. Their clothes were human in style and design according to Kaarali's drawings. Nevertheless, when it came out that the young *innersuit* woman offered in marriage to the shaman Naaja did not know how to sew correct human clothing, this irreparable defect settled the matter. The rule of dyadic relations with the "Others" got the upper hand. Most land spirits lived like humans in households of several generations. They each made a living by their species's more or less peculiar way of hunting using awkward tools. In contrast, the *innersuit* underneath foreshore and skerries, who shunned everything of the land, were magnificent sealers. They were equipped like human kayakers except for the very short hind part of their kayaks, which prevented them from turning around if they capsized. To repeat: perfect balance in body was a human prerogative.

---

figure, whereas the differing characteristics of the humanlike land spirits, such the dwarves and giants of the land as well as the pre-human *innersuit*, point to bird species. However, they do not appear in the plumage of birds, and seem to have been dressed more or less like humans.

In relation to life and death, animals were more like humans than spirits. The animals gave birth, grew in size and competence, and aged; when killed by humans, the latter saw to their reincarnation in ways resembling the burial and mourning rites of human relatives. The spirits and deceased humans did not reproduce, grow, age, and die, *in principle* (see again Oosten & Laugrand 2004–5). Like folktale types and comic-strip figures, they did not undergo any development. Nevertheless, when attached to a human shaman as helping spirits, their lives were dependent on his public performances, which permitted them, one at a time, to enter his body and become reenlivened by gaining some of his interior warmth. The presumably static lives of spirits were also a challenge to the imagination in storytelling as in practical thinking. You may remember this from the section on Kaassassuk, a particular stone-handling giant of the inland who multiplied beyond any thinkable measure (see p. 105).[30] The human shaman Taatsiarsuaq was kidnapped by *innersuit* in order to have him cure a young *innersuaq* who, having lost its hunting bladder, was on the point of dying (Sonne 2005: ID 1304, 1598). On the whole, trusting acculturated Aqajaq, the "rules" of the *innersuit* were contrary to humans', because they mourned only as long as a relative was dying but never after the death (ID 1598). In other words, *innersuit* were not exempt from dying, and the symbol of a human hunter's life, his hunting bladder, was apparently also in force among the *innersuit*. Spirits could definitely also be killed for good by other spirits, in that one of Missuarniannga's helping spirits had lost five sons that way. The medium-size giant, Uppiinnguaq, a helping spirit of Naaja, was killed by another helper among his spirits. Uppiinnguaq was buried the ordinary human way but revived by his father, who sang daily at his grave. During performances a *toornaarsuk* could be killed by a fart. The eternal life accorded the Devil/*Toornaarsuk* by the missionaries, would, if true, demand unthinkable powers, the Greenlanders pondered. Some dwarves possessed a somersaulting method of rejuvenation that could be repeated five times, but not six. And the dwarfish size of (human) Peter Ranthol was explained by his origin as a spirit dwarf. Sold by his biological father to a human shaman, he entered the womb of the shaman's wife. Thus he was born a human, but as he was still a dwarf in size, he was even credited a memory about the migration history of his ancestors. Indeed, eternal and eventless—that is, ahistorical—life exists only in the abstract, outside stories. Eternal life in the Other Worlds granted to humans by the Christian missionaries made the shamans go verify these claims on the contrasts between the lives in hell and heaven. The continuous happiness of the Christian heaven preached by the missionaries was likened to the euphoria of song duels by the Greenlanders, with one couple replacing the next continuously. These, of course, were repetitions that brought about no change. The sufferings of hell, however, could still be remedied by the shaman Maratsi on the verge of his baptism. His removal of the discomforts of individuals even brought about a significant *change*, in that from then on the dead dwelling down there could reunite with their relatives. Baptism was considered the key to reunion after death, a desired comfort partly overshadowed by the existence of two realms of death cutting one off eternally from some relatives. A solution to this problem has been mentioned several times above (e.g., pp. 167, 384). In principle this idea could not be new, but in pre-Christian practice, ideas of afterlife used to dominate less than a rebirth by being named (see also Sonne 2000a).

30. Since Inuit recognized that stones erode over time, in this case erosion seems to be explained by birth symbolism.

Essences

Mentally, all "Others" were sentient beings, capable not only of thinking but also of speaking, and their language, *taartaq*, is perhaps a remnant of Thule culture heritage, brought along by the Inuit of Canada and Greenland from the culture's origin in North Alaska. *Taartaq* presupposes a common perspective of all Others. They do not differ "multinaturally" as one could expect from the theory proposed by Viveiros de Castro. The salient opposition at work in *taartaq*, "belonging to darkness," is inside versus outside. From a human point of view, the "Others" dwell inside, in darkness—i.e., in invisibility. Their primary focus is on the interior throbbing life of the whole bodylike world (see Therrien 1987). Animals are differentiated by *their way of movement* in This World, not explicitly by their *puuat*, nor for that matter by peculiarities in their humanlike bodies. *Inua*, defined as a humanlike being by Victor and Robert-Lamblin, is not called *inua* in *taartaq*. It is called *taarda* and, in the meaning of a helping spirit, *tittarti* (Victor & Robert-Lamblin 1989–93, II: 255). So, their relations with humans are in focus. Turning to myth, some of the beings called *inuat* in ordinary language used to be ordinary human men or women who ended up in the Other World and retained their sexual identity. In myth, their humanlike but differing appearances by sex are expounded in detail. In *taartaq*, human men and women, the moon, and his sister, the sun, are all identified by their lack or possession of male genitals. Similarly, although no myth of origin was told, the four winds and the seasons were paired off by these terms as well. Among the other mythic *inuat*, some (but not every) *inua* are imagined in human shape, although "its human being" is the most common translation into Western languages. My proposed translations, "its life" or "its personality," pay regard to differentiations between *inuat*. And they allow for analysis of the perceptions behind its way of life. Take the example of the ringing sound of a cracking iceberg, transformed into a humanlike man. With his cracks and furrows all over his face, he was disliked beyond tolerance by his human mother-in-law. He left his pregnant human wife, whose son became an unsurpassed hunter of polar bears. In my understanding, icebergs, the polar bear's hunting ground, express their "life," "movements," by cracking sounds. They are "born," loudly, from the calving inland ice, and they change form by turning around with a deep sigh, or roar by breaking utterly asunder. Having a deep draft, in myth they connect with the lower world of *innersuit* and bring seals on its side when summoned by the shaman. This is how I understand *inua* as the personality (or characteristic way of life) of a being, be that of a species, an object, a sound, a phenomenon. Its eventual humanlike figure is marked by its character, and its characteristics, in this case associated with sealing, are inherited by its human son. All this goes to say that the definition of the cover, *pooq*, and the essence or spiritual body appear to be one and the same.

Nevertheless, the principle of an undifferentiated essence makes sense in some specific Inuit contexts. Animals and humans shared the same kind of life at birth and were accorded the same kind of a soul, *tarneq*; it was naming that made all the difference. As long as a newborn baby remained unnamed, it was not a social being and could be disposed of without danger of retaliation. Born in secrecy, however, such an exposed baby would turn into an *anngiaq*, who would kill its mother's male relatives. Similarly, deceased humans and killed animals, which were not attended to by the death rites and taboos in force, would transform into terrifying ghosts and monsters. The name(s) constituted the human baby's social identity in relation to both live and deceased relatives (as stressed in Oosten & Laugrand 2004–5). However, as soon as individual identity comes in, it remains and dominates the thoughts about essences. Navagiaq, for instance, who "sought a mother" in one animal species after another, came, from inside their bodies, to know the species's way of living. But he lost neither identity nor memory, and he did not want to stay put until he had gotten inside a human female body, been born, and received back his former human name. Eventually satisfied by regaining himself by way of his name, he stopped crying. "Searching for a mother" was also (believed to be) the possible practice of an unhappy deceased young person, who took possession of an ordinary live human body, preferably a woman. The intruder made her "hostess" sick until fed through her mouth by its parents, who were still alive. No doubt can be raised about the individual and social identity of that possessing "essence." Helping spirits, as we know, sought mothers as well. Their shaman, pressing down and under his breath, let them have his body one by one. Descended down under, however, he did not lose himself. Quite able to follow the happenings above in darkness, and sometimes seeing his interest in meddling, he ascended into his body and took over for a comment or two. Similarly, while traveling in spirit, the shaman lost none of his bodily senses, nor his mind and identity. Deceased humans, whether visited, called individually to the grave, or employed as helping spirits, were each recognizable in their immaterial appearances. All in all, immaculate essences are as hard to find as undifferentiated *puuat*, whereas, trusting *taartaq*, mutually differing perspectives are not put into words by the "Others." Maybe the latter did not bother, or better the Inuit did not insofar as it is their perspective on the "Others'" perspectives that find expression in *taartaq*.

Nonetheless, nonhumans' differing points of view did obtain in myth, where hunting and eating habits come to the fore. Some of these coincide with human habits and some do not; degrees of difference prevail. Thus, the polar bear, which hunts seals and hibernates in igloo-like dens, is considered by the Inuit to be very much like a human. Its flayed body looks like a copy. The gull, who knows how to serve a human visitor some delicious fish, seems quite close as well. But raven, which eats feces and sees it as the delicious loin of a woman, would be a cannibal in human terms. He arouses curiosity—there must be a reason why he sees excrement as the loin part of a woman and not of a man, or any other piece of meat. The explanation is not far-fetched because both raven and the loin part of a catch (the *kujak*) have sexual connotations in Greenland. Raven is accorded fertile power, just as a man and a woman sharing *kujak* at a meal signal a mutual desire.[31] The reason why raven sees twigs as dried capelins may have similar explanations that currently escape me, just as I do not know the probable rituals, sayings, or other connotations that might make the Amerindian jaguar see human blood as beer. Or, in other words, granted the compartments of multinaturalism did work, they make little sense per se in attempts at coming to grips with the symbolic meanings of the Inuit worldview. For my part the analysis of the human perspective of the perspectives of the "Others" yields more satisfying results.

31. I once happened to hear this saying in Greenland about such a couple.

■ ■ ■

Coda

Why and how did Greenlandic stories, ideas, rituals, sayings, etc. make sense within their own culture or worldview? The above analyses of Greenlandic/Inuit symbolism offer a great number of the answers I have been looking for since my early academic years, when the theories I was taught proved insufficient—that is, save those about coherences between ritual and myth. To take one instance, attention to the closing *ululoo* call of the successful *puulik* initiation asked for further investigations, which made my vague hypothesis of bearded seal as the third animal of the complex far more likely. Otherwise theories of body symbolism, together with those of natural and social environment, have yielded satisfying answers, and the theories of "new animism" have been a welcome challenge. The Anthropological Field Study method (AFS), which I recognized as similar to my own framed by cultural history, has now and then been widened beyond the Thule culture boundaries for inspiration. Looking to the world tree of Siberian people, for instance, sharpened my focus on the pillars upholding the Inuit world, and it added sense to the entire complex of New Year ceremonies. A fortuitous reading of the Tlingit raven myth about the tide drew my full attention to rituals at spring tide and, applied as a theory, it suddenly had the pieces of the puzzle, my hypothesis of balance, fall into place.

Stories vary and change according to multifarious factors of which several are out of scope, because the stories used are written texts, exclusively. No factors of communication with listeners, the occasion for telling the story, etc. could be considered (see above p. 16, note 15). The quality of a text has been considered, of course, but without many attempts at making explicit the vast amount of impacts from the way of recording, the competence of the teller, of the collector, etc. Solid competence in writing offers the author a greater liberty in my definition of mythopoetics: the way of making changes according to context, message, and/or changes in worldview. Aron is a strong case in point, and a patient, fine storyteller like Kristian—who let Rink take down his apparently complete stories word for word—speaks to the authenticity of oral storytelling. Amos Daniel writes at length, but unstructured. He combines well-known episodes in idiosyncratic ways, not worth the trouble to follow. Kaarali Andreassen, competent in literacy and conscious about his mission of presenting the traditions of his culture to educated people, Greenlanders and Danes, let people tell their stories, and he may have made his own mix of the variants. The writings by Kaarali published by Otto Rosing in Greenlandic are, as are the tape recordings made by Jens Rosing in Ammassalik in 1961–62, extremely well translated into Danish by Jens Rosing. Their sympathetic understanding has opened up to me the genius, thrill, and consequently the frame of reference of several pretty staged and performed séances.

My till-now secret ambition—to come up with a theory of mythopoetics regarding impacts from changes in worldview—has not been achieved. Key symbols are obvious vehicles. Perhaps they could be rephrased in the way of Lakoff and Turner (1989) into basic metaphors like "Life is an inflated bladder," or "Dress (cover, *pooq*) shows one's protected identity," or "Oscillating balance makes the world go round." Or definitely: "Seeing (by means of light) is knowledge." Still, the way a key symbol may simultaneously change and retain its meaning—and thus reveal the very process of change—makes Spink's tricksteresque T-point come to the fore: "where are nested the relations between the functional needs of older, but superseded order and those of a newer more inclusive order." Or as phrased by Connerton: "the present derives its meaning as a departure from earlier ways, but the latter are then dialectically implicated in the very idea of the new." The first metaphor about the inflated bladder has most probably lost its tricksteresque value with the decline in kayak hunting. The second (dress) and the third (balance) may still be at work. Research by fieldwork might reveal this.

■ ■ ■

Reference List

Atuagagdliutit (Greenlandic newspaper since 1861). http://www.aviisitoqqat.gl/listing_init.jsp?lang=da
KRH Knud Rasmussens Arkiv, (Archives of Knud Rasmussen) Hundested.
NKS *Ny Kongelig Samling.* Det kongelige Bibliotek (Royal Library), København.

Adams, Barbara
1994 Perceptions of Time. In Tim Ingold (ed.), *Companion Encyclopedia of Anthropology.* London and New York: Routledge.

Aitchison, Jean
2000 [1996] *The Seeds of Speech, Language Origin and Evolution.* Cambridge: Cambridge University Press.

Andreassen, Kârale
1961 En fangstrejse til omegnen af »Kialéq« (Skrækkens Bugt) i 1880'erne. Edited by Johannes Balle. *Tidsskriftet Grønland,* Årg. 1961, No. 4.

Anisimov, A. F.
1963 Cosmological Concepts of the Peoples of the North. In Henry N. Michael (ed.), *Studies in Siberian Shamanism.* Arctic Institute of North America, Anthropology of the North, Translations from Russian Sources, No. 4, University of Toronto Press.

Appelt, M., H. C. Gulløv, and H. Kapel
1998 De sidste palæoeskimoer i Grønland. Nyt lys over den gådefulde Dorsetkultur. *Nationalmuseets Arbejdsmark*: 11–26.

Appelt, Martin, and Hans Christian Gulløv
2009 *Tunit, Norsemen and Inuit in Thirteenth-Century Northwest Greenland: Dorset between the Devil and the Deep Blue Sea.* In Herbert Maschner, Owen Mason, and Robert McGhee (eds.), *The Northern World AD 900–1400.* Salt Lake City: University of Utah Press, 300–20.

Arneborg, Jette

1991 *Kulturmødet mellem nordboer og eskimoer: En kritisk analyse af kilderne til kulturmødet mellem nordboere og eskimoer. Vurderet i norrønt perspektiv.* Unpublished PhD thesis.

1996 Exchanges between Norsemen and Eskimos in Greenland. *Cultural and Social Research in Greenland, 95/96: Essays in Honour of Robert Petersen.* Nuuk: Ilisimatusarfik/Atuakkiorfik.

1997 Cultural Borders, Reflections on Norse-Eskimo Interaction, Fifty Years of Arctic Research, Anthropological Studies from Greenland to Siberia. Edited by R. Gilberg and H. C. Gulløv. *Ethnographical Series* 18, National Museum of Denmark.

Arneborg, J., N. Lynnerup, and J. Heinemeier

2012 Human Diet and Subsistence Patterns in Norse Greenland A.D. c. 980–A.D. c. 1450: Archaeological Interpretations. *Journal of the North Atlantic* Special Volume 3: 119–33.

Arnfred, Signe

1991 Kvinder, mænd, arbejde og seksualitet. In Lise Skifte and Marianne Lykke Thomsen (eds.), *Kvinder i Grønland.* Nuuk: Atuakkiorfik, 82–125.

Asmussen, J. P., and J. Læssøe (eds.)

1968 *Illustreret Religionshistorie*, I. København: Gad.

Atkinson, Jane Monnig

1992 Shamanism Today. *Annual Review of Anthropology* 21: 307–30.

Bak, Ove

1977 *Kujavarsiks rejse til månen Eventyr fra Grønland.* København: Hernov.

1979 *Troldbjørnen. Også isbjørne har en sjæl.* København: Hernov.

Balikci, Asen

1970 *The Netsilik Eskimo.* New York: The Natural History Press.

Barth, Fredrik

1995 [1987] *Cosmologies in the Making: A Generative Approach to Cultural Variation in Inner New Guinea.* Cambridge: Cambridge University Press.

Basso, Keith H.

1990 *Western Apache Language and Culture. Essays in Linguistic Anthropology.* Tuscon: University of Arizona Press, ch. 4 and 6.

Bauman, Richard, and Charles L. Briggs

1990 Poetics and Performance as Critical Perspectives on Language and Social Life. *Annual Review of Anthropology* 19: 59–88.

Bertelsen, A.

1914 Folkemedicin i Grønland. *Det grønlandske Selskabs Aarsskrift,* 22–57.

Berthelsen, Christian, and Per Langgård

1983 *Grønlandsk Litteratur. Kommenteret antologi.* Centrum.

Berthelsen, C., F. Nielsen, B. Jacobsen, R. Petersen, I. Kleivan, and J. Rischel

1990 *Oqaatsit, Kalaallisuumiit Qallunaatuumut. Grønlandsk Dansk Ordbog.* Nuuk: Attuakkiorfik.

Biesele, Megan

1986 How Hunter-Gatherers' Stories 'Make Sense.' *Cultural Anthropology* 1(2): 157–70.

Bilby, Julian
1923 *Among Unknown Eskimos*. London: Seeley Service and Co.

Birket-Smith, Kaj
1924 The Ethnography of the Egedesminde District. *Meddelelser om Grønland,* 66.
1953 The Chugach Eskimo. *Nationalmuseets Skrifter. Etnografisk Række* VI. København.
1959 [1936] *The Eskimos*. Rev. ed. Translated by W. E. Calvert, foreword by C. Daryll Forde. London: Methuen.
1961 *Eskimoerne*. København: Rhodos; Gyldendal, Copenhagen.

Blaisel, Xavier, and Jaypetee Arnakak
1993 Trajet rituel: du harponnage à la naissance dans le mythe d'Arnagtaaqtuq. *Études/Inuit/Studies* 17(1): 15–46.

Blaisel, Xavier, and J. Oosten
1997 La logique des échanges des fêtes d'hiver inuit. *Anthropologie et Societés* 21(2–3): 19–44.

Bloch, Maurice
1992 *Prey into hunter. The politics of religious experience.* Cambridge: Cambridge University Press.

Boas, Franz
1901–7 The Eskimo of Baffin Land and Hudson Bay, I–II. *Bulletin of the American Museum of Natural History,* 15. New York.
1964 [1888] *The Central Eskimo.* Introduction by Henry B. Collings. Lincoln: University of Nebraska Press.

Boddy, Janice
1994 Spirit Possession Revisited: Beyond Instrumentality. *Annual Review of Anthropology* 23: 407–34.

Bodenhorn, Barbara
1990 I'm Not the Great Hunter, My Wife Is: Iñupiat and Anthropology, Models of Gender. *Études/Inuit/Studies* 14(1–2): 55–74.
2000 It's good to know who your relatives are but we were taught to share with everybody: Shares and sharing among Iñupiaq households. In G.W. Wenzel, G. Hovelsrud-Broda, and N. Kishigami (eds), *The Social Economy of Sharing: Resource Allocation and Modern Hunter-Gatherers, Senri Ethnological Studies.* Osaka: National Museum of Ethnology, 53: 27–60.

Bogoras, V.G.
1907 *The Chukchee,* II, Religion. Jesup North Pacific Expedition VII. New York: Leiden.

Born, E. W., and A. Rosing-Arvid
1989 Isbjørnen (Ursus maritimus) i Grønland: En oversigt. *Grønlands Hjemmestyre, Miljø- og Naturforvaltning.* Teknisk Rapport No. 8 (November).

Bourdieu, Pierre
1972 *Esquisse d'une théorie de la practique, précédé de trois études d'ethnologie kabyle.* Librairie Droz.
1980 *Les sens practique.* Paris: Minuit.
1990a [1977] *Outline of a Theory of Practice.* Cambridge: Cambridge University Press.
1990b *The Logic of Practice.* Cambridge: Polity Press.

Bourguignon, Erika (ed.)
1973 *Religion, Altered States of Consciousness, and Social Change.* Ohio: Ohio University Press.

Boyer, Pascal
1990 *Tradition as Truth and Communication: A cognitive description of traditional discourse.* Cambridge: Cambridge University Press.

Brandt, Ole
1971 *Qooqa.* Nuuk: Det grønlandske Forlag.

Brehm, A.
1907 *Dyrenes Liv,* I–III. Ved J. O. Bøving-Petersen. København: Gyldendal.

Briggs, Jean L.
1974a [1970] *Never in Anger: Portrait of an Eskimo Family.* Cambridge, MA: Harvard University Press.
1974b Eskimo Women Makers of Men. In Carolyn J. Matthiasson (ed.), *Many Sisters: Women in Cross-Cultural Perspective.* New York: The Free Press, 261–304.

Brimnes, Niels
2004 Fra enerådende diskurs til flertydig dialog, E. W. Said's Orientalism og moderne kulturmødeteori. *Kontur, Tidsskrift for kulturstudier* 8: 26–29.

Bujis, Cunera
2003 Furs and Fabrics. Transformations, Clothing, and Identity in East Greenland (last draft).
2004 Furs and Fabrics. Transformations, Clothing, and Identity in East Greenland. *Mededelenen van het Rijskmuseum voor Volkenkunde Leiden*, The Netherlands.

Burch, Ernest S., Jr.
1971 The Nonempirical Environment of the Arctic Alaskan Eskimos. *Southwestern Journal of Anthropology* 27(2): 148–65.
1975 *Eskimo Kinsmen.* New York: West Publishing Company.
1978 Caribou Eskimo Origins: An Old Problem Reconsidered. *Arctic Anthropology* 15(1): 1–35.
1988a War and Trade. In William W. Fitzhugh and Aron Crowell (eds.), *Crossroads of Continents: Cultures of Siberia and Alaska.* Washington, DC: Smithsonian Institution Press.
1988b *The Eskimos.* London: Macdonald and Co. Ltd.

Butler, K. J.
1973–74 My Uncle Went to the Moon. Ed. by Kay Bridge. *Artscanada* 30: 154–58.

Carpenter, Edmund
1968 [1956] The Timeless Present in the Mythology of the Aivilik Eskimos. In Victor F. Valentine and Frank G. Vallee (eds.), *Eskimo of the Canadian Arctic.* Toronto: McClelland and Stewart, 39–42.

Christensen, Torben Hammersholt
2007 Mystik—et komparativt, kognitionsvidenskabeligt perspektiv. *Religionsvidenskabeligt Tidsskrift* 49: 49–73.

Cohen, Anthony P.
1994 *Self Consciousness: An Alternative Anthropology of Identity.* London and New York: Routledge.

Connerton, P.
1989 *How Societies Remember.* Cambridge: Cambridge University Press.

Cranz, David
1765–1770 *Historie von Grönland,* I–II. Barby.

1820 [1767] *The History of Greenland; including an account of the mission carried on by the United Brethren in that country*, I–II. London: Longman, Hurst, Rees, Orme and Brown.

Crépeau, Robert R.
1997 Le chamane croit-il vraiment à sez manipulations ét à leurs fondements intellectuels? *Recherches Amerindienne* 27(3–4): 7–17.

Curtis, Edward S.
1930 *The North American Indian*, XX. New York: London.

Czaplizka, M. A.
1914 *Aboriginal Siberia: A Study in Social Anthropology*. Oxford: The Clarendon Press.

Dahl, Jens
2000 *Saqqaq: An Inuit Hunting Community in the Modern World*. Toronto: University of Toronto Press.

Dalager, Lars
1915 [1752] *Grønlandske Relationer*. Edited by L. Bobé. *Det Grønlandske Selskabs Skrifter*, II.

Danielsen, Isak
2006 *Qanga Avannaamiunik* I. Nuuk: Atuakkiorfik.

de Heuss, L.
1971 *Pourquoi l'épouser? Et autres essais*. Paris: Gallimard.

Descola, Philippe
1986 *La nature domestique: symbolisme ét praxis dans l'écologie des Achuar*. Paris: Maison des Sciences de L'Homme.
1994 *In the Society of Nature: A native ecology in Amazonia*. Cambridge: Cambridge University Press.
1996 Constructing natures. Symbolic ecology and social practice. In Philippe Descola and Gísli Pálsson (eds.), *Nature and Society: Anthropological Perspectives*. London and New York: Routledge.
2005 *Par-delà nature ét culture*. Paris: Gallimard, Bibliothèque des sciences humaines.

Dolitsky, Alexander B. (ed.)
2000 *Tales and Legends of the Yupik Eskimos of Siberia*. Translated by Henry N. Michael. Juneau: Alaska-Siberia Research Center, Publication 11.

Dorais, L.-J
1988 Inuit Identity in Canada. *Folk* 30: 23–31.

Douglas, Mary
1970 *Natural Symbols, Explorations in Cosmology*. New York: Pantheon Books.

Dufour, R.
1975 Le phénomène du Sipiniq chez les Inuit d'Iglulik. *Recherches Amérindiennes au Québec* 5(3): 65–69.

Dumond, Don E.
1977 *The Eskimos and Aleuts*. London: Thames and Hudson Ltd.

Dybbroe, Susanne, and Poul Møller
1980 Kulturhistorisk forskning i det 20. århundrede. Chap. 1 of unpublished master's thesis, Kultur-og Samfundsforskning i Grønland.

Eber, Dorothy Harley

1989 *When the Whalers Were Up North: Inuit Memories from the Eastern Arctic.* Kingston: McGill-Queen's University Press.

Egede, Hans

1763 *Descriptions et histoire naturelle du Groenland.* Translated by DRDP, Copenhague et Geneva.

1818 *A Description of Greenland by Hans Egede, who was a missionary in that country for twenty-five years.* Translated from the Danish, new edition. London: T. and J. Allman.

1925 [1738–41] Relationer fra Grønland 1721–36 og Det gamle Grønlands nye Perlustration eller Naturel Historie. *Meddelelser om Grønland* 54.

1971 [1738–41] *Relation angaaende Den Grønlandske Mission* (1971, 1) *samt Det gamle Grønlands Nye Perlustration* (1971, 2). Edited by Finn Gad. København: Rosenkilde and Bagger.

Egede, Niels

1939 Poul og Niels Egede: Continuation af Hans Egedes Relationer fra Grønland. Edited by H. Ostermann. *Meddelelser om Grønland* 120: 127–206.

1943 Niels Egedes Dagbog. Edited by Louis Bobé. *Det grønlandske Selskabs Aarsskrift*: 7–61.

1971 [1741] *Tredie Continuation af Den Grønlandske Mission.* Edited by Finn Gad. København: Rosenkilde og Bagger. (Same publication as Poul Egede 1971.)

Egede, Poul

1750 *Dictionarium Grönlandico-Danico-Latinum.* Hafnia.

1939 Poul og Niels Egede: Continuation af Hans Egedes Relationer fra Grønland. Edited by H. Ostermann. *Meddelelser om Grønland* 120.

1971 [1741] *Continuation af Den Grønlandske Mission.* Edited by Finn Gad. København: Rosenkilde og Bagger.

1988 [1788] Efterretninger om Grønland, uddragne af en Journal holden fra 1721 til 1788. Edited by Mads Lidegaard. *Det Grl. Selskabs Skrifter* XXIX.

Eliade, M.

1964 *Shamanism: Archaic Technique of Ecstasy.* London: Routledge and Kegan Paul.

1971 *The Myth of the Eternal Return: Cosmos and History.* Princeton: Princeton University Press.

1975 *Rites and Symbols of Initiation: The Mysteries of Birth and Rebirth.* New York: Harper and Row.

Eriksen, Th. Hylland

1997 [1993] *Små Steder Store Spørgsmål. Innføring i sosialantropologi.* Oslo: Universitetesforlaget.

Evans-Pritchard, E. E.

1937 *Witchcraft, Oracles and Magic among the Azande.* Clarendon Press.

Fabricius, Otho

1804 *Den Grønlandske Ordbog.* København: Det Kongelige Vaisenhuses Bogtrykkeri.

1946 Otho Fabricius. Grønlandsbeskrivelse 1ste Bog. Edited by Hother Ostermann. *Meddelelser om Grønland* 129(4). Copenhagen: C. A. Reitzel.

Fausto, Carlos

2007 Feasting on People. Eating Animals and Humans in Amazonia. *Current Anthropology* 48(4): 497–530.

Fernandez, James W.

1991 Introduction, Confluence of Inquiry. The Cultural Basis of Metaphor. In James W. Fernandez (ed.), *Beyond Metaphor: The Theory of Tropes in Anthropology*. Stanford, CA: Stanford University Press, 1–13.

Fienup-Riordan, Ann

1983 *The Nelson Island Eskimo*. Anchorage: Alaska Pacific University Press.

1984 Regional Groups on the Yukon-Kuskokwim Delta. *Études/Inuit/Studies* 8 (Supplementary Issue): 63–93.

1990 *Eskimo Essays*. New Brunswick: Rutgers University Press.

1994 *Boundaries and Passages: Rules and Ritual in Yup'ik Eskimo Oral Tradition*. Norman: University of Oklahoma Press.

1996 *The Living Tradition of the Yup'ik Masks*. Seattle: University of Washington Press.

1997 Present Recollections of Past Shamanism. *Études/Inuit/Studies* 21(1–2): 229–44.

Fienup-Riordan, Ann, and Alice Rearden

2013 *Ellavut. Our Yup'ik World and Weather, Continuity and Change on the Bering Sea Coast*. Seattle: University of Washington Press.

Fitzhugh, William W., and Aron Crowell

1988 *Crossroads of Continents: Cultures of Siberia and Alaska*. Washington, DC: Smithsonian Institution Press.

Fortescue, Michael

1986 Thule- og Kobbereskimoisk. Om gensidig påvirkning mellem visse affikser og endelser i vestgrønlandsk set på baggrund af de vestlige dialekter i Inuktitut. In J. Rischel and Robert Petersen (eds.), *Vort sprog—vor kultur*. Nuuk: Ilisimatusarfik and Kalaallit Nunaata Katersugaasivia, 165–75.

1988 Eskimo orientation systems. *Meddelelser om Grønland, Man and Society* 11.

1998 *Language Relations Across Bering Strait: Reappraising the Archaeological and Linguistic Evidence*. London: Cassel.

Fortescue, M., S. Jacobson, and L. Kaplan

1994 Comparative Eskimo Dictionary with Aleut Cognates. *Alaska Native Language Center, Research Paper* 9, University of Alaska Fairbanks.

2010 Comparative Eskimo Dictionary with Aleut Cognates. *Alaska Native Language Center* 9, 2nd ed., University of Alaska Fairbanks.

Freuchen, Peter

1935 *Arctic Adventure: My Life in the Frozen North*. New York: Farrar and Rinehart Inc.

Gad, Finn

1967–76 *Grønlands Historie*, I–III. Copenhagen: Nyt Nordisk Forlag Arnold Busck.

1973–82 *The History of Greenland*, II–III. Montreal: McGill-Queen's University Press (translation of 1967–76).

1974 *Fire detailkomplekser I Grønlands historie 1782–1808. Sammenstilling og fortolkning af materiale*. København: Nyt Nordisk Forlag Arnold Busck.

Gagné, Raymond

1968 Spatial Concepts in the Eskimo Language. In Victor F. Valentine and Frank G. Vallee (eds.), *Eskimo of the Canadian Arctic*. Toronto: McClelland and Stewart, 30–38.

Garber, Clark M.

1975 *Stories and Legends of the Bering Strait Eskimos.* New York: AMS Press.

Geertsen, Ib

1990 *Kârale Andreassen. En østgrønlandsk kunstner.* Nuuk: Atuakkiorfik.

1994 *Grønlandske Masker.* Copenhagen: Rhodos.

Gessain, Robert

1970 [1969] *Ammassalik. Den påtvungne Civilisation.* København: Rhodos. Translated from the 1969 French edition (*Ammassalik.* Paris: Librairie Flammarion).

1975a Uizerq, L'Amant. Un personnage de la mythologie des Ammassalimiut. *Objets et Mondes* XV(3): 319–29.

1975b Essai sur l'éthnosociologie des Ammassalimiut au XIXe siècle d'après les notes de C. Ryder. *Objets et Mondes* XV(2): 129–48.

1978 L'homme-lune dans la mythologie des ammassalimiut. *Systèmes de Signes. Hommage à Germaine Dieterlen.* Paris: Harmann, 205–22.

1984 Dance Masks of Ammassalik (East Coast of Greenland). *Arctic Anthropology* 21(2): 81–107.

Gessain, R., and J. Robert-Lamblin

1974 Migrations des Ammassalimiut au XIXè Siècle d'apres les archives des Frères Moraves. *Cahiers du C.R.A. 13, Bull. et Mém. de la Soc. Anthrop. de Paris* (XIIè s.): 153–59.

Gessain, R. and P-É. Victor

1973 Le tambour chez les Ammassalimiut. *Objets et Mondes* XIII, Fasc. 3: 129–60.

Giesecke, K. L.

1910 Mineralogisches Reisejournal über Grönland 1806–1813. *Meddelelser om Grønland,* hæfte 35.

Gilberg, Rolf

1974–75 Changes in the Life of the Polar Eskimos Resulting from a Canadian Immigration into the Thule District, North Greenland in the 1860's. *Folk* 16–17: 159–70.

1978 *Ånder og mennesker.* København: Nationalmuseet.

1984 Polar Eskimo. In David Damas (ed.), *Handbook of North American Indians.* Vol. V, "The Arctic." Washington, DC: Smithsonian Institution Press, 577–94.

Glahn, H. C.

1771 *Anmærkninger til Cranz' Historie von Grönland.* København: Det Kongelige Vajsenhuses Bogtrykkeri.

1921 Henric Christoffer Glahns Dagbøger for Aarene 1763–64, 1766–67, og 1767–68. Edited by H. Ostermann. *Det grønlandske Selskabs Skrifter,* 4.

Goetz, Noah

1977 *The Inuit Print/L'Estampe inuit.* Ottawa: National Museum of Man.

Graah, W.

1932 [1832] *Undersøgelsesrejse til Østkysten af Grønland, efter kongelig Befaling udført i Aarene 1828–31.* Introduction and notes by Kaj Birket-Smith. København: Nordisk Forlag.

Grandorf, Marie Louise

2004 *Åndernes erobring. En analyse af de østgrønlandske shamaners initiationsfortællinger.* Unpublished master's thesis, Institut for Religionshistorie, Københavns Universitet.

2005 Åndernes erobring—eller hvordan man kan blive åndemaner af at blive ædt af en bjørn. *Tidsskriftet Grønland* 2–3: 99–104.

Grove, Arnaq

2000 *Nedskrivning af nyere grønlandsk mundtlig fortælletradition. En undersøgelse af det mundtlige fortællesprog og dets retoriske komponenter med udgangspunkt i Qivaaqiarsuk fortalt af Simon Nielsen, samt litterær analyse og tolkning af den.* Unpublished PhD thesis. Københavns Universitet.

Grønnow, Bjarne

1991 Vejen til Grønland. *Tidsskriftet Grønland* 4: 99–101.

1994 Qeqertasussuk—The Archaeology of a Frozen Saqqaq Site in Disko Bugt, West Greenland. In D. Morrison and J.-L. Pilon (eds.), Threads of Arctic Prehistory: Papers in honour of William E. Talor, Jr. *Archaeological Survey of Canada, Mercury Series*, Paper 149. Canadian Museum of Civilization: 197–238.

2009a Blessings and Horrors of the Interior: Ethno-Historical Studies of Inuit Perceptions Concerning the Inland Region of West Greenland. *Arctic Anthropology* 46(1–2): 191–201.

2009b (ed.) On the Track of the Thule Culture from Bering Strait to East Greenland, Papers in honour of H. C. Gulløv. *Publication from the National Museum Studies in Archaeology and History* 15.

2017 The Frozen Saqqaq Sites of Disko Bay, West Greenland Qeqertasussuk and Qajaa (2400–900 BC). Studies of Saqqaq Material Culture in an Eastern Arctic Perspective Series: Monographs on Greenland. *Meddelelser om Grønland* 356, *Man and Society* 45.

Grønnow, Bjarne, and Jens Fogh Jensen

2003 The northernmost ruins of the globe: Eigil Knuth's archaeological investigations in Peary Land and adjacent areas of high Arctic Greenland. Dansk Polarcenter. *Meddelelser om Grønland: Man and Society* 29.

Gubser, Nicholas J.

1965 *The Nunamiut: Hunters of Caribou.* New Haven: Yale University Press.

Gulløv, H. C.

1983 Herrnhuternes Grønlændere. *Tidsskriftet Grønland*, 247–59.

1986a Straat David's grønlændere og sydlændinge. In J. Rischel and Robert Petersen (eds.), *Vort Sprog—vor kultur.* Nuuk: Ilisimatusarfik and Kalaallit Nunaata Katersugaasivia, 101–12.

1986b The Revival at Pisugfik in 1768: An Ethnohistorical Approach. *Arctic Anthropology* 23(1–2): 151–75.

1987 Dutch Whaling and Its Influence on Eskimo Culture in Greenland. In Louwrens Hacquebord and Richard Waughan (eds.), *Between Greenland and America.* University of Groningen, The Netherlands: Arctic Centre, 75–93.

1995 'Olden times' in Southeast Greenland: New archaeological investigations and the oral tradition. *Études/Inuit/Studies* 19(1): 3–36.

1997 From Middle Ages to Colonial Times. Archaeological and Ethnohistorical Studies of the Thule Culture in South West Greenland 1300–1800 AD. *Meddelelser om Grønland, Man and Society* 23.

1999 Fra Beringstrædet til Grønland. En rejse i forhistorien. In Jørgen Lorentzen (ed.), *Inuit kultur og samfund—en grundbog i eskimologi.* Århus: Systime, 215–25.

2008 The Nature of Contact between Native Greenlanders and Norse. *Journal of the North Atlantic* 1: 16–24.

2012 Grønlands forhistorie og dialekterne. *Tidsskriftet Grønland*, 133–46.

2016 The Concepts of Paleo- and Neo-Eskimo Cultures: The Danish Tradition from H. P. Steensby and His Students, G. Hatt, K. Birket-Smith, and Th. Mathiassen to their Successors, H. Larsen and J. Meldgaard. In I. Krupnik (ed.), *Early Inuit Studies: Themes and Transitions, 1850s–1980s*. Washington, DC: Smithsonian Institution Scholarly Press.

Gulløv, H. C. (ed.)
2004 *Grønlands forhistorie*. København: Gyldendal.

Haase, Evelin
1987 *Der Schamanismus der Eskimos*. Aachen: Edition Herodot, Radar Verlag.

Hall, C. F
1970 [1865] *Life with the Esquimos, a narrative arctic experience in search of survivors of Sir John Franklin's expedition*. Rutland (VT) and Tokyo: Charles E. Tuttle.

Hallendy, Norman
2009 *Tukiliit. The stone people who live in the wind. Introduction to inuksuit and other stone figures of the north*. Fairbanks: University of Alaska Press.

Hallowell, A. Irving
1960 Ojibwa Ontology, Behavior, and World-view. In Stanley Diamond (ed.), *Culture and History*. London: Oxford University Press.

Hamayon, R.
1990 *La chasse à l'âme. Esquisse d'une théorie du chamanisme à partir d'exemples sibérien*. Nanterre: Société d'Ethnologie.

Hansen, Keld
1986 Kvindelige fangere. *Tusaat/Forskning i Grønland* 2.

Hansen, Kjeld
2001 *Farvel til Grønlands natur*. København: G.E.C. Gads forlag.
2002 *A farewell to Greenland's wild life*. Translated by Robin Worall. Copenhagen: G.E.C. Gad.

Hansen, Klaus Georg
1994 Kajaksvimmelhed.—Begrebshistoriske refleksioner over en særlig grønlandsk lidelse. *Grønlandsk Kultur- og Samfundsforskning* 94: 36–65.

Hastrup, Kirsten
2015 *Thule på tidens rand*. København: Lindhardt og Ringhof.

Hastrup, Kirsten (ed.)
2007 [2004] Introduktion. In Kirsten Hastrup (ed.), *Viden om Verden*. København: Gyldendal Akademisk.

Hawkes, E. W.
1913 *The Inviting-in Feast of the Alaskan Eskimo*. Ottawa: Government Printing Bureau.
1916 The Labrador Eskimo. *Canada Department of Mines, Geological Survey, Memoir 91, Anthropological Series 14*. Ottawa: Government Printing Bureau, 1–164.

Hessel, Ingo
1998 *Inuit Art, an Introduction*. British Museum Press.

Himmelheber, Hans
1951 *Der gefrorene Pfad*. Eisenach: Kassel.

1980 Ethnographische Notizen von den Nunivak-Eskimo. *Abhandlungen und Berichte des Staatlichen Museums für Völkerkunde, Dresden* 38: 5–45. (English translation in Himmelheber 2000, pp. 107–80.)

2000 *Where the Echo Began and Other Oral traditions from Southwestern Alaska Recorded by Hans Himmelheber.* Translated by Kurt and Ester Vitt, edited and annotated by Ann Fienup-Riordan. Fairbanks: University of Alaska Press.

Hindsberger, M.

1997 *Grønlandsk Livssyn i 1990'erne.* København: Museum Tusculanum.

Hobsbawm, Eric

1984 [1983] Introduction: Inventing Traditions. In Eric Hobsbawm and Terence Ranger (eds.), *The Invention of Tradition.* Cambridge: Cambridge University Press, 1–14.

Holland, Dorothy, and Naomi Quinn (eds.)

1987 *Cultural models in language and thought.* Cambridge: Cambridge University Press.

Holm, Gustav

1888 Den østgrønlandske Expedition udført i Aarene 1883–85, II. *Meddelelser om Grønland,* bind 10. Edited by F. Johnstrup. København.

1914 [1888] Ethnological Sketch of the Angmagsalik Eskimo, The Ammassalik Eskimo: Contributions to the Ethnology of the East Greenland Natives. Edited by W. Thalbitzer. *Meddelelser om Grønland* 39(1): 3–147.

1957 [1888+1989] Østgrønlændernes Sagn og Fortællinger. Edited by W. Thalbitzer, *Det grønlandske Selskabs Skrifter* XIX: 215–317.

1972 [1888] *Konebådsekspeditionen. Ethnologisk Skizze af Angmagsalikerne.* Edited by J. Meldgaard. København: Rhodos, 129–45.

Holm, Gustav, and Johan Petersen

1921 Angmagssalik Distrikt. *Meddelelser om Grønland* 61: 560–661.

Holtved, Erik

1951 The Polar Eskimos, Language and Folklore, I–II. *Meddelelser om Grønland* 152(1–2). Copenhagen: C. A. Reitzel.

1967 Contribution to Polar Ethnography. *Meddelelser om Grønland* 182(2): 1–180.

Honko, Lauri

1975 Zur Klassifikation der Riten. *Temenos* 11.

Hoppál, Mihály

1992 Pain in Shamanic Initiation. In M. Hoppál and Juha Pentikäinen (eds.), *Northern Religion and Shamanism, Ethnologica Uralia,* 3. Budapest: Akadémiai Kiadó; Helsinki: Finnish Literature Society, 151–57.

Hughes, Charles C.

1984 Siberian Eskimo. In David Damas (ed.), *Handbook of North American Indians.* Vol. V, "The Arctic." Washington, DC: Smithsonian Institution Press, 247–61.

Hultkrantz, Åke

1962 Die Religion Nordeurasiens und der amerikanischen Arktis, Doe Religionen der Menschheit, Band 3. Edited by Christel Matthias. Stuttgart: Schröder.

1973 A definition of Shamanism. *Temenos* 9: 25–37.

1978 Ecological and Phenomenological Aspects of Shamanism. In V. Dioszegi and M. Hoppál (eds.), *Shamanism in Siberia.* Budapest: Akadémia Kiadó, 27–58.

1989 The Place of Shamanism in the History of Religions. In M. Hoppál and O. J. von Sadovszky (eds.), *Shamanism Past and Present*, I. Budapest: Ethnographic Institute, Hungarian Academy of Sciences, 43–52.

Høiris, Ole

2009 William Thalbitzer. In Ole Høiris (ed.), *Grønland, en refleksiv udfordring*. Aarhus: Universitetsforlag, 211–37.

Ingold, Tim

1986 *Evolution and Social Life*. Cambridge: Cambridge University Press.

2000 *The Perception of the Environment: Essays in livelihood, dwelling and skill*. London and New York: Routledge.

Inuutersuaq, Ulloriaq

1976 *K'itdlarssuákúnik oKalualâK*. Nuuk: Det grønlandske Forlag.

1985 Beretningen om Qillarsuaq og hans lange rejse fra Canada til Nordgrønland i 1860'erne. *Det Grønlandske Selskabs Skrifter* XXVII.

Jacobson, Steven A.

1984 *Yup'ik Eskimo Dictionary*. Alaska Native Language Center, University of Alaska Fairbanks.

Jakobsen, Merete Demant

1999 *Shamanism: Traditional and contemporary approaches to the mastery of spirits and healing*. New York: Berghahn.

Jenness, Diamond

1922 The Life of the Copper Eskimos. *Report of the Canadian Arctic Expedition 1913–18*, XII, Ottawa.

Jensen, Anne M.

1987 Patterns of Bearded Seal Exploitation in Greenland. *Études/Inuit/Studies* 11(2): 91–116.

Jensen, Bent

1963 Notes on an Eskimo "Thanking Act." *Folk* V: 187–98.

1968 Pernarneq, den første fangst. *Jordens Folk* 4(2).

Jensen, E. Lund, Kristine Raahauge, and H. C. Gulløv

2011 Cultural Encounters at Cape Farewell. *Meddelelser om Grønland, Man and Society* 38.

2012 *Kulturmøder ved Kap Farvel. De østgrønlandske indvandrere og den tyske Brødremission i det 19. århundrede*. Københavns Universitet, Museum Tusculanums forlag.

Jochelson, W.

1910 The Yukaghir and the Yukaghirized Tungus. *The Jesup North Pacific Expedition*, IX(1). Leiden: Brill; New York: G. E. Stechert and Co.

Jones, Kirsten Gade, and Robert Petersen

2003 *Ordbogen*. Nuuk: Ilinniusiorfik, Undervisningsforlag.

Jørgensen, Lars, Bjarne Grønnow, Jette Arneborg, and Hans Christian Gulløv

2012 At ordne min verden—billeder af inuit og nordboernes mentale landskaber gennem 4500 år. In Marita Akhøj Nielsen (ed.), *Grønlands fascinationskraft, Fortællinger om polarforskningen*. Et festskrift til Hendes Majestæt Dronning Margrethe II ved 40-års-regeringsjubilæet 2012. Viborg: Specialtrykkeriet.

Kaalund, Bodil

1990 [1979] *Grønlands Kunst. Skulptur, Brugskunst, Maleri.* København: Gyldendal.

1983 *The art of Greenland: sculpture, crafts, painting.* Translated by Kenneth Tindall. Berkeley: University of California Press.

Kaalund, Bodil, Einar Lund Jensen, Inge Lynge, and Robert Petersen (eds.)

2006a *Hans Lynge. En grønlandsk kulturpioner.* København: Rhodos.

2006b *Hans Lynge. Kalaaleq kulturikkut aqqutissiuisoq.* København: Rhodos.

Kari, James, and Ben Potter (eds.)

2010 The Dené-Yeniseian Hypothesis. *Anthropological Papers of the University of Alaska, New Series*, vol. V.

Keesing, Roger

1987 Models, 'folk' and 'cultural': paradigms regained? In Dorothy Holland and Naomi Quinn (eds.), *Cultural models in language and thought.* Cambridge: Cambridge University Press, 369–93.

1993 'Earth' and 'path' as complex categories: semantics and symbolism in Kwaio culture. In Pascal Boyer (ed.), *Cognitive aspects of religious symbolism.* Cambridge: Cambridge University Press, 93–110.

Keithan, E. L.

1976 [1958] *Alaskan Igloo Tales.* Anchorage: Alaska Northwest Publishing Company.

Kielsen, Lene

1996 Mitaartut: An Inuit winter festival in Greenland. *Études/Inuit/Studies* 20(1): 123–29.

Kleinschmidt, Samuel

1871 *Den Grønlandske Ordbog.* Ministeriet for Kirke- og Undervisningsvæsenet. Kjøbenhavn: Louis Kleins Bogtrykkeri.

Kleivan, Inge

1960 Mitârtut, Vestiges of the Eskimo Sea-Woman Cult in West Greenland. *Meddelelser om Grønland* 161(5).

1962 The Swan Maiden Myth among the Eskimos. *Acta Arctica*, Fasc. XIII. Copenhagen: Ejnar Munksgaard.

1971a Song Duels in West Greenland: Joking Relationship and Avoidance. *Folk* 13: 9–36.

1971b Why Is the Raven Black? *Acta Arctica* XVII. København.

1982 Grønlandske sagn om nordboerne. *Tidsskriftet Grønland* 8–9: 314–30.

1984 History of the Norse in Greenland. In David Damas (ed.), *Handbook of North American Indians.* Vol. V, "The Arctic." Washington, DC: Smithsonian Institution Press, 549–55.

1986 The Virgin Mary of Tasiussaq. A Case of Feminism. *Arctic Anthropology* 23(1–2): 221–38.

1996 Inuit Oral Tradition About Tunit in Greenland. *Paleo-Eskimo Cultures of Greenland, New Perspective in Greenland Archaeology.* Edited by Bjarne Grønnow. Copenhagen: The Danish Polar Center, 215–36.

Kleivan, Inge, and Birgitte Sonne

1985 *Eskimos, Greenland and Canada. Iconography of Religions*, VIII (2). Leiden: J. E. Brill, 43 + XLVIII.

Kragh, Peter

1875 Udtog af Missionair P. Kraghs Dagbog. Haderslev, Sabroe's Boghandel.

Krauss, Michael E.
1988 Many Tongues—Ancient Tales. In William W. Fitzhugh and Aron Crowell (eds.), *Crossroads of Continents: Cultures of Siberia and Alaska*. Washington, DC: Smithsonian Institution, 145–50.

Kreutzmann, Jens
1997a *Fortællinger og Akvareller*. Translated and edited by Kirsten Thisted. Nuuk: Atuakkiorfik.
1997b *Oqaluttuat Assiliat*. Transcribed by Arnaq Grove, edited by Kirsten Thisted. Nuuk: Atuakkiorfik.

Kroeber, A. L
1899a The Eskimo of Smith Sound. *Bulletin of the American Museum of Natural History* 12.
1899b Tales of the Smith Sound Eskimo. *Journal of American Folk Lore* 12: 166–82.

Kruuse, C.
1912 Rejser og botaniske undersøgelser i Øst-Grønland mellem 65°30' og 67°20' i aarene 1898–1902, samt Angmagsalik-egnens vegetation. *Meddelelser om Grønland* 49.

Kublu, A., and J. G. Oosten
1999 Changing Perspectives of Name and Identity among the Inuit of Northeast Canada. In J. Oosten and C. Remie (eds.), *Arctic Identities*. Leiden: Universiteit Leiden, 56–78.

Lakoff, G., and M. Johnson
1980 *Metaphors we live by*. Chicago: University of Chicago Press.

Lakoff, G., and M. Turner
1989 *More than Cool Reason, A Field Guide to Poetic Metaphor*. Chicago and London: University of Chicago Press.

Langdon, E. J.
1989 Shamanism in the History of Anthropology. In Mihály Hoppál and Otto von Sadovszky (eds.), *Shamanism Past and Present*, pt. 1. Budapest Ethnographic Institute Hungarian Academy of Sciences, Los Angeles/Fullerton International Society for Trans-Oceanic Research, 53–68.

Lantis, Margaret
1946 The Social Culture of the Nunivak Eskimo. *Transactions of the American Philosophical Society* n.s. 35(3): 264–313.
1947 Alaskan Eskimo Ceremonialism. *Monographs of the American Ethnological Society*, 11. Edited by Marian W. Smith. Seattle and London.
1960 Eskimo Childhood and Interpersonal Relationships. Nunivak Biographies and Genealogies. *The American Ethnological Society*, Monograph 33. Seattle and London: University of Washington Press.

Larsen, Aviaja
2008 *Kaassassuk myten fra Aron til i dag*. Unpublished master's thesis at Eskimology and Arctic Studies, Department of Cross-Cultural and Regional Studies, University of Copenhagen.

Larsen, H., and F. Rainey
1948 Ipiutak and the Arctic Whale Hunting Culture. *Anthropological Papers of the American Museum of History*, no. 42.

Laugrand, Frédéric
1997 *Siqqitiqpuq: conversion ét réception du christianisme par les Inuit de l'Arctique de l'Est canadien (1890–1940)*. Québec: Université Laval, Département d'anthropologie.

Laugrand, Frédéric, and Jarich Oosten

2002a Canicide and Healing. The Position of the Dog in Inuit Cultures of the Canadian Arctic. *Anthropos* 97: 89–105.

2002b Quviasukvik, The celebration of an Inuit winter feast in the central Arctic. *Journal de la Societé des Américanistes* 88: 203–25.

2006 Connecting and Protecting: Lines and Belts in the Canadian Arctic. *Anthropological Papers of the University of Alaska* 4(1): 133–47.

2008a Reconnecting people and healing the land. Inuit Pentecostal and Evangelical movements in the Canadian Eastern Arctic. *Numen. International Review for the History of Religions* LIV(3): 229–69.

2008b *The Sea Woman: Sedna in Inuit Shamanism and Art in the Eastern Arctic.* Fairbanks: University of Alaska Press.

2010 *Qupirruit*: Insects and Worms in Inuit Tradition. *Arctic Anthropology* 47(1): 1–21.

2015 *Hunters, Predators and Prey: Inuit Perceptions of Animals.* New York and Oxford: Berghahn Books.

Laugrand, Frédéric, Jarich Oosten, Maaki Kakkik, and Alexina Kublu (eds.)

2003 *Keeping the Faith, Memory and History in Nunavut,* 3. Nunavut: Arctic College.

Laugrand, Frédéric, Jarich Oosten, and Francois Trudel (eds.)

2000 *Representing Tuurngait Memory and History in Nunavut,* vol. I. Iqaluit: Nunavut Arctic College.

2002 Hunters, Owners, and Givers of Light: The Tuurngait of South Baffin Island. *Arctic Anthropology* 39 (1–2): 27–40.

Lauridsen, Lena

2015 *Inussuk. Pejling mod Grønland.* Culture Crossing.

Leach, Edmund

1963 [1961] *Rethinking Anthropology.* London: Athelone Press.

Lehtisalo, T.

1924 Entwurf einer Mythologie der Jurak-Samojeden. *Mémoires de la Société Finno Ougrienne,* LIII. Helsinki.

1937 Der Tod und die Wiedergeburt des künftigen Schamanen. *Journal de la Societé Finno-Ougrienne,* 48(3). Helsinki: Der finnischen Literaturgeselschaft, 1–34.

Leonard, Stephen Pax

2014 The need to "belong": Social connectedness in Polar Eskimo settlements. *Polar Record* 50(253): 138–46.

Lévi-Strauss, C.

1953 Le sorcier et sa magie. *Anthropologie structurale.* Paris: Plon.

1963 [1958] *Structural Anthropology.* New York: Basic Books.

Lewis, I. M.

1975 [1971] *Ecstatic Religion.* Middlesex: Penguin Books.

1981 What is a shaman? *Folk* 23: 25–35.

1994–2002 *Encyclopedia Britannica.* https://www.britannica.com/topic/witchcraft,

Lidegaard, Mads

1986 *Hans—en eskimo.* København: Nyt Nordisk Forlag Arnold Busck.

1999 Pussimeq og Isseq. *Tidsskriftet Grønland* 6: 1–12.

Lyberth, Juaaka

2016 *Grønlandske før-kristne trosforestillinger i nutiden. Synkretistiske trostræk og–tendenser i det nyreligiøse felt i Grønland*. Unpublished master's thesis. 2016.

Lynge, Finn

1981 *Fugl og sæl—og menneskesjæl, kalâtdlit itsaq ússatait ugperissaitdlo*. Gylling: Nordiske Landes Bogforlag.

Lynge, Hans

1955 Inegpait. *Meddelelser om Grønland* 90(2).

1967 *Inugpât*. Godthåb: Det Grønlandske Forlag.

1978 *Nûk. Hvad der i vore dage huskes fra Godthåbs fortid*. Nuuk: Det Grønlandske Forlag.

1981–88 *Grønlands indre liv*, I–II. Nuuk: Atuakkiorfik.

Lynge, Kristoffer

1978 [1957] *Kalâtdlit oqalugtuait oqalualâvilo*. Godthåb.

Lyon, F. G.

1824 *The Private Journal of Captain F. G. Lyon*. London: J. Murray.

Lytzen, C.

1874 Grønlandske sagn. *Fra alle Lande*, XIX, Aarg. 1874 (1).

MacDonald, John

1998 *The Arctic Sky, Inuit Astronomy, Star Lore, and Legend*. Royal Ontario Museum/Nunavut Research Institute.

Marquardt, Ole

1992 Socio-økonomiske tilstande i Vestgrønland på Rinks tid: befolkningskoncentration i kolonibyer og dannelse af lokale 'Brædtmarkeder'. *Grønlandsk Kultur- og Samfundsforskning 92*. Ilisimatusarfik: Atuakkiorfik, 147–82.

1999 A critique of the common interpretation of the great socio-economic crisis in Greenland 1850–1880: The case of Nuuk and Qeqertarsuatsiaat. *Études/Inuit/Studies* 23(1.2): 9–34.

2009 H.J. Rink. In O. Høiris (ed.), *Grønland en refleksiv udfordring. Mission, kolonisation og udforskning*. Århus: Århus Universitetsforlag, 129–54.

Mary-Roussilière, Guy

1980 *Qitdlarssuaq—l'histoire d'une migration polaire*. Montréal: Les Presses de l'Univerité de Montréal.

Mauss, Marcel

1979 [1906] *Seasonal Variations of the Eskimo: A study in social morphology*. Introduction and translation by James J. Fox. London: Routledge and Kegan Paul (originally published in French in collaboration with Henri Beuchat).

McElroy, Ann

1975 Canadian Arctic Modernization and Change in Female Inuit Role Identification. *American Ethnologist* 2(4): 184–99.

McGhee, Robert

1974 Beluga Hunters. An archaeological reconstruction of the history and culture of the Mackenzie Delta Kittegaryumiut. *Newfoundland Social and Economic Studies* 13, Memorial University of Newfoundland.

1984 Thule Prehistory of Canada. In David Damas (ed.), *Handbook of North American Indians*, Vol. V, "The Arctic": 369–76.

Meldgaard, Jørgen
1960 *Eskimo Sculpture*. London: Methuen and Co. Ltd.
1982 *Aron. En af de mærkværdigste Billedsamlinger i Verden*. København: Nationalmuseet.

Meldgaard, Morten
1986 The Greenland caribou-zoogeography, taxonomy, and population dynamics. *Meddelelser om Grønland, Bioscience* 20.

Merkur, Daniel
1985 Becoming Half Hidden. Shamanism and Initiation among the Inuit. *Acta Universitatis Stockholmiensis/Stockholm Studies in Comparative Religion* 24. Stockholm.
1991 *Powers Which We Do Not Know. The Gods and Spirits of the Inuit*. Moscow, ID: University of Idaho Press.

Métayer, Maurice
1973 *Unipkat: Tradition esquimaude de Coppermine, Territoires-du-Nord-Ouest, Canada*. Première partie, Tome 1–3. Québec: Université Laval.

Michelsen, Knud
2014 *Vejen til Thule. Knud Rasmussen belyst gennem breve og andre kilder 1902–1910*. Forlaget Falcon.

Mishler, Craig
2013 *The Blind Man and the Loon: The story of a tale*. Lincoln: University of Nebraska Press.

Morrison, David
2001 Radiocarbon Dating the Birnirk-Thule Transition. *Anthropological Papers of the University of Alaska* n.s. 1(1): 73–85.

Morrow, Phyllis
1984 It Is Time for Drumming: A Summary of Recent Research on Yup'ik Ceremonialism. *Études/Inuit/Studies* 8 (Supplementary Issue): 113–40.

Morrow, Phyllis, and Alice Volkman Toby
1975 The Loon with the Ivory Eyes: A Study in Symbolic Archaeology. *Journal of American Folklore* 88(348): 143–50.

Mousalimas, S. A.
1989 Shamans-Of-Old in Southern Alaska. In Mihály Hoppál and Otto von Sadovszky (eds.), *Shamanism Past and Present*. Budapest, 307–16.

Munn, Nancy D.
1992 The Cultural Anthropology of Time: A critical essay. *Annual Review of Anthropology*, 93–123.

Muus, B., F. Salomonsen, and C. Vibe
1981 *Grønlands Fauna*. Copenhagen: Gyldendal.

Müller-Wille, Ludger
1998 *Franz Boas among the Inuit of Baffin Island, 1883–1884: journals and letters*. Toronto: University of Toronto Press.

Mylius-Erichsen, Ludvig, and H. Moltke
1906 *Grønland*. Copenhagen: Gyldendalske Boghandel, Nordisk Forlag.

Møbjerg, Tinna
1994 Ammassalik i 4000 år. *Tidsskriftet Grønland*, 125–44.

Nagy, Murielle

2006 Time, Space, and Memory. In Pamela Stern and Lisa Stevenson (eds.), *Critical Inuit Studies: An Anthology of Contemporary Arctic Ethnography*. Lincoln: University of Nebraska Press.

Napolskikh, V. V.

1992 Proto-Uralic World Picture: A Reconstuction [*sic*]. In M. Hoppál and J. Pentikäinen (eds.), *Northern Religions and Shamanism, Ethnologica Uralica* 3. Budapest; Helsinki, 3–20.

Narayan, Kirin

1989 *Storytellers, Saints, and Scoundrels: Folk narrative in Indian religious teaching*. Philadelphia: University of Pennsylvania Press.

Nellemann, George

1960 Sådan var det dengang. *Tidsskriftet Grønland* 1.

1962 De stærke drikkes historie i Grønland. *Tidsskriftet Grønland* 5.

Nelson, E. W.

1899 The Eskimo about the Bering Strait. *18th Annual Report of the Bureau of American Ethnology*, 1. Washington, DC.

Neu, J.

1975 Lévi-Strauss on Shamanism. *Man* 10(2): 285–92.

Nooter, G. W.

1975 Mitârtut, winter feast in Greenland. *Objets et Mondes* XV(2): 159–68.

1976 Leadership and Headship. Changing authority patterns in an East-Greenland hunting community. Leiden, *Mededelingen van het Rijksmuseum voor Volkenkunde*, 20.

1978 Traditionelt lederskab og grønlandsk selvforvaltning. *Tidsskriftet Grønland* 9.

Nuttall, Mark

1992 *Arctic Homeland, Kinship, Community and Development in Northwest Greenland*. London: Belhaven Press.

2000 Choosing Kin. In Peter Schweitzer (ed.), *Dividends of Kinship*. London: Routledge.

Nørlund, Poul

1967 [1934] *De gamle Nordbobygder ved Verdens Ende*. Nationalmuseet.

Olsen, Lars-Henrik

2009 *Isbjørn mod hvalros*. Edited by Astrid Petersen. Alinea.

Ong, Walter J.

1969 World as view and world as event. *American Anthropologist* 71: 634–47.

1982 *Orality and Literacy: The technologizing of the word*. New York and London: Methuen and Co. Ltd.

Oosten, J. G.

1976 *The Theoretical Structure of the Religion of the Netsilik and Iglulik*. Rijksuniversitet Te Groningen, Krips repro-Meppel.

1989 Theoretical Problems in the Study of Inuit Shamanism. In M. Hoppál and O. J. von Sadovszky (eds.), *Shamanism Past and Present*. Budapest, 331–41.

1990 Cosmological cycles and the constituents of the person. *Inuit Studies Conference Occasional Papers* 4: 185–96.

2002 Kiviuq: une épopée en devenir? *Anthropologie et Société* 26(2–3): 71–90.

2006 A privileged field of study: Marcel Mauss and structural anthropology in Leiden. *Études/Inuit/Studies* 30(2): 51–71.

Oosten, Jarich, Frédéric Laugrand, and Wim Rasing (eds.)

1999 Perspectives on Inuit Law. *Interviewing Inuit Elders*, 2. Iqaluit: Nunavut Arctic College.

Oosten, Jarich, and Frédéric Laugrand

2004–5 Time and Space in the Perception of Non-human beings among the Inuit of Northeast Canada. *Folk* 46/47: 85–120.

2006 The bringer of light: the raven in Inuit tradition. *Polar Record* 42(222): 187–204.

Oosten, Jarich, and Frédéric Laugrand (eds.).

1999 The Transition to Christianity. *Inuit Perspectives on the 20th Century*, 1. Iqaluit: Nunavut Arctic College (informants: Victor Tungilik and Rachel Uyarasuk).

Oosten, J. G., and Cornelius H. W. Remie

1997 *Angakkut* and reproduction: Social and symbolic aspects of Netsilik shamanism. *Études/Inuit/Studies* 21(1–2): 75–100.

Orr, E. C., and Ben Orr (eds.)

1995 *Qanemcikarluni Tekitnarqelartuq. One Must Arrive with a Story to Tell, Traditional Narratives by the Elders of Tununak, Alaska.* Lower Kuskokwin School District, Alaska Native Language Center, University of Alaska Fairbanks.

Ortner, Sherry B.

1973 On Key Symbols. *American Anthropologist* 75(5): 1338–46.

Pedersen, Birgit Kleist

2002 Gysergenren—gru eller trøst? Grønlandsk Kultur- og Samfundsforskning, Forlaget Atuagkat.

2006–7 Gysets anatomi—børn og unges behov for skrækfortællinger. Grønlandsk Kultur- og Samfundsforskning, Forlaget Atuagkat.

Pedersen, Morten A.

2001 Totemism, Animism and North Asian Indigenous Ontologies. *Journal of the Royal Anthropological Institute* (n.s.) 7: 411–27.

Petersen, Johan

1957 Ujuâts Dagbøger. + Østgrønlændernes Sagn og Fortællinger. Edited by W. Thalbitzer. *Det Grl. Selskabs Skrifter*, XIX.

Petersen, N.-K.

2013 Fra 'Kvinden som vasker' til 'Opus 5. Eja med sælen.' *Tidsskriftet Grønland*, 214–17.

Petersen, Robert

1963 Family Ownership and Right of Disposition in Sukkertoppen District, West Greenland. *Folk* 5: 269–81.

1966/67 Burial Forms and Death Cult among the Eskimos. *Folk* 8–9: 259–80.

1984 East Greenland before 1950. In David Damas (ed.), *Handbook of North American Indians.* Vol. V, "The Arctic." Washington, DC: Smithsonian Institution Press, 622–39.

n.p. *Fangst og Bosættelse. Studie fra to grønlandske fangersamfund*, I–II. Institut for Eskimologi, Københavns Universitet.

1990 On the Material Element in the Supernatural Aspect of the Former Greenlandic Religion. *Temenos* 26: 95–103.

1993 Samfund uden overhoveder—og dem med. Hvordan det traditionelle grønlandske samfund fungerede og hvordan det bl.a. påvirker fremtiden. *Grønlandsk Kultur- og Samfundsforskning* 93: 121–38.

1996 Administration of justice in the traditional Greenlandic community. In Gudmundur Alfredsson and Peter Macalister-Smith (eds.), *The Living Law of Nations; Essays on refugees, minorities, indigenous peoples and the human rights of other vulnerable groups In memory of Alte Grahl Madsen*. Kehl, 279–86.

2000 Om grønlandske slægtssagaer. *Tidsskriftet Grønland*, 299–311.

2003a Settlements, kinship and hunting grounds in traditional Greenland. A comparative study of local experiences from Upernavik and Ammassalik. *Meddelelser om Grønland. Man and Society* 27.

2003b *Om Grønlandsk (Inuit-) Syn på Verden og Livet*. Ilisimatusarfik. Not published.

Petterson, Christina

2008 Moses and Abraham go Arctic. *Biblical Interpretation* 16: 363–74.

Qaavigaq, David, and Torben Diklev

2000 Inughuaq/Inughuit. *Tidsskriftet Grønland*, 5.

Qúpersimân, Georg

1972 *Taimane gûtimik nalussûgama*. Godthåb: Det Grønlandske Forlag.

1982 *Min eskimoiske fortid*. Godthåb: Det grønlandske Forlag.

Rainey, Froelich G.

1947 The Whale Hunters of Tigara. *Anthropological Papers of the American Museum of Natural History* I(1): 227–83.

Randa, Vladimir

1986 Au croisement des espaces et des destins: *nanuq* 'marginal exemplaire'—Un cas de médiation animale dans l'Arctique central canadien. *Études/Inuit/Studies* 10(1–2): 159–69.

Rasmussen, Knud

1905 *Nye Mennesker*. København: Nordisk Forlag.

1906 *Under Nordenvindens Svøbe*. Kjøbenhavn and Kristiania: Gyldendalske Boghandel, Nordisk Forlag.

1908 *The People of the Polar North*. London: Kegan Paul, Trench, Trübner and Co.

1915 *Min Rejsedagbog, Skildringer fra den første Thuleekspedition*. København: Gyldendal.

1921 Beskrivelse af Thule Distrikt. *Meddelelser om Grønland* 60: 517–67.

1921–25 *Myter og Sagn fra Grønland* I–III. København: Gyldendal.

1925–26 *Fra Grønland til Stillehavet, Rejser og Mennesker fra 5. Thuleekspedition*, I–II. København: Gyldendal.

1927 *Across Arctic America: Narrative of the Fifth Thule Expedition*. New York: G. P. Putnam's Sons.

1929 The Intellectual Culture of the Iglulik Eskimos. *Report of the 5th Thule Expedition 1921–24*, 7(1). Copenhagen: Gyldendal.

1930a Observations on the Intellectual Culture of the Caribou Eskimos. *Report of the 5th Thule Expedition 1921–24*, 7(2). Copenhagen: Gyldendal.

1930b Iglulik and Caribou Eskimo Texts. *Report of the 5th Thule Expedition 1921–24*, 7(3). Copenhagen: Gyldendal.

1931 The Netsilik Eskimos, Social Life and Spiritual Culture. *Report of the 5th Thule Expedition 1921–24*, 8. Copenhagen: Gyldendal.

1932 Intellectual Culture of the Copper Eskimos. *Report of the 5th Thule Expedition 1921–24*, 9. Copenhagen: Gyldendal.

1938 Knud Rasmussen's Posthumous Notes on the Life and Doings of the East Greenlanders in Olden Times. Edited by H. Ostermann. *Meddelelser om Grønland* 109(1).

1939 Knud Rasmussen's Posthumous Notes on East Greenland, Legends and Myths. Edited by H. Ostermann. *Meddelelser om Grønland* 109(3).

1942 The MacKenzie Eskimos. Edited by H. Ostermann. *Report of the 5th Thule Expedition 1921–24,* 10(2). Copenhagen: Gyldendal.

1952 The Alaskan Eskimos as Described in the Posthumous Notes of Dr. Knud Rasmussen. Edited by H. Ostermann. *Report of the 5th Thule Expedition 1921–24,* 10(3). Copenhagen: Gyldendal.

1967 *Kâgssagssuk: The legend of the orphan boy.* Illustrated by Jakob Danielsen, taken down by Knud Rasmussen. *Kâgssagssuk, sagnet om den forældreløse.* Lyngby: Lyngby Kunstforening (trilingual edition).

1979 500 leveregler, Gamle Ord og Varsler fra Vestgrønland. Edited by Regitze M. Søby. *Det Grl. Selskabs Skrifter,* XXIII. Skjern.

1981 *Inuit Fortæller,* I–III. Edited by Regitze Søby. Lynge: Bogan.

1981–82 *Oqlugtuat oqalualâtdlo,* I–IV. Edited by Regitze M. Søby. Nuuk: Atuakkiorfik (for references see the relevant IDs in Sonne 2005).

1988 Agayut. Eskimo Masks from the 5th Thule Expedition. *Report of the 5th Thule Expedition 1921–24,* 10(4). Edited and analyzed by Birgitte Sonne. Copenhagen: Gyldendal. (Same publication as Sonne 1988a.)

Remie, H. W.

1988 Flying like a butterfly, or Knud Rasmussen among the Netsilingmiut. *Études/Inuit/Studies* 12(1–2): 101–27.

Riches, David

1994 Shamanism: the key to religion. *Man* (n.s.) 29.

Rink, H. J.

1859–63 *Kaladlit oqaluktualliait/Grønlandske Folkesagn* I–IV. Nunnap Nalagata Naqiteriviane Naqitat, Nuuk. (Fotoprint 1972.)

1866–71 *Eskimoiske Eventyr og Sagn,* I–II. København: C. A. Reitzel.

1875 *Tales and Traditions of the Eskimo.* Edinburgh and London: W. Blackwood and Sons. (For references see relevant IDs in Sonne 2005.)

1878a Grønlænderen og Polarsfareren Hans Hendriks Erindringer. *Fra alle Lande.* København, 269–391.

1878b *Hans Hendrik 1834–1889, Memoirs of Hans Hendrik, the Arctic Traveler.* Edited by George Stephens. London: Trübner.

1881 Om grønlandske Skikke og Vedtægter. Copenhagen: Carl Lund.

1887–91 The Eskimo Tribes: their distribution and characteristics, specially in regard to language, I–II. *Meddelelser om Grønland* 11(1–2).

1974 [1877] *Danish Greenland, its people and products.* Montreal: McGill/Queen's University Press.

1975 [1875] *Tales and Traditions of the Eskimo; with a sketch of their Habits, Religion, Language and other Peculiarities.* New York: AMS Press. (The "sketch" is a translation of Rink 1866–71, II: "Tillæg, Om Eskimoerne," pp. 150–253.)

Rischel, Jørgen

1986a Geografisk dialektfordeling og lydforandringer i grønlandsk. In J. Rischel and Robert Petersen (eds.), *Vort sprog—vor kultur.* Nuuk: Ilisimatusarfik og Kalaallit Nunaata Katersugaasivia, 123–41.

1986b Kalaallisut sumiorpaluutit agguataarnerat nipillu allanngorarnerat. In J. Rischel and Robert Petersen (eds.), *Oqaatsivut kulturerpullu*. Nuuk: Pilersuiffik, 127–43.

Robbe, Pierre

1981 Les noms de personnes chez les Ammassalimiut. *Études/Inuit/Studies* 5(1): 45–82.

1994 Les Inuit d'Ammassalik, Chasseurs de l'Arctique. *Memories du Muséum National d'Histoire Naturelle*, 159, Ethnologie.

Robbe, Pierre, and Louis-Jacque Dorais

1986 Tunuamiit Oraasiat, Tunuamiut oqaasii, Det østgrønlandske sprog, The East Greenlandic Inuit Language, La langue inuit du Groenland de l'Est. *Nordicana* 49. Québec: Université Laval.

Robert-Lamblin, Joëlle

1981 Changement de sexe de certains enfants d'Ammassalik (est Groenland): Un rééquilibrage du sex ratio familial? *Études/Inuit/Studies* 5(1): 117–25.

1986 Ammassalik, East Greenland—end or persistence of an isolate? Anthropological and demographical study on change. *Meddelelser om Grønland, Man and Society* 10.

1988 Le saga des Maratse ou la petite histoire des habitants de Sermiligaaq au Groenland oriental. *Objets et Mondes* 25, Fasc. 3–4: 103–10.

1996 Les dernières manifestations du chamanisme au Groenland oriental. *Boreales* 66/69: 115–30.

1997 Les chamane du Groenland Oriental: éléments biographiques et généalogiques. *Études/Inuit/Studies* 21(1–2): 269–92.

Roepstorff, Andreas

2003 Clashing cosmologies: Contrasting knowledge in the Greenlandic fishery. In Andreas Roepstorff, Nils Bubant, and Kalevi Kull (eds.), *Imagining Nature, Practices of Cosmology and Identity*. Aarhus University Press, 117–42.

Rosing, C.

1906 *Tunuamiut kalâdlit Gûtimik nalussut ugperissáinik ilerkunigdlo inûsiáningdlo*. Nûngme: Ilíniarfigssûp naKiterivigtâne naKitigkat.

1946 [1906] *Østgrønlænderne/Tunuamiut*. Translated by Karl Rosing, edited by W. Thalbitzer. *Det grønlandske Selskabs Skrifter*, 15.

Rosing, Emil

1994 *Tunuamiut aarnuaat. Østgrønlandske amuletter*. Nuuk: Atuakkiorfik.

Rosing, Jens

1957 Den østgrønlandske "maskekultur." *Tidsskriftet Grønland*, 241–51.

1963 *Sagn og Saga fra Angmagssalik*. København: Rhodos.

1970 *Kimilik*. København: Rhodos.

1993 *Hvis vi vågner til havblik. En slægtssaga fra Østgrønland*. Valby: Borgen.

Rosing, Otto

1957–61 *Angákortaligssuit*, I–II. Nuuk/Godthåb: Grønlands Forlagip naqitertitai.

1989 *Aassuutit: stjernerne der forhindrede solen i at gå til bunds*. Nuuk: NAPA/Nordens Institut i Grønland.

1990 [1957–61] *Angakkortalissuit*. Nuuk: Atuakkiorfik.

Ross, W. Gillies

1975 Whaling and Eskimos: Hudson Bay 1860–1915. *Canada, National Museum of Man, Publications in Ethnology* 10, Ottawa.

Rowley, Susan
1985 Population Movements in the Canadian Arctic. *Études/Inuit/Studies* 9(1): 3–21.

Rüttel, F.C.P.
1917 *Ti Aar blandt Østgrønlands Hedninger*. København and Kristiania: Gyldendalske Boghandel.

Saabye, Hans Egede
1942 [1816] Brudstykker af en Dagbog holden i Grønland. *Meddelelser om Grønland* 129, 2.

Sahlins, Marshall
1976 *Culture and practical reason*. Chicago: University of Chicago Press.

Saladin d'Anglure, B.
1977 Iqallijuq ou les réminiscences d'une âme-nom inuit. *Études/Inuit/Studies* 1(1): 33–63.
1978 L'homme (angut), le fils (irniq) et la lumière (qau), 'Mélanges offerts à Claude Lévi-Strauss à l'occasion de son 70e anniversaire de naissance.' *Anthropologica* n.s. XX(1–2): 101–44.
1980a Nanuq Super-Mâle: L'ours blanc dans l'espace imanigaire et le temps social des Inuit de l'Arctique canadien. *Études Mongoles* 11: 63–94.
1980b Petit-ventre, l'enfant-géant du cosmos inuit. *L'Homme* 20 (1): 7–46.
1983 Ijiqqat: voyage au pays the l'invisible inuit. *Études/Inuit/Studies* 7(1): 67–79.
1984 Inuit of Quebec. In David Damas (ed.), *Handbook of North American Indians*. Vol. V, "The Arctic." Washington, DC: Smithsonian Institution Press, 476–507.
1986 Du fœtus au chamane: la construction d'un "troisième sexe" inuit. *Études/Inuit/Studies* 10(1–2): 25–113.
1990a Frère-lune (Taqqiq), seur-soleil (Siqiniq) et l'intelligence du Monde (Sila). *Études/Inuit/Studies* 14(1–2): 75–140.
1990b Nanook, Super-male: the polar bear in the imaginary space and social time of the Inuit of the Canadian Arctic. In Roy Willis (ed.), *Signifying Animals: Human meaning in the natural world.* London: Unwin Hyman, 178–95.
1991 The Mythology of the Inuit of the Central Arctic. In Y. Bonnefoy (ed.) and W. Doniger (tr.), *American, African and Old European Mythologies*. Chicago: University of Chicago Press.
1993 The Shaman's Share, or Inuit Sexual Communism in the Canadian Central Arctic. *Anthropologica* XXXV: 59–103.
1997 Pour un nouveau regard ethnographique sur le chamanisme inuit ou la circulation des noms (*atiit*), des âmes (*tarniit*), des dons (*tunijjutit*) et des esprits (*tuurngait*). *Études/Inuit/Studies* 21(1–2): 5–36.
2001 *Cosmology and Shamanism, Interviewing Inuit Elders,* 4. Edited by Bernard Saladin d'Anglure. Iqaluit: Nunavut Arctic College.
2007 Troisème sexe sociale, atome familial et mèdiations chamaniques. Pour un anthropologie holiste (Entretien). *Anthropologie et Sociétés* 31(3): 165–84.

Saladin d'Anglure, B., and Francoise Morin
1998 Mariage Mystique et Pouvoir Chamanique chez les Shipibo D'Amazonie Péruvienne et les Inuit du Nunavut Canadien. *Anthropologie et Sociétés* 22(2): 49–74.

Sand, Erik Reenberg
2005 Helligt rum i indisk perspektiv. Rituelt rum mellem krop og kosmos. *Chaos* 44: 39–5.

Sandgreen, Otto
1967 *Isse issimik kigutdlo kigúmik*, I–I. Godthåb: Kalâtdlit-nunãne naqiterisitsissafik, Det Grønlandske Forlag.

1987 *Øje for øje og tand for tand.* Translation, introduction, and notes by Birgitte Sonne. Nuuk: Otto Sandgreens Forlag.

Schjødt, Jens Peter
1986 Initiation and Classification of Rituals. *Temenos* 22.

Schneider, Lucien
1985 *Ulilirnaisirgutiit. An Inuktitut English Dictionary of Northern Quebec, Labrador and Eastern Arctic Dialects.* Québec: Université Laval. Schultz-Lorentzen, C. W.
1927 Dictionary of the West Greenland Eskimo Language. *Meddelelser om Grønland* LXIX. Copenhagen: Reitzel, Bianco Luno.
1967 [1926] *Den Grønlandske Ordbog. Grønlandsk-Dansk.* Copenhagen: S. L. Møller.
1969 *Det Vestgrønlandske Sprog i Grammatisk Fremstilling.* København: Ministeriet for Grønland.

Seiding, Inge
n.p. Married the Daughters of the Country: intermarriage and intimacy in Northwest Greenland ca. 1750–1850. Unpublished Phd thesis. Nuuk: Ilisimatusarfik.

Sejersen, Frank
2001 Hunting and management of beluga whales in Greenland: Changing strategies to cope with new national and local interests. *Arctic* 54(4): 431–43.

Siikala, Anna Leena
1978 The rite technique of the Siberian shaman. *FF Communications* 220. Helsinki.

Smidt, Carsten M.
1989 Nekrolog over Sofie Jørgensen. *Atuagagdliutit* 39.

Sokolova, P.
1989 A survey of Ob-Ugrian Shamanism. In M. Hoppál and O. J. von Sadovszky (eds.), *Shamanism Past and Present.* Budapest, 155–66.

Sonne, Birgitte
1975 Den besudlede kvinde. Havkvinden i ritual og myte. *Tidsskriftet Grønland* 4: 104–17.
1978 Ritual Bonds between the Living and the Dead in Yukon Eskimo Society. *Temenos* 14: 127–83.
1980 *Eskimoiske Døderitualer. Religiøse betydninger og sociale funktioner.* Institut for Religionssociologi, Københavns Universitet.
1982a The Professional Ecstatic in His Social and Ritual Position. *Scripta Instituti Donneriani Aboensis*, XI: "Religious Ecstasy," 129–50.
1982b The ideology and practice of blood feuds in East and West Greenland. *Études/Inuit/Studies* 6: 21–50.
1984 Eskimoerne. In B. Alster and C. Lindtner (eds.), *Gads religionshistoriske tekster.* København: G.E.C. Gad, 469–86.
1985 Toornaarsuks forvandlinger. *Chaos.* Dansk Tidsskrift for Religionshistoriske Studier - Særnummer: "Religionssociologiske perspektiver": 117–36.
1986a Angakkut puullit i Grønland og Alaska. In J. Rischel and Robert Petersen (eds.), *Vort sprog—vor kultur.* Nuuk: Ilisimatusarfik og Kalaallit Nunaata Katersugaasivia, 143–56.
1986b Toornaarsuk, An Historical Proteus. *Arctic Anthropology* 23(1–2): 199–219.
1988a Agayut. Eskimo Masks from The 5th Thule Expedition. *Report of the 5th Thule Expedition 1921–24,* 10(4). Viborg: Gyldendal. (Same title as Rasmussen 1988.)
1988b In Love with Eskimo Imagination and Intelligence. *Études/Inuit/Studies* 12(1–2), "The Work of Knud Rasmussen": 21–44.

1990 The Acculturative Role of Sea Woman. Early contact relations between Inuit and Whites as revealed in the Origin Myth of Sea Woman. *Meddelelser om Grønland, Man and Society* 13.

1996 Genuine Humans and "Others", Criteria of "otherness" at the beginning of colonization in Greenland. *Cultural and Social Research in Greenland 95/96, Essays in Honour of Robert Petersen*, 241–52.

1997 Kontrasten mellem Sila som mytisk skikkelse og opdragelsens ideal hos inuit I Canada og Grønland. In Lene Buck et al. (eds.), *Idealernes rolle i religion og religionsvidenskab*. Københavns Universitet, Museum Tusculanum, 49–67.

2000a Heaven negotiated. The realms of death in early colonial West Greenland. *Études/Inuit/Studies* 24(2): 65–87.

2000b *Gender Perspectives in Greenlandic stories*. Unpublished paper read at a conference on Folklore in Leiden, May 2000.

2001a Sources of Greenland Shamanism: survey and ethnohistorical implications. *North Atlantic Studies* 4(1,2): 31–38.

2001b Krop og klæ'r, bare ben og kamikker. *Tidsskriftet Grønland*, 186–92.

2003 Er tavshed guld? Hemmeligholdelse i Østgrønland, før—og endnu? *Grønlandsk Kultur- og Samfundsforskning*.

2005 *Sonnesbase 2004*. http://sonne.arktiskleksikon.dk/index.php?id=50

2007 La vie est un sac rempli d'air. Polysémie de *pooq* et autres notions associées. *Anthropologie et Sociétés* 31(3): 15–36.

2010 Who is afraid of Kaassassuk? Writing as a tool in coping with changing cosmology. *Études/Inuit/Studies* 34(2): 107–27.

2017 *Pooq, en metafor for livet*. In press.

Spinks, C. W.

1991 The Laughter of Signs: Semiosis as Trickster. In *Semiosis, Marginal Signs and Trickster, a dagger of the mind*. London: Palgrave Macmillan, 1–17.

Steenhoven, Geert van

1962 *Leadership and Law among the Eskimos of the Keewatin District, Northwest Territories*. The Hague, Rijswijk.

Steiner, Franz

1967 [1956] *Taboo*. Middlesex: Penguin Books.

Swanton, John R.

1970 [1909] *Tlingit Myths and Texts*. Washington DC: Johnson Reprinting Corporations.

Søby, Regitze

1969/70 The Eskimo Animal Cult. *Folk* 11–12: 43–78.

1973 Uddrag af Martéraqs selvbiografi. *Tidsskriftet Grønland*, 6.

1983 Førstefangstfesten for småbørn. En overset rite. *Tidsskriftet Grønland*, 149–56.

Sørensen, M., and H.C. Gulløv

2012 The Prehistory of Inuit in Northeast Greenland. *Arctic Anthropology* 49(1): 88–104.

Tejsner, Pelle

2013 Historier fra kysten eller klima-krise narrativer. *Tidsskriftet Grønland*, 162–72.

Taylor, J. Garth

1989 Shamanic Sex Roles in Traditional Labrador Inuit Society. In M. Hoppál and O. J. von Sadovszky (eds.), *Shamanism Past and Present*. Budapest, 297–306.

1997 Deconstructing deities: *Tuurngatsuak* and *Turngaatsuk* in Labrador Inuit Religion. *Études/Inuit/Studies* 21(1–2): 141–58.

Tersis, Nicole
2008 *Formes et Sens des Mots du Tunumiisut. Lexique inuit du Groenland oriental.* Arctique 9, SELAF, no. 445. Paris: Peters.

Tester, Frank James
2010 Mad dogs and (mostly) Englishmen: Colonial relations, commodities, and the fate of Inuit sled dogs. *Études/Inuit/Studies* 34(2): 129–47.

Thalbitzer, William
1909 Østgrønlands Hedenske Præster (Angakut). *Nordisk Tidsskrift för Vetenskap, Konst och Industri*, 91–100.
1914 The Ammassalik Eskimo, I. *Meddelelser om Grønland* 39(7): 319–755.
1923 The Ammassalik Eskimo, II(1). *Meddelelser om Grønland* 40: 115–563.
1926 Eskimoernes Kultiske Guddomme. *Studier for Sprog og Oldtidsforskning* 143. København.
1928 Die kultischen Gottheiten der Eskimos. *Archiv für Religionswissenschaft* XXXVI. Leipzig: 364–430.
1930 Les magiciens esquimaux, leur conceptions du monde, de l'ame et de la vie. *Journal de la Société des Américanistes de Paris* (n.s.) 22: 73–106.
1931 *Tunuamiut taigdliait.* Sinersissap Kujatdliup Naqiterivani.
1932 Grønland Nu og För. *Nordisk Tidsskrift för Vetenskap, Konst och Industri*, 8.
1941 The Ammasalik Eskimo, II(2). *Meddelelser om Grønland* 40: 565–740.
2014 Dagbog Østgrønland, Juni 1905–September 1906. Edited by Ole Lund. *Det grønlandske Selskabs særskrifter, No. XLIV*. Copenhagen: Narayana Press.

Thalbitzer, William (ed.)
1933 Den Grønlandske Kateket Hansêraq's Dagbog. Translated by O. K. Skaarup. *Det Grønlandske Selskabs Skrifter*, 8.

Therrien, Michèle
1987 *Les corps inuit.* Paris: SELAF. Arctique 1.
1996 Les Expériences premières et la notion de dynamique généralisée. In Nicole Tersis and Michèle Therrien (eds.), *La Dynamique dans la langue et de la culture inuit.* Paris: Peeters, coll. Arctique 4, 22–41.

Therrien, Michèle, and Frédéric Laugrand (eds.)
2001 Perspectives on Traditional Health. *Interviewing Inuit Elders* 5. Language and Culture Program of Nunavut Arctic College, Iqaluit.

Thisted, Kirsten
1994 *Som perler på en snor.... Fortællestrukturer i grønlandsk fortælletradition—med særligt henblik på forskellen mellem de originale og de udgivne versioner.* PhD thesis, Ilisimatusarfik.
1997 Dengang i de ikke rigtig gamle dage. Grønlandsk fortælletradition som kilde til 1700-tallets kulturmøde. In Marianne Alenius, Pil Dahlerup, Søren Peter Hansen, Hans Hertel and Peter Meislin (eds.), *Digternes Paryk. Studier i 1700-tallet.* Museum Tusculanum, Københavns Universitet, 73–85.
1999 *Således skriver jeg, Aron*, I–II. Nuuk: Atuakkiorfik. (References in Sonne 2005.)
2001 On Narrative Expectations: Greenlandic Oral Traditions about the Cultural Encounter between Inuit and Norsemen. *Scandinavian Studies* 73(3): 253–96.

2008 Åndernes kraft og kristendommen—fire film om inuits religion. *Religion, Tidsskrift for Religionslærerforeningen for Gymnasiet og HF* 2: 26–50.

Thisted, Kirsten, and Gâba Thorning
1996 *Oqalualaartussaqaraluarnerpoq ...Oqluttuat H. J. Rinkip katersai. Måske nogen kunne fortælle ...Fortællinger indsamlet af H. J. Rink*. Nuuk: Atuakkiorfik.

Thorning, Gâbâ, Arnaq Grove, and Kirsten Thisted
1999 *Taamma allattunga, Aron,* I–II. Nuuk: Atuakkiorfik.

Thuesen, Søren
1988 *Fremad, opad, Kampen for en moderne grønlandsk identitet*. Copenhagen: Rhodos.

Thuesen, Søren, and Birgitte Sonne
2005 Eskimologi og Religionsvidenskab. In Kirsten Thisted (ed.), Grønlandsforskning, *Det Grønlandske Selskabs Skrifter*, XXXVIII, 253–76.

Tróndheim, Gitte
2010 *Slægtskab og Køn i grønlandske Bysamfund—Følelser af Forbundethed*. Unpublished PhD thesis. Ilisimatusarfik, University of Greenland, Nuuk.

Trondhjem, Naja Blytman
2009 Marking of pasttime in Kalaallitsut, the Greenlandic language. *Typological Studies in Language* 86: 171–82.

Trott, Christopher G.
2005 *Ilagiit and Tuquraqtuq: Inuit Understandings of Kinship and social Relatedness*. Paper prepared for First Nations, First Thoughts, Centre of Canadian Studies, University of Edinburgh.
2006 The gender of the bear. *Études/Inuit/Studies* 30(1): 89–109.

Turner, Lucien M.
1894 Ethnology of the Ungava District, Hudson Bay Territory. *Bureau of American Ethnology, Annual Report* 11(2): 159–350.

Turner, Terence
1977 Transformation, Hierarchy, and Transcendence: A Reformulation of van Gennep's Model of the structure of Rites de Passsage. In S. F. Moore and B. G. Meyerhoff (eds.), *Secular Ritual*. Amsterdam: Assen.
1991 "We Are Parrots," "Twins Are Birds": Play of Tropes as Operational Structure. In James W. Fernandez (ed.), *Beyond Metaphor. The Theory of Tropes in Anthropology*. Stanford, CA: Stanford University Press, 121–58.
2009 The Crisis of Late Structuralism, Perspectivism and Animism: Rethinking Culture, Nature, Spirit, and Bodiliness. *Tipití* 7(1): 3–42.

Turner, Victor
1964 *The Forest of Symbols. Aspects of Ndembu Ritual*. Ithaca, NY: Cornell University Press.
1974 *Dramas, Fields and Metaphors*. Ithaca, NY: Cornell University Press.

Tybjerg, Tove
2008 Trickster og kaos/kosmos. *Chaos*, Dansk-norsk tidsskrift for religionshistoriske studier 49: 95–112.

Underbjerg, Niels
1984 E Åndemanerens værktøj. In *Tasiilaq, Angmagssalik*. Edited by Jørgen Fisker. Tasiilaq, Ammassalik, Gylling.

Usher, Peter

1971 The Canadian Western Arctic: A Century of Change, Pilot not Commander. Essays in Memory of Diamond Jenness. *Anthropologica* 13(1–2): 169–83.

Vahl, Martin, F. C. Amdrup, L. Bobé, and A. S. Jensen (eds.)

1928–29 *Greenland*, I–III. Copenhagen: C. A. Reitzel; London: Oxford University Press.

van Gennep, A.

1909 *Les Rites de passage*. Paris.

van Londen, Selma M.

1999 Mythology and Identity Construction among the Inuit. In Jarich Oosten and Cornelius Remie (eds.), *Arctic Identities*. Leiden: Leiden University, Research School CNWS, 109–34.

VanStone, Jim W.

1983 Protective hide body armor of the Historic Chukchi and Siberian Eskimos. *Études/Inuit/Studies* 7(2): 3–24.

Vasilevic, G. M.

1968 The Acquisition of Shamanistic Ability among the Evenki (Tungus). In Vilmos Diószegi, *Popular Beliefs and Folklore Tradition in Siberia*. The Hague: Mouton and Company, 339–49.

Vebæk, M.

1990 *Navaranaaq og andre. De grønlandske kvinders historie*. København: Gyldendal.

2006 The Southernmost People of Greenland—Dialects and Memories. Qavaat—Oqalunneri Eqqaamassaallu. *Meddelelser om Grønland, Man and Society* 33.

Veniaminov, I.

1984 *Notes on the Islands of the Unalaska District*. Translated by L. T. Black and R. H. Geoghegan, edited by R. A. Pierce. Kingston, Ontario: The Limestone Press.

Victor, Poul-Émile

1991 Chants d'Ammassalik. *Meddelelser om Grønland, Man and Society* 16.

Victor, Poul-Émile, and Jöelle Robert-Lamblin

1989–93 *La Civilisation du Phoque*, I–II. (Vol I: Jeux, gestes et techniques des Eskimo d'Ammassalik; Vol. II: Légendes, rites et croyances des Eskimo d'Ammassalik). Bayonne.

Villadsen, Villads

1996 [1965] *Nalusuunerup taarnerani: taallatut allagaq* (In the darkness of paganism). Nuuk: Atuakkiorfik.

Viveiros de Castro, Eduard

2002 [1998] Cosmological Deixis and Amerindian Perspectivism. In M. Lambek (ed.), *A Reader of Anthropology of Religion*. Oxford: Blackwell Publishers, 306–26.

Wenger, Hubert

2001 Eskimo Database. http://www.wengereskimodb.uaf.edu. University of Alaska Fairbanks.

Wentzel, Knud

1990 *Thule I Hjertet. Nærbillede af Knud Rasmussen*. Viborg: Munksgaard.

Weyer, E. M.

1932 *The Eskimos, Their Environment and Folkways*. New Haven, London.

Willerslev, Rane

2001 The Hunter as a Human "Kind": Hunting and shamanism among the Upper Kolyma Yukaghirs of Siberia. *North Atlantic Studies* 4(1,2): 44–50.

2007 *Soul Hunters. Hunting, Animism, and Personhood Among the Siberian Yukaghirs.* Berkeley: University of California Press.

Williamson, Robert

1974 Eskimo Underground. Socio-Cultural Change in the Canadian Central Arctic. *Institutionen för allmän och jämnförande etnografi vid Uppsala Universitetet.* Occasional Papers, II, Uppsala.

Zeilich-Jensen, Leif

1974 Den centraleskimåiska Världsbilden. Huvuddragen av eskimåisk religion mod bakrunden af termerna för orientering. *Acta Universitatis Stockholmiensis, Stockholm Studies in Comparative Religion*, 12, Västerås.

■ ■ ■

Index

Acknowledgments

My thanks are due to a good number of colleagues and former teachers. Throughout the many years of my research into the topics of this book, Robert Petersen has been a continuous support and help in cultural and linguistic matters. Long ago, the late Margaret Lantis welcomed my interest in Yup'ik Southwest Alaska, which was stirred by some curious correspondences of myths between Nunivak Island and East Greenland. Michael Fortescue and Naja Trondhjem helped me solve linguistic problems. Inge Kleivan, H. C. Gulløv, and Kennet Pedersen contributed on other issues. Michèle Therrien commented on parts of early drafts, and both Michèle Therrien and Phyllis Morrow on the entire penultimate draft. Phyllis Morrow went into a discussion of details that proved immensely useful and proposed one of the book's main hypotheses. Jens Dahl, who kindly offered to serve as the ignorant, educated reader, proposed a series of welcome questions and requests for explanations. In addition to the many experts on Inuit and Yup'ik issues, I am indebted in particular to the writings of Bernard Saladin d'Anglure, Jarich Oosten, Frédéric Laugrand, Ann Fienup-Riordan, and Phyllis Morrow. Their interpretations have quite often guided me into finding otherwise undiscovered issues of my Greenlandic sources.

Jenanne Kirsten Ferguson patiently corrected my English of the penultimate draft. Copy editor Rachel Fudge has cleaned up many a clumsy Danish-English phrase and solved editorial computer problems. My thanks are due also to University of Alaska Press's former editorial director, James Engelhardt, who was the first to read the manuscript; to his successor, Amy Simpson, who saw to my academic well-being while I was anticipating the final decision about publication; and finally to Krista West, for following me patiently to the end.

And last but not least, my husband, late poet Jørgen Sonne, was my eager and intent listener and interlocutor throughout our married life. I so regret he did not live for only one more month, as he would have been immensely pleased that the manuscript was accepted for publication.

Birgitte Sonne

Tyvelse, 2017

■ ■ ■

About the Author

Photo by Zsuzsanna Willkan

Birgitte Sonne holds a Danish M.A. in the Sociology of Religion. She studied and taught Inuit Culture and Society at the Institute of Eskimology at the University of Copenhagen. Sonne retired in 2006 and spent the next eleven years writing this book.